ENGAGING WITH FOREIGN LAW

This book presents a developed theory of how national lawyers can approach, understand, and make use of foreign law. Its theme is pursued through a set of detailed essays which look at the courts as well as business practice and, with the help of statistics, demonstrate what type of academic work has any impact on the 'real' world. Engaging with Foreign Law thus aims to carve out a new niche for comparative law in this era of globalisation, and may also be the only book which deals in some depth with both private and public law in countries such as England, Germany, France, South Africa, and the United States.

Engaging with Foreign Law

Sir Basil Markesinis QC, FBA
in co-operation with
Professor Jörg Fedtke

·HART·
PUBLISHING

OXFORD AND PORTLAND, OREGON
2009

Published in North America (US and Canada) by
Hart Publishing
c/o International Specialized Book Services
920 NE 58th Avenue, Suite 300
Portland, OR 97213-3786
USA
Tel: +1 503 287 3093 or toll-free: (1) 800 944 6190
Fax: +1 503 280 8832
E-mail: orders@isbs.com
Website: http://www.isbs.com

Hart Publishing Ltd, 16C Worcester Place, Oxford, OX1 2JW
Telephone: +44 (0)1865 517530 Fax: +44 (0)1865 510710
E-mail: mail@hartpub.co.uk
Website: http://www.hartpub.co.uk

British Library Cataloguing in Publication Data
Data Available

ISBN: 978-1-84113-947-0

Typeset by Hope Services, Abingdon
Printed and bound in Great Britain by
TJ International Ltd, Padstow, Cornwall

PREFACE

This book is about foreign law, ie the law of a country other than that of the observer (here frequently referred to as the 'national' lawyer), and how to engage with it. There are many reasons why one may wish to find out more about foreign law. It may be that this is the 'proper' (ie applicable) law for the dispute in question. Alternatively, it may be needed if one is interpreting an international convention (or other legal instrument) which calls for a more or less similar interpretation and application. Local law may also be underdeveloped, unclear or (arguably) deficient, and recourse to foreign law may help strengthen the conviction that change is needed—and even suggest what form it should take. Finally, recourse may also be sought out of intellectual curiosity; an attribute which is found not only among academics but also among the most learned of judges and the most enlightened of legislators. Whatever the reason—we regard the advantages of exchanges of ideas so axiomatically important and desirable that we do not find it necessary to pursue this point further. Only the most narrow-minded will be contemptuous of such exercises, or arrogant enough to believe that in these days when people, capital, goods and (alas) even drugs and terrorism travel so easily, cultural differences will impede the exchange of legal ideas.

The number of books about foreign law or comparative law or comparative methodology (the terms are not synonymous but they are often used interchangeably) has grown in recent years as the interest in the subject has increased—in Europe because of European integration, the world over because of the globalisation phenomenon. But these publications tend to fall into one of three categories, and we feel that there is room for a fourth.

The first kind of book is the 'cases and materials book'. Written by authors with impeccable credentials, they contain—as the subtitle usually suggests—a selection of materials, often translated by the authors themselves and provided for teachers to use, annotate, expand, and amplify for the benefit of their students in the way each thinks most appropriate. These books work better where their authors have annotated their material in a way that promotes its further use and assists those teaching from the book, especially if their expertise is not entirely coterminous with that of the authors.

The second type of book can come in two variants. The first takes the form of a collection of essays produced by different authors but trying to bring together scholars who have a minimum of common basic beliefs about the amplitude and form that the teaching of the subject should take. The second variant wishes to be broader in its coverage, open to various ideologies rather than committed to one, and is consequently more inclusive in selecting its contributors. It also ends up being larger as a result.

The third category is exemplified by the Zweigert and Kötz textbook *An Introduction to Comparative Law*. These books tend to be divided into two parts. The first provides a general introduction about the legal systems covered in the text, usually grouped in families, then talks about their histories and sources of law, and finally emphasises some of their peculiarities. The second moves on to discuss the law of obligations by looking in turn at the Germanic systems, the Romanesque, and then the common law. Though the presentation owes much to Rabel's functionalist method, this kind of book is more concerned with providing fairly detailed information presented in comparative juxtaposition than to argue a thesis or theses of the kind one finds in monographs or learned articles.

We have attempted to create a fourth category of book, which we hope can be treated as a textbook and not as monograph, but which differs from the others in the following ways.

First, this book is not really interested, as others have been, in merely *describing* foreign law—even though its reader will garner much 'pure' information if he reads the book carefully—but in showing how to analyse foreign ideas, concepts and institutions (so as not to feel overwhelmed by their—often only apparent—difference) and then explaining how to 'package' or 're-package' them so as to make the material (thus 'discovered') usable in one's own environment. This book is then about *legal methodology* (and more particularly *comparative* methodology) as well as substantive foreign law, and in this it goes a step further than the other types of work alluded to above—both in terms of content and philosophy.

In this book, the authors provide, secondly, personal impressions and background information about the subject and its protagonists—not only in order to give this account a more lively dimension but also to demonstrate to the reader how much comparative law has developed and changed during the last 40 years, a point often missed by those who have held the approach in low esteem during this time. In the chapters that follow we thus discuss the reasons—related to persons and, above all, the modern phenomenon of globalisation—that may explain this change; but also warn (politely, we hope, but with deliberate bluntness) of the dangers which threaten to slow down (if not halt) this growth.

Thirdly, the book's aim being to help those lawyers who are interested in detail and not in generalities, it has also tried to avoid the often bland, generalised and (to most users) ultimately useless descriptions of foreign law. In what follows we thus identify the writings of others which fall into this category, and make at least those who know something about the subject ask the question: what new has such work brought to the subject? This lack of originality may be due to the fact that many who teach it these days treat it as a secondary or tertiary interest rather than the passion it can become to those who can see it as a way to unlock access to other countries and different mindsets.

From the little already said it will have been noticed that this book does not hesitate to express personal views, to present them in a strong (though, we hope, courteous) manner, and to back the various theses it advances through the use of extensive empirical research. To strengthen its message, it has thus made increased use of statistical information in order to familiarise the reader with the need to use, wherever possible, the tools and techniques of other disciplines. This statistical information, however, has also been added to show how wrong some have been in claiming that (a) the study of foreign law is not in a state of crisis, and (b) to move both scholars and students towards the realisation that the future of the subject depends on how we all use the knowledge we can derive from it.

This is yet another of the many theses promoted here for the purposes of further discussion in the classroom. The book thus criticises the old tendency to link comparative law too closely to Roman law, lest the decaying features of the latter also infect the former. It also warns its readers to avoid flirting with contemporary attempts to bring into the study of the law political correctness, postmodernism, deconstructionalism and the like. All of these ideas and approaches, shaped by unsavoury language, would sound the death knell of the subject since they have nothing to offer to those who are likely to use foreign law—namely legislators, courts, law reformers, administrators, not to mention practitioners (especially those working in the growing number of international law firms).

The above observations, brief though they may be, will have revealed the last main difference between the kind of book that we have tried to produce and those which fall into the other categories previously identified. For here we have not just given information (in the form of primary materials) to the teacher and asked him to 'fatten it up' as best he can; we have given him our own interpretation—along with plentiful further references—and, time again, invite him or her to agree, to disagree, or to come up with a different view or explanation of what *is* happening around us. For it is of no use to argue that 'cultural' reasons prevent us from getting together and learning from each other when this is precisely what *is* happening or, to take an opposite example, that legal reasoning can benefit from literal reasoning. In one sense our way of presenting our thesis may metaphorically amount to 'assaulting the intellect' of the student and his teacher, and forcing them both to think. We know of no better way to sharpen the readers' reactions than by provoking them to think and then giving them the chance to agree or to disagree. In the same way, the book differs from the collections of essays, since it gives the student a unified view of the subject and then, in the hands of a skilful guide, asks him to work out variants which, though mentioning, we have chosen not to promote.

The reader of this work should thus be prepared for a book which will not only inform but also provoke and, one hopes, prove fun to use in the classroom. Yet we have to state the obvious (since artificially created misunderstandings are a speciality of our times): that such provoking as we have attempted has been in good faith, based in the belief that in the classroom and in books, those who 'speak' should help generate *new* thought and not just repeat and describe what others have said before. If we have gone beyond the limits, we apologise in advance—though, as TS Elliot once put it, you do not know what the limits are until you have passed them.

Sir Basil Markesinis QC FBA

Jörg Fedtke

PS: After this manuscript was completed, we received a long letter from Dr Nicolas David, second son of the late René David. It contained a number of points and reactions to some of our earlier writings about the work of his father. All his comments were expressed with impeccable style and were based on his recollections of his father's views, the conditions which prevailed in Paris when the 'great man' was a professor there, and his own long years of experience as leading counsel at Elf Petroleum. Following an exchange of views, Dr David authorised us to use as much or as little of his comments as we wished when considering his suggestions for this book. We have done this with deep appreciation, sent him advance copies of the chapters which deal with his father, and invited his further comments. The text published here may not represent in its entirety the son's views; but we repeat not only our admiration at the tactful and stylish way he explained his father's position but also hope that, with his assistance, we may have placed our own observations about René David's work in a better and more correct perspective. We thereby wish to stress that academic disagreement does *not* imply (particularly in the case of René David!) lack of respect and admiration. Our criticism is only meant to express our sincere belief that the work of all of us dates, and that the time comes (sooner or later) when it has to be replaced. Dr David's letters indicate that his father, too, was fully aware of how this law of nature affected his own *Les grands systèmes des droits contemporain.*

ABOUT THE AUTHORS

Sir Basil Markesinis was born into a family which, from his father's side, was for more than 10 generations involved in politics, law, and the world of letters, first in Venice and later in Greece. He holds a Doctor Iuris from the University of Athens, a PhD and an LLD from the University of Cambridge, and a DCL from the University of Oxford. He is also an honorary doctor of the universities of Paris I (Sorbonne), Ghent, Munich, and Athens. He has held tenured posts at the universities of Cambridge, London, and Oxford (where he was Professor of Comparative Law), held the Chair of Anglo-American Law at the University of Leiden/Netherlands, and has taught for many years at Cornell and Michigan. At various times, he also held the Francqui Chair of the University of Ghent. He currently holds the Jamail Regents Chair at The University of Texas at Austin. He has given lectures or held seminars in over 25 universities on three continents.

In pursuit of greater intellectual co-operation and understanding between lawyers of different legal systems, Sir Basil has founded (in chronological order) the Institute of Anglo-American Law at the University of Leiden (1987), the Institute of European and Comparative Law at the University of Oxford (1995), the Institute of Global Law at University College London (2000), and the Institute of Transnational Law at the University of Texas at Austin (2000). His website of leading translated German and French legal materials is now housed at Texas.

As a scholar, Sir Basil has authored (or co-authored) over 30 legal books and over 120 articles. A Bencher at Gray's Inn since 1991, he also practises law from Essex Court Chambers, having been appointed Queen's Counsel in 1997. He specialises in tort litigation with an international element.

His scholarly work has been recognised internationally by his election as Fellow of the British Academy; a Foreign Fellow of the Accademia dei Lincei of Rome, the Royal Belgian Academy of Arts and Sciences in Brussels, and the Royal Netherlands Academy of Arts and Sciences in Amsterdam; and as Corresponding Member of the *Institut de France* (Académie des Sciences Morales et Politiques) and the Academy of Athens. He is also a Member of the American Law Institute. In 2005 he was knighted by HM the Queen for 'services to international legal relations' while, over the years, his work on European law and integration has received many high civic honours from the Presidents of France, Germany, Greece, and Italy.

Professor Jörg Fedtke was born in Tanzania, educated at schools in Zambia, the Philippines and Germany, and went on to study law and political science at the University of Hamburg in Germany. He was awarded a PhD *summa cum laude* for a ground-breaking analysis of constitutional legal transplants in South Africa. Entitled *Legal Transplants in Constitutional Law* and written largely at the Institute of Foreign and Comparative Law at the University of South Africa in Tshwane (then Pretoria), this project brought him in close contact with judges at the newly founded Constitutional Court of South Africa and academic experts involved in the drafting of the two South African Constitutions of 1993 and 1996.

Dr Fedtke joined the Institute for Foreign and International Private Law and Law of Procedure at the University of Hamburg in 2000, where he worked as a researcher and collaborator (with Professor Ulrich Magnus) for the Vienna-based European Group on Tort Law, which published its *Principles of European Tort Law* in April 2005. He is a Fellow of the European Centre of Tort and Insurance Law in Vienna and the German reporter at the Centre's annual conferences on developments in European tort law.

Dr Fedtke joined University College London in September 2001 as Clifford Chance/DAAD Lecturer in German Law. He was promoted to a Readership in 2004 and, in 2007, to the Chair for Comparative Law. He was Director of UCL's prestigious Institute of Global Law from 2001 to 2008. Dr Fedtke joins Tulane University as A N Yiauupoulos Professor in Comparative Law in January 2009.

Dr Fedtke was invited to act as an external adviser in the constitutional negotiations in Iraq and has in this context participated in conferences and workshops organised by the German Foreign Office and the United Nations on several occasions since 2005. He is also a Visiting Professor at the University of Texas at Austin since 2003, where he regularly teaches courses on comparative constitutional law and European Union law. Dr Fedtke, who specialises in both comparative public and private law, has written extensively in both areas. Most recently he co-edited and contributed to volumes on *Patterns of Federalism and Regionalism* (with Sir Basil, Hart Publishing) and *Human Rights and the Private Sphere* (with Dawn Oliver, Routledge-Cavendish).

CONTENTS

ABBREVIATIONS

A 2d	Atlantic Reporter (Second Series)
AC	Law Reports, Appeal Cases (House of Lords and Privy Council from 1891)
All ER	All England Law Reports
Amer J Comp L	American Journal of Comparative Law
AöR	Archiv des öffentlichen Rechts
BCLR	Butterworth's Constitutional Law Reports (South Africa)
BGB	Bürgerliches Gesetzbuch (German Civil Code)
BGBl	Bundesgesetzblatt (German Government Gazette)
BGH	Bundesgerichtshof (Germany's Federal/Supreme Court)
BGHSt	Entscheidungen des Bundesgerichtshofs in Strafsachen (Decisions of the German Supreme Court in criminal matters)
BGHZ	Entscheidungen des Bundesgerichtshofs in Zivilsachen (Decisions of the German Supreme Court in civil matters)
BR-Drucks	Bundesrats-Drucksache (printed matter of the German Bundesrat)
BT-Drucks	Bundestags-Drucksache (printed matter of the German Bundestag)
BVerfG	Bundesverfassungsgericht (Germany's Federal Constitutional Court)
BVerfGE	Entscheidungen des Bundesverfassungsgerichts (Decisions of the German Federal Constitutional Court)
BVerwGE	Entscheidungen des Bundesverwaltungsgerichts (Decisions of the German Federal Administrative Court)
Ca App	California Court of Appeal
California L Rev	California Law Review
Cambridge LJ	Cambridge Law Journal
Can Bar Rev	The Canadian Bar Review
Cardozo L Rev	Cardozo Law Review
CC	Constitutional Court (South Africa)
CE	Conseil d'Etat
Ch D	Law Reports, Chancery Division (1875–90)
Chi-Kent L Rev	Chicago-Kentucky Law Review
CISG	UN Convention on the International Sale of Goods
Civ Just Q	Civil Justice Quarterly
CLJ	Cambridge Law Journal
CLP	Current Legal Problems
Colum J Eur L	Columbia Journal of European Law
Columbia J Transnat'l L	Columbia Journal of Transnational Law

Colum L Rev	Columbia Law Review
Copyright Rev	Copyright Review
Cornell L Rev	Cornell Law Review
Denning LJ	Denning Law Journal
EGBGB	Einführungsgesetz zum BGB (introductory law to the BGB)
Fam L Q	Family Law Quarterly
FED App	Federal Appeal
F Supp	Federal Supplement
GRUR Int	Gewerblicher Rechtsschutz und Urheberrecht, Internationaler Teil
Harv L Rev	Harvard Law Review
Hastings Int'l & Comp L Rev	Hastings International and Comparative Law Review
Hastings L Journal	Hastings Law Journal
ICLQ	International and Comparative Law Quarterly
ILJ	Indiana Law Journal
Ill App	Illinois Court of Appeal
ILR	Iowa Law Review
JBl	Juristische Blätter
JCL	Journal of Comparative Legislation and International Law
JCP	Juris-Classeur Périodique (also referred to as SJ—La Semaine juridique)
J Legal Stud	Journal of Legal Studies
JSPTL	Journal of the Society of Public Teachers of Law
JZ	Juristenzeitung
KB	Law Reports, King's Bench
Law Com No	Law Commission Paper (number)
LG	Landgericht
LMCLQ	Lloyds Maritime and Commercial Law Quarterly
Lloyd's Rep	Lloyd's (List) Law Reports
LS	Legal Studies
LQR	Law Quarterly Review
Maryland L Rev	Maryland Law Review
MLR	Modern Law Review
NCL Rev	North Carolina Law Review
NE 2d	North Eastern Reporter (American law reports)
NJW	Neue Juristische Wochenschrift
NLJ	New Law Journal
New York University L Rev	New York University Law Review
Northw J Int L B	Northwestern Journal of International Law and Business
NW 2d	North Western Reporter (Second Series)
NYS 2d	New York Supplement (Second Series)
OGH	Oberster Gerichtshof (Austrian Supreme Court)
OLG	Oberlandesgericht (German Court of Appeal)
OJLS	Oxford Journal of Legal Studies
OUP	Oxford University Press
OVGE	Entscheidungen der Oberverwaltungsgerichte (Decisions of the German Administrative Courts of Appeal)

PL	Public Law
P 2d	Pacific Reporter (Second Series)
QB	Law Reports, Queen's Bench (1891–1900; 1952–)
RabelsZ	Rabels Zeitschrift für ausländisches und internationales Recht
RdA	Recht der Arbeit
Revue dr unif	Revue de droit uniforme
Rev int dr comp	Revue international de droit comparé
Rev trim dr civ	Revue trimestrielle de droit civil
Rev trim dr com	Revue trimestrielle de droit commerciale
RGZ	Entscheidungen des Reichsgerichts in Zivilsachen (Decisions of the German Imperial Court in civil matters)
RVO	Reichsversicherungsordnung (Imperial Insurance Act)
SAJHR	South African Journal on Human Rights
SJ	La Semaine juridique (also referred to as JCP—Juris-Classeur Périodique)
RLR	Restitution Law Review
SLT	Scots Law Times
Tul Eur & Civ L Forum	Tulane European and Civil Law Forum
Tulane L Rev	Tulane Law Review
UBCL Rev	University of British Columbia Law Review
UCL	University College London
UNIDROIT	L'Unification du droit
Va L Rev	Virginia Law Review
VersR	Versicherungsrecht
Wall St J	Wall Street Journal
WLR	Weekly Law Reports
Yale L Journ	Yale Law Journal
ZaöRV	Zeitschrift für ausländisches öffentliches Recht und Völkerrecht
ZEuP	Zeitschrift für Europäisches Privatrecht
ZfRV	Zeitschrift für Rechtsvergleichung, Internationales Privatrecht und Europarecht
ZGR	Zeitschrift für Unternehmens- und Gesellschaftsrecht
ZIP	Zeitschrift für Wirtschaftsrecht und Insolvenzpraxis

LIST OF TABLES

1

REFLECTIONS ON THE STATE OF COMPARATIVE LAW I: THE TWILIGHT OF THE HEROES

1. OF GHETTOS AND SMART NEIGHBOURHOODS

As one enters the final stretch of one's professional life as a law teacher one is tempted to ask, with a considerable measure of personal self-doubt, the question: what value have I added to my product (for which read 'subject') during the years that I ran the shop? For, as Montaigne rightly stressed,[1] '[I]t is a misfortune that wisdom forbids you to be satisfied with yourself and always sends you away dissatisfied and fearful'. The leading author asked himself that question when first entertaining the idea of writing a book on comparative law which was more than a monograph or textbook but also contained his personal experiences of writing and teaching this subject for so long. The need to re-examine this question has, in recent years, been keenly felt, especially in the light of new and multi-faceted material on the subject. For contemporary writing on comparative law reflects 'old' and 'new', 'conservative' and 'liberal', 'traditional' and 'trendy' ideas in such a mix of good and bad as to call for a critical and (so far as is humanly possible) objective assessment. It is difficult, of course, to attain the desired degree of objectivity in describing the above in a subject in which one has been so active for so long. For, inevitably, the describers, the older more than the younger one, carry with them their own intellectual baggage of views, opinions and biases. On the other hand, the leading author has now retired from some of his academic duties and thus feels like the famous Cretan writer Nikos Kazantzakis, who once expressed his feelings of intellectual liberation by writing: 'I fear nothing, I hope for nothing: I am free'.[2]

Contrary to a widely held view, not all academics strive for objectivity. Even fewer are prone to self-doubt. In his Francis Mann Lecture, Professor Peter Birks,[3] a keen and eloquent advocate of an enriched legal curriculum, had no doubts that one of our subjects—comparative law—remained 'in the ghetto'. Referring to the first of us, he added, this was despite 'all [his] energy'. Since one of Peter Birks' own subjects, Roman law, would appear to share the same fate—indeed, as we shall argue in this book, it may well be the prime example of a subject dying 'on its feet'—he would have known how it feels having to try to operate from an (apparently) disadvantaged neighbourhood. More importantly, however, if he was right in saying what he said about the state of affairs in 1997, one wonders how he would have described the neighbourhood of comparative law at the time the first of us embarked on his career in England four decades ago. Was comparative law then Chelsea?

[1] 'On the art of conversation' in *The Complete Essays*, translated and edited with an introduction and notes by MA Screech (1991), pp 1062 *f*.

[2] Epitaph on the tomb of Nikos Kazantzakis in Heraklion, Crete.

[3] 'The Academic and the Practitioner,' 18 [1998] Legal Studies 397 at 408.

Or was it always Brixton? And if it was in a better condition then than it is now, is he one (of many) who, having inhabited it for so long, contributed to the decline? Peter Birks did not suggest that; but we must ask the question. As the many theses expounded in this book develop, the reader may come to share our view that the Birks aphorism was a 'throwaway line', intended more for effect than to be taken seriously. For, if anything, comparative law is, at the time of writing, enjoying in Europe, the United States, and other countries such as South Africa, Israel and Canada an unprecedented attention by judges, legislators and academics, an attention which has resulted in a literature across the world which in terms of volume (if not always in terms of quality) is unmanageable by one author alone. But to appreciate the current renaissance, one must begin with the scene as Birks and the first of the present authors found it at the beginning of their university careers in the mid-1960s.

In many respects these years were, we think, a golden era inhabited by heroic figures.[4] André Tunc and René Rodière, both strong personalities,[5] held the relevant chairs in Paris with René David, his best years by now behind him, having retreated to Aix after *les événements* of 1968 had broken up his favourite faculty into fragments. Konrad Zweigert, Hans Stoll, Wolfgang Fikentscher and Werner Lorenz were among the main protagonists in Germany, while a generation of other distinguished colleagues such the elegant writer Hein Kötz, the atypical and inventive Bernhard Grossfeld, and the meticulous polymath Ulrich Drobnig were coming on stream. Gino Gorla, that finest of Italian minds and the embodiment of a 'cultured' man, was reigning undisputed in Italy, with Rodolfo Sacco closely at his heels. In Britain, Sir Otto Kahn-Freund was displaying his pulverising personality[6] to the Oxford Law Faculty, which—surprisingly, some might argue, given the Oxbridge dislike

[4] Most comparatists (especially the French) would probably reserve this title for the belle époque of the Congress of Paris of 1900 when the subject was launched in its present form and the scene was dominated by French figures such as Gény, Saleilles, Lambert and (a little later in the area of public law) Esmein. We would regard the work done in the 1920s and 1930s at the Kaiser Wilhelm Institute as work which is more relevant to our times and impressive in its detailed attempt to understand and describe foreign systems. No wonder, then, that many of the scholars who worked there later colonised a good number of European and American universities. Either way, to go back to this 'prehistoric' era in a book dealing with comparative law in our times would transform it into a history of comparative law. This is not what we think is needed nor what we wish to write about. Besides, it would be making the assumption that these indisputably great figures of 100 years ago are still known to modern audiences, and their work still used as building blocks towards constructing new ideas and exploring new directions which, we submit, is patently not true. Time, as Sophocles put it in Ajax, 'shrivels everything'—even grandeur.

[5] We stress their strong personalities for we will argue that academics, in their majority, are not bold or adventurous by nature. In addition, as their social status in society has declined over the years (the proliferation of universities and chairs being an important contributory factor), their abilities are so penned in by the restrictive environments they inhabit that it encourages them to release their energy in the form of personal antagonisms of the kind that once (apparently) led Dr Henry Kissinger to remark that 'academics are bitchy because the stakes [in the academic world] are so low'. Nowadays, therefore, those parts of the university world which are experiencing the greatest increase in influence are their so-called human resources departments. How 'human' or 'resourceful' their inhabitants are is, however, highly debatable. The above sketch, appropriate for England and, to some extent, the Continental European scene, is less accurate as far as the United States is concerned. For there, growing wealth, professorial involvement in real-life activities—for lawyers this often means acting as advisors of high-powered interests or people—and impressive facilities are rapidly giving that country's institutions of higher learning an incredible advantage over their European competitors. Their Achilles heel thus remains the race and political correctness issues which, as we explain below, are threatening the pursuit of excellence under the guise of equality or fairness. One must, finally, also note the paradox (and for a country which dislikes regulation so much it is a *huge* paradox) of growing administrative burdens and direct or indirect state interference, especially on matters of recruitment. This strikes us as increasing, in particular, at state universities where control of the university budget encourages growing interference.

[6] This expression and idea belong to Lord Annan (though expressed in a slightly different context); see 'The Victorian Intellectual Aristocracy' in JH Plumb (ed), *Studies in Social History: A Tribute to GM Trevelyan* (1955), ch 8.

(fear?) for *openly* forceful personalities—was not only putting up with it but also, apparently, liking it! The late Jack Hamson—a man endowed with a subtle (and mischievous) mind and a unique turn of phrase (alas rarely committed to paper)—having alerted his compatriots to the neglected advantages of French administrative law—was on the verge of passing on the baton to the mild-mannered and constantly self-doubting Kurt Lipstein, the last of the learned émigrés bequeathed to the Anglo-Saxon world by the Hitlerian madness. Last but by no means least, a young Tony Weir had just completed with Pierre Catala of the University of Paris one of the most stimulating pieces on foreign law and comparative methodology ever to be written.

At present, we say little of the scene across the Atlantic since we shall survey it later in greater detail. Though how can one ignore recalling that Max Rheinstein, in our view the civilian who most penetrated the common law mind, was still teaching at Chicago, while Rudi Schlesinger was captivating successive generations of law students at Cornell, having just completed his most unusual scholarly endeavour with a score of eminent or rising European luminaries. And then there were the formidable Jack Dawson and John Fleming—the latter, after some hiccups, having managed in 1960 to transfer to Berkeley the talent that has earned him such renown in the antipodes (and in Canada).

The first was a truly erudite comparative legal historian and restitution lawyer. Both he and Fleming did not suffer fools gladly—happily they lived before the era of political correctness, otherwise they would surely have landed in trouble. Both were polymaths but were mostly interested in the common law of obligations. But they also kept weaving into American law Germanic ideas with learning and effect surpassed, in our view, only by the more overt efforts of Karl Llewellyn and Roscoe Pound some 50 years earlier. It would thus be a mistake to regard Dawson and Fleming as purely 'national' lawyers though, as we shall note in Chapter Three, their work poses some problems of classification for the purposes of counting citations.[7]

The above list needs no amplification. In terms of *personalities* this was, indeed, a unique era; and the first of the authors of this book was privileged to have grown up in such an environment, to have met all the above, and (in varying ways) to have worked with most of them. Indeed, he has such vivid memories of this time that he fully sympathises with a statement made by Goethe to Johann Eckermann at the end of the former's long life.[8] For it reflects on the value of the German poet's *first-hand exposure* to important events and people, which subsequent generations will only attempt to understand through books.[9] The experience is simply not the same.

So whatever the value of Birks' ghetto theory for the mid-1990s, clearly it was inapplicable to the situation that existed in the mid-1960s. If decline followed (which it *did*) and still persists (which, we shall argue, it does *not*)—what brought it about? The search for reasons stems not only from a wish to test the veracity of a provocative statement, but from suspicions about some structural weakness of the university system which, in our view, contributed to the undoubted problems we shall discuss in the two opening Chapters. If some of these problems can be correctly identified and exposed, this enquiry may even hold lessons for the future. What follows, then, inevitably contains 'fragments of a great confession'.[10] However, a more

[7] A problem shared by their disciples/successors Professor Mary Ann Glendon (Harvard) and John Langbein (now Yale), both undoubtedly learned comparatists.

[8] And recorded in the latter's *Gespräche mit Goethe* on 25 February 1824.

[9] See the Insel Verlag edition (1992) at p 83.

[10] *Goethes Werke* (Hamburger Ausgabe), vol IX, 283.

empirical and doctrinal examination of the subject, its methodology, and its state of health, will come in the 10 Chapters that follow, where many sections of substantive law will be examined along with the kind of methodology which can help promote learning and professionally benefit from those who know how to use it.

2. DECLINE

Decline seems only mildly less damning than *decay*; and to claim that either occurred courts controversy. Serious dispute may erupt if one actually succeeds in identifying *and* naming the agents and causes of such decay. Yet this has to be done frankly if it is to be handled effectively. Let us therefore look at this possibility under a number of headings, bearing in mind that the ideas expounded under each cannot be strictly kept apart.

(a) The Absence of a Defining Treatise, an Inspiring Thesis, or a New Methodology

(i) France

Any account of textbooks, treatises, or influential monographs of that period must start with France and René David's *Les Grands Systèmes de droit contemporains*, even though it dates from an earlier time than that which we are taking as the starting point of our enquiry. The way this book came about reflects the personality of its author: larger than life, full of charm and *bonhomie*, but no less tough and ambitious.[11]

Yet, with all its originality, David's book suffered from a number of defects, some detectable when the work first appeared in print but all magnified with the passage of time. Here are five.

First, its attempt to divide systems into legal families, though original at the time, was and has remained fuzzy at the fringes. Though the taxonomy of the systems of the world continues to attract academic attention,[12] the work done on it can no longer be described as being on the cutting edge of modern comparative law, which is now fighting two main battles: will it survive the globalisation phenomenon (and, if so, in what form); and will it be taken over by the Critical Legal Studies movement (CLS) and, in our view, then lose its practical appeal?

Secondly, his groupings always struck us (and others) as defective, since they were entirely devised on the basis of *private* law and ignored the different arrangements that might result if *public* law had served as the yardstick.

Both these objections were, we think, valid even at the time when the book appeared.

[11] Our correspondence with Dr Nicolas David make it abundantly clear that not much love was lost between these two men though, by contrast, David and Sacco were linked by a close friendship. This lack of friendship seems to have been accompanied by a lack of appreciation of each other's work. The first is probably explicable in 'personality' terms if nothing else. The second, however, is difficult to explain but worth exploring further. For the 'psychology' of any artistic creator can always help understand his work better; and this psychological background invariably acquires a more prominent role when it comes to writers who try to understand, analyse and explain foreign cultures to their own people. Such a delicate task, however, is yet another addition to the list of things that comparatists of the future may have to do.

[12] See, eg, H Patrick Glenn, 'Comparative Legal Families and Comparative Legal Traditions' in Mathias Reimann and Reinhard Zimmermann (eds), *The Oxford Handbook of Comparative Law* (2006), pp 421 *ff.*

Thirdly, one must mention David's aims. Vis-a-vis the then Soviet bloc, for instance, they prompted ideas which had to be revised with subsequent editions. Towards the rest of the world, they hardly concealed his attempts to place French law in a pre-eminence that was neither easily acceptable to all nor likely to be proved correct with time. It could be said that both these undercurrents allowed his philosophical position as a citizen to cloud his judgment as a scholar. Yet that is not the reason why we offer this interpretation which, in any event, may be misguided. Rather, we wish to flag the concealed but no less real political thrust of his work since we think non-politicised comparative law loses some of its shine.[13] In any event, law and politics are rarely separable. Political aims were clearly discernable in Rabel's very influential work, and political motives are openly declared by those in the opposite camp, namely CLS protagonists (who repeatedly declare their leftist, anti-establishment, and anti-Eurocentric beliefs).

Fourthly, the classification of legal systems into more or less recognisable legal families can no longer easily accommodate a fascinating and (relatively) recent trend. This is the mutation of some systems which have deviated, or even departed, from their genealogical ancestors and moved, partially or more substantially, in the direction of 'rival systems'. Portugal and the Netherlands offer examples of systems which have moved away from their Roman and—later—French origins, and have either turned towards Germanic notions or created their own (mixed) systems, impregnated by Germanic concepts and the ideas found in German literature.[14] Others (like Canada in some areas, for example human rights—especially after the introduction of the Charter of 1985) moved away from the English model towards that found in the United States while remaining closely linked to 'paternal' ideas in areas such as the law of obligations. South Africa is yet another instance since its constitutional law (in may respects more novel and thus more fascinating to outsiders) has made extensive use of Germanic and other ideas, and not only concepts drawn from the American experience. These 'shifts' (sketched here but looked at in somewhat greater detail in subsequent Chapters) raise a series of fascinating questions—legal, methodological, and political—all of which attest to the revived vitality of comparative law.

Finally and most importantly, David's book treated comparative law at such a level of generalities that it slowly became downright unappealing to the more demanding requirements of practice-oriented law students while never being useful in the courtroom for the very same reason. These changes, some of which were discernible from the earliest days (discernible, one should add, especially to those more familiar with the Germanic approach to foreign law), have come more to the fore in the last one or two decades.

Yet none of the above criticisms or doubts were, by themselves, enough to shift attention away from the David method, and this is largely because for those who wish to teach a general course there was no other book available to serve as a teaching tool. Indeed, the book's

[13] We shall return to this theme in Chapter Twelve but here we also note that another great contemporary of David's, Jean Carbonnier, also saw in the growing internationalisation of the law a threat to French law. See *Droit civil. Introduction* (2002), pp 79 *ff.* The fear that internationalisation (or Europeanisation) might dilute the vitality and vibrancy of a great system has also been shared by English authors (and politicians) but it is not one found in the legal communities of the smaller European countries (such as the Netherlands, Belgium or Greece) which in this sense have stronger credentials in championing the cultural side of the European cause. The unique work of Olé Lando, a cosmopolitan Dane, offers a good illustration for this thesis.

[14] The view that the final product reflects mixed influences is, inter alia, put forward by Professor Ulrich Drobnig in 'Das neue niederländische bürgerliche Gesetzbuch aus vergleichender und deutscher Sicht', *Revuew européenne de droit privé* (1993), 171 (at 187). More generally see Ewoud Hondius, 'Les Bases Doctrinales du Nouveau Code Néerlandais' in Claude Ophèle and Philippe Rémy (eds), *Traditions savantes et codifications*, Colloque Poitiers of 8, 9, and 10 September 2005, pp 257 *ff.*

grip even strengthened for a while after Brierly produced in Canada in the mid-1980s an English version of the text. For 30 years before Birks made his 'ghetto' speech, English students (and more advanced lawyers) thus had little to consult in the shape of a textbook, let alone a treatise, that came from British pens—even though, as we noted, there was no shortage of great names.

So the book survived—too long for its own good. For however marvellous in the 1950s, the book and the 'method' for which it stood began to age rapidly by the 1980s. In the 1950s it filled a gap (as David rightly sensed, and wrote precisely in order to fill).[15] 30 or 40 years later it became an obstacle to new thinking, especially in France, as David's reputation was by then so unshakeable in his own country that few had the guts to rebel. For it is a phenomenon well observed and widely studied that great men cast a bright light and a long shadow that few who follow in their footsteps can avoid. Thus, even the formidable André Tunc, who was at the time we are talking about so skilfully laying the foundations of his great crusade on traffic accident law, ignored his own prescription when it came to teaching his general class on comparative law at Paris I. For whereas in his own research on specific topics Tunc made skilful use of detailed foreign and interdisciplinary information, in his main contacts with his students (which the first of us attended avidly in the early 1980s when working in Paris as visiting professor), he substantially followed the David method. And this, at least in so far as it was encapsulated in David's best-known work, was happy to present the 'great lines' of foreign laws and ascribe to the subject primarily a *mission civilisatrice.* This attitude also spread to the common law world, where the idea that the main purpose of comparative law as a university subject was its *mission civilisatrice* was, in the main, shared by Tony Jolowicz, Professor of Comparative Law at the University of Cambridge during the second half of the 1970s and the 1980s.

We subscribe to these views even after having read with great interest the long note sent to us by Dr Nicolas David alluded to in the Preface. This exceedingly interesting document, written with great moderation and style, makes a number of points which either tie in with the thesis of this book or call for some minor but necessary adjustments of our text in order to do better justice to David's work. From the letter we thus select the following three points to make public and, where necessary, to offer our own responses.

First, Dr David claims that in our account we failed to pay adequate attention to the 'time factor' (that is, to the conditions prevailing in France in the 1950s and 1960s). We were under the impression that we had done this, though we may have failed to do so sufficiently strongly and in a manner that revealed *the difficulties which René David must have faced in his time in getting his subject established.* This last point (put in italics) is a crucial one so we stress these adversities now, in particular the extremely poor linguistic abilities possessed at that time by French law students studying at the Sorbonne (and, a fortiori, one would suspect, in provincial French universities). However, to this observation we also add a rider in the form of a question to which we have no obvious answer: were these conditions different or worse from those which prevailed in Germany at the time (or during the Halcyon days of the Kaiser Wilhelm Institute)? To put it differently, is it only the French who were (are?) committed monoglots?

Secondly, Dr David claims that plunging students straight into cases, especially the Delphic decisions of the French Court of Cassation, without a proper introduction can lead them to 'drown'—that is, get lost in the mysteries and obscurities of a foreign system. Left at

[15] He tells the story himself in *Les Avatars d'un Comparatiste* (1982), p 144.

that, his point amounts to powerful and justified criticism of what we have tried to do in our professional careers. Yet, first, did René David's book(s) *really* explain to foreigners how French decisions should be read and understood or, alternatively, how English or American decisions should be handled? Secondly, and more importantly, we have never advocated reliance on cases alone. All we have suggested (in different fora and in different contexts and with a differing amount of detail) is that the careful selection of cases, dealing with factual configurations found in most legal systems, can provide an excellent *entry point* for the study of a foreign system by 'calming' the fears of a novice lawyer about the strangeness (real or apparent) of a foreign system. For beginning with cases which deal with familiar problems shows such novices that they are invariably similar across national borders, as are the answers analogous if not identical. It also shows that the real differences lie in different-sounding and different-meaning concepts, hence our preference for the *functional* rather than *conceptual* approach proposed by Rabel. Otherwise, our writing shows amply how, starting with litigated situations, we lead our readers progressively into the details of the system, the relationship of the compared rules of law with their wider political and economic environment, and other branches of the law in which one may at times find unexpected solutions to a problem. In short, our approach, as the Chapters that follow clearly show, does not separate the foreign legal rules from the wider context; it just 'eases' the novice comparatist into this material in a focused and systematic manner rather than giving him very broad statements conveying real or (not in David's case) pretended learning.

Thirdly, Dr David accepts a point made by us when quoting his father's preface to the 9th edition of his *Grands systèmes* where he admitted that his book 'had corresponded to a certain era' (now gone). Dr David emphasises this point by saying, for instance, that 'comparative law should enter into details as done in the Zweigert and Kötz book' (first published in Germany in 1971); that *Les Grands systèmes* was a work which his father considered as 'a work largely dated' (oeuvre dépassée au début des années 1980'); and that his father 'was a man who moved, not a man who was interested to see always the same ideas repeated' so that he would have understood (if not shared) the position we adopt here. We thus agree that subsequent editors of this classic book missed the opportunity to *change* rather than to *update* it. In fairness to them, however, one must add that changing a great book by a great predecessor must be a daunting task.

In summary, it would thus seem that René David wrote for his times, just as we are writing for ours—and that we must be right in trying to cater for different needs and stressing our disagreements with older approaches. Whether our own responses and proposals will endure for as long as David's did is quite another (and as yet undecided) matter; but his ideas and methods *did* hold centre stage for a long time, and that is why we placed him from the outset among our list of heroes.

(ii) The Germanic World

Enough has been said about the French attempts to further the study of foreign law through the publication of a major book. Though we shall return to other aspects of French law in Chapters Six, Seven and Eleven below, the time has now come to ask how, if at all, did the Germanic world fill the gap? Were they able to produce a book which dealt with the subject in a more concrete and idea-inspiring manner? More importantly, did they give us a *method* that could help us approach, understand and, ultimately, use the ideas of another legal system? As it happened, in 1970 they *did* produce not *one* but *two* books, though, in the end, only one was to capture the imagination of the common law world. Both, as we shall explain in the next Chapter, draw much of their inspiration and methodology from the earlier work of Ernst Rabel.

The first of these books was by Wolfgang Fikentscher, Professor at the University of Munich. Fikentscher, a man of great culture and style, gave his book a broad sweep, covering not only the Romanistic tradition and the common law but also religious systems. The chapters, some very long, discussed the work of especially important authors (such as Rudolf von Jhering) in Germanic detail, while others, revealing the author's wide learning, reviewed the American Realist School. But there was a problem: thoroughly Germanic, the work came in an epic size—five volumes. Notwithstanding its learning, the above-mentioned features proved its downfall on the international stage as attempts to have the work translated into English had failed by the mid-1970s. An important piece of comparative law scholarship was thus never made available to the non-German-speaking world.

This failure, however, opened up the way for the second work to 'make it'. Written by Konrad Zweigert and Hein Kötz (who joined in later), compact in size, and more easily readable in German and renderable into English, the book was lucky enough to fall into the hands of Tony Weir. The door to an international market was thus opened in 1977 and, indeed, it was further facilitated when 10 years later a new publisher took it over, priced it more moderately than the first had done, and even decided to merge its two volumes into one.[16] As far as the translation is concerned, John Fleming was right to describe Tony Weir as the Boswell of Zweigert and Kötz! We shall return to the methodological approach of the German school in Chapter Two.

(iii) England

In England, as indeed in France, comparative law was treated throughout the 1960s and 1970s as an ancillary subject and taught, if at all, with the help of two general works of modest size and ambitions. The first was by Amos and Walton and entitled *French Law*. The second was by the late Professor Cohn—a German, not an Englishman—entitled *Manual of German Law*. Both were good books, the latter in our view more perceptive than the former but too cursory to be of any real practical value, a disadvantage that was enhanced by the fact that both of these books began to show their age from about the mid-1970s onwards.

Neither of these works was really a fully blown work on comparative methodology, though they did give a moderately detailed account of foreign law as it stood at the time they were written. With the more demanding hindsight we now have of comparative law works, the truth is that both books were content to offer readable descriptions of the basic branches of two major foreign legal systems with more or less frequent cross-references to English law.[17] Indeed, on reflection, both these books—and the bulk of the periodical literature of the time—give the impression that the French terminology of *droit comparé* had prevailed over the more accurate German *Rechtsvergleichung*. For, in reality, these books (and most

[16] This book was blessed by happy coincidences. Oxford University Press was at the time not interested in publishing books about comparative law, so it would not have been taken over from its first publisher had it not been for Richard Hart (then law editor at OUP), who saw its potential for the European market and secured it for the Press. Hart was later to prove instrumental in getting van Gerven's *Ius commune* Series for his own publishing house (Hart Publishing) and turning it into an important feature of the modern comparative law library. The whole story again shows the importance of marketability, packaging, and (above all) the presence at the right time of charismatic personalities who see opportunities and seize them.

[17] One must not forget that Cohn's manual had started life as a longish pamphlet meant to assist the allied forces occupying defeated Germany after 1945.

of the articles of that period, as well as many which still appear nowadays) were not works on comparative methodology or even comparative law but contented themselves with describing the approach of a foreign system to a particular topic which happened to catch the author's attention. It would thus appear that comparative law was seen as a medium of providing elementary knowledge of a foreign legal system, and little more. This is more than a point of mere terminology. On the contrary, it reflects a conception that was destined to have a *continuing* effect on the way the subject is researched, taught, and used in this country. It may also explain in part its limited appeal.

The only truly English comparative textbook that one can mention from this period is Buckland and MacNair's *Roman Law and Common Law*. And it was no coincidence that its last edition was brought up to date by England's foremost comparatist—the late Harry Lawson. Common lawyers of that generation thus had no books on comparative law since even the ground-breaking *Einführung* of Zweigert and Kötz had not yet seen the light of day in its homeland. But Lawson cannot take all the credit for the excellence of this book since both Buckland and MacNair, though not primarily comparative lawyers, were possessed of a very broad legal culture. MacNair's comparative learning is thus very visible in his work *The Legal Effects of War*, which contained one of the best comparative accounts of the concept of frustration (or subsequent change of circumstances).

The inability or unwillingness to attempt a fully blown treatise or monograph on comparative law and methodology continued during the end of the 20th century and beyond. The preferred way of presenting foreign law thus remains through books usually subtitled 'Cases and Materials' (of which we think von Mehren and Gordley is the best) or compilations of large essay collections of which the fullest is *The Oxford Handbook of Comparative Law*, recently edited by Professors Reinhard Zimmermann and Mathias Reimann.

As a teaching tool the first type raises a number of concerns, the most important of which, in our view, are linked to the breadth of knowledge expected from those who use it as a teaching instrument. For without it being supplemented by notes and questions written by the expert, that is, widely read scholars, the true richness of the material (such as that found in the von Mehren and Gordley *Casebook*) will elude most of its readers. Its success or failure will thus largely depend on how those who use it as a tool will compose their cadenzas.

This is a conclusion we have reached about other casebooks as well; but in the area of comparative law it has made us agonise a great deal since the average student reading about foreign law comes to this vast topic with minimal preparation. How one should teach foreign law and how to attempt the comparison of systems is thus, in our view, a topic which has not been adequately addressed by Anglo-American comparatists. The answer to this key question is closely linked to another (equally un-answered and equally un-discussed): who are we primarily trying to interest and instruct—the student or the practitioner or the judge? Or all three (though in different ways and for different reasons)? The von Mehren/Gordley work provides one type of book which is primarily aimed at students. What other alternatives do we have for this audience? And what if we wish to reach and influence also the other targets mentioned a few lines above?

Teaching comparative law through a collection of essays seems another—the second—alternative adopted by lawyers targeting anglophone audiences. We shall soon explain why we are not convinced that this is the better (and certainly not the best) method. Still, it is beyond doubt that it is fashionable these days to produce large tomes which encompass within their covers collections of essays written about different systems or different aspects of the wider questions of comparative law. How does one understand a foreign system? Why do different societies tend to produce systems that cannot converge? How can deconstructionalism enter the study of comparative law? What is the role of sociology in such exercises? These essays, though written by different authors, may be linked by the desire to assemble around the editors like-minded writers, anxious to promote (more or less) the same kind of theme or approach to the study of foreign law. Paradoxically, this theme can sometimes be that it is not even worth trying to bring the systems closer together because their societies make such convergence impossible.

A variant of the above is to adopt a wider approach and to divide the voluminous collection of assembled essays under headings dealing with countries (for example, comparative law in France, Germany and England), purposes, aims, or techniques. These books *do* express belief in convergence, harmonisation, or (at the very least) enhanced understanding. Unfortunately, they also believe that in entrusting this task to 20 or 30 authors the advantages that flow from the use of multiple talents will outweigh the absence of thematic cohesion. The *Oxford Handbook* is probably the best example of this genre. Its aim is clearly to be as inclusive as possible of ideologies and approaches and thus (partly) to satisfy the desire of its editors to be as complete as one can afford to be, giving teachers using the book enough material for each to use whichever part of it best suits their own interests. As stated, this approach does *not* assist the internal cohesion of the book, nor guarantee contributions of equal merit; but it *can* satisfy the publisher's desire to try and reach as large a market as possible.

Both types of collections of essays suffer from the insurmountable problem that affects all books the contents of which come from different pens: the various parts are unequal in quality, some purely descriptive, others more thought-provoking, yet others rehashed versions of papers given elsewhere or essays which fly academic kites rather than attempt a definitive presentation of the author's view. Above all, however, such assembled pieces, unless subjected to severe editorial intervention, are rarely ideologically consistent with each other, and even more rarely do they have *a message* to convey—let alone one shared by all the authors. These ideological or political differences may not always be discernible to students but they are to the expert eye. As if these defects were not enough, such works suffer from another serious flaw: large though they are, the component pieces are rarely specific, focused, and detailed enough to be of any real use to the practitioner, judge, or lawmaker. One example is again the Zimmermann/Reimann magnum opus, which is largely a summary of widely known facts about, say, the story of comparative law in France. For someone who knows nothing about this topic, books of this kind may be of some interest; but for someone who needs reliable, specific information about a foreign system, this material is close to being of no use. Those who are interested in citology studies will thus confirm that the kind of works that are noted, cited, and used as inspiration are detailed, precise and practical (and not general, chatty and descriptive), and that a large part of the essays in these books do not meet these criteria. To say all of this in an age which dislikes meritocratic distinctions and believes in (unearned) equality of result may be unpopular; but we think our view contains a part at least of the truth, so it may be worth putting it in writing for others to consider and, if need be, reject *in a reasoned and specific manner.*

(b) The Human Factor

By this we mean the role performed by the 'high priests' of the subject during the period which interests us. This (as so often is the case with human endeavours of some significance) was shaped by their background, their education, and their training—in brief: their outlook and mentality. To these factors we owe their greatness; and to these we must also attribute their failings (at any rate those failings that have affected the growth of comparative law).

The fact is that in England during the years we are mainly studying there were some very learned comparatists.[18] They wrote with erudition and elegance of style. Their work, like the best of that period of English writing, was lean and muscular; and anyone who has tried to edit the texts of this period will soon discover how difficult it is to try and displace even one word in some very compact sentences. With such qualities, why did not their work train minds, create schools, and secure continuity of interest in what the greats had started *in the domain of comparative law*? Over the years, it increasingly became obvious to us that these great men fell into two categories; and that—probably unconsciously—both groups failed to address the questions of methodology and transferable techniques in using foreign law.

Incidentally, their learning and the extent of their influence on subsequent generations (disputed in some cases), has attracted our attention and led to the distinction we explore in Chapter Three, namely that between scholarship, reputation of scholarship, and legacy. This categorisation, which we feel has not hitherto been studied and applied to legal writings and legal activity in general (and comparative law in particular), is an important one. For it suggests that one can doubt or even challenge the 'impact' or 'influence' which a colleague's work has had on his own and subsequent generations *without* doubting the thoroughness or originality of his research. The statistical information given in the Chapters below thus reposes on this distinction; and colleagues dissatisfied with what the figures suggest about their own influence or legacy should not treat them as putting in doubt the scholarly merits of their work.

But let us return to these two groups.

The first generation of English comparatists[19] (with the notable exception of Harold Gutteridge, who was also a successful practising barrister) were academic purists. Many were linked to the dying scholarship of Roman law and remained unable and, we think it is fair to say, intellectually unwilling to shake it off completely and focus on its new incarnation: European law, modern French, German or Italian law, or comparative methodology. This applied also to Kurt Lipstein, who was one of the first to write a book on Community law and yet also remained fastened to the Roman law tradition in which he had grown up. In this sense one might even argue that though these colleagues were endowed with much

[18] Professor John W Cairns gives a fuller account of the 'Development of Comparative Law in England' in Mathias Reimann and Reinhard Zimmermann (eds), *The Oxford Handbook of Comparative Law* (2006), pp 131 *ff*. This piece is not only most readable but preserves details which are increasingly unavailable to most lawyers. On the 'minus' side, however, it is not the kind of work that either rectifies the omission of the 'greats' to leave us with a transferable methodology or gives us a prescription of its own. The same lack of guidance about how foreign law should be used in the contemporary world (especially by the courts) is found in the equally learned but descriptive essay 'Sources of Law and Legal Method in Comparative Law' by Professor Stefan Vogenauer, also included in *The Oxford Handbook* at pp 869 *ff*.

[19] 'First' may here appear somewhat misleading for there were many jurists—judges as well as practitioners—who showed a keen interest in foreign law during the 19th century. Here, however, we are focusing on the last four decades, which is for us the crucial period for understanding the state of comparative law in our times.

learning and many insights, they lacked the political vision to see where the interest in foreign law, which they had helped create, was leading.

Thus, the writings of the best of this (English) group—and here we unhesitantly include the late Harry Lawson and his masterpieces *The Rational Strength of English Law*[20] and *A Common Lawyer Looks at the Civil Law*—are classics that still repay reading as much for their pithy style as for the originality of their ideas (even though they constantly harp back to Roman law of the classical or mediaeval times). It thus came to pass that in England, the European country least connected with Roman law, the link between comparative law and Roman law (as well as legal history) was more than kept alive: it remained dominant. Dominant in the texts these scholars produced;[21] dominant in the share it claimed of their work; and—we submit: most unfortunately—dominant in the creation of an 'establishment' mentality that continued to control the subject well into the 1970s and treated Romanists almost as the only natural holders of chairs of comparative law.[22] Indeed, it is not just the blending of Roman and modern material, which nowadays seems less accessible or relevant, that is obvious from the writings of this era. One also gets from the writings of these authors the same impression found mostly in legal history: the author is mainly addressing a small circle of acolytes—academics of the purest kind. These scholars thus, obviously, believed that their scholarship—undoubted by the harshest of standards—would also attract others to study, teach, and then propagate further the subject. The statistics we give below cruelly show how misplaced this hope has been.

The clinging to Roman texts and legal history, though undoubtedly adding enviable erudition to their work, and in some instances explicable by reference to the authors' own personal history and training, did not, however, further the future of comparative law *in a rapidly changing world.* For one thing, much of classical Roman law (for example, the position of women, the status and powers of the paterfamilias, or slavery) has been turned on its head and largely become irrelevant to public law as much as private law. Other long references to Roman law add little (if anything) to the understanding of the common law, which has developed oblivious of parallel Roman ideas, and thus seems to creep into modern writings for some extraneous but not 'functional' reason.[23] Thus, in our view, such

[20] Hamlyn Lecture (1951).

[21] For instance in Lawson's *Negligence in the Civil Law* (1951) as well as his Cooley lectures entitled *A Common Lawyer Looks at the Civil Law* (1955).

[22] Of the 'British' comparatists of the second half of the 20th century, four thus began their academic lives as Romanists (Lawson, Lipstein, Honoré and Nicholas) and a further two (Rudden and Weir) taught Roman law for much of their academic careers. Gutteridge was primarily a commercial lawyer and John Bell came to the subject via philosophy. And matters did not stop there. The first of us recalls a senior colleague at the British Academy complaining that the election criteria where being 'diluted' since 'it was no longer considered necessary to be a Roman lawyer or maintain a strong interest in legal history before one was considered for membership'. The question of finding objective ways of electing the Academy's fellowship is currently one of the thorniest issues reviewed by Britain's most senior society for arts and humanities in an attempt (in our view well overdue) to ensure that (a) female colleagues of merit are properly represented and (b) colleagues from all of Britain's universities are fairly considered. The same is true of the Royal Society.

[23] How interesting and (more crucially) useful is it to explain, as Professor Vogenauer does, that all legal rules 'flow' or 'emerge' from a particular 'source'? Citing Pomponius and Cicero for such a statement (and for the idea behind it) will neither be understood by most readers (if cited, as it is, in Latin) nor retained in their memory. Nor, finally, will it be used in any professional or social context, for it is meaningless to have a citation for such a proposition. Paraphrasing Professor John Merryman in 'The Italian Style III: Interpretation' (1996) 18 *Stanford LR* 583 (at 585), it would seem that inserting such citations 'demonstrably' serve[s] no purpose but 'persist because they are firmly rooted in the culture'. For further examples see Stefan Vogenauer, 'Sources of Law and Legal Method' in Reinhard Zimmermann and Mathias Reimann (eds), *The Oxford Handbook of Comparative Law* (2006) at pp 869, 883 or 887.

exercises only helped distance their authors and their ideas slowly but steadily from the real world of practice which, particularly in the common law world, is the bloodline of survival and regeneration. As comparative law (and later European Community law) de facto pushed Roman law aside, the surviving Romanists began to whine and actively promote the members of their dwindling group, but to no avail.[24]

Our law is thus increasingly public law in its character, regulation-oriented in its structure and ambit, concerned with the manifold problems arising from the power of the modern press, information technology, patents and copyrights, and deeply affected by social security and modern insurance practices (not to mention the fact that in almost all its branches it is exposed to international pressures and influences). Add to these some contemporary challenges such as the globalisation of the financial markets and the needs of modern, multinational law firms, and we think it is easy to understand why the study of the legal past is likely to become less relevant and less prevalent in the future.

In the midst of this romanistic vogue just described, one exception stands out in the English Pantheon. This exception is Kahn-Freund, an equal (we think) of Lawson in intellectual terms, who also managed to create a school and leave a methodology for approaching foreign law—a tradition to see law in its wider sociological context and a most practical (even if not always prevalent) view of making use of foreign practices in the field of labour law. Moreover, and this is little known in England, he remained influential as a writer in his country of origin, thus being the only 'English' comparatist who played successfully on both tableaux. He was, however, *not* a Roman lawyer but first and foremost a legal sociologist and labour lawyer. The statistical information given in Chapter Three confirms his broad and enduring influence. He was, in short, a scholar who also left a legacy (both in terms of methodology and students) unmatched by the others.

In this Chapter we must thus focus on the effect the academic predilection for Roman law had on the scholarship of so many authors, especially in its comparative dimensions. This can best be done by looking at this topic under three sub-headings: (i) the continued utility of studying Roman law; (ii) how its continued study harmed both its high priests and their work; and (iii) the more modern attempts to salvage parts of Roman law.

(i) The Continued Utility of Studying Roman Law

In England, unlike Italy or Germany, Roman law has not been a major ingredient in the development of local law. Law here is original, and forms a distinct legal family precisely because of the fact that its growth has been, as so many other English institutions, autochthonous. This is not to deny that during certain periods of its history and in certain areas of its law there has been no influence of Roman law. But the argument that you cannot understand English law without understanding Roman law has never had many adherents (notwithstanding the fact that there were a number of significant Germanophiles among the 19th century English and American jurists). So what have been the original

[24] See, eg, the bitter comments made by Lord Rodger of Earlsferry in *The John Maurice Kelly Memorial Lecture* 'Savigny in the Strand' published by University College Dublin in 1995, especially pp 23 *f.* The same attitude can be found in Italy, an understandable bastion of Roman law. On this see Monateri, 'Critique et Différence: Le Droit Comparé en Italie', *Rev intern dr comp* 1999, 989 (at 996). Interestingly enough, Jhering, one of the greatest Romanists of the 19th century, thought that the loss of Roman law was a blessing in disguise as it opened up a new way towards universality via the medium of comparative law; see *Geist des römischen Rechts auf den verschiedenen Stufen seiner Entwicklung* I (7th edn 1924) at p 15.

arguments in favour of according to Roman law the semi-protected status of an obligatory subject which it has enjoyed for so long? Three deserve special scrutiny, for though we have heard them uttered repeatedly they appear (to an objective observer at least) increasingly contrived and unconvincing.

First, *Roman law gives our students a summary view of another system early on in their studies, allowing them to gain both awareness that problems are capable of different answers and also a global view of a legal system as their learning of English law progresses in a fragmented manner from branch to branch.* A study of one of the major modern European legal systems—French or German—can, in our view, achieve the same result. Moreover, *and this is more than can be said of Roman law*, it can act as a good stepping stone towards a greater familiarity with that system before our students go abroad—as more and more of them do—to enhance their knowledge of that (living) legal system and, generally, widen their experiences in law. This need is growing given the inflow of European ideas into English law via the case law of Luxembourg and Strasbourg. We say nothing about the possible counter-argument that one does not prevent the other, for we all know how over-burdened the modern law curriculum is, with more and more subjects claiming a protected status. If something has to go, Roman law seems to be a very good candidate.

Secondly, *understanding modern institutions and concepts can, at times, be facilitated by knowledge of the past.* As already stated, this has been particularly true of the German Code—especially in its early days, given its strong Roman antecedents. But it is less convincing in England, notwithstanding the fact that legal historians of great repute (such as Professors Helmholz and Zimmermann) have, at times, tried to establish a Roman law influence on the earlier developments of English law or on certain topics linked, for instance, to ecclesiastical or maritime law. But no one even remotely aware of modern English case law and practice or, indeed, of student or practitioners' literature, will ever be convinced that either students or practitioners are today likely to seek enlightenment in the texts of past times or empires defunct for millennia. It is arguing otherwise that helps perpetuate the phrase 'living in ivory towers' as a sign not just of luxury, but also of being 'out of touch with reality'. Besides, some of the greatest problems now occupying our courts (dealing with, say, matters of intellectual property, human rights, in vitro fertilisation, Community case law, or media law) were—mischievous ingenuity apart—unknown to the Romans. More often than not, their answers lie in modern textual analysis and considerations of policy, and to pretend otherwise would simply amount to wasting the time of the court on flights of antiquarianism. If some argue that seeking guidance from the contemporary practices of the supreme courts of, say, South Africa, Germany, the United States, Canada or Israel is a waste of time and money, what should be said of the time spent on trying to reconstruct a text from the Digest, probably corrupted by the work of many subsequent lawyers?

Lord Rodger's invocation of Roman law in his judgment in *Fairchild*[25] could be seen as an illustration of this rearguard action. But leaving apart the question how many of those who have read this judgment retain anything but the faintest memory of his use of Roman law, it is, we submit, extremely unlikely that anyone will make use of it in the future. For how does it help a modern practitioner to be told that the problem they are asked to solve 'had begun to exercise the minds of the Roman jurists not later than the first century BC?'

[25] *Fairchild v Glenhaven Funeral Services Ltd* [2002] 3 WLR 89, §§ 156 *ff.*

'Imagine that!' may be the politest answer one may get in a real setting. This is gratuitous antiquarianism. Much more important, by contrast, is the citation given by Lord Rodger to the *Motive* of the German Bürgerliches Gesetzbuch and the cases decided under § 830 BGB, which he not only used but went to the trouble to reproduce both in the original German and in a translated form. This material is focused; it comes from factual configurations which are recognisable by English judges and is thus usable; it shows that a particular solution works; it finally shows how policy rather than the strict application of concepts or notions is more likely to give a better result to the problem at hand. Thus both Lord Rodger and, before him, Lord Bingham showed how much more fruitful it is to look at the German casuistry, richer, more fact-sensitive, more likely to serve as the starting point of inspiration, and untouched by the kind of problems that affect Roman law (for example, missing texts, interpolations, or the impact of time on an old rule).[26]

Of course, however powerful these arguments may be to most contemporary lawyers, one should not allow oneself to be deluded into believing that because we advance the above-mentioned rational arguments, those who do not wish to be convinced about the new realities will ever accept to face them. The defenders of the old faith will thus not only seek comfort in Professor Zimmermann's pronouncements; they will also redouble their efforts to produce more illustrations to support their thesis.

(ii) How the Continued Study of Roman Law has Harmed both its High Priests and their Work

Roman lawyers, sometimes like comparatists who have not learnt the art of adapting the way they treat their own subject, resemble Pirandellian characters in search not of a writer but an audience. For what they write may be (a) abstrusely scholarly, of interest only to a minute section of the academic population, or (b) it may be contrived to bring into their treatment Roman law but ends up doing this in a most artificial manner. Lord Rodger's article 'Objections and Exceptions: The Palingenesia of D. 43.24.17'[27] or his more recent 'A Very Good Reason for Buying a Slave Woman?'[28] are examples of the first genre. A textual analysis bearing all the hallmarks of the scholarship of its author, manifesting his knowledge of the subject which, for a second generation now, he is continuing from where his late father—also a scholar of Roman law—left it. Yet the unanswered question is: 'Does anyone read these pieces since, it would appear, hardly anyone cites them?' If the answer is, as we suspect it may well be, *very few*, then why do the editors of these journals publish them? Is it because of the eminence of the author or is it because they wish to project the journals as covering 'all parts of the law'—including branches which are nowadays of interest only to a tiny minority of readers?

An illustration of the second can be found in the late Peter Birks' Kelly Memorial Lecture, which set out to examine *Hubris and Harassment* in comparative juxtaposition. At first sight, the attempt is admirable since it not only pays tribute to a great Irish lawyer who contributed both to Roman law and to contemporary Irish legal developments but also satisfied Birks' own interests in old and modern law. Birks' text embodied this belief. *Hubris* (Latin) and *Harassment* (English) appeared in the title; and an account of Roman law took up about one third of the entire, adapted, written version of his speech; the remainder was

[26] Lord Rodger alludes to them himself in § 160 of his judgment.
[27] 64 [2005] CLJ 79.
[28] 123 (2007) LQR 447.

on 'un-reconstructed' (as he put it) common law. Yet the question remains: did this attempt, laudable in theory, work in practice? Or did it merely reveal Birks' learning? We submit the answer to the first question is 'no' and to the second 'yes'—but then both of these answers were known from the outset.

The futility of the Birks enterprise is enhanced by the fact that Roman law did not influence the development of the common law nor the recent English Act. Roman law was not cited in any of the cases Birks discussed. Birks himself gave no link between the two in his conclusion, though there exist some interspersed sentences, suggesting here and there superiority in the Roman law thinking. We also doubt that the idea of punitive damages, which Birks finds in Roman law and approves of heartily, is likely to make a comeback in our law. But most important of all, however, is another point which Birks himself stresses in his lecture: the common law managed to reach the same position *on its own*. So why was so much space really given to an account of the position taken by Roman law, given that it had no direct impact on the topic under discussion, nor is likely to have any in the future? Views on this may, of course, differ. But ours is that Birks' learned account of Roman law was an attempt to keep Roman law in the front of our minds while also being an elegant historiographical tribute to a great jurist who had once taught Birks.

Our criticism of this piece does, however, not end there. For one critical development was also passed over in the article: the *reality* that John Kelly's Chair of Roman law and Jurisprudence now exists in Dublin as a Chair of Jurisprudence—pure and simple. To us that provides the concluding argument most succinctly: notwithstanding the honoured man's contribution, and the learned pupil's tribute, the subject—Roman law—no longer justifies an independent chair!

Fierce supporter as he was of the need to keep up the study of Roman law, Birks himself would have never accepted such an analysis. Yet it is arguable that indirectly he felt that this decline was unstoppable and hence devoted most of his own writings to modern law and not Roman law. More importantly, the citation rates received for his work clearly show that the ones which were read, or at least cited (and, dare one argue from there, left the greatest impact), were the works on *restitution*. Birks, in other words, will, when the dust settles, be remembered as a modern lawyer and *not* as a Roman lawyer. This point must be driven home clearly—and how better to do it than through figures, numbers, and statistics which make our point strongly arguable.

Thus Birks' work—as is already well known—covered modern law (mainly restitution and legal education) and Roman law. A survey of five of England's leading law journals (*Cambridge Law Journal, Law Quarterly Review, Modern Law Review, Oxford Journal of Legal Science* and *Legal Studies*) during the period 1980–2000 revealed a total of 143 academic citations. Birks' citation record increased during the last years of his life, no doubt reflecting the growth of his standing. Thus, for the years 2001, 2002, 2003 and 2004 one gleans 163 citations from the same journals plus one in the *International and Comparative Law Journal* (that is, from a slightly broader base). Finally, a search of the Westlaw JLR database 2001–2005, covering the vast bulk of American law journals plus some foreign journals (thus creating a possible small area of overlap), shows a total of 352 citations during these five years.

What is remarkable from these *extensive* figures, incomplete though they are insofar as they do not include *all* legal (and *historical*) journals worldwide, is the ratio of citation they show for modern versus Roman law writings. Thus, for the first period we note that out of a total of 143 citations received, 136 were to his modern writings and seven were to his

Roman law pieces.[29] For the second period surveyed (2001–2004 inclusive) the figures for the citations gleaned from the seven major journals already mentioned suggest that 156 were to his modern law works while seven were to Roman law writings. The citations made to his Roman law materials seems higher, at any rate if one adopts a more *generous* interpretation of what should count as a 'Roman law' article and what should count as a 'modern law' essay. If one does that, Birks receives 307 citations for his work on modern law and up to 45 citations for works solely or predominantly looking at Roman law. This means that 12.5 per cent of these references are to Roman law instead of just under 5 per cent.[30]

One must complete these rough calculations with two caveats in the hope that they will assist the reader to interpret the authors' methodological errors in evaluating these figures in a way most favourable to Birks.

First, these numbers do not reflect Roman law material or ideas found in Birks' overtly modern law works; nor do they reveal the influence that Roman law had on the formation of his legal mind. Yet they *do* show unequivocally that the bulk of his writing was on modern law or modern legal themes. Whether this is because Roman law held out less fascination for him than modern law (despite his protestations) or whether this was due to the realisation that restitution was really the subject that could help make his name and career is a matter of speculation. The reader can decide this for himself.

The Birks figures are duplicated in the citation record of other Romanists. Professor Tony Honoré, for instance, who between 1980 and 2000 received 89 citations in the five major English law journals reviewed in this survey, had 39 citations to his (co-authored) book on *Causation in the Law* and only a single citation to his purely Roman law monograph *Studies in the Roman Law of Sales* published in 1959. The preference for his 'modern' work remained unabated in the statistics for the years 2001–2005 (inclusive). Thus, for this period he received a total of 39 citations, all for modern tort or jurisprudential works, and only one citation to his monograph on *Tribonian.*

Of course, these figures must be qualified carefully in order to become truly meaningful. His causation book, for instance, makes use of foreign law; and, no doubt, many of its ideas contained in it can be traced back to the considerable German learning on this subject. Yet this uniquely learned book is cited mainly as a *modern* tort monograph dealing with troublesome issues of causation, and can thus not be treated as representing either a comparative, and even less Roman law, resource.

The citation of his Roman law material also suggests that it has left 'indifferent' the readers of the leading general law journals, though one might object that these figures do not include references found in articles published in specialised history journals. This, undoubtedly, is an argument that must be given due weight when evaluating the overall impact of Honoré's scholarship on the legal profession. For a search of historical journals might alter the overall picture. Yet, our figures (notwithstanding this *possible* limitation)

[29] This does not take into account the fact that his modern writings would, occasionally, have references to Roman law texts or literature. Nor was any attempt made to qualify how numerous these references were so as to justify describing the piece as hybrid (modern/roman). Our overall impression is that for most of the citations no such claim can be made.

[30] The almost total irrelevance of Roman law to judges and practitioners can be seen from the fact that none of Birks' Roman law writings are cited in court decisions. Thus, for the UK, the Westlaw UK-RPTS-All database for the years 2001–2005 reveals 31 citations, all to his works on modern law. For the United States the Westlaw ALL-CASES database citations suggests a total of five citations for the years 2001–2005 of which four were to 'Unjust Enrichment and Wrongful Enrichment', 79 *Tex L Rev* 1767 (2001), and one to *Justinian's Institutes* (1987). These figures, incidentally, also suggest a considerable difference in appeal on the basis of geographical distribution.

also support our thesis, namely that non-contemporary works receive little (if any) attention from the bulk of lawyers. So, if one were forced to formulate a judgment about Honoré's impact on law and other colleagues, judicial as well as academic, it would have to be that this has mainly been through his work on causation (in England) and his very learned treatise on the South African law of trusts. This, of course, in no way diminishes the standing of a quite remarkably widely read and productive scholar; but it does confirm our pessimistic prognosis of the 'pulling power' that Roman law has in our times. The figures in fact suggest that it is close to zero.

Such speculation may provoke counter-arguments and encourage a different interpretation. We would welcome such a development. That is what scholarship is all about: debate and exchange of views. And that is what we wish to stimulate (provided the replies are as specifically formulated as are our own assertions and not limited to generalisations). But what we suggest above surely is prima facie plausible. To the extent that it is also correct, it would reinforce the strength of the *suggestions* made earlier on, namely that (a) work on Roman law is appealing to an ever-*decreasing* circle of people; (b) that Birks and others in his position, while vocal supporters of Roman law, realised the above and, in practice (and notwithstanding the rhetoric), focused their writing efforts on modern law since this gave them the greatest satisfaction, or exposure, or both; and, finally, (c) the continued association of comparative law (a subject of growing importance) with Roman law (a subject experiencing the slow death suggested by the above figures) is harmful to the former because of the decreasing appeal of the latter to modern audiences. It is this last point which most concerns us in this book, and not the decline of Roman law.

(iii) Modern Attempts to Salvage Parts of Roman Law

The harm thus (unwillingly) done to comparative law by linking it to Roman law is minimised (though not eliminated) wherever a shift along the lines of Zimmermann's work has been attempted. For here the emphasis is on the influence that history (including Roman law) has had on the development of the modern codal structures by providing the foundations of a common European legal culture. The argument has thus been of a seductive simplicity: to understand what we have now, we must understand what we had yesterday—in short, how the past evolved into the present. This shift of emphasis is shrewd and it is executed in the erudite manner which one would expect from Zimmerman and the growing number of disciples he is placing in so many universities. It is also helped by the fact that the tenacity with which Zimmermann is pursuing this agenda, though as admirable and determined as that of Birks, is much less confrontational in style.

Thus, fairly recently, Zimmermann, in his desire to show the continued relevance of legal history for modern law, has also argued how post-codification (early 20th century) judicial decisions in Germany continued to make use of the Romanist work of the 19th century. Though we admire (for the reasons given) the attempted shift, we do not find his thesis surprising since a clean break in 1900 onwards with the (immediate) past was neither desired nor possible. Radbruch, after all, called the BGB 'more cadence of the nineteenth century than the upbeat of the twentieth'.[31] But we also feel that the continuity which he so stresses is, in fact, exaggerated, since we do not believe that this kind of argument will hold any sway as the 21st century gets going and we move further and further away from the Roman origins and controversies of the 19th. To put it differently, the continued influence of Roman

[31] Cited by Zweigert and Kötz, *An Introduction to Comparative Law* (3rd edn 1998), p 148.

law on the Reichsgericht of the early 1900s was inevitable. Equally inevitable, however, is the fact that the new and major influence on Germany's supreme courts is not going to be Roman law but European law in all its shapes and forms.

The recent codal reforms in Germany must strengthen the trend we predict. And despite Zimmermann's very latest eloquent attempt to argue that French law, as well,[32] is indebted to Roman law (and without it can never really be understood properly), this suggests (to us at least) that he is writing as if in an ivory tower and not conversing daily with contemporary French practitioners of private law (let alone other modern areas of French law completely unrelated to Roman law) where the search for answers lies in the modern treatises. If these take any notice of foreign law, it is almost exclusively that of Luxembourg and Strasbourg, and it is certainly not Roman law. And to this we add a minor but interesting postscript. Relying on Dr David's letter (discussed earlier on) we repeat his assertion that, in his view, Roman law played a minimal influence in France even in the days when he was a law student in Paris.

More importantly (to return to Germany), contemporary German private law is, in our view, steadily moving away from the individualistic principles of the Code and towards a spirit of consumerism and socialisation of risks which makes the divorce with the past even more pronounced and inevitable. If correct, this assessment will, in our view, convince more to study this (private) law in conjunction with contemporary German constitutional law, European Union law, and economic theory, than try to keep it tied to legal history. In any event, this latest work of Zimmermann carries, again, little force with English students and English law.

So, whatever the value of such an approach in Germany, where the link with Roman law was, at a certain time in the history of this country, undoubted and strong, we do not believe that in the end these efforts will succeed in England. Indeed, one might be bolder and dare to suggest that they may even be doomed in Zimmermann's own country despite his Germanic ability to produce disciples who then find positions in law faculties.

The reasons for such a bold prediction are not just the practical and financial ones that form a recurring theme of this book, and which academic purists simply cannot wish away. The reasons are also intellectual, among which we include the undoubted decline of Latin as a subject studied at school or 'demanded' at law faculties these days—the current (German) and very conservative Pope being one of the 'rare' examples of individuals who think otherwise. Additionally, whatever the influence of Roman law on the German Civil Code of 1900 or the (earlier) French Code of 1804, the fact is that the Roman texts were never asked to address a plethora of issues which nowadays have come to occupy a central role in the legal curriculum.

We shall return to this theme. Suffice it to say here that the overall view must be getting clearer to all but the most short-sighted. The beginning of the 21st century is very different to that of the 20th. The nature and extent of the changes—globalisation of markets; new technologies; the importance of insurance and social security; the emergence of the consumer as a litigating party (and the effect this has had on traditional contract law); press regulation and freedom of expression—represent a marked departure from the past. Indeed, not just *marked* but so *radical* as to make the invocation of German jurisprudence at the turn of the last century as an example of continuity and of what can go on happening in the future appear weak and unconvincing. The changes we are thus experiencing increasingly

[32] 'Römisches Recht und europäische Kultur', 2007 JZ 1 *ff.*

make the linking with the Roman past as meaningful as referring a modern nuclear scientist to Democritus as the father of the atom theory. The Delphic pronouncement given to the Byzantine Emperor Julian enquiring about his attempts to restore the old pagan order (cited at the outset of this Chapter) contains the message that Romanists cannot bring themselves to accept. But it is no less true for being unpalatable.

(iv) Other English Reasons for the Decline of Comparative Law

We already noted that one of the reasons for the (temporary) decline of comparative law in England was the lack of an enduring methodology as well as the lack of schools of thought telling us why and how we should be using foreign law. Why was there no urge to encourage the creation of schools of thought in England? We are, of course, thinking of comparative law, though parts of what we say may be of wider import. Whatever the reason, it seems undeniable that few of those of us who, at the time of writing, profess an interest in comparative law can be treated as intellectual heirs to Gutteridge, Hamson, Lipstein, Lawson, Honoré, Nicholas or Rudden. We make this point in all honesty and despite considerable admiration for much of the work of these learned colleagues. For judging from ourselves we cannot say how much we owe to them in *methodological* terms, even though we have undoubtedly benefited from their learning, their company, and the invaluable support which many of them gave to the leading author of this book.

On the other hand, if we have incurred 'literary debts' (as the Germans so aptly call them), we feel that they are towards the Germans, especially to Rabel and his Zweigert and Kötz progenies, as well as Werner Lorenz. And these debts are as much for what these scholars said as for the way they put what they thought in writing. This does not mean, of course, that the Rabel school does not have its less developed parts or even weaknesses. We shall mention a few in the next Chapter, and say how we tried to cope with them ourselves.

Declarations of intellectual indebtedness serve no wider purpose save to satisfy the personal need of retrospection and reminiscence to which older people are more prone, so we shall say no more on this subject. But speculating why the 'greats' (especially those who operated in England) did not ensure that their subject and the approach flourished after their passing or retirement *may* reveal something that goes beyond what was said about their work, their mentality, or outlook—something interesting about the wider English academic scene that has to be considered, even if the thoughts here expressed will not, once again, please everyone.

Noel Annan, in the last book published just before his death and entitled *The Dons*, allows many useful clues on this subject to drift on the surface of his oceanic but elegant name-dropping. For in the world he describes, apart from such gigantic personalities as John Henry Newman, Benjamin Jowett, Lord Rutherford, and Isaiah Berlin, one finds the core of the Oxbridge don. His sketches of many of the Oxbridge greats reveal invariable homosexuality, prevalent loneliness (especially at the end of their lives), and wit only barely less developed than egos—all topped up by a heavy dose of dilettantism and cynicism.

We are emphatically *not* saying *nor* implying that these were features shared by the great British comparatists who figure prominently in this work. What we *are* saying, however, is that this was the prevalent mentality in the environment in which they operated and which the first of us experienced during his years as a Cambridge and Oxford don (even though he came at the tail end of this epoch). And what he noticed—since it stood out so clearly from the different world across the Channel—was a cynical, self-conscious superiority that often stemmed from personal insecurities and invariably led to loneliness. One writes with concrete examples in mind, not figments of the imagination (though names, of course, are best left to the imagination of the readers since each will easily have his own candidates that slot into these categories).

In scholarly terms the mentality and characters we are referring to, and the overall environment (much more prevalent, we think, in arts rather than in sciences), tolerated the above. In one's experience, but also from reading autobiographical works such as Annan's, this rarefied environment far-too-frequently resulted in unhappy lives being led in the loneliness of private College rooms once the last glass of port had been consumed in Hall and the post-prandial mirth had subsided.

More importantly, it led to a serious deficit in written work. This last point is really quite striking if one considers some Oxbridge law chair-holders between, say, 1920 and 1970. For, if one looks at the record, one cannot help but notice that some of the dons who obtained chairs in the 1950s or 1960s would have never have come remotely close to holding chairs in any respectable Continental European university while the claims of other, worthier colleagues, were left unsatisfied.[33] But the Oxbridge preference for the teacher rather than the writing scholar, for wit rather than the disciplined and sombre polymath, for the effervescent quip rather than the premeditated but almost inevitably dull response, had, on the whole, a deleterious effect on scholarship.[34] And to this day it has not entirely been removed. By this we do *not* mean that it is still possible to get a chair in a leading university on the basis of an (unpublished) fellowship dissertation, as was the case with the late Patrick Duff, Regius Professor of Law at the University of Cambridge, who was reputed for his brilliance and the grip he once held over the politics of his College.[35] What we *are* referring to is the deliberate killing of the writing ethos—at least until the Research Assessment Exercises shook the foundations of the lethargic existence of the English don. We suspect things were different for scientists, especially those who worked in labs and were forced, as it were, to a greater interchange of ideas.

Still more opposed to the creation of a writing ethos and the idea of scholarly continuity has been the exploitative teaching imposed by the Oxbridge 'system' on young colleagues. This, again, is linked to the preference of teaching over writing and research. And it has blighted the career of many a young don because it resulted in (and at times even cynically encouraged) writing sterility. The years in Cambridge and Oxford have still left the first of us aghast at the way the system can destroy young talent. For it subjects brilliant youngsters to impossible teaching and committee demands (often to discuss matters such as fund raising, for which they are totally unsuited).

The amateur and the anti-federalist (by which we mean the College-centred don) thus combine to make the English university less efficient than its American counterpart, which is regarded in the Oxbridge the first of us got to know fairly well with a mixture of envy and disdain. The one-to-one teaching is an amazing experience; but it also has its drawbacks beyond the obvious one: cost. And one which one should regret particularly is the fact that

[33] Which, of course, is not to say that academic careers on the Continent are not subject to their own hazards and influenced by equally capricious factors.

[34] It is thus difficult to imagine a German sharing (even as a joke) Cecily's view of Dr Chasuble as 'a most learned man. He has never written a single book, so you can imagine how much he knows' (Act II, *The Importance of Being Earnest*).

[35] Though appointments through patronage, even with growing consultations that the democratic age has fostered, still lack transparency and have not always carried conviction, especially when ever-decreasing clans desperately promote their own to selected posts.

one can sail through Oxford without ever having sat at the feet of Patrick Atiyah, Roy Goode, Ronnie Dworkin, or Gunter Treitel but, instead, having received training by brilliant (in many cases) but (invariably) inexperienced youngsters. The English university system is only in appearances less hierarchical than the German or the Italian. But what it gains in appearances it loses in the kind of duties and responsibilities that the senior/junior relationship can impose on the former.

All of this is very different to the environment that Rabel created at his institute, where the search for talent was exceeded only by the effort to bring it out by, among other things, facilitating the interchange of ideas and cultivating an *esprit de corps* that those who tasted kept alive even when they were scattered in the four corners of the world. Coupled with this was the constant encouragement to commit research to paper, first in the form of a short note, later, perhaps, as an article, and then by means of longer pieces which would earn the candidate his higher doctoral degree and *venia docendi.*

How good this was—not just for the science of comparative law but also for those who were trained there—can be noted simply by mentioning randomly the names of Ernst von Caemmerer, Wolfgang Kegel, Friedrich Kessler, Max Rheinstein and so many more in so many other countries in the world. And before this is dismissed as a Germanic phenomenon—using the term in a pejorative way—let us recall that the same compliment could be paid to Rodolfo Sacco and, to a lesser extent, Mauro Cappelletti. For though their cliquish attitudes have not left many eyebrows unraised in their native country, the fact is that both these colleagues have done more to establish their subject in Italy than our greats did in England. This environment still lives on in Germany.

The current English fad to create centres and institutes in every law faculty should in no way be compared with the German prototype, which is a veritable hothouse of ideas and co-operation (and sometimes also rivalries), and not the 'phantom centre' which one encounters in the modern English academic world where 'centres' and 'institutes' (most of them without funds, real structure, or internal cohesion) are springing up like spring flowers—attractive to begin with but doomed to a short life. English academics have much catching up to do if they wish to be serious about the centres or institutes they create or claim to run.

Finally, mention must be made, we think, of the absence in England of the *prolonged*[36] partnership between the older and experienced scholar and the young novice, which is fostered in Germany by the doctorate and then the gruelling *Habilitation* process, both nurtured in that uniquely German environment of *das Institut* (the same is true of Italy, less so in France). Thus, the long and systematic imparting of knowledge and the gradual shaping of the mind (through example as much as instruction and advice) has been deliberately sacrificed in England to the altar of dazzling wit, attraction to paradox, brief university studies, and the idea that any hierarchical relationship is necessarily exploitative in nature and must thus be avoided.

[36] We stress *prolonged* because in the two universities where the tutorial still exists in its traditional form, namely as a one-to-one/two/three teaching session, a bond of sorts *does* emerge between teacher (especially those who are charismatic in character and/or take their tutorial tasks seriously) and pupil. But it is different in intensity and duration than the one built up, say, in Germany between doctoral father and student or *Habilitant*; and it is the latter which leads to what we have called 'schools' of thought. This relationship can, of course, be exploited by some teachers who rely on their PhD students to do an enormous amount of primary research and delegate to them much secondary teaching and examining. One must on the other hand stress that this relationship also gives rise to reciprocal obligations, which in Germany, Italy and Greece (less so in France) impose a moral obligation on the teacher eventually to place his student in as good a 'first' chair as possible.

But that is only one side of the coin; and there is, of course, another. Max Perutz, the distinguished Austrian-born molecular biologist who, because of his Jewish background, found himself exiled in that country, thus wrote in later life that:

> creativity in science, as in the arts, cannot be organised. It arises spontaneously from individual talent. Well-run laboratories can foster it, but hierarchical organisation, inflexible bureaucratic rules, and mountains of futile paperwork can kill it. Discoveries cannot be planned: they pop up like Puck, in unexpected corners.[37]

This seems to argue *against* what we just said. To some extent it does, proving that this is a debatable issue. But Perutz's sentences are also carefully crafted. They contain caveats which suggest that both approaches towards academic regeneration can be dangerous if their key features are taken to extremes. The extreme opposite of Perutz's hierarchically structured laboratory can be College insularity (leaving everyone to do their own thing), which Oxford even more than Cambridge tolerates (especially in the arts subjects). Those who have experienced it first hand know that it can encourage administrative paralysis, and also lead to the kind of extreme form of dilettantism which one found in the late Warden of All Souls, Charles Sparrow.[38] The latter feature is more relevant to the theme of this book than the former. For to oppress a younger colleague (as can happen in Germany) is just as much a crime as it is a sin to allow (as in the case of Oxbridge) a talented one to frit away his intelligence and end his life lonely (if not abandoned), with the shadow of his past intelligence as the only memory.

The final verdict thus calls for a *careful balance.* No comparatist, especially no one who has experienced both the English and Continental approach as a student and as a teacher, can thus condemn outright either model. Instead, he must try to understand both, weigh their respective strengths and weaknesses, and devise a mixture of his own that combines the best features of both systems.[39] But the English model—and this is our conclusion—has not favoured comparative law. For, at the end of the day, the brevity of the teaching relationship in the English law faculty, its emphasis on the tutorial rather than the writing of a dissertation, and its being conducted in an atmosphere of *apparent* equality, have not been conducive to the creation of schools of thoughts, of intellectual heirs or, even, a planned continuity of ideas or inventions. The absence of assistantships, an institution fiercely criticised by English purists conscious of its occasional abuses in Germany, has also come at a price. For on the Continent this academic relationship fostered, at its best, a complex set of mutual duties and obligations—social as well as intellectual—which, in the end, worked well for the younger colleague whose career was thus promoted. And it also worked well for the older man, whose ideas continued to be refined, improved, or altered, but rarely died with retirement.

All in all, therefore, in England and America, the chances of the substance and glitter of the golden age surviving the death of the last émigrés were not good. As we shall note further down, what is bringing the subject out of decline is politics *not* geniuses; practical needs *not* academic hothouses; private enterprise *not* government-structured education; business-related law *not* philosophy (not to mention the gold at the end of the American

[37] Taken from his Obituary in *The Times* (2002).

[38] Subject of a sad essay by Lord Annan in *The Dons* (1999).

[39] See B Markesinis, 'Tutorial and Repetitorium: Parallel and Different techniques of teaching Law in England and Germany' in Basil Markesinis (ed), *The British Contribution to the Europe of the Twenty-First century. The British Academy Centenary Lectures* (2002), pp 63 *ff.*

rainbow, which is triggering off westwards a new—and this time voluntary—immigration of young talent).[40]

(c) The Comparatists in Germany and the United States

By contrast to the British comparatists, their German counterparts did not display the same weakness towards Roman law (even though the average German lawyer knows much more about Roman law than his English or American counterpart).[41] For they made this switch from Roman law to modern law in droves, especially after the end of the First World War; and the Max Planck Institute in Hamburg (founded in 1926, effectively as the successor of the Kaiser Wilhelm Institute in Berlin) gave them a welcoming home. An unprecedented flourish of comparative activity took place in the mid-1920s and early 1930s, interrupted only by the advent of the Hitlerian storm which pushed so many of these scholars to England and, more so, the United States. Their sufferings and tribulations thus proved beneficial for the study of foreign law in America; and it was not until the mid-1950s and later that Germany began to regain its old glory in this branch of the law.

The role and influence in the developing science of comparative law in Germany is too important to deal with summarily in the introduction so we shall examine the German scene in a chapter of its own and see what impact it had on the various legislative agencies of the state. It is interesting, however, to note that the same tendencies found in the work of German comparatists can also be seen in the work and approach of their American counterparts—the indigenous (who are nowadays gaining the upper hand) as well as the central European émigrés who dominated the American scene in the 1950s, 1960s, and a large part of the 1970s.

Obviously, there is something not easily identifiable in the United States which led these émigré scholars, though mostly trained in Roman law, to put their talents to a more local and practical use, and employ their learning of foreign law either in the context of private international law or (more so these days) to public law (especially human rights law), as well as the problems associated with judicial review. Our guess is that one important reason for this is the conception of the American law school as a graduate school for professional preparation and, in this context, there appeared to be little or no room for a purely intellectual pre-occupation with the past, except in the older and richer schools which were subject to European influences for a longer period of time. Little that resembles this 'shift' can be found in England, which may, conversely, be partly due to the fact that the cloistered Oxbridge environment in which many of these escaping scholars found refuge did not put them under the kind of pressures which they had to respond to in America if they wished to survive.

Across the Atlantic the picture was thus different from that found in England, German émigrés propagating their subject differently than they did in the old world. Roman law has thus survived, in an ever-enfeebled state, in the history faculties, most indigenous comparatists referring to it (if at all) as a sentimental relic. For present purposes, the account in the United States must thus start with Rudy Schlesinger.

[40] For a glimpse into the very different (but not necessarily worse) Italian world see Grossi, *Scienza giuridica italian. Un profilo storico 1860–1959* (2000).

[41] The same may be true of Italian colleagues but much less so of the French, in whose life Roman law has for some time now played a decreasing role.

Schlesinger shared Rabel's interest in the 'real world'. This was a most fortunate predilection given that he had been forced, because of his Jewish background, to settle in the 'New World' which favoured the channelling of his knowledge in a practical way. The professional nature of the American law curriculum did not in those days (and in our view *still* does not) tolerate easily philosophising or generalities in its courses. Schlesinger thus perceptively gave his subject his own, *practical* twist. His book, though entitled *Comparative Law*,[42] is really and in the main devoted to foreign law as pleaded and used in American courts and is not a 'theoretical' or 'philosophical' work on comparative law nor a fully fledged thesis on comparative methodology in general. These attributes made *Comparative Law* the only textbook cum casebook of its kind. They also enabled its charismatic author to draw the crowds into the classroom in a way that no other comparative law teacher in the United States (or, come to that, in England) has since managed to achieve.

Yet the book's strength was also its weakness. The impact which the book has thus had in England—and the European Continent more generally[43]—has been much smaller than the influence it exerted on its home turf; and as one moved further eastwards into the Continent of Europe its relevance became minuscule. The statistics given below attest to this.

The same, we think, can also be said of Schlesinger's other undoubtedly great venture, his *Formation of Contracts: A Study of The Common Core of Legal Systems*,[44] though here one must adopt a more nuanced approach. Once again the idea to assemble a distinguished team of foreign lawyers to discuss common factual situations in a way that would bring out the common threads that ran through the various legal systems was brilliantly conceived and meticulously executed. But though it was rightly praised for its many innovations, its basic premise—a fact-oriented analysis—appears much more original to Europeans than it does to common lawyers who are accustomed to their law being presented to them through decisions dealing with narrow factual situations.

Other, 'lesser' objections were levelled against it at the time, mainly by some (French) reviewers. But by far its greatest weakness was, in our view, the fact that, though it produced some immensely useful information (gathered by its carefully drafted and fact-oriented questionnaire), the project never tested its main premises beyond the easiest part of contract law—offer and acceptance. According to Professor Werner Lorenz (who took part in the exercise), it deliberately avoided grappling with some of the doctrinally nightmarish issues such as consideration, reliance, mistake, and breach, which have really separated common and civil law of contract.

But the Schlesinger project *did* have one visible effect on Europeans, which in much later years (and thanks to an intricate network of personal links) bore some fruits. For, devised at Cornell and in an American fact-oriented environment, it has led others to study foreign systems by setting them in comparable factual settings and then examining them in logical juxtaposition. This novelty is thus visible in the so-called Trento Project, which has been animated by some able former pupils of Rodolfo Sacco and borrows largely on the Schlesinger approach since key protagonists also happened to have had links with Schlesinger. The fact-oriented approach also seems to have had some bearing on the

[42] Now in its 6th edition by Hans Baade, Peter Herzog and Edward Wise.

[43] Though later, Schlesinger seems to have acquired a following among some contemporary Italian academics. Thus see U Mattei, 'The Comparative Jurisprudence of Schlesinger and Sacco: A Study on Legal Influence' in Annelise Riles (ed), *Rethinking the Masters of Comparative law* (2001), pp 238 *ff.*

[44] Two vols (1968).

structure of the more systematic and voluminous work sponsored, edited, or co-authored by the eminent Viennese comparatist Helmut Koziol, which has also tried to discover the solutions given by various European legal systems to a fairly large number of typical factual situations.

Both of these works search for the principles of (mainly tort) law common to the whole of modern Europe; and they are united in the mistrust, shared by many others (including ourselves) of the so-called 'von Bar attempts to draw up draft European codes' that may one day be 'imposed from above' on European citizens by the fiat of the European Commission. These appear to many as unattractive Germanic structures, incompatible with the pragmatic and casuistic common law way of thinking, while they are also unpopular with a sizeable section of the French legal community, which sees them as a rather crude attempt at European harmonisation, undertaken by academics who often have little to do with the real world of legal practice, politics, insurance, and other areas which need to be consulted when reforms of this magnitude are being contemplated.

In their desire to avoid these pitfalls but to discover the principles common to Europe's contemporary law, the Trento and Koziol projects thus admirably provide a broad and useful substratum of factual information. Admirable also is their (successful) attempt to bring together at regular intervals European specialists to discuss the topic under review. But such major undertakings, a clear sign that the slowly progressing idea of European integration has generated a huge amount of activity in the area of foreign law and comparative methodology, obviously also have their weaker points.

Thus, like most collective works written by many different authors, the contributions are unequal in terms of language and academic quality. More importantly for the purposes of this work, they are unlikely to serve as teaching tools in the classroom (as opposed to the smaller and ever-improving books in the Ius commune casebook series driven by Walter van Gerven). How useful they may thus prove in the courtroom remains to be seen; but their visible neglect to try and explain the differences and, above all, to answer the question how one can use foreign solutions with a reasonable degree of confidence by transplanting them into a different system, has yet to make them a useful tool for judicial law builders. Thus, though this kind of work obviously displays the learning of most of its participating authors, the statistical information we provide below supports the contention that they have yet to make their mark on judges (even though in the fullness of time they may prove useful sources of information to potential transnational legislators).

Next to Schlesinger, Fleming was another German émigré with a penchant for comparative law and the linguistic ability to satisfy it. Though he was widely respected by the American comparatist world during his time at Berkeley and, indeed, was for that reason asked to act for many years as the editor of *The American Journal of Comparative Law*, he, too, failed to leave a magnum opus in comparative law. Such traces as we thus have of the kind of methodology he favoured derives from articles and even very short case notes. All of them, however, suggest that he favoured comparison at the level of *functional specificity*, distrusted sweeping statements, felt Roman law had become an encumbrance to modern comparative law, and invariably drew most of his ideas from German law. Thus, despite his formidable knowledge of different legal systems, which he weaved (often imperceptibly) into his tort book and the incisive case notes he wrote for the *Law Quarterly Review* towards the end of his life, his excursus into foreign law were brief and not connected to any central theme. His name will thus endure mainly through his quite unique textbook and the impressions which he made through his learning and jovial character on his many friends.

His textbook—unlikely (if it *is* kept alive) to retain the signs of his unique learning, personality, and outspokenness—thus constantly blended the solutions and ideas of at least three major common law systems (the Australian, the American, and the English) *and in that sense was a masterpiece of comparative law in practice* but gave (understandably) no clues on comparative methodology. What brought this (often) disparate material together was Fleming's command of detail that could be displayed to full effect by his pithy language. The comparatist, however, who is looking to learn from the master just gets the finished product and no instructions as to how to get there himself. For these reasons, a Fleming legacy in the area of comparative law is unlikely to remain alive for long.

Methodologically speaking, the greatest praise must thus go to Max Rheinstein and his mentor Ernest Rabel, who bequeathed both to European and American comparative lawyers the most workable method to date—and this notwithstanding the fact that with the passage of time and, particularly, the consitutionalisation of private law, many even prima facie sympathetic readers have come to express doubts about his approach to the subject. Yet for us Rabel still stands out as a giant of the subject—as the indisputable creator of an enduring methodology. More about his work and method will be said in the next Chapter. Here, however, one must stress one of the important characteristics which make him stand out from those who shaped comparative law in England. For though Rabel started out as a pupil of the great Austrian Romanist Ludwig Mitteis (to whom he remained indebted for the discipline and methodological precision which he instilled in him[45] from 1916 onwards, when he moved to Munich and took over the direction of their Institute for Foreign and International Law[46]) he shifted his attention to modern law. While never disclaiming the intellectual rigour of Roman law and acknowledging the role it has played in his own formation, Rabel (unlike his British counterparts) thus consciously chose (mostly) not to link his comparative studies to history or philosophy but to the interests and needs of the practitioners of his time; and he saw to it that his disciples did the same. This change had, in fact, been predicted earlier by another famous (but adaptable) Roman lawyer, Rudolf Jhering, who has famously called for a shift of emphasis from Roman law to the real life problems beyond Roman law.[47] This was a world that he got to know and admire since he, himself, was to act as a judge, as an arbitrator, and as a consultant of big business and which, later in his life, he was to reinforce as a result of studying the common law.[48] Though one finds hints in his work suggesting an interest in theory and philosophy (and legal history when it helps put a living rule in its proper context), on the whole these themes take second place in Rabel's work. Instead, the man becomes pre-occupied by the task of focusing on (relatively) narrow topics and, in pursuit of his wider political agenda, presenting them in a way that might be useful to practitioners of all kinds. To do this, he pioneered another break with German tradition: he set aside language and concepts and tried instead to focus on the function the rules under consideration were meant to achieve. It is thus a great misfortune that his work never really became widely accessible to the English common law world (which, by definition, shares with him an interest in specifics and a dislike in theorising). Indeed, we often wonder what would the state of comparative law have been in England had Rabel chosen to migrate there and created, rather than on the other side of the Atlantic, the generation of disciples that were to give his German work its common law facet? On further

[45] 'In der Schule von Ludwig Mitteis', 7–8 *Juristic Papyrology* 157 (1954) at 159.
[46] With Max Rheinstein employed as assistant librarian!
[47] *Geist des römischen Rechts auf den verschiedenen Stufen seiner Entwicklung I* (3rd edn 1873), p 14.
[48] 'Deutsches und Amerikanisches Recht', 16 *Rabels Zeitschrift* 340 (1951).

reflection, and judging from the shabby way the Oxford establishment of the late 1940s and early 1950s treated another great German émigré (Martin Wolf), Rabel may have been wise to choose America.[49]

(d) The Practitioner Comparatist: An Untapped Gold Mine

We have already noted that the first major British figure in comparative law—Harold Gutteridge—was not only the first holder of a chair of comparative law at an English university; he was also a successful commercial silk. But during the chronological period we are discussing in this book, there was another cohort of lawyers with strong comparative credentials but who were mainly devoted to the world of practice even though they also wrote works containing an element of foreign law.

This second group of the golden era were primary émigré practitioners and only part-time academics (though no less admirable or learned for that). This group comprised those who practised foreign law in the international field and who made skilful use of the foreign expertise in their daily work, taking full advantage of their linguistic abilities and their indomitable energies. We include here men like Ernst Stiefel in New York[50] and Francis Mann and Clive Schmithoff in London. Of the English group, the former became more recognised than the latter, in part perhaps because he chose to (over-) emphasise his newly founded 'Englishness' and remained exceptionally severe towards his German background—something which must have appealed to some of his hosts.[51] But this group confined the use of their knowledge of foreign law to writing specialised legal pieces mainly connected with the law they practised,[52] and failed to show their contemporaries and their successors *how* to interest the English in their foreign learning. The way they exploited their Janus-type personalities was thus left to be described anecdotally by those who worked with

[49] Fritz Pringsheim, who had fought bravely for Germany on both the Eastern and Western fronts during the First World War, also found himself an exile in Oxford because of his Jewish background. Thanks to the exertions of his former pupil Harry Lawson, Merton gave him some meagre assistance; but otherwise he was essentially ignored (indeed even interned after an amusing incident) and was thus eager to return to Freiburg the moment fighting ended. Albert Ehrenzweig was another of the émigrés who fared badly in England and found no recognition until he moved to the United States. John Fleming's services to the common law were not rewarded by this country until the British Academy made him a Corresponding Fellow towards the very end of his life. Trinity, where he spent a year in the 1980s as Arthur Goodhart Professor, could for technical reasons not even bring itself to give him a Visiting Fellowship, and simply described him as a Visiting Fellow Commoner.

[50] Stiefel is not known in England and is probably now forgotten in the United States, where he lived about half of his long and quite remarkable life. Its beginnings were inauspicious, even sad. For his Jewish origins forced him to flee Germany in the mid-1930s and begin a peregrinating life in France and England, picking up legal qualifications before settling in America. But after the War he became a member of various commissions charged with the economic reconstruction of Germany, and was able to give many valuable services to the country that had earlier forced him to flee its borders. This earned Stiefel the gratitude of important representatives of the German industry, laid the foundations of a successful practice in New York and Germany, and earned him a high decoration from the German State just a year before his death. Stiefel's writings were largely in the area of comparative procedure.

[51] Emigrés who pandered to English tastes and illusions of grandeur have, invariably, done better in their new country than those who remained faithful to their cultural heritage. In her celebrated *Britons Forging the Nation 1707–1837* (1992), Professor Lynda Colley offers the examples of Händel and Canaletto who, as a result, became 'national institutions'. Francis Mann neither pandered nor did he become a 'national institution'. But his oft-proclaimed preference of English over German law strengthened further his appeal among certain sections of the English legal establishment.

[52] Though both Mann and Schmitthoff produced some excellent books and many articles which also appeared in collections of essays. Mann's 'The Legal Aspect of Money' is the work that clinched his fame as a practitioner with impeccable academic credentials.

them, and benefited or (often) suffered as a result of their quirks and (abundant) energy, rather than be studied through texts that made their expertise and their insights transferable to others.

The inability of the British greats to leave a methodology that could clearly be identified with one of them was not their only failure. Both groups failed to leave successors to continue their tradition even though the academics supervised scores of DPhil students. Their scholarship, in short, did not translate into an enduring legacy. There was thus no Sacco,[53] Cappelletti,[54] Schlesinger or Rheinstein[55] among the above. Kahn-Freund is (in our view) the only exception; but then he was not at all English. His strong Germanic accent, like that of another influential émigré, Sir Leon Radzinowicz (who also left a legacy by creating the Cambridge Institute of Criminology), reminded everyone of that—if any reminding was ever needed! Unlike some of their kind—Jack Hamson, Kurt Lipstein and Francis Mann, for example—these two jurists did not even try to blend into their new environment. Their self-confidence ensured their individuality and, ultimately, sealed their success.

In this sense the British 'greats' differed, as a group, to what happened consciously in Berlin at the Kaiser Wilhelm Institute and (from the mid 1920s) in its successor in Hamburg and in most other research institutes in Germany (for example, Frankfurt, Heidelberg or Munich). To be sure, Rabel's shaping comparative law into a science (and inculcating the special mentality it needs into the minds of young scholars) was to some extent dictated by his political agenda to make German industry competitive again in the midst of the Weimar depression. No such agenda existed, of course, in England (though, as we noted, something not dissimilar had crossed David's mind since he was always anxious to promote, through law, French influence abroad). But in England even talk about promoting political agendas through cultural means was seen as an unacademic (even vulgar) exercise. Yet such statements must be taken with a pinch of salt, for empire building is not a dream that many British academics have not had. The real reasons for the omission we refer to are much wider; and they go to the Oxbridge ethos as it was shaped during the golden era of these two centres of learning, namely between the two Wars and until about the end of the 1950s.

3. NOT LEAVING A WORKING METHOD

The 1960s, as pointed out at the beginning of this Chapter, were populated by charismatic comparatists; and yet they left us with no workable directions how to produce the kind of goods they did.

[53] Sacco's ability to multiply the chairs of comparative law in Italy and help place on them protégés such as Professors Bussani, Gambaro, Mattei, and Monateri is a matter of both admiration (mainly abroad) and criticism (in his own country). That said, one must also note that his judgment was often excellent.

[54] His followers included Professors De Vitta, Trocker, Varano, Vigoritti and (in the United States) Merryman. Pizzorusso, originally a scholar within the gravitational force of the late Professor Mortati and later a judge, was also for a time with the Cappelletti empire.

[55] Rheinstein largely influenced the work and careers of such learned colleagues as Mary Ann Glendon and John Langbein. David's method of perpetuating his approach was more ingenious. For early in his career, he persuaded the French Ministry of Education to make the teaching of comparative law compulsory and then set about writing what, in effect, has remained the main textbook since. See his own account in *Les Avatars d'un Comparatiste* (1982), p 144.

Are we alone in complaining that whatever the value of their writing, the works of these masters are thin on leaving us a comparative methodology and telling us whom to target, how to present foreign law to home audiences, and how to put it to practical use? Professor John C. Reitz recently gave the answer we have been mulling over for a very long time—*no.* In fact he put it more elegantly when he wrote:

> Most of us who teach and write in the field of comparative law [. . .] were not taught formally how to do comparative law. Rather, we have for the most part worked out our own methods based on an amalgam of the scholarship we thought effective for our particular purposes at that time.[56]

Earlier, Sacco, a leading Italian comparatist, had come up with a similar (negative) conclusion—if only to claim that he had provided the missing link himself. Referring to the generation of David, Schlesinger, and Gorla, he made essentially the same point as Reitz when he described (one suspects with a touch of false modesty) his own contribution to comparative scholarship as being similar to the 'act [of a] notary that [. . .] puts things [thought of by the previous generation] in writing, using some neologism when necessary'. Sacco then concluded as follows:[57]

> I have been forced to do so because the three masters who taught me what I know curiously, indeed, very curiously, have forgotten to spell out at the end of their works the formulas that allowed them to reach the magical results of their researches. They never seemed to have noticed the work of restating their methodology that I have done.

Sacco's point about David, Schlesinger, and Gorla, and of the relationship of his own work to theirs, strikes us as ambivalently phrased. If there is an implication in the above statement that none of his masters really devised a transferable methodology, we think he may be correct. And if we are wrong to read such an implication, we think he also is wrong not to make it. More importantly, such an accusatory implication applies with greater force to the English greats—Lawson, Honoré, Nicholas, Rudden, Hamson, and Lispstein. Our express extension of Sacco's view to the English school, with which the Italian comparatist (not an English speaker) never seemed to have much affinity, would probably please him. For it makes his contribution through his theory of *legal formants*[58] even more important (even if one allows for some influence from Schlesinger's work on *Formation of Contracts*).

But if Sacco was right in claiming that his 'heroes' left no prescription as to how to do comparative law, he was wrong not to mention Rabel in his list of 'masters'. On reflection, the omission is not surprising given how different these two men must have been. But whatever the reason for omitting Rabel, the failure to bequeath a methodology for comparative law is not an accusation that can be placed at his doorstep. For Rabel *did* leave a method with which some contemporary comparatists have sought to find faults but which, nonetheless, may well be the one that has dominated serious comparative work ever since it was devised in the 1920s and 1930s. It is thus more plausible to suggest that Sacco's greater intellectual affinity with David, explicable on a variety of grounds including their shared use of the French language, almost dictated the omission of the German who was so bent on

[56] 'How to do Comparative Law', 46 *Am J Comp L* 617–18 (1998). The view seems to be shared by Mattei and Reimann, 'Introduction' (Symposium on New Directions in Comparative Law), 46 *Am J Comp L* 597 (1998).

[57] *Che cos'e'il diritto comparato* (1992), p 285—cited and translated by U Mattei in 'The Comparative Jurisprudence of Schlesinger and Sacco: A Study in Legal Influence' in Annelise Riles (ed), *Rethinking the Masters of Comparative Law* (2001), p 250.

[58] Developed in many Italian works and available to English speakers as 'Legal Formants: A Dynamic Approach to Comparative Law', 39 *Am J Comp L*, 1 *ff* and 343 *ff* (1991).

detail and particularism, and seemed to abhor philosophising. We do not see these last two features as prominent characteristics of Sacco's approach; nor is the latter's tendency to invent neologisms something which, we suspect, would have appealed to the German (or, more accurately, Austrian) genius.

But as we stated earlier on, England can boast one exception: Kahn-Freund.

In comparative law terms the book of his that breaks the (English) mould just described are his Hamlyn Lectures published under the title *Labour and the Law*. The work had all that is needed to become an immediate success. It was small and readable; and instantly got onto the reading list of every labour law teacher. It came at the right time, namely when labour unrest was to become a particularly strong feature of English life and was to remain so until the end of round one of the Thatcher anti-labour reaction of the first half of the 1980s. It was a book with a theme and, what is more, a theme that was relevant to English society at the time that it appeared. Intellectually, the book innovated by bringing sociological (especially German) thinking into English law in general and labour law in particular; but it did so in a way that recognised that law (and not sociology) had to be at the core or, at any rate, the starting point of the enquiry. For Kahn-Freund (like Rabel) was in many ways shaped by the Germany of Weimar and drew heavily on the sociological writings of the time as well as the post-War German industrial and labour scene, which had taken such a different (and less confrontational) path to the English.

In both these senses, the practical and the theoretical, the book and his other writings thus set a trend: it started a way of looking at labour law which was German in many ways but could also work in England. To be sure, some of his ideas are now dated (though some might wonder whether parts might become fashionable again). The approach, for those who still follow it, has also been modified, fine-tuned here and there. But he left a school and left a method and left people who are still willing to swear by his name. It is easy, indeed imperative, to say of him that he taught a succession of scholars who were interested in foreign law. Extending such a compliment to his successors in his chair at Oxford is distinctly more debatable. Debatable but not surprising, since genius is not inheritable—biologically or through the intervention of electoral boards.

The worst that can thus be levied against Kahn Freund's legacy was that it was not as well developed in the wider context of comparative law. And yet, again, his individual articles contain gems that show how practical and concrete his mind was. Thus, to give but one example, consider his 'Common Law and Civil Law—Imaginary and Real Obstacles to Assimilation'.[59] There, at one point, he refers to Maitland's aphorism that 'taught law is tough law'. Having then reminded himself and others that 'what is taught are primarily the general doctrinal foundations to which in after life the lawyer will cling as he may cling to the religious beliefs he learned at his mother's knees', he concludes with a vintage sentence which gives away his practical and focused mind. For he adds:[60]

> Practical details are negotiable. Fortunately, for the future of Europe what matters are the practical details, and the diverse doctrinal foundations can look after themselves.

Kahn-Freund, in our view, is the only exception in the English group of comparatists who went a long way towards devising a comparative methodology and keeping it firmly linked to the problems of the society of his time. That he managed to do this while not losing the ability to write black letter law works on labour law, family law, and conflicts, is

[59] Mauro Cappelletti (ed), *New Perspectives for a Common Law of Europe* (1978), pp 137 *ff*.
[60] *Ibid* at p 147.

a sign of his true genius. And the fact that his writings remain cited in both his countries further attests to the uniqueness of his achievement.

4. AN EPILOGUE TO THE IDEA OF DECLINE

The very gifted men we have referred to thus far undoubtedly kept the flag of comparative law flying high. They did so in the way they thought best for their times. We must do the same for ours. Yet, apart from Rabel, Rheinstein, Kahn-Freund and, possibly, Sacco (the latter mainly within Italian boundaries), they did little to teach those of us who followed in their footsteps how to present foreign law to national audiences, how to put foreign learning to practical use, and how to ensure its survival in the classroom without giving it a purely descriptive appearance. The price for this omission is becoming clear and was very high.

For the subject became the property of charismatic preachers instead of an instrument to satisfy societal needs.[61] It thus flourished while the preachers were around, because of their personalities and their charisma, but on foundations that were too insecure to survive their fall. If, therefore, comparative law is nowadays in a ghetto—and by the end of this book we will be refuting this assertion—the causes of this decay are, in part, traceable to the golden era. Why do we place so much of the blame at their doorstep? The answer, to us, is obvious. To think of Roman law, Hindu law or even Sanskrit law during the height of the 19th century and, even, the first half of the 20th century was only natural where, as far as Germany is concerned, Roman law was still (more or less) alive and Great Britain's Empire (and thus active links with India) intact. On the other hand, for those who lived and worked in the 1950s and 1960s (in both these countries) these links must have been much weaker. On the contrary, the coming changes must have been foreseeable. What, then, kept them back from adapting to this new world? Inertia? Why not? Or inability to adapt to a new world? That, too, is plausible. But whatever the reason (or reasons), the fact is that they failed to re-orient their own subject towards Europe, America, international human rights, and globalisation. Those who have every reason to admire and be grateful to them cannot pass in silence this failure of the greats. For being truly great entails not only reflecting one's times correctly but also being able to see ahead.

So, if a ghetto *did* emerge after the death or retirement of the generation of scholars we have referred to, it was, in part, a *self-generated* ghetto and not one externally imposed as ghettos historically are. Worse still, it was a ghetto that seemed to thrive on the separation of academic and practising law, even though each side of the profession had its share of gifted comparatists. This was a separation which was not only helping keep academics and practitioners and judges apart. This was a separation which was allowing scholars to cultivate a kind of research and writing which they knew would never appeal to practitioners. What a contrast with the views exchanged between Lord Atkin and Professor Gutteridge in a correspondence which took place over 70 years ago but which is even more relevant now than it was when it took place. What a contrast to the views proclaimed by Professor E. M. Meijers, the intellectual father of the current Civil Code of the Netherlands, who, apparently, found it 'useless ever to cite [in the codification discussions] foreign sources of

[61] The latest book, in the form of a collection of essays by comparatists with a link to the United States confirms this; see Annelise Riles (ed), *Rethinking the Masters of Comparative Law* (2001).

law if they did not lead to concrete ideas'.[62] By ignoring and, at times, even suspecting each other, the two groups (academics and practitioners) pushed—unconsciously we think—comparative law down the path of Roman law, old law, inaccessibility, and gradual decline. The subject was thus wilting for all perhaps except the most academically inclined and linguistically gifted. The revival was to come not by heroes but by a politically and economically transformed world that received further impetus by the end of the cold war and by growing confidence in the European idea as well as an increasing interest in the subject, mainly in the rather neglected areas of public law and human rights. The future looks as if the study of foreign law will be event-driven and not hero-dependent.

[62] Cited by Ewoud Hondius, 'Les Bases Doctrinales de Nouveau Code Neerlandais' in Claude Ophèle et Philippe Rémy (eds), *Traditions savantes et codifications*, LGDJ (2005), 257 at 261.

2

REFLECTIONS ON THE STATE OF COMPARATIVE LAW II: THE ERA OF SOCIETAL NEEDS

1. THE EMERGENCE OF A STRATEGY

The contours of our efforts to combat what we regard as shortcomings of the older school of writers, especially of the David variety, should by now have become clear. Specific examples covering private and public law can be found in other Chapters of this volume; and a broader collection of the leading author's essays fleshing out this method have appeared in two earlier publications.[1] Our approach is in most respects influenced by the Rabel philosophy, which avoided comparing concepts and chose instead to adopt a functional approach. Nothing more need be added at this stage about this work since it is available to anyone interested in further elaboration. The need for practicalities—or, better, *functional* practicalities—should, however, be emphasised. Our efforts have thus focused on making foreign material first and foremost attractive to national judges while academics were treated as secondary players. But since English judges rely heavily on information and argument coming from practitioners, a second aim has been to encourage as far as possible co-operation between the academic and practising sides of the legal profession in order to help judges look at foreign ideas whenever deciding novel or difficult cases.[2] Ultimately, we thus see the relationship in triangular terms, with academics playing an assisting but useful—and at times crucial—role by making the material (which they are best equipped to assemble) user-friendly and clear for the ultimate consumer: the judge. We call this *packaging*. This may sound, if not pejorative, then certainly very commercial in tone. Yet who can deny the fact that the package often sells the product? And these ideas *must* be sold to others just as much as any other commodity. Being highbrow does not help in the task that we are trying to achieve.

The *Greatorex* decision, discussed in one of the subsequent Chapters of this volume, offers a perfect—if incomplete—example of the approach. English lawyers had to wait a long time for it, but this is hardly surprising. For the approach advocated here marks a conscious effort, based on Continental European experience and with effects that go far beyond comparative law, to weaken the prevalent position—so eloquently expressed by Sir Robert Megarry[3]—that judges and academics perform *entirely* different tasks. However right

[1] *Foreign Law and Comparative Methodology: A Subject and a Thesis* (1967) and *Always on the Same Path* (2001).

[2] See Basil Markesinis and Jörg Fedtke, *Foreign Law in National Courts: A New Source of Inspiration?* (2006).

[3] 'The process of authorship is entirely different from that of a judicial decision. The author, no doubt, has the benefit of a *broad and comprehensive survey of his chosen subject as a whole*, together with a lengthy period of gestation, and intermittent opportunities for reconsideration. *But he is exposed to the peril of yielding to preconceptions*, and he lacks the advantage of that impact and sharpening of focus which the detailed facts of a particular case bring to the judge. Above all, he has to form his ideas without the aid of the purifying ordeal of skilled argument on the specific facts of a contested case. Argued law is tough law.' *Cordell v Second Clanfield Properties* [1969] 2 Ch. D. 9, 16 *ff*.

Megarry may have been when he made the pronouncement, with the passage of time it seems to be less attractive, calling for fine-tuning. For different though the roles may be, it does not follow that they must also be pursued in splendid isolation from each other. Lord Goff's Maccabean and Denning Lectures of the 1980s encourage one further down this path of thought even though his texts did not steer too far away from the crucial part of Megarry's message. But his subsequent judicial and extra-judicial forays into foreign law have proven that if judges like Lord Goff are helped with suitably packaged material, the study of foreign law could become a more acceptable method of interpreting and making law. Interestingly enough, this wider issue has also been confronted in Germany, and we will return to it again at a later point. It is raised here merely to stress that some of the most 'basic issues' we wish the reader to consider appear in all systems and are not excluded by different national histories or other local peculiarities.

The strategy developed here is today made more palatable to the courts by the growing shift of emphasis away from Roman to modern European law. It is complex; and it clearly requires more time. In the end, however, it can and will be shown to work, given that it is designed to serve current practical needs. The fact that by the end of the 1990s Lord Goff was no longer the only senior judge willing to cite judicially modern civil legal systems gave further impetus to those who like us had turned their efforts to this area of comparative law. Lords Woolf, Bingham, Steyn, Hope, Clyde, Sedley, and even Lord Irvine (Lord Chancellor in the late 1990s) were joining the experiment. The references to modern civil law were growing at a reasonable rate and were exceeded only by the number of extra-judicial pronouncements made by English top judges stressing that the differences between Common and civil law were not as great as they had been thought to be. Indeed, the phenomenon of British judges producing a growing volume of extra-judicial papers, usually based on lectures they have been asked to deliver, gave many of them the chance of using foreign law, an opportunity which some were still reluctant to seize in the judgments themselves. One can only speculate that this greater openness with regard to foreign law was, first, due to a lessened fear of the consequences of getting it wrong and, secondly, the fact that in their extra-judicial writings they did not have to involve in the exercise counsel for the parties appearing before them (with whatever economic consequences this might entail for litigation). Intellectually, however, this greater willingness to refer to foreign law and learning was equivalent to dipping the judicial toe in the water: it was, in short, an important first step!

Two further issues concerning our agenda and methodology now require closer attention. The first is concerned with the alleged shortcomings of the Rabel method, which has proved the starting point of our work. The second is to look at the kind of problems we encounter in Chapters Six, Seven and Eight, which epitomise the method and the strategy just described, and which must be read in conjunction with the material in Appendix 1. We use this as an example of the rigours of the proposed method—linguistic, conceptual, and methodological—but also as an illustration of how something that begins as a detailed study of a narrow topic can *organically* grow into a wider enquiry about another legal system. Finally, we use these examples as illustrations of how focused and practical the method is compared to the more sociological and 'trendy' theories which have emerged in recent times in the United States, and which we criticise severely at the end of this Chapter. For a cosmopolitan approach to law need not, as Professor Twinning once remarked, 'lack in depth'.[4]

[4] 'A cosmopolitan discipline? Some implications of "globalisation" for legal education', *International Journal of the Legal Profession*, vol 8, No 1, 2001, 23 at p 24.

2. THE RABEL METHOD OVER TIME

So how has the Rabel approach fared over time?

First, we must note that though many comparatists (beyond Rabel's immediate pupils) have followed it, their indebtedness to it is not always recorded. The answer, of course, is that such acknowledgements are not called for on a routine basis. Still, the 'omission' (if not the indebtedness) cannot be allowed to pass unnoticed. For, if nothing else, it contrasts with the 'cliquish' cross-referencing in which some (especially Italian) comparatists (belonging to the same 'school') seem to over-indulge. Indeed, in Chapter Three of this volume we hope to show that a fair percentage of the references to the comparative literature of the Italian scholars is due to their technique of auto-citation and cross-citation. This does not, of course, detract from the intrinsic value of some of the contemporary Italian writings; on the contrary, we regard ourselves as admirers of the Italian legal culture in all its manifestations, including comparative law. Nonetheless, this practice *does* mean that one must read this literature with caution. Additionally, one must recall Judge Posner's warning[5]

> . . . that reputation is conferred by the people doing the reputing rather than produced by the reputed one—and it is conferred for their purposes, not his.

Secondly, Rabel's method has not escaped criticism. Here, we shall look briefly at four points, mainly in order to show how one can try to address them in one's own work. They are: (i) *particularism*, (ii) *statics*, (iii) *process*, and (iv) *neglect of public law*. Unless otherwise stated, all but the last of these headings, and the summary form of the criticisms that follow, come from Professor Gerber's piece; and this is cited once only in order to avoid the unnecessary multiplication of notes, and not to belittle its importance or his learning.[6] Where others have shared these doubts, we give references in the notes.

(a) Particularism

Professor Gerber first argues that the knowledge derived from the Rabel-type of approach is 'particularist [. . .], largely independent of and un-related to other knowledge'. If that means, as he suggests himself, that Rabel is not interested in theorising and generalisations, then Professor Gerber is broadly right. But we see no reason why a researcher or an author cannot set out his own parameters and then work within them. Professor Gerber's accusation, however, could be more serious if the statement that the Rabel product was 'unrelated to other knowledge' is meant to suggest that his approach was legalistic and his results unrelated to the socio-economic circumstances that dictated them. Though Rabel may not have refined how one was to set about understanding the 'problem' that was being investigated, he was fully conscious of the need to see it in its proper and wider context. This meant—and means—investigating all the factors that played a part in the production of the

[5] Richard A Posner, *Cardozo. A Study in Reputation* (1990), p 59.

[6] Gerber, 'Sculpting the agenda of comparative law: Ernst Rabel and the façade of language,' in Annelise Riles (ed), *Rethinking the Masters of Comparative Law* (2001), pp 190, esp. at pp 204 *ff.* Gerber's piece attracts by its condensed learning as much as its moderate tones. 'Towards a Language of Comparative Law', 46 *The Amer. J. Comp. L.*, 719 (1998), an earlier piece of his, foreshadows some of these ideas but also pursues different paths which deserve attention.

problem being studied and the solution it received. Anyone reading Rabel's seminal *Aufgabe und Notwendigkeit der Rechtsvergleichung*[7] can pick up immediately the importance of this point, which his disciples developed further in their own work. Rheinstein, for instance, did this elegantly and, we think, effectively (especially considering the time when this work was being produced) in areas such as family law. Mary Ann Glendon, a Rheinstein disciple, applied these teachings to her powerful (but controversial) *Abortion and Divorce in Western Law: American Failures, European Challenges* (published in 1987), where philosophy and law were intertwined in a masterly but also specific manner. And Langbein did the same with the help of either history or civil procedure in his own prolific work, especially on criminal law. Works such as these suggest that the Rabel emphasis on looking at rules 'in their context' encourages a multi-dimensional approach to law even if Rabel did not *always*[8] do it himself.

Hein Kötz has equally shown great sensitivity to the wider setting of the rules, and has done so both in his masterly treatise with Konrad Zweigert and in his many articles written both in German and English.[9] But this study of the law in its context can also be seen in the excellent recent edition of his German (*not* comparative) tort textbook.[10] For not only does the book have the courage to ascribe a radically different emphasis to the parts of the law of torts that it regards as important in practice, and relegate others to a few lines or paragraphs. It also presents its German material constantly supported by cross-references to insurance law, social security, and statistical data. For a book which is meant to teach German students the rudiments of their tort law, it thus breaks new ground (though we add, for the sake of completeness, that we know that not all of our German colleagues share our admiration for Kötz' work). And, in our view, its uniqueness owes much to the fact that both the current authors—Kötz and Gerhard Wagner—are comparatists with long exposures to the Anglo-American legal culture.

So, while not denying the fact that the Rabel teachings are capable of improvement and refinement, we do not see them as having acted as brakes upon those who have used their main tenets some 60 years after they were designed.

(b) Statics

But what about the second critique, namely that the 'knowledge [derived from a Rabel study] is largely static'? 'The Method', says Professor Gerber (no doubt echoing others), 'creates a careful still photograph, a snapshot [. . .]. Change is not its concern.' Even if the conclusion of analysing a detailed problem does, indeed, create a 'snapshot', this can be an extraordinarily useful product in the light of the reasons that prompted the analysis: law

[7] Written in 1925 and reprinted in his *Gesammelte Aufsätze*, vol III, 1967 (edited by HG Leser).

[8] *Always* is the operative word; for Rabel made brilliant use of multiple factors when explaining the difference between the German and common law of contract in general and sales in particular in *Das Recht des Warenkaufs*, vol I (1936/1957) and vol II (1958). Rheinstein did the same in *Die Struktur des vertraglichen Schuldverhältnisses im anglo-amerikanischen Recht* (1932), a work written under the guidance of Rabel and full of magnificent insights into both common and civil law.

[9] Of his numerous writings we pick here his address to the Trento Circle, where he points out succinctly how 'the doctrinal development of a country's contract law typically depends on the types of contracts litigated before the country's higher courts'. His point is made with the aid of statistics, which in turn support knowledge that emerges from history and the knowledge of different societies; and it is presented devoid of neologisms or opaque jargon. See 'The Common Core of European Private Law: Presented at the Third General Meeting of the Trento Project', 21 *Hastings Int'l & Comp L Rev* 803, esp at 805–6.

[10] Hein Kötz and Gerhard Wagner, *Deliktsrecht* (9th edn 2001).

reform, judicial inspiration, or some other cause. But the 'snapshot accusation' seems, again, unfair (if not inaccurate) if one puts together the individual pictures collected by such method. The Zweigert/Kötz treatise, again, gives the illustration we need. For if a pictorial image is needed, panorama rather than snapshot is the word that springs to mind when looking at this book. A panorama, moreover, which (though wide in its coverage) also remains extraordinarily detailed and usable. The commercial and academic success of the book must surely reduce the appeal of the criticism. Moreover, Rabel's work is invaluable mainly not for its particular solutions—even though in his lifetime he hit quite a few nails on the head—but for the *methodology* he suggested and to a large extent developed in the course of his own life.

(c) Process

Professor Gerber also regrets that Rabel paid little attention to 'the processes that created the artefacts of the law'. Certainly those who, like us, have approved in general of the approach have tried to investigate insurance issues and other economic factors that led to the results. We have thus recently examined the liability of local authorities for the gross negligence of their employees[11] and were able to show, using the Rabel kind of approach, how the answer to the problem may lie not in the substantive tort law but the law of damages. We have done the same in other areas such as the developing law of privacy, and even disparate areas of medical law where—with the help of judicial dicta—we have tried to stress how solutions must be explained against the social background of their time. The large comparative treatise on the *German Law of Torts*[12] (co-authored by the first of the present authors) is also replete of examples which show how German judges (sensitive, *almost to excess*, of their recent experience under the National Socialist regime) have gone down paths unimagined by other systems. This is, for instance, what has happened in the area of medical law in the sensitive questions of 'informed consent' or actions for wrongful life. And we stress 'almost to excess' for in our (laudable) eagerness to condemn the human experiments conducted by the Nazis we may have at times forgotten another school of thought that goes back over 2,000 years and which refused to adopt the view that life was in all cases preferable to death, or that impaired life should always be seen as a gift.[13] This underlying philosophy may be extraordinarily important when discussing such legal issues as abortion, claims for failed sterilisations, or wrongful birth and life. If that is not law emerging from a particular social context, what is? And many more examples can be given in the context of womens' or workers' rights. Again, the Rabel method in no way stops us from giving credit to these 'extra-legal' factors if and when they help shape the content of legal rules. In our view, it is this method that alerts us to the need to enquire whether it is good enough for the child if the system only compensates the mother for its needs and costs. And it does so by helping us link narrowly phrased and concrete rules found in different parts of a legal system. No fluffy jargon here but 'law in context' in the best possible sense of these words.

[11] Sir Basil Markesinis and Jörg Fedtke, 'Authority or Reason? The Economic Consequences of Liability for Breach of Statutory Duty in a Comparative Perspective', [2007] EBLR 1, 5–75.

[12] Basil Markesinis and Hannes Unberath, *The German Law of Torts: A Comparative Treatise* (4th edn 2002).

[13] See Basil Markesinis, 'Réflexions d'un comparatiste anglais sur et à partir de l'arrêt Perruche', *RTD civ* (1) janv.–mars 2001, 77 *ff.*

Gerber's discussion of the importance of the 'process' (as he puts it in his 1998 article)—how legal actors think, talk, process information, interpret conduct, and make decisions—totally ignores two works which we find extraordinarily useful. Chronologically the first is *Form and Substance in Anglo-American Law* published by Patrick Atiyah and Robert Summers in 1987. A year later came John Fleming's *The American Tort Process.* Between them, these books reveal an enormous amount of information about how 'back-drop' factors—such as the presence or absence of social security, the method of financing litigation, the wider constitutional framework, or the structure and mentality of the judiciary—can account for substantial differences in outcome to emerge in the solutions of systems that belong to the same legal family. Both these books deal with English and American law. But, as stated, we have drawn on the methodology (and ideology) both in our writings and international practice. The piece in this volume on the potential liability of public authorities for the failure to provide adequate educational training to the citizens confirms, we hope, our view that one *can* combine the Rabel method of 'snapshots' (to use Gerber's term) with the lessons taught by Atiyah, Summers, and Fleming. In our view, the comparison of Anglo-American law revealed (surprisingly, some would say) English law to be more 'frank' and more 'complete' in its judicial reasoning than the American. John Fleming in particular, with whom we have had endless discussions about judicial styles, was invariably critical of the long and 'uninformative' English judgments (as he often described them). Yet here, as stated, we have an example that supports the opposite conclusion. We also have an illustration where wider factors (which Fleming in particular explored in his book) might prevent the transplantation of the English result—assuming it was deemed to be superior. It would be a shame if this were to prove the last word on the matter, for we still believe that Lord Nicholls's opinion in *Phelps v Hillingdon LBC*[14] is as replete of wider ideas about the notion of duty of care as it is stylistically attractive.

If we have laboured this point more than others it is not only because we feel that studies such as these go some way towards showing that Professor Gerber's concerns can be addressed by neo-Rabelists (such as ourselves) but also because we feel that they show how traditional comparative law can, with suitable adaptations, be of use to the contemporary American scene. And, conversely, studies of 'American law in action' should provide useful warnings to those who are sometimes too eager to bring it to Europe. In a sense, these thoughts also provide a limited reply to Professor Reimann's assessment that 'legislators and judges [in the USA pay] . . . scant attention to foreign ideas'.[15] But though the assertion is correct, the reason (blame?) for such contemporary insularity must, to a large extent, lie with the so-called 'full-time comparatists' as well as the neo-conservative climate which has gripped American politics—and most unfortunately US foreign policy—during the last 10 years or so. For it is up to them to show American judges why the fruits of their efforts are worthy of some consideration. To this tack the answer, of course, will be 'I still bet it won't happen in the States'. But if the approach we favour fails to move an American court, we doubt that any of the alternatives on offer—such as 'postmodernism'—will hold out any more appeal. So, if no one is singing our tune, it may be because we have failed to come up with something really catching. More about this later.

14 [2000] 3 WLR 776.

15 'Stepping Out of the European Shadow: Why Comparative Law in the United States Must Develop its Own Agenda,' 46 *The Amer J Comp L*, 637 at 644 (1998).

(d) Neglect of Public Law

Apparently, Rabel's 'methods' have also 'tended to exclude issues of public law'. This is the last of Professor Gerber's positions with which we feel uncomfortable. This point is, likewise, adopted by Professor Reimann,[16] who cites Zweigert and Kötz as an illustration of this sinful tendency of comparatists. But (unforgivably) he forgets the superb work done in his (adopted) country in the area of public comparative law by Professors Curry (Chicago), Kommers (Notre Dame), Markovitz (Texas), and Quint (Maryland), and—in his own fatherland (indeed, his former university!)—the learned work of Professor Jürgen Schwarze. More importantly, Reimann seems to pass in silence the many American comparatists—Ann Marie Slaughter, Mary Ann Glendon, Cass Sunstein, Mark Tushnet, and Vicki Jackson, to mention but a few—who have recently revived in the United States an interest in comparative methodology by focusing on issues of public law. Calling these colleagues 'neo-Rabelists' may not be what really matters. Labels are important—but only to a point. What is really important is that the work of these colleagues is focused on specific aspects, is functional in approach, displays great and detailed knowledge of foreign law, and avoids all the generalisations so typical of the David school—qualities which not only bring their work very much in line with the methodology we wish to encourage but also makes the Reimann silence inexplicable if not unforgivable.

All this, of course, does not deny the fact that Rabel focused largely on issues related to contract and trade *because they were so relevant to him and his country during the Weimar period.* But this is not the same as saying that his pragmatic and particularist *method*, focusing on specifics and avoiding (unless absolutely necessary) legal history and generalities, does not work in the area of public law. We have ourselves tried to use it in a number of areas of public law proper, or public law that lies on the borderline of tort law, and feel that it has worked well. The rich extra-judicial work of former Judge Tim Koopmans is probably the best example of such use of comparative public law in Continental Europe.

Take, for instance, the discussion on *Drittwirkung*, which is now receiving much coverage in England[17] but was first brought to the attention of the English public by a thesis of a human rights lawyer and the third edition of *The German Law of Torts.* We think that the collective work done on this subject shows how right Rabel was to suspect language and try, instead, to reach the core of the problem by means of a factual and contextual analysis. The attempts of the first of us to compare[18] a leading decision of the German Federal Labour Court[19] with *Novosel v Nationwide Insurance Company*[20] shows, we think, how approaching the problem in a Rabel kind of way can reveal similarities seriously hidden by language. Such an approach can further give the writer the opportunity to try to explain the differences by reference to the wider context and also suggest to him and his students ways of comparing issues which, at first glance, appear to be incapable of proper comparison. We think the same could be said about the work done in the context of privacy where, though starting with factual equivalents in a very narrow context, one has been able to address wider issues and fears that underlie the

[16] 'Stepping out of the European shadow: why comparative law in the United States must develop its own agenda', 46 *The Amer J Comp L*, 637 (1998), 639 *ff.*

[17] See, eg, Dawn Oliver and Jörg Fedtke, *Human Rights and the Private Sphere—A Comparative Analysis* (2007).

[18] 'Our Debt to Europe: Past, Present and Future' in *The Clifford Chance Millennium Lectures: The Coming Together of the Common Law and the Civil Law* (2000), 37, 57 *ff.*

[19] BArbGE 1, 185 (1954).

[20] 721 2d 894 (1983).

debate. If Professor Reimann familiarised himself with the current English literature on human rights and public law, we think he would find a shining example of comparative law that brings together American, Continental European, and Commonwealth ideas. A glance at the case law of the South African Constitutional Court would also show him that the method we favour is also working in the courtroom. A brief allusion to this phenomenon will, again, be made in Chapter Three. In any event, we belong to those who keep saying that the distinction between private and public law is becoming increasingly tenuous.

And one concluding thought. We are not convinced that the Rabel approach has exhausted its utility. This does not mean that its scope should not be widened or, more crucially, its targets redefined. Method, in the broad sense of thinking about how to achieve one's goals, may also necessitate a recalibration of these goals. For Rabel, as a German mainly active in the period between the First and Second World Wars, internationalisation of trade was the paramount idea. His desire to improve the German practitioner's ability to operate effectively in a new and unstable socio-economic environment greatly influenced his goals and his targets. Our main variation to this theme has been to switch most of our attention to judges in the belief that if they become interested, the practitioner will have to cite to him foreign law. And since he cannot do this on his own, he will be forced to seek the assistance of the academic. But this does not mean that the legislator or the civil servant should be ignored—or that they are less likely to be persuaded by detailed, pragmatic and inter-disciplinary studies rather than trendy language and theorising.

3. FUNCTIONAL SPECIFICITY: MORE OF THE SAME MEDICINE

Let us now turn to our second issue: the difficulties associated with our approach. Here we would like to point out two things.

First we wish to show in the context of a very concrete example how the co-operation of academics, practitioners, and judges can further the study of different laws and their comparison. Secondly, we are anxious to underline yet again how our emphasis on practical issues does not strip our method of intellectual or even philosophical content. Our search for a method of presenting foreign law to practitioners may thus not only be useful to the real world—especially if others can be persuaded to continue and refine it. It may also be educationally (if not even philosophically) a stimulating, additional, way at looking at the law.[21] For like Montaigne, whose name and example we invoke out of admiration and not presumption, we feel one can start from one particular example (or individual) and end up by discovering 'the whole of human kind'.[22] In our case this meant remaining faithful to the

[21] Rabel and his school, though not enamoured of the kind of work that philosophers tend to do to comparative law, were quick to acknowledge—even to novices—that their preoccupation with the practical utility of their method did not deprive it of intellectual challenge; see, eg, Rheinstein, 'Comparative Law—Its Functions, Methods and Usages', 22 *Arkansas Law Review and Bar Association Journal*, 415, 424 (1968).

[22] See MA Screech, *Montaigne & Melancholy. The Wisdom of the Essays* (1999), especially at pp 162 *ff*—an incomparable example of condensed and yet lucid English academic writing at its best. In law, Harry Lawson wrote in the same manner, making subsequent editing of his work almost impossible. My generation cannot write like that; and I often get the impression, especially in the USA, that my younger colleagues are not even conscious of the appeal of such pithy language. The contrast with those who have resorted to what they call 'post-modernist' language and ideas, and have tried to bring them into law is, aesthetically at least, most unattractive. For an illustration see Mattei and di Robilant, 'The Art and Science of Critical Scholarship: Postmodernism and International Style in the Legal Architecture of Europe', 75 *Tulane L Rev* 1054 (2001).

idea of teaching foreign law from specific litigated situations and then slowly fanning out towards a bolder attempt to better understand a foreign system. We readily accept that, at best, we have only partially succeeded in this aim. But this kind of attempt is crucial. For what we have advocated and tried to do is what separates the comparative lawyer from the expert in foreign law.

Finally, we repeat that what we are offering here (and in many of the remaining Chapters that follow) are guidelines as to how to select the subject of one's comparative study, how to approach and analyse the foreign material in the classroom, and, finally, how to present to potential users (be they judges, legislators, or other law reformers) the material so sifted and processed in order to make it usable by those who belong to a different jurisdiction. To put it differently, our ideas are repeatedly presented in this work from different angles and in different contexts to demonstrate that they work for most branches of the law, but are always geared to facilitate the exchange of ideas with lawyers coming from other systems.

Our focused (some might even call it 'narrow') approach can be seen at work in our comparative account of the *Greatorex* litigation in Chapter Nine of this book. Yet even that short commentary does not reveal all the difficulties and benefits that lie from this meticulous approach to foreign law. This is too detailed an observation to merit elaboration for the average Common law reader using this book; but it will be patently obvious to any German lawyer reading our analysis of his highly complex (and sophisticated) law.

The Chapter on *Greatorex* is based on the belief that the best use of foreign law came from academics making suitable foreign material available to practitioners, who could then use it in court to mould the law when, in its present state, it was either unclear, unsatisfactory or contradictory. *Greatorex* is important not simply because it used foreign law; *Greatorex* is important for it showed how the foreign material could *slide into national law if properly packaged.* It also showed how the problem the court had to confront was only partially solved because of the special facts of that case. The German decisions mentioned in our account deal with a further and un-resolved part of the problem. Simply put it is this: can the primary defendant (the person we henceforth call D1) claim a contribution from the secondary defendant (henceforth D2) for any damages which he may have paid to the claimant (henceforth P)? Or should he carry the consequences himself? A third possibility would be for him, alone, to be liable *but then only to the extent that his personal fault contributed to the claimant's loss.* At one level the problem appears to be a straightforward problem of joint debtors or, as we would call them, joint tortfeasors (the two terms in the two systems are not identical, but for present purposes this need not be pursued). In reality, however, the waters are muddied in those cases where D2 enjoys some immunity or privilege vis-a-vis P. This factor can (should?) 'distort' the normal rules about internal contribution, and that is why the Germans refer to this problem as 'disturbed internal settlement between joint debtors' (*gestörter Gesamtschuldnerausgleich*).

The German approach is sketched below; and the crucial and most recent decision by the Federal Supreme Court in this context was translated and reproduced in a previous volume.[23] Readers of the original and the translation might wish to change the English version here and there. Such changes might improve readability, perhaps by sacrificing something to complete accuracy. But apart from raising the perennial problems of what a translation—

[23] Basil Markesinis, *Comparative Law in the Courtroom and Classroom* (2003).

especially one of a legal text—should aim to achieve, the fact is that the German text remains heavy going. The problem of making it 'usable' requires more than linguistic talents: it requires *packaging* it (linguistically, conceptually and functionally) in a way that makes it usable. Some colleagues (such as Pierre Legrand) cringe at these efforts to anglicise sensibly foreign law. Our own view has always been that if we do not attempt them, we shall never benefit from foreign law nor will foreign lawyers ever see their legal ideas spread further than their national boundaries. We have both worked long enough in France and Germany to be able to say with confidence that the French and the Germans would love to see their law studied abroad, especially in *les pays anglo-saxons.* And we have also worked and spoken with many learned English and French judges in the very highest echelons of the judiciaries of these two major legal systems, and have always found them eager to borrow good ideas from wherever they came if and when the need presented itself—provided they were packaged in a way that made them usable. Legrand's objections may thus contribute to his high visibility as a controversial scholar; but (in our honest opinion) they are not what our shrinking world nowadays seems to require.

Are we exaggerating the importance of this crusade? Or is our method so 'British' as to be of little use to other countries and their systems? Let us stick to *Greatorex* and ask a simple question: why was German law used there instead of French or Italian? The first of us was asked that question by colleagues who teach the subject in both Oxford and Cambridge when his comments on *Greatorex* first saw the light of day. Now, even those who admire German legal science would be slow to suggest that it was used because it was 'better' than the others. But it was nonetheless used; and the reason supports our thesis perfectly: it was used because its material and its ideas had been made available to English counsel and he, in turn, could make it work to his advantage. That, in short, is comparative law in practice, and not academic ideas tucked away in little-used books.

Let us amplify this point by inviting the reader to consider our thoughts and observations further, alongside the text of a decision of the German Federal Supreme Court of 1 March 1988. For this decision of the BGH is, in a sense, the logical sequel to the *Greatorex* problem, and might even have undermined part of the rationale of BGHZ 56, 163 on which *Greatorex* relied so much. English lawyers should consider it, especially its second part, however taxing the text of the case may be.[24] For *Greatorex* decided that P could not sue D2—the primary victim of the accident in question. But because of its unusual facts, it did not have to consider the liability of D1 (in most cases the main tortfeasor), for there was no D1 in that case. Nor, as a result, were D1's rights considered for contribution and indemnity from D2. Nor, finally, was any thought given to another intriguing question, namely whether D2, if he was a 'privileged victim' (that is, one enjoying vis-a-vis P protection because of a contractual clause or a legal immunity), could rely on these immunities to avoid liability, even if sued by D1. The German decision deals with all these questions—directly or indirectly (if one sees it in conjunction with the case it appeared to overrule:

[24] P stands for plaintiff/claimant (or creditor in German law since this system looks at substance rather than procedure). He is also the secondary victim of the accident that provoked the litigation, his damage in a sense flowing from that suffered by the primary victim, referred to as D2. D1 is the tortfeasor and primary defendant in the action. Finally, D2 is the primary victim of the tortfeasor. But because he may have contributed through his own negligence to the accident leading to P's loss, he may also be sued by the tortfeasor. German lawyers may also refer to D2 as the 'privileged defendant' because he may enjoy some protection vis-a-vis the claimant should he chose to sue him. This may stem from a contractual exemption clause or it may offer an immunity of sorts conferred *ex lege.*

BGHZ 35, 317). The English Common law answer would probably be that if D2 were not liable to P, D1 would be unable to claim any contribution. The American position that D1 might be liable, but only to the extent of his fault, would probably be unsupportable under English law. And the German reasoning why this is the best answer would remain unknown. Those who can consult German material would not easily get much further, or, at any rate, find the right answer because the Germans themselves have not agreed on one yet. The German decision is obviously written against this background of intense academic discussion. This, in itself, is interesting for the teacher of comparative law, as he can develop this theme of judicial/academic co-operation both in historical terms as well as comparatively. More importantly, however, the injustice—in our view—reached by the German decision in making the local authority/defendant (D1) solely liable for the claimant's injuries even though his father was also careless in looking after him must make one check the policy reasons behind such a result. One can even go further and ask if it is right that such immunity for D2 (the father in this case) should exist because of his status as a married man but denied if he was merely cohabiting with the mother. The approach of BGHZ 56, 163 is certainly wider in this respect than §1359 BGB and, perhaps, better for that reason. But even this case depends largely on the closeness of the relationship and would not work at all if P and D2 were strangers.

So what should a Common lawyer in search for new ideas do? The easy solution, no doubt taken by most, is to abandon German law and, indeed, run away from it. Legrand would, in essence, probably advocate this, though he would do it in his forceful but also broadly educated manner. But the problem that has to be addressed will *not* go away; and American literature, the other huge source of material, is not very clear on this point. So the answer is to return to the three-sided partnership—the judge, practitioner, and academic—and see how the junior can help the middleman to convince the senior. If the work is done properly, the process commenced in *Greatorex* will be brought to a successful conclusion. Learning, inventiveness, and fairness will be brought into some kind of balance; and a solution may even emerge, backed by the assertion that it has been tested elsewhere and not found wanting.

4. OLD (BAD) HABITS AND NEW (SILLY) THREATS

In the first Chapter we spoke of some old (and, in our view, bad) habits, and how they have adversely affected, certainly in England, the survival and growth of our subject. The critical references were to Roman law; and our view was that if it were to survive at all, it should find its niche in those few universities which can afford the luxury of chairs on culturally stimulating but defunct subjects. In any event, they should not burden the budgets of law faculties or clutter their curriculum, which is always under pressure to accommodate new subjects. History faculties may thus be a right home for Roman law; and this is what has happened in the United States and seems to be happening even in Germany, where the subject once formed the first building block for the study of private law.

This threat, namely the threat of Roman law dragging down comparative law, has not been a feature of the American legal scene. The latter, however, has been subject to a different, newer, and potentially even more devastating threat or, more precisely, a set of threats. These must be examined even by Europeans since the experience of the last 30 or 40 years shows that what happens in the United States arrives in Europe with a time lag of about 10 to 20 years.[25] The threats are two.

The first is political correctness; and it is affecting not just law but also the entire university world in the sense that it is influencing what is taught, how it is taught, and what is banned (often challenging openly even the sanctity of the First Amendment). Political correctness in its various shapes and forms, which include militant feminism, has also been trying to give a new twist to comparative law, its content, and its aims. One aspect of this movement—its most unattractive if not down-right opaque language—will occupy us further down, for it simply cannot be left unchallenged given the harm which, in our view, it is causing to true scholarship.

The second threat or challenge is mixing—confusing, one is tempted to say—the study and comparison of advanced legal systems with the wish to include in such studies systems which are less developed than those found in the modern and technologically advanced societies which have traditionally attracted the attention of comparatists. These are systems—and even 'system' is a word which implies a degree of structure and sophistication that is often absent in these legal orders—which are more appropriately left to anthropologists and sociologists rather than to lawyers proper.[26] We suppose it might be technically correct to describe them as 'primitive' systems, especially since one of the CLS gurus has referred to countries such as Columbia—indisputably a society with a more developed legal system than some tribal areas of Africa—as 'peripheral'.[27]

Though the old (European) threat and the new (American) threats to comparative law have different origins and objectives, they do have at least one thing in common: they both ignore the realities of the world we inhabit. And as the ancient Greeks used to argue, even the Gods give in to reality! This message, with which we shall conclude this Chapter, will not be popular. Yet free speech makes it possible; and freedom of conscience requires that our concerns be flagged for serious discussion.

(a) Eurocentrism—Is it a Vice?

The first 'trendy' accusation levied against traditional comparative law is that it is too Eurocentric for its own good and that it should, therefore, be re-oriented in its focus.[28] Consider the following statements from two American comparatists (joined here to reflect the essence of the trend):

[25] French lawyers seem to be among those who fear this phenomenon most; see, eg, *L'Américanisation du droit*, Archives de philosophie du droit (2001). Their German counterparts, especially the comparative public lawyers—judges and practitioners—have, on the other hand, made good use of American material in their scholarly writings.

[26] It may be objected that an inter-disciplinary exchange of ideas could be useful to all concerned. We agree that in many cases this may well be so. What is less obvious to us, however, is why those interested in these other 'disciplines' should form part of the law faculties. Collaboration can be forged even if they inhabit different buildings; though admittedly, those belonging to 'other' faculties may not then benefit from the higher salaries which they enjoy when they are also associated with law faculties. This last point is particularly important in the United States where the salary differentials between law and liberal arts faculties can be considerable.

[27] Duncan Kennedy, 'Two Globalizations of Law & Legal Thought: 1850–1968', 36 *Suffolk UL Rev* 631 (2003).

[28] Mathias Reimann, 'Stepping out of the European Shadow: Why Comparative Law in the United States Must Develop its own Agenda', 46 *Am J Comp L* 637 (1998). See also Monateri, 'Black Gaius: A Quest for the Multicultural Origins of the "Western Legal Tradition"', 51 *Hastings L Journ* 479–55 (2000) and Hondius, 'The Supremacy of Western Law' in *Viva Vox Iuris Romani*, Essays in Honour of Johannes Emil Spruit (2002), 337 *ff.*

> Colonialism and Social Darwinism were the primary contributors to the ethnocentric illusion of the superiority of . . . Western law. Today, the presumption seems to be that legal systems [which ones?] . . . jostle with one another in a market-place of possibilities.

Another American comparatist of repute who subscribes to this view is Professor Mathias Reimann of the University of Michigan. Despite his Germanic origins and impeccable training received in his home country he, too, has castigated the dominant influence that European legal thought has had on comparatists of his new country.[29] The position he adopts is indisputably in line with current trends in the United States (though no one is even implying that this is the reason which has prompted the learned colleague to adopt such a posture!). But if one reads his work carefully, especially the second of the above-mentioned articles, one will see how much he has to struggle—unconvincingly, it is submitted—to reconcile his own call to move the subject away from Europe with the 'impressive success' with which the subject has met in Europe in recent years as a result of the European movement. 'From an American perspective', Reimann continues,

> one can indeed look across the Atlantic with envy [sic] . . . Comparative law in Europe is a hot topic. It is *practically relevant, self confident, and enjoys a high profile.*[30]

Why get out of the 'shadow' of Europe—his word, not ours—if Europe is not, in fact, casting shadows but radiates 'practically relevant' ideas and is producing practical and relevant rules? The whinging that follows on pages 692–93 of Reimann's said article thus simply does not tally with his earlier words (italicised in our text) assuming they are to be taken literally. If anything, it might even suggest that the status achieved in Europe was achieved precisely because one did *not* follow Professor Reimann's predilections. So, if the state of learning in Europe is enviable, a sentence which presumably includes the idea of containing original thoughts and solutions, why ignore it? In intellectual terms, such a 'closed eyes' attitude is hardly commendable. Professor Reimann must either re-think his views or find a way to reconcile them where they are (or appear to be) in conflict with each other.

The generalisations about the uselessness of European culture, however externalised, thus strike us as of very dubious value, not just because of their ponderous tone, not even because they have not been thought out fully, but also for two further practical reasons.

First, in the European world—which is also present (physically and intellectually) in the Australian and Northern and Southern American worlds, and (to a considerable extent) in the legal systems of mixed (and highly advanced) jurisdictions such as South Africa and Israel—one finds the most developed ideas likely to deserve careful study. *Is it really suggested that this is not a fact?* And if it is not, why do hugely important countries such as China, Korea, and systems of the former Eastern European bloc invest so much in studying these major Western European and American systems, and are trying to import their notions and their institutions[31] as they build up their own financial markets and the legal infrastructure that goes with them? One could ask the same question differently. Have Chinese lawyers turned to Fiji (as some anthropologists have urged Westerners to do) or looked in the direction of African tribes (as a sociologist in New York has advised his compatriots to attempt) in order to find inspiration for their legal systems and bring them into

[29] Reimann, *ibid*, at p 644. Professor Reimann returned to this theme ('fashionable' in the United States) in 'The Progress and Failure of Comparative Law in the Second Half of the Twentieth Century', 50 *The Amer J Comp L*, 670 (2002).

[30] *Ibid*, at p 691 (emphasis added).

[31] Subject to inevitable adaptations to meet local needs.

line with the growth of liberalism and capitalism in these countries? These anthropologists should perhaps go and tell these people what they are missing out by not doing this. Alternatively, these nations—we are now thinking of China—may be as wise as tradition has them to be, and are thus consciously and deliberately ignoring the 'fads' which are hitting the 'old' world.

Secondly, even if we were convinced that other models should be jostling for our attention, we must remind ourselves of Professor Bernard Brodie's admonition[32] that '(R)eading time, even for the most favored, is a sharply limited commodity'. This is a warning which applies equally to the legislator, the judge and the academic.

The warning must be taken even more seriously when we digest fully the implications of what we are being asked to do. For we are not just advised to read the extra book or article about the laws and customs of such 'less developed' systems. We are asked to try and immerse ourselves in completely different legal cultures in order to understand them and learn from them. Is our life span so long and are our library resources so unlimited to allow us the luxury suddenly to shift direction and start studying, say, African law, native American law, or religious law as a first priority? We fully accept that some colleagues may have such interests; and, of course, they should be free to pursue them. But the call for funds to support such posts must, by necessity, be weighed against other, more pressing, university priorities. The wider call for comparative scholarship to become 'mostly . . . devoted to radically different cultures'[33] seems to us utopia of the worst kind.

In any event—should we develop such tastes, through trendiness, political correctness, or even genuine intellectual curiosity, would any students follow us in the classroom? We say nothing of practitioners, judges, or businessmen investing in different countries. Of course, we pose the question rhetorically, for we have no doubt whatsoever what the answer is.

(b) Why Focus on Some Systems Only?

This question is often linked to the previous one, the assumption being that traditional comparative law has tended to limit its interest to the major European systems. So, why them—and them only? Why not broaden the scope of research? Indeed, why not include as many systems as possible in the name of thoroughness or objectivity?

At first sight, such answer may be appealing; on reflection, it is not, and this is so for a number of reasons.

History supplies the first answer. These major legal systems have provided some of the key notions of law—the rule of law, obligations, property, equity, justice, fairness, and the like; and de facto they served for a very long time as sources of inspiration for the legal orders of most countries of the world. Additionally, the economic and technological superiority that has existed in countries that operated under these legal rules has given them an obvious place of pride in any comparative exercise. To put it bluntly: these systems worked; and just as one does not mend something that is not broken, one does not re-invent the wheel if it has already been invented and is suitable for the purposes at hand.

But this no longer means (and, indeed, for some time now has not been taken to mean) that our interest should be limited to the study of the Common law, French law, and German law, the three main progenitors of what was once known as the Western world.

[32] Bernhard Brodie and Sir Michael Howard, *Carl von Clausewitz On War* (1989), at p 49.

[33] Mattei, 'An Opportunity Not to be Missed: The Future of Comparative Law in the United States,' 46 *The Amer J Comp L*, 709, 711, note 7.

This is partly because the pre-eminence once enjoyed by these systems has, to some extent, been dented; but it is also partly linked to the fact that recently (if a time scale were required, one would hazard the figure of 20 or 30 years) courts of smaller countries have, through their openness, hard work, and ingenuity, come to play an important part in the worldwide exchange of ideas. Israel, Canada, and South Africa are countries and systems which one should include in this constantly changing (but *not* closed) group of 'influential' systems. For that reason we have included in this book a new Chapter dealing with South Africa, especially in the area of constitutional law and human rights, and but for our linguistic limitations would have also included the secular law of the State of Israel.

So if the idea of limiting one's interest in comparison to one or two systems must be seen as totally *dépassé*, it does not mean that we should, for reasons of political correctness or even good old-fashioned intellectual curiosity, attempt to include in our purview the legal system of every country in the world. Indeed, for the reasons we explain in great detail in Chapter Ten, in the case of the subject there discussed we saw compelling reasons to chose a particular system (the German) and compare its practice to that of the English courts.

Our point therefore is that if what we ask for is to be done *properly*, it must be done *selectively*. The study, in other words, must start in a focused manner—and by that we mean not only have a focus *ratione materiae* but also select the range of systems from which the inspiration may be sought. Let us look at these two issues separately, starting with the second since, in practice, it will usually arise first.

Relevance requires that a choice be made at an early stage of one's research as to which systems should be examined.[34] Of course, the researcher's knowledge being limited, the chances are that this choice may *begin* by being made in too restrictive a manner. But the intellectually honest researcher will, as his work progresses, feel obliged to revisit some of his starting premises. This may lead him to develop an interest in another system to which, initially, he had paid little attention.

Yet even this desire will not be easy to satisfy and may force him to draw a blank. For, first and foremost, research in this area must always be conscious of the fact that borrowing, even at the level of ideas and not solutions, will often work better when the systems compared are of the same socio-economic level of advancement. Secondly, linguistic difficulties will loom larger and larger as the desire to study and use a foreign system expands to include those countries whose language the researcher may not speak and whose legal materials may be unavailable even in the best libraries of the world. The suggestion that one should research if not literally *all* but certainly the *majority* of legal systems is, as stated, plain utopia. And the accusation of 'bias' which post-modernists will be quick to levy against such an assertion, or the claim that the researcher is cherry picking, will easily be shown to be totally unconvincing.[35]

For one is not picking the systems because one expects them to be on the side of the view one favours. By definition the researcher—be he judge or academic—will often be unaware

[34] Though Professor Jackson is one of the few who have touched upon the subject of 'relevance', we do not *think* that it has been studied by her or anyone else in any detail. On the European side the only author who, to our knowledge, seems to have escaped from this tendency to treat all systems as if they were of the same importance is Professor Raymond Legeais in his *Grands systèmes de droit contemporains. Approche comparative* (2004)—though he, too, cannot escape the tradition so prevalent in his country to describe here and there (in a very short space) other legal systems beyond the common law, French law and German law, which form the bulk of his presentation.

[35] As Judge Posner seems to assume in 'Argument: Could I Interest you in Some Foreign Law? No Thanks, We Already Have our own Laws', 2004-AUG *Legal Aff* 40, 41–2.

of the exact solution the foreign system gives to his problem before he has completed his research;[36] nor, in an adversarial system, will he be allowed to do so with impunity. But one will—indeed *should*—pick a system on the basis of its prima facie richness, development, relevance, and transplantability. We stress these words because, for a variety of reasons, *not* all legal systems can serve as models and cannot thus be deemed, in most cases, to be 'relevant'. Just as people in the world are of different height, intelligence, and health, so do legal systems enjoy differing degrees of sophistication and richness of material. This is why the wish to move away from the major legal systems of the world, advocated by some American lawyers, strikes us as being motivated either by excessive idealism or political trendiness, or both, and would not prove feasible in practice. We maintain this for two further reasons.

The first is, as so often with our arguments, pragmatic and not theoretical. Look at all the new states which are emerging from socialism, communism, or racism, and entering the new world of today. Where do they seek their inspiration from? Well, with all respect to Fiji, the Azande tribe[37] (now dispersed over the Central African Republic, the Sudan and the Congo), or other 'minor' legal systems—they are not looking at their customs, their laws, their rituals, or their modus operandi. What they are studying is the way the more advanced systems are organising markets, devising bankruptcy laws, dealing with securitisation, handling issues of intellectual property, providing compensation for accidents, or handling international sales.[38] Of course, this does not mean that the advanced solution, if prima facie attractive, can or will be introduced without taking into account local customs and traditions. Adaptation, in order to take account of local cultural and legal factors, can be found even in the case where one advanced legal system is borrowing an idea from another equally advanced system;[39] and it is only right that it should also happen when the borrower is less advanced than the state from which ideas are borrowed but which may be unusable without due adaptation.

But even more interesting is not *from where* these countries are cherry picking *but how*—through their own ability and perseverance, and without the 'hang ups' that weigh so heav-

[36] Cherry picking could occur if the researcher found a system or an authority in a particular system which went counter to his views and values and then decided to conceal it. But quite apart from the intellectual dishonesty of such a modus operandi, the thrashing out of foreign law in open court would minimise this risk considerably. More generally, however, one must also note that cherry picking is not something that happens/could happen only in the area of foreign law, so this objection may have been given more force than it deserves.

[37] *Apparently* made a central theme by Professor Oscar G Chase, *Law, Culture, and Ritual. Dispute Systems in Cross-Cultural Context* (2005). We say *apparently*, for after the tribal practices of this race are described in a 15-page chapter (which derives most of its 'key' information largely from an anthropological study conducted in the mid- to late-1920s), the Azande tribe and their dispute-settling rituals do not really appear again until the end of the book in an equally short (three- to four-page) *afterword*. The central theme/thesis of the book is 'the deep and reciprocal connection between a people's disputing institutions and their culture'. We have no difficulty with this though we would, respectfully, suggest that it is hardly novel since comparative lawyers, among others, have referred to this factor as one which can (legitimately) impede transplantation of solutions or even ideas. But the second part of his thesis, namely that the study of such material 'liberates the mind and makes it conscious that there can be different ways of handling similar problems, is lamely made, *at any rate to the extent that it is connected with the Azande rituals.* For we do not have to study such 'less developed' systems (if 'primitive' is a politically incorrect way of describing them), operating in an environment which is so alien to ours and where primary information is hard to come by, in order to grasp the author's main point. For we can do this more easily and, it is submitted, more profitably, by studying systems closer to our own where deeper understanding may be easier to obtain and where the lessons learnt might be of practical use.

[38] Even Professor Chase, who makes so much of his excursus into the realm of Azande rituals, at the end of the day makes his thesis (with which we have most serious doubts) more credible by focusing in the main chapter of his book on the comparison of American and contemporary European (mainly German) law.

[39] This, eg, occurred when the Scandinavian institution of the ombudsman was introduced in England in the 1960s but had to be adapted to the special features of English parliamentary practices.

ily in the post-modernist psyche—*they are now themselves becoming centres for inspiration to others.* South Africa offers such an example, and in the Chapter devoted to its constitutional practice we shall observe its remarkable willingness to borrow from German constitutional law. We predict that China, currently thirsting for Western legal ideas as much as Western technology, will also reach one day—and the day may be nearer than many think—a similar stage after it has absorbed in its own way (and not been forced to do so under outside pressures) foreign ideas, assimilated them into its own ancient and modern culture, and then made them ready for re-exportation. Like anything that has to do with the emerging Chinese power, this thought must scare the living daylights out of many. Yet we believe it to be arguable, and we are thus putting it forward for our readers to consider.

A particular custom of a 'primitive' race may thus be of scholarly interest (especially to social anthropologists), just as the laws of a small state will be of importance to anyone living or wishing to do business there. Indeed, one could go further by referring to the civil code of a small country such as Greece, and invoke it as an example of a system which began with the German BGB of 1900 as its basis but in the process of drafting its own code included provisions which reflected new ideas and rectified defects found in its model. Yet even allowing for this, how realistic is the claim that an emerging country in Eastern Europe (let alone the Far East) will turn to Greek law and not to American law for inspiration? A claim that the codes, laws, and judicial decisions of all systems are of equal intellectual value and practical utility can only be made by those who wish to be politically correct or otherwise gain some 'favour' from such proclaimed open-mindedness.

Secondly, another reason why an interest in such 'secondary or lesser' systems is unlikely ever to gain any *substantial* following is the fact that few scholars and even fewer practitioners will ever be able to access this material in a linguistic or even tactile manner. Those who subscribe to the view that comparative law is 'superficial' (for the reasons given above) are only making it even more superficial by insisting that one must broaden one's search to include all legal systems. To put it differently (and more pragmatically)—if the Scalias of the world distrust the relevance of English law (as the judge did with force and, it must be added, some reason in his *Roper* dissent[40]), are they not likely to be even more reluctant to look at 'minor' systems or customary laws or practices coming from, say, Fiji,[41] primitive central African tribes, customs from the Polynesian islands, Aboriginal, or even native American tribes (unless specific circumstances made it necessary to know their rules)? Though every rule has its exceptions, we are here concerned with the norm which will dictate what is most likely to be used in the classroom and the courtroom.

We make this point strongly albeit politely (and in entire good faith) because in the United States (and increasingly also Europe) political correctness has forced us all to express our lifetime beliefs and values in bland and thus uninteresting terms—something which is happening across the board and not just in the domain of law. No wonder that electorates are bored by debates which are as sanitised as they are too long; that students become blasé at the end of their first year by lectures which rarely dare to 'provoke' different thinking lest they be followed by official complaints; and that oratory has disappeared from politics, the courtroom, and the classroom, since emphasis on style matters so little in an era where writing consists in putting thoughts in 'bullet' form, or takes the form of

[40] 125 S Ct 1183, 1228 (2004), demonstrating an impressive personal (or clerk-derived) knowledge of the relevant English (and Franco-English) legal literature.

[41] As Professor Anneliese Riles seems to suggest in 'The Empty Place: Legal Formalities and the Cultural State.' The paper is available online at http://papers.ssrn.com/sol3/papers.cfm?abstract_id=302156.

'highlighting' and then 'dragging' the borrowed text into one's own. Selection of legal systems on the basis of their *intrinsic* and time-tested value is thus the first step, and will remain so for any serious comparative study. But the step that follows can be even more complex.

This involves testing relevance *ratione materiae*; and, again, the selection may to start with be somewhat haphazard since the researcher, unless particularly knowledgeable, may not be able to determine whether this part of foreign law lends itself to inspiration or even transfer. This is because at this stage of the enquiry one may be forced to undertake a wider examination of the foreign system before the compatibility or incompatibility of a particular solution can become obvious, and this may mean restricting further the group from which inspiration is sought. Our point is best made through a concrete example.

Justice Breyer's recourse to foreign law in his dissenting judgment in *Printz v United States*[42] (though a well-intended exercise in 'empirical testing') may offer a good illustration since it has provoked in the United States some sceptical academic responses. What makes this writing noteworthy is that it comes from those who are, in principle, well disposed to the use of foreign law. The reason for this cautious scepticism is what we call here relevance ratione materiae. Could the learned Justice perhaps have paid inadequate attention to some structural differences between the American and German versions of federalism?[43] If this point can be proved, the comparison may have been misguided, however good motives behind it.

The difficulties here are clearly linked with the subject matter, not the intrinsic value of the system used as a guide (which is beyond dispute). They arise not only because some federal systems may, for historical reasons, have built-in 'centralising' tendencies while others are more 'devolutionary' in their aims,[44] but could also be linked to the fact that the political settlement contained in a federal compromise can potentially also reflect an interrelated set of rules which—as Professor Jackson rightly observes[45]—then obliges one to undertake a 'task that is even more difficult' to perform. This exercise could become near-impossible for a monolingual judge or busy practitioner to undertake on his own and without the help of trained comparatists; but then that is precisely why we have suggested a closer interrelationship of these different agents of the law-making process.

At this point it is crucial to clarify that our concern here is not the search for the 'right' answer *to this particular question*. We raise it merely as an example of the difficulties in comparison which a judge by himself will not normally be able to address. But we are suggesting that critical (albeit reasoned) comments such as those expressed against Breyer's attempt to use foreign law in the domain of federalism are much more valid and convincing than the blunt statement of Justice Scalia in that very same case, where comparison was dismissed outright and without the slightest attempt to justify it on the grounds that it is 'inappropriate to the task of interpreting the Constitution, though it was quite relevant to the task of writing one'.[46] Thus, while Scalia's rejection of Breyer's approach does not deserve a sequel, the more sophisticated doubts found in academic literature should resur-

[42] 521 US 898 at pp 976–7 (1997), provoking an unusually 'limp' riposte by Justice Scalia, 921, n 11.

[43] See Professor Jackson's interesting observations in 'Narratives of Federalism: Of Continuities and Comparative Constitutional Experience', 51 *Duke L J* 223, 268 *ff* (2001) and, more generally, Professor Daniel Halberstam, 'Of Power and Responsibility: The Political Morality of Federal Systems', 90 *Va L Rev* 731 (2004).

[44] See Bruce Ackerman 'The Rise of World Constitutionalism', 83 *Va L Rev* 771 (1997); Peter Schuck, 'Citizenship in Federal Systems', 48 *Am J Comp Law*, 195 (2000).

[45] Jackson, n 43, at 273 and note 207 (2001). See also 'Ambivalent resistance and Comparative Constitutionalism: Opening Up the Conversation on 'Proportionality', Rights and Federalism', 1 *U Pa J Const* 583 (1999).

[46] 521 US 898 at 935 n 11.

face the next time a question touching on different types of federalism comes before the US Supreme Court.

It is a moot point but one which must be raised nevertheless—whether such attempts at 'functional comparison' should also be accompanied by a general warning that in issues of federalism (unlike human rights) the possibilities of legal borrowing may be more limited. A learned Canadian Supreme Court Justice, Claire Heureux-Dubé, has thus observed in fairly general terms that[47]

> [D]ecisions on federalism, which are necessarily focused on the particularities of the United States Constitution, [may be less influential] than principles that are more universal.

Coming from a former Justice of a country which has not shied away from judicial dialogue, this statement warrants special attention. For it demonstrates a healthy awareness of the need to know where borrowing may be viable and where it is better avoided. This careful stance should not, however, be taken to extremes by simply excluding all comparisons on matters of federalism, especially given the fact that contemporary lawyers have a variety of federal models from which to draw inspiration.

(c) The Opacity of Post-Modernism

In the United States, comparative law has, in our view, been threatened by a number of modern trends that figure under a variety of names which seem more appropriate to the heyday of Critical Legal Studies (or its offshoot, militant feminism) than to what is happening in today's legal world. For the adherents of these schools, comparative law[48] should come closer to literary theory, or be associated with modern ideas of deconstruction, post-modernism, critical legal feminism,[49] or anthropology. Most of those who are associated with these trends also believe that comparative law should shed its Eurocentric tendencies, a point already considered and refuted. Like all those who 'destroy'[50] however, the Critical

[47] 'The Importance of Dialogue: Globalization and the International Impact of the Rhenquist Court', *Tulsa L J* 15, 35 (1998).

[48] Indeed some doubt themselves whether their work really has any connection with comparative law—a doubt, however, which does not prevent them from pontificating about the subject and its future orientation. See, eg, Brenda Crossman, 'Turning the Gaze Back on Itself: Comparative Law, Feminist Legal Studies, and the Postcolonial Project', 2 *Utah L Rev* 525, 527, 529 (1997).

[49] In terms of quality, the literature under this heading is in reverse proportion to its quantity. Picking out the most influential is not easy but we would include the following: Kate Millett, *Sexual Politics* (1977); Catherine MacKinnon, *Towards a Feminist Theory of State* (1989); Robin West, 'Jurisprudence and Gender', 55 *Univ of Chicago L Rev* 1072 (1988); and Susan Estrich, *Real Rape* (1987). The best (in the sense of a critical but moderately phrased and well documented account of this movement and its effect on the law) is Professor Ian Ward, *Law and Literature. Possibilities and Perspectives* (1995), at p 126.

[50] CLS scholars seem anxious to show that their approach can be seen as representing trends of thought that pre-date the movement's real appearance in comparative law—roughly in the 1990s—and also a completely new way of 'leftist anti-hegemonic' thinking. To the extent that the latter element prevails it must, by necessity, involve the invention of a new approach which probably means the demise or weakening of the one which they are trying to replace. Yet reading Professor Hugo Mattei's latest attempt to glorify the success of the movement to which he belongs—'Comparative Law and Critical Legal Studies' in Mathias Reimann and Reinhard Zimmermann (eds), *The Oxford Handbook of Comparative Law* (2006), pp 815 *ff*—one cannot help noticing how often words such as *disruption, rupture, invention of a new vocabulary, avoidance*, or *full fledged assault* figure in his text, which makes one wonder what is the reason for so much 'penned in' frustration. It would be taking amateur psychology to extremes to try and find an explanation for this desire to destroy. But if, in our search for an explanation for such vocabulary, we adopt instead a political angle the answer may well be found in the collective and individual psychology which people excluded from power or mainstream thinking tend to adopt. Professor Mattei's constant references to Harvard being the centre of this school, used to substantiate the legitimacy and prestige of the

Legal Studies Group finds it more difficult to agree on what to put in the place of the culture or institution that is being assaulted. Indeed, no one has put it more elegantly than one of the members of this group, the Italian-American Professor Ugo Mattei, when he observed that their

> contributions are sometimes difficult to fully appreciate [sic] and are easily misunderstood. The main reason for the resulting miscommunication is that the Critical Legal Studies comparatists often write and reason at high levels of abstraction and frequently borrow freely from particular intellectual traditions in neighbouring social sciences, putting the resulting scholarship well beyond the ken of many, if not most readers.[51]

In plain and concise English, the school and the writings of its members are opaque (hence the title of this sub-section, inspired by one of the keenest followers of the movement).

Our *personal* objection to this kind of thinking and writing can be summed up as follows: (a) much (though not all) could be seen as a short-cut to easy theorising, parading as scholarship;[52] (b) the language used is stylistically unattractive, cannot be easily integrated into the existing legal discourse, and is thus destined to have no impact on law in general and comparative law in particular; and (c) this new material is not likely to be of any use to 'applied research' of the kind that judges, legislators, and practitioners would ever wish to consult, and is thus not likely to promote one of the core purposes of our subject: discourse among lawyers. *If* this literature has any role whatsoever to play for 'basic' research (in or outside a law school) we will discuss briefly in one or two points further down. But this is not the main utility *we* see in comparative studies, and for us it is therefore a *secondary* concern.[53]

The closest the post-modernists have ever reached to drafting a manifesto must surely be the collection of essays published in Volume 2 of the *Utah Law Review* of 1997. In our eyes it encapsulates perfectly their interests (often opaque), their writing style (to us unattractive), their general perception of comparative *law* (in our eyes utopian), and the twisting of the basically just (and for a long time inexcusably neglected) idea of improving the legal position of women into a sometimes absurdly worded dogma.[54] Moreover, even the most

movement, also strikes us as an oversimplification in so far as it largely draws on the reputation of Duncan Kennedy and Morton Horowitch, and tends to ignore the counterbalancing importance and prestige of such important figures as Jack Dawson, Mary Ann Glendon or Ann Marie Slaughter, all of whom have done some very highly regarded work in the area of comparative law.

[51] 'Comparative Law and Critical Legal Studies' in Mathias Reimann and Reinhard Zimmermann (eds), *The Oxford Handbook of Comparative Law* (2006), pp 815, 822.

[52] For a critical overview of this literature, raising in greater detail the same objection, see Ann Peters and Heiner Schwenke, 'Comparative Law Beyond Post-Modernism', 49 *Int and Comp L Q*, 800 (2000).

[53] We have italicised some words to emphasise that these are personal views which others may not share. We are, however, more emphatic when it comes to the audience we are targeting: judges, legislators and practitioners. Here we have no doubts that the post-modernist approach will have no impact.

[54] Professor Susan McClary, a well educated but, arguably, even more controversial musicologist, may well have coined one the most controversial examples of critical feminism in the context of music. In 'Getting Down Off the Beanstalk', *Minnesota Composers Forum Newsletter* (January 1987), pp 7 *ff*, she thus had this to say about Beethoven's Ninth Symphony: 'The point of recapitulation in the first movement of the Ninth is one of the most horrifying moments in music, as the carefully prepared cadence is frustrated, *damming up energy which finally explodes in the throttling murderous rage of a rapist incapable of attaining release.*' This may have nothing to do with law; but it does illustrate to lawyers not aware of this feminist literature the frequency with which some critical feminist writers introduce rape images as the basis of some of their thinking. We venture to suggest that this language and imagery will strike the vast majority of readers as entirely gratuitous and unconvincing, and will, almost certainly, leave most lawyers totally unmoved. To see how extreme this tendency can be, consider Professor Sandra Harding's claim in *The Science Question in Feminism* (1986) at p 113 that Newton's *Mathematica Principia* could/should be seen as 'Newton's rape manual'.

untrained mind in matters of human psychology will detect from the way these authors write about the subject, their adversaries, and themselves, that they are aware—troubled one might even say—that they are operating on the margins of comparative law, and perhaps even law in general. Even before it has started, this school of thought thus suggests (to us at least) that it has a 'chip on its shoulder'. That is rarely, if ever, a good starting point for objective criticism—and even less so for the construction of a theory, let alone a school of thought!

This is not the place to single out one or more of these 'gems' for further discussion. But given this book's main theme—the need to make the intellectual advantages that flow from comparison more obvious to practitioners of all kinds—we find in Professor Günter Frankenburg's piece[55] an excellent illustration of the kind of comparative law writing which, in our view, will leave the audiences we are targeting *totally* unmoved. Of course, his speech may appeal to different audiences, for instance those who attended the Utah conference. His narrative, as the next speaker suggested[56] (it must be said with some wit), could have made 'a fine script for a play'. Yet we would bet a good lunch at one of London's best restaurants that it will never affect the contents of any legislation, it will never help shape the outcome of any judicial decision, nor, finally, will it ever help draw aspiring lawyers into the classroom of an American law school or, come to that, in his native Germany.

What is left for comparative law once you remove these groups of potential users? Are we wrong in saying that the post-modernists, as indeed those of the antiquarianist predisposition described in the first Chapter, are thus writing for each other's delectation? We think not, and the *only* argument that can plausibly be made for this group or type of writing is that in the academic world we need both 'basic' and 'applied' research, and that sacrificing this wider writing would deprive us of the former. In other words: we should not only tolerate but encourage them, for though what they are doing today may strike some of us as useless, it may well prove important tomorrow. We are, however, in no way convinced that this would be the case if post-modernism were allowed to die. Our reasons for saying this are two.

The first is theoretical. We do not see in most of these works signs of convincing scholarship,[57] evidence of detailed and reliable information about other systems, or traces of knowledge transferable to other branches of legal learning. Our practical objection is that even if we *are* wrong, which we may well be, we feel that we cannot ignore the fact that every human endeavour comes at a cost, and so we should pursue those efforts which give us the greatest marginal returns. We have explained many times before, and try to do so again in this Chapter and book, why our method can offer tangible returns, in practical *as well intellectual terms.* In our view, the returns we will get from the survival and extension of post-modernist theories about foreign law and comparative methodology have yet to be shown to exist.

Let us move from substance to imagery, impressions, and wider appeal, for it is not enough to have good ideas—they must, like all other products of human endeavour, be properly packaged in order to be sold.

The imagery of the adherents of this school reinforces our negative gut feelings. Consider, for instance, the following extract from an article jointly written by Professors Mattei and di Robilant:[58]

[55] 'Stranger than Paradise: Identity & Politics in Comparative Law', 2 *Utah L Rev*, 259 *ff* (1997).

[56] Frances Olsen, 'The Drama of Comparative Law', *ibid*, 275 *ff.*

[57] A point made more fully by Ann Peters and Heiner Schwenke, 'Comparative Law Beyond Post-Modernism', 49 *Int and Comp L Q*, 800 (2000).

[58] 'The Art and Science of Critical Scholarship: Postmodernism and International Style in the Legal Architecture of Europe', 75 *Tulane L Rev* 1053, 1055 (2001).

> This article discusses the political implications of postmodern conditions in the making of European law. It looks at contemporary movements in art and architecture to understand and gain perspective in the postmodern condition of European law.

If you are a judge, or a practitioner, or even a law student (knowledgeable or ignorant of Le Corbusier, Kandylis, Frank Lloyd Wright, or any other innovator of 20th-century architecture), would such an introduction spur you on to read further, assuming the title itself had not already led you to skip this piece altogether? In the contemporary market of ideas, a badly packaged thought will simply not attract attention. We submit that this is precisely the kind of phrase that would be covered by Professor Mattei's subsequently written description of the opacity of writing that characterises this school.

The language in which the post-modernists express their thoughts is also a cause for concern. This is not simply a matter of taste and style on which, after all, personal views and predilections differ legitimately; it is also a question whether this way of externalising thoughts can ever be integrated into the legal discourse of the law book, the judgment, or the statute. To put it differently, can anyone imagine any of these texts 'highlighted' and then 'dragged' into a legal text proper? We think not; and we say this for two reasons.

The first is that it tends to be verbose (Professor Mattei described it himself as sometimes being '*carnavalesque*'[59]), externalising its ideas through the medium of opaque or impenetrable neologisms or downright plainly fabricated words.[60] But a text that has to be read two or three times before one even begins to get its message will simply not be read! One has to be specific to make a point with conviction, even at the cost of causing offence—*which we most certainly do not wish to do.*

So let the reader glance at a paper recently given by Professor Riles at the University of Texas School of Law entitled 'Rethinking Realism: Lessons from Anthropological Research among Financial Lawyers' (apparently soon to appear as part of a book entitled *Collateral Knowledge: Instrumental Reason, Market Sociality, Legal Subjectivity*[61]).

Leaving aside the fact that her 'encounter' with Wigmore has already appeared in at least three pieces of hers that we have read already, and ignoring for a moment the question why the anthropological information she has assembled about the Japanese attitude towards 'derivatives' will ever be of use to those highly specialised practitioners who deal with such matters,[62] one wonders why one has to read in this piece *a few pages* describing her wonderings in the empty halls of Northwestern Law School during her early years there?[63]

Since this has little to do with her arguments (other than to tell us how she came upon Wigmore's writings), it is plausible to suppose that the aim of these long passages must stem from her desire to create style and atmosphere in her narrative. Such an apparent attempt to create 'atmosphere' might be acceptable, indeed appreciated, in a novel; but in a piece

[59] 'Comparative Law and Critical Legal Studies,' in *The Oxford Handbook of Comparative Law* (2006) at p 834.

[60] Again quoting Mattei, *ibid* at p 825, who explains that the members of his school like 'inventing new vocabulary'. These, in other words, are not only reformers; they would also be bad tacticians since they are trying to sell a product without any serious thought as to how one should make it understandable and thus desirable.

[61] This was the subject of a colloquium recently given at UT which, unfortunately, we were unable to attend but which seems to have left our colleagues who did somewhat perplexed. This raises the point which she, herself, disarmingly mentions in her paper: 'What does all this have to do with a Law School?'

[62] Colleagues highly knowledgeable in this complex area of law have assured us that they would not.

[63] For instance: 'I walk down the hall, back toward my office. It is a dark, wood panelled hallway, built when Wigmore was Dean. It has always felt cold and slightly depressing to me. Boring, old, conservative, alien territory. For the first time, I slow down enough to glance at the lithographs hung at three-foot intervals on the walls . . . I end up spending most of the night wandering the halls, noticing the spoofs of crests of arms built into mouldings, or the faux facsimile of the American declaration of Independence posted in a case'.

allegedly directed to lawyers, we cannot help feeling that it is unlikely to leave this audience impressed, and has only survived the editorial process because American law journals and books do not force their authors to be economical with their texts. To put it differently, those who (like Justice Cardozo[64] or, in England, Lord Denning[65]) have attempted to create 'style' or 'atmosphere' in law did so with economy *and* with a clear *legal* aim in mind. Unfortunately, very few jurists can claim the unique talents of Cardozo or Denning, and most should thus stay away from this kind of writing.

The language used in some of these writings can also be problematic in terms of its ability to merge in the normal discourse which one finds in law and among lawyers. Consider, for instance, the following text from Nathaniel Berman's contribution to the Utah 'manifesto'[66]:

> Critical comparativism requires strategic redeployment of . . . familiar techniques: in those contexts where the tradition would exoticize; in those contexts where it would normalize, exoticize; in those contexts where it finds infinite depths of meaning, formalize and fragment. Above all, refuse the homogenizing and essentializing gestures of the tradition: instead, show how all cultural formations are split, hybrid, and embedded in contexts of power. These kinds of transformative strategies can restore the critical edge to a field living in the aftershocks of the traumas suffered by three familiar anchors of progressive critique: nationalism, assimilationism, and interpretivism.

Texts such as these must make professionals ask themselves a number of questions. Does this kind of writing draw the crowds into one's class? Or will they stimulate a torrent of ideas in the works of other legal academics?[67] Will thoughts such as these, expressed in language replete with (if we may be frank) acoustically abhorrent neologisms,[68] appeal to a judge[69] or the legislator?[70]

[64] From his many examples we mention here *Wood v Lucy, Lady Duff-Gordon*, 222 NY 88, 118 NE 214 (1913), for it became the subject of a fascinating but little-known commentary by Karl Llewellyn, 'A Lecture on Appellate Advocacy', *University of Chicago Law Rev* 29 (1962), 627, esp 637, showing how style can, in the hands of a true master, be used to usher in the desired result.

[65] *Beswick v Beswick* [1966] Ch 538. As Professor Dennis R Klinck has observed in '"Criticising the Judges". Some Preliminary Reflections on Style', 31 *Revue de Droit de McGill* (1986), 655 at 680, 'The simplicity [of the language] . . . is almost certainly part of a deliberate rhetorical strategy . . . Lord Denning . . . win[s] over his audience. Most of the appeal is emotional, not intellectual'.

[66] 'Aftershocks: Exoticization, Normalization, and the Hermeneutic Compulsion', 2 *Utah L Rev* 281 (1997).

[67] It does not seem to have a huge appeal on legal academics. Professor Riles' fairly prolific output thus gets 111 citations in all American journals included in the Westlaw data bank during the years 1995 to 2005. Of these, 14 citations are found in journals which we would not regard as being prime hunting grounds for lawyers: *Law and Society Review* (4), *Law and Social Inquiry* (2), and *The Political and Legal Anthropology Review*, of which Professor Riles is the General Editor (8). This 'mixed' trend is visible even when one asks *who* is doing the citing: a lawyer or a scholar from another discipline (eg, anthropology or politics)? The above 111 citations came from 67 persons, of whom 49 were legal academics, three law students, one PhD student, four attorneys, one judge (writing extra-judicially), and nine non-legal academics.

[68] We cannot help quoting from Brian Garner's *Modern American Usage* (2003), where he advises that neologisms ending in 'ize' 'are generally to be avoided for they are usually ungainly and often superfluous' (at p 471). Not to be outdone by this growing trend, Professor Duncan Kennedy, *le vieillard terrible* of the ageing CLS movement, offers his own collection such as 'hybridity', 'hybridized' and 'crittish' theories. See his 'Three Papers on Four Boards', 2 *Utah Law Review*, 371, 373, 375, 373 (1997).

[69] It thus comes as no surprise to note that a search of all published American and English court decisions between 1995 and 2005 reveals no citation to any of the works of Riles, Lasser or Mattei. Our search of the raw data concerning other 'modernists' is continuing but on the basis of work done thus far we would be surprised if the final outcome was different.

[70] In her own contribution to Reimann and Zimmermann's *The Oxford Handbook of Comparative Law* (2006) entitled 'Comparative Law and Socio-Legal Studies', Professor Riles, as always, urges the countries of South Eastern Asia to do further socio-legal studies in the process of developing their own legal institutions. However, she then observes with surprise (at p 786) that 'ironically, in the last ten years, as the legal institutions of some

If this criticism is on target, one is only left with one 'maybe': maybe something will eventually survive out of all this post-modernist writing, germinate, and, who knows, flower one day. We are reminded that this has happened in science a number of times. But for us that 'maybe' is not only a very tentative one in the area of contemporary legal education; it is also bought at too high a price. At a time of economic restraint, even in American law schools (except perhaps the very rich), we must decide our priorities and let them dictate how we spend tuition and alumni money.

Inextricably, one is thus led to the conclusion that whatever the significance of the likes of Derrida, Unger, and other deconstructionists and thinkers in the world of literature—and however justified the post-modernists may be in their dissatisfaction with the comparative law 'establishment'—this kind of thinking and writing cannot easily work in the realm of law. So in at least one thing we find ourselves agreeing with Professor Riles, and that is when she writes that[71]

> These writers [that is, of the new school of comparatists] do not pretend to 'solve' real problems. Rather, in the spirit of 'Arts for Art's Sake', they present comparative law as an entirely academic (by which they mean theoretical) pursuit, more similar to cultural studies or comparative literature than a technocratic set of skills.

This strikes us as the kiss of death; and since some of her own work (despite the obvious breadth of her reading) displays the same characteristics, we are happy it is not we who have administered it. However, in stating this (as we must in order to explain and defend the orientation we wish to give to our subject) we repeat that we are not doubting the sincerity of the beliefs of these colleagues, undervaluing their intelligence or learning, or remaining always impervious to their ingenuity. Indeed, in one important area we find ourselves agreeing with them, namely that political aims always seep into juridical adjudication.[72] All we are saying is that this simply will not do for the method we feel has to be pursued in order to encourage the study of foreign law.

(d) Law and Philosophy, and How to Use the Latter in Conjunction with Comparative Law

The thoughts expressed in the previous sub-sections bring us to another question, namely 'What is the relationship between comparative law and philosophy of law?' Consistent with the thesis we are propounding in this book, we would like to narrow it somewhat: how best can one combine the two branches of the law?

To make comparative law captive to the theorising prevalent in a *certain type* of philosophy would be a mistake. Here is how Professor Fletcher, Cardozo Professor of Jurisprudence at Columbia University Law School (and also a learned comparative lawyer), puts it:

East Asian countries have developed [they have turned] in the direction of Euro-American legal institutions'. We suspect she must be among the very few who feel surprised by such a trend. Earlier, when criticising the anti-Eurocentric (and American) recommendation, we gave our reasons why. We fear that Professor Riles may have to wait for some time yet before she manages to interest lawyers in the law of the Fiji islands, a subject which has enthralled her so much.

[71] 'Wigmore's Treasure Box: Comparative Law in the Era of Information', 40 *Harv Int'l L J* 221, 247 (1991); italics added.

[72] We have made this a central theme of a recent article, 'The Judge as Comparatist', 80 *Tulane L Rev* 11–167 (2005), trying to explain and often criticising modern American exceptionalism. But what is new about this? By contrast, Judge Posner in his recent article 'The Supreme Court, 2004 Term: Foreword: A Political Court,' 119 *Harvard Law Review* 31 (2005) appears to present this point as being at the centre of his (presumably new) thesis.

> The great challenge for comparative lawyers is to probe our legal culture for its sources of resistance, for its implicit judgments about the normal way of doing things, for the way in which our identity is bound up with our practices.

In the same article Fletcher gives examples of things that could be done and questions that could be asked in order to help rehabilitate the subject—comparative law—which he, too, regards as being marginalised. Yet nowhere in his enticement to be 'subversive'—and he admits he is using the term in the title of his article in a 'playful' way—do we find a single word about making the subject more appealing to practitioners and the courts. His own position is quite clear—he is targeting 'the inner circles of the academe'. For courts he seems to have no time. 'One can understand', he writes (as if it were the most natural thing to say), 'why lawyers [*sic*] and judges pay little attention to foreign law. They have a job to do.'[73]

Frankly, we are worried by the optic he adopts in order to examine the 'malaise' affecting the subject; and we are just as unhappy by the way he phrases his thoughts in the above-mentioned quotation. In our view, academics *in general* and comparatists *in particular* (including philosophers) should be showing the courts that *their* discipline is linked to the 'job' *they* have to do. If this mission ever crossed the learned Professor's mind, there are few visible signs of it in his article. No wonder then that our subject is suffering (or is seen to be suffering) when colleagues tell us that we should be writing for those in the cloisters and not those in the boardroom or the courtroom or the legislative chamber. Writing from Columbia (locked in fierce competition with NYU), Professor Fletcher should have been able to appreciate the force of globalisation, the power of fundraising, the challenge from competition, and the importance of reaching the constituency of practitioners of all kinds, and his approach should have thus been somewhat more worldly than it is.

So let philosophers use the information comparatists unearth and weave it into their theories; but do not allow them the chance to shape either the agenda or the methodology of comparatists unless it is in order to show how philosophical ideas can shape better practical solutions. For if they do not, they will only help separate the subject from the world of practice and thus not further its wider use. If we were to use one example to support this view, by no means shared by everyone, we would point to Professor James Whitman's contribution in the Legrand and Munday collection of essays.[74] We chose this piece for we see it as an example of scholarship, style, and polemical but (on the whole) restrained language.

Whitman's thesis is that all the modern comparatists who are preoccupied with understanding 'otherness'—if not declaring in various forms of extreme language that it is either 'unconquerable'[75] or one of 'potentially irreducible complexity'[76]—are in fact following (consciously or unconsciously, one is not clear) the teachings of great German philosophers such as Johan Gottfried Herder, Hans Georg Gadamer, or the more extreme Wilhelm Dithley. As stated, his narrative summary of their views is done in a way that displays his knowledge and elegant style. But beyond showing that 'there is nothing new under the sun' or wisely advising the successors of this school not to over-stress that the systems can never converge, what practical use will this learning bring to modern lawyers? In his own essay, Professor Lasser accuses (anonymously) fellow comparatists for choosing the audience

[73] 'Comparative Law as a Subversive Discipline', 46 *The Amer J Comp L* 683, 690 (1998).

[74] 'The neo-Romantic turn', *Comparative Legal Studies: Traditions and Transitions* (2003), pp 312 *ff.*

[75] Professor Nora Demleitner, 'Combating Legal Ethnocentrism: Comparative Law Sets Boundaries', 31 *Arizona State L J* 737 (1999).

[76] 'The question of understanding', in Pierre Legrand and Roderick Munday, *Comparative Legal Studies: Traditions and Transitions* (2003), 197, 216.

which we wish to target, and in this he sees a clear sign of lack of objectivity, even bias in the presentation that follows. So how does one choose one's audience?

We have always stated clearly which audiences we target; and why should not an author (a fortiori an author who is also a practising lawyer) determine himself which audience matters most in his view? Anyway, which are the potential audiences for any university writer? Students, practitioners, judges, and law-makers (mainly state or transnational legislators).[77] Now take any of the above. How many have heard of Dithley or Herder, or are likely to read their work? Is it the kind of learning which will help a practitioner give an inventive twist in their advocacy or provide a judge with a readily available argument for his judgment?

Or take Whitman's long argument in the second half of his essay about old aristocratic traditions lying behind the modern tendency of European law to protect honour and reputation, thus belittling the more often invoked explanation that this part of (mainly) German law represents a reaction to the Nazi excesses. Though the first of us has clearly indicated this in *The German Law of Torts*,[78] Professor Whitman is right to elaborate it, daring this time on his own earlier work. But how important is this to, say, an English judge struggling (as most of them are) to decide the limits of protection afforded to human privacy? For him the questions that have to be answered are whether the time has come to stop calling privacy breach of confidence? To what extent the latest *Caroline* decision of the European Court of Human Rights affects English law? Whether these modern trends will suppress speech to an unacceptable extent? Whether there will be an explosion of litigation? And (though they will never admit this openly) whether the English tabloid press has gone too far in making money out of other persons' sufferings and trying to be protected for such publications by invoking the sacred right of free speech? An academic, just as much as an advocate, has a right to target his audience; he has a right to invoke figures and statistics to disperse irrational fears; and he has the right show how other systems have achieved the balance between the values protected by articles 8 and 10 of the European Convention on Human Rights by means of rational criteria and not by over-stretching medieval torts. The motives are openly declared; the work is available for scrutiny; its accuracy has been vouchsafed by eminent German scholars; and the approach and analysis is shared by real heavyweights of the subject such as, for instance, Professors van Gerven, Kötz or Zimmermann, and eminent judges such as Lord Bingham or Lord Justice Sedely. So where is the impropriety, or Professor Legrand's unacceptably defamatory accusation of a 'duplicitous strategy'? The most that authors such as him can say is that they disagree. Beyond that good judgment gives way to inelegance.

Not all legal philosophers, however, have displayed their wares in this way. The work that Professor James Gordley has been producing over the years[79] shows how legal history, philosophy, and comparative law can profitably be combined so long as one does not try to make one dominate the agenda of the other. His tracing of the impact which the Aristotelian ethics—mainly through the *Nichomachean Ethics*—have had on the development of legal doctrine is fascinating. And it is not only doctrine, concepts, and legal notions which have been shaped on the basis of philosophical beliefs but also court decisions. Lord Steyn in England has thus been one of the few who has repeatedly invoked the notion of dis-

[77] We have not included in our list fellow academics, for targeting our colleagues is not the best way of promoting comparative law. Authors who write for each other's delectation is not something we are interested in.

[78] Co-authored with Professor Hannes Unberath, 4th edn (2004) at p 74, citing the Protokolle of the Second Draft of the Code.

[79] See, eg, *Foundations of Private Law* (2006).

tributive justice to buttress other, more positivistic concepts and precedents in order to justify his own final conclusion in a case.[80]

Much of this has happened in the context of actions for wrongful life and death, which have multiplied as abortion regimes have been liberalised the world over. The starting points in all these cases has been Christian thought, reinforced by the legacy of the Nazi atrocities, that life is always valuable—even when burdened by grave impairments. Theological teaching has even tried to move the notion as far back as the second week of conception, when the fertilised cells first divide into two. The result is not only an affirmation that life is always preferable to death but also that it begins at a much earlier phase than currently attracts the protection of the law.

This is a debatable proposition; and has been so ever since some of the greatest Greek law-givers (Solon), dramatists (Sophocles), and philosophers (such as Plato and Aristotle) have questioned its validity. It could and thus has been argued, for instance by Aristotle, that what matters is not life but good (quality of) life. This, thinking, too, is a—substantial—part of our Western civilisation, but its impact on cases dealing with wrongful life and death, euthanasia, abortion, and other such issues has not been studied as carefully as one would have liked nor has it prevailed—arguably because the 'pro life' lobbies all over the world have been so well organised and active.

More importantly for present purposes, when we talk about all these legal issues, we must not only consider the diverging philosophical views but also see how these divergences have been handled subtly by different legal systems. Dismissing philosophy out of hand would thus impoverish the law curriculum; but using it in conjunction with comparative law and, as often as possible, demonstrating its practical applications and utility, would help strengthen both disciplines.

(e) Comparative Law and Sociology

The leading contemporary English legal sociologist Roger Cotterrell has repeatedly argued in favour of the close co-existence and collaboration of comparative law and sociology or, at the very least, legal sociology.[81] His argument is scholarly, his tone calm and conciliatory; his work thus invites further discussion, even favourable consideration. Unfortunately, the history of the literature on the possible overlap of the subjects has not, up to now, favoured such a constructive co-existence. The future might be different if the work done by legal sociologists is less keen on excessive abstractions, more empirical in its orientation, and more likely to help applied comparative law. But are they willing to adopt such an approach?

In earlier times, these prospects looked bright. When comparative law was launched as a subject during the Paris Congress of 1900, some of its protagonists, like Eduard Lambert, imbued by the ideas of Emile Durkheim, the father of French sociology, favoured such collaboration. Indeed, in many respects comparative law was so obviously a new 'science' that comparative legal history was almost seen as a branch of sociology.[82]

[80] Lord Steyn in particular has made frequent references to these notions, eg, in *MacFarlane v Tayside Health Board* [2000] 2 AC 59, 83 D.

[81] 'Is There a Logic of Legal Transplants?' in David Nelken and Johannes Feest (eds), *Adapting Legal Cultures* (2001), pp 71–92; 'Comparatists and Sociologists' in Pierre Legrand and Roderick Munday (eds), *Comparative Legal Studies: Traditions and Transitions* (2003), pp 131–53; 'Comparative Law and Legal Culture' in Mathias Reimann and Reinhard Zimmermann (eds), *The Oxford Handbook of Comparative Law* (2006), pp 709–37.

[82] Emile Durkheim, reviewing Lambert's *La function du droit comparé* (1903), pp 913–16 in *Textes*, vol III (1975), p 266. More generally see Roger Cotterrell, *Emile Durkheim: Law in a Moral Domain* (1999), pp 7–8.

The next great figure of legal sociology in France, Jean Carbonnier, a man of wide culture, strong French-centred views (as was still understandable in the de Gaulle years) and an even wider influence on the French legal scene, was more ambivalent towards the subject. For though his work was peppered with references to foreign law, leading one to believe that he would have encouraged the growth of comparative law as an autonomous discipline, he in fact caused the subject much harm. For his pre-occupation with legal sociology, coupled with his fear of legal distortions resulting from the bad use of comparative law and the (excessive, in his view) Europeanisation of French law,[83] led him to relegate comparative law to the status of a 'collateral subject'.[84]

Great men have strong ideas; and history teaches us that it is also great men who make the biggest mistakes. When they come in twos, the mistakes may take a generation to eradicate; and that is, indeed, what happened in this case. For Carbonnier was a near contemporary of David's; and we have already noted how the latter allowed little breathing space around him for lesser men to thrive or diverge from his positions.

The loss of opportunities is even more regrettable since the mid-1960s were years of exceptional legislative reform under the guidance of Jean Foyer, General de Gaulle's reforming Minister of Justice. Yet, according to Professor François Terré (at that time Chef de Cabinet of Foyer), repeated attempts to convince either or both of these men to set up for the government a permanent source of information on foreign law were never actively pursued. This may not be that surprising as far as David goes, for, we are told, he was never a team player. But Carbonnier, notwithstanding his views about comparative law as an autonomous discipline, actually *did* believe that, as a subject, it could assist the task of legislative reform.

Carbonnier's indifference towards comparative law was mirrored, but in the reverse form, in Alan Watson's work, which showed near contempt for sociology. For him law was made by its own 'internal' forces and in a way responded to societal pressures or changes. Watson's classic work on *Legal Transplants*[85] has held a dominant position in the literature of comparative law; but, though it ascribed an important role to legal history—understandably, given that Watson was first and foremost a Roman lawyer—and philosophy, it banished sociology from the comparative law scene. Watson's basic tenets were that legal changes are controlled *internally*, within the legal system and by its elites; and, secondly, that law was insulated from politics, economics, and societal changes.

Those who refused to find common ground for comparative law and sociology were also helped in keeping the subjects apart by a scholar who tried to bring them closer to one another. He was Jerome Hall, who in 1963 argued in his *Comparative Law and Social Theory*

[83] A phenomenon he described as 'acculturation juridique'; see *Droit civil, Introduction* (2002), 79 *ff.* In this Carbonnier was no different than most 'grand' figures of the subject who, though supportive of the emerging European idea, still believed that their own countries and systems could dominate but not be seriously distorted by Europeanisation. The difficulties experienced by the French and German courts in accepting the dominance of Community law illustrates the same phenomenon in the context of court practice. This touches on the wider and truly fascinating question of how genuinely 'European' are the great European powers? This is not the place to discuss this issue but, arguably, the most genuine supporters of European integration are the smaller countries of the European Union—Belgium, Ireland, Greece, Luxembourg, Netherlands, or Portugal—possibly because they stand to gain (and in financial terms have gained) more than others.

[84] His complex but always intriguing (and beautifully expressed) views are scattered in his many works, among which see (in chronological order): 'L'apport du droit comparé à la sociologie juridique', *Livre du centenaire* (1969), 75 *ff*; 'A beau mentir qui vient de loin', *Essais sur les lois* (1995), 227 *ff*; *Droit et passion du droit sous la V[85] République* (2000).

[85] *Legal Transplants: An Approach to Comparative Law* (1974).

that the former could be of assistance in the development of social history. Hall's insistence on the idea that comparative law's main role in the curriculum was to assist in the understanding of societies had the same effect as the work of others who openly opposed any idea of *rapprochement.* Comparative law was suffering because of disagreement over its proper aims and functions; and this disagreement also had an impact on its relations with legal sociology. Hall thus over-focused on one aim, in our view the wrong one at that, and did nothing to foster mutual understanding and co-operation.

For those who, like us, see a mainly practical purpose for comparative law, the interrelationship with sociology is likely to remain underdeveloped. But *under*developed rather than *un*developed is the operative word. For, unlike Watson who preaches with such force the idea of total autonomy of law from society, we do not think it is still plausible to argue such a thesis in times when law develops rapidly under many different pressures which even the legal elites cannot ignore. The modern sources of law are also so multi-polar in their origins, and societal pressures can (with the help of the media and modern technology) be exercised on legislators and judges in so many different and powerful ways, that it seems unconvincing to put so much emphasis on the power of the 'internal' legal elites—not least because they are now to be found in different bodies, different countries, and operating in a very global setting. At the very least, Watson's over-emphasis on the reforming power of internal elites needs reconsideration and re-setting in today's wider and much more complex legal world.

If developments affecting foreign law and comparative methodology are seen from such an optic, it becomes wrong to deny the need to study how all these factors operate within contemporary and interrelated societies of similar political and economic development.[86] The functional approach we have recommended may find in concrete litigated situations a good point to *begin* the comparative journey but has never stopped there nor excluded the weighing of other factors before reaching a final conclusion. But all this—the 'general' as well as the 'specific'—must be attempted in a focused way. It must follow a systematic route, have a manageable aim, and avoid excessive abstraction, generalisation and conceptualism. For the first (the general) makes comparisons, whether they tend to show similarities or differences, meaningless,[87] while the second (the technical or specific)—being the product of a particular language and legal tradition—obscures rather than illuminates what is really happening beneath the surface.

[86] Our interest in the study of tribal or primitive cultures is minimal. We accept, however, that 'local' sociological or anthropological work may be necessary to advise these primitive cultures to what extent the importation of the more developed law of advanced societies is compatible with strongly opposed customary law. Such 'respect' for local traditions was shown in the case of the Malagasy codification process but was brutally set aside by David's codification of the Ethiopian Civil Code. On the latter see his 'Considerations on the Codification of the Civil Law in African Countries', 37 *Tul L Rev* 188 *ff* (1962–63) and, more generally, the comments of Professor TW Bennett, 'Comparative Law and African Customary Law', in Mathias Reimann and Reinhard Zimmermann (eds), *The Oxford Handbook of Comparative Law* (2006), at 641 *ff.* But the above observations are of little interest to the exporting country/system unless it has a vested interest of its own to ensure that the exportation of its ideas takes root.

[87] For these reasons we feel equally uncomfortable with generalisations like those of Pierre Legrand—in *Fragments on Law-as-Culture* (1999)—encouraging 'empathy for alterity' or Franz Wieacker—'Foundations of European Culture', 38 (1) *Amer J Comp L*, 20–5 (1990)—stressing similarities. Cotterrell, referring to Wieacker's list of similarities, rightly criticises 'such a level of abstraction [as taking us] only a short distance'—see 'Comparative Law and Legal Culture', in Mathias Reimann and Reinhard Zimmermann (eds), *The Oxford Handbook of Comparative Law* (2006), 709, at 714—but fails to emphasise (as he did in his earlier work) the need for sociologists studying culture and trying to combine their learning with that of comparatists to be specific, focused and, whenever possible, present their conclusions with the aid of empirical studies.

For these reasons, repeatedly examined from different angles in this book, we feel equally uncomfortable with generalisations like those of Pierre Legrand[88] (who talks of irreconcilable cultural differences) or Franz Wieacker[89] (stressing cultural similarities). Roger Cotterrell thus rightly criticises Wieacker's 'level of abstraction [as taking us] only a short distance'. [90] Yet, Legrand is just as guilty of the same sin. But Cotterrell, drawn as he is into the gravitational orbit of Legrand, fails to criticise his generalities as well as failing to emphasise the need for sociologists who study the importance of culture and society to try and combine their learning with that of comparatists by being specific, focused, and (whenever possible) presenting their conclusions with the aid of empirical studies. Thus, most of the authors he cites come nowhere near to meeting the kind of criteria of specificity which we think would help explain cultural difference in a way that would allow a judge or legislator to decide whether he can use sociological or comparative legal data.

Take, for instance, the German sociologist Volkmar Gessner, who incidentally does not believe that there exists a common European legal culture. Cotterrell cites some of the indicators which Gessner thinks will help facilitate comparison of European legal cultures. Among them, Gessner includes, for example, the 'frequency of illegal . . . behaviour of public officials, knowledge of law in the general population, attitudes towards state regulation'.[91]

We claim no expertise in sociology but do declare a lawyer's inability to understand how (a) the above indicators could be 'meaningfully' measured or evaluated, and then (b) 'usefully' introduced in a legal discussion involving, for instance, the violation of privacy rights, remedies for breach of contract, or the highly technical issues which must be addressed in cases involving a violation of intellectual property rights or unjust enrichment (to give but a few examples).

Cotterrell, however, seems to regard the above indicators as 'concrete behavioural and attitudinal indicators, detectable in the activities and opinions of lawyers and other [*sic*] citizens'.[92] Again, he may be seeing things we cannot see. No doubt he does, since he seems to quote with approval Legrand's aphorism that culture is 'the framework of intangibles [*sic*] within which an interpretative community operates'. We (again) feel lost as to how such matters can be *measured* and how they can be presented in a *usable* manner to a legislator or judge unless amplified and fleshed out with concrete examples. No doubt, therefore, the only way to understand such things is through *empathy*, appropriately Legrand's word for understanding *differences* (naturally he omits *similarities*). But, given that 'empathy' is defined by the Oxford Dictionary 'as the power of projecting one's personality into, and so fully understanding, the object of contemplation', the process must be psychological, presumably self-induced, and not necessarily dependent on facts, figures, or empirically provided specific evidence. This is for the legal mind simply too 'fuzzy' a way of thinking and analysing, though it may well appeal to sociologists and like-minded lawyers.

Be that as it may, in Chapter Ten we thus give one of three examples amplified in this book, and show how *we* understand functionality and specificity. In equal measure, however, we also demonstrate how we try to take into account in the discussion of a very specialised problem the wider and special features of a particular legal and philosophical

[88] In *Fragments on Law-as-Culture* (1999), encouraging 'empathy for alterity'.

[89] 'Foundations of European Culture', 38 (1) *Amer J Comp L*, 20–5 (1990).

[90] See 'Comparative Law and Legal Culture', in Mathias Reimann and Reinhard Zimmermann (eds), *The Oxford Handbook of Comparative Law* (2006), p 714.

[91] 'Global Legal Interaction and Legal Cultures', 7 *Ratio Juris*, 132–4 (1994).

[92] 'Comparative Law and Legal Culture', in Mathias Reimann and Reinhard Zimmermann (eds), *The Oxford Handbook of Comparative Law* (2006), p 716.

environment before presenting our complex data to an inexpert audience, as well as suggesting ways for making this knowledge transferable from one society to another. Our presentation is extremely detailed; it is aided by empirical evidence never before submitted on this topic; and, finally, it invokes the views of eminent 'insiders'—suggesting that our method of transferring knowledge from one system to another is conceptually and philosophically acceptable by the national lawyers of the potential borrowing system. In plain and simple English: this is not a theoretical model but one which shows how information and experience from one system can be transferred to another.

Sociologists should take account of the above 'worries' and become ready to review their own optic as well as their tendency towards abstraction and generalisation before they can hope to establish a genuine working link with *all* sections of the comparative law community. Until then, traditional comparatists may be tempted to consider applying in reverse the Carbonnier aphorism and treat sociology as a 'collateral subject' to applied comparative law. That may not be an ideal solution; but it is preferable to marginalising them outright.

(f) Comparative Law and Anthropology—A Suffocating Embrace?

In this sub-section we discuss the comparison (or attempted comparison) involving more primitive or peripheral systems, typically tribal law or customary law of, say, African nations. The rich variety of them has been noted by many specialists, even when we are talking of one and the same area which now forms a modern state. Also noted is the often uncertain nature of identifying correctly the content of these practices or customs. It is a work normally left to anthropologists, some of whom (and certainly those who contribute the most original work) spend years on location studying their chosen topic or subject.

Here, by contrast to the (on the whole doubting) comments made in the previous sub-section, the cohabitation with contemporary and applied comparative law is even more difficult to justify. This is especially so in a world of restricted finances and cluttered curricula, which cannot keep growing without a willingness to shed off from time to time courses which, for whatever reason, have become less necessary. This, therefore, is our verdict about the advantages and possibilities of anthropology, whether it appears linked to comparative law or not. In the university world more than anywhere else, every proposal for reform invariably meets with opposition. 'Howls of anguish' is often a better term; and these are emitted in the names of academic freedom, cultural richness and the like. Not surprisingly, therefore, anthropologists will not agree with our ideas and proposals.

Scholars such as Professors Chase (NYU) and Riles (Cornell) are thus among those who have stressed the important contribution which anthropological and sociological research can make to the contemporary study of comparative law. Of course, to deal with these views one must (again) remind oneself of the purposes which comparative law can *effectively* pursue. As stated, some authors have discovered many such aims or targets;[93] we maintain throughout this book that what is *useful* to the legal profession is what will keep the subject alive; otherwise it will wither on the vine, as has happened with Roman law.

Chase's account of the Azanda tribe, already briefly referred to above, is the best example why the study of such sociological material is inappropriate to a law school, especially the professional law schools usually found in America.

[93] Eg Professor Roger Cotterell in 'Comparatists and Sociology', in Pierre Legrand and Roderick Munday (eds), *Comparative Legal Studies: Traditions and Transitions* (2003), pp 134 *ff.*

From beginning to end, the book proves our point—though Professor Chase would (naturally) claim the opposite. Here are five reasons why we find what he advocates unconvincing.

First, the tribe he studies has dispersed if not disappeared. We are thus not just talking of hardly relevant law but literally non-existent law.

Secondly, the material he has about it, and discusses in some detail in his book, is (as he himself admits) largely secondary information derived from the work of an English anthropologist. In short, the raw material for the thesis is not new; what is (presumably) new is the way in which it has been used.

Thirdly, not only is the material second-hand; it is also old, since the field research was actually done some 60 years ago.

Fourthly, the language of the dispersed or disappeared tribe is also hardly understood by many (if any) European scholars; and we suspect that those who could use it would not be lawyers.

Finally, the punishments which the tribe had devised for the crimes they disapproved are hardly conceivable in any advanced society.

This list of doubts about the utility and feasibility of such research could go on forever. What we can do here is only express our personal views about such work: material of this kind will not help one iota an aspiring lawyer in the United States; for many it will be seen as a 'soft' option to gain a few missing credits; and in a world of shrinking financial resources (which nowadays affects even the rich American law schools), using public or private money to fund such posts would strike many as a waste. As for the subject itself, in the courtroom or the legislative chamber, it would mark the death knell of comparative law. Embraced by modern anthropology, comparative law would die even more quickly than if it remained faithful to its historical links with Roman law. For dated the latter subject may have become, but its intellectual rigour in its heyday cannot be denied by anyone; it is certainly not denied by us.

(g) The Shared Error of the Old and New Schools

The above indifference for the real world is, in our view, the main reason why legal history in general and Roman law in particular have lost and, more importantly, *deserve* to lose their decisive grip over comparative law and their (semi-) protected or, in the eyes of some, prestigious status in the law curriculum in general. Let us back this assertion with a specific example since the first of us was once involved in teaching Roman and Byzantine law.

Consider, for instance, the lex Aquilia—a topic that once took up much of the leading author's time. Today, the average English lawyer cannot be asked even to reflect on the wording and scope of its third chapter (even in translation) for he has almost certainly never heard of it. And if he happens to be one of those who read law during his Cambridge days and took, as a third year option, Roman Law II (as it was called in those days), he will, almost certainly, have forgotten everything.

Our hypothetical contemporary reader of the lex Aquilia—for how many are there these days that fall into this category?—may be even more surprised to be told that the preoccupation with the chapter's 31 words has been a particularly British hobby-horse, having attracted the attention of such great jurists as David Daube and Felix Jolowicz—not to mention Harry Lawson and Tony Honoré. Great they all were—but their work on such subjects is no longer part of the collective psyche of lawyers; it is rarely (if ever) cited; and no one would dream of using it in a courtroom or as part of a legislative reform agenda. It represents a piece of true scholarship that remains fossilised by the passage of time. It forms part of the palaeontology of law.

But Roman law, even though it once had at its service some of the finest legal minds in the land, could not bring itself to accept that the world had changed or sense the imperious need to address the demands of our times. Like Goethe's frustrated student, its scholars resided in halls of learning, devoid of hearing, sight, or sense of the real world.[94] Unlike him, however, they seem to be unaware of their isolation. On the 'live and let live' principle, we would not have been too worried about so much effort being expended on such subjects were it not for the fact that in our time it affected adversely—or at the very least slowed down—the growth of comparative law. For this cohabitation of Roman law with comparative law harmed the latter by preventing it from turning its attention to contemporary, practical, issues rather than cultivating assiduously an air of excessive intellectuality and separateness, thus boxing itself into a corner. For Roman law, the consequence had to be one and one only: gradual atrophy. We do not wish to see the same happen to comparative law.

But our argument goes beyond this thought. If Roman law, one of the finest creations of human endeavour, did not avoid this decay, surely the same will happen to the ephemeral contemporary material which appears with excessive regularity mainly in some American law journals and is desperately trying to dominate the comparative law agenda. These 'killing' habits must not be allowed to affect the study of contemporary foreign law and the science of comparative methodology. The very full statistics provided in Chapter Three support the view/complaint that Roman law (a) took up a disproportionate amount of the time and effort of British comparatists, diverting them from comparative law; (b) affected—for what it is worth—adversely the citation rates of these authors; and (c) diminished, as a result, the legacy they could have left to posterity.[95]

The above arguments and, more importantly, the lessons that must be drawn from the statistical survey attempted in the next Chapter, are not to be dismissed lightly. In purely intellectual terms, however, there is no doubt that the practical slant that we chose to give to our work will strike many—Professor Sacco[96] and like-minded purists are an excellent contemporary example—as a sad negation of what true scholarship should stand for. For these colleagues believe that the accumulation and systematisation of knowledge is more important than finding a way of putting this knowledge—even eventually—to wider use. This view represents an ideal—an ideal that was, in fact, practised in the days when there were few universities, the number of students was small, and the cost of legal education a fraction of what it is now. The problem is that this ideal is dead.

This conflict between the 'elegant' and the 'utilitarian' represents, of course, a clash of philosophies as regrettable as it is old. We once thought that in law ways could be found to breach the chasm. In striving for reconciliation we have experienced in a very real sense the Faustian agony (which can, we think, be read in a non-theological way) that follows when 'two souls dwell within one breast'. That beautiful passage can show how being pulled in

[94] 'Und in den Sälen auf den Bänken Vergeht mir, Hören, Sehn und Denken'. Faust, Part I (Insel edn), p 57.

[95] Though as the leading author explained in his John Maurice Kelly Memorial Lecture, published by the Faculty of Law of University College Dublin (2003), scholarship, reputation of scholarship, and legacy are not made up by the same ingredients.

[96] 'Legal Formants: A Dynamic Approach to Comparative Law', 39 *Am J Comp L* 1, 4 (1991).

opposite directions can tear a soul apart.[97] Between us we have clocked over 50 years of teaching in some of the world's leading law faculties; and this experience makes us less hopeful now than in our earlier days that a complete reconciliation can be achieved. And since we are, *above all*, anxious to play our part in keeping our subject alive, we are trying to find ways to ensure its survival, jettisoning if need be anything that weighs it down. The orientation we have tried to give to our subject is thus a compromise born of our life's experience in teaching on both sides of the Atlantic and both sides of the Channel, and not in all of its aspects one of first choice.

This personal agonising runs deeper than most readers might think by reading our text and reflecting on our substitute solutions. Misunderstanding our text will come more easily than weighing it carefully in order to understand it properly. For the sadness that our conclusions generate can only be measured against a lifetime's experience.

The first of us thus recalls how, less than 20 years ago, he joined the famous Leiden Law Faculty as a tenured part-time member. He found there a second Professor of Comparative Law, a Professor (and a flourishing Institute) of Eastern European Law, two and a half Chairs of Roman Law, a Chair in Ecclesiastical Law, and two posts in papyrology (ancient and modern)—not to mention a fully fledged Department in European Community Law! By the time he resigned in the late 1990s, the Professor of Roman Law was doing some teaching in English law; the University could not fill the chair of English Law except on a (very) part-time basis; and the other posts had disappeared—all except the European Community Law section. The same is true of most chairs of Roman law as far apart as Scotland and South Africa, not to forget Ireland. Increasingly they stand empty or are filled by colleagues who claim Roman law as a secondary string in their bow. How in such circumstances some Dutch colleagues can entitle a collection of essays *Viva Vox Iuris Romani* defeats us since for years we experienced at first hand the stranglehold that public finances have placed on Dutch law faculties. The gradual disappearance of Latin as an A-level option in English schools must also point in the same direction.

Though legal history is not our immediate concern it, too, has sometimes followed this pattern. When, as far back as 1888, William Maitland gave his inaugural lecture at the University of Cambridge under the title 'Why the History of English Law Has Not been Written', he pinned his hopes in completing the necessary research for writing it on ten 'failed barristers'. In return for a modest stipend, he thought, they would be willing to edit a goodly number of yearbooks. Professor John Baker, the current holder of the Maitland Chair and one of the most erudite legal historians of our times, is still making the same appeal,[98] but in an environment that is no longer likely to see it as quaint but as unrealistic.

Funds, or lack of funds, played a key part in ensuring the failure of Maitland's own appeal. Can we—must we?—avoid asking the question whether they are, nowadays, likely to be more forthcoming? And who in today's world can attract talent if his manifesto appeals to 'failed' lawyers to whom 'modest' pay is promised? The inevitable contrast must thus be drawn with the attractive offers made to students who are high achievers—not failures—willing to work in multinational law firms, banks, and the industry. One may regret the decline in interest in such topics just as much as one regrets—the leading author more than many—the dying of languages (such as ancient Greek) in which the founding values of our civilisation were once expressed with great economy of words. But as university

[97] Faust, Part I (Insel edn), p 37.

[98] 'Why the History of English Law Has Not Been Finished', [2000] 59 *CLJ* 62, 73.

leaders we must come to realise that our agendas, unlike our dreams, must be shaped in the light of the current financial condition of European law faculties. If this means adjusting the optic of our subjects to save what we can in the interests of a broader legal education, we should do it. Emulating Julian the Apostate is as successful a strategy as is the ostrich's burying of his head in the sand and wishing the danger away.

To sum up, the environment we live in has little time left for flirting with legal history and Roman law except as optional subjects[99]; and it has even less need for politically correct orientations. Likewise, it will not tolerate comparative law falling into the hands of philosophers, anthropologists, and incomprehensible 'post-modernists'—assuming that these disciplines can offer anything to the subject.[100] For the reasons we have just sketched out, these trendy approaches have little chance of becoming the orthodoxy of tomorrow, though in a country such as the United States, the super-abundance of law journals will always offer such ideas the chance to break out in print. In Pirandellian terms, however, their authors are producing a subject doomed to spend its life in search of an audience.

Yet even those who sympathise with our views might look at the number of American-based authors agitating for such changes in favour of post-modernism and come to the conclusion that we are the *vox clamantis in deserto*. But when one reflects deeply on the above-mentioned politically trendy literature in the area of comparative law, one is spurred on by Montaigne's remark that in times such as these '[W]e can only improve ourselves by walking backwards, by discord not by harmony, by being different not by being like'.[101] Academics, on the whole, are a cowardly lot, despite the security given to them by 'tenure'. For our part we share the view expressed by one of Bulgakov's characters who denounces '[C]owardice [as] one of the most terrible *sins*'.[102] It would be cowardice not to make a stand and denounce past practices and emerging trends which one honestly believes to be bad.

But if, in this instance, we wish to 'walk backwards', could we not only be different but also wrong? Could our emphasis on practice and the real world be entirely misconceived? It has been said, for instance, that the American scene is showing us how the emphasis in law is shifting from the judge to the scholar.[103] Between us, however, we have been teaching in the United States for nearly 30 years and we honestly doubt that this represents an accurate reading of the current scene. Our view remains unchanged even if one makes allowance for the fact that American academics have been more actively involved than their English counterparts in the shaping of the policy of the law and, nowadays, comparative public law.

For as long as American legal education retains its professional features, aims to train lawyers—and not just civil servants, bankers, or merely provide a general degree—the concrete, the pragmatic, the utilitarian method we have advocated will thus find a fertile soil to germinate. And the American approach, aided by the spreading dominance of the English

[99] The fact that many of our best faculties make the subject a compulsory one shows how little faith they have in its ability to draw in the crowds.

[100] See, eg, 'The Art and Science of Critical Scholarship: Postmodernism and International Style in the Legal Architecture of Europe', by Ugo Mattei and Anna di Robilant, 75 *Tulane L Rev* 1053 (2001).

[101] 'On the Art of Conversation', *The Complete Essays*, translated and edited with an introduction and notes by MA Screech (1991).

[102] *The Master and Margarita* (1969) at p 336 (our emphasis). In an earlier section of the book (p 322) the thought is more openly attributed to Jesus.

[103] Ugo Mattei, 'Why the Wind Changes: Intellectual Leadership in Western Law', 42 *Am J Comp L* 195, 207 *ff* (1994).

language and the fact that the financial world (in all its forms) remains largely Anglo-Saxon in mentality, provides the background which *needs* our method. Not, it must be stressed again, that this ignores either the principles or the interests of the jurist. On the contrary, it is an approach that believes that by engaging the attention of the judge, the practitioner, and the law reformer, it will force greater and fruitful collaboration between the practitioner and the academic, and thus secure the survival of the subject. How right we think we are can be seen by looking at the figures assembled in the next Chapter. Bluntly, they paint a simple picture: most of the comparatists included in our survey have left courts and practitioners totally unmoved. In this sense, and maybe in this sense alone, Birks may have been right when he implied that comparative law, in the state it was in when he made his speech, seemed irrelevant to the real world.

Yet if this was the case when he made his speech, it was largely the fault of its high priests including himself. That is our verdict; and that is our *j'accuse*. But that is not the end of the story. For Birks' statement totally missed the signs of revival which the move towards European integration was already manifesting at the time. And he seemed to ignore completely the volume of American and international scholarship which dealt—and deals—with human rights and comparative public law. Of course, Birks was not a comparative lawyer—and even less a comparative public lawyer. Notwithstanding his broad learning, he clearly could not keep his eye on so many balls. But the signs already existed at the time of his writing, and they have since then become stronger. The extent to which the use of foreign law is nowadays discussed in the United States is considerable, lively, and showing no signs of abatement, especially since it has become so closely intertwined with contemporary political debates. Comparative law, if ever it was in a ghetto, no longer is. And this is so even though some of its contemporary priests, in England or in France, as well as some amateurs who feel the urge to enter a debate they know little about,[104] are doing their best to tell us that for cultural, linguistic[105] or other reasons, it simply cannot succeed. The crude and simple answer is that it *is* succeeding, even though it still has to iron out many creases in the methodology it is trying to develop.

5. FROM HEROES TO MOVEMENTS OF CONTEMPORARY GLOBALISATION

So let us return to the starting point of the first Chapter: is comparative law in a ghetto and, moreover, doomed to stay there? Clearly there have been signs of unease and restlessness. Some have voiced their concerns in an even gloomier imagery. Professor Merryman, writing at the same time as Birks did, observed that[106] 'Comparative law languishes in a narrow dungeon of its own construction, deprived of light and air by a conversely constricted academic vision'. Yet others expressed their hopes in millenarian terms, claiming that

[104] See, eg, Jane Stapleton, 'Benefits of Comparative Tort Reasoning: Lost in Translation', Journal of Tort Law, vol 1 [2007], Iss 3, Art 6 (online version available at http://www.bepress.com/jtl/vol1/iss3/art6).

[105] One of the leading legal translators of our times, Tony Weir, has so argued; see 'Die Sprachen des europäischen Rechts: Eine skeptische Betrachtung', (1995) 3 *Zeitschrift für Europäisches Privatrecht*, 368 *ff*. But the validity of this argument has been doubted by Zimmermann, 'Savigny's Legacy. Legal History, Comparative Law, and the Emergence of a European Legal Science', 112 (1996) *LQR*, 576, esp 595–6.

[106] 'Comparative Law Scholarship', 21 *Hastings Int'l & Comp L Rev* 771, 784 [1998].

comparative law 'desperately' needed the intervention of 'towering figures'.[107] But it *has* had towering figures who, along with great achievements, have also committed grave errors.

To react to such views intelligently one must first note that these cries of distress were emitted at the same time. This coincidence in time is intriguing; and we are not sure that it would be improper to see them as reflecting the frustrations felt at the end of the barren years (roughly speaking the 1980s and part of the 1990s), years barren as much in England as they were in the United States, and for which (as suggested) some of the earlier writers may have borne some responsibility themselves since this 'constricted academic vision' had materialised during their watch. After all, Merryman admitted that the 'dungeon' was 'of its own construction'.

Secondly, and without any doubt, these writers showed no signs of foreseeing the renaissance of interest generated by a variety of factors (to which they cannot claim any credit themselves) in the last 10 years or so on both sides of the Atlantic. These were factors linked to world events, not individuals—a point to which we shall return below.

Thirdly, we should ascertain to what exactly these cries of despair refer. Are those who are making these claims referring, for instance, to the fact that fewer universities are offering courses on foreign and comparative law? If they are, it is submitted that they are wrong; and this expansion of teaching of comparative law, to be sure of varying quality, has, in Europe, been facilitated by numerous student and research programmes originating from Brussels. Are the grumblers, alternatively, saying that fewer students are taking such classes? Again, we think, the answer is probably no, especially if one looks at the earlier years of the period we have chosen to study in greater detail. Is it, then, the quantity of writing on the subject, which is in decline? To this question a negative answer can here be entered with even greater assurance than in the previous one. Are the citations that comparatists are getting for their work (as a measure of their wider reputation) substantially lower than those made to writers of mainstream subjects? The information provided in the next Chapter suggests that this may be the case in the United States but is not true for English authors, where the non-comparatists are not scoring that much better than the comparatists. Finally, are the personal and intellectual exchanges between lawyers of different countries weakening instead of strengthening? This question, in our view, cannot even be posed. For the last 10 or 15 years have witnessed a veritable explosion of intellectual co-operation and exchange,[108] even at judicial levels, which our heroes of yesterday could not have anticipated to come about so rapidly. All these changes have created a real need for *applied* comparative law. It is difficult to argue, at least by looking at things with hindsight, that the 'grumblers' saw matters clearly. If their gaze was accurate, it was to the extent that it was directed backwards, to the end of their own era. To the extent that it was directed forward, they simply got things wrong.

Yet, despite the above-described (undoubted) progress, which gives the lie to the ghetto theory, it would be difficult to deny that something 'marginal' remains about the subject.

Marginal, first, in the sense that those who devote their energy to it attract little attention from the general educated public (and their faculties) compared to those who devote their minds to 'core' or 'trendy' subjects. The emphasis is thus on building up a stronger presence in commercial law, intellectual property law, and public law, and much less in

[107] Ugo Mattei, 46 *The Amer J Comp L*, 709, 711 (1998).

[108] How far we have come in this field of endeavour can be seen by reading von Bar, Lando and Swann, 'Communication on European Contract Law: Joint Responses of the Commission on European Contract Law and the Study Group on a European Civil Code', *European Rev of Private Law* 2, 183–48 (2002).

international networking and introducing into the existing curriculum the strengths of modern comparative law.

Marginal, secondly, because their work has failed to attract the attention of practitioners and the courts in the way that the great treatise writers have.

Marginal, finally, because the greater understanding of foreign law has yet to be exploited by the globalisation of trade, finance, and social intercourse. To the extent that this has happened, it has occurred in the major international law firms, not the universities.

The marginalisation, however, that we have described above seems to us to be radically different from the one the critics of the subject have in mind. It is also a marginalisation that is very different in kind from that experienced by Roman law, which is much more terminal in nature. Finally, to the extent that marginalisation in any of the above forms is continuing, it remains self-inflicted by the past generation, which allowed its subject to be hijacked by legal history and Roman law, and is casting a long shadow which few seem to have the courage to remove. And it is likely to remain self-inflicted again by some of our contemporary comparatists who threaten to marginalise the subject further by placing it at the service of trendy causes. If there is thus (to change the metaphor) a cloud on the horizon, it is caused by those who identify a crisis in the American academic scene and propose remedies which, in reality, would enhance and not solve it. For these American 'grumblers' cannot see what world-shrinking is bringing in its wake—just as many of their English counterparts do not understand that universities are increasingly driven by the needs of the real world and cannot be dominated by dead disciplines.

Before we elaborate our views on these rebel dogmas, let us return briefly to our earlier image of a golden era, inhabited by fallible heroes. Greek mythology shows us how the heroes often brought about their own demise. Hercules did; and so did Achilles. The light of contemporary scrutiny can be even more destructive when it comes to some of the old reputations, especially of those comparatists who ran the show in the 1980s and early 1990s.

Each age, we think, has the tendency to idolise the one that preceded it; to see it in terms of a *belle époque*. We have slipped into such elegiacal moods ourselves in the previous Chapter, though we have also tried to guard against them. But in our case one must do more than guard against them; one must try to understand why such elegies must be restrained.

First of all, we think that behind this admiration is hidden some kind of psychological need to inflate the past in order to bolster greater confidence in the present. In our next Chapter we will try to show with the help of statistics (and some references) how some comparatists have, to use Judge Posner's words, promoted 'their own . . . interests by hitching their wagon to a star'[109] and for this reason endeavoured to enhance even further the reputation of the past master. Our own attitude has been to admire (and learn) from past masters but not to idolise them and, above all, not to treat their beliefs as immutable or untouchable. Post-1960s scepticism towards all canonical figures and phenomena could not leave comparative law or its heroes untouched; and in this book we are doing some demystifying and criticising of our own, especially with respect to the legacy of those who came at the tail end of the great era. But demystifying or deconstructing is not all that happens with the passage of time. Even those who are not 'un-pegged' simply get forgotten.

In one sense, this is much worse than has been commonly realised. We are, for instance, constantly surprised to see how few contemporary comparatists have read Lord Macmillan's *Two Ways of Reasoning* even though it is as relevant today as it was 60 years ago

[109] *Cardozo. A Study in Reputation* (1990), p 60.

when it was delivered as a lecture at the University of Cambridge.[110] And the leading author will never forget the case of a German student of his who had never heard of Rudolf von Jhering and mistook his (Austrian) title of nobility[111] as a being a *versus* not a *von*, and treated him as a case: the case of Rudolf against Jhering! If this can happen to Jhering—the man who saw Roman law not as an end in itself but as a means towards a new legal order—what does the future hold for most of us ordinary mortals? It is salutary (and not painful) to accept the inevitable answer: nothing![112]

So the images of ghettos and good neighbourhoods, towering figures and mortal descendants, should not be over-used. For though, as individuals, we may fade into the background, and our work becomes blurred and even extinguished with time, we still exist as parts of movements. This sobering thought fits in well with the current anti-heroic academic culture of our times. A culture in which committees have replaced leaders, political correctness robust and clear language, trendiness sound judgment, and research assessment exercises the slow but inevitable accolade of peer recognition that time invariably (but not always) brought to those who deserved but did not seek it. We make no secret of the fact that we regret some of these shifts. We also see in them dangers for our subject (and, worse still, for academia as a whole). For those criticising the state of comparative law in the United States are, it seems to us, consciously rebelling against the philosophy of the heroes of the golden era which, with all its faults,[113] we found had some attractions.

And yet in this 'de-personalisation' of academic life we also see the chance for a real breakthrough for comparative law. It is this new environment which will make law faculties discover the true utility of studying foreign law and comparative methodology. And it is again this environment which will defeat the calls to give the subject the trendy apparel which the American-based reformers wish for it but which we find most unattractive.

So it is the political and economic realities that prevail at the turn of the 21st century—European integration, world trade, globalisation of human rights, multi-national law firms, and enhanced career opportunities for those who speak foreign languages and know something about other systems—that have changed the background and created the right conditions for the survival, indeed, expansion of our subject. It is these conditions that largely account for the revival that started slowly in the mid- to late-1990s and brought the subject out of the ghetto to which it was being consigned. It is these changes which enabled the study of foreign law to replace Roman law as the only medium of becoming aware of another legal system in the course of an ever shortening period of legal study.

[110] See *Law and Other Things* (1935).

[111] In his letters to Windscheid, Jhering describes how, on his departure from Vienna in the early 1870s, the Austrian Emperor bestowed upon him the Knight's Cross of the Order of Leopold, which carried with it the nobility title of *von* which, henceforth, Jhering would religiously incorporate in his signature. See Karl Kroeschell (ed), *Jherings Briefe an Windscheid 1880–1891* (1988).

[112] An even more dramatic example emerged from a recent 'survey of students of German literature at Cologne University [*sic*] [who] believed Schiller to be a play by Goethe'. See Lesley Sharpe, *The Cambridge Companion to Goethe* (2002) at p 4.

[113] A 'fault' that Merryman has pointed out is the neglect of Italian law. But leaving aside the fact that Italian is the fourth foreign language in order of priority of study at English schools, the conclusion is still too pessimistic. For first, Professor Merryman and others have, in recent years, supplied casebooks and textbooks about Italian law. Secondly, also in the last 10 years or so, at least two major law faculties in the UK, Oxford and UCL, have started offering courses in Italian law (in Italian). Thirdly, a new wave of travelling Italian scholars have done much to give us a new picture of Italian scholarship both in the area of comparative and public international law. Finally, the other missing major system is that of the Hispanic world (old and new). To some (small) extent, however, this ignorance is made up by some knowledge of the underlying French legal ideas. One wonders, therefore, whether allusions to prisons lacking light or air are not over-dramatisations!

For they embedded European law into the modern syllabus in England and progressively (even in the United States) brought comparative law indirectly into the syllabus of many specialist subjects. It is political developments and changes in the social environment which have brought about the changes that are making the study of foreign law necessary. In short, it is *events* and not *heroic figures* (as in the past) that are determining our subject and will shape its future. Among these causes or developments or events we include 'Europe'—the Brussels-inspired (often unwise but invariably imaginative) initiatives to facilitate European integration are among the most significant. And that is another reason why the 'Eurocentric' approach of comparative law has not yet gasped its last breath. On the contrary, it is forcing others to study and learn from its successes as well as its mistakes.

Then there has been 'Europe' in the form of the output of the courts in Luxembourg and Strasbourg, which has brought new ideas, new concepts, and new doctrines into subjects which 30 years ago had a distinctly parochial if not stale look about them. Ideas, incidentally, which should make English lawyers appreciate that on all the major legal issues of our times—human rights, patterns of federalism, or individualism versus socialisation of risks—there exist plausible European alternatives, and America and the Commonwealth are not the only source of attractive ideas.

Europe, thirdly, as an idea that has already captured the imagination of English judges more so than the country's politicians. Since the pioneering Hamlyn lectures of Lord Scarman[114] some 30 years ago, numerous articles have been written by some of our leading judges which bear deep marks of European legal thinking. We are thinking, for instance, of judges such as Goff,[115] Mustill,[116] Bingham,[117] Hoffmann,[118] Woolf,[119] Steyn,[120] Sedley,[121] Laws[122] and, indeed, the former Lord Chancellor,[123] making England (proportionately to its population) the country with the most academically oriented judges in the Western world. Though in their judgments as well as their extra-judicial pronouncements one finds the whole gamut of emotions from the most pro-European to the most sceptical, all are infinitely more open-minded in accepting the impact of European law than many of our academic colleagues. Through their example they have also created the trend of the writing judge, which in its own way will also contribute to breaking down the old barriers that separated bench and academic cloister as well as the barrier which the Channel used to present. For all of the above (and we could give more names and illustrations) have in their work dwelled in comparative law, or foreign law, or both, and used it intelligently to shape, inspire, and even change national law.

[114] His seminal Hamlyn Lectures, *English Law the New Dimension* (1974), could be credited for having started this whole debate in its contemporary form.

[115] For instance his classic 'The Search for Principle', (1983) 69 *Proceedings of the British Academy*, 169; 'Judge, Jurist and Legislature', (1987) 2 *Denning L Jo* 79; 'Coming Together—The Future', *The Clifford Chance Millennium Lectures, The Coming Together of the Common Law and the Civil Law* (2000), 239 *ff.*

[116] 'Negligence in the World of Finance', 5 *The Supreme Court [Malaysia] Journal*, 1 (1992); 'What do Judges do?', *Särtryck ur Juridisk Tidskrift*, 1995–96, Nr 3, 611.

[117] *The Business of Judging* (2000).

[118] 'A Sense of Proportion', F Jacobs and M Andenas (eds), *Community Law in English Courts* (1998).

[119] *Protection of the Public: A New Challenge* (1990), Hamlyn Lectures. See also his FA Mann Lecture entitled 'Droit Public—English Style', [1995] *PL* 57 *ff.*

[120] For instance, Perspectives of Corrective and Distributive Justice in Tort Law', *John Maurice Kelly Memorial Lecture*, University College Dublin (2002).

[121] 'The Sound of Silence: Constitutional Law Without a Constitution', (1994) 110 *LQR* 270. 'Human Rights: A TwentyFirst century Agenda', [1995] 1 *PL* 386 *ff.*

[122] 'The Ghost in the Machine: Principle in Public Law', [1989] *PL* 27 *ff*; 'Is the High Court the Guardian of Fundamental Constitutional Rights?', [1993] *PL* 59; 'Law and Democracy', [1995] *PL* 72.

[123] 'Judges and Decision-Makers: The Theory and Practice of *Wednesbury* Review', [1996] *PL* 59.

And Europe, finally, because it is increasingly (not decreasingly) going to occupy American business and its legal advisers as they realise the size of the new emerging market and wish to stake a claim in it. And this market, from the Atlantic to the Urals, will need practitioners to draw contracts, shape the language of transactions, and sort out the mess when things go wrong (as they are bound to). These lawyers will not be shaped by sociological or anthropological theories but by an environment which will require pragmatic and focused thinking, training in languages, a talent not to be chauvinistic, and the need to be mentally agile. And when, perhaps, comparative law ceases one (distant) day to be a separate subject and becomes an integral part of employment law, enterprise law, corporations law, defamation law, immigration law, and so on, it may—finally—also have achieved its double intellectual aims of teaching foreign law and making us think about our own. We see these paramount aims as being interlinked; and as scholars resolutely unwilling to commit themselves to one culture and ignore others, we see also in these qualities another great merit of our subject: that it only works if it is seen as a two-way street.

Europe, the end of the cold war, and trade globalisation have thus been some of the 'causes', the 'catalysts', and 'needs that have to be addressed'. Indeed, they were first recognised by multinational law firms—not universities—as issues that need to be tackled. It was thus major City firms which in diverse ways helped lead London law schools to expand their ambitions in the direction of Europe and indirectly encouraged the ever growing number of joint courses by eagerly employing those who took them as part of their university degrees, or offering scholarships to students spending time abroad. It is events such as the above which are in the process of rejuvenating a subject which once existed only because a bunch of talented émigrés and a handful of local scholars saw its intellectual appeal. The 'de-personification' of the subject is its salvation, *not* its nemesis. Necessity, practical *commercial* necessity, is what will make the study of foreign law grow further and deeper, not trendy preachers such as one finds in the United States—the country which will always find followers for even the most eccentric of prophets. And we have it on the good authority of one of the seven sages of antiquity that 'even the Gods do not fight against necessity'.[124]

[124] Pittacus of Mitylene, RD Hicks (ed), *Lives of Eminent Philosophers*, I, 79 (1925), cited also by Plato in *Protagoras*.

3

SPREADING THE GOSPEL (AND THE NAME OF THE EVANGELIST)

1. AIMS TO BE PURSUED

Judge Richard Posner was not the first to use statistical information to measure reputation by reference to the number of citations an author receives to his works.[1] Yet his biography of Benjamin Cardozo[2] gave an impetus to other lawyers to develop what one of them has since called the science of 'reputology'.[3] The word 'science' may, in fact, be exaggerating the status of this new branch of learning since the conclusions one can draw are hedged by numerous (yet necessary) qualifications that must be made to the raw material and the way it is assembled and interpreted. At times, these qualifications make the resulting lessons vague, perhaps even tenuous; and the language in which some of these pieces are written is not one which will either be familiar or attractive to many lawyers, at any rate those operating in the European area.

Yet, as ways of measuring 'a "quality" that is socially defined, reflecting the utility of the writing in question to other scholars, rather than gauging its intrinsic merit',[4] these guides may be useful exercises. Moreover, despite the limitations in the methodology, the new topic is undoubtedly gaining in popularity and sophistication in the United States,[5] so it may be safe to assume that it will not be long before we begin to see its European counterparts. For American ideas and tastes, ingenious or crude, on average tend to reach Europe with a time lag of about 10 years. Indeed, the Royal Dutch Academy's Research Fellowships and the Blaise Pascal Chairs awarded by the prestigious Ecole Nationale Superieure of France use this method, among others, to evaluate the standing of competing professors.[6]

[1] See, eg, Wade, 'Citation Analysis: A New Tool for Science Administrators', 188 *Science* 429 (1975); Stigler and Friedland, 'The Pattern of Citation Practices in Economics', 11 *History of Political Economy* 1 (1979); Robey, 'Reputations vs Citations: Who Are the Top Scholars in Political Science?', 15 *PS* 199 (1982); Shapiro, 'The Most Cited Law Review Article', 73 *California L Rev* 1540 (1985).

[2] *A Study in Reputation* (1990).

[3] William Powers, 'Reputology', 12 *Cardozo L Rev* 1941 (1991). Two other Texas colleagues, JM Balkin and Sanford Levinson, coined the acoustically equally unattractive term 'citology'. See 'How to Win Cites and Influence People', *71 Chi-Kent L Rev* 843 (1996). The corruptive effect of American linguistic inventiveness seems already to have acquired a foothold in England. See *The Guardian*, 'Glossary for the 1990s', 10 May 1997.

[4] Shapiro, 'The Most cited legal Scholars', 29 *J Legal Stud* 409, 412 (2000).

[5] Thus see Barrett, '"Citology". The Study of Footnotes Sweeps the Law Schools', *Wall St J*, 22 January 1997 and, more recently, the collection of essays published in vol 29 of *The Journal of Legal Studies* (2000), especially the articles by Professor Fred Shapiro at pp 389 *ff*, 397 *ff* and 409 *ff*, and William M Landes and Richard A Posner at pp 319 *ff*.

[6] Interestingly, the Higher Education Funding Council for England (HEFCE) is currently considering the potential for using bibliometric analysis, that is, analysis of how frequently a piece of research is cited by other researchers, in the evaluation of academic research in the context of HEFCE's current work to develop a new research assessment and funding framework to replace the Research Assessment Exercise after 2008; see http://www.hefce.ac.uk/pubs/rdreports/2007/rd18_07/.

In this Chapter we shall be putting this method to a narrow and less ambitious use. To that extent our use of this material may thus prove more acceptable. On the other hand, we have broadened the scope to include more than one system, and in this sense the exercise is the first of its kind in so far as it is trying to indicate 'reputation of scholarship' at an international level. To this end one must draw information from many countries and legal systems, and this is what makes this attempt riddled with difficulties. At the very least, therefore, we hope that our efforts will prompt further investigation along the lines we are suggesting (which remain insufficiently explored by our predecessors) with a view to refining or refuting our arguments. Thus, in the context of comparative law, three points in our view need to be explored further with the aid of this method.

(a) The Importance of Language

First, reputation of scholarship in foreign and comparative law is greatly enhanced if the writer makes some (if not most) of his work available in the English language. Professor Rodolfo Sacco of Turin University offers an excellent illustration since the bulk of the citations he receives in the American literature come from one (of two) articles of his which have been translated into English by Professor James Gordley.[7] Whether this is sufficient to support the statement that he has thus had some tangible impact on the American (academic) scene is open to doubt. Our view is that he has not; and his impact in England has, if anything, been even smaller. Yet this is as good a moment as any to repeat what has already been said, namely that what we are here trying to measure is how much the work of a particular author has been used by other colleagues, especially outside his own country (in this case Italy), and not the quality and originality of his learning—which, in Sacco's case, is beyond dispute. Something of the same lesson emerges from the American citations to René David's chief work, *Les grands systèmes de droit contemporain*.[8] This suggests that a foreign scholar runs a very real risk of remaining out of reach of a substantial part of the world's legal readership if he does not write in English. The danger is greater, of course, the less widely used is his own language.

In a shrinking world this is a serious drawback, especially for comparatists. Foreign scholars who rightly feel proud of their respective languages and rich cultural heritage may regret this growing domination of the English language. But it is also a reflection of the fact that English is increasingly the *lingua franca* of the business, financial, and (by extension) legal worlds, having replaced French and, more importantly, Latin.

The above observations also underline another point, namely that reputation and scholarly merit are not co-terminous, the former depending on such fortuitous factors as

[7] 'Legal Formants: A Dynamic Approach to Comparative Law', 39 *Amer J Comp L*, 1 *ff* and 344 *ff* (1991). This article is cited 64 times in 50 documents. No other work of his approaches this level. His *Introduzione al diritto comparato* (5th edn 1992), possibly his magnum opus, appears 10 times in 10 documents. For a man who, in the space of a long and productive career, has written extensively in Italian (and less so in French), this is a very poor showing though, in my view, this reflects more adversely on American legal academe, which rarely goes beyond English texts, than on Sacco. But how language has 'disadvantaged' Sacco (and other Italians) can be seen if one compares the number of his citations in the American literature (106) to those given to another Italian—Cappelletti (514)—writing mainly in English.

[8] *Major Legal Systems in the World Today*. The Spanish and Portuguese versions of the same book received three citations. David's other major monograph, written in English and entitled *English Law and French Law* (1980), receives a total of 17 citations. All of his remaining works receive 195 citations, each of them usually receiving citations in single figures.

language and also being in many ways easier to manipulate than the latter, for reasons which Posner himself explores with his usual clarity.[9] Moreover, scholarly merit may be great but undiscovered, precisely because the language element has hindered it becoming known and thus impeded its recognition beyond its natural and national frontiers. Scholars who have 'suffered' from not being accessible for linguistic reasons to Anglo-Saxon audiences include such eminent Continental European jurists as Ernst von Caemmerer and, to some extent, Hans Stoll (both Germany), Gino Gorla, Rodolfo Sacco and Benedetto Conforti (all Italy), and Gérard Cornu, Francois Terré and Genevieve Viney (all France)—to mention but a few. Others, of course, could be added to this list. But overall, and in national terms, those who seem to have suffered most are, arguably, our Italian colleagues, something which represents a great loss to international legal science given the originality of the Italian mind—in law as, indeed, in other matters.

(b) Where One is Cited

Secondly, in this piece we have, inter alia, been anxious to explore the validity of the thesis developed in the first two chapters of this book. There, our quest was for the *kind* of comparative law that has the best chance of attracting the attention of the courts and strengthening the position of the subject in the law curriculum. Though we think what follows supports this thesis, the figures reproduced must, again, be read with caution, even though our efforts at updating the material, analysed in the second part of this Chapter, suggest that the trend described here is continuing if not strengthening. The same is true of the propositions they are meant to support.

Still, some caution is required here, partly because the figures collected are (relatively) modest. More importantly, however, in some countries (like France and Italy) the collection of statistical data is seriously impeded by the fact that their courts (unlike the German and, nowadays, the English) do not cite academic literature in their opinions. It is, therefore, difficult to demonstrate an overt link between academic ideas and judicial results.[10] A third and final reason why it is difficult to assert with confidence whether the method we have championed (of 'targeting' judges and not, simply, fellow academics) is working in practice is due to the fact that the approach is relatively new; it has not yet had sufficient time to produce any statistically significant evidence as to whether it is leading to the desired co-operation between the two parts of the legal profession. The most that one can say is thus that the overall picture is evolving and incomplete. Still, for the reasons we give below, we feel it is, generally speaking, supportive of our views.

Of course, we must never let out of sight the fact that many scholars would dispute our claim that targeting the judge is the best way of ensuring the success of our subject. Our own doubts about the validity of this objection were given in the previous Chapters, and all we need repeat here is our conviction that our subject will only take root when it has proved its worth to practitioners (of all kinds). We must, however, add one point at the very outset of our discussion, and that is that even though we are talking of targeting judges, we feel that the guidelines we offer to attract their interest are also applicable if we are trying to interest

[9] See Chapter 4 in general.

[10] We have, for instance, spoken to both Italian judges and academics and asked them whether prior to writing a judgment they would occasionally consult leading academics. Both replied in the affirmative; but the link between what was read and what appeared in the subsequent judgment cannot be proved by anything published. Yet those who know a particular author's theory can sometimes identify it in a judgment.

other agents of law reform. Our advice as to how foreign law should be looked at, studied, and applied, works equally well if one is targeting the legislator or a law reform body such as the Law Commission for England and Wales. If the latter has not made sufficient use of foreign law—and by this we mean non-Common law—it is partly because not all of its members have been that anxious to receive it, fewer scholars still have tried to present material to it, and when they have they have not, in our view, done this in the way that would best make the foreign ideas usable and instructive. Our methodology about using foreign law is thus applicable across the board even though, as lawyers operating in a Common law country, we are giving pride of place to the courts.

Let, us, however, return briefly to the disappointment produced by the French and Italian courts by not revealing their sources of inspiration. This disappointment can, in fact, be minimised somewhat if one consults the conclusions of the *avocats généraux*, the *conseillers rapporteurs*, and the *commissaires du gouvernement* of the French courts. For these major trial protagonists *do* cite literature; and, as we shall explain below, this trend is growing fairly fast in France. These writings thus show that academic literature *is* brought to the attention of the judges even though it is concealed in the judgment itself. Incidentally, they also reveal the close and constructive co-operation that exists between the *arrêtiste* (who in the French legal world fleshes out the opaque decisions of the highest courts) and the court itself.

A random selection of leading French cases confirms the accuracy of the above. Even more importantly, recent decisions show that the *Cour de cassation* has nowadays acquired an almost insatiable taste for references to foreign literature and judicial practice.[11] We are also informed that, as a result of the close co-operation that exists between France and Germany, both countries have a 'national judge' attached to the equivalent foreign court. On at least one occasion we have been shown the kind of summary reports these French judges send 'back home' and confess considerable admiration at the way the German material was reported back. But the ways of demonstrating the above in a statistically interesting manner are non-existent, since carrying out electronically the kind of checks we did with the American material is simply not possible. To attempt to do this work manually by looking at each reported case would, on the other hand, require an enormous investment of time which none of us could make. So here suffice it to say that this second structural deficiency again disadvantages European scholars compared to those who operate in the United States and publish in English, especially in American journals.

[11] The controversial decision of the plenum of the French court of cassation in the *Perruche* case of 17 November 2000 demonstrates this most clearly. The documentation can be found in *JCP* 13 Dec 2000, no 50, pp 2293 *ff*. Even more remarkable is the most recent decision of the Court of cassation in the *Chapin* case, Decision number 511 FP-P+B+R+1 of 13 March 2007 (dealing with the question whether 'marriage' between homosexuals was permissible by the French Civil Code and deciding that it was not), in which a remarkable opinion clarifying the attitude of other legal systems towards this topic was commissioned from the Centre of Comparative Law Eduard Lambert of the University of Lyon. Thus, the Supreme Court (and the advocates who appeared before it) considered not only the wording and history of the French Code, the impact that various European documents (such as the Strasbourg Convention) had on it, but also a detailed report on the law in Canada, Belgium, England, the Netherlands, Spain, and the United States. This decision, with others in between the Perruche judgment and itself, shows how far the French Supreme Court has gone towards using foreign law in the process of forming its own conclusions. That this is happening on an issue as sensitive as marriage, linked to religious and other factors, ideas and misconceptions about homosexuality, shows that the movement of ideas is becoming a reality—no doubt to the extreme annoyance of those who keep telling us that cross-culture dialogues cannot happen and will not work. But that is the second point that arises from such decisions: does one pay attention to what the courts are doing or listen to academics following a theory they have developed even if it is daily being proved to be inapplicable in real life?

(c) *Inflating Reputation*

Our *third* and last point is based on a hunch (but not, we would like to believe, a wild one or one which is entirely unsupported by reliable evidence). Though developed from our own personal experience, we are both, nonetheless, intrigued to see that this hunch also finds its place in Posner's work. Thus, in a more general context, he rightly observes that

> (R)eputation is conferred by the people doing the reputing rather than produced by the reputed one—*and it is conferred for their purposes, not his.*[12]

The italicised section of the quotation is immensely important, especially given the way Posner amplifies this point further on in his treatment of the subject by giving it a cynical and almost sinister twist. He thus observes that

> the reputers may be promoting their own selfish interests by hitching their wagon to a star.[13]

Unfortunately, this interesting observation is not pursued further by Posner. In this piece, we will return to it and attempt to give our own interpretation based on what we believe to be typically Continental European habits. Once again, the suggestions are made to provoke more reflection rather than to be taken in any definitive way. For a subject is best cultivated through more detailed research and discussion rather than plain assertion.

2. WARNINGS AND CAVEATS

So let us start by mentioning some of the caveats that have to be borne in mind when reading the figures that we have managed to assemble as part of a first attempt to address the above points. This task was made possible thanks to the invaluable assistance of three younger colleagues[14] and the library staff of the Tarlton Law Library of the University of Texas and the Cornell Law Library.[15]

In this Chapter we have, *first*, tried to apply the citation method mainly to (a) a number of lawyers who held chairs of comparative law or (b) professed a strong interest in the subject, and, finally, (c) were active (approximately) during the last quarter of the last century. Though the total number of scholars looked at with the aid of Lexis, Westlaw and Juris searches (supplemented by manual counts) is not insignificant—49 to be precise—and come from five countries—England, France, Germany, Italy and the United States—it is by no means complete. The omission of worthy colleagues, especially from the United States (where the numbers are greater than in Europe), was dictated by considerations of time and space as well as our estimation of how widely cited they were outside their country of origin. Regrettable though these omissions are, we stuck to the original decision in the belief

[12] Richard A. Posner, *A Study in Reputation* (University of Chicago Press 1990), p 59.

[13] *Ibid* p 60.

[14] Mr Underwood (who manually and with exceptional patience tracked down academic references in five major English law journals for the period 1980–2001 and, again, 2001–2005); Dr Marino, who undertook a similar task in Italy; and last, but by no means least, Miss Kathryn Ritcheske JD, who carried the bulk of the burden of checking and re-checking the searches for 1980 to 2000 (using a new and more extensive database) but also doing those for 2001–2005.

[15] Thanks are thus due to Professor Roy Mersky (UT) and Claire Germaine (Cornell).

that the overall conclusions would not be affected if instead of looking at 50 names we had looked at 60 or even 70.

The restriction of this preliminary survey to a small, albeit important, number of legal systems is also immediately obvious and regrettable. Here, however, the time factor (though playing a part) was not the main reason for the omission. Inability to gain electronic access to material was the prime obstacle that stopped us from even attempting this challenge. For in most cases nothing short of manual searches was possible. We particularly regret the omission from our tables of countries such as Canada, Japan, South Africa and Israel (though in the case of the last, the work of most of its comparatists has received indirect attention by virtue of the fact that colleagues of Jewish ancestry have traditionally dominated this field of law). We hope that one day we may find the practical means to expand our survey.

Secondly, the reader will soon notice that some authors appear with ratings which are significantly higher than others. This discrepancy could, of course, have been attributed to some authors receiving significantly higher citation rates than others. Yet, it soon also became clear that we had to dwell deeper and to explain this marked deviation from what appeared to be normal. Our preliminary conclusions are mentioned later on in this Chapter; but the exercise clearly showed that the counting of citations must be adjusted downwards to take into account some factors indicated below. Doing this has not been easy; but the need at least to attempt the task was necessary since the citation tables were not only meant to show the citation rates of scholars interested in comparative law but, just as importantly, the rates received for their work which was genuinely devoted to foreign or comparative law. Once this adjustment has been made, the conclusion is that the contribution which most of our comparative lawyers have made *to their subject and the real world of practice* is smaller than most—certainly we—would have expected. We shall return to this point in several parts of this Chapter since, again, it must be seen in the context of other readings before it can be evaluated correctly.

Thirdly, the time of commencement and 'cut off' of this statistical survey was, originally, 1980 and 2000 respectively. The choice of these dates was not entirely arbitrary for it was meant to coincide with the period of active work done by the principal author's generation of comparatists as contrasted with that of the 'greats' of the golden era.[16] Yet we have included in our search list some proponents of the previous generation if either they were still active or their works widely used. And yet, clearly, the figures given above do injustice to the older generation for they do not include citations made while these people were at their peak. Some allowance thus has to be made for this fact, though we are not sure how this can be done in figures. The interested reader can find more guidance about how the age factor can skew results (in both directions) in the Landes and Posner article in *The Journal of Legal Studies* cited above. Additionally, modern surveys suggest that, in most cases, the citation rate of works declines sharply after a period of time, indeed citations, apparently, peak four years after publication.[17]

The validity of this observation is confirmed by the figures covering the years 2001 to 2005, and provides humbling evidence for those of us still 'around' and with large egos. For it shows that not only we are, but also our work is, ephemeral. As teachers dedicated to preparing new generations to take over from where we left, we find the thought that all of

[16] This must be read in conjunction with the points we make in Chapters One and Two above.
[17] Ayres and Vars, 'Determinants of Citations to Articles in Elite Law Reviews', 29 *J Legal Stud* 427, 436 (2000).

us have a 'sell-by' date natural and even pleasing. For it does not allow us to fall into the wonderful trap of thinking, as an old Greek saying puts it, that 'we are all as big as our shadows'; additionally, it makes us conscious of the need to prepare our students to take over from where we get off. True endurance of scholarly reputation is thus the reserve of an extremely small number of scholars, and that is true not only of law.

A *fourth* and important proviso is related to electronically available data. This is excellent in the United States, moderate in Canada, limited in England (to courts but not legal journals), even more limited in Australia (to some courts) and almost totally unobtainable as one moves across the Channel into the Continent of Europe.[18] This, again, does great injustice to the Continental comparatists, especially those who have written in less popular languages (such as Scandinavian, Flemish, Greek or Portuguese). But we have tried to indicate these limitations by stating, whenever appropriate, where these figures come from or, alternatively, to which courts or journals they are limited. A glance at Appendix 3 may thus be advisable to anyone who wishes to become fully conscious of the difficulties we encountered in assembling the data as well as its limitations. As far as courts are concerned, however, we repeat once again the general practice of the highest French and Italian judges not to cite academic authors. The position is different in Germany so, in this context, some information has been provided mainly derived from court citations. But, again, it is (largely) limited to court citations since there is no way one can access (with few exceptions) electronically the periodical literature—a great loss given that the Germans are prolific citators. These limitations accentuate the point made above about the importance of writing in English; they also underscore the limitations of our data.

Fifthly, and relatedly, the figures given in these charts have been collected from court reports and legal journals but have not included searches of the web or newspapers. Such citations are evidence of notoriety rather than reputation and, even less so, scholarly achievement. As Landes and Posner have shown,[19] these citations are, effectively, limited to a small number of academics; and their showing is minuscule by reference to politicians and members of the sports and arts world. It would thus be futile to extend such research to include a small branch of the legal profession such as the comparatists.

Sixthly, we regard the citation ratings in court decisions as more important than the citations by fellow academics. But then again, this is only an acceptable argument to those who, like us, believe that attracting the attention of the judge and the practitioner is the best way of keeping the subject alive and well. But we fully accept that this is certainly not likely to be the view taken in modern civil law systems. For there, research and writing are often justified on the principle of *ars gratia artis* and, in any event, attracting the attention of the legislator or the academic community would, it seems, be seen as a more worthwhile activity than influencing the courts.[20] Nonetheless, we remind our readers of our belief that a method that is focused and detailed, and not platitudinous, vaguely sociological, or anthropological in nature, is likely to appeal to legislators and law reformers as well, even though we do not at present have ways of showing this in a statistically meaningful manner. However, having said this one notes that some statistical support for this comes from our section on contemporary practices of the German legislator. Though the data we have collected and reproduced is indicative of a number of trends and attitudes discussed in this

18 The Juris system for German decisions is an exception.

19 'Citations, Age, Fame, and the Web', *Journal of Legal Studies*, vol 29, pp 319, 330 (2000).

20 We return to this point when we make some observations about the German figures.

and the previous Chapters, the figures remain, on the whole, too slender to support anything more than suggestions as to how they could be interpreted.

Let us, however, return to citations by courts. These are difficult to evaluate for another reason. The full value of such citations can only be assessed by finding out how the foreign reference was used: as secondary supporting evidence of a solution reached by other means, or by playing a more important part in the production of the final decision. The quick answer is likely to veer towards the first suggestion rather than the second; but our feeling is that even this modest use is a novelty, characteristic of roughly the period of time covered by this study, and thus likely to be still in its infancy. But decisions are also beginning to appear in the Common law world where the use of the comparative method has played a crucial and not just supportive role.

The commercially important decision of the United States Court of Appeals for the Sixth Circuit *In re: Dow Corning Corporation (debtors)*[21] provides an excellent illustration for comparative law in practice in the context of a very important, world-wide legal dispute literally worth billions of dollars. The *Greatorex* case[22] of the English High Court is another example of how the skilful presentation of foreign law can tempt a national court to have recourse to it. Though in practical terms the *Greatorex* decision is nowhere near as significant as the *Dow Corning* litigation, the interest it presents from a methodological point of view is great, as we have tried to show in a separate, subsequent part of this volume. A House of Lords decision[23] in an asbestos case provides a kind of high-water mark of use of comparative law by the highest court of the land. In many ways, its significance for comparative law is likely to be more long-lived and fundamental than the earlier exercise in *White v Jones*.[24] Finally, however, we note the most recent examples coming out of the French Cour de cassation where, thanks to the personal interest shown in this matter by its then First President M. Guy Canivet, that court may now be giving a fine example of how European judges can make real and effective use of foreign material in order to shape its new law.

Court citations may call for another adjustment mentioned earlier on, namely that some high courts (the Italian and French) never cite authors whereas others, such as the German courts, have traditionally resorted to academic citation at a much higher rate than their English and American counterparts. We could think of no way of making any allowance in our tables for these different practices. However, we do refer the reader to some specialist literature that discusses this phenomenon.[25]

Seventhly, a further refinement of these statistics is important if one is to derive some concrete lessons from them. One such aspect that still remains to be investigated is who is citing whom. Auto-citation, for instance, in our view seems to be more frequent in the civilian traditions than it is in the Common law systems. This is because in the latter—at any rate in the English world—authors tend to restrain themselves in the number of notes they insert in their texts, especially to their own work. Whether this is due to the real or assumed attitudes of modesty of the English we cannot say. But the fact remains that the English, unlike the Germans and the Italians, are less likely to inflate the number of citations to their own work. But we repeat, in our view this is an English and not a Common law habit, and

[21] Electronic citation: 2002 FED App. 0043P (6th Cir) File Name 02a0043p.o6.

[22] *Greatorex v Greatorex* [2000] 1 WLR 1976.

[23] *Fairchild v Glenhaven.*

[24] [1995] 2 AC 207.

[25] For instance Kötz, 'Scholarship and the Courts: A Comparative Survey' in *Comparative and Private International Law. Essays in Honor of John Merryman on his Seventieth Birthday* (1990), pp 183 *ff.*

Australian authors, for instance, do not appear to share this kind of self-control. At the other end of the spectrum one finds American authors who seem to have a taste for long (and sometimes even useless) footnotes. In this context, we also note in passing the habit of young Continental academics to (over-) cite their 'doctoral fathers'. This deferential attitude (the result of tradition, intellectual indebtedness, and reverence towards authority—the latter often confused with age) is deeply regrettable, though in our 'equalising' society this unfortunate habit may not have a bright future ahead of it.

While the last point made above must be treated as being open to further discussion, a related issue—important for the purposes of the ideas found in this essay—needs to be flagged up. What we have in mind here is a citation through which the reputer is seeking to enlarge the image of the school of his master to which he, naturally, belongs. In such instances we have, in other words, a double aim: to enhance one's own image through an association with a 'grand master' but, secondly, also to go on flattering the grand master who, despite the passing of the years, remains for his school the main or only true beacon. Likewise, adherents of one school tend to cite more those who share the same broad philosophical attitude towards the subject that they subscribe to, and even exaggerate the value of the movement.

The above-described phenomenon is particularly prevalent in Italy but can also be found in other European countries such as Germany and Greece, where the idea of 'leading professors'—in Germany somewhat pejoratively but most colourfully referred to as 'Platzhirsche'[26]—create their own territories of influence in which they rule supreme. To the extent that these tendencies generate an esprit de corps and closer sense of identity and camaraderie it must be welcome. But there is, potentially, a darker side to this phenomenon; and it comes closer to Posner's pejorative reference to self-interested reputing. Quite simply it is this. Repeated cross-citation by members of a group or a circle can create to the unwary an impression of importance which is not reflected by other indicators.

Finally, one technical warning about the way we searched for the names of those on whom we chose to focus. Invariably, the search was made primarily on the basis of how the author uses his own name. John G Fleming is how the late Professor Fleming signed his books. But courts have sometimes cited him as JG Fleming; and in academic literature, references also appear in the form of 'According to Fleming so and so is right whereas . . .'. Searches using surnames, alone, have not been conducted for they would obviously produce false positives. Other difficulties with electronic searches, associated with 'local' ways of citing authors, are described in greater detail in the Appendix. Fleming, incidentally, like Professor Langbein in the United States and Professors Honoré and Jolowicz in the United Kingdom, raises a particular difficulty when counting citation rates. For all of these colleagues have also written books on the core subject of tort law; and if we are trying to assess their reputation and legacy as comparative lawyers, we must somehow deduct from their total figures citations to some of their non-comparative law works.

[26] 'Hirsch' is the male deer; and the idea that he has 'marked out' his territory—his 'Platz'—in which no other dominant male can enter, is beautiful imagery and very close to what happens in German law schools where these grandees of the law suffered little interference.

3. SOME RAW DATA[27]

Table 3.1: Citations of comparatists in academic literature (1980–2000)

Americans				
Country	England	Germany	Italy	USA
Author				
Hans W Baade	6	6	1	434
George A Bermann	4	0	1	552
John P Dawson	28	2	4	633[28]
John G Fleming	84	7	13	315
Mary Ann Glendon	24	4	18	2,097
James Gordley	9	0	16	398
John Langbein	0	0	0	1,799[29]
Ugo Mattei	4	0	53	128
John Henry Merryman	15	9	14	1,081
Matthias Reimann	5	2	1	150
Rudolf B Schlesinger	5	9	15	392
Arthur T von Mehren	21	3	3	881
Alan Watson	24	9	9	560[30]

British				
Country	England	Germany	Italy	USA
Author				
John Bell	51	6	5	109
Tony Honoré	89	0	1	491[31]
JA Jolowicz	88	1	18	95
Otto Kahn-Freund	96	7	10	235
FH Lawson	53	0	9	169
Kurt Lipstein	21	8	2	58

[27] A detailed author-by-author breakdown of our data is available on the website of the University of Texas at Austin, Institute for Transnational Law (www.utexas.edu/law/academics/centers/transnational).

[28] 116 documents citing his *Oracles of the Law* and 50 his *Gifts and Promises.* The rest of the citations were to other works by the author. Searching for Dawson was not easy, and the overall figure includes results for the name 'J Dawson'—which inevitably includes some false positives. However, a survey of the 633 citations indicates that the vast majority of documents in the Westlaw JLR database with a citation to 'J Dawson' did, in fact, refer to John P Dawson.

[29] 959 of 1,799 citations were to Langbein's comparative law works.

[30] 377 of 560 citations were to Watson's comparative law works, chiefly to *Legal Transplants* (1974). Most of the remaining 183 citations are to Watson's works on Roman law. Works that overlap the categories (such as *Roman Law and Comparative Law* (1991) are included in the comparative law total.

[31] *Causation in the Law* (with Hart): 252; 'Ownership' in Guest (ed), *Oxford Essays in Jurisprudence* (1961): 74. The remaining articles cite a range of works in the areas of Roman law, tort law, and jurisprudence.

British (*cont.*)				
Country	England	Germany	Italy	USA
Author				
FA Mann	83	11[32]	4	340
Basil S Markesinis	114	6	12	169
Barry Nicholas	26	4	10	241
Bernard Rudden	41	1	1	106
Tony Weir	78	8	6	246[33]

German				
Country	England	Germany	Italy	USA
Author				
Ulrich Drobnig	6	58	9	136
Eric Jayme	7	0	24	90
Hein Kötz	65	73	54	326
Werner Lorenz	14	0	2	22
Marcus Lutter	0	0	12	82
Peter-Christian Müller-Graf	2	11	8	32
Peter Schlechtriem	9	0	16	102
Christian von Bar	6	0	3	25
Reinhard Zimmermann	33	0	17	150
Konrad Zweigert	57	0	31	268

French				
Country	England	Germany	Italy	USA
Author				
Xavier Blanc-Jouvain	3	0	4	17
René David	31	0	48	381
Mireille Delmas-Marty	6	20	10	46
Pierre Legrand	17	3	18	72
Horatia Muir Watt	0	6	8	3
Denis Tallon	14	5	27	77
André Tunc	29	3	31	147

[32] These hits were only found in the commentaries searched. The number of hits in journals (above 400), by far most of which are false positives due to the ambiguous meaning of 'Mann' in German, was too large to analyse.

[33] Translations account for citations in 204 documents.

	Italian			
Country	England	Germany	Italy	USA
Author				
Guido Alpa	0	8	189	22
Michael Joachim Bonell	3	25	25	196
Mauro Bussani	0	0	28	17
Mauro Cappelletti	38	11	59	514
Antonio Gambaro	0	0	54	32
Gino Gorla	2	0	100	35
Maurizio Lupoi	2	0	10	10
Rodolfo Sacco	4	3	230	106

Table 3.2: Citations of comparatists by courts (1980–2000)

	American				
Country	Australia	Canada	England	Germany	USA
Author					
Hans W Baade	0	0	0	0	11
George A Bermann	0	1	0	0	19
John P Dawson	1	0	1	0	21
John G Fleming	81[34]	678[35]	32[36]	1	12[37]
Mary-Ann Glendon	0	9	1	0	12
James Gordley	0	1	0	0	10
John Langbein	6	2	0	0	93
Ugo Mattei	0	0	0	0	1
John Henry Merryman	0	1	1	0	16
Mathias Reimann	0	0	1	0	0
Rudolf B Schlesinger	0	0	0	0	8[38]
Arthur T von Mehren	0	1	0	0	30
Alan Watson	0	0	0	0	1

[34] Of which 77 refer to the *Law of Torts* (various editions).

[35] A record 671 of these citations are to his *Law of Torts* (various editions).

[36] Of which 30 refer to the *Law of Torts* (various editions).

[37] Because the forms are common and therefore generated large numbers of false positives, we did not search on either 'John Fleming' or 'J Fleming.' This means that inevitably some true positives were missed.

[38] All but two of the citations are to *Comparative Law: Cases—Text—Materials*, edited with Baade, Damaska and Herzog (1988).

British					
Country	Australia	Canada	England	Germany	USA
Author					
John Bell	0	5[39]	1	0	0
Tony Honoré	23	1	16[40]	0	13[41]
JA Jolowicz	20	58	38[42]	0	7
Otto Kahn-Freund	10	5	2	0	4
FH Lawson	0	0	4	0	4
Kurt Lipstein	0	0	2	0	4
FA Mann	12	7	24	0	1
Basil S Markesinis	11	6	26	0	12
Barry Nicholas	0	0	0[43]	1	26
Bernard Rudden	2	0	0	0	0
Tony Weir	1	2	6	0	2

German					
Country	Australia	Canada	England	Germany	USA
Author					
Ulrich Drobnig	1	0	0	0	1
Eric Jayme	0	0	0	3	1
Hein Kötz	0	2	7	0	3
Werner Lorenz	0	0	2	0	0
Marcus Lutter	0	0	0	0	0
Peter-Christian Müller-Graf	0	0	0	0	0
Peter Schlechtriem	0	0	0	4	5
Christian von Bar	1	0	5	1	0
Reinhard Zimmermann	0	0	3	0	0
Konrad Zweigert	0	2	4	2	5

[39] Owing to the number of false positives it was possible to search only on the full name 'John Bell'.

[40] All but one are citations to *Causation in the Law* with HLA Hart (1st or 2nd edns).

[41] Every citation is to *Causation in the Law* with HLA Hart (1st or 2nd edns).

[42] 36 out of the 38 citations are to various editions of *Winfield and Jolowicz on Tort.*

[43] An electronic search using Professor Nicholas' initials or the name 'Barry' revealed no hits. The use of the surname 'Nicholas' alone revealed over 2,000 documents which, because of their volume, could not be searched but theoretically could contain 'true positives'. The figure given in the chart must thus be read with the above qualification in mind.

French					
Country	Australia	Canada	England	Germany	USA
Author					
Xavier Blanc-Jouvain	0	0	0	0	0
René David	0	3	4	0	3
Mireille Delmas-Marty	0	0	0	0	0
Pierre Legrand	0	11	0	0	0
Horatia Muir Watt	0	0	0	0	1
Denis Tallon	0	1	1	1	0
André Tunc	0	3	0	1	2

Italian					
Country	Australia	Canada	England	Germany	USA
Author					
Guido Alpa	0	0	0	0	0
Michael Joachim Bonell	0	0	0	0	0
Mauro Bussani	0	0	0	0	0
Mauro Cappelletti	0	1	0	0	1
Antonio Gambaro	0	0	0	0	0
Gino Gorla	0	0	0	0	0
Maurizio Lupoi	0	0	0	0	0
Ugo Mattei		[see American table]			
Rodolfo Sacco	0	0	0	0	0

4. DRAWING THE FIRST LESSONS

(a) Lesson One—Citations Need to be Adjusted Downwards; Each Author Needs to be Given Individual Attention

The first thing that became evident to us as the figures contained in the tables began to settle down in their final form was that, as far as British comparatists were concerned, their citation records were no less impressive than those of other British leading scholars who wrote on mainstream subjects. The mini-table in the notes shows this most clearly.[44] For

[44] The following mini-table makes this surprising assertion very plausible.

Author	USA literature	English literature	USA courts	English courts
Ashworth, A	164	95	4	7
Atiyah, P	894	207	16	31
Birks, PBH	153	144	0	14
Goode RM	143	69	0	51
Treitel, G	99	118	2	71

the citation rates for such eminent colleagues as Sir Roy Goode can boast 143 citations in the academic literature of the five leading journals actually searched (manually) while Professor Birks' own figure (153) is at a roughly comparable level. So, too, is the first of the present authors with 114 citations (reduced to 97 once the references to his English tort textbook are removed). This leaves only Patrick Atiyah way ahead of the pack with a record 894 citations. This is a significant assertion made not out of vanity—one did not have the slightest clue how these figures would turn out before the research began—not only because the comparison is between an (émigré) comparative lawyer and the father of English commercial law or the greatest theoretician of the recently discovered law of restitution, but for the impact it has on the 'ghetto theory'. Further on, we shall note that the figures—not theories—suggest the same picture when we compare citation rates found in court judgments. American comparatists, on the other hand, who had thus far not been measured in the way we have done here, revealed a much less substantial citation record than American core-subject writers whose figures are given in the Shapiro/Landes and Posner articles. To put it differently: American comparatists, apart from a handful of exceptions, did less well when compared to their mainstream American colleagues than the English comparatists did when compared with their core subject writers.

What is also interesting to note is how well English comparatists did on the American scene. Apart from five or six notable exceptions, the American figures were higher, but not substantially so, than those received by their British counterparts competing for attention on American turf. This is not really surprising since this competition was taking place at home. On the other hand, it must be admitted that the big hitters in the United States—notably Glendon, Langbein, von Mehren, Dawson and Watson—have received a significant number of citations, approaching the high levels of their non-comparatist colleagues.

Two tentative explanations can be advanced for this discrepancy between citation rates of comparatists versus non-comparatists in England and the United States.

The first is that British comparatists seem to have spread their writing efforts over a wider range of topics than their American counterparts. Seen in this way, the higher citation records were, on the whole, earned by their wider work and *not* by their comparative law endeavours. This explanation brings the British scene more into line with the American. For, once the British figures are adjusted downwards by removing citations to non-comparative work, the difference between (British) comparatists and (British) non-comparatists becomes more significant and seems to fall in line with that found in the United States.

The second is that the American comparatists have not yet been subject to a reputology study as a group or individually (on the basis of a breakdown of their figures) since they never made it into Shapiro's list of top one hundred.[45] Looking at them more closely, however, reveals significant variations—some, like Mary Ann Glendon and (less so) John Langbein, John Merryman, Jack Dawson and Alan Watson, attaining very high totals. Before we look at the citation records of the two with the highest score—Glendon and Langbein—and then, for reasons which will become obvious, examine the citation record of Alan Watson, two general observations are necessary.

First, high figures such as the above made us dwell more on these colleagues and their work, and try to discover which pieces in particular, written by these authors, had attracted

[45] Shapiro, 'The Most cited legal Scholars', 29 *J Legal Stud* 409, 412 (2000).

high attention. In other words we felt that for the purposes of our study it was not enough to record total numbers of citations; a breakdown also had to be attempted to weed out the comparative from the non-comparative. This proved an extremely time-consuming exercise where such high figures are involved. But the enquiry suggested that a fair number of citations (in some cases the majority) made to some of these highly cited authors *should not be counted as citations for the purposes of foreign law and comparative methodology.* This was, of course, in general terms no different to what we found in England. Still, in this case the size of the figures made this adjustment process very important and presented the 'presence' of these colleagues in the comparative arena as impressive but not as astounding as it had appeared at first sight.

Secondly, for reasons explained more fully below, we do not feel able to recommend a scientifically correct way to attempt such downward adjustment that would work across the board and that would suit the richly varied work of some of our authors. For even if one looks at each piece individually, which in many cases we had to do, classifying it as comparative or not (and distinguishing comparative from, say, conflicts of laws), the procedure often presents problems of a particular kind. Thus, is a piece that describes a foreign system (for example, the German) a comparative piece? And what if it is primarily concerned with national law, but the text is peppered with references, mainly in the notes, to another system or systems? This type of questioning can be further multiplied but enough has, perhaps, been hinted at to show the difficulties one encounters in such an exercise.

In the end we therefore decided to try and slot our scholars into four sub-categories, each of which may call for a different appreciation. Because our statements and our assessments may (inadvertently) be debatable, if not wrong, we thus supplemented these observations with references, especially to Tables 3.1 and 3.3, which show which of our authors' works attracted judicial attention.[46] This material makes for boring reading. But the information it contains will be essential for those (few) of our readers who might wish to see what exactly has been cited and make up their own minds as to whether these works can be classified as contributions to the study of foreign law and the development of a comparative methodology or whether, on the contrary, they represent a contribution to some other branch of the law—typically conflicts of laws, legal history, Roman law, jurisprudence, or torts. The aim, however, has once again been the same: to test the 'ghetto theory' as well as the veracity of our thesis advanced in this book, namely that the comparatists, themselves, have brought about their own neglect by those who shape law on a daily basis.

The sub-categories into which our authors seemed to fall were the following.

First, we find some authors with a mind-boggling number of citations. Mary-Ann Glendon comes under this category with citations at the phenomenally high rate of 2,273. Closer scrutiny of the figures shows that her prolific activities as a writer of books have contributed to this distinction. Thus, her *Rights Talk: The Impoverishment of Political Discourse* (1991) earns her citations in 503 documents; her *Abortion and Divorce in Western Law* (1987) 314; *A Nation Under Lawyers* (1994) 293; *The New Family and the New Property* (1981) 164; while her jointly co-authored casebook on *Comparative Legal Traditions* (2nd edn 1994) comes out at 56. In the light of her total number of citations, we question her non-inclusion in Fred Shapiro's list and must assume that she had not attained such levels

[46] These references are available online at the Institute of Transnational Law of the University of Texas at Austin and the Institute of Global Law at University College London.

at the time when he collected his data for the well-known article 'The Most Cited Legal Scholars'.[47]

Glendon's work calls for another caveat. Though the spirit of comparative law runs through her veins, not all of her works can be easily classified as works on pure comparative law. Her large citation score may thus reveal more about her broad learning and its overall impact on American academic literature than, say, her individual input in the creation of either a school of comparatists or a particular comparative methodology. A cognate reason may be the fact that most of her books could be brought under the more cited headings of jurisprudence, constitutional law, and family law rather than pure comparative law. These, we readily admit, may be more debatable propositions. Thus, though Glendon's work needs some downward adjustment, there is no denying the fact that she remains a very highly cited author as well as one whose scholarship has been widely admired and (dare one add?) envied.

The problem raised by the overall classification of Glendon's work becomes more acute in the second category of scholars which, likewise, includes some eminent figures. For here the bulk of citations come from works which are *obviously* linked to other branches of the law but, tenuously, *may* also present a link with comparative law. We include here John Fleming's *The Law of Torts*,[48] which in United States legal literature earns him citations in 122 documents out of a total of 315. His more recent *The American Tort Process* is cited in 42 documents but is less easily described as a work on comparative law. For though this is an inspiring book, especially for non-American lawyers, it is, essentially, a sociological and statistical survey of American tort law in practice and thus cannot be counted as a pure or traditional work of comparative law. The remainder of Fleming's citations go to a variety of articles, many dealing with particular problems of tort law and only very few of his truly comparative law pieces receive passing attention—academic or judicial. In the light of the above, it is again necessary to adjust downwards (probably substantially) Fleming's overall figures given in Table 3.1 to reflect the fact that much of his cited work was of national and not comparative interest. Yet many of his colleagues regarded Fleming, especially during the last quarter of his life, as one of America's most knowledgeable comparatists. The statistics do not reflect this belief. Still, we suspect that because of technical difficulties (his name is so common that it gives rise to a serious risk of false positives) we may still have underestimated his total record.

John Langbein, with a phenomenal total of 1,799 citations to his credit, comes second after Mary Ann Glendon but should be slotted into this category rather than hers. For though his citation record reflects both the extent of his publications and their breadth, a fair number of them do not display comparative features, which make one hesitate as to how to classify them. Thus, nearly half of the citations (850 out 1,799) are to his works on wills and trust, and about 950 are to his various comparative law works or works with comparative elements or information about foreign law. The difference from Glendon, however, is that in his case the separation between comparative and non-comparative work (subject to the difficulties already alluded to) seems to be clearer. Langbein, however,

[47] 29 *J Legal Stud* 409 (2000). Shapiro has kindly informed us (email dated 22 May 2002) that Mary Ann Glendon 'fell just short of the 1,000-citation minimum needed to make' his list when he completed his searches in January 1999. But if that is so, and our figures are right, that means that Glendon almost doubled her citations in about two years. Since this seems difficult to believe, one is forced to consider another possibility, namely that Shapiro's database is less complete than ours (see Appendix 1 for further details).

[48] 9th edn (1998, published posthumously).

deserves one more general observation which might even justify an independent article which could explore a fascinating but never discussed underlying point.

In Langbein's case it is particularly interesting to note that his 'The German Advantage in Civil Procedure' alone earns him 217 citations, that is, about 12 per cent of his total number. This long and highly documented piece nonetheless had a very mixed reception in the United States, and even attracted a measure of rather inelegantly expressed criticism. In a sense this is not the point that matters. But what *does* matter is whether—and here we are just flying a kite—a particularly or deliberately controversial piece attracts a reaction and thus enhances the citation record of an author. Langbein's work was certainly controversial in the sense that it challenged (as he saw it and wished it to) established practices of the American legal profession, so the point made here may deserve closer scrutiny: does being controversial enhance one's visibility? The answer must almost certainly be affirmative. But further questions then arise: do such pieces also raise their author's academic visibility? Do they increase his chances of being 'poached' by another ('better') law school—a favourite pastime of American legal academics? Finally, and more difficult to answer, does it advance academic debate? These are all interesting subsidiary questions to which we give in this book clues as to how to try to find answers but do not offer (yet) a conclusive solution of our own.

Alan Watson deserves special mention in this list, and this not only because his work has attracted a good number of citations. Once again, however, we remind our readers that we are not commenting on the quality of scholarship or the extent of his erudition, both of which are beyond all doubt. The reasons why we think Watson's case deserves special notice are two.

First, Watson, the Roman lawyer, escaped the pattern followed by his British Romanists and comparatists who 'stayed at home', remained essentially Roman lawyers or Roman legal historians, and made a rather small contribution to the study of comparative law and methodology. We shall explain below that this is, in our view, the case of Barry Nicholas and, overall, his imprint has been less impressive. Not so with Watson who, like Zimmermann, chose to make different use of his expertise as a Roman lawyer as well as a talented linguist.

With his *Legal Transplants*, which alone earns him 377 out of his 560 citations, Watson not only produced a monograph which combined Roman law, modern law, and comparative methodology; he also helped set the tone for much of the comparative law debate during the period here examined. This success, his high standards, and his reputed inability to suffer fools easily, may have made him some powerful enemies; but those who build something, especially if it is new, tend to attract jealousy and criticism, and Watson did not escape this fate. We are among those who inadequately assessed Watson's contribution to the debate about modern comparative law and feel we have to make amends in public.

A variant of the above category—the third group—includes jurists who held chairs of comparative law but wrote pieces which are primarily works about their own national legal system and thus formed a secondary part of their work. The connection here with comparative law was either weak or came too late in their lives to leave a permanent mark on the subject. In this sub-category, Professor Tony Jolowicz, formerly Professor of Comparative law at the University of Cambridge, furnishes an excellent illustration. His citation rates confirm our assessment.

In American legal journals, Jolowicz is cited in 95 documents. Ten of these are for articles on purely English law. A further 45 citations are to *Winfield and Jolowicz on Tort*, which

Professor Jolowicz successfully transformed (and not merely updated) over 40 years ago while he acted as its editor between its 7th and 9th editions (the book is now in its 17th edition). Unlike Fleming's tort textbook, however, which can lay *some* claims to being a comparative work (since it looks at tort law simultaneously from the optics of English, Australian, New Zealand, and American law), Jolowicz' textbook is a straightforward textbook on English law. These two figures (45 + 10) thus suggest that about 61 per cent of his total citations are dedicated to non-comparative work. A downward adjustment of his original figure of 95 to 40 thus seems more necessary than in Fleming's case. The discounting process, however, cannot stop there. For it must also be noted that a fair number of the remaining 40 citations are to works which contain a 'foreign' element which is neither predominant nor does it embody an attempt to formulate a comparative technique or methodology. Interestingly enough, the overall pattern (in this as in so many of our other examples) does not change if one looks at Jolowicz's citations in English journals. For here one finds that 57 citations out of 88 (that is, 64.77 per cent of the total) are to writings on English law.

So where does all this leave Jolowicz as a *comparative* lawyer if he is to be judged by which of his works have been noted by or (maybe) influenced his Anglo-American colleagues? If one is to go by statistics alone, the impact of Jolowicz's work on other comparative lawyers and their literature seems small, though curiously enough it is slightly greater in the United States than in his own country. Smaller still, as Table 3.3 demonstrates, is the impact of his comparative writings on the courts. At the end of the day, it is therefore difficult to say what lasting contribution this (indisputably solid and reliable) scholar has made to the study and use of foreign law even though he held the Cambridge (ad hominem) Chair for 17 years.

Why this is so is difficult to explain; but reputology helps bring to the surface many questions which might not have otherwise been asked. Perhaps one reason is the fact that Jolowicz came to comparative law late in life. Another reason may be that he, himself, largely saw in the subject a *mission civilisatrice* and never tried to promote its appeal by making it appear as useful and relevant. Yet another reason may be that he devoted most of his time to civil procedure—a subject to which he has devoted much energy but which arguably (and one should add: wrongly) has not yet attained the prominence it deserves in the academic curriculum in England. If this last point were indeed a factor in the overall (pessimistic) assessment we have advanced about his long-term impact, it is little short of ironic and unfair. For in his writing on that subject, alone or with his friend Mauro Cappelletti, Jolowicz helped give civil procedure in England a greater academic presence than it had had before his time.

Finally, the analogous observation could be made of the work of Professor Guido Alpa in Italy. For like Mary Ann Glendon, Alpa has been extraordinarily prolific, having written extensively on most aspects of Italian private and commercial law. Though the bulk of this work is, again, of a dogmatic nature and deals with a particular legal system (the Italian) increasingly as it has come under the influence of the two European courts, it has, in the latter years of his life, been supplemented by articles and books which aim to make known abroad the richness of Italian law. Notwithstanding the intellectual interest which Italian law presents, non-Italian lawyers have been slow to respond to his laudable efforts and to put to use this information. In any event, Alpa's work falls more easily under the category of 'foreign law' than comparative law so, overall, he has not (yet) managed to challenge the pre-eminent position reached by some of his Italian 'seniors'—for example, Sacco, Taruffo or Gambaro—or his 'juniors'—such as Mattei, Bussani, or Ranieri (all of whom who have found better ways to introduce the international learning into the study of comparative law in Italy). Once again, therefore, assessments and evaluations of Alpa's work as a comparatist must be made with caution, his overall impressive figures in the charts calling for a substantial downward adjustment if one is looking at his publications purely from the angle of comparative law. Yet, given his productivity and energy, this assessment must only be a temporary one.

A different (downward) adjustment must be made for another holder of a chair of comparative law, Professor Barry Nicholas, who receives in United States literature 241 citations. Here, the reason is closely linked to the English 'practice' of entrusting comparative law to Romanists. This adjustment is necessitated by the fact that over half of all Nicholas' citations in legal literature go to his work on Roman law. In the American legal literature, his edition of (Felix) Jolowicz's *Historical Introduction to Roman Law*[49] thus receives citations in 31 documents whilst his own (smaller) and elegant *Introduction to Roman Law* accounts for citations in 94 documents. By contrast, his very readable student textbook on *French Law of Contract*[50] earns him citations in 46 documents. These statistics again indicate strongly what most colleagues operating on the English scene would probably readily admit—namely that when the dust settles Nicholas' main contribution to law will be seen to be more in the area of Roman rather than comparative law. This (preliminary) assessment receives some support from the citations he has received (or, more accurately, *not* received) for one of his most scholarly articles on foreign law,[51] which boldly predicted a great future for the French *Conseil constitutionnel* at a time when established wisdom thought otherwise. This remarkable piece, full of comparative insights, has met with an even more remarkable lack of appreciation on both sides of the Channel, perhaps because it was a prophetic, speculative piece rather than one which could be put to some immediate, practical use. His many loyal pupils may not like the conclusion; but that is what the figures suggest until someone can interpret them differently.

Finally, a group of comparatists seem to have earned the vast majority of their citations on the strength of one work which contains elements of comparative law but cannot be described as a straightforward example of comparative literature. They are, instead, dogmatic accounts of a difficult part of national law which have received particular attention in a foreign system. Tony Honoré pre-eminently falls into this category, with a large number of citations (252 out of a total of 491) coming from his widely (and rightly) admired book on *Causation in the Law* (co-authored with HLA Hart). Other works of his which receive attention include *Morality of Tort Law—Questions and Answers* (1995), *Responsibility and Fault* (1999), *Responsibility and Luck: The Moral Basis of Strict Liability*,[52] *Making Law Bind* (1987), *Emperors and Lawyers* (2nd edn 1994), *Law in the Crisis of Empire* (1998) and *Tribonian* (1978). It will, of course, not escape the attention of the careful reader that this former Regius Professor of Roman Law at the University of Oxford thus spent most of his time writing on matters of contemporary law—torts in England and trusts in South Africa—and certainly received most of his citations for these works.

A moment's reflection over these titles will thus suggest that his *enduring* scholarly legacy will be found mainly in the areas of jurisprudence, tort law, and trusts (though on the latter topic, his impact seems to be more localised in South Africa). Honoré's equally

[49] 3rd edn 1972.

[50] 1st edn 1982; 2nd edn 1992.

[51] 'Fundamental Rights and Judicial Review in France', [1978] *PL* 82 with only two citations in the English literature of the last 20 years.

[52] 104 *LQR* 530 (1988).

phenomenal erudition in Roman law, found par excellence in his two monographs on Tribonian (1978) and Ulpian (1982), receive between them 16 citations. It is difficult to see in these figures the conclusion that these days Roman law, notwithstanding the intellectual rigour of the subject is, quite simply, *not* a way to create a school and to influence other law colleagues.

Honoré's main contribution to the literature of comparative law—the comparative variation of his causation monograph published in the *Encyclopaedia of Comparative Law* and his elegantly and tightly argued Hamlyn Lectures, which made constant use of French and German material—have been almost entirely ignored by authors and courts alike. Like Nicholas's work on the *Conseil Constitutionnel* or Weir's essay on 'Friendships in the Law' (one of the most elegant pieces of legal literature of recent times), these works confirm the trend: a scholarly piece without potential practical utility bites the dust. Even a polymath like Honoré cannot buck this trend.

Yet what is really so surprising about these figures is that the citation rates in academic publications suggest that such pieces not only leave the courts, the legislator, and practitioners totally unmoved; they also seem to have a minuscule impact on other academic writings. We readily confess to our own astonishment; and even find the emerging picture quite disturbing. If the reason for this very low rate of use is another than the fact that Roman law is slowly dying, we await with interest to hear what it is.

In the world of Anglo-American legal literature, the great German comparatists Konrad Zweigert and Hein Kötz fall into the same sub-category in the sense that about 66 per cent of the citations they receive (203 out of 326) come from their jointly written *An Introduction to Comparative Law*,[53] a credit which nowadays probably goes mostly to Kötz since his co-author has been out of the picture for a long time during which the book has grown in detail and elegance.

Unlike the other authors in this category, however, the *Introduction* is clearly a comparative law masterpiece, which, moreover, reflects in practice the enduring appeal of Rabel's approach. Here the picture is thus the reverse of that given above; for authors such as Zweigert and Kötz have in the Anglo-American law made their reputation on the strength of one masterpiece. Nonetheless, this book also presents us with a peculiarity. For popular though it has proved in the United States and England, the citation rates by courts are markedly lower than those found in legal literature. This 'neglect' extends to the German courts (though, as we explain later on, this may be due to particular local factors). By contrast, Professor Kötz's German law-oriented works have fared much better with the courts of his own country, something which may, again, be linked to the interpretative techniques prevalent among German courts. Here we simply note the paradox, namely that an author mainly known as a comparative lawyer abroad is in his own country cited largely as a national lawyer.

At this point it is also necessary to say something about the Weir 'phenomenon'. In American legal literature, Weir receives citations in an impressive 246 documents. 204 of these, however, refer to him as the translator of the Zweigert and Kötz and four other German books which he has rendered into English with consummate style. That leaves 42 documents—a mere 17 per cent of his total—citing him for his own works, and of these only a handful are to comparative law and not works on the English law of torts (such as his

[53] Which earns Tony Weir (as translator) the bulk of his citations.

tort casebook). This figure is so minute when compared with that of his translations that it calls for a comment.

On the positive side, it shows the importance which a translator has in making significant works of foreign authors known and cited in the Anglo-Saxon world. For Weir's efforts are undoubtedly the single most important factor in making Zweigert and Kötz known in the Anglo-Saxon world. Without it, these colleagues, two of Germany's finest comparatists, would be substantially less influential in the Common law than they are at present. The late Professor Fleming was thus right in referring to Tony Weir as the Boswell of the German comparatists. This is no mean service to the science of comparative law; and the detailed analysis of his figures should not be seen as attempting to belittle his learning or his sui generis service to comparative law.

On the negative side, the citations to Weir's personal work demonstrate that some of his most erudite publications have remained substantially unnoticed, his wit and learning notwithstanding. The Catala and Weir pieces in the *Tulane Law Review* have already been cited as a paradigm of comparative methodology and pithy formulation, and yet in the United States, where it first appeared just over 30 years ago, it receives a mere nine citations. How devastatingly low this is can only be appreciated by the fact that our database includes over 1,000 American law journals; and the search covered a period of 20 years! It is thus greatly to be regretted that not only has it not found scholarly imitators as a method of examining foreign law, as the authors of this great series of articles had wished, but also that it has failed to impress the literature in the United States[54] and England.[55] The fate (in citation terms: four) of Weir's 'Friendships in the Law'[56] supports the (sad but, it seems, unassailable) argument that pure research has no impact on the visibility of the subject or its utility in the courtroom. We stress the fate of Weir's learning in this last piece for it is as impressive in its breadth of reading as it is for the beauty of some of its sentences.

The Weir phenomenon thus reveals in stark terms the perpetual clash between the 'elegant' and 'utilitarian' approach to comparative law. It also reconfirms the picture that has been revealed by the earlier statistics. One is thus inescapably forced either to reappraise the lessons that a statistical survey of an author's work tell us about its value to other authors and courts or, alternatively, draw the lessons that emerge from such neglect of their orientation and message.

The above observations can help draw two main conclusions. Both are put forward in a tentative manner.

The first is that the raw data thus far assembled suggests that, few exceptions apart, the scholars included in our sample have had a very modest impact on courts, legislators, and practitioners. The citation exercise lends some considerable support to the thesis advanced in the first two Chapters of this volume. For the majority of what these indisputably eminent scholars chose to write about has left the courts and practitioners almost totally unmoved. Where, by contrast, they write something with a practical slant, it is used even if the author's point of view is not entirely understood! This is, apparently, what happened with Professor Nicholas' early piece on unjust enrichment in the civil law and the law of Louisiana. Notwithstanding these misunderstandings, it was immediately snatched up by the courts, accounting for over half of the judicial citations he has received in the United

[54] Judging from the fact that it is only cited in nine documents.
[55] Where only one document seems to have cited these articles.
[56] 6/7 *Tul Civ L Forum* 61 (1991–92).

States. Give the courts something that seems to help them in their daily work and they will use the material (even if they sometimes make a mess of it). Practicality once again wins over elegance and learning.

If the above has been the fate of some very learned writers producing some very elegant pieces, the mind boggles at what impact (if any) will the new, trendy, deconsturctionalist, politically correct literature have on those who make law either as legislators or judges?

The second conclusion is that citation studies are not a measure of scholarship but only of reputation of scholarship. Yet even that must be treated with caution. For citation references are not, by themselves, convincing evidence of reputation. Some figures given by Landes and Posner support this scepticism.[57] For it is debatable, to say the least, to claim that Rawls' reputation is greater than Bentham's because the first receives 618 citations compared to the second's 499; or that Dworkin with 1,031 citations dwarfs Aristotle with 356.[58]

On the other hand, they *do* tell us something as to what is used and read. If Dworkin is thus more read than Aristotle, it may say something about the general education and discernment of modern readers. Such figures and comparisons must thus lead us to scrutinise not only the way in which the data is collected (are we limiting our searches to references in legal journals?) or the impact of topicality and how it may wane with time, but also the general level of education provided in the centres of modern academic excellence. Likewise, the extraordinary high number of citations of highly accurate and usable treatises such as those written by Professor Tribe or Dean Prosser[59] can hardly suggest that the reputation of these scholars is higher than the less widely cited but intellectually more thoughtful works of such jurists as Bruce Ackerman, Guido Calabresi, or Mary Ann Glendon. Judge Posner makes a similar point when he writes: 'Citations are thus an imperfect proxy for reputation, and reputation itself an imperfect proxy for quality'.

(b) Lesson Two—Reputation and Legacy in Comparative Law

What we have said about scholarship and reputation of scholarship does not complete our study. We have to complement the questions asked thus far with one more: have the above scholars, otherwise than through their work and the citation rates it has received, left a quantifiable impact on their subject?

A thought which emerges clearly from the careful reflection of the figures given above is that the frequency of citation of an author's work gives a fairly good picture of the impact that it has on others. But this may be only part of the wider picture that deals with his contribution to the successful establishment of his subject. As against that, however, we must weigh the fact that an author's influence wanes with time as he ceases to produce or dies, and as his works (once noted and cited) age and lose their appeal (and certainly their

[57] 29 *Journal of Legal Studies* 319 (2000).

[58] These figures come from Posner's *Cardozo* (p 78) and cover citations in legal articles over a much shorter period (1982–89) than that covered by Shapiro's later works.

[59] According to Shapiro, 'The Most Cited Legal Scholars', 29 *J Legal Stud* 409, 424 *et seq* (2000) Tribe's *Constitutional Law* treatise earns him 5,351 citations, and Prosser's similarly popular tort law book earns him 4,984. Though these figures also include citations of important articles, these authors seem to be 'primarily cited for one or two standard treatises' (*ibid* at p 414). Bruce Ackerman comes in with a healthy but less impressive 2,547 while Guido Calabresi overtakes him by some 300 citations with 2,887 to his credit.

novelty). Few, very few indeed, ever escape from this impact that time has on their work. So can anything else achieved during one's life-time survive the test of time? We are now looking at a different idea—legacy—and immediately note that this can created only in part by the author's literary output.

For a jurist may contribute to his subject in ways other than writing scholarly pieces in his chosen area or being cited in what he has to say about it. This point deserves its own reflections. An author may thus have played a determinant role in establishing comparative law in his country even though this is not (or only inadequately) reflected by the citation studies or an enhanced personal profile. The ways this can come about are many. For instance—and we offer these only as illustrations—a scholar may (a) leave successors to continue his work; (b) create a methodology which others follow; (c) create (or run successfully) institutes or centres which then act as research and teaching hubs; or (d) otherwise help the subject acquire roots in the law curriculum of his country by creating novel networks with other institutions. Incidentally, none of these achievements need be linked to the length of tenure since there exist plentiful examples of academics who held their chairs for long periods of time but left no impact on their environments.

We discussed (b) in the first Chapter and said as much as we wish to at this stage about (c). Under (d) we would include such projects as the Tunc/Chloros creation of the double maîtrise programme between Paris I and King's College, London—in our view the most successful double qualification programme in the United Kingdom today and the product of two men who, through their imaginative action, locked their respective institutions into a long-term and profitable link. So let us say a few words about the form a legacy can take, noting what is, probably, the obvious—namely that few persons have combined all of the above-mentioned talents. Indeed, if we were pressed to choose one out of the Pantheon of comparatists who came close to achieving all four of these aims, we suspect we would end up—again—with the name of Ernst Rabel.

Yet let us, instead, return to Professor Rodolfo Sacco, for he satisfied points (a) and (d) almost to perfection. He was the moving force behind the establishment of most modern chairs of comparative law in Italy and thus played a key role in strengthening its roots. Citation studies do not demonstrate this directly. But it is a fact and actually also affects indirectly citology. For Sacco skilfully succeeded in appointing to these chairs many of his former pupils who are now handsomely repaying both him and his method with frequent citations. In the long term, Sacco's virtual colonisation of the Italian law schools thus proved more successful than a similar attempt made by Mauro Cappelletti in the 1970s and 1980s—partly, perhaps, because the former managed to maintain the loyalty of his disciples (to him, personally, as well as to his method), but partly also because the restless peripatetic life of Cappelletti did not allow him to control sufficiently his Italian fiefdom.

Those who know something of the Italian scene must also complement this picture with a postscript. This must take the form of noting the opposition and even resentment which the forceful pursuit of Sacco's empire-building has also brought in its wake. But if the final verdict on his scholarly standing compared to that of Gino Gorla remains to be handed down by the collective judgment of his peers, his success in progressively dominating the Italian academic scene—from about the late 1960s onwards—cannot be in doubt. Though in citation terms Cappelletti thus beats Sacco by a ratio of 5 to 1 (in the American literature at any rate), indisputably due to the fact that the former wrote most of his later work in English, Sacco's role as a great figure of the Italian comparative legal scene is secure. Sacco the scholar undoubtedly helped create this legacy; Sacco the teacher undoubtedly magnetised scores of pupils in continuing his work; but it was Sacco the (academic) politician who created his school and his legacy.

The above observations about legacy and the different ways it is conferred are, in some respects, self-evident. What is interesting is finding illustrations that support them in different countries. The Sacco example for instance (good or bad is not the point here) for structural reasons could not have been duplicated in England—or even in Germany, where federal fragmentation makes the pursuit of such a *national* policy impossible. In each country, the ways of leaving a legacy are thus to some extent shaped by the conditions of university life appropriate to that system. But it is also important to make—indeed stress!—these points here in order to help dispel the impression that we may have over-emphasised the citation criterion for the purposes of determining the contribution a particular comparative law scholar has made to his subject. We have instead tried to adopt a multi-faceted approach to the problem we set ourselves to examine. What, then, is the conclusion that emerges from such effort?

For the reasons suggested earlier, British comparatists have not been particularly adept in pursuing targets such as the above in order to secure a strong position for the subject in the law curriculum. The world they worked in, it must be stressed, did not favour such strategies. It was not, and indeed is still not, a world of institutes, collaborative ventures, schools of thought, or closely linked junior colleagues, but a world, essentially, of 'loners'. To be sure, institutes have mushroomed in England in recent years just as the practice of *Festschriften* has, alas, also invaded our shores.

The above-mentioned 'novelties' of English academic life are only pale reflections of their Germanic models. For the centres and institutes which can now be found in many English law faculties are really little more than paper entities, devoid in most cases of their own funds, lacking internal cohesion and the kind of esprit de corps which one encounters in their German counterparts. For the entire period that we both served at UCL, the so-called Vinogradoff Institute at University College London thus had no physical space of its own and, so far as we know, no funds, no staff, no collective publications, and no collaborative programmes or institutional presence. In a manner which Louis XIV would have recognised, the Institute was its Director, and the Director was the Institute. Comparison with the Kaiser-Wilhelm-Institute or any of the current Max Planck Institutes thus reveals immediately that the only thing the German model shares with the English copy is the name. In England, promoting comparative law as a subject through the activities of institutes is very far from being a reality, though there is a centre which, especially at its peak, came close to attaining such heights: the Centre for Commercial Law Studies of Queen Mary College London, founded by Sir Roy Goode.

English comparatists not only turned their backs on the kind of institutional framework which could have helped them promote their subject. They also shot themselves in the foot by splitting their efforts between Roman law and foreign law and, for the better part of the 20th century, treating the latter as an outgrowth of the former. This prevented them from looking at foreign law in a practical manner and discovering how its cultivation could be of assistance to our courts. Instead, a doctrinal, historical, approach was chosen. One which lacked the desire to show how modern European law had grown beyond Roman law (and not just out of it) or to examine the emerging features of contemporary European law as it responded to new challenges coming from within (Luxembourg and Strasbourg for instance) as well as from without (for example, the United States). Watson's insistence to pursue the idea of transplants or Zimmermann's equally original idea to stress the common features found in both the civil law and Common law are among the few examples where a serious attempt was made to combine 'old and new' and present it in a new and relevant manner. Neither happened in England.

For comparative law in England, the consequences of such a lack of imagination or strategic errors—one may talk indefinitely about what mental blocks stopped English comparatists from following the routes set out by Zimmermann or Watson—were very considerable. For, first, we note how some extremely interesting and learned works of English comparatists either remained little noticed or are fast becoming forgotten. Secondly, now that the globalisation of markets expects from us to know how to handle foreign law (and lawyers), scholars at English universities are beginning to feel the fact that their predecessors did not furnish them with the means to facilitate it. And what was happening at the universities was spilling over to the practice of the law, where equally old professional habits were instilling into the minds of the young lawyers of the 1960s, 1970s and 1980s that we could safely go on ignoring what was happening elsewhere.

It is thus becoming imperative for English comparatists to draw conclusions from the evidence and to re-think a survival strategy for the subject. For the lack of judicial attention accorded to their work, combined with a minuscule number of references in legal literature, should make them wonder whether the targeting of a different audience would not make their knowledge more wide-spread and their subject more central to university studies. We tentatively express our doubt that the lessons that have to be learnt are being learnt. The appearance of huge multi-authored volumes lacking internal cohesion, philosophy, or aim suggests as much. If they are appearing in English, it is not because they are English but because the English publishing houses that are willing to publish them give their authors access to the English-speaking markets.

Our own effort has gone down a different route. Neither do we endorse insularity nor have we embraced the rush to draft European codes before discovering and digesting what (a) the Common law shares with Continental law, and (b) how we can put it to best use when talking to national practitioners. For us this means interesting the courts; through them, those who practice there; and, through them, forcing a reappraisal at university level of what we teach and how we teach it. We envisage a close but complex interrelationship between the different parts of the legal profession; and one has to ask whether it is working. Slowly we think it is beginning to do so. And how does one prove this? Not with arguments and counter-arguments but the beginnings of empirical evidence that suggests that the method can work *if we wish it to work*. It is thus important to point out (though only with a sense of embarrassment since the comparison involves one of the present co-authors) that, during this period in question, Markesinis has been quoted by English courts 26 times as compared to Birks' 14.

Making the point may strike some as the height of personal arrogance. It was not meant to be seen in that light though of course it may. What it wishes to highlight is the fact that despite the 'low standing' of comparative law—after all we were told that it was in a ghetto—properly used it can outflank Birks (the comparator) at the peak of his fame, writing on one of the most topical issues of contemporary private law (restitution). The ghetto theory can be consigned to the bin if *The German Law of Torts* alone receives nine citations while the total track record of Birks is 14, that of Ashworth is seven, and that of Atiyah is 31. However unattractive reputology may be to English academics, they will have to get used to taking into account the hard lessons it teaches us all. Given that the British Academy, that bastion of intellectual conservatism, is about to adopt this criterion as one of many which may be used to evaluate the worth of one's work, the signs that change is round the corner cannot be ignored.

Yet it would be wrong to blame for such introverted attitudes only the academic community. The role our judges have played in promoting international dialogue has also been mixed. When in the mid-1970s Lord Scarman raised the European banner with his Hamlyn Lectures, he remained respected but also alone for a long time. For there were—and still are—some judges whose (undoubted) intelligence has led them to reject (or give the impression that they are rejecting) the possibility that they can ever learn from either comparative law or trained comparatists. This 'reverse snobbery'—we are not sure how else to describe it—is all the more remarkable when it comes from judges who began their life in academe. As against such judges, however, one must also pit others who have declared their keenness to engage in an intellectual dialogue with their foreign counterparts. The list is so long and so distinguished that we content ourselves to mention just a few, namely Lords Goff, Bingham, Steyn, Phillips, Hope, and Lord Justice Sedeley (all from Britain); the former First President of the Cour de cassation Canivet (France); Justices Ackermann and Goldstone (both South Africa); Chief Justice Barak (Israel); Constitutional Court Judges Grimm, Hoffman-Riem, and Bryde (all Germany); Justices Breyer, Ginsburg, and O'Connor (all United States) and Chief Justices Maclachlin and former Justice Heureux Dubé (Canada).

We have looked at the work of judges as comparatists in another monograph[60] and thus need not return to this topic here. We merely mention it as evidence against those, be they judges or insular academics, who refuse to see what is happening and where the future lies. And if one retorts that the figures we have produced seem slender, the answer is *yes, they are slender, but the citation record of non-comparatists (for example, Birks) is weak.* In any event, what comparatists such as us are trying to do is to innovate; and at the beginning of any innovative process the existing hard evidence can always be interpreted in different ways. Our submission, however, remains that comparative law, almost the world over, has now moved out of the hands of academics and into the judicial sphere, and with this shift we are seeing not only an enhanced interest in foreign law but also the need to research it, to teach it, and to use it in a different way than was done until now. No wonder that those who build their comparative law around Jacques Derrida's ideas see themselves left 'out in the cold'. For how else can one explain their attacks on distinguished colleagues, inter alia on the grounds that they do not reply to their criticisms? Ignorance, it would seem, hurts these people more than attack; and ignored are those who cannot move with the times.

(c) Lesson Three—The Power of School Citation and Exaggeration

Thirdly, we return to a point touched on at the beginning of this Chapter, which, we noted, Judge Posner raised but left undeveloped. This is the power of auto-citation, or 'school' citation, or even 'plain propaganda' citation. In our view, some indication for this phenomenon comes from the activities of a new generation of Italian comparatists currently working within the United States. This group has overcome the 'drawback of language' and is making up for lost time by constantly citing like-minded scholars, again largely of Italian

[60] Basil Markesinis and Jörg Fedtke, *Foreign Law in National Courts: A New Source of Inspiration?*, Routledge-Cavendish (2006).

origin. Thus, of Sacco's 89 citations in American journals, 25 per cent come from his closest pupils. More precisely: 13 come from Professor Mattei, three from Professor Bussani and three from Professor Monateri. A handful of authors (Gordley, Gerber, Kasirer) cite him in two documents each. The remainder are single citations in different documents. This interesting 'Italian habit' seems to be reflected in Italy itself, and the Italian literature, on an even larger scale. For there, too, it would appear that a substantial number of citations to the Sacco group—some these days like to be known as the 'Trento circle' (and the two terms are by no means co-terminous)—come from each other but far less so from other Italian colleagues.

Finally, Table 3.3 below suggests a slightly different aspect of the same phenomenon, namely that scholars also tend to receive most of their citations from their own national colleagues. Table 3.3 shows that, for instance, Professor Cappelletti receives 59.4 per cent (35 out of 59) of his citations from his fellow countrymen, Professor Sacco receives a hefty 64 per cent of his from Italians (39 out of 61), whilst Professor Alpa a staggering 71.4 per cent (25 of his 35). The sample is, once again, too small to justify safe conclusions; and there may be an alternative and equally plausible explanation for it—for example, they are more cited by their countrymen because that is where they are mostly known. On the other hand one must note that, first, these figures come from a truly comparative law journal and, secondly, that they do not deviate markedly from the pattern of citations that these same authors received in the samples collected from individual countries. Moreover, one must note the pattern of other scholars—for example, Professors Kötz, Zimmermann, David, and the editor of the latest editions of his grand oeuvre, Professor Jauffret Spinosi—who seem to receive equal attention from the writers in most major legal systems.

Such patterns and cross-referencing by adherents of the same school could prove misleading, especially to those who have only a faint acquaintance of the comparative law scene in countries other than their own. Such techniques can even exaggerate the importance of particular pieces by investing them with an aura of importance that is not really deserved. An example of this can, in our opinion, be found in Professor Mattei's assertion[61] that 'Schlesinger's work in Europe *has been extensively cited* and I believe that the volume on Formation of Contracts has received more book reviews in the old continent than any other book published in the United States'. If the statement is taken literally to refer to *book reviews* it may well be true. On the other hand, the first part of the statement—the one *we* (not the author) have printed in italics—is so open-ended that we were unable to check its

[61] In Annelise Riles (ed), *Rethinking the Masters of Comparative Law* (2001), at p 256. We were originally tempted to attribute such exaggeration to the Mediterranean predilection for well-intended hyperbole. The phenomenon is, however (like so many other patterns of human behaviour) nowadays also encountered in the United Kingdom. Thus, to give one example, Barry Nicholas' obituary in *The Times* of 7 March 2002 referred to his student textbook on *The French Law of Contract* as showing comparative law at its best. This may strike some as excessive praise; but then that is reserved for his *Introduction to Roman Law*, which is described as 'quite simply the best introduction *to law* [*sic*] that has ever been written'. The fellow Romanist who wrote these words (widely believed to have been the late Peter Birks) might have achieved his aim more plausibly had he at least added the word *Roman* before the word *law*; but then, if indeed it was Birks who wrote the text, he must have been restrained from composing a more measured piece by the infectious enthusiasm that made him such a passionate speaker. Nevertheless, putting these incidents in true perspective (not always available to outsiders) we note for the record that, talking to the first of us, the country's leading Roman lawyer seemed even more reserved in his reactions towards this introductory book. The statistics in this Chapter could be seen as supporting him and not the author, whoever it was, of the obituary notice.

accuracy given the difficulties one encounters in counting citations across Europe. Still, the statistics we have managed to assemble make it highly problematic. In fact, as presently advised, we think it is wrong.

For the figures of Table 3.3, composed from France's leading comparative law journal—the *Revue Internationale de Droit Comparé*—of the years 1980–2001 do not suggest any particular prominence of Schlesinger's work (indeed quite the opposite: a comparative neglect). And the same picture emerges from Table 3.1, giving citation figures in legal literature in four countries. This table places Schlesinger 10th out of a list of 13—even in his own (second) country and when compared with his American peers. Schlesinger's two-volume work *Formation of Contracts. A Study of the Common Core of Legal Systems* (1968), which particularly attracts Mattei's attention, receives a mere 23 citations in the entire American legal literature of the last 20 years, and a single one in England during the same period. According to the same table, the picture in England and Germany is hardly different. Table 3.3 completes the picture by measuring the impact which a scholar's work has had on courts of law and, again, Schlesinger fares poorly. The inability to give European-wide figures with scientific accuracy has been noted; and we have to live with it. But what we do have is hardly compatible with Professor Mattei's statement. Given his energy, maybe now that he is about to become a co-author of this book he may succeed in reversing this trend.

The above comments on the work of one author reinforce, in our view, the feeling that the scholarly evaluation of one's work cannot be assessed solely by looking at citation rates. The point was made before and is repeated here for greater emphasis. But statistics *can* help question hyperbolic statements about a work when (allegedly) based on quantitative assessments. More generally, though they cannot 'make' scholarly reputations, they can help cut down to size claims made by others about them, giving a sense of dry reality to hagiographic treatment of certain authors. The particular example we looked at—and others could be added—may also offer a concrete illustration of Posner's theory that some citations do little more than promote the citator's own intellectual agenda. This then, as stated earlier on, is a facet of the science of reputology that needs more research.

This somewhat cynical attitude towards such multiplication of citations can be tested if we compare the citation rates of some of the above-mentioned Italian scholars with that of another—some would say the greatest—of Italian comparatists: Gino Gorla. For Gorla suffers not only as a result of not writing in English but also from the fact that none of his disciples chose to pursue a career in the United States and make his name known there or create an international 'Gorla school'. Gorla's work is thus hardly known in the Anglo-Saxon world, which is a great loss to knowledge since many in the know would probably regard him as a methodologist of the first order, especially in the way he combined the task of contemporary comparison and historical research. Yet if one talks to Italian colleagues one does not come across a single interlocutor who has failed to place Gorla on top of his list of learned comparatists. *Opinio communis*, even if ascertained in such an unscientific manner, thus also counts in forming as objective a view as one can about a fellow colleague and his impact on others.

Table 3.3: Citations of comparatists in *Revue Internationale de Droit Comparé* 1980 to 2001 (on the basis of the country of the citator[62])

American						
	Canada	England	France	Germany	Italy	USA
Cited Author						
Hans W Baade	0	0	1	0	0	0
George A Bermann	0	0	1	0	2	0
John P Dawson	0	0	2	0	0	0
John G Fleming	2	0	6	0	2	0
Mary Ann Glendon	0	0	8	4	4	0
James Gordley	2	0	8	2	8	1
John Henry Merryman	0	0	8	3	6	0
Mathias Reimann	0	0	1	0	0	0
Rudolf B Schlesinger	0	0	2	0	0	0
Arthur T von Mehren	0	0	4	1	1	0
Alan Watson	3	0	5	3	2	4

British						
	Canada	England	France	Germany	Italy	USA
Cited Author						
John Bell	0	1	6	0	0	0
Tony Honoré	0	0	1	0	0	0
JA Jolowicz	0	7	8	7	0	0
Otto Kahn-Freund	0	0	5	4	1	0
FH Lawson	0	1	4	3	0	2
Kurt Lipstein	0	0	2	1	0	0
FA Mann	0	0	3	1	4	0
Basil S Markesinis	0	6	14	1	6	0
Barry Nicholas	0	1	3	0	2	0
Bernhard Rudden	0	0	1	0	0	0
Tony Weir	0	0	2	0	0	1

62 The country used is not necessarily the country of origin but the country in which the university of the author is located at the time of writing.

German						
	Canada	England	France	Germany	Italy	USA
Cited Author						
Ulrich Drobnig	2	0	3	3	2	1
Eric Jayme	0	0	2	3	1	0
Hein Kötz	0	0	19	12	18	0
Werner Lorenz	0	0	1	0	0	0
Marcus Lutter	0	0	1	1	0	0
Peter Müller-Graf	0	0	3	5	2	0
Peter Schlechtriem	0	0	3	2	6	0
Christian von Bar	0	0	3	2	0	0
Reinhard Zimmermann	0	0	7	6	10	0
Konrad Zweigert	0	1	9	6	2	0

French						
	Canada	England	France	Germany	Italy	USA
Cited Author						
Xavier Blanc-Jouvain	0	0	13	1	4	0
René David	1	23	31	6	12	2
Mireille Delmas-Marty	0	0	13	1	4	2
Pierre Legrand	2	6	16	2	5	0
Horatia Muir-Watt	0	0	12	1	0	0
Jauffret Spinosi	0	2	11	5	8	2
Denis Tallon	0	0	24	9	7	1
André Tunc	3	7	42	3	6	4

Italian						
	Canada	England	France	Germany	Italy	USA
Cited Author						
Guido Alpa	0	0	9	1	25	0
Michael Joachim Bonell	0	0	6	4	9	0
Mauro Bussani	0	0	1	0	4	0
Mauro Cappelletti	0	1	13	10	35	0
Antonio Gambaro	0	0	0	0	4	0
Gino Gorla	0	0	7	0	18	0
Maurizio Lupoi	0	0	2	0	12	0
Ugo Mattei	0	4	13	0	16	0
Rodolfo Sacco	0	2	16	2	39	2
Anna De Vita	0	0	2	0	11	0

5. FIRST CONCLUSIONS

Statistics can kill intuitive evaluations of facts and other physical phenomena. That is one of their drawbacks. For intuition and imagination—and even myth—also play a useful role in our lives, besides being, invariably, more attractive to read than a dry set of figures. The world of statistics is not only dull: it is also slippery. In the present case this is largely because of the way the data is collected. We thus spent much time—too much, any true propagandist would say—setting out the caveats which we thought were necessary for our readers. It could be argued that in stressing them too much, we may have drained our own conclusions of much of their force. Others might argue more broadly and say that the statistical method cannot be applied easily to an area of law such as comparative law because it is not a coherent enough field to stand up to this kind of analysis. We 'hear' these arguments but disagree with both.

For first, the data we have collected, despite its limitations, is broad and rich enough to suggest patterns that repeat themselves in many systems and may thus be a good indication of what is actually happening out there. To put it differently, we are not convinced that if more detailed studies were carried out concerning additional jurists, more countries, and more journals, the overall picture we have presented would be affected significantly.

Secondly, as already stated, the figures collected for the next five years following the first collection of data for 1980 to 2000 fully confirm our conclusions. Indeed, the figures given in this Chapter, slightly increased to reflect the enlarged database we used when revisiting them for this book, have in no way affected our various arguments.

Thirdly, what impact have comparatists had on comparative law, its teaching, and its use by the courts and the legislator? Here the data needs to be analysed carefully; and because the figures involved are rather low, the conclusions must be phrased with appropriate caution. Overall, we feel that our data corroborates the view that comparatists, with few notable exceptions of colleagues whose work has set the comparative law agenda for the last 20 years or so (and we are here thinking of Watson, Kötz, Sacco and Zimmermann) the remainder have had a small impact both on the worlds of academe and of practice. The reasons we have already discussed; and though they may not meet with everyone's approval, they do at least provide a basis for a new and more focused discussion than that which we have had so far.

Fourthly, notwithstanding the above, we feel that we may have opened up a new path for measuring the reputation of scholarship through statistics in the area of comparative law. This is because the use of the assembled figures suggests that a distinction has to be drawn between the apparent and real citation rate of some scholars, which means discounting from their totals citations not referring to foreign and comparative law work. If one is looking for the comparatists' impact on scholarship, this is a crucial point; and in making it, our use of statistics may have destroyed myths and diminished reputations.

The figures of the late Professor Schlesinger offer one example of what we referred to above and which one could call 'adjustment' of reputation. Eminent and charismatic though he was, his citation figures simply do not support the image which his supporters have tried to create for him—that his influence has been unique and is now radiating back to Europe.[63]

[63] The so-called Trento project seems to be the major exception, but then it is run by the very same people who belong to the Sacco/Schlesinger schools.

The figures support a range of similar or analogous propositions for other 'greats'. In one sense, these may not be earth-shattering conclusions; but they do help build up the truer picture about comparative law during the last 30 years or so, and help us separate myth from reality. Finally, we regard as not unimportant the preliminary data and interpretation we provided about the reception of foreign ideas in contemporary South Africa, not least because it suggests how governments and scholars can combine in the spreading of legal ideas emanating from a particular legal culture.

The significance goes beyond what one chooses to make of the figures given above. For one, citation breeds citation, as authors who are encountered frequently will sooner or later attract the attention of readers who might not have otherwise become aware of their work. Citation, even auto-citation, if repeated over a period of time and geographical space will add to the reputation and perhaps the kudos of the author cited. The same goes for what, for lack of a better term, one could call 'mischievous' citation.

It is tempting to say that negative, that is, critical citation may also have this effect (somewhat along the lines of the well-known argument that even adverse publicity is good publicity). Of course, this does not eliminate the possibility that when the dust settles, many of these reputations may vanish into thin air. But then given the somewhat pessimistic attitude expressed by the longevity of academic reputation (even the good ones), in 99 per cent of all cases this may not be so significant after all.

Fifthly, we feel that the attempt to generate an interest in judges to become involved in the use of foreign law may have made some headway over the past decades. Though this is a highly controversial issue in the United States, especially in the area of constitutional law, judicial review, and human rights, in the rest of the world it is actually happening. Our guess as much as our wish is that it will continue to grow, not least because contemporary economic and commercial realities require this.

Finally, allowing for differences of size (country, numbers of universities, journals, etc) we note a certain consistency of result in the citation figures of comparatists across borders. We already noted for instance that Professor Jolowicz' work has had the same reception on both sides of the Atlantic. This is consistent with our view that a true comparatist has an audience that goes beyond his national borders, and only if he is afraid to reach out will he shut himself off such rejuvenating sources of ideas.

So, when all is said and done, and the various provisos have been weighed carefully and found wanting or in need of further refinement, one thing seems to be reasonably clear. The statement that comparative law is nowadays in a ghetto is *not* substantiated by fact. At best, the proposition must be advanced with qualifications, limited perhaps to the 1980s and part of the 1990s, and the state of affairs attributed to the proponents' own fault. For the number of scholars nowadays teaching the subject is growing; the citations that comparatists attract to their work are going up not down (at any rate if one looks solely at academic literature); and there are strong judicial stirrings in favour of an exchange of ideas, enhanced mutual understanding, and even legal borrowing. Thus, some of the comparatists in our lists can almost claim a place among the 100 or so best cited authors in the United States. Others, with a smaller number of citations in any one system, more significantly end up with a substantial intellectual presence in a number of continents, not a mean achievement for people meant to be inhabiting ghettos.

The statistics can also be taken to support the view that the linkage for comparative law with Roman law (or legal history) has harmed, or at the very least not benefited, the interests of the former while helping prolong the condemned life of the latter. Note, for instance, the point made about professors of comparative law having hitherto devoted the substance of their energies to keeping their Roman law scholarship alive. Since time is a most precious commodity, this was achieved at the expense of more effort being put into the study of contemporary foreign law. The danger of that happening in the future has now receded as European law, in its Community, human rights, or comparative law incarnation, has almost everywhere in Europe supplanted Roman law as the course that gives us a glimpse of another system and thus helps us understand our own better.

There was a second and costlier price tag that this 'back to the past' habit carried with it; and it will also affect the new trends mentioned earlier. For it produced (and if we are not careful it could produce again in the future) works that had little or no impact on the courts and the real world. The statistics, modest though they are, support placing this hypothesis on our agenda. Comparatists who get a fair number of citations in the literature are totally absent from the real world of practice. The disproportion in the figures given in Tables 3.1 and 3.2 is staggering. Here, for once, the inadequacy of raw data cannot be used as an excuse to weaken the conclusion. But this, clearly, is not because of lack of ability but because of a wrong focus. Professor Nicholas' example shows that when his great talents were put to a contemporary and relevant purpose, the courts—even courts which he felt misunderstood what he had written—made use of his ideas. When, by contrast, these colleagues remained restricted to Roman law, they earned the respect of the dwindling number of like-minded peers, along (perhaps) with a beautiful obituary by a fellow Romanist. But that, we submit, is not legacy; not at any rate as we defined it above. The fact of the matter is that the Rabels and the Kötzes and the Saccos and the Zimmermanns and the Stolls of the subject can be counted on one hand. And the successors are more likely to come from Germany, the United States (especially in comparative public law), or Italy than from England or France. The examination of the entrails at the time of writing gives little room for more hope.

Though much more work still remains to be done on the path we have cleared up with this Chapter, such work will prove even more useful if it looks at the use *legislative* bodies make of foreign and comparative law. Our hunch is that there, as well, concrete, focused, detailed and practically relevant studies are used rather than work which looks at the past or at other areas of human knowledge *unless it can be shown to have a close bearing on the subject under scrutiny.* Our suspicion also is that the legislator, when using information about foreign law, derives it through the writings of his 'own' scholars writing in his 'own' language. The ability to move across borders and across languages is still limited to a few jurists; and the limits are not imposed so much by language barriers or poor libraries or lack of opportunities for travel but by the most insurmountable of barriers: human mentality. In our subject it is of an inward type; arrogant in nature and stubborn in its attachment to past glories; failing to recognise new realities and yet, sometimes, apparently eager to embrace new fads. Academics who wish to break down the mentality barriers we alluded to will only do so if they can attract the support of business and the courts; and they will only succeed in this if they make their work relevant to both.

6. REPUTOLOGY FOR THE YEARS 2001 TO 2005

In the following sections we re-visit the basic statistical information given for the years 1980 to 2000 but now look at what has happened in the five years that followed, namely

2001–2005. Our general conclusion is that the assumptions made or opinions expressed previously survive unscathed the influx of the new figures. These are not just updated figures but are also enlarged through the use of a more extensive database (which includes approximately 100 more law journals) and by the addition of two new American colleagues, included in our list as representatives of the new (but not extreme) tendencies in comparative law. This is a fairly extensive source of raw material, and the picture described fairly representative of the actual state of affairs in the United States. The English figures, though derived from a much smaller database (six leading journals manually searched) confirm the patterns emerging from across the Atlantic.

7. CITATION FIGURES OF BRITISH COMPARATISTS AND NON-COMPARATISTS

Since the argument has been made that non-comparatists fare much better in the attention they receive from fellow scholars as compared to 'proper' comparatists, we begin by looking at the citation rates of *five* 'major legal figures' of the contemporary British scene. As always, one may object to the selection of authors—why is X included rather than Y? Though the substitution of one set of names for another would, in our view, make no difference to our observations or conclusions, the fact is that no English colleague would, we believe, argue that the names we have selected are not among the leaders of our profession. All, for instance, are (or were) Fellows of the British Academy, supposedly the supreme academic accolade one can receive in Britain. All also taught (or teach) core subjects, and are thus the kind of scholars who are most likely to attract maximum attention both from other scholars and the courts. The summary for previous years, we remind our readers, read as follows:

Table 3.4: Non-comparatists—citation rates for 1980 to 2000

Author	US literature	English literature	US courts	English courts
Ashworth, A	164	95	4	7
Atiyah, P	894	207	16	31
Birks, PB	153	144	0	14
Goode RM	143	69	0	51
Treitel, G	99	118	2	71

The English figures for these scholars were assembled on the basis of manual searches of *six* major journals. The journals searched from 2001 to 2005 are: *Modern Law Review*; *Oxford Journal of Legal Studies*; *International and Comparative Law Quarterly*; *Cambridge Law Journal*; *Legal Studies*; and *Law Quarterly Review*. Though these journals are among the major law journals circulating in the United Kingdom, the list is not complete; and the exclusion of such publications as the *Criminal Law Review* and *Public Law* represent omissions which may have distorted the final showing of learned colleagues. This is especially true of Professor Andrew Ashworth who, almost certainly, would have been the prime beneficiary of a search of the *Criminal Law Review.* Manual searches are, however, very time-consuming, so we can only explain what we have done and why we have done it, and warn that, if an electronic search of all journals published in the United Kingdom had been possible, all these figures (possibly for all colleagues) would have been higher. For the reasons already explained previously, we still maintain that what follows represents a reasonable sample from which one can test the ideas, hypotheses, and conclusions mentioned earlier and in the paragraphs which follow. All other figures supplied were obtained electronically.[64]

Table 3.5: Non-comparatists—citation rates for 2001 to 2005[65]

Author	US literature	English literature	US courts	English courts
Ashworth, A	182	77	1	9
Atiyah, P	259	51	1	23
Birks, PB	139	193	4	11
Goode RM	12	40	0	3
Treitel, G	62	24	1	54

When comparing Tables 3.1 and 3.2 one must not allow it to slip one's mind that the second set of figures cover only one quarter of the time of the first, that is five years instead of 20. If one were thus to attempt a downward and purely mathematical adjustment by 75 per cent to account for the reduced period of time shown in the new table, that should produce, for this new five-year period, the following figures, rounded up for the sake of convenience (in parentheses are added the actual figures obtained): Ashworth = 24 (77); Atiyah = 52 (51); Birks = 36 (193); Goode = 17 (40); and Treitel = 25 (24).

This mathematical adjustment is, indisputably, a crass and arbitrary test; and it is further weakened by the fact that the new chart gives figures taken from six journals and not, as in the previous case, five. It is only attempted to give us a rough guideline on how these colleagues should be faring, five years after, on the basis of their previous figures and if all other conditions remained unchanged. In practice, we find that (almost) all have done better in absolute terms; and this conclusion is reinforced by their American figures which show that there, too, they have on the whole done better than their original figures would have suggested. Thus, on the basis of the previous performance, Ashworth should have obtained 41 citations but actually obtained 182; Atiyah should have had 227 but received 254; Birks could have expected 38 but received 153; Goode was due for 36 but ended up with 12; and Treitel was expected to end up with 23 but received 62. These statistics follow the pattern of the English figures by showing an increase in the United States, with the sole exception of Professor Goode, who recorded a drop.

These combined figures provide evidence (in varying degrees of strength) for the following propositions: (i) that the citation rates both in the United States and England have gone up, possibly because of our increased databases; (ii) that authors who are at the pinnacle of their careers during this period show a dramatic increase in citation rates compared to their

[64] Details are supplied in Appendix 3.

[65] Details of the cited publications are again available online at the websites of the Institute of Transnational Law at the University of Texas at Austin and the Institute of Global Law at University College London.

earlier scores, especially if compared to other 'big hitters' who have retired; and (iii) that some of those who belong to this last group may be beginning to show signs of 'stabilisation' of their citation rates, perhaps even indicating the beginning of a decline. If this proves to be so, it will be in line with other figures given below, which suggest that retirement (especially if accompanied by a reduction in publishing) hastens one's 'disappearance' from the citation charts.

Though this is a plausible prediction, supported by hard figures in more detailed surveys of this kind in the United States, the fulfilment of this prophecy may, to some extent, be affected if the main works of the above-mentioned eminent colleagues are successfully taken over by able disciples. Professor Peter Caine's re-vamping of Patrick Atiyah's *Accidents, Compensation and the Law* is an example of a new lease of life given to a famous work. The book (and its authors) are thus certain to remain in the citation charts. On the other hand, this is unlikely to happen with all of Atiyah's major publications, though, having said this, one must note with admiration the high rate of attention which he continues to receive in the United States well over 15 years after his premature retirement. Besides, in America and elsewhere, Atiyah has always been perceived as an 'ideas man' and not just as a treatise writer, and has thus readily come to mind to anyone writing in his field. In our experience, this is the image he also has in Italy and Germany, though we suspect that he is less known in France.

That said, we note once again that the citation figures achieved in the six major English law journals by five of our major non-comparatists compare favourably with the top five English comparatists. The comparison, which needs to be made to test in yet another way the validity of the 'ghetto theory', thus shows the following:

Table 3.6: Citation rates of comparatists and non-comparatists in English law journals from 2001 to 2005 (in order of citation figures)

Birks	193	Markesinis	72
Ashworth	77	Andenas	34
Atiyah	51	Honoré	29
Goode	40	Bell	25
Treitel	24	Weir	24
		Lawson	21

When, however, we move to citations by courts and compare non-comparatists to comparatists, the former gain the upper hand. The only exception seems to be provided by Markesinis's figures, something which could be taken to lend support for the thesis that courts are only likely to be interested in comparative law literature if it is focused and of potential practical use to them. We must, however, also note that the figures are rather slender (equally for comparatists and non-comparatists), so that it would be dangerous to try and draw firm conclusions from them. Thus, the situation has to be revisited in about five years time.

Table 3.7: Citation rates of comparatists and non-comparatists by English courts for 2001 to 2005

Treitel	54	Markesinis	27
Atiyah	23	Andenas	7
Birks	11	Mann	6
		Honoré	3[66]

We leave it to our readers to continue the evaluation undertaken, in *tentative* terms, in the first part of this Chapter, and let each decide if, in the light of the above figures, comparatists have done so much worse than their non-comparatist colleagues. We do, however, draw the reader's attention to the 'performance' of Professor Mads Andenas, whose work has attracted the attention of the courts much more than that of well-established figures in the comparative *and* non-comparative scene. For, notwithstanding the fact that the *overall* figures are low—preventing the formulation of firm conclusions—Andenas' citation rate deserves closer attention for two reasons. First, because his work is *pure, practical comparative law*—untouched by Roman law or comparative historical references—and is thus precisely the kind of work we urge comparative lawyers to undertake if they wish to be noticed *and used.* Secondly, because his overall citation figures come only slightly below the number of references made to the impressive oeuvre of, say, the late Peter Birks. For a younger Norwegian/English lawyer, writing on a subject which is meant to be marginalised, this is an impressive performance and one which, again, lends some support to our theories and questions of accepted wisdom.

8. THE COMPARATISTS DURING THE YEARS 2001 TO 2005

Table 3.8: Citation of comparatists in academic literature for the years 2001 to 2005

Americans

Country	England	Germany	USA
Author			
Hans W Baade	1	3	96
George A Bermann	0	0	291
John P Dawson	7	0	231
John G Fleming	19	1	90
Mary Ann Glendon	3	2	872
James Gordley	8	2	242

[66] That is because we have not counted his 13 references to *Causation in the Law* as comparative citations. If one does, then he takes second place with 16 and Mann comes third with six.

Americans (*cont.*)

Country	England	Germany	USA
Author			
John Langbein	0	0	1020
Mitch Lasser	0	0[67]	57
Ugo Mattei	3	1	273
John Henry Merryman	12	1	553
Matthias Reimann	8	0[68]	204
Annelise Riles		0	79
Rudolf B Schlesinger	0	5	109
Arthur T von Mehren	0	3	412
Alan Watson	12	1	408

British

Country	England	Germany	USA
Author			
Mads Andenas	34	22	88
John Bell	25	0	99
Tony Honoré	28	3	184
JA Jolowicz	9	0	52
Otto Kahn-Freund	12	3	72
FH Lawson	21	3	46
Kurt Lipstein	4	10	29
FA Mann	6	16[69]	0
Basil S Markesinis	72	10	190
Barry Nicholas	13	5	90
Bernard Rudden	4	1	47
Tony Weir	24	6	149

[67] The number of hits in journals (above 400), by far most of which are false positives attracted by the entry 'Lasser', was too large to analyse. The search for 'Mitch Lasser' did not return any hits.

[68] The returns for 'Reimann' (over 400), most of them false positives due to the frequency of this name in the German language, was too large to analyse. The entry 'Mathias Reiman' did not return any hits. Specific searches were carried out for a number of works but did not return any hits.

[69] The number of hits in journals (above 400), by far most of which are false positives due to the ambiguous meaning of 'Mann' in German, was too large to analyse. Searches were conducted for a number of specific works.

German

Country	England	Germany	USA
Author			
Ulrich Drobnig	0	116[70]	65
Eric Jayme	5	>400[71]	70
Hein Kötz	22	157[72]	225
Werner Lorenz	5	26[73]	13
Marcus Lutter	0	17[74]	41
Peter-Christian	0	0	0
Müller-Graff	1	46[75]	4
Peter Schlechtriem	6	7[76]	44
Christian von Bar	1	34[77]	61
Reinhard Zimmermann	24	51[78]	226
Konrad Zweigert	16	73	159

French

Country	England	Germany	USA
Author			
Xavier Blanc-Jouvain	0	0	1
René David	2	2	153
Mireille Delmas-Marty	6	7	52
Pierre Legrand	24	4	197
Horatia Muir-Watt	6	1	55
Denis Tallon	3	10	34
André Tunc	1	0[79]	53

[70] Of which roughly 25% each seem to be comparative or on private international law.

[71] The search for 'Jayme' returned more than 400 hits, the vast majority of which were to his work on private international law or (comparative) family law.

[72] We estimate that Kötz is cited at least as much for his comparative work as for his work on purely national law.

[73] The search for 'Lorenz' returned over 400 hits, many false positives due to the frequency of the name in Germany. The search for 'Werner Lorenz' returned eight references to the *Festschrift Werner Lorenz* (1991). Searches were conducted for a number of specific works.

[74] The search for 'Lutter' returned over 400 hits, many false positives due to the frequency of the name in Germany. The search for 'Marcus Lutter' returned fewer than 10 references to Lutter's work in the area of (mainly German) company law. Searches were conducted for a number of specific works.

[75] Of which more than 50% are to his work on Community law. A single comparative piece attracts four citations: *Rechtliche Auswirkungen einer laufenden Geschäftsverbindung im amerikanischen und deutschen Recht* (1974).

[76] The search for 'Schlechtriem' returned more than 400 hits, most of which are positives. Owing to the large number of hits we were, however, not able to discount multiple citations to single works of Schlechtriem by the same author; the actual number of hits is therefore bound to be substantially lower. The search for 'Peter Schlechtriem' did not return citations by other authors. Searches were conducted for a number of specific works.

[77] The search for 'von Bar' returned more than 400 hits, most of which are positives. Owing to the large number of hits we were, however, not able to discount multiple citations to single works of von Bar by the same author; the actual number of hits is therefore bound to be substantially lower. The search for 'Christian von Bar' did not return citations by other authors. Searches were conducted for a number of specific works.

[78] The search for 'Zimmermann' returned over 400 hits, many false positives due to the frequency of the name in Germany. The search for 'Reinhard Zimmermann' returned two reviews of Zimmermann's work and a single reference to *Zivilrechtswissenschaft und Schuldrechtsreform* (with Ernst, 2001). Searches were conducted for a number of specific works.

[79] The number of hits in journals (above 400), by far most of which are false positives due to the ambiguous

Italian

Country	England	Germany	USA
Author			
Guido Alpa	0	5	18
Michael Joachim Bonell	0	21	142
Mauro Bussani	0	1	61
Mauro Cappelletti	1	1	225
Antonio Gambaro	0	1	27
Gino Gorla	0	0	16
Maurizio Lupoi	1	4	24
Rodolfo Sacco	4	4	114

9. COMMENTARY: SHOWING IN LITERATURE

The citation performance of the scholars reviewed for the years 2001 to 2005 must again, in purely mathematical terms, be compared to 25 per cent of the citations they received during the preceding longer period. On that basis—and we have already stressed that it does not represent a scientific way of comparing their 'progress or decline' but only a rough and ready method of reflecting on their performance—we note that our comparatists have either held their ground or improved their performance.

First, the comparatist 'heavy hitters' have in no way lost their appeal on the rest of their colleagues; if anything they have improved their performance. Wherever this has happened, two reasons can explain this across the board—continued appeal of existing major works and new output. Remaining active/productive and, failing that, finding a younger colleague to take over your major work[s] is an important way of ensuring that one remains noticed and cited. In both cases, of course, the established reputation of the older author helps the younger attract readers by making him, *ab initio* as it were, 'respectable'. In this sense, these co-authors begin with an inbuilt advantage since the 'pressure' or temptation to cite a newcomer is, for better or worse, less great. This, of course, also applies to non-comparatists and, in both cases, it is 'unfair' in so far as it means that good pieces from newcomers take time to be noted. But there is no guarantee that the older and well-established figures will continue to dominate the scene, for we know from experience that few contemporary works have the enduring appeal of, say, OW Holmes' *The Common Law* or Benjamin Cardozo's *The Nature of the Judicial Process.* Even such classics, however, tend to be ignored by the modern generation of students, whose reading is increasingly determined by notions of practicality and necessity.

Among our two top-cited comparatists, Langbein has, during the last five years, overtaken Glendon in absolute numbers, though one must again note that just over half (maybe closer to 60 per cent) of his citations (depending how one draws the distinction between national and foreign/comparative work) are on topics of national law concerning mainly probate and employment. Langbein's *Chicago Law Review* essay on 'The German Advantage in Civil Procedure' also continues to earn him about 9 per cent of his total

meaning of 'Tunc' in the German legal language (eg '*ex tunc*'), was too large to analyse. The search for 'André Tunc' did not result in any hits.

citations, a slight drop from his earlier 12 per cent but still a figure showing an interest in his ideas on procedural reform, much though they were opposed by legal sociologists (such as Professor Chase) and practice-oriented lawyers. The remainder of his considerable citations is distributed in much smaller numbers among other pieces, many related to criminal law and procedure combined with legal history (a feature which we find in all the breakdowns we have done for this Chapter). This point deserves a small excursus.

To our knowledge little noticed, but to varying degrees affecting most authors who receive decent-to-good citation showings, overall citation rates may hover at high levels but not be due to one book but to many works. This could suggest that a prolific author sooner or later gets 'picked up' by other colleagues. On the other hand, it could be seen as indicating that high visibility is due to the fact that an author is prolific and less to the production of a blockbuster text. It is difficult to determine whether, in evaluative terms, this is a 'plus' or a 'minus' for the author in question. We note, however, that in this category we find many known comparatists, among them Bell, Gordley, Legrand, Markesinis, Reimann, Watson and Zimmermann.

Other national and international law scholars (like Langbein and von Mehren), though fully fledged members of the comparatist community, receive a substantial percentage of their citations for works on national law or conflicts of law. The first category (found in Langbein for instance) reduces somewhat his comparative law 'colours'—something which is less obvious for those who (like von Mehren) have spent much time writing on conflicts, a subject very close to comparative law. Professor Gordley also falls into this grouping with an equally good showing across his three interrelated fields of comparative law, comparative legal history, and jurisprudence, while Markesinis' work is—apart from his *Tort Law* textbook—almost entirely devoted to comparative law and methodology.

Nicholas' somewhat 'odd' situation was already noted above. The latest figures confirm that though his interests covered ancient and modern civil law, his reputation remains (fairly) solidly that of a Roman lawyer, with 60 out of 90 of his new citations going to his two main Roman law textbooks. Apart from his French law student book (which still receives 15 citations, that is, about 16 per cent of his total), his other comparative law articles (or contributions in books) earn him single figure citations as do some other (and very interesting) works on restitution and international sales.

This fate has been avoided by Watson, whose *Legal Transplants* still earns him 92 of his 409 citations. Among the remainder, 180 citations go to works which are comparative (or mixed comparative and Roman law) while 137 are reserved for pure Roman law. As stated, therefore, Watson has managed to attain a better combination of Roman law and comparative law than other Romanists. Honoré, likewise, remains an author widely cited by scholars interested in different branches of the law (and our survey is seriously deficient in not showing his South African profile in the law of trusts). Otherwise, however, his *Causation in the Law* still earns him one third of his total citations (65 out of 184) while the bulk of the remainder go to his latest works, which are on the borderline of jurisprudence and tort law. However, like Birks (and unlike Watson) Honoré's—pure and historical—work on Roman law seems to have fallen off the radar screen. Given the author's erudition we again see the lack of citations indicating a lack of interest in the subject or a poor number of scholars writing on Roman law. One can, indeed, tentatively go further and suggest that, in later life, Honoré (like Birks) seems *de facto* to have transformed the Regius Chair at the University of Oxford into a chair of contemporary law. Innate conservatism, aided by the persuasive force of the few remaining high priests of the subject, must thus be the only reason for insisting upon appointing Roman law scholars to this prestigious chair. Though conservatism is the hallmark of old institutions it cannot, forever, defy 'market' forces.

Jolowicz, though once a Professor of Comparative Law at the University of Cambridge, continues to be cited mainly for the English tort textbook that he co-authored many years ago.[80] For this reason, and because there are signs that his citation rates are trailing off, we have ceased producing a detailed breakdown of the references he has received. Weir, too, remains in a category of his own, but for a reason which is probably unique. For he must be the only comparatist who still exercised a great influence on the study of comparative law but does so mainly through his translation work. This continues to earn him over 78 per cent of his total citations (119 out of 140).

In this search, two further colleagues have been added to our list: Anneliese Riles and Mitch Lasser, both of the Cornell Law School. The reason we have included them here is to show how the 'new school' of comparative law is doing on the citation front. To this group one should, of course, add Professor Ugo Mattei and, more hesitantly it would seem, Professor Mathias Reimann ('classically' educated but with some leanings towards the group we describe as being 'more trendy'). In terms of total citation numbers, Mattei and Reimann come around the middle/second half of the American list (seventh and 11th out of the top 15, respectively) whereas Riles and Lasser come penultimate and last, respectively.

Though we do not find ourselves to be in sympathy with the (intellectual) approach towards comparative law which the last two choose, we hasten to note that neither has adopted the strident language of the more extreme post-modernists. We also note that there is insufficient evidence for us to attribute (critically or otherwise) their (lower) citation figures to the kind of angle they have adopted in their work. Other explanations could for instance be that they have been around for a shorter period of time than most of their colleagues/competitors and/or that their work also receives attention in non-legal journals—a likely possibility for Riles, given that she is (in our eyes at least) active primarily as an anthropologist—which we have not, however, considered in our searches.[81] The 'problem' which Riles raises is, however, a much wider one, which cannot be addressed in this book—namely should anthropology be represented with a post in law faculties if combined with the study of foreign law? Certainly, the holders of such posts will see educational as well as financial advantages by forging such links. We remain to be convinced, especially in times of economic restraint affecting even the priorities of rich American law faculties.

Moving to the foreign scene we note, without surprise, that the two big hitters in Germany are Hein Kötz and Reinhard Zimmerman, followed by Konrad Zweigert—though the latter's figures very largely duplicate those of Kötz since their names appear cited together every time their famous textbook is used. *Introduction to Comparative Law* thus earns them 134 citations in the American journals for this five-year period. Worth noting, however, is the fact that in the case of Kötz, who is still active in writing, 134 citations represent approximately 58 per cent of his total citation record, which means that his other

[80] It is important at this point to make an observation which may apply equally to other authors in our list who have ceased being 'active' participants in newer editions of their work. In such cases, is it convincing to attribute citations to new editions to the original authors? Professor Jolowicz, for instance, worked on the 7th, 8th and 9th editions of Winfield's classic textbook; eight editions have followed since then, all the exclusive work of Professor WVH Rogers. Given the rapidity of change in this (and other) fields of law, how much 'credit' for these 'new' works can still be given to the original authors (or co-authors)? A quantitively reliable way of answering this question seems to be impossible; but the temptation to transfer credit exclusively to the new author (or editor) must be real.

[81] On the other hand, one should also stress (out of fairness to Roman lawyers and legal historians) that in our searches we have not included purely historical journals. We must thus at least entertain the possibility that some of these publications would also contain references to their Roman/historical work.

works also attract proper attention. In Professor Zweigert's case, however, 134 citations to the (co-authored) text represent just under 85 per cent of his total citations. Notwithstanding his distinction as both a writer and a Constitutional Court judge, Zweigert thus seems to be clearly affected by the syndrome alluded to earlier on: 'You get old, you cease writing, and you gradually get forgotten.' Zweigert died in 1996.

By contrast to these three German colleagues, the citation figures for Professor von Bar seem surprisingly low. Indeed, we feel not just 'surprised' but also unable to explain this somewhat poor showing given how much he has done through his own initiative to drive breath into the European debate about the desirability of a common civil (or at least contract law) code. The (relative) paucity of the von Bar citations in English academic literature is also surprising given that his treatise on the European law of torts had met with some success with a few English judges. Perhaps one explanation is that his preoccupation with coordinating his team's drafting efforts have temporarily taken him out of writing scholarly works. Not having done a detailed breakdown of his publications, we can only put this forward as a supposition.

On the French side, David *Les grands systems* remains highly quoted, earning him 82 citations out of a total of 153—that is, just over 50 per cent of his total number. Of these, a large numer are to the English edition (even though it has not been kept up-to-date, as the French one has, confirming the adverse effect that writing in a non-English language can have on the citation fortunes of a foreign scholar). Incidentally, we alluded to the French edition being updated at more or less regular intervals. Yet these have been mere updates, not substantial re-writings and re-formulations (as David had himself predicted were necessary in the 9th edition). That the book thus survives this 'deficiency' and, more critically, the appearance of more attractive alternatives, must to some extent be attributed to teacher conservatism, that is, our colleagues' reluctance to move to new books from the ones they have become accustomed to using.

On the other hand, one must note that David has for the first time lost the first place on the citation listings of French colleagues. Professor Legrand has now claimed the crown; and it is possible that his productivity and controversial style have combined to bring him to the attention of comparatists, especially those who believe that they can introduce into law the 'Derrida jargon' on deconstructionalism. Yet again, whether one agrees with what he writes or not is, as a matter of personal taste and preference, relatively secondary to the fact that his rise must be seen to indicate that the general readership is looking—thirsting—for new approaches to a subject they increasingly see as important.

The Italian scene, finally, holds no surprises with Professors Cappelletti, Bonnel and Sacco topping the team of eight scholars for whom we conducted searches.[82] Sacco's figures, however, call for an interesting addendum. We thus noted about his citation rates for the years 1980 to 2000 that his work had not been sufficiently noticed in the United States because little of it had ever appeared in English. Sacco's new figures suggest that 56 citations go to his article on 'Legal Formants' (translated by James Gordley and published in *The American Journal of Comparative Law*). Though this article was both interesting and expertly translated by Professor Gordley (who is proficient in Italian) it is, for those who know Professor Sacco's prolific work, only a pale reflection of his theses, fully elaborated in his Italian books (or their French or German versions). Nonetheless, this single translation was sufficient to stimulate interest in the work of the notable Italian colleague; and this is shown by the

[82] There are, in fact, three Italian nationals who are making their presence mainly felt under the American or German flags. Professors Merryman and Mattei come under the first category while Professor Ranieri of the University of Saarbrücken comes under the second.

remaining 58 citations which the rest of his work has attracted during the last five years.

Speaking more generally, all of the 'big hitters' in the Italian contingent have earned their spurs, though different reasons may lie behind each success story. Cappelletti, for instance, was greatly helped by the fact that he was active in the United States for so long prior to his untimely death. Bonell's citations must clearly be linked to the excellent work he has done in the context of Unidroit, and the third because of his undoubted intellectual merit. Merryman we have, of course, counted among the Americans. Individual explanations can easily be found for the positive or negative performance of all our scholars. The point already made about the richness of the Italian activity in the domain of comparative law is still not reflected, however, on the international plane in a manner that it deserves. Those of us who have worked in Italy and with Italian colleagues can thus attest to a remarkable production line of monographs by younger Italian colleagues showing considerable awareness of Anglo-Saxon literature and great imagination. Yet the profile of these authors and of their country remains lower than it should—which we are inclined to attribute to the fact that few foreign scholars read Italian. Some have bucked this trend, among them Professor Michele Taruffo, who has a considerable reputation in the United States for his work on comparative procedural law (authored on his own or with Professor Hazard) and Professor Antonio Gambaro of the University of Milano I.

On the whole, however, many very interesting and promising young Italian scholars have not had any impact on Anglo-American literature because their work has been written in their mother tongue. Professor Mauro Bussani may be a further exception, producing a steady stream of well-informed and moderately phrased pieces which should soon bring him to the top list of activist comparatists. Overall, we are eager to urge the Italian Centre for Scientific Research, a State-run and funded body, to consider having some of the best examples of Italian comparative literature translated into English and made available to a non-Italian speaking public.

Table 3.9: Citation of comparatists by courts for the years 2001 to 2005

American

Country	Australia	Canada	England	Germany	USA
Author					
Hans W Baade	0	0	0	0	4
George A Bermann	0	0	0	0	3
John P Dawson	0	0	1	0	9
John G Fleming	19	65	21	0	2
Mary-Ann Glendon	0	2	1	0	4
James Gordley	0	0	0	0	0
John Langbein	7	0	2	0	42
Mitch Lasser	0	0	0	0	0
Ugo Mattei	0	0	0	0	1
John Henry Merryman	0	0	0	0	4
Annelise Riles	0	0	0	0	0
Mathias Reimann	0	0	0	0	1
Rudolf B Schlesinger	0	0	0	0	2
Arthur T von Mehren	0	0	0	0	6
Alan Watson	0	0	0	0	1

British

Country					
Author	Australia	Canada	England	Germany	USA
Mads Andenas	0	0	7	0	0
John Bell	0	3	2	0	0
Tony Honoré	27	1	16	0	3
JA Jolowicz	14	8	17	0	2
Otto Kahn-Freund	8	13	1	0	0
FH Lawson	0	1	3	0	0
Kurt Lipstein	0	0	2	0	0
FA Mann	3	2	6	(0)[83]	0
Basil S Markesinis	9	1	27	0	1
Barry Nicholas	0	0	1	0	1
Bernard Rudden	3	0	0	0	0
Tony Weir	4	0	9	0	0

German

Country	Australia	Canada	England	Germany	USA
Author					
Ulrich Drobnig	0	0	0	6[84]	0
Eric Jayme	0	0	0	41[85]	0
Hein Kötz	1	0	0	13[86]	0
Werner Lorenz	0	0	0	7[87]	0
Marcus Lutter	0	0	0	0[88]	0
Peter-Christian Müller-Graff	0	0	0	19[89]	0
Peter Schlechtriem	0	0	1	60[90]	2
Christian von Bar	0	0	2	1[91]	0

[83] The number of hits (above 400), by far most of which are false positives due to the ambiguous meaning of 'Mann' in German, was too large to analyse. Searches were conducted for a number of specific works.

[84] All of which are to work on German law.

[85] Of which 37 are to work on private international law. Three citations refer to work on Italian and one to work on Portuguese family law.

[86] Of which 12 are to his German work and one (by the Bundesgerichtshof) is to Zweigert and Kötz, *Introduction to Comparative Law.*

[87] The returns for 'Lorenz' (over 400), most of them false positives due to the frequency of this name in the German language, was too large to analyse. The entry 'Werner Lorenz' produced a single positive citation to Lorenz' work on restitution. Searches were conducted for a number of specific works.

[88] The returns for 'Lutter' (over 400), most of them false positives due to the frequency of this name in the German language, was too large to analyse. The entry 'Marcus Lutter' did not return any hits. Searches were conducted for a number of specific works.

[89] Of which 17 are to work on Community law and two to work on German law.

[90] Of which 29 are to work on CISG and 31 to work on German law.

[91] The returns for 'von Bar' (over 400), most of them false positives due to the ambiguous meaning of 'Bar/bar' in the German language, was too large to analyse. The entry 'Christian von Bar' did not return any hits. Searches were conducted for a number of specific works.

German (*cont.*)

Country	Australia	Canada	England	Germany	USA
Author					
Reinhard Zimmermann	0	0	2	1[92]	0
Konrad Zweigert	0	0	0	2	0

French

Country	Australia	Canada	England	Germany	USA
Author					
Xavier Blanc-Jouvain	0	0	0	0	0
René David	0	1	0	0	0
Mireille Delmas-Marty	0	0	1	0	1
Pierre Legrand	0	3	0	0	0
Horatia Muir-Watt	0	0	1	0	1
Denis Tallon	0	1	0	0	0
André Tunc	0	1	0	0	1

Italian

Country	Australia	Canada	England	Germany	USA
Author					
Guido Alpa	0	0	0	0	0
Michael Joachim Bonell	0	0	0	0	0
Mauro Bussani	0	0	0	0	0
Mauro Cappelletti	0	0	0	0	0
Antonio Gambaro	0	0	0	0	0
Gino Gorla	0	0	0	0	0
Maurizio Lupoi	0	0	0	0	0
Rodolfo Sacco	0	0	0	0	0

10. COMMENTARY (BIS): SHOWING IN THE COURTS

This section will, alas, be short since it reveals a bad if not dismal presence of comparative writing in court decisions. This may well be—in the absence of, in volume, more substantial empirical evidence one cannot assert it with confidence—a sign of what we are

[92] The returns for 'Zimmermann' (over 400), most of them false positives due to the frequency of this name in the German language, was too large to analyse. The entry 'Reinhard Zimmermann' did not return any hits. Searches were conducted for a number of specific works.

complaining about, namely that what comparative lawyers write is of little interest to practitioners. Yet some evidence to support this exists in both a positive and negative form. The positive side can be found in the kind of works by the leading author of this book that the courts have chosen to cite. As already stated, the bulk of his citations go to comparative works; these have been geared towards giving information about foreign law and making the common law courts contemplate in a realistic manner alternative solutions. It has, in short, been practical in character. Indirect (or negative) evidence of this comes from Weir's court citations. For if we compare these with the citations he receives by academics we note an interesting difference. For in the latter he is, mainly, referred to as translator and otherwise receives slender references to his purely scholarly works. His court citations (though mainly to his works on national law and not his comparative law writings) are by contrast to works which address difficult issues in the practice of the law. Where he has done that in his writings, he is noticed.

The fact that the same fate—ignorance—has been reserved to important *American* writers neither explains the phenomenon nor provides any comfort for non-American lawyers. In the absence of a convincing alternative explanation we are inclined to return to the point which for us is obvious: you write something of potential use to the courts, and they will cite and use it in one way or another; you choose instead to write elegant historical pieces or less stylistically attractive 'trendy' pieces, and you will ignored.

Three additional—and more general—points deserve to be highlighted here.

We deliberately italicised the word *American*, for the situation in the United States needs to be refined in two important ways.

First, we note the contrast between the practice of American courts compared with those from other countries such as South Africa, Canada, Israel and, in particular, England and Australia (from which we were able to obtain electronic data). The information derived from the three systems in question suggests that those smaller jurisdictions have not shown the same indifference towards this literature that the American courts have demonstrated. Certainly, the jurists included under the British heading have registered a respectable presence in the court decisions of these countries, and the breakdown of the figures (which we have not reproduced in the book) suggest that the work cited is of a practical, useful nature rather than purely doctrinal or speculative.

Secondly, and still staying with the United States, it will have been noticed that our data has largely focused on what could freely be called the domain of private law. This was done deliberately, partly because in another work we looked at the comparative human rights scene[93] but mainly because conducting these searches is so extraordinarily time-consuming that to extend their amplitude to include public law and human rights would have delayed inordinately the publication of this survey. Yet these are precisely the branches of the law which nowadays generate the liveliest contributions on comparative law in the United States. Even if this unusual intellectual activity has not yet been adequately reflected in the decisions of the US Supreme Court because of its internal political and ideological divisions, the fact remains that it is here that we find the most interesting and informed debate about the study of foreign law, how it should be done, and how the information thus gleaned can then be used by the national courts. Though this dimension is not reflected here, its importance for comparative law and its gradual elevation to the status of an important subject for the law curriculum must thus not be forgotten.

[93] Basil Markesinis and Jörg Fedtke, *Foreign Law in National Courts: A New Source of Inspiration?*, Routledge-Cavendish (2006).

The final ray of light in this domain of court interest in foreign law comes from France. The recent forays of the French Supreme Court into foreign law and its growing desire to engage in an intellectual dialogue with its foreign counterparts will be the subject of closer study below, so we need add nothing further here. We note, however, that though this influence of foreign law does not figure in the judgments themselves (since such express references are prohibited by the rules of civil procedure), the evidence that this is nonetheless taking place is beginning to be documented in other official materials of the Court.

11. A POSTSCRIPT

As we have seen, reputology is gaining acceptance and can, notwithstanding many limitations in the discovery of the raw data, justify some interesting (if tentative) conclusions. Is there, however, an overall lesson that can be said to emerge from our copious attempts to gather and evaluate the statistical use of the work of our colleagues (and ourselves)? The answer is 'yes'—and it is one which seems to be reinforced with the passage of time.

The lesson is relevant more to legacy or 'long-term impact' of the work of a particular author than the temporary interest which an 'intelligent' or 'unorthodox' piece may attract. It is, however, a pessimistic one, though entirely understandable and not unexpected. Thus, with very few exceptions—and we do mean *very few*—the work of most of us is extremely ephemeral. This realisation puts our egos and the in-fighting and intrigue that so dominate academic life in a salutary (but rarely noticed) context, reducing the importance of our work to the area of individual assistance and, more rarely, inspiration provided to a few willing and receptive students.

How great and ruthless is this onset of 'insignificance' can be seen by talking to one's students—and both of us have taught in many universities in many different countries—and asking them if they have read or even heard of great names of the past such as Maine, Dicey, Anson, Pollock, Jhering, Windscheid, Rabel, Gorla, Chiovenda, Storey, Holmes, Llewellyn, Jack Dawson and others. In our experience, the best students have heard of some of these great scholars (not all), but very few indeed have read any of their works unless these happen to have been updated regularly by subsequent authors (in which case all they have heard of is a name—for example, Dicey on Conflicts—but know next to nothing about the man, his life, and his original ideas). Even 'giants' like Oliver Wendell Holmes are beginning to be placed under the microscope, their reputations re-evaluated, their own contribution in 'making' them criticised, and their character increasingly questioned. So, outside the realm of physical sciences, where the works of the likes of Newton, Einstein, Pasteur or Currie remains inescapably with us, what real impact can lawyers expect to have on their profession and their subject?

The impact on individual students and their career has already been noted; and though it comes more under the heading of teaching and pastoral duties than research, it is no less important for that. The impact of beautiful writing (of the kind which, for instance, added so much to the reputations of Holmes and Cardozo) is also appreciated by some, though one gets the impression that the numbers are decreasing as interest in linguistic talent wanes and communication and legal intercourse are increasingly shaped by the techniques and practices of computer jargon, 'bullet-form' presentations, and the like. This leaves us with innovations that re-orient the interests, teaching, and use of our subject. We would include here the work of authors who created intellectual movements—such as the 'Realist movement' or the 'law and economics movement'—since in various shapes and forms they have affected what subsequent generations of lawyers write and promote. Likewise, a very small number of authors have also managed to create a special niche in the curriculum for their own scholarly interests. The late Sir William Wade and Professor Stanley de Smith would come under this category as far as English administrative law is concerned, and Lord Goff and Professor Gareth Jones for making (through the timely appearance of the classic monograph on restitution) unjust enrichment an essential part of the modern law curriculum.

Can one, perhaps, add here the internationalisation of law as part of the globalisation movement? Though national laws are slowly acquiring an international significance since they can matter so much in the context of trade and greater mobility of work, the subject has still to acquire suitable academic underpinnings in order to give it an essential position in the law curriculum. The innovation and its innovators have thus not yet appeared on the scene. Time, alone, will tell when that happens.

4

SOUTH AFRICA

South Africa deserves a chapter of its own due to the innovative approach that the country and its system have adopted towards foreign law and comparative methodology following the demise of apartheid. We have chosen to focus on the country's constitutional developments over the past two decades because they exemplify three of the issues highlighted in the previous sections of this volume: (1) courts have proved willing to make use of foreign material if *suitably assisted* in this task; (2) they have welcomed comparative methodology as a tool for analysis when it has helped them address *practically* relevant questions; and (3) empirical evidence corroborates the *importance of language* and our assertion that the work of foreign scholars suffers if it is not presented in English. This does not mean that the country's private law presents a lesser interest, not least because of its double allegiance to both the Common law and civil law (old and new); it merely means that, because of lack of space, choices have to be made. For the reasons given above we regard the developments in the public law area as more interesting and, arguably, more original.

Despite the enormous practical impact of our subject on contemporary South Africa, the system also provides illustrations of *failed* attempts to make use of foreign legal ideas. These failures are just as worthy of careful study as 'showcase' successes, for they help us identify problems and further refine the method of 'applied' comparative law presented in this book.

1. LEGAL TRANSPLANTS

The main focus of this Chapter is on legal transplants, both by the legislator and the judge. One of the 'big themes' in comparative law, borrowing has attracted the attention of comparatists for such a long time that it may seem difficult to add a new dimension to the topic. We nevertheless see three distinct reasons for revisiting the phenomenon in the context of the South African experience.

First, as already hinted, much of the research that has been done in this area concerns private law. This in itself should not worry constitutional lawyers too much. Comparative methodology will in many cases encounter the same hurdles, and yield similar rewards, on both sides of the public–private law divide. Much of our own work is dedicated to the considerable space where one area blends into the other, and where it is at the very least prudent—and in some cases even necessary—to combine the ideas of private lawyers such as Otto Kahn-Freund, Konrad Zweigert, Hein Kötz, or Alan Watson with insights provided by the work of public lawyers such as Peter Häberle, Jürgen Schwarze, or John Bell. 'Probe everything and retain the best.'[1]

[1] St Paul's exhortation to the Thessalonians.

Borrowing constitutional ideas nevertheless poses particular challenges. Modern constitutions perform functions within societies which private law will only address marginally, and which may render legal transplants in this area more difficult.

Constitutional settlements thus strive to provide legitimacy and moral authority to the state, and are often—especially in post-conflict settings such as those found in South Africa or Iraq—designed to foster national identity. They define the political structures of legally organised societies, and thus contain the blueprints for the exercise of power and hold the keys to future change. Human rights, an important feature of nearly every constitutional text in force today, shape the relationship between the state and the individual, and are often a carefully balanced expression of a society's basic values and aspirations. Albie Sachs, before becoming a judge of the Constitutional Court in South Africa, thus insisted that an effective bill of rights 'comes from inside the historical process, not outside', and that it 'reflects a set of values gained in the course of a struggle and rooted in the consciousness of the people, not one imported from other contexts'.[2] This is a warning which is as important as it is wise—especially in times such as ours where nations, their Presidents, and their foreign ministers proclaim a human rights-based foreign policy based on the (utopian) idea that democracy can be built from the top downwards, or (more generally) an 'ethical' foreign policy that can never be applied with even a modest measure of consistency. Constitutions also differ from private law in that they are usually given a superior legal status, and are more difficult to amend. Their provisions are at the same time often fairly brief, and require extensive interpretation when put into practice.

These factors can turn the borrowing of constitutional ideas into an unpredictable and potentially even hazardous activity. We need only think of the European Union, which is in effect a legal system that has borrowed many elements from its constituent societies. Despite the regular emphasis of 'common' values and 'mutual' legal traditions, tensions between local approaches and what are often regarded as ideas imposed from the outside require constant attention both by those involved in the political process and the courts. Embracing foreign notions of human rights protection or the power of judges to declare void parliamentary legislation is thus arguably more difficult than to agree on common solutions to the many problems found in the domain of commercial and private law. This is, in short, another reason to distinguish between comparative law and methodology in the domains of private and public law.

A second reason to revisit legal transplants is the observation that the borrowing of ideas can attract much attention at the outset, but that this initial excitement tends to fade rather quickly once the plant is in the ground and the tools back in the shed. Comparatists often rush to new locations—much like paparazzi hunting their next celebrity shot—rather than staying *in situ* (at least intellectually) and watching the development of a particular transplant over longer periods of time. This is unfortunate, for the success or failure of legal borrowing will rarely (if ever) be immediately obvious. The transplantation of law is a *dynamic* process. The initial phase involves the identification of an appropriate model and (in most cases) more or less comprehensive adjustments of the chosen material in order to merge it successfully with related rules of the new legal environment. Even mere translation can increase the differences between the original and its new incarnation, can cause considerable difficulties in practice, and requires one to proceed with caution.

[2] Albie Sachs, *Protecting Human Rights* (1991), p 14.

More importantly, the borrowing system is in no way bound by the interpretation of the model provision in its country of origin, and courts are thus free to ignore or to take into account related foreign case law or academic literature. This begs the question how foreign ideas develop once they have found their way into a new legal and factual setting, and how legislators and courts interact when it comes to borrowed ideas. Closely related is the question whether judges are authorised to utilise comparative methodology and become transplanting legal gardeners themselves (assuming, of course, that they are able to carry out this task on their own).

We will address some of these issues by returning to South Africa several years after the major constitutional reforms of 1993 and 1996 in an attempt to assess whether its foreign plants have taken root in the new legal and social soil, whether—and if so, how—they have changed, or whether foreign ideas have by now withered away.

All of this we hope to do for one, final, reason. Legal transplants continue to be extremely important in practice. Alan Watson observed in 1974 that borrowing is 'the most common form of legal change',[3] and this is as true for constitutional ideas today as it has been for private and commercial law in the past. The demise of the former socialist systems in Eastern Europe, the desire of many countries to join the European Union, the democratisation of many societies, and efforts to improve human rights protection around the world have further strengthened the trend towards a global spread of constitutional ideas.

Legal transplants are often justified by the quality of a given foreign solution. Other, at times overlapping, reasons include the harmonisation of law within the framework of international agreements; the influence of successful (or at least glamorous) political concepts; special economic, judicial, or cultural ties that exist between particular societies[4]; the general influence that many 'parent' legal systems continue to exert on their former colonies[5]; or demands of donor countries calling for the observance of democratic standards and the respect for human rights by nations receiving from them development aid.[6] The unequal distribution of economic power creates further incentives not only for the introduction of changes based on foreign commercial law but also, for example, foreign approaches to the constitutional protection of property interests or the creation of an effective court system. Military intervention, finally, followed by the reconstruction of societies on the basis of 'imported' legal principles (today often called 'system change'), has re-emerged as yet another scenario favouring constitutional legal transplants.

All of the above have increased the attraction of what can arguably be called the most successful 'product' that comparative lawyers have to offer. Legions of experts in foreign constitutional law are these days touring the globe in order to provide model solutions for the large number of systems currently in transition. International organisations such as the Venice Commission provide substantial support in this respect, and even the United Nations have very recently responded to the need by creating a permanent stand-by team of experts to provide comparative legal advice in all UN-led mediation exercises (quite an unusual step given that the UN's main modus operandi is to rely on ad hoc solutions).

[3] Alan Watson, *Legal Origins and Legal Change* (1991), p 73.
[4] One such close relationship which has led to a number of mutual influences is that between Germany and Austria.
[5] Zweigert/Kötz, *Introduction to Comparative Law* (3rd edn 1998), p 65 *f*.
[6] Decalo, 'The Process, Prospects and Constraints of Democratization in Africa', [1992] African Affairs 7, 16 *ff*.

There is, however, still a gap between the *practical* importance of legal transplants and what we currently really *know* about the phenomenon, both in methodological terms and with respect to the potential utility of single legal ideas outside their country of origin.

With this background in mind, we will look at seven constitutional transplants of German origin—two early casualties, three examples from the area of human rights protection where the courts have played a particularly active role in subsequent developments, and, finally, two transplants of organisational structures rather than substantive rules of law.

2. CONSTITUTIONAL TRANSITION AND FOREIGN INFLUENCE

Before focusing on these particular examples, it is necessary to recall briefly the remarkable constitutional transition that South Africa has gone through over the past 18 years. Since the former President Fredrik Willem de Klerk officially announced the opening of negotiations between the white apartheid government and the African National Congress (ANC) and its allies in November 1990, the country has lived under no fewer than three constitutional settlements—the last apartheid Constitution of 1983,[7] the so-called 'Interim' Constitution of 1993 (IC),[8] and the current 'Final' Constitution of 1996 (FC).[9]

Constitutional change on this scale is a challenge for any society. For the comparatist, the transition from apartheid to present-day South Africa has been particularly interesting. The last decade and a half has seen the country borrow, discard, and modify transplanted constitutional ideas and concepts from a wide range of systems, with the legislator paving the way and open-minded judges seizing the opportunity to blend local traditions and experience with foreign approaches.

South Africa was particularly open for legal transplants due to a number of special local conditions which are rarely found elsewhere.

Perhaps the most interesting factor from a methodological point of view is procedural. The competing political parties, while restructuring the country's new legal order in the early 1990s, agreed on a two-stage reform process. This led to the negotiation of the Interim Constitution (which entered into force in 1994) and—following the first free elections in May 1994—the final constitutional settlement of 1996/1997. Foreign ideas adopted in the first phase could thus be tested in practice and subsequently retained or discarded in the second.

Both documents were strongly influenced by foreign constitutional ideas, the German Basic Law of 1949 proving one important source. Other influential systems and legal instruments were the United States, Canada, India, Namibia, the European Union, and the European Convention on Human Rights. This remarkable reception of foreign ideas was mainly fostered by political parties and individual influential academics offering legal advice to the Multi-Party Negotiating Process (MPNP) at Kempton Park outside Johannesburg in 1993 and to the newly elected Parliament, subsequently convened as a Constitutional Assembly, between 1994 and 1996.

As the examples we shall discuss show, the South African judiciary was (and remains) the third—and perhaps the most important—catalyst in this development. The Constitutional Court in particular (itself a new element previously unknown in South Africa) has repeat-

[7] Republic of South Africa Constitution Act 110 of 1983.
[8] Constitution of the Republic of South Africa Act 200 of 1993.
[9] Republic of South Africa Constitution Act 108 (FC) of 1996.

edly referred to foreign material in order to shape the country's new and developing body of constitutional doctrine. Judges have thereby not restricted themselves to foreign case law; references to foreign legislation and, more importantly, to academic work feature prominently in many judgments. This is a break with the past, when South African judges 'did not value academic writing highly',[10] and is a change initially necessitated by the absence of South African precedents in this field of law.

The scale of comparative work in South African courtrooms is indeed staggering. Supreme Court and Constitutional Court judgments between July 1994 and August 1998 feature more than 1,200 references to the decisions of American, Canadian, British, German, European, and Indian courts alone.[11] The influence that some of these legal systems exert today has changed, but the overall volume of references remains incredibly high. These little-known statistics also demonstrate that Germany is the only civil law system which has had a significant input in this development (ranking fourth with 72 citations out of the total 1,258). More importantly, it is the only major legal system in which courts do not deliver their judgments in English.

This last statement calls for some explanation, and our research has shown that most of this influence is due to translations of court judgments made available through the work of a limited number of (non-German!) academics.[12] This basic comparative work is obviously one important key which enables South African judges to take advantage of German ideas, especially in the area of human rights. A precondition is thereby the open-minded approach which some judges—such as the former Constitutional Court Justice Laurie Ackermann—take towards the use of foreign material. Challenged by colleagues taking a more conservative stance towards comparative law in the judicial sphere,[13] the views of these judges do not

[10] Susan Scott, 'Evaluation of securities by means of moveables: Problems and possible solutions. Section C: Codification of the law of cession', (1997) Tydskrif vir Hedendaagse Romeins-Hollandse Reg 633 at 638.

[11] See Jörg Fedtke, *Die Rezeption von Verfassungsrecht. Südafrika 1993–1996* (2000), p 446.

[12] See, eg, the death penalty decision of the South African Constitutional Court, *S v Makwanyane and Another*, 1995 (6) BCLR 665 (CC). In *Makwanyane*, the Court referred to the Grundgesetz and various judgments of the Bundesverfassungsgericht mainly with the help of two American sources: Donald P Kommers, *The Constitutional Jurisprudence of the Federal Republic of Germany* (1989) and David P Currie, *The Constitution of the Federal Republic of Germany* (1994). Kommers and Currie are thus cited three and five times respectively by the court. Professor Dieter Grimm (at that time a member of the German Constitutional Court) is also cited twice, but for one of his English publications, namely 'Human Rights and Judicial Review in Germany' in Beatty (ed), *Human Rights and Judicial Review: A Comparative Perspective*, pp 267 *ff.* (1994). Original German sources (judicial and academic) are referred to only indirectly. The judgments of the Bundesverfassungsgericht were accessed through the works of Kommers and Currie; and a reference to Maunz/Dürig, *Grundgesetz* (one of the leading commentaries on the German Basic Law) can also be found via Currie. This and other such cases, which we do not cite because of lack of space, confirm the validity of one of the theses of this book: academics can help judges, thus not only ensuring better co-operation between the different parts of the legal profession but also promoting the use of foreign law. Studying these cases can also offer comparatists the opportunity to fine-tune the methodology proposed in this book.

[13] See the following dictum by Justice Kriegler in *Bernstein and Others v Bester NO and Others*, 1996 (4) BCLR 449 (CC): 'I agree with the identification and the logical analysis of the principle . . . but prefer to express no view on the possible lessons to be learnt from other jurisdictions. That I do, not because of a disregard for section 35 (1) of the Constitution, or in a spirit of parochialism. My reason is twofold. First, because the subtleties of foreign jurisdictions, their practices and terminology require more intensive study than I have been able to conduct. Even on a superficial view, there seem to me to be differences of substance between the statutory, jurisprudential and societal contexts prevailing in those countries and in South Africa as to render ostensible analogies dangerous without thorough understanding of the foreign systems. For the present I cannot claim that degree of proficiency . . . The second reason is that I wish to discourage the frequent—and, I suspect, often facile—resort to foreign 'authorities'. Far too often one sees citation by counsel of, for instance, an American judgment in support of a proposition relating to our Constitution, without any attempt to explain why it is said to be in point. Comparative study is always useful, particularly where the courts in exemplary jurisdictions have grappled with universal issues confronting us. Likewise, where a provision in our Constitution is manifestly modelled on a particular provision

always prevail; but their dicta nonetheless infuse the South African legal system with a treasure trove of potentially useful foreign ideas.

The degree of German influence is quite remarkable given that this system was the only country outside the Common law world and the English-speaking legal community which received such attention from the framers of the new South African constitutional order. The reasons why German constitutional law proved to be such a successful model are of interest in our context.

Parts of the German fundamental rights doctrine had already found their way into South Africa prior to the political changes in Pretoria, having permeated its borders via the Constitutions of Boputhatswana—one of the now defunct satellite states of apartheid South Africa—and Namibia. The Supreme Court of South Africa, exercising final judicial authority in Boputhatswana until 1982 and in Namibia as late as 1990, found itself confronted with cases of constitutional review many years before the first judgments of South African courts were handed down following the enactment of the Interim Constitution. These judgments referred to German law on several occasions, and were discussed by South African academics, fuelling the local fundamental rights debate and opening the doors for further German influence in the subsequent constitution-making process.

A second reason can be found in the fact that a number of (mostly Afrikaans-speaking) academics found opportunities for comparative studies in Germany at a time when universities and other academic research facilities in the more traditional target countries were closed to South African scholars due to the political isolation of the system. The close linguistic relationship between Afrikaans and German must also have served as an important bridge for legal ideas; many key German terms such as *Rechtsstaat*, *Wechselwirkung*, *Wesensgehalt*, *Drittwirkung*, or *Bundestreue* are often not even translated by South African courts and academics.

Other factors explaining the role of German law during the negotiation process include the international reputation of the *Grundgesetz* and the support rendered by the German government, politically affiliated foundations, and academic institutions to the emerging new state.[14]

Finally, one could point out that a legal system (the German) that had itself been confronted in the post-1945 period with a traumatic past must have appeared as especially relevant to a country struggling to put behind it its own experience with apartheid.

3. THE 'CONSTITUTIONAL STATE PRINCIPLE' OR RECHTSSTAATSPRINZIP

This last factor explains the inclusion of the Rechtsstaatsprinzip, or constitutional state principle, in the Preamble of the Interim Constitution. The Preamble was drafted literally overnight by Professor François Venter, one of the legal experts at Kempton Park, and was

in another country's constitution, it would be folly not to ascertain how the jurists of that country have interpreted their precedential provision. The prescripts of section 35 (1) of the Constitution are also very clear: where applicable, public international law in the field of human rights must be considered, and regard may be had to comparative foreign case law. But that is a far cry from blithe adoption of alien concepts or inappropriate precedents'.

[14] See Jörg Fedtke, above note 11, pp 433 *f.*

accepted at the 11th hour by the political negotiators without further amendment. It defined South Africa as a sovereign and democratic constitutional state.

The Constitutional Court subsequently utilised this brief reference to German law in a number of important cases. Among these are the death penalty[15] and *Hugo*[16] decisions, the latter concerning the judicial review of a presidential pardon for imprisoned mothers of young children issued by Nelson Mandela. On both occasions, the constitutional state principle was identified as a safeguard against the arbitrary or unequal exercise of public authority. Another example is the *Bernstein*[17] case, which involved the duty of particular officers to disclose potentially incriminating information about companies in liquidation. Here, the existence of and access to an independent and impartial judiciary featured as a core element of the Rechtsstaat. Finally, Justice Ackermann put on record in *Du Plessis*,[18] a decision on the effect of human rights in the private sphere, that the direct application of basic rights by judges in ordinary civil proceedings would make the law vague and uncertain, and again run counter to the notion of a constitutional state. The principle thus emerged as a fundamental structural feature of the Interim Constitution, and was on several occasions used by judges as an important interpretative guideline.

Despite this success, the Constitutional Assembly chose to substitute the principle by a reference to the rule of law in s 1(c) of the Final Constitution. Legal tradition seems to have been the main reason why the transplant suffered an early death in its new legal environment. The rule of law was, simply put, the more familiar concept in South Africa. Rechtsstaat, as Venter himself subsequently pointed out, cannot be translated directly into English, and even academics well familiar with German law struggle to come up with a term that reflects adequately the conceptual differences between the two approaches.[19] While indeed quite similar in respect to many *formal* legal safeguards, the Rechtsstaat in Germany also provides the conceptual basis of a supreme constitution and (in *substantive* terms) of enforceable human rights, including the principle of proportionality.

That said, there is no doubt that South Africa today *is* indeed a Rechtsstaat. The supremacy of the Constitution, human dignity, the achievement of equality, and the advancement of human rights and freedoms are all identified as founding values in the opening section of the final settlement, and given enhanced protection from constitutional amendment.[20]

The conceptual change has nevertheless resulted in two subtle differences. A distinct feature of the Rechtsstaat principle in Germany lies in its potential to create both formal and substantive obligations for, and place restrictions on, government bodies *which are not otherwise expressly prescribed by the constitutional text*, and case law in the interim phase indicates that South African judges were willing to utilise the constitutional state principle in a similar fashion. Whether courts will be able to draw on the fundamental values enshrined in s 1 of the Final Constitution with a similar amount of flexibility remains to be seen.

What *has* already become apparent, however, is that South African judges and scholars have changed their preferred source of inspiration. The link to German constitutional doctrine surrounding the Rechtsstaat—very much noticeable both in court decisions and

15 See note 12 above.

16 *Hugo v State President of the Republic of South Africa and Another*, 1996 (6) BCLR 876 (D) and *President of the Republic of South Africa and Another v Hugo*, 1997 (6) BCLR 708 (CC).

17 *Bernstein and Others v Berster NO and Others*, 1996 (4) BCLR 449 (CC).

18 *Du Plessis and Others v De Klerk and Another*, 1996 (5) BCLR 658 (CC).

19 Examples are *constitutional state, law state, law-based state*, or *just state*.

20 Any amendment of these principles would require a 75% majority in the National Assembly and the support of six of the nine provinces represented in the second legislative chamber, the National Council of Provinces.

academic writing before 1990 and during the interim phase—is much weaker today, and Anglo-American ideas are set to take its place.

4. HUMAN RIGHTS PROTECTION

The Bill of Rights in South Africa is extensive,[21] covering a wide range of classical liberal rights such as human dignity, life, freedom and security of the person, privacy, freedom of religion, belief and opinion, freedom of expression, freedom of assembly and association, political rights, and the protection of property. The Constitution also features extensive socio-economic rights such as the right to fair labour practices, a healthy environment, rights to housing, health care, food, water and social security, special children's rights, and the right to basic education. Access to information held not only by the state but also—where required for the exercise or protection of any rights—private individuals, a right to just administrative action and access to courts, and a number of rights for arrested, detained and accused persons are also guaranteed. Equality is protected both as a general principle and in the form of two special anti-discrimination clauses addressed both to the state and private parties.

The introduction of the (interim) Bill of Rights in 1994 had an immediate impact on litigation. Courts on all levels of the system, usually exercising general jurisdiction (the Constitutional Court being the most important exception), have been confronted with a wide variety of human rights issues from day one of the post-apartheid era. This development has continued under the Final Constitution, and is characterised by frequent references to foreign legal ideas.

German law was particularly influential in what can be called the 'general' part of the South African Bill of Rights. The limitation clause, the effect of constitutionally enshrined human rights on private relationships (horizontal effect or *Drittwirkung*), and the constitutional protection of juristic persons were all influenced by German thinking. A striking example of a *substantive* legal transplant is s 22 FC, protecting economic activity, which is a direct translation of article 12 BL.

(a) The Essential Content Clause

A second early casualty in this area is the so-called essential content clause. Under the Interim Constitution, a limitation of human rights and freedoms was permissible only by a law of general application and to the extent that it was, first, reasonable and justifiable in an open and democratic society based on freedom and equality, and, second, did not negate the essential content of the right in question.[22] The latter element was borrowed from article 19(2) of the German Basic Law. Similarly phrased constitutional safeguards can again be found in Namibia and in former Boputhatswana, and in the limitation clauses proposed by the ANC,[23] the Inkatha Freedom Party,[24] and the South African Law Commission.[25]

[21] Chapter 2 FC.
[22] Section 33(1)(b) IC.
[23] Art 16(4)(b) ANC Draft Bill of Rights (May 1992).
[24] Section 17 IFP Draft Constitution of the Federal Republic of South Africa of 18 June 1993.
[25] Art 34(1) Bill of Rights, South African Law Commission, *Project 58: Group and Human Rights—Interim Report* (1991), p 697.

Academic opinion was from the very outset critical of this transplant. Discussions focused mainly on the difficulty in determining this 'essence' of a right and the uncertain relationship between the essential content test and the proportionality analysis prescribed by the same section of the Interim Constitution. The clause was generally accepted—in the words of Stuart Woolmann—as a 'bright prophylactic line that will suffer no trespass'[26] but at the same time regarded as a poorly drafted paper tiger, which would in all likelihood cause unnecessary confusion and be of little practical relevance in the South African context.

Case law in the interim phase confirmed these negative predictions.

In a 1995 decision concerning access of accused individuals to information held by police authorities and the public prosecutor, the Cape Town Provincial Division of the Supreme Court criticised the essential content clause as establishing a too far-reaching level of human rights protection.[27] The Court thus noted that

> [I]n their understandable zeal to ensure that the fundamental rights . . . remain undiluted as far as possible, the framers of [the limitation clause] . . . appear to have brought about a rigidity and inflexibility which society may come to regret . . . The assimilation into our Constitution of disparate provisions to be found in other constitutions and bills of rights has resulted . . . in a limitation provision which may be found to frustrate the achievement of entirely respectable and legitimate goals.[28]

The Court in this case felt that the right of access to information held by the state was indeed affected in its core by the challenged Common law privilege of disclosure.

The Constitutional Court had to deal with the essential content test only a few months later in its famous death penalty decision. The leading judgment of President Chaskalson engaged only briefly with the interpretation of the provision, raising but not answering the question whether the essential content of a right should be defined with respect to the prisoners on death row or its continued enjoyment by the rest of society.[29] The case was, however, solved through application of the principle of proportionality; only Justice Sachs applied the essential content test, pointing out that 'life by its very nature cannot be restricted, qualified, abridged, limited or derogated from . . . You are either alive or dead'.[30]

The essential content clause, in any case, was dead at this point. It played no role in case law after the death penalty decision, and was subsequently dropped by the Constitutional Assembly. Only the Democratic Party endorsed the provision in its original form, while the National Party demanded that the concept be clarified and the ANC suggested to delete the clause altogether. The Technical Committee on Fundamental Rights emphasised that most rights *do* have a core content that may not be destroyed by limitation, but acknowledged that the test was not a useful component of the South African limitation clause. 'It is a test', said the Committee in an explanatory memorandum of October 1995, 'that is not easily loosened from its German moorings, and courts are likely to devote too much of their interpretative energies to ascertaining the meanings of this phrase in German law'. Developed as an ultimate safeguard against the erosion of human rights as experienced under Nazi rule

[26] Stuart Woolmann, 'Limitations' in Matthew Chaskalson et al, *Constitutional Law of South Africa* (1996/1998), pp 12–30 at note 1.

[27] *Nortje and Another v Attorney-General of the Cape and Another*, 1995 (2) BCLR 236 (C).

[28] *Ibid* at p 257 *f.*

[29] *S v Makwanyane and Another*, 1995 (6) BCLR 665 (CC) at p 718 *f.*

[30] *Ibid* at p 782 *f.*

in Germany, it was probably the least successful attempt at transplanting foreign law to South Africa.

This experience nevertheless holds a lesson. Complex constitutional change which involves the introduction of foreign ideas will profit from a phased process in which a legal system can test out new concepts for a limited period of time. The two-stage transition in South Africa allowed the Constitutional Assembly to review the practical effect of the essential content clause in the light of local experience, and to discard a highly symbolic but ultimately superfluous provision, which today is little more than a sleeping beauty even in its own country of origin.

(b) Horizontal Effect or Drittwirkung

Horizontal effect or *Drittwirkung* concerns the question whether human rights should apply in the private sphere.

There are clear signs that the political parties negotiating the constitutional settlement of 1993 had already contemplated various solutions found abroad when discussing this issue. Noting the considerable differences of influence and power which can exist in private relationships and the international trend towards a stronger effect of constitutional rights in the private sphere, the Technical Committee on Fundamental Rights in its 5th Report of June 1993 had proposed to make human rights binding, 'where appropriate, on all social institutions and persons'.[31] This approach was inspired by the Constitution of Namibia[32] and reflected the proposals of the African National Congress (ANC)[33] and the Democratic Party (DP).[34] The de Klerk Government, on the other hand, tried to limit the operation of human rights to vertical relationships, conceding only an indirect effect through inherent limitations (rights should, for example, not be exercised to the detriment of others), the interpretation of existing private law in the light of constitutional values, and the binding effect of a supreme constitutional settlement for future legislation.[35]

The Technical Committee initially tried to bridge this gap between the parties by proposing to identify in the text of the Interim Constitution specific rights which were to have direct effect, but eventually suggested to insert a qualification into the application clause declaring that non-State actors would only be bound by human rights where this was

[31] Technical Committee on Fundamental Rights, 5th Report of June 1993 (11 June 1993) at 3.1.

[32] Which declares in Art 5 that the fundamental rights and freedoms enshrined in that document 'shall be respected and upheld by the Executive, Legislature and Judiciary and all organs of the Government, its agencies and, where applicable to them, by all natural and legal persons in Namibia, and shall be enforceable by the Courts in the manner hereinafter prescribed'.

[33] Art 17(1) of the ANC Proposal of 1992 declared: 'The terms of the Bill of Rights shall be binding upon the State and organs of government at all levels, and where appropriate, on all social institutions and persons'.

[34] Art 1 of the DP proposal of 1993 declared: 'This Bill of Rights guarantees the rights enshrined in it. They shall be respected and upheld by all organs of the State and government, whether legislative, executive or judicial, and, where applicable, by all persons in South Africa, and shall be enforceable by the Supreme Court of South Africa'.

[35] See the *Republic of South Africa Government's Proposal on a Charter of Fundamental Rights,* (1993) *African Journal of International and Comparative Law* 436 *f.* 'The Draft Charter is based on four principles. Firstly, the principle of verticality. This means that the Charter primarily regulates legal relations between the State and the subject. It does not directly regulate relations among citizens themselves, although the Charter will have an "over-flow" effect on such horizontal relations. For instance rights are required by the Charter to be exercised responsibly with due regard to the rights of others. Also, the principles of the Charter will serve as guidelines in the interpretation of statutes dealing with legal relations among subjects. These principles will also materially influence the substance of future laws'.

deemed 'just and equitable'.[36] The latter approach relied heavily on the courts to achieve an appropriate level of protection in the private sphere. The Committee put on record that the Interim Constitution should 'not . . . be prescriptive as regards the horizontal application of fundamental rights during the transition' and argued in favour of an 'evolutionary and natural development of the concept of the horizontal enforcement of rights in the jurisprudence of the designated judicial authority.'[37]

This solution was rejected not only by the South African Communist Party (SACP)[38] but also, and more importantly, by the judiciary, which came out strongly against a direct effect of constitutional rights on the Common law for fear of 'great legal uncertainty and social insecurity'. Judges also felt that the courts should not become embroiled in the task of distinguishing constitutional rights which have direct effect in the private sphere from those that do not. The question was regarded as a 'policy issue' rather than one which should be allocated to the judiciary.[39]

The approach eventually codified in the Interim Constitution was a political compromise which involved a careful balancing of several provisions and which, in effect, left the question undecided.

The judiciary was, on the one hand, excluded from the binding effect of the Bill of Rights, while the interpretation clause was, on the other, expanded by a provision which opened the door to an indirect effect of constitutional rights along the lines developed by the German Federal Constitutional Court in its famous *Lüth* decision of 1958.[40] Section 35(3) IC thus declared that '[I]n the interpretation of any law and the application and development of the common law and customary law, a court shall have due regard to the spirit, purport and objects' of the Bill of Rights. Similar provisions had previously been suggested by the South African Law Commission (with specific reference to the German model)[41] and by the de Klerk Government.[42] The Interim Constitution also acknowledged the indirect influence of human rights via legislation in s 7(2) IC, declaring that the Bill of Rights shall

[36] 7. Report (29 July 1993).

[37] *Ibid* at 1(1)(b).

[38] See L du Plessis and H Corder, *Understanding South Africa's Transitional Bill of Rights* (1994), p 111.

[39] See M Corbett, *Memorandum submitted on behalf of the Judiciary of South Africa on the Draft Interim Bill of Rights* (3 September 1993) at 3: 'This clause will create great uncertainty and confusion. The reference to the application of the Bill to 'other bodies and persons' implies the horizontal application of the Bill. This entails the application of the Bill to, inter alia, the actions of companies and corporations (whether public or private), partnerships, societies and clubs, and all individuals. In consequence, all private relationships will be governed by the Bill of Rights. The phrase quoted above can, and notionally will, be interpreted to mean that the provisions of the Bill override the common law. For example, clause 9 entrenches freedom of speech. If clause 1(1)(b) remains, it may be construed as meaning that A can defame B freely; B's common law protections and remedies are nullified by A's constitutional rights. Is this the intention? If so, it must be realised that the effect of the Bill may be to supersede large parts of our established common law, and that it may well lead to great legal uncertainty and social insecurity. We suggest that what the drafters of the interim Bill probably had in mind was to eliminate privatised discrimination, ie unfair discrimination by legal entities and individuals in private affairs. If so, it is necessary to demarcate, clearly and unambiguously, the precise field of impermissible discrimination (eg, employment) from those areas of highly personal affairs where one should be free to choose one's own associates (eg, religion, cultural organisations, private home life, etc).'

[40] BVerfGE 7, 198 of 15 January 1958.

[41] Above note 25, section 39.

[42] In 1993, the Government proposed the following provision under the heading *Operation of the Charter Against Third Parties*: '(1) No provision of this Charter shall be construed so as to create or regulate legal relations other than those between the State and a person as contemplated in Section 1. (2) In the interpretation of any law regarding legal relations among persons *inter se*, the spirit, objects and purport of this Charter shall be taken into account. (3) Where a person exercises or enjoys a right recognised by this Charter, such a person shall do so in a manner which will not infringe the rights of any other person'.

apply to all law in force, and s 33(4) IC, a provision which specifically addressed the possibility of legislation designed to prohibit unfair discrimination by private parties. Section 33(2) IC, finally, specifically prohibited any law—'whether a rule of the common law, customary law or legislation'—from limiting constitutional rights unless the limitation was, in particular, proportionate.

How did this complex solution work in practice?

Academic opinion was divided on the matter, some authors suggesting an indirect effect similar to the German model while others argued in favour of a direct application of human rights in the private sphere.

The first group felt that constitutional rights should influence private relationships by 'seepage' or, closer to German vocabulary, a 'radiating effect'.[43] Policy considerations and open-ended standards or principles were identified as the most appropriate links between private law and constitutional values. Fairness, justice and good faith, or the notion of an equitable compensation of loss in ideally balanced contractual relationships are, according to this view, examples of suitably flexible elements of private law through which constitutional rights can be made operational; wrongfulness, legal causation, remoteness and negligence were suggested in the area of tort law. The effect of these 'gateways' was, however, to be limited; only in exceptional circumstances should human rights call for judicial intervention.[44] The main reason for this careful approach was the fear of the negative consequences which a more direct effect could have on the principle of private autonomy.[45] The importance of legal certainty, a value stressed in particular by the judiciary, also played a strong role.[46]

These fears were not shared by the 'horizontalists'.[47] Apart from arguments based on the wording of the Interim Constitution, three important points were raised in favour of direct effect.

[43] See, eg, L du Plessis and H Corder, *Understanding South Africa's Transitional Bill of Rights* (1994), pp 113 *f* and 116; L du Plessis, 'A Background to Drafting the Chapter on Fundamental Rights' in B de Villiers (ed), *Birth of a Constitution* (1994), pp 93 *ff*; D Basson, 'South Africa's Interim Constitution: the Challenges to Diversity and Identity', (1995) *Verfassung und Recht in Übersee* 421 *ff*, at p 16; J Kruger, 'Is interpretation a question of common sense? Some reflections on value judgments and section 35', (1995) *Comparative and International Law Journal of South Africa* 1 *ff*, at 7; A Henderson, 'Operation of the constitution between private actors', (1995) *De Rebus* 439 *ff*, at 440; G Erasmus, 'Limitation and Suspension', in D van Wyk *et al* (eds), *Rights and Constitutionalism* (1994), p 632.

[44] See Annél van Aswegen, 'The Implications of a Bill of Rights for the Law of Contract and Delict', (1995) *South African Journal on Human Rights* 50 *ff*, at 56 and 60: 'Policy considerations are usually applied in instances where the traditional area of application of a settled rule has to be expanded to meet changed social, scientific or technological circumstances, or where settled rules apparently conflict or give rise to contradictory consequences, and occasionally where settled rules have to be altered to accommodate novel factual circumstances . . . Obviously, legal rules formulated with reference to policy considerations furnish the most effective method of incorporating the values underlying the protection of fundamental rights into the fabric of private law. It can be assumed that the bill of rights reflects the fundamental values accepted in a society, and as such it represents a crystallised form of public policy. The policy considerations determining the contents and application of open-ended rules can therefore to a significant extent be extracted from the provisions of the Bill of Rights.'

[45] E de Wet, 'Indirect Drittwirkung and the Application Clause', (1995) *South African Journal on Human Rights* 610 *ff*, at 613.

[46] J de Waal, 'A Comparative Analysis of the provisions of German Origin in the Interim Bill of Rights', (1995) *South African Journal on Human Rights* 1 *ff*, at 14.

[47] See, eg, JD van der Vyver, 'The private sphere in constitutional litigation', (1994) *Tydskrif vir Hedendaagse Romeins-Hollandse Reg* 47 *ff*; D Davis, 'Equality and Equal Protection' in D van Wyk *et al* (eds), *Rights and Constitutionalism* (1994), pp 210 *f*; HA Strydom, 'The private domain and the bill of rights', (1995) *South African Public Law* 52 *ff*; A Cachalia *et al* (eds), *Fundamental Rights in the New Constitution* (1994), p 122.

There was, first, much criticism of the uneven distribution of (private) power and wealth in post-apartheid South Africa, and, coupled with this, the fear that past discrimination by the state might continue within the sanctuary of private law. Full application of human rights in the private sphere was regarded as the most appropriate safeguard against 'privatised apartheid'.[48]

Direct effect was, second, deemed preferable in terms of legal certainty because it renders unnecessary the difficult distinction between public and private action.[49]

Finally, supporters of direct effect felt that a limited impact of human rights on judge-made Common law would be a contradiction to the full subordination of the legislator to human rights considerations.[50] Some academics thereby accepted that particular areas of private law might be insulated from the effect of constitutional rights; the internal rules of private organisations or purely private transactions such as the sale of a house or the contractual relationships between a hotel and its guests could thus be regarded as an 'a-constitutional private sphere'[51] in which human rights considerations could become effective only through specific anti-discrimination laws.

The courts, confronted with this highly ambiguous constitutional text, adopted very different solutions. Two divisions of the Supreme Court restricted, in principle, the effect of human rights to vertical relationships between the state and its citizens while at the same time accepting that

> the fragrance of values in which the Constitution is anchored [could] permeate [the] judicial approach to interpretation of statutes and the development of the common law.[52]

This restrictive approach was justified mainly with the traditional argument that human rights operate first and foremost between the state and the citizen. The legislator of 1993, so the argument went, had been aware of this but had nevertheless opted against an expansion of human rights considerations into the private sphere. Some judges also felt that this was in line with the historical experience of the country, where individuals had suffered primarily at the hands of public authorities.[53] The broad language of constitutional rights was, finally, regarded as too imprecise; well-developed principles of private law could not readily be modified or even exchanged by the direct application of the Bill of Rights. The court in *De Klerk* thus held that

> [T]he alternative, that it was intended that the Bill of Rights have horizontal effect, is extremely unattractive. It entails that all private rights, contracts and relationships are henceforth to be tested by the Constitutional Court against broad and vaguely defined principles. Legal uncertainty on an unprecedented scale would be the result.[54]

[48] A Cachalia *et al*, *ibid*, p 20; JWG van der Walt, 'Justice Kriegler's disconcerting judgment in *Du Plessis v De Klerk*: Much ado about direct horizontal application (read nothing)', (1996) *Tydskrif vir die Suid-Afrikaanse Reg* 732 *ff*, at 733.

[49] S Woolmann, above note 26, pp 10–15.

[50] S Woolmann, *ibid*, pp 10–14 *ff* and 11–2; F Naude and V Terblanche, 'The Interim Constitution—Effect on private litigation on our common law', (1994) *De Rebus* 609 *ff*, at 613; D Spitz, 'Eschewing Silence coerced by Law: The Political Core and Protected Periphery of Freedom of Expression', (1994) *South African Journal on Human Rights* 301 *ff*, at 317.

[51] JD van der Vyver, above note 47, at pp 389 *f* and 393 *f*; E de Wet, above note 45, at p 614.

[52] *De Klerk and Another v Du Plessis and Others*, 1994 (6) BCLR 124 (T) at p 133.

[53] *Ibid*, at p 130 *f*.

[54] *Ibid*, at p 131.

Most other courts, however, came out in favour of direct effect. The most influential of these decisions was *Gardener v Whitaker* of the Eastern Cape Division of the Supreme Court,[55] which identified three distinct areas of private activity with different levels of judicial scrutiny in terms of human rights considerations. 'Societal activities not directly prescribed by law' were thus not subject to human rights, and could only be affected by constitutional values through legislative intervention aimed specifically at the prohibition of certain forms of discrimination.[56] Direct effect, however, was assumed for most parts of the legal system. The courts, according to this view, were thus obliged to protect individuals against threats to their constitutional freedoms by direct application of human rights in private relationships.[57] 'Merely apparent and insubstantial conflicts' should, finally, be resolved by adapting the Common law to constitutional values as envisaged by the interpretation clause.[58] Interestingly, the Court acknowledged the values of the new constitutional settlement while at the same time calling for a cautious approach to the review of long-standing Common law rules. Not all human rights provisions would, moreover, lend themselves to direct effect. There is, in the words of the Court,

> no uniform and single answer to the question whether an alleged breach of a fundamental right contained in Chapter 3 of the Constitution can found an action between private individuals and entities, or whether it only applies between individuals and State organs. It all depends on the nature and extent of the particular right, the values that underlie it, and the context in which the alleged breach of the right occurs.[59]

An intermediate position was, finally, adopted by the Witwatersrand Local Division of the Supreme Court, which rejected the notion of an unqualified horizontal effect of human rights in *Holomisa v Argus Newspapers Ltd.*[60] Much emphasis was, however, placed on s 35(3) IC, which—in the eyes of the Court—could even justify a complete overhaul of pre-Constitutional law.

The issue was eventually resolved by the Constitutional Court in *Du Plessis and others v De Klerk and another.*[61] A defamation case involving the Pretoria News, the judgment resolved the question in favour of indirect effect.

In 1993, the Pretoria News had published a series of six articles dealing with the supply of weapons and other material to the Angolan rebel movement UNITA. In a nutshell, the paper wrote that South African citizens were involved in these covert operations, which were conducted in contravention of air traffic control regulations. The Pretoria News criticised the supply of arms to UNITA, and suggested that those responsible for organising the flights were fuelling the war in Angola for personal gain.

The last two articles of the series mentioned Gerd de Klerk and his company, Wonder Air (Pty) Ltd, as one of several private air operators which the South African Department of Foreign Affairs had called in for questioning in the context of these illegal flights. De Klerk issued a combined summons claiming damages of 750,000 rand for injury to his reputation

[55] 1994 (5) BCLR 19 (E).

[56] At p 28 with specific reference to JD van der Vyver, above note 47.

[57] The indirect effect of human rights on the private sphere through their binding effect on legislation was already emphasised in an earlier decision of the Orange Free State Provincial Division of the Supreme Court in *Walton's Stationary Co (Edms) Bpk v Fourie and Another*, 1994 (1) BCLR 50 (O).

[58] 1994 (5) BCLR 19 (E) at p 30.

[59] *Ibid*, at p 31.

[60] 1996 (6) BCLR 836 (W).

[61] *Du Plessis and Another v De Klerk and Another*, 1996 (3) SA 850.

and feelings; Wonder Air claimed a total of 5 million rand for loss of business and damage to its commercial reputation.

The Pretoria News admitted to publishing the articles but denied that the material had presented de Klerk and his company as being involved in illegal activities or that it was, indeed, defamatory. The newspaper also invoked the public interest defence of fair comment; as far as the articles were an expression of opinion, these constituted a fair comment made in good faith on matters of public interest, and were based on facts truly stated in the articles themselves.

More importantly, the exercise of the constitutional right to free speech as enshrined in s 15(1) IC was later added to the defence after the coming into force of the Interim Constitution on 27 April 1994. This last aspect was at issue in the Constitutional Court. Not only had the Transvaal Provincial Division decided that the case was to proceed without reference to the Interim Constitution since it had been filed before the enactment of the new constitutional settlement; the lower court had also accepted the argument of the plaintiffs that the new Bill of Rights could not, in principle, be applied to horizontal relationships.

The leading judgment of Kentridge AJ emphasised, first, that the Bill of Rights was binding only on the executive and legislative branches of government. The courts, in applying statutory law and developing the Common law, are bound only indirectly by virtue of the interpretative rule contained in s 35(3) IC, which would be redundant if constitutional rights were to be understood as having direct effect. Human rights are thus directly relevant in private law disputes only insofar as they form a constitutional standard with which all law has to comply.[62]

Interestingly, Kentridge also invoked procedural considerations in this context. Section 98 IC thus restricted the jurisdiction of the newly created Constitutional Court to the invalidation of formal statutes, while it was left to the Supreme Court to develop and, if necessary, adapt the Common law to the values of the new constitutional order. Final and overarching (constitutional) control by the Constitutional Court would, in the view of the majority, have run counter to the logic of the new court structure established by the Interim Constitution.[63]

Other judges such as Sachs and Ackermann supported this line of argument, the latter pointing out that direct application of human rights by the Constitutional Court would deprive the system of its necessary flexibility and infringe the division of powers principle.[64] An indirect effect of constitutional rights on the development of the Common law by the Supreme Court would thus preserve the right of the legislator to shape private relationships through the enactment of statutes, while final and binding judgments of the Constitutional Court precluded further legislative intervention short of constitutional amendments.[65] This approach maintained the Common law jurisdiction of the Appellate Division of the Supreme Court.[66]

[62] 1996 (3) SA 850, at p 879.

[63] He thus remarked at p 883 that '[T]he consequence would be that appeals in all such cases would lie to the Constitutional Court and the Appellate Division [of the Supreme Court] would be deprived of a substantial part of what has hitherto been seen as its regular civil jurisdiction. At the very least, appeals to the Appellate Division would routinely result in referrals of common law cases to the Constitutional Court. I do not believe that such a state of affairs could ever have been intended by the framers of the Constitution.'

[64] *Ibid*, at p 906.

[65] *Ibid*, at p 931 *f*.

[66] In *National Media Ltd v Bogoshi*, 1999 (1) BCLR 1 (SCA), the Appellate Division thus heard an appeal based on the alleged unconstitutionality of a common law rule on defamation, and adjusted its own past jurisprudence on the matter without directly applying constitutional rights but rather examining the compatibility of the new rule with the spirit, purport and objects of the Bill of Rights.

The majority of the Court thus opted for an indirect horizontal effect of human rights. In line with the new specialised jurisdiction of the Constitutional Court, the German model was thereby regarded as particularly relevant. A flexible interpretation of all law in the light of constitutional values, as envisaged in s 35(3) IC, was deemed preferable to a control of the Common law by the court, which could only invalidate but not constructively shape the private legal order. Indirect effect would, by contrast, allow

> the development of the common law and customary law by the Supreme Court in accordance with the objects of [the Bill of Rights]. This is provided for in section 35(3) . . . The presence of this subsection ensures that the values embodied in [the Bill of Rights] will permeate the common law in all its aspects, including private litigation.[67]

Individuals are therefore not directly bound by the constitutional rights of others but the courts were under an obligation to interpret and develop the Common law in the spirit of the Bill of Rights. The Court was, however, anxious only to exclude '*general* direct horizontal application' of the Bill of Rights, and acknowledged that single constitutional rights could in certain circumstances exert a more direct effect.

Two judges, however, took a different view and argued forcefully in favour of direct effect. The opinion of Kriegler J, in particular, focused on the historical background of the Interim Constitution and emphasised the need for fundamental changes in the South African legal order.[68] Any resolution of private disputes with the help of legal instruments activates, in Kriegler J's view, the supremacy of the Constitution: 'All organs of the State in all their decisions and actions are bound by the terms of the rights. So, too, are any resorts to law by anybody.'[69] Freedom to organise one's private life beyond the ambit of constitutional values existed only in areas not regulated by any law unless the legislator decided to intervene in order to prevent discrimination. This did not, in Justice Kriegler's view, render s 35(3) IC superfluous. The provision thus established a duty of the courts to take constitutional values into account even where the parties had chosen not to invoke them in private law disputes.[70] Madala J, finally, suggested that the question of direct or indirect effect

[67] *National Media Ltd v Bogoshi*, 1999 (1) BCLR 1 (SCA), at p 885. Ackermann J saw in s 35(3) IC a legal transplant of the German theory of indirect effect and invoked the German counterpart of the rule of law, the *Rechtsstaatsprinzip*, to reject direct effect as a too unpredictable mechanism in the area of private law. Indirect effect, made operational through general clauses and concepts such as public policy considerations, the *boni mores*, unlawfulness, reasonableness, fairness and the like, would, by contrast, allow a gentle seepage of constitutional values into all areas of the law (*ibid*, at p 903).

[68] Writing at [127]: 'It is therefore no spirit of isolationism which leads me to say that our Constitution is unique in its origins, concepts and aspirations. Nor am I a chauvinist when I describe the negotiation process which gave birth to that Constitution as unique; so, too, the leap from minority rule to representative democracy founded on universal adult suffrage; the Damascene about-turn from executive directed parliamentary supremacy to justiciable constitutionalism and a specialist constitutional court, the ingathering of discarded fragments of the country and the creation of new provinces; and the entrenchment of a true separation and devolution of powers. Nowhere in the world that I am aware of have enemies agreed on a transitional coalition and a controlled two-stage process of constitution building. Therefore, although it is always instructive to see how other countries have arranged their constitutional affairs, I do not start there. And when I do conduct comparative study, I do so with great caution. The survey is conducted from the point of vantage afforded by the South African Constitution, constructed on unique foundations, built according to a unique design and intended for unique purposes.'

[69] *Ibid*, at p 916.

[70] *Ibid*, at p 917: 'Section 35(3) answers the question what courts do when there is no direct infringement or claim of an infringement of a right protected under [the Bill of Rights]. This includes cases dealing with statutory law, common law and customary law. It mandates that all courts . . . in interpreting statutory law and when applying and developing common and customary law, always have regard to the spirit, purport and objects of [the Bill of Rights]. This includes courts with constitutional jurisdiction and courts without constitutional jurisdiction. The purpose is that this Constitution is to permeate all that judges do, just as it is to permeate all that the legislature and the executive do, conformably under section 7(1) . . .'.

should be reviewed on a case-by-case basis and with a view to the particular constitutional right involved.

Du Plessis is probably one of the most comparative judgments ever published. The method was used for two reasons.

There were, as discussed above, clear signs that the political parties negotiating the constitutional settlement of 1993 had contemplated various solutions found abroad. For political reasons, the agreement eventually found was highly ambiguous, and in interpreting this text it made good sense for the judges of the Constitutional Court to apply their minds to the arguments put forward in the drafting process.

The issue had, second, been left undecided by the legislator. Here, we encounter a similarity with the well-known death penalty dispute,[71] an issue which was equally left for the courts to resolve. In both cases, South African judges were thus indirectly given a mandate by the political process—a mandate, one could argue, not only to apply traditional *judicial* but also *legislative* techniques, which no doubt include the use of comparative law. The judges thereby had to deal with an ambiguous textual framework which was already influenced by comparative arguments raised by politicians and academics alike. The Constitutional Court was thus, in a way, merely completing a puzzle, many parts of which were already foreign in origin.

Foreign law also had exceptional impact on the reasoning of the judges because the issue at hand has, at one time or the other, riddled most societies with a system of human rights protection.[72] Before embarking on an extensive analysis of US, Irish, Canadian, and German law, as well as the work of Chief Justice Barak in Israel, Kentridge J nevertheless emphasised the need to bear in mind the specific characteristics of the South African setting:

> There can be no doubt that the resolution of the issue must ultimately depend on an analysis of the specific provisions of the Constitution. It is nonetheless illuminating to examine the solutions arrived at by the courts of other countries. The Court was referred to judgments of the courts of the United States, Canada, Germany and Ireland. I would not presume to attempt a detailed description, or even a summary, of the relevant law of those countries, but in each case some broad features are apparent to the outside observer. A comparative examination shows at once that there is no universal answer to the problem of vertical or horizontal application of a Bill of Rights.[73]

Another element which specifically enhanced the influence of German law on the thinking of some judges is the close genealogical relationship between South African law and the German legal system. The provisions of the 1993 Constitution relevant in *Du Plessis* may not have been *direct* legal transplants (as indicated by Ackermann) but there *was* certainly substantial influence of German legal thinking on the work of the Multi-Party Negotiating Process related to the question of *Drittwirkung*. This thinking continued to exert its influence in *Du Plessis*.[74]

[71] See note 12 above.

[72] As Kentridge J emphasises in the leading opinion at no [8] of the judgment: 'The question whether Chapter 3 of the Constitution (Fundamental Rights) has only a "vertical" application or has in addition a "horizontal" application has been the subject of considerable debate by commentators on the Constitution. There have been similar debates, both academic and judicial, in other countries with constitutional Bills of Rights.' And at no [32]: 'The "horizontality" issue has arisen in other countries with entrenched Bills of Rights and the parties have supplied us with a wealth of comparative material both judicial and extra-judicial, for which we are grateful.'

[73] At no [33].

[74] One can see this clearly from the following passage from the opinion of Ackermann J: 'That the drafters of our Constitution had recourse to or were influenced by certain features of the German BL in drafting our Constitution is evident from various of its provisions. The marked similarity between the provisions of section 35(3), enjoining courts "[i]n the interpretation of any law and the application and development of the common

As in other decisions of the Court, there thus seems to be a balance between a line of reasoning which focuses on the provisions of the 1993 Constitution and the discussion of foreign ideas. The latter are, however, not only used to *confirm* a 'South African' solution; references to, in particular, German and Canadian law show that foreign ideas were actually used to *shape* the result in *Du Plessis*. Kentridge thus emphasised that

> [T]he model of indirect application or, if you will, indirect horizontality, seems peculiarly appropriate to a judicial system which, as in Germany, separates constitutional jurisdiction from ordinary jurisdiction. This does not mean that the principles evolved by the German Constitutional Court must be slavishly followed. They do however afford an example of how the process of influencing the common law may work in practice.[75]

Du Plessis was heavily criticised by a number of academic authors. Besides invoking those sections of the Interim Constitution which could be read as establishing direct effect, the inability of indirect *Drittwirkung* to address discrimination effectively in the private sphere was a frequently voiced concern. Many commentators also rejected the comparative approach of the Constitutional Court; Germany and Canada, the two most important models for *Du Plessis*, were regarded as too different in terms of their socio-economic environment to provide workable templates for South Africa.[76]

The approach developed in *Du Plessis* was later nevertheless confirmed by the Constitutional Court in *Gardener v Whitaker*,[77] and applied by the lower courts in a series of subsequent cases.[78]

By that time, transition had, however, already moved on. The two-stage process leading from the 1983 Constitution to the final settlement of 1996 gave the newly elected Parliament (convened as a Constitutional Assembly between 1994 and 1996) an opportunity to revisit the matter both in the light of judicial developments and changed political majorities.

The first free elections held in April 1994 had shifted the balance of power in favour of those parties which supported direct effect; the National Party (NP) was now the only political group to promote a more restrictive approach, arguing that the application of constitutional rights to private relationships would limit the ability of the private legal order to function properly.[79] Most other parties represented in the Constitutional Assembly felt that a restriction of human rights to vertical relationships would undermine seriously the trust of South Africa's citizens in the final constitutional settlement.[80]

law and customary law" to "have due regard to the spirit, purport and objects of [Chapter 3]", and the indirect horizontal application of the basic rights in the German BL in German jurisprudence cannot, in my view, simply be a coincidence. It provides a final powerful indication that the framers of our Constitution did not intend that the Chapter 3 fundamental rights should, save where the formulation of a particular right expressly or by necessary implication otherwise indicates, apply directly to legal relations between private persons.'

[75] At no [60].

[76] See, eg, S Woolmann and D Davis, 'The Last Laugh: *Du Plessis v De Klerk*, Classical Liberalism, Creole Liberalism and the Application of Fundamental Rights under the Interim and Final Constitution', (1996) *South African Journal on Human Rights* 361, at pp 363 *ff*; H Cheadle and D Davis, 'The Application of the 1996 Constitution in the Private Sphere', (1997) *South African Journal on Human Rights* 44, at pp 51 *ff*; S Woolmann, 'Application' in Chaskalson *et al* (eds), *Constitutional Law of South Africa* (2nd edn, Original Service: 02-05), pp 31–23 *ff*.

[77] 1996 (6) BCLR 775 (CC).

[78] See, eg, *Ryland v Edros*, 1997 (1) BCLR 77 (C); *Rivett-Carnac v Wiggins*, 1997 (4) BCLR 562 (C); *McNally v M and G Media (Pty) Limited and Others*, 1997 (6) BCLR 818 (W); *Mistry v Interim National Medical and Dental Council of South Africa and Others*, 1997 (7) BCLR 933 (D); *Buthelezi v South African Broadcasting Corporation*, 1997 (12) BCLR 1733 (D).

[79] Theme Committee 4, *Explanatory Memorandum* (9 October 1995), p 266.

[80] See Theme Committee 4, *Report on Nature and Application of the Bill of Rights* (May 1995).

Regardless of this shift, political opposition against direct effect nevertheless continued. Uncertainty concerning the possible consequences of one or the other approach eventually prompted the Technical Committee advising the Constitutional Assembly on human rights issues to present a further report as late as October 1996, in which it put on record that the differences between indirect and direct effect were, in fact, negligible in practice. The Committee supported its position with four arguments.

Constitutional and Common law values were, first, in most cases very similar (if not identical), so that courts would usually continue to apply private law without recourse to the Constitution. If, however, constitutional rights indeed required a different solution in single cases, even a horizontal approach would, second, in all likelihood utilise the open-ended clauses of the Common law to cover the situation. The notion of *boni mores* had, third, always been used to introduce considerations of the public good into South African contract, tort, and inheritance law. As long as the Final Constitution offered access to the courts in cases of human rights infringements, judges would probably continue to use this mechanism and come to very similar results as the German concept of indirect effect. Finally, conflicts between competing constitutional values could be resolved through a balancing of interests, a technique already well-known to common lawyers.[81]

The Committee nevertheless proposed to qualify the new application clause by inserting the caveat 'where applicable' into the text. It also suggested binding the judiciary to the Bill of Rights (as is the case in Namibia and Germany). Courts confronted with private disputes, so the argument ran, would in any case be bound by human rights considerations only to the extent to which these are, in principle, applicable to private relationships, while certain constitutional rights such as the right to a fair trial are clearly addressed to judicial activity.[82]

These suggestions of the Committee were eventually incorporated in s 8(1) FC, dealing with the effect of human rights on vertical relationships, and s 8(2) FC, which establishes direct horizontal application. Section 8(3) FC was designed to reflect the more active role of the judge in Common law jurisdictions by specifying that a court, when applying a provision of the Bill of Rights to a natural or juristic person, must apply, or if necessary develop, the Common law to the extent that legislation does not give effect to that right, and may develop rules of the Common law to limit a right, provided that such limitation is in accordance with the general limitation clause and, in particular, the principle of proportionality.

These late additions to the text of the Final Constitution were clearly meant to protect in particular the Common law from the potentially disruptive effects of horizontally applicable constitutional rights. The substance of s 35(3) IC was maintained as an 'interpretational directive'[83] in s 39(2) FC. The provision has subsequently been understood *not* as an expression of the German theory of indirect effect but rather as a general guideline for the courts to respect human rights in all cases and irrespective of whether the parties actually invoke them or not. The provision also addresses the procedural concern voiced by a number of judges in *Du Plessis*, namely that the Constitutional Court had no jurisdiction to develop the Common law in order to give effect to constitutional rights in the private sphere.[84]

[81] Theme Committee 4, above note 79, pp 270 *f.*

[82] See Theme Committee 4, above note 79, p 272 *f.* 'Including the judiciary in the binding clause does not imply that it is bound to apply the Bill of Rights in a totally unqualified way. The judiciary in deciding on matters concerning relationships between private parties (like the legislature in making laws, and the executive in their execution) can only be bound by the Bill of Rights to the extent that the Bill of Rights can be applied to such relationships.'

[83] Constitutional Committee, *Supplementary Memorandum on the Bill of Rights and Party Submissions* (9 November 1995), section 38 at 1.2.

[84] I Rautenbach and EFJ Malherbe, *Constitutional Law* (1994), p 314.

Finally, the 1996 Constitution removed the procedural obstacle to direct application of human rights specifically identified by the Constitutional Court in *Du Plessis*. The High Courts, the Supreme Court of Appeal and the Constitutional Court now exercise a shared jurisdiction over constitutional matters. This had a knock-on effect on the whole structure of the legal system in that constitutional law and Common law are now no longer regarded as distinct areas (with constitutional values affecting private law indirectly) but rather as one unified system of law with the Constitution at its apex.[85]

As far as the substantive provisions of the Bill of Rights themselves are concerned, it is important to note that some rights are expressly designed to regulate private relationships while others, by virtue of their content, operate only vertically. Section 9(4) FC thus provides that no person may unfairly discriminate directly or indirectly against anyone on one or more of the grounds identified in s 9(3) FC, and therefore has an immediate impact on the private sphere. The same is true for s 32(1)(b) FC, which establishes the right of access to information held by another person and required for the exercise and protection of any rights. A person's right to citizenship, just administrative action, or the rights of arrested, detained and accused persons are, by contrast, obviously limited to the relationship between the state and its citizens.

Direct effect will, moreover, also depend on the protective scope of a right, which may be limited to particular individuals such as adult citizens, children, workers and employers, or persons belonging to a cultural, religious or linguistic community. Academic commentators have also stressed the danger of compiling a formal list of rights and duties that can have an effect in the private sphere and those which cannot; the details of the particular case under consideration should always be taken into account.

Direct effect of human rights has subsequently been invoked in a large variety of situations including defamation cases,[86] the freedom not to attend religious observances in private schools,[87] or the contractual undertaking not to use loudspeakers to broadcast calls to prayer from a suburban mosque.[88] It is, however, important to note that the notion of directly enforceable human rights has in practice been rendered practically redundant. The Constitutional Court spoke of 'horizontal application' when dealing with s 8 FC in its Second Certification Judgment,[89] but since *Du Plessis*, courts have routinely tackled the problem of *Drittwirkung* through the indirect application of constitutional values to the Common law. The reasons for this could lie in the very similar—if not equal—outcome of cases under both regimes,[90] the flexibility of Common law remedies, and the fact that indirect effect has since *Du Plessis* offered a familiar template for the resolution of human rights issues in private disputes.

One exception is the decision of the Constitutional Court in *Khumalo v Holomisa*,[91] a defamation case involving the leader of the United Democratic Movement (Bantu

[85] See *Pharmaceutical Manufacturers Association of South Africa: In re: ex parte President of the Republic of South Africa*, 2000 (2) SA 674 (CC), where the Constitutional Court held that '(T)here are not two systems of law, each dealing with the same subject matter, each having similar requirements, each operating in its own field with its own highest court. There is only one system of law. It is shaped by the Constitution which is the supreme law, and all law, including the common law, derives its force from the Constitution and is subject to constitutional control'.

[86] *National Media Ltd v Bogoshi*, 1999 (1) BCLR 1 (SCA).

[87] *Wittmann v Deutscher Schülerverein, Pretoria*, 1998 (4) SA 423 (T).

[88] *Garden Cities Incorporated Association Not for Gain v Northpine Islamic Society*, 1999 (2) SA 268 (C).

[89] *In re Certification of the Amended Text of the Constitution of the Republic of South Africa, 1996*, 1997 (2) SA 97 (CC).

[90] See, eg, Christopher Roederer, 'Post-Matrix Legal Reasoning: Horizontality and the Rule of Values in South African Law', (2003) 19 South African Journal on Human Rights 57 *ff.*

[91] 2002 (5) SA 401 (CC).

Holomisa) and the newspaper Sunday World over a report that alleged that Holomisa was involved in criminal activities and under police investigation. The Court held that the Bill of Rights must find direct application to the Common law wherever appropriate and, in balancing the Final Constitution's commitment to human dignity with freedom of expression, came out in favour of Holomisa. The Constitutional Court did not, however, provide a workable approach to the application of s 8(2) FC, in particular as far as the distinction between direct horizontal application and the binding effect of human rights on all law (including the Common law) is concerned,[92] and it remains to be seen whether the case will indeed have a long-term effect on the development of *Drittwirkung* in South Africa.

Drittwirkung, a judicial legal transplant, is thus our first German survivor. *Du Plessis* not only answered for the interim phase an important question left open by the political negotiations in Kempton Park; the decision provided an authoritative methodological framework, strongly influenced by foreign law, which has thus far prevailed in legal practice despite attempts of the Constitutional Assembly to increase the horizontal effect of human rights protection in the final constitutional settlement.[93]

Two final points should be made in this respect.

The 1996 Constitution, first, does not expressly provide a new constitutional remedy for the infringement of human rights in private relationships. Making constitutional rights operational in the private sphere remains an interpretative—and thus, structurally, 'indirect'—task in the sense that the Common law as a whole provides the link between constitutional values and the private sphere. Constitutional 'action' in private disputes is thus in most cases still mediated through the Common law, which must be applied and, if necessary, developed in order to give effect to human rights. The difference between the South African approach and its German model is thus one of degree rather than substance. By limiting the radiating effect of human rights mainly (though not exclusively) to general clauses contained in the German Civil Code, German indirect *Drittwirkung* tends to be more restrictive. This is, however, largely a consequence of the structural differences between Common law and civilian systems of private law.

Second, the South African legislator, too, is (vertically) bound by the Bill of Rights. The mere existence of a supreme constitution will thus in itself have a strong impact on the private sphere through judicial review of an ever increasing amount of parliamentary legislation regulating private relationships. The practical relevance of the problem might thus well diminish—if not disappear—over time.

(c) The Protection of Economic Activity

The next transplant we wish to discuss is a model case in the sense that the legislator copied two provisions practically verbatim from a foreign constitutional text; the desired effect was, however, strongly diluted by subsequent judicial interpretation.

The right to freedom of trade, occupation, and profession guaranteed by s 22 of the 1996 Constitution was drafted on the basis of the German *Berufsfreiheit* protected by article 12(1)

[92] See the criticism by S Woolmann, above note 26, pp 31–42 *ff* and I Currie and J de Waal, The Bill of Rights Handbook (5th edn 2005), p 51 *f*.

[93] See, eg, Johan van der Walt, 'Progressive Indirect Horizontal Application of the Bill of Rights: Towards a Co-operative Relation between Common-law and Constitutional Jurisprudence', (2001) 17 South African Journal on Human Rights 341 *ff*; Marius Pieterse, 'Indirect Horizontal Application of the Right to have Access to Health Care', (2007) 23 South African Journal on Human Rights 157 *ff*.

of the Basic Law. A simple textual comparison immediately reveals the close relationship. Both norms establish the right to choose freely an occupation or profession, and allow the practice of such activities to be regulated by law. Both systems restrict the protective scope of this right to nationals.

Table 4.1: Freedom of occupation in Germany and South Africa

Article 12(1) BL[94]	Section 22 of the 1996 Constitution
[1] All Germans shall have the right freely to choose their occupation or profession, their place of work, and their place of training.	[1] Every citizen has the right to choose their trade, occupation or profession freely.
[2] The practice of an occupation or profession may be regulated by or pursuant to a law.	[2] The practice of a trade, occupation or profession may be regulated by law.

The two provisions nevertheless display some differences in detail. The German text includes a reference to the place of training and specifies that the *practice* of an occupation or profession may also be regulated *pursuant* to a law. In South Africa, trade is singled out as a separate category of protected activity.

Closer analysis shows, however, that these differences in wording are not substantial. The term 'occupation' (*Beruf*) is generally acknowledged to mean any permanent activity designed to create and safeguard the economical basis of earning a livelihood in Germany and covers all forms of commercial activity, including trade. The choice of a place of training is thereby not more than a sub-category of the right to choose freely an occupation for which such training is necessary or desirable. Finally, the ability of the South African executive to regulate the practice of a trade, occupation, or profession *pursuant* to a law is contained in the right to regulate *by* law. As in Germany, laws which meet the constitutional requirements of a limitation can authorise the executive to take further action within the limits of the empowering statute.

These first indications that the South African provision was, indeed, drafted along the lines of the German model are further strengthened by a contextual analysis of the South African Bill of Rights.

The 1996 Constitution relies on a general limitation clause contained in s 36.[95] A similar provision was included in s 33 of the 1993 Constitution, but was accompanied there by a number of specific limitation clauses located *within* the various human rights provisions *themselves*—again much in the style of the German Basic Law, which—unlike the Canadian Charter of Rights and Freedoms—does not contain a general limitation clause. This super-

[94] Translation by Tomuschat/Curry in: Press and Information Office of the Federal Government, *Basic Law for the Federal Republic of Germany* (1998). The German text of Art 12 (1) BL declares: 'Alle Deutschen haben das Recht, Beruf, Arbeitsplatz und Ausbildungsstätte frei zu wählen. Die Berufsausübung kann durch Gesetz oder auf Grund eines Gesetzes geregelt werden'.

[95] Section 36 Republic of South Africa Constitution Act 1996 declares: '(1) The rights in the Bill of Rights may be limited only in terms of law of general application to the extent that the limitation is reasonable and justifiable in an open and democratic society based on human dignity, equality and freedom, taking into account all relevant factors, including—(a) the nature of the right; (b) the importance of the purpose of the limitation; (c) the nature and extent of the limitation; (d) the relation between the limitation and its purpose; and (e) less restrictive means to achieve this purpose. (2) Except as provided in subsection (1) or in any other provision of the Constitution, no law may limit any right entrenched in the Bill of Rights.'

fluous system of 'internal limitation clauses' fell away in 1996. The right to freedom of trade, occupation, and profession, however, a latecomer in the drafting process which substituted a similar right to engage in economic activity and to pursue a livelihood anywhere in the national territory under the 1993 Constitution, obviously retained in its second sentence the limitation clause which the draftsmen had found in its German counterpart. This second sentence seems to be redundant for the purposes of limiting the right safeguarded by s 22, which is already possible on the basis of the general limitation clause.[96]

We feel that its existence can only be explained in one of two ways.

It could simply be an editorial error, which is rather unlikely given the omission of the words 'or pursuant to [a law]' in preliminary drafts of the text and, more importantly, the deliberate removal of all the other internal limitation clauses contained in the 1993 Constitution. Given the intense discussion surrounding the limitation of rights, this does not look like a cut and paste mistake.

Alternatively, the retention of the second sentence could be a sign that the draftsmen wanted to emulate the German provision for a particular reason. The distinction between the *choice* of a trade, occupation or profession and the *practice* of such activities is a prominent feature of article 12(1) BL and has influenced the approach of German courts when reviewing legislative or administrative measures. Varying degrees of judicial scrutiny apply, depending on the type of limitation. The regulation of practice will thus require *reasonable* considerations of the common good, while limitations of choice are only justified if *particularly important* community interests are at stake. In the light of the conflict between adherents of a free market economy and supporters of strong state intervention, it is quite likely that this sliding scale of protection, which is not immediately apparent on a mere reading of article 12(1) BL itself, motivated the legislator to retain the special limitation clause.

The German origin of s 22 is, finally, confirmed by contemporary accounts of the drafting process. Peter Leon, one of the experts intimately involved in the negotiations leading to both Constitutions, recalls that the stalemate between those in favour of giving the state more latitude to engage in the socio-economic reconstruction of the country and those who stressed the protection of individual freedom, property, and economic activity was overcome by a proposal of the late Professor Etienne Mureinik, who pointed to the German approach as a possible compromise.[97]

How did this legal transplant fare in practice?

The close relationship between article 12(1) BL and s 22 of the 1996 Constitution was first acknowledged in *City of Cape Town v Ad Outpost (Pty) Ltd*,[98] a case where the plaintiff (a commercial firm) challenged a municipal by-law which placed restrictions on the use of billboards for commercial purposes. It is worthwhile to quote the relevant passage of the judgment. The Court thus explained that

[96] This is also pointed out by Ignus Rautenbach and EFJ Malherbe, *Constitutional Law* (2nd edn 1998), p 328 ('the clause does not seem to serve any purpose') and Devenish, *A Commentary on the South African Constitution* (1998), p 65 ('internal modifier'). The latter, however, seems to have had second thoughts when writing in 1999: 'At the very least, it is obviously intended to provide some kind of ideological comfort for those persons who wish to see the free market economy system entrenched, without offending those who are strongly committed to socialism, or at least social democracy. What is however clear is that legislation regulating trades, occupations or professions must comply with the general limitation clause.' See Devenish, *A commentary on the South African bill of rights* (1999) at p 304.

[97] Peter Leon, 'A Personal Perspective on Etienne Mureinik's Contribution to South Africa's Final Constitution', (1998) *South African Journal of Human Rights* 201, 203.

[98] *City of Cape Town v Ad Outpost (Pty) Ltd and Others*, 2000 (2) *BCLR* (Butterworths Constitutional Law Reports) 130 (C) at 141F.

> [S]ection 22 appears to be modelled on article 12(1) of the German Basic Law which provides that all Germans have the right freely to choose their occupation and profession, their place of work, study or training. The practice of an occupation may be regulated by law. The German courts have interpreted article 12 to provide a considerable amount of constitutional protection for commercial activities. Thus in the Pharmacy case 7 BVerfGE 377 article 12(1) was interpreted to empower the legislator to regulate the practice as well as the choice of an occupation. Regulations dealing with the latter are greatly circumscribed by the article. The practice of an occupation which is the relevant issue in the present case may be 'restricted by reasonable regulations predicated on considerations of the common good'. In short an uncritical application of German jurisprudence would afford some assistance to respondent's attempt to attack the by-law in terms of section 22 of the Constitution.

The German approach does, indeed, differentiate between the *choice* and the *practice* of an occupation, establishing a higher level of judicial scrutiny for limitations of the former. But (as correctly indicated in the South African judgment) *both* types of limitation are subject to the principle of proportionality, which is regarded as a basic constitutional safeguard usually derived from the *Rechtsstaatsprinzip* but not found in the text of the Basic Law itself. Under German law, limitations such as the restrictions imposed by the City of Cape Town regarding billboards would thus have to be capable of achieving the legislative or administrative aim (*Geeignetheit*), they would have to be the mildest means by which this aim can be achieved (*Erforderlichkeit*), and they would have to be reasonable when balancing the adverse effects of the measure on the individual citizen with the positive effects for the particular public interest in question (*Verhältnismäßigkeit*). The different structure of the South African Constitution, which contains the principle of proportionality as part of its *general* limitation clause, led to a different result regarding the appropriate standard of judicial scrutiny in this case. While the German approach to article 12 BL—if applied to s 22—would have required a proportionality analysis, the court thus held that South African authorities only need to show a *rational connection* between the desired measure and a legitimate public interest:

> [T]here is always a great danger in the uncritical employment of foreign law in the process of domestic interpretation. Notwithstanding that article 12 and section 22 are similar in wording the latter must be interpreted in the context of the South African constitutional text and its own pedigree . . . [T]he interpretation of section 22 must take account of the difference in wording between section 22 of the Constitution and section 26 of the interim Constitution . . . The purpose of section 22 would thus appear to be to ensure that regulations which control a citizen's right to choose a trade and occupation or profession should be implemented in a rational manner.

According to this interpretation, the special internal limitation clause taken from the Basic Law—specifically introduced in an attempt to strike a balance between necessary state intervention and the protection of the individual on the basis of the German model[99]—thus leads to a distinctly lower level of protection in what is probably the great majority of all cases involving regulatory intervention in this area. A proportionality analysis on the basis of the general limitation clause is only activated if the *choice* of a trade, occupation, or profession is in question; mere regulation of commercial practice will only require a rational connection. For purely structural reasons—one is even tempted to say by coincidence!—the flexible and sliding scale of judicial scrutiny which determines the specific character of

[99] In which the *importance* of the public interest and the *degree of danger* to this interest play a crucial role in the application of the principle of proportionality.

the German model, and which formed the basis of the political compromise in South Africa during the negotiations in 1996, is thus exchanged for an all-or-nothing approach which draws a rigid line between these two types of limitation. German experience again suggests that this may not be an easy distinction to make. South African courts will have to define the two areas, and may provide citizens with more protection in single cases which fall into the grey zone between choice and practice if they regard a particular measure as so onerous that it amounts to a restriction of choice.

The Constitutional Court had to deal with the interpretation of s 22 four years after the *City of Cape Town* decision.[100] In that case—involving the introduction of specific requirements for the dispensation of medicines by medical practitioners (rather than pharmacists)—Justice Ngcobo, delivering the judgment of the Court, again reflected on the close similarity between the South African provision and its German counterpart. The Court confirmed the approach taken in *City of Cape Town v Ad Outpost (Pty) Ltd* by distinguishing between choice and practice of a profession (as in Germany), and requiring a *reasonable*—that is proportionate—limitation in the first but only an *objectively rational* regulation in the second alternative. This marks, as just explained, an important difference to the German model. Interestingly, though, the judgment leaves open a back door through which the Court could, in the future, still introduce a stricter form of inquiry. It is again worthwhile to quote the relevant passage verbatim:

> [T]he scope of permissible regulation that we adopt here is not entirely inconsistent with the German approach. It recognises that it is not always possible to draw a clear line of distinction between regulation that affects the practice of a profession on the one hand and one that affects choice on the other. It requires that where, objectively viewed, the regulation of the practice of a profession impacts negatively on choice such regulation must be tested under section 36(1). Such regulation does not fall within the purview of section 22, and must therefore meet, amongst other requirements, the standard of reasonableness, of which proportionality analysis is an important component . . . However where, as here, the regulation, objectively viewed, does not impact negatively on choice, it need only satisfy the rationality test. In the result, restrictions on the right to practise a profession are subject to a less stringent test than restrictions on the choice of a profession.[101]

It is worthwhile noting, however, that the general limitation clause has thus far not been applied in the context of s 22. What remains, then, is the fact that the very same text has produced very different results in the two systems, and that the main reason for these differences is not the political will as expressed in the negotiations leading to the adoption of the German idea but rather the differences between both systems when it comes to the limitation of human rights in general. The irony of the matter is that the desire of the legislator to capture the essence of the German approach by copying the Basic Law practically verbatim led to a very different result in the majority of cases because it failed to take into account the difference between proportionality as an overarching constitutional principle and proportionality as a component of a general limitation clause. Structure prevailed over original intent.

[100] *The Affordable Medicines Trust and Others v The Minister of Health of the Republic of South Africa and Others*, Case CCT 27/04 of 11 March 2005.

[101] At no [93] of the judgment.

(d) Juristic Persons

The *City of Cape Town* case is interesting to illustrate yet another area where German thinking has had significant influence on the application of human rights—the treatment of juristic persons. Again we find a close textual relationship between the model, in this case article 19(3) BL, and the transplant found in South Africa. In Germany, basic rights apply to domestic corporations to the extent that the nature of such rights permits. Famous cases triggered by companies are the so-called *Solange I* and *Solange II* cases. The South African counterpart to article 19(3) BL is again very similar in wording. According to s 7(3) of the Interim Constitution, juristic persons shall be entitled to the rights contained in the Interim Bill of Rights where, and to the extent that, the nature of the right permits. Slightly modified, the principle is now expressed in s 8(4) of the Final Constitution, which declares that a juristic person is entitled to the rights in the Bill of Rights to the extent required by the nature of the rights and the nature of that juristic person.

Table 4.2: Juristic persons in Germany and South Africa

Article 19(3) BL	Section 8(4) of the 1996 Constitution
Basic rights also apply to domestic corporations to the extent that the nature of the right permits.	A juristic person is entitled to the rights in the Bill of Rights to the extent required by the nature of the rights and the nature of that juristic person.

The Court in *City of Cape Town* held that the company could not rely on the protection offered by the freedom of trade, occupation, and profession. The provision, the Court held,

> introduces a constitutional protection to be enjoyed by individual citizens as opposed to juristic bodies. The right ensures that each citizen will have the right to choose how to employ his or her labour and skills without irrational governmental restriction. It is not a provision which should be extended to the regulation of economic intercourse as undertaken by enterprises owned by juristic bodies which might otherwise fall within the description of economic activity.[102]

This is a surprisingly brief verdict bearing in mind, first, that article 12 BL—the counterpart, as we have seen, of s 22—offers *full* protection to juristic persons formed under German law and, second, that the rule dealing with the application of human rights to juristic persons in South Africa—s 8(4) of the 1996 Constitution—is, again, a *legal transplant* based on the *German* approach. Under these circumstances, the arguments which led German courts to expand the scope of protection to legal entities when it comes to commercial activity must surely have been of interest to a South African judge confronted with the very same question. This is especially true since a textual analysis of the 1996 Constitution *itself* raises serious doubts concerning the restrictive approach of the South African court in *City of Cape Town.*

The decision is very much influenced by the use of the term *citizen* in s 22. But did the draftsmen really intend to limit the protective scope of the norm to natural persons, or was the outcome of the drafting exercise—yet again—influenced by the German model?

[102] *City of Cape Town v AD Outpost (Pty) Ltd and Others* 2000 (2) BCLR 130 (C).

It is useful to look at the other provisions of the 1996 Constitution which give rights to citizens. At first glance, the list would seem to support the result in *City of Cape Town.* All other rights which are linked to citizenship can only be exercised by natural persons: political rights such as the right to form, participate in the activities of, or recruit members for, a political party, the right to free, fair, and regular elections, and the right to vote and to stand for public office[103]; the right not to be deprived of citizenship[104]; the right to enter, to remain in, and to reside anywhere in the Republic; and, finally, the right to a passport.[105]

The difference from s 22 is easy to spot—economic activities of the kind envisaged by article 12 BL can obviously be pursued by a large variety of commercial entities as well as individual natural persons. This observation is confirmed by the fact that s 26 of the Interim Constitution, the direct predecessor of s 22, granted the right to freely engage in economic activity to *every person,* and that an earlier version of s 22 itself gave the right to pursue a livelihood, including the right to freely choose an occupation or profession, the place of work and the place of training, to *everyone.* The latter term is the most common category of beneficiary in the South African Bill of Rights, and is usually taken to refer to both natural and juristic persons. The protection of property, access to information, and the right to just administrative action are, for example, granted to everyone—including juristic persons.

Why then did the framers of the 1996 Constitution eventually opt for the term 'citizen'? The link between the rights which are granted to citizens is not the distinction between natural persons and juristic bodies but rather the distinction between rights which the framers of the Constitution wished to restrict to *nationals* and those which were to be granted to everyone including *foreigners.* This is equally true for the German model, which indeed refers to 'all Germans' and distinguishes in practice between *German* and *foreign* natural and juristic persons. A comparative analysis could have clarified this wider background.

Whether the restrictive approach in *City of Cape Town* will have a long-term effect on the question whether juristic persons can invoke s 22 in the future is not yet clear. In the *Affordable Medicines Trust* decision of 2005 it was not necessary for the Constitutional Court to discuss whether the Trust and the National Convention on Dispensing could rely on the freedom of trade, occupation or profession as both applicants had standing as associations acting in the interests of their members under s 38 of the Constitution. The third applicant in that case was a natural person.

It is important at this point to again emphasise that foreign law can never be a binding guideline for the national judge—not even in the case of closely related legal transplants. In this instance, therefore, the South African courts are not in any way bound by a German 'copyright' concerning the interpretation of their 'own' versions of article 12 and article 19 of the Basic Law. On the contrary, the different socio-economic parameters prevalent in both countries actually call for a very careful assessment of the transplanted solution and may justify an interpretation which gives South African authorities more latitude in the regulation of economic activity or restricts freedom of trade, occupation or profession to natural persons.

The two last examples, however, highlight the difficulty of moving foreign plants into very different constitutional environments, and beg the question to what extent (if at all) courts are bound by the political intentions of the legislative gardener. It would also seem that comparative law can provide valuable additional angles from which to analyse a legal

[103] Section 19 FC.
[104] Section 20 FC.
[105] Section 21 FC.

system. Especially in the case of legal transplants, the method may thus lead to a more informed result, and there is no reason why it should be restricted to the legislator. In the case of s 22 FC, German law provided guidance for specific reasons, and it is doubtful whether the solution adopted by the courts regarding the low level of justification required for a limitation of the practice of a trade, occupation, or profession can be reconciled with the original intent of the Constitutional Assembly.

The application of the right to juristic persons may be a different matter. Historical evidence suggests that the political parties did have corporate entities in mind when discussing the provision in 1996 but in the absence of a clear constitutional decision, the judge was bound to apply the criteria established by s 8(4) in order to determine whether the respondent was entitled to the protection provided by s 22. German experience could have been of particular interest in this context, and would certainly have facilitated a more profound discussion of this important point. That said, the South African result could *still* have been different.

(e) Allgemeine Handlungsfreiheit—*A General Right to Freedom?*

Our last example from the area of human rights protection is different from the previous cases in that a foreign approach was proposed although the text of the 1993 Constitution and the background material of the drafting process offer no indication that its framers had in any way discussed such a possibility. The foreign idea (which would, if used, have amounted to a judicial legal transplant) was rejected by the majority of the Constitutional Court.

In *Ferreira,*[106] the Court dealt with the statutory duty of company employees to disclose confidential business information under circumstances specified by s 417 of the South African Companies Act[107] *notwithstanding* the risk that this information might incriminate them and subsequently be used as evidence in criminal proceedings. Justice Ackermann proposed to expand the protective scope of s 11(1) of the 1993 Constitution[108] to include—beyond the limits of the constitutional text—a *general* right to freedom. Referring to Sir Isaiah Berlin and the opinion of Dickson CJC in the Canadian case *R v Big M Drug Mart,*[109] he defined this freedom as the right of individuals not to have obstacles to possible choices and activities placed in their way by the state.[110]

Ackermann justified this interpretation, first, by emphasising the vast number, extent, and variety of limitations which had been placed on the personal freedom of citizens under the *apartheid* regime; second, by reference to the values underlying an 'open and democratic society based on freedom and equality'[111]; and, finally, by arguing that the new constitutional order required the state to justify any limitation of the citizens' freedoms. A broad interpretation of s 11(1) would help to create a 'culture of justification', while comparative experience had shown that it would not subject the courts to a flood of frivolous complaints or unduly restrict state legislation.[112]

[106] *Ferreira v Levin NO and Others,* 1996 (1) BCLR 1.

[107] Act 61 of 1973.

[108] Entitled 'freedom and security of the person'. The provision grants everyone the right 'to freedom and security of the person, which shall include the right not to be detained without trial'.

[109] (1985) 13 CRR 64.

[110] At no [54].

[111] At no [50].

[112] At nos [61] *ff.*

Despite references to foreign legal systems such as the United States and Canada, Ackermann developed these ideas and addressed possible objections to his proposal in this part of the opinion primarily within the framework of *South African* constitutional law and the country's *own* history.

He then, however, focused his attention to foreign law and analysed in great detail Canadian, American, and German experience, as well as the International Covenant on Civil and Political Rights and the European Convention on Human Rights. These reflections were introduced by the following passage, which seems to indicate that Ackermann was using comparative law mainly (but not exclusively) to *support* a result reached through other means. He thus wrote:

> It is appropriate to consider whether comparable foreign case law would lead to a different conclusion. Direct comparison is of course difficult and needs to be done with circumspection because the right to personal freedom is formulated differently in the constitutions of other countries and in the international and regional instruments. Nevertheless, s 33(1) of our Constitution enjoins us to consider, *inter alia*, what would be 'justifiable in an open and democratic society based on freedom and equality' and s 35(1) obliges us to promote the values underlying such a society when we interpret Chapter 3 and encourages us to have regard to comparable case law. In construing and applying our Constitution, we are dealing with fundamental legal norms which are steadily becoming more universal in character. When, for example, the United States Supreme Court finds that a statutory provision is or is not in accordance with the 'due process of law' or when the Canadian Supreme Court decides that a deprivation of liberty is not 'in accordance with the principles of fundamental justice' . . . we have regard to these findings, not in order to draw direct analogies, but to identify the underlying reasoning with a view to establishing the norms that apply in other open and democratic societies based on freedom and equality.[113]

This, then, is a good example of the open-minded approach that many South African judges take when dealing with questions of national law—societies which broadly operate on the basis of a similar set of values are taken as an additional point of reference in order to determine the validity of their own solution. What is surprising, though, is the amount of space invested for this purpose (judges in other countries such as Germany, the United States or England would—at most—add a throwaway line or a footnote indicating that their solution is confirmed by the approaches found abroad). We thus suspect that Ackermann J's reflections served an *additional* purpose beyond mere confirmation 'whether comparable foreign case law would lead to a different conclusion', and the final paragraph dealing with the interpretation of s 11(1) indicates that foreign ideas are indeed part of his *ratio decidendi*.[114]

The attempt to expand s 11(1)[115] was, admittedly, difficult. Neither the text of the 1993 Constitution nor the negotiations at Kempton Park indicate that the political parties contemplated the introduction of any such right; and only during the later work of the Constitutional Assembly do we find references to a broad residual right in the positions of the African National Congress and the Freedom Front.[116]

[113] At no [72].

[114] At no [90], Ackermann J includes these ideas in his 'end result'.

[115] Along the lines, eg, of the German *allgemeine Handlungsfreiheit*. This notion, derived from Art 2(1) BL, provides a residual right to individual self-fulfilment (*freie Entfaltung der Persönlichkeit*) subject to the rights of others and subject to the constitutional order and morality. Article 2(1) BL is a general clause establishing freedom from *any* kind of State intervention but plaintiffs will only invoke the provision successfully in the absence of a more specific fundamental right.

[116] Constitutional Assembly, Theme Committee 4, *Schematic Report on Freedom and Security of the Person* of August 1995, at 2.2.1 and 2.2.2.

These textual differences between the 1993 Constitution and its foreign counterparts are an important counter-argument for the majority of the court. Though in agreement with Ackermann that the relevant provision of the Companies Act *is* unconstitutional (though for different reasons), Chaskalson—then President of the Court—felt the need to explain why s 11(1) should be interpreted primarily as a protection of the *physical* integrity of every person. For this purpose, he, too, relied on comparative evidence:

> This is how a guarantee of 'freedom (liberty) and security of the person' would ordinarily be understood. It is also the primary sense in which the phrase, 'freedom and security of the person' is used in public international law. The American Declaration of the Rights and Duties of Man, the International Covenant on Civil and Political Rights, the European Convention for the Protection of Human Rights and Fundamental Freedoms, and the African Charter on Human and People's Rights, all use the phrase 'liberty and security of the person' in a context which shows that it relates to detention or other physical constraints. Sieghart notes that although '. . . all the instruments protect these two rights jointly in virtually identical terms, they have been interpreted as being separate and independent rights', and that the European Commission of Human Rights and the European Court of Human Rights have found that what is protected is 'physical liberty' and 'physical security'. There is nothing to suggest that the primary purpose of section 11(1) of our Constitution is different.[117]

He then emphasised the differences in wording between the foreign constitutions specifically discussed by Ackermann,[118] and responded to the arguments drawn from American, Canadian, and German law. Focusing particularly on the *Lochner* decision of the US Supreme Court, Chaskalson noted the dangers of a broad interpretation of s 11(1) for the workload of the courts and rejected (at least for the time being) the solution proposed by Ackermann.

Three points are worth emphasising in this context.

First, Ackermann emerged from this judicial dialogue with some success *despite* the rejection of his approach by the majority of the court. The opinion of Chaskalson concedes that the text could be interpreted differently in other factual circumstances, and O'Regan J already took the middle ground in the subsequent *Bernstein* decision of 1996.[119] Ackermann's interpretation could thus still bear fruit in the future.[120]

[117] At no [170].

[118] At no 175 he thus notes: 'Reference is made in the judgment of Ackermann J to the manner in which the courts have construed the Constitutions of the United States of America, Canada and Germany. It is important to appreciate—as Ackermann J is at pains to point out—that these Constitutions are formulated in different terms, and the rights protected under them are not dealt with in the same way as the rights protected in Chapter 3 of our Constitution are'.

[119] *Bernstein and Others v Bester NO and Others*, 1996 (4) BCLR 449 (CC). O'Regan J thus wrote: 'Section 11(1), however, will protect a residual area of freedom. I do not believe that this residual scope of the right should be interpreted as broadly and generously as possible. To this extent I disagree, respectfully, with Ackermann J. I also disagree, respectfully, with Mokgoro J that the right to freedom in section 11(1) should be limited to physical freedom. It is likely, given the clear entrenchment of freedoms such as expression, belief and association, that the residual scope of section 11(1) will largely concern physical freedom, but I am unconvinced that it should be limited to physical freedom.'

[120] A historical interpretation of s 12 of the 1996 Constitution would thus have to consider the following passage in the *Explanatory Memorandum* of the Technical Committee to Theme Committee 4 (of 9 October 1996): 'The right to freedom refers in this context to physical deprivation of liberty, not other dimensions of freedom which are protected by other rights, eg, freedom of assembly, religion, conscience, speech etc' (at p 35 note 2). A major concern of the majority in *Ferreira*, the strict requirements for a limitation of s 11(1), has, on the other hand, been mitigated by the Constitutional Assembly's sole reliance on a general limitation clause in the 1996 Constitution.

Second, Chaskalson did not reject the solution proposed by Ackermann J *simply because it was strongly influenced by foreign law.* Both sides used comparative law to argue their respective positions.

Finally, Ackermann's approach would have amounted to a full legal transplant, not just an expansion or development of the law on the basis of constitutional principles already contained in the 1993 text. Such 'freestanding' use of comparative law in the courtroom must be particularly controversial as judges who venture into hitherto uncharted constitutional waters inevitably slip into a highly legislative function.

5. FEDERALISM

The last example we wish to mention briefly differs from the previous transplants in that it concerns constitutional *structures* rather than rules of *substantive law.*

While governmental activity was already organised on different levels prior to 1994, South Africa was in practice under apartheid a highly centralised state in which all important decisions were concentrated at the national level. This has changed considerably under the new constitutional dispensation. Stopping short of establishing a fully federalised system, the country is today divided into nine provinces which enjoy considerable autonomy and are represented on the national level through a second legislative chamber, the National Council of Provinces (previously called the Senate under the Interim Constitution). The details of a third, municipal tier of government are set out in Chapter 7 of the Final Constitution.

Disassembling state power—as federalised, regionalised or devolved systems do in varying degrees—inevitably results in the need for some form of interaction between the various players. Kempton Park gave little thought to the problem of intergovernmental relations as negotiations focused very much on the question whether South Africa should be a federal state at all, or, as preferred by the ANC, be organised in a more unitary fashion. The lack of experience with multi-tiered forms of government may have been a second reason to neglect the issue in 1993.[121]

German experience was, however, utilised in the interim phase. The distribution of legislative competence between the national and provincial levels, the resolution of disputes within a bicameral legislature, and the composition and functions of the National Council of Provinces, itself, strongly reflect structures found in the German Basic Law.

Sections 40 and 41 of the Final Constitution are particularly interesting in that they contain principles designed to promote co-ordination, rather than competition, between the various tiers of government. This approach is very similar to the German notion of co-operative federalism (*kooperativer Föderalismus*), which is not expressly entrenched in the Basic Law but has evolved over time in constitutional practice and through decisions of the German Constitutional Court.[122]

[121] See, eg, Bertus de Villiers, 'Intergovernmental relations in South Africa', (1997) 12 South African Public Law 197, 198.

[122] See, eg, BVerfGE 1, 14 (Südweststaat) of October 1951 (competence of the Federation to restructure the south-western parts of Germany but no authority to interfere with the constitutional structures of the existing Länder as long as they are in existence); BVerfGE 8, 104 and 122 (Atomwaffen-Volksbefragung) of July 1958 (Bundestreue—mutual trust and good faith—prevents the Länder and municipalities from conducting formal consultations of their citizens on issues falling within the federal competence; Länder and municipalities are,

The Final Constitution, amongst other things, also demands respect for the constitutional status, institutions, powers and functions of government on other vertical tiers of the system and, horizontally, other provinces or municipalities, and establishes a duty to co-operate in a spirit of mutual trust and good faith. These principles are aspects of federal comity, or *Bundestreue*, which mirror the German approach to the resolution of disputes within a federal system, and have been utilised by South African courts in a number of intergovernmental disputes.[123] Examples are provided by the Final Constitution itself—the duty to foster friendly relations; to provide assistance and support; to inform of, and consult on, matters of mutual interest; to co-ordinate executive action and legislative activity; to adhere to agreed procedures; and to make every reasonable effort to avoid litigation by exhausting all other available options.[124]

The Final Constitution also calls for the establishment of structures and institutions to promote and facilitate intergovernmental relations, as well as formal dispute resolution mechanisms. The National Council of Provinces is perhaps the most important body in this respect, but additional structures were formally put in place in 2005 following gentle indications that continued legislative inactivity might otherwise prompt the Constitutional Court to play a more proactive role in the definition of appropriate rules of engagement.[125] The Intergovernmental Relations Framework Act 2005 thus provides for a number of councils which bring together key figures of the National Government and the nine provinces in order to consult on matters of common interest and co-ordinate policy approaches in specific areas.[126] These structures are replicated on the provincial and municipal tiers, and supplemented by dispute resolution mechanisms in Chapter 4 of the Act.

The notions of co-operative federalism and *Bundestreue* are thus still very much alive in South Africa today. They have, of course, taken on a different guise in structural detail and political practice, but have survived as new elements in the South African constitutional landscape. The main threat for these legal transplants is a political one. International experience suggests that co-operative governance only becomes a real issue when different

however, political entities in their own right; discussion of federal issues is part and parcel of their position as separate and distinct entities); BVerfGE 12, 205 (Deutschlandfernsehen) of February 1961 (the federation may not encroach on the competence of the Länder in cultural matters—here: broadcasting; more importantly, the Federal Government under Konrad Adenauer had infringed the principle of Bundestreue by the way it had conducted the negotiations with some Länder and set up unilaterally the legal structure for the development of a new broadcasting station); BVerfGE 61, 149 (Staatshaftung) of October 1982 (no federal competence for state liability; no legislative action despite the subsequent introduction of such a competence in 1994); BVerfGE 86, 146 (Länderfinanzausgleich III) of May 1992 (one of several decisions dealing with financial equalisation; the Federation is authorised to grant long-term financial aid to single Länder; if necessary, a restructuring of the federal territory may become necessary in order to overcome the economical disparities between the 16 Länder); BVerfGE 92, 203 (Fernsehrichtlinie) of March 1995 (strengthens the influence of the Bundesrat in decisions on the EU level).

[123] For a closer analysis see, eg, Rassie Malherbe, 'The role of the Constitutional Court in the development of provincial autonomy', (2001) 16 South African Public Law 255 *ff*; Nico Steyler, Concurrency and co-operative government: The law and practice in South Africa', (2001) 16 South African Public Law 241 *ff*; George E. Devenish, 'Federalism Revisited: The South African Paradigm', Stellenbosch Law Review 2006 (1) 129 *ff*; Dirk Brand, 'The South African Constitution—Three Crucial Issues for Future Development', Stellenbosch Law Review 1998 (2) 182 *ff*.

[124] See s 41(1).

[125] See *In re: Certification of the Constitution of the Republic of South Africa, 1996*, 1996 (10) BCLR 1253 (CC); *In re: The National Education Policy Bill No 83 of 1995*, 1996 (4) BCLR 518 (CC); *Premier of the Province of the Western Cape v President of the Republic of South Africa*, 1999 (4) BCLR 382 (CC); and *National Gambling Board v Premier of KwaZulu Natal*, 2002 (2) BCLR 156 (CC).

[126] Intergovernmental Relations Framework Act 13 of 2005.

political parties control different parts of a multi-tiered system.[127] The dominant position of the African National Congress on all levels of government in South Africa has thus far prevented serious conflicts, but as the most recent clashes within the party leadership itself show, co-operative governance may yet have a more important role to play even under these very unique political circumstances. A recent initiative of the Department for Provincial and Local Government, which in 2007 launched a campaign to explain how intergovernmental disputes should be settled, suggests as much.[128]

6. LESSONS FROM THE SOUTH AFRICAN EXPERIENCE

South Africa is today certainly located at the very top end of the scale as far as the use of comparative law is concerned. Court decisions of this country are a showcase for comparative law *in action*, providing exceptional insights into the opportunities, dangers, and practical difficulties inherent to the method. This gradual evolution was achieved through a subtle and complex interplay of legislator and judge, which is a key to the understanding of the judicial attempts to use foreign ideas to shape contemporary South African law.

Elements of German origin were used mainly in the context of human rights protection and federalism. Of the examples discussed in this Chapter, two transplants have died, two are still struggling, and two seem to be in relatively good condition. One attempt, the residual right to individual freedom proposed by Justice Ackermann, has thus far not come off the ground.

Is there a pattern which might explain these outcomes?

In terms of the *type* of law which was transplanted, the examples seem to fall into three categories—first, *substantive rules* such as the essential content clause, the application of human rights to juristic persons, the freedom of trade, occupation and profession, and a general right to freedom; second, *broad principles* such as the Rechtsstaat concept, indirect horizontal effect, or the principles of co-operative federalism and federal comity; and, finally, *institutional structures* such as the National Council of Provinces, modelled along the lines of the second legislative chamber in Germany, or the intergovernmental bodies envisaged by s 41 FC.[129] It would seem that substantive rules, though appealing because they promise to solve a particular problem also encountered in the borrowing system, are the most difficult to transplant successfully. Broader conceptual ideas offer considerable flexibility and will thus be more adaptable to their new legal environment, while institutional structures—once put in place—are the most resistant simply because of their factual existence in constitutional reality.

A second point to make concerns the importance of taking into account the wider constitutional context of a provision. The South African version of article 12 BL hit the rocks in its new constitutional context simply because its internal limitation clause runs counter to the general approach of the Final Constitution when it comes to the limitation of human

[127] On this point see Bertus de Villiers, 'National-provincial co-operation—the potential role of provincial interest offices: the German experience', (1999) 14 South African Public Law 381, 383 *f.*

[128] See the following documents published by the Department for Provincial and Local Government: *Working Together for Development. Understanding Intergovernmental Relations* (2006); *Practitioner's Guide to Intergovernmental Relations in South Africa* (2007); *Intergovernmental Dispute Prevention and Settlement* (2007); and *Intergovernmental Relations Toolkit. A Policy, Advocacy & Information Resource* (2007).

[129] The creation of a specialised constitutional court also falls into this category.

rights. Paradoxically, the legislative intent behind the transplant would probably have fared much better if the framers of the Final Constitution had redrafted the German idea in their own words rather than relying on a direct copy of the German text.

The continued use of comparative methodology as an interpretative tool in judicial practice is, third, a precondition for the survival of legal transplants. Foreign models were in many cases referred to in the submissions of the political parties involved in the transition process, and independent legal advice, including that provided by the South African Law Commission, greatly facilitated recourse to foreign law in both drafting exercises—to the point that single transplants, such as the adoption of the Rechtsstaatsprinzip and the freedom of trade, occupation and profession can be traced to the interventions of single individuals. Judges, however, by interpreting and applying law based on foreign models, ultimately emerged as the key players.

Three points should be emphasised in this context.

Within the borrowing system, legal transplants require, first, a dialogue between legislator and judge. Such dialogue can develop best under the conditions of a phased transition, which, as in South Africa, provides more opportunity for trial and error than the one-off enactment of a new constitution which will subsequently be more difficult to amend. The rejection of the essential content test by the Constitutional Assembly in 1996 and the gradual development of a local approach to the problem of Drittwirkung in South Africa provide excellent examples.

Second, comparative law offers an ideal methodological framework within which to interpret legal transplants. Foreign experience is of enormous potential here, and courts should not hesitate to look in detail at the historical background of particular provisions, and seek the insights that foreign law can perhaps provide. The court in *City of Cape Town* missed this opportunity, though one must concede that the working conditions of judges in terms of time constraints, library resources, research staff, or the opportunity to discuss the wider background of cases with experienced colleagues differ strongly on the various levels of a legal system.

The consideration of foreign law can, finally, also lead to its rejection. In *Du Plessis*, Kriegler J emphasised the unique character of the South African constitutional arrangements, and cautioned against too much reliance on foreign experience. At no [144] he added:

> Nor does the advent of the Constitution . . . warrant the wholesale importation of foreign doctrines or precedents. To be true we are to promote values not yet rooted in our traditions and we must have regard to applicable public international law. We are also permitted to have regard to foreign case law. But that does not amount to a wholesale importation of doctrines from foreign jurisdictions.

We accept this criticism, which has also featured in the opinions of judges in other legal systems. At the same time, we believe that our survey has shown the colleagues of Kriegler J to be fairly balanced in their use of foreign law. The *Ferreira* decision in particular is an example where the majority of the Constitutional Court carefully weighed the comparative arguments put forward by Ackermann J—only to reject them with a view to the specific features of South African constitutional law.

A second criticism of Kriegler J seems to be, however, more substantial. At no [147] of the *Du Plessis* decision he thus remarked:

> I find it unnecessary to engage in a debate with my colleagues on the merits or demerits of the approaches adopted by the courts in the United States, Canada or Germany. That pleases me, for I

have enough difficulty with our Constitution not to want to become embroiled in the intricacies of the state action doctrine, Drittwirkung and the like.

Kriegler J is referring here to the basic precondition of any comparative exercise, which is adequate knowledge about foreign law. He later further elaborates this point in the *Bernstein* case, criticising the depth of comparative analysis as conducted in South African courtrooms. Again we feel that both *Ferreira* and *Du Plessis* do not fall foul of the standards rightly invoked by Kriegler J, though we do concede that especially lower courts may have difficulties in this respect.

That said, not even the strongest critics of comparative law in the courtroom could deny that there are, indeed, good reasons for judges to look at foreign material. For lawyers operating in a legal system which attaches importance to the legislative intent, a comparison will not only help to show why a particular foreign model was chosen; by highlighting possible differences between that model and the national version, the meaning of one's own law may also become clearer. More importantly, foreign case law dealing with a very similar (or even identical) provision will be likely to display a range of possible solutions for disputes with a similar factual background. At the end of the day, that does not absolve judges from forming their own opinion; it may, however, expand the 'argumentative horizon' for the solution of their case and thus, sometimes, even save precious court time.

Our final observations concern the future of German constitutional law in South Africa.

Notwithstanding the fact that the conditions for the reception of foreign ideas were good, we would not be surprised to witness in the years to come a decline of German influence. The main reason for this negative prognosis is the language barrier and (closely connected to it) the limited accessibility of German case law and academic work. As pointed out, our research clearly shows that much of the influence of German law depends on the translation of German court decisions. Equally, academic input will only penetrate the system if it is presented in English; even short pieces of less well-known authors will find an audience if written in the prevailing legal language.[130] One of the most interesting results of our inquiry into the South African situation is thereby the important role of non-German authors—both South African[131] and foreign—presenting German legal ideas. These findings again support the thesis that comparative law is nowadays highly dependent on English as the emerging *lingua franca* of the legal world. If this is not recognised by German comparatists, their work (and the rich ideas which the German system as a whole has to offer) will be of limited effect in the future. This of course will take time and effort. Thus, apart from turning to its own legal roots, South Africa is, in the years ahead, more likely to have recourse to readily available comparative material from Anglo-American, Canadian or neighbouring African legal systems when it comes to the interpretation of constitutional norms originating from Germany.[132]

A legacy, unique in comparative law terms, may thus not last for long unless Germany harnesses to its advantage the power of the English language. If such a thing happened, it would, indeed, be a fascinating twist in the history of comparative methodology but not out of line with the themes explored in this book.

[130] See, eg, the frequent references to the Occasional Papers series of the Konrad Adenauer Stiftung.

[131] See, eg, the frequent citations of Blaauw, 'The Rechtsstaat Idea Compared with the Rule of Law as a Paradigm for Protecting Rights', *South African Law Journal* 1990, 76 *ff*; de Waal, 'A Comparative Analysis of the Provisions of German Origin in the Interim Bill of Rights' ; de Wet, 'Can the Social State Principle in Germany Guide State Action in the Field of Social and Economic Rights?' *South African Journal of Human Rights* 1995, 30 ff.

[132] This is recognised by South African academics such as Professors HA Strydom, André van der Walt and Venter.

5

THE SITUATION IN GERMANY

1. THE LIMITED RADIATING EFFECT OF GERMAN LAW

The presentation of German law calls for an introduction of its own, for in terms of geographical spread the system has historically never rivalled either the Common law world or French law.[1] Language difficulties as well as an inchoate suspicion or even dislike of things German still present considerable hurdles even in present times, and prevent German legal ideas from achieving the wider radiance they deserve. Its long pedigree and undoubted intellectual robustness have nevertheless earned German law not just admirers the world over but also increased attention in some quarters.

Though England has been slow to take up this challenge, South African courts, as we have seen above, have for a variety of reasons met German approaches head on and greatly benefited from them.[2]

The relationship with America is more complex, indeed in some respects intriguing, for the links are mainly of an academic rather than a judicial kind. Its traces can thus be found mainly in the American legal literature[3] and (this is one of its fascinating aspects!) more often in the works of *political scientists* whose work has a bearing on constitutional law than *lawyers proper*. The revived interest in the work of Carl Schmitt, a brilliant German scholar severely compromised by his pro-Nazi and overtly anti-Semitic tendencies, is one example that we briefly touched upon in the first Chapter.

This American interest in German 'theorising' is to a more limited extent returned by German Constitutional Court judges, for their writings and (if not as frequently as one would wish) judgments display some measure of interest in American law. German federalism is another example where one finds a (mutual) interest and even potential competition for 'new' countries seeking to imitate one or the other model. Both German and US ideas were thus considered in South Africa (where the German model arguably prevailed) and Iraq (where the outcome is still undecided). On the other hand, the truly

[1] For information on the influence of German private law on various foreign legal systems see Michael Martinek and Patrick Sellier (eds), *100 Jahre BGB—100 Jahre Staudinger* (1999). The countries covered in this volume include Austria (discussed by Theo Mayer-Maly), Italy (discussed by Giovanni Gabrielli), the United States (discussed by Joseph J Darby), Japan (discussed by Akira Ishikawa), Poland (discussed by Inetta Jedrasik-Jankowska), and the Benelux countries (discussed by Walter Pintens).

[2] For a detailed discussion of the influence of German constitutional ideas on South Africa see Jörg Fedtke, *Die Rezeption von Verfassungsrecht—Südafrika 1993–1996* (2000).

[3] For a discussion of this covert influence of German ideas on American legal thinking see J Darby, above note 1, pp 101 *ff.* Darby mentions a number of leading US scholars, including Karl Llewellyn and Joseph Beale, whose work was affected by German private law. See also Stefan Riesenfeld, 'The Impact of German Legal Thought and Institutions in the United States' in Mathias Reimann (ed), *The Reception of Continental Ideas in the Common Law World 1820–1920* (1993) and James Whitman, 'Commercial Law and the American Volk', 97 *Yale Law Journal* 156 (1987). The influence of German emigrés on US law is covered by Marcus Lutter (ed), Der Einfluß Deutscher Emigranten auf die Rechtsentwicklung in den USA und in Deutschland (1993).

amazing case law of the German Federal Constitutional Court on human rights issues remains to be discovered, though single cases—such as the decision to declare void a federal statute authorising the downing of hijacked commercial airliners by the German military[4]—have attracted considerable international attention.

Closer to its own borders, German law is more influential—if only due to the country's large population and overwhelming economic weight within the European Union. In matters of private law, current attempts to produce a European private code[5] or at least to establish common principles of law[6] are thus basically in 'German' hands (though one must also mention the 'Trento Project' run mainly from Italy). These examples—mentioned indicatively—strengthen our view, expressed here and elsewhere, that at least in matters of pure *university* scholarship there is little doubt that Italian and German comparatists dominate the scene. From the outset, and with strong *practical* effects, the German legal system was also able to exert considerable influence on the constitutional development of the European Union. The preliminary reference from national courts to the European Court of Justice on questions of Community law,[7] the principle of proportionality as developed in the case law of the ECJ and subsequently integrated in the European Treaties,[8] and distinct features of the Charter of Fundamental Rights and Freedoms[9] are examples of German thinking which have at times even permeated through the EU level and affected the purely *national* legal systems of the country's European neighbours.

But let us now turn to some specifics.

2. JUDICIAL RECOURSE TO FOREIGN LAW IN GERMANY

What follows, and which to some extent draws on the research of our German colleagues, again focuses mainly on the 'true' types of comparative law (that is, *not* situations where a court is 'obliged' by the nature of the subject or rules of conflict to look at foreign law). One must also note that in Germany the plethora of different, specialised courts means that one must distinguish between the practices of each of them. For practical purposes, however, what is of most interest are the Federal Constitutional Court (or Bundesverfassungsgericht[10]) and the Federal Supreme Court (or Bundesgerichtshof[11]), which decides cases in the areas of private, commercial, company, and criminal law.

More than half a century after Zweigert's much-cited inaugural lecture on comparative law as a universal method of statutory interpretation in Tübingen,[12] Hein Kötz, one of

[4] Case 1BvR 357/05 of 15 February 2006.

[5] See the von Bar-project.

[6] For the area of tort law see the work of the European Group on Tort Law headed by, inter alia, Professors Helmut Koziol from Vienna and Ulrich Magnus from Hamburg.

[7] See the similarities between Art 234 EC Treaty and Art 100 of the German Basic Law.

[8] For more information on the use of 'foreign' law (both that of EU Member States and countries like the United States) see Sir Basil Markesinis and Jörg Fedtke, *Judicial Recourse to Foreign Law—A New Source of Inspiration* (2006), pp 109 *ff* and Konrad Schiemann, 'The Judge as Comparatist' (in the same volume), pp 358 *ff.*

[9] Document 2000/C 364/01.

[10] BVerfG or FCC.

[11] BGH.

[12] Konrad Zweigert, 'Rechtsvergleichung als universale Interpretationsmethode', (1949/1950) 15 RabelsZ 5–21.

Germany's most respected comparatists, continues to recommend the use of comparative law by judges. But his analysis of Bundesgerichtshof decisions conducted in 2000[13] has shown little more use of foreign reasoning than did a count conducted by Ulrich Drobnig some 14 years earlier.[14] As we shall see below, both counts are disappointing. In German law and practice we thus note a picture similar in mentality but dissimilar in emphasis and intensity to that found in England.

Comparing figures from different courts is of course a dangerous exercise; and at the very least it must take into account the far larger number of judgments handed down annually by the higher German courts as compared to their English counterparts.[15] Nonetheless, on this score, it is tempting to give the lead to the recent generation of British judges, for they have proved to be more open-minded than their German counterparts. The above assertion must, nonetheless, be further qualified by proposing some important distinctions.

Taking a closer look at the use of comparative law by Germany's highest civil court, both Drobnig and Kötz identify two basic categories of decisions.

Areas in which the court *has* shown itself willing to turn to comparative law include transportation and maritime issues,[16] international commercial transactions based on the Convention on the International Sale of Goods (CISG),[17] cases dealing with international private law (for example, family law disputes),[18] and German provisions which have their origin in international treaties.[19] A further area expected to join this category includes a wide array of rules which were introduced in the wake of European legislation and explicitly aim at harmonisation (although the BGH thus far does not appear to have used comparative material in this context).[20] The common denominator of these decisions—their subject proximity to internationally harmonised rules or the conflict of laws—clearly forces judges to look out of the national window, otherwise obscured by the curtains of legal tradition. It could be argued that in this context comparative law has established itself as an essential requirement in the evaluation of many cases. The analysis of Drobnig thus shows that approximately 50% of the decisions of the Bundesgerichtshof and the Oberlandesgerichte (higher courts of appeal) dealing with the major international treaties (for example, the Warsaw Convention) make use of foreign material. Interestingly, the percentage of cases dealing with such material is significantly lower (approximately 3 per cent) with the two conventions on cheques and bills of exchange signed in Geneva in 1930/1931. This can be explained by the fact that these two conventions were *fully incorporated* into German law, whereas the other treaties were only ratified by Germany and thus remain distinctly international in character.[21] As the next part of this section will show, German law (or provisions which are at least *regarded* as genuinely German) will attract much less comparative attention by practitioners.

[13] Hein Kötz, 'Der Bundesgerichtshof und die Rechtsvergleichung' in: Heldrich/Hopt (ed), *50 Jahre Bundesgerichtshof, Festgabe der Wissenschaft, Band II* (2000), 825 *ff.*

[14] Ulrich Drobnig, 'Rechtsvergleichung in der Deutschen Rechtsprechung', RabelsZ 50 (1986), 610 *ff.*

[15] For statistical data on the caseload on German courts see Chapter Eight below.

[16] Which has been influenced by English contract law.

[17] See Art 7 CISG, which explicitly calls for comparative considerations.

[18] Art 36 EGBGB again requires comparative work.

[19] Such as the Warsaw Convention.

[20] Marcus Lutter, 'Die Auslegung angeglichenen Rechts', JZ 1992, 593 (604); Peter Mansel, 'Rechtsvergleichung und europäische Rechtseinheit', in JZ 1991, 529 (531); Walter Odersky, 'Harmonisierende Auslegung und europäische Rechtskultur', ZEuP 1994, 1 (2).

[21] Ulrich Drobnig, 'Rechtsvergleichung in der Deutschen Rechtsprechung', (1986) 50 RabelsZ 610 (615).

The second category involves cases which lack the inherent link to foreign law shared by the first group. It is this field of 'genuine' German law that most comparatists regard as the true test (*Kürprogramm*[22]) for the willingness of courts to look beyond the boundaries of their own legal system.[23] In this category of cases, the findings are meagre.

Drobnig thus identified seven decisions of the Bundesgerichtshof, one decision of the Federal Administrative Court (or Bundesverwaltungsgericht), and two decisions of the Bundesverfassungsgericht resorting to foreign law.[24] Fourteen years later, Kötz pointed to seven additional decisions of the Bundesgerichtshof, and concluded that the voluntary use of the comparative method is still confined to exceptional cases in Germany.[25] These decisions referred to issues of tort law,[26] family law,[27] labour law,[28] criminal law,[29] and administrative law.[30] Interestingly enough, Professor Bernhard Aubin, writing in 1970,[31] argued that the Imperial Supreme Court (Reichsgericht) had been more open to the use of comparative material than its republican successor.[32] Thus, 17 decisions—handed down between 1909 and 1928—made use of foreign legal material, a large number of these cases dealing with issues related to limited liability companies.[33] In another study on the use of foreign material in cases involving only constitutional issues, Professor Jörg Manfred Mössner counted 24 decisions of the Bundesverfassungsgericht which had recourse to comparative law. To these he adds two further decisions from State constitutional courts, two decisions of the Bundesgerichtshof, and one decision of the Landgericht Lübeck.[34] All these judgments involved a 'voluntary' use of comparative law and dealt with the interpretation of basic concepts of the German Constitution with the help of foreign material.[35]

[22] H Kötz, above note 13, p 832.

[23] K Zweigert, above note 12, p 9; Bernhard Aubin, 'Die Rechtsvergleichende Interpretation autonom-internen Rechts in der deutschen Rechtsprechung', (1970) 34 RabelsZ 458/459.

[24] U Drobnig, above note 21, p 611.

[25] H Kötz, above note 13, p 842.

[26] Infringement of personality rights: BGHZ 35, 363 *ff* (of 1961); BGHZ 39, 124 *ff* (of 1963); BGHZ 131, 332 *ff* (of 1995); BVerfGE 34, 269 *ff* (of 1973). Compensation for damage suffered in the course of dangerous sports activities: BGHZ 63, 140 *ff* (of 1974). Wrongful life: BGHZ 86, 240 *ff* (of 1983). Rescue doctrine: BGHZ 101, 215 *ff* (of 1987). Claims based on tort if the requirements of claims based on sales contracts are precluded: BGHZ 101, 337 *ff* (of 1987). Duty of a tortfeasor to pay compensation although the victim continues to be paid by an employer during sick leave on the basis of § 616 BGB: BGHZ 21, 112 *ff* (of 1956).

[27] BVerfGE 36, 146 *ff* (of 1973).

[28] BGHZ 24, 214 *ff* (of 1957).

[29] BGHSt 1, 293 *ff* (of 1951); BGHSt 9, 385 *ff* (of 1956); BGHSt 32, 345 *ff* (of 1984); BGHSt 38, 214 *ff* (of 1992); BGHSt 44, 308 *ff* (of 1998).

[30] BVerwGE 12, 42 *ff* (of 1961).

[31] B Aubin, above note 23.

[32] English and American lawyers (judges and academics) were also more comparatively minded during the 19th century, especially its second half, than most of their successors were during the middle years of the 20th century. One reason for this may have been the effects of the First and, even more so, the Second World War. But this can explain only the reduction in interest in German law, and the whole subject still awaits a more comprehensive examination.

[33] RGZ 74, 276 *ff* (of 1910); RGZ 77, 152 *ff* (of 1911); RGZ 79, 332 *ff* (of 1912); RGZ 80, 385 *ff* (of 1912); RGZ 82, 116 *ff* (of 1913); RGZ 84, 419 *ff* (of 1915); RGZ 123, 102 *ff* (of 1928).

[34] Jörg Manfred Mössner, 'Rechtsvergleichung und Verfassungsrechtsprechung', (1974) AöR 193 *ff*.

[35] Parliamentary system: BVerfGE 1, 144 *ff* (of 1952) on parliamentary procedures concerning money bills; BVerfGE 1, 208 *ff* (of 1952) on election principles; OVGE 12, 470 *ff* on the participation of cabinet members in parliamentary commissions of inquiry; BVerfGE 4, 144 *ff* (of 1955) and BVerfGE 32, 157 *ff* (of 1971) on the expenses of MPs. Social state principle (Sozialstaatsprinzip): BVerfGE 1, 97 *ff* (of 1951). Division of powers: BVerfGE 3, 225 *ff* (of 1953); BGHZ 10, 266 *ff* (of 1953) and LG Lübeck NJW 1953, 907 *ff*. Definition of political treaties within the meaning of Art 59(2) Basic Law: BVerfGE 1, 372 *ff* (of 1952). Prohibition of political parties: BVerfGE 5, 85 *ff* (of 1956). Extradition: BVerfGE 4, 299 *ff* (of 1955) and BVerfGE 18, 112 *ff* (of 1964). Adjudication of law enacted by the Allies during their occupation of Germany after 1945 (so-called Besatzungsrecht): BVerfGE

Just as interesting is to see which (foreign) legal systems served as models for inspiration for the German courts. In the decisions looked at by Mössner, the United States headed the list with nine examples. It was followed by Switzerland with eight, France with four, the United Kingdom with three, Austria with three, Italy with two, and the Netherlands, Norway, and Sweden each having one. The International Court of Justice was also used in one instance. Eleven cases referred to 'foreign experience' in general without identifying a particular country.[36]

These statistics suggest that courts seem more willing to look at systems outside Germany's own (private law) legal family when dealing with constitutional issues than they are in matters pertaining to private law (where comparative material is more often taken from Austria and Switzerland).[37] This would suggest that the language barrier may play a part in this 'reluctance' to consult foreign material, but that it is by no means an *insurmountable* obstacle. Especially in the early years of the Constitutional Court language proved less of an inhibiting factor since a substantial number of the justices had either studied or taught in the United States and England, or even lived there as political refugees. The studies also indicate that German courts use the comparative method with considerable caution and, in some instances, even with an undesirable (and, one might add: unexpected) degree of uncertainty. Many comparative observations are thus left undocumented, with decisions often referring vaguely and without further qualification to 'the situation in other legal systems'[38] or making use of unspecified quotations.[39] Given the German punctiliousness this is a somewhat surprising practice and may suggest lack of confidence on the part of the citing judge in the thoroughness and reliability of his understanding of foreign law. A recent decision of the OLG Celle[40] (dealing with the legality of freely negotiated fees for attorneys) gives a particularly good summary of the view that many German judges take when it comes to the scope of comparative law in court practice:

> Comparative law can reveal similarities and differences between legal systems. As a 'fifth interpretative method' [references to Peter Häberle and Konrad Zweigert omitted[41]], it can also be of assistance to the judge. The practical relevance of such an approach has, however, been very limited. Conflict of laws aside, any knowledge gained through comparative work can only have an impact where local law is 'open' and thus leaves room for interpretation [reference to Bernhard Grossfeld omitted]. Judges are, moreover, constitutionally bound by the law (Article 20 III Basic Law). This principle cannot be put in question. Finally, it must be emphasised that transplanting

2, 181 *ff* (of 1953). Analogous application of time limits: BVerfGE 4, 31 *ff* (of 1954). Validity of penal judgments pronounced in the absence of the accused: BVerfGE 1, 332 *ff* (of 1952) and BGH NJW 1965, 1146 *ff*. Right of members of the press to give evidence in criminal proceedings concerning treason: BVerfGE 20, 162 *ff* (of 1966). Freedom of expression: BVerfGE 1, 198 *ff* (of 1951). Nature of laws dealing with press delicts (State laws, not federal criminal law): BVerfGE 7, 29 *ff* (of 1957). Family law: BVerfGE 10, 59 *ff* (of 1959). Freedom of artistic opinion: BVerfGE 30, 173 *ff* (of 1971). Freedom of occupation: BVerfGE 7, 377 *ff* (of 1958) and BVerfGE 21, 245 *ff* (of 1967). Constitutional complaint (Verfassungsbeschwerde): BVerfGE 1, 97 *ff* (of 1951).

[36] JM Mössner, above note 34, p 228.

[37] U Drobnig, above note 21, p 626. We, may, by the way, be faced with a similar pattern in South Africa which in public law matters seems to be more adventurous than it is when dealing with private law.

[38] Mössner has counted 11 unspecified comparative arguments in 29 decisions. These decisions frequently use phrases such as 'the development of this area of law in other countries' or refer to 'international developments'.

[39] One example is the unspecified quotation of Cardozo in the famous *Lüth* decision of the Bundesverfassungsgericht (BVerfGE 7, 198 at p 208).

[40] OLG Celle, Beschluß vom 26. 11. 2004 (Case 3 U 250/04), NJW 2005, 2160.

[41] See our discussion of the German approach to statutory interpretation below.

legal ideas from a foreign system, especially if this system belongs to a different legal family, must be done with great caution.

Equally understandable, but perhaps also surprising, is the degree of 'mistrust' towards material from a different legal family which becomes apparent towards the end of this excerpt. This problem already emerged in one of the early leading 'wrongful life' decisions, where the Bundesgerichtshof mentioned English and American case law but cautioned against an unqualified reliance on these decisions. After emphasising the absence of comparable German cases the court thus stated:

It appears that foreign experience, which can already be of only limited value to national law because of the different legal foundations [in other countries], can be found in England and the United States.[42]

The BGH noted that the claim of the child against the doctor had been rejected in *McKay v Essex Health Authority and Another*,[43] and that legislation in Great Britain, passed a few years earlier,[44] had, similarly, excluded claims of this nature. When the Bundesgerichtshof, on the other hand, turned its attention to US law, the judges were, arguably, less accurate in their use of foreign law when citing *Curlender v Bio-Science*[45] as a decision awarding compensation to the child but failing to mention the subsequent decision of *Turpin v Sortini*,[46] which had overruled *Curlender* and given the child 'special' damages only. Nonetheless, the most surprising (and indeed disappointing) feature of this decision is the suspicion shown by the BGH towards foreign, especially non-Germanic law. We stress this since the issue before the Court was not one that depends for its solution on a specific legal provision of the German Civil Code but deals with a wider philosophical issue that transcends state borders (and even religious beliefs), and thus makes legal borrowing instructive—if not even necessary. This critical approach to comparative methodology is also apparent in a more recent judgment of the Federal Administrative Court, which stressed in 1993 that 'law is a national science'.[47]

The German legislator, by contrast, seems to be more open to the use of foreign law by judges. While not expressly *encouraged* to look abroad (as South African judges are in cases involving human rights issues[48]), German private law courts at least enjoy *full freedom* to inquire into the law of other countries wherever appropriate. § 293 of the Code of Civil Procedure (Zivilprozessordnung) thus declares that

[T]he law in force in another nation, customary law, or international conventions require proof only insofar as the court is not aware of them. In determining the content of these sources of law, the court is not restricted to the material provided by the parties; *it is authorised to also make use of other sources of knowledge, and to order any measures necessary to exploit such sources.*

The Federal Constitutional Court, too, has shown itself more open to comparative law *in general* than its private and administrative law counterparts (and again we note a certain parallel with South Africa!). Commenting in December 1953 on the rapid development of

42 BGHZ 86, 240 at p 250 (our emphasis).
43 [1982] 2 WLR 890.
44 Congenital Disabilities (Civil Liability) Act 1976.
45 106 Call App 3d 811, 165 Cal Rptr 477 (1980).
46 31 Cal Rptr 3rd 220, 643 P 2d 954 (1982).
47 See BVerwG NJW 1993, 276: 'eine national geprägte Wissenschaft'.
48 See s 39(1)(c) of the South African Constitution.

family law by German courts over the preceding eight months,[49] the FCC thus expressly included comparative law in its list of accepted and well-proven judicial techniques. The judgment stated that

> [T]he courts have quite rightly not seen it as their task to completely restructure the area of matrimonial and family law. They have rather felt themselves bound by the existing laws insofar as they are not incompatible with Article 3(2) BL. On this basis, a number of issues could easily be resolved by the judges through the adoption of quite obvious solutions. In all other cases, courts have made use of the tried and tested judicial techniques, ie legal interpretation and the closing of gaps in the law, *also with help of the comparative method*, and have taken into particular consideration the essentially unanimous demands concerning the equality of man and woman—crucial also for the purposes of legal interpretation—which have been voiced in the discussion over the past five decades.[50]

This clear, if brief, endorsement of comparative work by German judges is one of the rare cases in which the Bundesverfassungsgericht has actually indicated—in abstract terms—a position on the *methodological* status of foreign law in German judgments. This may be surprising (especially in the light of the open discussions about the merits and dangers of comparative law in contemporary US, English, and South African judgments). Yet, in part at least, it can be explained by the different style of German decisions, which are traditionally focused on the solution of a case, and will not often feature abstract methodological discussion, for example on the role of foreign law in the work of a court. One must also bear in mind that the general 'climate' in 1953 regarding comparative law was, the world over, certainly a different one than it is today.

The famous *Spiegel*-decision of 1966[51]—politically a highly controversial case which also led to divided opinions within the Court—offers more insights into the use of the method by the FCC. Here, four judges referred to foreign material in answering the question whether members of the press can refuse to give evidence in criminal proceedings involving treason, and opted against such a right. Drawing on papers presented at an international conference on the legal position of the Press in criminal proceedings,[52] the Court stated:

> The German and Swiss contributors concluded that the right [of members of the press] to refuse to give evidence should recede if information is [itself] gained through criminal conduct or if the criminal proceedings in question involve one of the (political) offences identified by the law. This corresponds to the legal approaches found in other democratic countries [reference to Swiss law omitted]. It can hardly be the aim of the Basic Law to tolerate an abuse of the freedom of the Press, a great liberal achievement designed to further a more objective approach to politics through the free and public debate of responsible citizens, in order to obstruct inquiries into serious crimes directed against the security of the State and its free basic order. Such farreaching interpretations of Press freedom must also have a negative effect on the trustworthiness of the Federal Republic

[49] This judicial 'hyperactivity' was caused by the fact that the Federal Parliament had failed to adapt all provisions of the Civil Code which contravened the principle of equality established by the Constitution of 1949. Art 117 BL had given the Federal Parliament up until 31 March 1953 to do this, and when the date passed without this task being accomplished, the Federal Supreme Court began to unpick one provision of the Civil Code after the other and re-fashion the law on a case law basis. For an account in English see BS Markesinis and S Enchelmeier, 'The Applicability of Human Rights as between Individuals under German Constitutional Law' in BS Markesinis (ed), *Always on the Same Path. Essays in Foreign Law and Comparative Methodology* (2001), vol II, ch 8.

[50] BVerfGE 3, 225 at p 244 (our emphasis).

[51] BVerfGE 20, 162 *ff.*

[52] Organised by the Gesellschaft für Rechtsvergleichung barely a year earlier.

> within an integrated alliance such as NATO, where all other members, despite the fact that their legal orders are based on essentially the same intellectual-historical traditions, regard a far more intensive protection of military secrets as something perfectly natural.[53]

This argument, which not only drew parallels to other (unspecified) 'democratic countries'—only Switzerland was mentioned by name—but also made a highly *political* case for a solution compatible with the approaches adopted by Germany's military partners, was openly rejected by the other four judges of the Senate. Interestingly, their criticism was not directed against the use of comparative law *as such* but rather at the slim factual foundation on which the comparative argument was based in this particular case. They thus pointed out:

> A comparison with the legal systems of other democratic countries is equally incapable of providing convincing arguments against the opinion presented here if this comparison is reduced to the existence or absence of one particular legal provision and fails to evaluate the other legal system as a whole—such as England and the federal law of the United States, which do not grant a right to refuse to give evidence to any profession—or to take into consideration court decisions or the democratic convictions of these societies in general.[54]

This passage indicates that the depth of comparative analysis conducted behind a court's closed doors and eventually culminating in a forceful reference to 'other' legal systems in the final draft of a judgment may in fact often not be state-of-the-art in methodological terms.

Finally, it seems noteworthy that over 80 per cent of the decisions identified by Mössner (in 1973), Drobnig (in 1986), and Kötz (in 2000) were delivered by the Bundesgerichtshof and the Bundesverfassungsgericht between 1951 and 1974; only three decisions with comparative input were identified over the past 14 years. Subject to further analysis (especially of constitutional and labour law cases), this could be an indication that the use of comparative arguments has become less frequent in German court decisions over the past three decades than was the case in earlier times. This would suggest a development which is directly in opposition with what we find in England and other countries (such as Israel and South Africa).

How can this reluctance of German judges to use foreign material—labelled as a kind of 'horror alieni juris' by Professor Hans Dölle[55]—be explained?

Apart from the influence exerted by the traditional canon of interpretative methods indicated earlier and discussed in more detail below, limited judicial time and lack of comparative input on the side of counsel might be part of the answer.[56] More importantly, it could (even in Germany) be the dearth of up-to-date comparative material, carefully compiled by specialists and packaged to meet the needs of practitioners, which might lie at the heart of the matter. Pointedly (and much in line with the views presented in this book), Hein Kötz regards the provision of such material by comparatists as 'a debt overdue to the science of

[53] At pp 220/221.

[54] At p 208. The lack of a coherent comparative methodology in court decisions is also noted by U Drobnig, above note 14, p 625.

[55] Hans Dölle, 'Der Beitrag der Rechtsvergleichung zum deutschen Recht' in: *Hundert Jahre Deutsches Rechtsleben* (Festschrift Deutscher Juristentag), Band 2 (1960), 19 (34).

[56] W Odersky, above note 20, p 4; H Kötz, above note 13, p 840.

comparative law' (*Bringschuld der rechtsvergleichenden Wissenschaft*).[57] Finally, it might also be the traditional caution of German judges to assume the role of the lawgiver wherever the rules of the system fail to provide answers.[58] Their tendency to look for solutions within the framework of positive law or acknowledged academic literature might thus make it difficult for them to use comparative law where the method is at its best. Yet doubts as to the validity of this last explanation remain. The famous decisions of the BGH and the Bundesverfassungsgericht concerning the recovery of damages for non-pecuniary loss (§ 253 BGB) are clear examples of judge-made law *contra legem*, and it is today well established that the freedom of German judges to creatively develop codified law ('die Freiheit zur schöpferischen Rechtsfortbildung'[59]) increases over time.

While a convincing explanation for the recent decline in the number of references to foreign law in German judgments would thus merit more research than was possible for us to conduct at this stage, the 'ups and downs' of comparative law in German courtrooms may ultimately be due more to the influence of individual judges or special historical circumstances rather than to any wider reason connected with the use of comparative methodology in courts. This interpretation may appear to provide an 'easy' way out of the dilemma; but it is supported by the study of Bernhard Aubin, who identified three (partially overlapping) 'waves' of private law decisions with comparative input. The first covers the years 1910 to 1924, with a sequence of six decisions of the Reichsgericht on limited liability companies within five years alone, and two further decisions on § 7 Road Traffic Act[60] and family law[61] (all eight decisions focusing on Austrian law). The second phase is between 1920 and 1928, with four Reichsgericht decisions on § 315 BGB,[62] trademarks,[63] insolvency law,[64] and § 138 BGB[65] (these decisions involve French, English, and Swiss law). The third period, finally, covers 1951 to 1961 and has a total of 11 decisions on private, criminal, and public law issues.[66] The same explanation would also be compatible with the thesis which sees in exceptional individuals—be they politicians, legislators, judges, or academics—a crucial factor for innovation, be it political or legal.[67]

Closer analysis of the material provided by our German colleagues also reveals that Bundesgerichtshof decisions with comparative input, though less numerous, are fairly evenly distributed over the decades (with a decline in the area of private law beginning only in the 1990s) whereas by far the most 'comparative' Bundesverfassungsgericht decisions were handed down in the first decade of the FCC's existence. After this initial flurry of comparative interest, the number of Constitutional Court judgments making references to foreign law dropped abruptly by approximately 66 per cent, putting the FCC roughly on par with the rate of the BGH. This particular decline of cases involving constitutional issues is likely to find its explanation in the fact that the Bundesverfassungsgericht was still

[57] H Kötz, above note 13, p 841.
[58] This is noted by U Drobnig, above note 14, p 611.
[59] BVerfGE 34, 269 = NJW 1973, 1221 (at C IV 2).
[60] RGZ 91, 269 *ff* (of 1917).
[61] RGZ 109, 243 *ff* (of 1924).
[62] RGZ 99, 105 *ff* (of 1920).
[63] RGZ 103, 359 *ff* (of 1921).
[64] RGZ 120, 205 *ff* (of 1928).
[65] RGZ 123, 102 *ff* (of 1928).
[66] See B Aubin, above note 23, pp 463 *ff*.
[67] See Sir Basil Markesinis and Jörg Fedtke, above note 8, pp 173 *ff*.

developing its jurisprudence in the early days of the Federal Republic. Called to interpret a new constitutional document born under the watchful eyes of the United States, Great Britain, and France, it seems quite logical that the court would have been particularly open to the experience of western democracies in the initial post-war phase. If this is, indeed, the answer (or at least part of it), then this could prove a pattern that could be followed by other (new) courts (such as the South African Constitutional Court) as their local jurisprudence gradually grows in diversity and sophistication. On the other hand, it is worth noting the continued vitality of comparative law in the Canadian courts.

The German Constitutional Court has also used comparative law on at least one occasion falling into this period in order to justify a constitutional provision which *distinguishes* the Federal Republic from its western neighbours.

In the famous *KPD* case of 1956, where the FCC banned the West German Communist Party on the basis of Article 21(2) BL,[68] the unanimous judgment thus held:[69]

> So it is no coincidence that the liberal democracies of the West do not have provisions banning political parties comparable to Article 21(2) BL, which was equally unknown to the Weimar Constitution of 1919 and the contemporary constitutions of the German States. The constitutional logic of these [Western] democracies—which equally, it must be noted, lack the strong legal institutionalisation and protection of political parties as offered by the Basic Law—lies in the fact that citizens are free or, as under the Italian Constitution of 1947, even encouraged to form political parties without limitation, and that the risk of a party opposing the existing constitutional order is consciously accepted; in cases of extreme danger to the existence of the State criminal sanctions will be brought to bear against the responsible individuals. This approach may be due to the optimistic conception that the best guarantee for a free democratic State lies in the views of its citizens; where there are free elections, the fight against hostile political parties can and should express itself in the denial of votes. These parties are thus excluded from influencing the political future of the State in a way consistent with the logic of democracy. During the Weimar Republic political parties could operate unfettered in Germany and fight against State institutions in every possible form although courts had ascertained that they were aiming for the violent abolition of the existing order and its replacement by their own constitutional concepts.

At the same time, the judges were also eager to find some foreign experience which could help 'soften' this seemingly harsh German approach. The same court thus continued:

> Recent developments have, however, shown that free democracies can equally not ignore the practical and political problems of excluding parties from public life which are hostile to the constitutional order if the threat to the State reaches a certain level of intensity. The solutions are not always the same. If the hostility of a certain party towards the constitutional order can already be safely concluded from historical experience, parties might sometimes already be prohibited by the constitution, itself (eg, the Fascist Party in Italy); more often—aside from interventions on the basis of criminal law, which are limited to extreme cases—administrative action against parties hostile towards the constitution will be authorised by special statutes or on the basis of

[68] Article 21 BL currently declares: '(1) The political parties participate in the forming of the political will of the people. They may be freely established. Their internal organization shall conform to democratic principles. They shall publicly account for the sources of their funds and for their assets. (2) Parties which, by reason of their aims or the behavior of their adherents, seek or impair or destroy the free democratic basic order or to endanger the existence of the Federal Republic of Germany shall be unconstitutional. The Federal Constitutional Court decides on the question of unconstitutionality. (3) Details will be regulated by Federal legislation.'

[69] BVerfGE 5, 85 at pp 135/136.

general constitutional powers. The Communist Party was thus prohibited in France and Switzerland in 1939 and 1940 by government regulations. In the United States the party was required to register in order to allow public authorities to efficiently monitor its activities as a subversive organisation.

It should also be noted that German judges use comparative arguments mainly to further *support* solutions they already seem to have reached by *traditional* ways of reasoning; foreign material is thus often mentioned only as an afterthought.[70] In this sense, the practice of the German judges seems to be comparable to their British counterparts. We have found no German equivalent to *Greatorex* (discussed in greater detail in Chapter Nine below).

Our final observations, on matters already touched upon at various points of this Chapter, concern the influence of history on constitutional interpretation (and, more specifically, the use of comparative methodology by judges).

We have argued elsewhere[71] that the German approach to statutory interpretation is more developed than that found in other systems—certainly the American. This may explain the fact that the German Constitutional Court, while not having avoided controversy itself,[72] may have not divided its citizens as much (or as often) as its American counterpart has done. On the matter of recourse to foreign law and ideas, the German rules of statutory interpretation do not, however, seem to have had any effect internally, partly perhaps because those who advocated recourse to foreign ideas failed, in practice, to carry judicial opinion with them. For the analysis of German case law presented in this Chapter has shown that the *open* use of comparative law is still a fairly rare event, both within and outside the area of constitutional litigation. Thus, though more willing to look abroad in the first years of its existence, even the FCC has, apparently, adjusted its initial outlook to the more national perspective of the Bundesgerichtshof. Whatever the reasons, and clearly many could be invoked, this is quite surprising given the historical circumstances under which the Basic Law was drafted in the late 1940s—and, indeed, even earlier. For there can be no doubt that foreign ideas exerted much influence on German thinking ever since American constitutionalism inspired the discussions in the *Frankfurter Paulskirchenversammlung* of 1848/1849.[73] Though less conspicuous in the Constitution of Weimar (1919), this influence survived both World Wars and, if at all, was further strengthened by the conditions laid down in the *Frankfurt Documents* for the eventual Allied approval of the Basic Law drafted in 1948/1949. For at that time, though refraining from an open prescription of particular provisions, the victorious countries made it clear that the new West German Constitution should be democratic, provide for a federal type of governmental structure (including the distribution of financial resources to the various levels and, more specifically, the allocation of police powers to the *Länder*), and should contain guarantees of individual rights and freedoms.[74] Even if historical analysis is only given the

[70] H Dölle, above note 55, p 37; H Kötz, above note 13, p 835; JM Mössner, above note 34, p 220; B Aubin, above note 23, p 470.[71] See Sir Basil Markesinis and Jörg Fedtke, above note 8, pp 13 *ff.*

[72] As we ourselves stress in various parts of this book by making references to specific decisions of the Constitutional Court.

[73] For more detailed information see Helmut Steinberger, 'American Constitutionalism and German Constitutional Development' in Louis Henkin and Albert J Rosenthal (eds), *Constitutionalism and Rights* (1990), pp 199 *ff.*

[74] See the text of the Frankfurt Documents in JöR 1951, 1 *ff.*

status of an additional tool and not regarded as the main method in statutory interpretation, one would therefore expect to find more comparative law in German courtrooms, especially in constitutional cases.

The answer to this riddle may, again, lie in the existence of much comparative work hidden 'behind the scenes'. Professor Alexander Somek has thus drawn attention to the influence of American thinking on judges like Gerhard Leibholz and Konrad Hesse in the development of the German equality doctrine,[75] an influence confirmed by some German observers and also alluded to ourselves when referring above to the extra-judicial writings of some contemporary German Justices.[76] Though giving this 'comparative account' some credit, Somek himself thereby challenges the view that German law has, beyond the initial identification of two levels of judicial scrutiny, indeed gone through more than a superficial phase of 'Americanisation', and that the (German) principle of proportionality could provide a better matrix for the understanding of German case law in this area.[77] This is certainly not the place to dwell on the intricacies of the German equal protection doctrine and its possible roots in American law. The degree of borrowing or, to put it in a more interesting way, the degree of resemblance or difference is, in our view, incapable of being set out clearly in a few lines since the reality is very nuanced. We do, however, submit that the true potential of comparative law in practice (beyond the inevitable influence that the experience or knowledge of individual judges must have) lies in the *open* discussion of specific points of law rather than the 'hidden' use of foreign doctrine in general.

3. JUDICIAL RECOURSE TO COMPARATIVE LITERATURE

This subsection begins with a table showing which of our comparatists has been cited by the Bundesgerichtshof and for which of their works. The figures and other information derived from this chart are, we readily admit, surprising. What is surprising is not only the low overall number of citations (in a country where judges are known for their willingness to cite academic works!) but also the almost non-existent citations to these scholars' *comparative* work.

[75] See Konrad Hesse, 'Der Gleichheitssatz in der neueren deutschen Verfassungsentwicklung', 109 Archiv des öffentlichen Rechts 1984, 174 at pp 188 *ff*; Gerhard Leibholz, *Die Gleichheit vor dem Gesetz: Eine Studie auf rechtsvergleichender und rechtsphilosophischer Grundlage* (1959), pp 36–38 and 79–81.

[76] Former Justices Dieter Grimm (a regular visitor to the Yale Law School) and Hoffmann-Riem, as well as Justice Brun-Otto Bryde are examples of contemporary judges who are fluent English speakers, have strong links with the United States, and (as former law professors) have despite their judicial duties maintained an active presence on the scholarly/academic front.

[77] See Alexander Somek, 'The deadweight of formulae: What might have been the second Germanization of American equal protection review', 1 *U Pa J Const L* 284 at 296.

Table 5.1: Authors cited by German Federal Supreme Court (BGH)

Author/country	Comparative	IPR (international private law)	German
John G Fleming (USA)	1[78]	0	0
Barry Nicholas (GB)	0	1[79]	0
Denis Tallon (F)	0	1[80]	0
André Tunc (F)	0	1	0
Ulrich Drobnig (FRG)	0	7	1
Erik Jayme (FRG)	3	14	6
Hein Kötz (FRG)	0	2	53[81]
Werner Lorenz (FRG)	0	1[82]	32[83]
Lorenz	0	6	30
Marcus Lutter[84] (FRG)	0	0	0
Peter-Christian	0	0	0
Müller-Graf (FRG)	0	0	1
Peter Schlechtriem (FRG)	4[85]	7[86]	34[87]
Christian von Bar (FRG)	1[88]	17[89]	6
Zimmermann[90] (FRG)	0	0	0
Konrad Zweigert (FRG)	2[91]	3	16

Given the very healthy state of comparative law studies in Germany and the fact that it is host to some of the best institutes for foreign and comparative law in the world, we feel that the phenomenon needs further investigation. Until such a survey is carried out in a detailed manner we tentatively offer three possible explanations.

[78] *The American Tort Process* (1988).

[79] 'Impracticability and Impossibility in the UN Convention on Contracts for the International Sales of Goods' in Galston/Smit, *International Sales* (1984).

[80] Contribution to Bianca/Bonell (eds), *Commentary on the International Sales Law* (1987).

[81] *Deliktsrecht* (now with Gerhard Wagner in its 10th edn): 3; *Münchner Kommentar*, Allgemeine Geschäftsbedingungen: 46; other: 4.

[82] Contribution to Ernst von Caemmerer (ed), *Vorschläge und Gutachten zur Reform des deutschen internationalen Privatrechts der außervertraglichen Schuldverhältnisse* (1983).

[83] Of which 31 citations to Staudinger, *Kommentar zum Bürgerlichen Gesetzbuch* (various editions).

[84] There are no citations of Marcus Lutter. 'Lutter' is cited in 127 cases, of which 125 deal with German law only (mostly company law) and two with EEC law.

[85] *Festschrift für Rheinstein* (1969): 2 and *Festschrift für von Caemmerer* (1978): 2.

[86] Citations in the context of CISG.

[87] Of which 17 citations to Jauernig/Schlechtriem, *Bürgerliches Gesetzbuch* (various editions).

[88] On comparative Swiss, Austrian, English and French international private law.

[89] *Staudinger*-von Bar, EGBGB: 4; *Internationales Privatrecht* (Bände 1 und 2): 8; *Europäisches Gemeinschaftsrecht und Internationales Privatrecht*: 1; other: 6.

[90] There are no hits for 'Reinhard Zimmermann'; 'Zimmermann' is cited in 50 cases, of which only one citation is comparative (Swiss law).

[91] Both citations refer to: Möhring/Schulze/Ulmer/Zweigert, *Quellen des Urheberrechts, Länderberichte* (Stand 30.VI.1971).

(a) Positivistic Tradition

First is the German positivistic tradition, which requires that court decisions are based, so far as possible, on the written German legal texts. These texts, though more detailed than, say, their French counterparts, inevitably require further exegesis and elaboration. This interpretative work is done with the help of the major (German) commentaries, monographs, and quite regularly even leading student textbooks. The figures we have been able to collect thus support the view that it is to this kind of text that the German judges turn to for further enlightenment. The need to go beyond their borders for elaboration or inspiration is thus not evidenced by citation of works on foreign on comparative law.

Table 5.1, which contains the most cited works of the German comparatists, shows how true this statement is. Citations of two very practical works by Professors Barry Nicholas and Denis Tallon also suggest that this pattern is broken only when a court can find guidance in an intensely practical and useful work on comparative law or conflicts of law. These findings conform to the thesis consistently advanced in this book. The perennial meagreness of statistical data prevents us, however, from using these figures as conclusive evidence of the wider thesis that comparatists are themselves to blame for not having any impact on the real world of law because of the nature of the things they write about. But the temptation is obviously there!

(b) The Prevailing Methods of Interpretation

Secondly, in Germany comparative methodology is generally not recognised as a tool for the interpretation of legal provisions (Gesetzesauslegung). Most German academics (both in private and public law) rather focus on the wording of statutes (grammatikalische Auslegung), the discovery of the lawgiver's intention (teleologische Auslegung), the legal context of a given provision (systematische Auslegung), and the historical background of a piece of legislation (historische Auslegung).[92] This traditional canon of legal interpretation is adhered to even if German law has not addressed a particular question, and only dedicated comparatists will openly point to foreign solutions as a source of inspiration and to comparative law as an accepted interpretative tool.

In the field of private law, Konrad Zweigert argued 50 years ago in favour of comparative law as a universal method of interpretation (universale Interpretationsmethode);[93] and Peter Häberle is perhaps the most prominent contemporary constitutional expert to consistently promote comparative law as a 'fifth interpretative method' (fünfte Auslegungsmethode).[94] But as Ulrich Drobnig pointed out in 1986, the conservative attitude of mainstream academic opinion (so-called herrschende Lehre) has influenced generations of lawyers in Germany, and is clearly reflected by the approach generally taken by the courts in the interpretation of the law.[95]

[92] See, eg, Hans Brox, *Allgemeiner Teil des BGB* (25th edn 2001), pp 38–44; Ingo von Münch, *Staatsrecht* (6th edn), pp 11–13.

[93] K Zweigert, above note 12.

[94] Peter Häberle, *Rechtsvergleichung im Kraftfeld des Verfassungsstaates* (1992), pp 27 *ff.*

[95] U Drobnig, above note 14, p 611.

(c) Competing Sources of Comparative Material

We have, moreover, already noted in the previous Chapters the important role that various academic institutes have played in developing both the study of foreign law and comparative methodology in Germany. Paradoxically, these institutions may also have contributed indirectly to the poor citation record of foreign material by German courts. This is because of the widespread practice of obtaining from academics written opinions about the state of foreign law whenever such knowledge is required by the rules of private international law, and many court libraries have over time acquired extensive collections of such expert opinions.[96] Similarly, the Bundesverfassungsgericht has on many occasions asked the German Foreign Office to provide reports on foreign legal systems (which subsequently do not appear in the text of the judgment itself),[97] and has even invited foreign experts to report directly to the Court.[98]

4. COMPARATIVE LAW IN THE FIELD OF LEGISLATIVE LAW REFORM

Finally, we note that the suspicion towards foreign law described above is not reflected in the law reform process when undertaken by the legislator.[99] Hans Dölle has thus demonstrated that the German lawgiver has made extensive use of foreign material over the past 100 years. Starting with the preparation of the Commercial Code (*Handelsgesetzbuch*) of 1897, which was influenced by an Austrian proposal as well as Dutch, Spanish and French ideas, Germany has constantly turned to other countries (including the United Kingdom, France, Spain, Norway, Sweden, Switzerland, Austria, and the United States) in order to gather new ideas for codification. This has occurred in such diverse areas as commercial law, design patents and copyright law, bankruptcy law, civil procedure, anti-trust legislation, criminal law, and the regulation of nuclear energy. The *Bürgerliches Gesetzbuch* of 1900 and the *Grundgesetz* of 1949, undoubtedly the two most prominent pieces of German legislation, were both influenced by comparative work.[100]

This obvious difference between the use of foreign material in the course of legislation as contrasted to adjudication by German courts can be explained by the freedom (and indeed the function!) of the lawgiver to mould society according to the prevailing political convictions of the time. Courts of law, on the other hand, must respect the notion of legal certainty (Rechtssicherheit) and are thus less free to import foreign solutions to a given problem.[101]

Notwithstanding this greater openness, one must also note that in such exercises the German legislator tends to rely on what *German* academics have said about foreign law *in*

[96] H Dölle, above note 55, p 47.

[97] BVerfGE 49, 286. A subsequent legislative initiative relates to the material gathered for the proceedings (see BT-Drucks. 8/2947, p 13).

[98] BVerfGE 7, 377 (415/416).

[99] JM Mössner, above note 34, p 204; Helmut Coing, 'Aufgaben der Rechtsvergleichung in unserer Zeit', NJW 1981, 2601 (2603); P Mansel, above note 20, p 531.

[100] H Dölle, above note 55, pp 22 *f.*

[101] JM Mössner, above note 34, pp 208 and 211.

German, and seems reluctant to make open use of the original material which emanates from other jurisdictions. This is confirmed by our own research, which was focused on the three pieces of legislation shown in the chart below—the regulation of standard contract terms in 1975,[102] the reform of the German law of obligations in 2001,[103] and the reform of German tort law in 2002.[104] We stress that our analysis is restricted to the explanatory sections of the respective government proposals. It can therefore only serve as a starting-point for a more detailed survey, which would have to include, inter alia, the preparatory work conducted within the ministries responsible for individual reform projects, the work invested by single legislators, the results of ministerial or parliamentary commissions and hearings, and any written opinions submitted by external experts, institutes, or pressure groups.[105] This material could in fact reveal direct access to foreign material.

On first glance, references to foreign law found in these important reform projects can be classified into three distinct categories.

The first category consists of *general references* to the situation in other legal systems. These are not attributed to any particular author, and include statements on the law in specific countries or regions. Though not appearing in the table, it is significant to note that the explanatory sections of many German bills refer to the legal situation in 'other systems' or (with regard to the European Union) in 'other Member States' *without* pinpointing particular jurisdictions. These generalised statements indicate that more comparative work has, in fact, been done behind the scenes even though it is not apparent from the published material, itself.

The second category contains references to the situation in other legal systems as described in *German* sources.

Finally, foreign law is also taken into account by the direct use of *foreign* authors and research projects. The following table may thus be of use.

Table 5.2: References to comparative law in selected German reform projects

	General references	German sources	Foreign sources
Contract terms	France Israel Italy Sweden United States Yardin **Council of Europe**	Hauss Neumayer Quittnat Raiser von Hippel	None

[102] Entwurf eines Gesetzes zur Regelung des Rechts der Allgemeinen Geschäftsbedingungen, Deutscher Bundesrat, Drucksache 360/75.

[103] Entwurf eines Gesetzes zur Modernisierung des Schuldrechts, Deutscher Bundestag, Drucksache 14/6040.

[104] Entwurf eines Zweiten Gesetzes zur Änderung schadensersatzrechtlicher Vorschriften, Deutscher Bundestag Drucksache 14/7752.

[105] See, eg, Wilhelm Consulting, *Study on the possible economic impact of the proposal for a directive on the sale of consumer goods and associated guaranties* (1998) and the extensive material published by the Federal Ministry of Justice on the reform of the German law of obligations: *Gutachten und Vorschläge zur Überarbeitung des Schuldrechts* (1981) and *Abschlußbericht der Kommission zur Überarbeitung des Schuldrechts* (1992).

	General references	German sources	Foreign sources
Obligations	Austria France GDR Greece Italy Netherlands Scandinavia Switzerland United Kingdom European Court of Justice European Union UN Sales Law	Basedow Kessler Stoll von Caemmerer Zimmermann Zweigert/Kötz	Bucher (Switzerland) Jud/Welser (Austria) Lando Lando/Beale Saleilles Treitel Viney Lando-Commission Unidroit
Tort law	ADR Treaty CRTD Treaty EC Directive 2407/92 EC Directive 2027/97	Braschos Diedrich von Bar	None

A closer look at these references reveals that the kind of foreign material that has been used for information and inspiration is in all cases specific, focused and informative rather than speculative, sociological or anthropological—further confirmation of the theses found in this book about the kind of comparative work which has a tangible impact on legal practice.

Comparative considerations found in the *Schuldrechtsreform* (triggered by the need to give effect to several European Union directives, but also designed to address some significant structural defects of the German Civil Code) thus focus largely on five key areas—pre-contractual liability (*culpa in contrahendo*), the collapse of the basis of a contractual agreement (*Wegfall der Geschäftsgrundlage*), standard contract terms (*allgemeine Geschäftsbedingungen*), irregularities of performance (*Leistungsstörungen*), and rules on prescription (*Verjährung*). As the following three examples show, foreign law is often used to argue in favour of an *overall change* in approach or structure, whereas German law is drawn upon as far as the *specific details* of a reform proposal are concerned.

Thus, the idea to codify pre-contractual liability (§ 311 BGB) is discussed with references to developments in France as described by authors as old as Raymond Saleilles and as contemporary as Geneviève Viney. Similar concepts in the United States are invoked by reference to Friedrich Kessler. The Swiss approach is described by Andreas Bucher, who also gives a reference to Article 1337 of the Italian Codice civile. The final solution, however, is exclusively based on German case law.[106]

This is also true of the references to foreign law found in the context of the reformed § 313 BGB, which codifies the doctrine of *Wegfall der Geschäftsgrundlage*. While drawing attention to Italian, Greek, and Dutch law as an argument for the proposed codification of the doctrine, the draft clearly attempts to develop the substance of the notion along the lines of German case law. Codification is thereby set in contrast to the situation in England, the United States, Switzerland and France as described by Konrad Zweigert and Hein Kötz.

[106] Deutscher Bundestag, Drucksache 14/6040, pp 161–3.

These countries rely on case law to resolve problems resulting from a drastic change in the basis of a transaction (as Germany did until the enactment of the *Schuldrechtsreform*).[107]

Similarly, the inclusion of standard contract terms in the BGB,[108] until recently regulated in a separate statute, is justified by reference to the Dutch Nieuw Burgerlijk Wetboek of 1992 and similar recommendations put forward by the Lando Commission. Despite this *structural* change, the *content* of this new section reflects German law.[109]

In other areas, foreign sources are used as a guideline for quite substantial changes. This is true, for example, for the new system of *Leistungsstörungen* (irregularities of performance). Impossibility (*Unmöglichkeit*), late performance (*Verzug*), faulty performance (*Schlechterfüllung*), and the so-called 'positive breach of contract' (*positive Forderungsverletzung*) are now substituted by a unitary notion (*Pflichtverletzung*) codified in the new § 280 BGB. This substantial change is justified by references to international developments in general, the work of the Lando Commission, as well as the approach taken by the UN Convention on the International Sale of Goods.[110] Another example is the introduction of a rule dealing with the termination of long-term contracts (*Dauerschuldverhältnisse*) in § 314 BGB. The extensive reference to Articles 1559–1570 Codice civile and Article 73 of the UN Convention on the International Sale of Goods indicate that these two codifications have had a strong influence on the German solution.[111] Further areas where foreign sources functioned as a model in the reform of the German law of obligations include the termination of contracts (*Rücktritt*),[112] the reform of § 321 BGB (dealing with the significant deterioration of a party's financial position in mutual contracts),[113] and the rules on prescription.[114]

Finally, comparative considerations in some instances serve to *confirm* the German position, and foreign solutions are openly *rejected.* This is true, for example, for the decision to uphold the notion of fault as a central requirement for contractual liability. The issue was discussed in the Government proposal on the *Schuldrechtsreform* and contrasted to the Anglo-American approach as outlined by Konrad Zweigert and Hein Kötz.[115]

As far as the reform of tort law is concerned, comparative considerations feature in two areas. The introduction of a general claim for pain and suffering (*Schmerzensgeld*) in situations covered by strict liability and in contractual relationships is justified with references to the situation in other European countries as presented by Franz-Joseph Braschos, Christian von Bar, and Frank Diedrich.[116] It must be stressed, however, that this comparative input merely serves as an *additional* argument to underscore a change already initiated by German developments.[117] A second reference to international trends as described by von Bar deals with the protection of passengers in the course of non-commercial and free transportation,[118] a problem already addressed and solved by French courts some 30 years ago.

[107] Deutscher Bundestag, Drucksache 14/6040, pp 174–6.
[108] §§ 305–310 BGB.
[109] Deutscher Bundestag, Drucksache 14/6040, pp 92, 149–60.
[110] Deutscher Bundestag, Drucksache 14/6040, pp 133–7.
[111] Deutscher Bundestag, Drucksache 14/6040, pp 176–8.
[112] Deutscher Bundestag, Drucksache 14/6040, pp. 180–189.
[113] Deutscher Bundestag, Drucksache 14/6040, pp 178–80.
[114] Deutscher Bundestag, Drucksache 14/6040, pp 98–125.
[115] Deutscher Bundestag, Drucksache 14/6040, p 131.
[116] Deutscher Bundestag, Drucksache 14/7752, p 15.
[117] Deutscher Bundestag, Drucksache 14/7752, pp 24–26.
[118] Deutscher Bundestag, Drucksache 14/7752, p 31.

In line with its solutions, the draft proposes to include this category of victims in the existing strict liability regime.

Some final observations can be made on the sources used in the process of comparative law reform. For (obvious) legal and (less apparent) political reasons,[119] the *Schuldrechtsreform* in particular draws heavily on international material. As pointed out above, solutions offered by the UN Convention on the International Sale of Goods, the Principles of European Contract Law published by UNIDROIT, and the work of the Lando Commission were adopted by the Government proposal in a great number of cases. Without endorsing excessive harmonisation, we think that this tendency of the German lawgiver to resort to refined concepts as found in model codes or principles of law marks the way for any comparative effort. To have impact, comparative work must be focused on clearly defined issues and produce ideas which can be easily used in the process of law reform or in the decision of cases.

A second observation concerns the language of the foreign material used in the process of German law reform. As stated, most references concern material which is presented in German. Apart from the German sources (for example, on American, English, French, and Swiss law), this is true of the general references to Austria, Switzerland, and the German Democratic Republic, as well as the specific references to Andreas Bucher (on Swiss law) and Brigitta Jud and Rudolf Welser (on Austrian law). The large number of unspecified references to the UN Convention on the International Sale of Goods found in the explanatory section of the *Schuldrechtsreform* can equally be counted to this category, as it seems that exclusively German authors writing on this corpus of law were consulted in developing the draft.[120] The close legal and cultural ties between Germany, Austria and Switzerland thereby only explain the frequent use of material from these two countries, and the fact that American, English, French or Israeli law is accessed by reference to *German* academics rather than original sources calls for other explanations. A number of these citations probably result from practical factors, such as the accessibility of German material or limited linguistic resources (as in the case of the reference to Israeli law as described by Joachim Quittnat[121]). In other cases, it might be the condensed form in which some prominent German authors have presented a fairly wide range of foreign material. This observation is especially true for *Einführung in die Rechtsvergleichung* by Konrad Zweigert and Hein Kötz and *Gemeineuropäisches Deliktsrecht* by Christian von Bar. Yet other German comparatists are cited because they discuss foreign law in direct context with the topic of a given reform project; this is obvious in the case of *Die Reform des Deutschen Kaufrechts* by Jürgen Basedow, who is cited frequently in connection with the *Schuldrechtsreform*. Though difficult to ascertain on the basis of this limited survey, the impulse to rely on information which has been converted into familiar terminology and concepts, and the effects of national reputation and influence of acknowledged German academics, might be additional factors which influence the choice of comparative sources by the German legislator.

To conclude this short excursion into the realm of law reform on a cautious note, we again stress that our observations merely serve to open the door to a fairly unexplored terrain. The influence of comparative law on legislation deserves closer analysis, which will,

[119] Transforming a number of European directives into German law, the Schuldrechtsreform is also a move to secure the position of the BGB as a model for a future European codification.

[120] Authors mentioned in this context include Hans Dölle, Johannes Huber, Peter Schlechtriem and Hermann Weitnauer.

[121] Deutscher Bundesrat, Drucksache 360/75, p 11.

hopefully, reveal more intricate patterns than was possible on the basis of the 300 very condensed pages of legislative explanation that we were able to look into at this stage.

5. 'APPLIED' COMPARATIVE LAW IN GERMANY—SOME TENTATIVE CONCLUSIONS

We have in this Chapter tried to assess the relevance of 'applied' comparative law mainly in the areas of litigation—with emphasis on the jurisprudence of the Federal Constitutional Court and the BGH—and (legislative) law reform. Different conclusions need to be drawn for each sphere.

The results are fairly disappointing when it comes to the use of comparative methodology in German courtrooms, though it would seem that the difficulties stem less from fundamental objections of the kind found, for example, in the opinions of Justice Antonin Scalia of the US Supreme Court but have their roots, rather, in a legal tradition which instinctively seeks to discover most (but not all) solutions in indigenous sources of law and their exegesis via the four well-trodden paths of German statutory interpretation (wording, legislative intent, context, and historical background). Despite this limitation, there thus exists a space that comparative law can *legitimately* occupy in German court practice, and it is for those dedicated to applied comparative work to fully unlock the potential of their subject by identifying gaps or contradictions in the law (Interpretationsspielräume[122]) and offering practically relevant solutions with the help of foreign ideas.

European integration, to which Germany is more open than most other countries in the region, will in many cases provide considerable assistance in this quest. We thus predict that—given time—the trenches between legal systems (and any corresponding unwillingness of local traditionalists to engage with foreign approaches to particular legal problems) will be determined less by the affiliation of single countries with legal families (an increasingly questionable private law concept of the past) but rather their status or not as members of the European Union; decades of convergence will eventually render, in principle, French or English solutions just as acceptable, to German eyes, as Austrian or Swiss answers. A closely related factor is the increased need for a more extensive and systematic horizontal judicial dialogue between courts across the European Union (in addition to the rather lively vertical dialogue between national courts and the European Court of Justice). In the absence of a dual court structure as it exists in the United States, harmonisation and/or the unification of law in Europe will only work if national courts start taking into account on a regular basis the interpretation of Community law by their counterparts in other Member States. This will inevitably lead to closer and better organised judicial co-operation, the wider spread of knowledge about foreign law, and a greater appreciation of the fact that better answers can sometimes be found—ready for use—beyond the national borders of a legal system. These changes might even spill over to areas which at present still lie outside the ever widening ambit of Union competence.

More importantly, even the most entrenched judicial instincts can change over time. John Henry Merryman and Rogelio Pérez-Perdomo in their third edition of *The Civil Law Tradition* thus maintain that 'the judge [in civil law systems] is a functionary, a civil servant;

[122] OLG Celle, above note 40, p 2161.

the judicial function is narrow, mechanical, and uncreative'.[123] This view may have been an accurate description of civil law judges and their modus operandi when the first edition of the book was published in 1969; the amount of creative judicial work not only in the constitutional field but also, for example, in the areas of tort law, family law, labour law, and social security have, however, fundamentally changed German (and French!) court practice over the past decades. Palandt, a thick practitioner's guide to the Bürgerliches Gesetzbuch, is thus published on an annual basis *not* because the German legislator is so active in amending the BGB (the 31 provisions of the Code dealing with tort law were, for example, left unchanged for over a century) but rather because of the need to make accessible to legal practice the immensely important *case law* of courts on all levels of the system. To think that the Code, itself, provides the answers to all legal problems was never true, a fact that is today openly acknowledged. This profound change in the role of German judges as 'oracles of the law' is fully endorsed by the Federal Constitutional Court, which declared that the separation of powers principle certainly precluded

> courts from assuming authority which the Constitution clearly allocates to the legislator. Article 20(3) BL binds the judiciary to law and justice. It would contradict this principle if the courts were to shift their role in applying the law [Normanwender] to a position involving the creation of law [normsetzende Instanz]—objectively releasing them from the abovementioned restrictions of law and justice. *These constitutional principles do not, however, prohibit the judge from developing the law. In the light of the increasing pace of societal change and the limited ability of the legislator to react to this change, as well as the open-ended language of many legal provisions, adaptation of the existing law to changed circumstances must, on the contrary, be regarded as a function of the judicial branch.*[124]

So German courts may, in principle, develop the law; their freedom to go beyond or even against the black letters of a statute gradually increases with the age of a given piece of legislation; and in doing so judges need not restrict themselves to traditional methods of interpretation but can also utilise foreign law without risking the kind of attacks that have been launched against some of their more open-minded American colleagues by politically conservative hardliners in the US Senate and House of Representatives.[125] That said, we also predict that the breathing space for applied comparative law in day-to-day litigation will always remain a more limited one in Germany than in many courtrooms across the Common law world. Despite the changes outlined in the previous paragraph, the spirit of codification—and the complex (if not *complete*) constitutional, administrative, social security, private, or commercial law infrastructures that come with it—inevitably reduces the number of cases in which foreign ideas should be given due consideration.

The remaining differences seem to disappear, however, as far as the legislator is concerned. Justice Scalia himself thus argued in *Printz v United States*[126] that comparative analysis was

> inappropriate to the task of interpreting a constitution, though it was of course quite relevant to the task of writing one.

And US Attorney General Alberto Gonzales (as he was then), an outspoken critic of comparative methodology in the courtroom, finds it

[123] John Henry Merryman and Rogelio Pérez-Perdomo, *The Civil Law Tradition. An Introduction to the Legal Systems of Europe and Latin America* (3rd edn 2007), p 38.

[124] BVerfGE 96, 394 *ff* (emphasis added). See also the recent decision of the Federal Constitutional Court in the Marlene Dietrich decision, NJW 2006, 3409.

[125] For an account of the conservative reaction to the use of foreign law by judges of the US Supreme Court see Jeffrey Toobin, *The Nine* (2007), pp 191–9.

[126] *Printz v United States*, 521 US 898 (1997).

entirely appropriate for our elected representatives in the Congress or the State legislatures to consider how lawmakers in other countries have approached problems when our representatives write the laws of the United States.[127]

This corresponds to the situation we found in Germany, where foreign ideas seem to influence legislative decisions on a regular basis, and the position in England, where the Law Commissions Act of 1965, for example, authorises the English Law Commission to 'obtain such information as to the legal systems of other countries as appears to the Commissioners likely to facilitate the performance of any of their functions'.[128] The overall impact of foreign ideas on the legislative output in these three systems may still be very different in practice, of course, but there is at least some agreement on both sides of the Atlantic that comparative experience may—in principle—be used by the legislator.

The contrast to the bitter controversy surrounding comparative methodology as an interpretative tool in the United States (and here particularly in the field of constitutional law) and the relatively calm reactions that we find in Europe calls for an explanation. Subject to further research, we suspect that the *real* distinction between 'the task of interpreting a constitution' and 'the task of writing one' may well lie in the ability of the legislator to control the final outcome of important societal conflicts. The *appointed* judge may well be a less legitimate 'clearing house' for foreign influence than the *elected* lawmaker, and the greater the power of courts to provide authoritative answers to core political and moral questions, the more we can expect other 'local' players (the legislator in particular, but also academics or the media) to criticise any recourse to foreign ideas in the courtroom by invoking democratic principles and division of power arguments. This is currently true of the United States. If the legislator, however, retains the potential to overrule the judiciary via constitutional amendment, as in South Africa under the political dominance of the African National Congress or in the United Kingdom with its unwritten and highly flexible constitution, we can expect far less tension to arise if judges do look abroad for inspiration. In this respect, Germany—with its *entrenched* but nevertheless *amendable* constitutional arrangements, which place only a limited number of core values beyond the legislative reach—seems to represent the middle ground.

Another point, which will be covered in greater detail in a separate Chapter, is the use of comparative law in German commercial practice. Here, Europe is (yet again) a strong stimulant, and German entrepreneurs seem to have embraced the opportunities that come with greater legal mobility within the European Union—for example in the areas of company and insolvency law. At the same time, national legal systems continue to place considerable limits on cross-border activities, and require companies with an international reach to build up in-house expertise or to seek specialised outside legal counsel on a wide range of issues including foreign data protection legislation, environmental law, labour law, and consumer protection. These barriers are of course particularly onerous for countries with a strong focus on export. Germany has been able to quite regularly claim top positions when it comes to the total value of its exported goods over the past decades, and it is this particular characteristic of the German economy which will in the future continue to create a high demand for lawyers with a solid grounding in foreign law and comparative methodology.

[127] Alberto Gonzales, Attorney General, Prepared Remarks at the University of Chicago Law School (9 November 2005), available at http://www.usdoj.gov/ag/speeches/2005/ag_speech_0511092.html.

[128] Sec 3(1) English Law Commissions Act (1965).

The final question, then, is whether the German *academic* world has adapted to the various challenges posed by the increasing globalisation of our world. Despite the low citation rate that comparatists currently enjoy in German courtrooms, the starting point is certainly a strong one due to the long tradition of comparative law at German universities and—more importantly—the extensive network of specialised institutes that spans the country. We were not able to conduct a detailed quantitative analysis of the German research output over the past years, and remain sceptical as to the insights that may be gleaned from such assessments[129]; as close observers of that particular academic scene, we do however get the impression that the overall volume of publications with a comparative focus (journal articles, monographs and postgraduate work) is currently at a fairly high level. A more important indicator for the status of comparative law as an *applied* discipline, however, is the fact that two of the most prestigious commentaries on the German Civil Code—the *Münchner Kommentar* and *Staudinger's Bürgerliches Gesetzbuch*—now feature in their respective sections on the BGB surprisingly extensive reflections on the legal situation in foreign (predominantly European and American) jurisdictions. So while it is certainly true that 'of the six or so most authoritative and extensive commentaries on the German Civil Code and extra-code law of obligations, none has been translated into English',[130] the opposite is not: German students, academics, judges and practitioners enjoy a constant flow of accessible and regularly updated contextual information about selected legal issues in the most important foreign jurisdictions.

While this openness strikes us as indefinitely more attractive from an intellectual point of view than the rather provincial thinking endorsed by Professor Jane Stapleton when she laments about the 'mono-linguist's problems' and, in essence, encourages Common lawyers to make do with whatever ideas and innovation can be found within the limited confines of the English-speaking world,[131] there are also a number of practical considerations which militate for a more enlightened approach. We wish to highlight two. There is, as indicated above, the need to cater to the needs of an internationally competitive economy, which requires a great amount of knowledge about the legal approaches relevant for the development of trade relations with a large number of systems across the globe. And there is, second, also a competitive advantage when it comes to the survival of national ideas on the global and, more importantly, the European stage. As Professor Ulrich Magnus put it on occasion of a colloquium organised by the publishers of the *Staudinger* commentary in 1998:

> Only if we are ready to take into consideration foreign solutions when commenting [the German Civil Code], to incorporate them in our work, and to use their standards to compare and test our own [German] solutions, will . . . the core elements of the BGB stand a chance to survive the next 100 years.[132]

This is an excellent starting point from which to revive the interest in comparative law as an applied discipline, and can only help to cultivate the practical approach to the subject as presented in this volume.

[129] For some information on the use of particular terms such as law, droit and Rechtsvergleichung in the *Neue Juristische Wochenschrift* (a leading—general—German law journal) see Mathias S Siems, 'The End of Comparative Law', Center for Business Research, University of Cambridge Working Paper 340.

[130] Jane Stapleton, 'Benefits of Comparative Tort Reasoning: Lost in Translation', Journal of Tort Law, vol 1 [2007], Iss 3, Art 6, p 34 of the online version (http://www.bepress.com/jtl/vol1/iss3/art6).

[131] *Ibid*, pp 33 *ff*.

[132] Ulrich Magnus in *J von Staudingers Kommentar zum Bürgerlichen Gesetzbuch mit Einführungsgesetz und Nebengesetzen. 100 Jahre BGB—100 Jahre Staudinger. Beiträge zum Symposion 1998* (1999), p 158.

6

THE RELUCTANCE TO BORROW IDEAS FROM ABROAD: TWO STRANGE BEDFELLOWS— THE UNITED STATES AND FRANCE

1. OPENING REMARKS

In this Chapter we focus mainly on comparative public law, this time putting under the microscope the United States and comparing its practices with those found in France. This is a mighty task incapable of being achieved in a satisfactory manner in such a short space. The aim, however, is not to exhaust the inexhaustible material but to suggest one or two themes worthy of further investigation, and voice some personal doubts and criticisms. We have thus attempted this task because we believe that what we touch upon here can help illustrate even more vividly than the previous Chapter the importance of the political background when attempting to understand judicial decisions, especially in the domain of public law.

This does not mean that political differences, which we suppose one would bracket under the rubric *cultural differences*, impede comparison or lend credence to Legrand's thesis that differences in mentality and culture make it impossible for legal borrowing to take place, or for rules to converge. The fact that some of these political or cultural attitudes have changed backwards and forwards in both countries (dragging with them the attitudes of lawyers towards foreign law) helps demonstrates this essential fluidity. This, in turn, means that the system may vacillate between phases of greater convergence or marked divergence. This is particularly true of France at the time of writing. For approximately half of the country seems to be experiencing the euphoria brought by a new and hyperactive new President who promises to introduce changes—including in the way higher education is organised, run, and funded—that could entail legal changes in the direction advocated here and, above all, in a way which would suggest convergence and not divergence with Anglo-American ideas. The emphasis on this different (but constantly evolving) socio-political background merely means that one must weigh it carefully when attempting to understand, describe, and then compare foreign law with one's own.

The comparison with France will also point out some surprising (and disturbing) partial similarities between the current approach which the two systems take towards foreign law and the comparative method. Nonetheless, as we shall suggest, the shared suspicion towards using foreign law may stem from different psychological attitudes. Thus, while the American neglect of foreign law may, in the past at least, be linked to the self-confidence (some might even describe it as arrogance) that has taken grip of the American scene since the neo-conservatives came to power (and may only die down if the setbacks in Iraq and Afghanistan grow further in number and intensity), the French suspicion towards non-French ideas may be nourished by the very opposite feelings of doubt, fear, and even lack of self-confidence. For their attachment to the French language (admirable), educational system (in need of modernisation), and regulatory framework (in need of replacement), may explain the disappearance of a public consensus as to France's future economic and international orientation.

In the case of France, therefore, the 'foreign' is not ignored because it is useless or irrelevant but because of the fear that it could absorb and dilute what is 'French'. The French have, after all, already suffered (unacceptable) challenges by the appearance of the American fast food industry on some of their most famous avenues, which now display the signs of that industry, not to mention the direct challenge to their (old) predominance in matters of dress styles, music, theatre, and cinema—in short, an all-out assault on the whole front of aesthetic values which by common consent formed for centuries a core element of the so-called 'western' civilisation.

The excursus into wider cultural attitudes apart, this Chapter remains true to the general spirit of this book. For it stresses the need for greater use of foreign law; it invokes, again, the important role—negative or positive—played by judges in this exchange of ideas; and it also underlines the many challenges which face those who wish to promote international dialogue, which can only be achieved if the task is undertaken in a positive frame of mind and with the emphasis being placed on concrete situations, especially those which call for similar answers. This is another way of saying that what follows will neither appeal to nor be adopted by those (few) contemporary comparatists who see nothing but difficulties and unbridgeable gaps separating the legal systems of today.

The authors of the present work do not share this starting point; and the growing literature on the subject discussed here demonstrates that the international dialogue, with the partial exception of the United States, is gaining momentum. We shall suggest, tentatively and for the sake of further exploration, that such signs of revival as we find in the contemporary French scene are coming from the courts and not the academics who, on the whole, remain handicapped by restrictive educational practices, as well as their (national?) preference to look at the broad picture and describe the current globalisation debate in rather sweeping terms. The expression 'the devil is in the detail' thus seems to be ignored in France, so far as we can judge being unknown even as a figure of speech.

2. THE UNITED STATES—THE OPEN SOCIETY

The United States is one of those countries where societal and cultural factors have changed and with them have also changed the attitudes towards having an intellectual dialogue with foreign colleagues. Countries go through open and closed phases, and the legal history of the United States shows this most clearly. During the periods of expansion and openness they are ready to seek inspiration from abroad; during the periods of introspection or self-sufficiency they close themselves into themselves.

Many reasons account for this. They can be political, ideological, or economic. Introverted or extroverted outlook may be determined by a constitution (the American coming under the first category, the South African under the second). Alternatively, these attitudes may depend upon the presence or absence of charismatic personalities, active as legislators, judges or (occasionally) academics. France has not been immune to this pattern; but here we begin by focusing on the United States, currently the only truly global power.

One aim is to explore the links between legal attitudes and political trends, especially in the area of foreign relations; another is to touch upon how countries such as France may be affected by the above.

During the 18th and 19th centuries American law was open to foreign influences. The draftsmen of its Constitution took advantage of foreign ideas, legal as well as philosophical. One suspects ideology as well as pragmatism—the need to re-assure the international community that the new state was not going to behave like a rebel and unruly regime—played their part in forming such an open mind. In the 19th century foreign creativity, especially judicial creativity, was welcomed and not seen as an attempt to interfere with American life. English statutes, mainly on matters of private law, would thus reach the westward expanding United States with a time lag of anything between 10 and 20 years.[1] Decisions of the highest English courts would also be followed, within about the same period of time, unless local conditions made their adoption undesirable.[2]

The same applied to Pothier, and even the Code civil, as America—for political, ideological as well as aesthetic reasons—often found itself admiring things French. Occasionally (and increasingly), local courts also developed the courage to challenge the wisdom of the progenitor system, displaying not only growing intellectual confidence but also the flexibility that is found in societies which have the mixed blessing of a shorter tradition.[3] The reasons given for distinguishing or rejecting the parent model were thereby often informative about both systems—the imitator and the imitated.

Initially, the relative 'poverty' of American law was undoubtedly an additional reason for this willingness to borrow; but, as stated, it was not the only one. Throughout the 19th century we find American jurists of very high intellectual standing progressively interested in both the laws of France and Germany, and not only England. This interest was not limited to the writings of the great Continental jurists but also extended to innovative legislative schemes introduced by European states.[4] By the turn of the 20th century, the German professoriate was, as an institution, one that came to be held in high esteem among many jurists of renown in the United States (as it was in France), while the celebration of the first centenary of the Code civil attracted a fair amount of discussion (Napoleon, himself, coming in for much praise).[5] Even the (short-lived) German school of 'free thinking' found adherents in the United States, notably in Roscoe Pound, long-serving Dean of the Harvard Law School.

This interest in German thinking received further and very concrete impetus from the mid 1920s onwards as Karl Llewellyn's teaching experiences in Germany gradually began to

[1] For instance, Lord Campbell's Act of 1846. For the American statutes see Speiser, Recovery for Wrongful Death (2nd edn 1975).

[2] For instance *Rylands v Fletcher*, 1865, 3 H & C 774, 159 ER 737, reversed in *Fletcher v Rylands*, 1866, LR 1 Ex 265, affirmed in *Rylands v Fletcher*, 1868, LR, 3 HL 330, a decision establishing a general rule of strict liability for the accumulation of any substance on the defendant's land likely to do mischief if it escaped. In the case in question, the substance accumulated was water (to assist a local milling industry), which escaped through some disused mine shafts and flooded the land of the plaintiff. In Texas, where water was and is a scarce commodity and its accumulation should be encouraged and not penalised, the courts refused to follow the English ruling. See *Turner v Big Lake Oil Co*, 96 SW 2d 221 (1936) and Leon Green in 38 *Texas L Rev* (1959), 5.

[3] Eg, *Lawrence v Fox* 20 NY 268 (1859) where the New York Court of Appeals essentially decided to depart from the traditional common law doctrine of privity and recognise contracts in favour of third parties.

[4] As, for instance, Bismarck's social legislation of the 1880s, which attracted much attention in the State of New York.

[5] A website search of the articles that appeared in American law journals on the centenary of the Code civil shows them to be more than double in number than those that were published on occasion of its 150th year, while the number of articles mentioning, let alone celebrating, the (recent) bicentenary was a mere trickle.

be imported into American law and even reflected in the Uniform Commercial Code. Though this flirting with Continental Europe decreased rapidly as the Second World War approached and placed Germany under the grip of the Nazis, the end of the War brought to the United States many first-class minds. They represented a second, unwilling, and more concealed wave of Germanic ideas crossing the Atlantic and enriching many law schools such as Harvard, Yale, Chicago, Columbia and, later, Berkeley and Texas—to mention but a few. At the same time law schools such as Tulane, respectably anchored in the civilian tradition, did a good job in keeping interest in French law alive, especially in the days of Professor Ferdinand Stone, who proved a most genial ambassador for the study of comparative law in the United States. In this climate, even the Digest found its way into a number of American decisions as 'supportive' authority used to alter existing American law in the context of claims brought by the injured foetus,[6] though the borrowing was not always complete or well understood. This transatlantic movement of ideas has been documented by various authors and need not occupy us further.[7] Towards the end of this Chapter, however, we shall express our concerns about its current decline.

3. THE UNITED STATES—CONSTITUTIONAL LAW AND STATUTORY INTERPRETATION

Unlike the developments briefly sketched in the previous section, which concerned the domain of Common law (Europeans might, in this case, use the word 'private' law with equal accuracy), the same pattern of imitative thought was not to be found in the domain of constitutional law and statutory interpretation,[8] not at any rate as the 20th century began to wane. The radical difference of the American Constitution as a single, written and entrenched document made it immediately distinguishable from that of England; but the differences in judicial interpretation were to become even more obvious in the area of judicial review of legislation—an indigenous development which has no real parallel in England and France, found an approximate equivalent in post-Second World War Germany, but which in more recent times was destined to serve as a model of exportation to most modern democracies.[9] This was, indeed, one of the 'triumph' areas of indigenous law and proved highly exportable in practice (though the success of judicial review in contemporary German constitutional law has not yet been adequately noted—largely, we suspect, due to language-related difficulties).

In the United States, judicial review became more than an issue of legal interpretation in the years that followed the Second World War—it became so seriously intertwined with political arguments and philosophy, especially during the years of the Warren and Burger Courts,[10] that foreign commentators run the risk of seriously misunderstanding American

[6] *Bonbrest v Kotz*, 65 F Supp 138 (DDC 1946).

[7] For an excellent collection of essays see Mathias Reimann (ed), *The Reception of Continental Ideas in the Common Law World 1820–1920* (1993).

[8] Justice Scalia makes the point with great clarity in *A Matter of Interpretation. Federal Courts and the Law* (Princeton University Press 1997).

[9] Among the rich literature see Anthony (now Lord) Lester, 'The Overseas Trade in the American Bill of Rights', (1988) 88 *Columb L Rev* 537 *ff.*

[10] Earl Warren was appointed by President Eisenhower and held office between 1953 and 1969; Warren E Burger was appointed by President Nixon and was at the Supreme Court between 1969 and 1986.

constitutional law books and judicial decisions if they do not learn to appreciate the influence of contemporary American political debates and the importance of the main judicial protagonists of that period. Judicial review was thus increasingly seen by the Right as undemocratic, as it allowed unelected judges to marginalise the powers of Congress.

The importance of the Warren and Burger Courts lies, of course, in the series of liberalising decisions announced in the 1960s and 1970s, which greatly extended civil rights in a whole range of areas of daily life. The American 'Right'[11] hated many of these liberty-enhancing decisions of the Supreme Court, especially *Roe v Wade*,[12] which they always believed had no roots in the Constitution. Even liberals like Professor John Hart Ely have described *Roe* as 'not law and not making any effort to pretend to be law'.[13] Of course there are theories by which *Roe* is derived from the Constitution, but the Right utterly rejects those explanations. So the problem the Right diagnosed to lie at the root of American society was unbridled judicial discretion leading to constitutionalising the political preferences of the Left,[14] and the remedy was to end (or try to end) judicial discretion and tie judicial power to a narrow and formalistic theory of interpretation. If the Founding Fathers of the American Constitution did not say it, the judges could not do it. The theory of 'originalism' or 'textualism'—expounded by academics such as Robert Bork (Yale Law School) and now finding its most consistent and forceful proponent in Justice Antonin Scalia of the United States Supreme Court[15]—was thus born. Nowadays, it finds strong support in the neo-conservatives who are increasing their grip on the American political establishment.[16] Outsiders find this emphasis on original intent or understanding enormously perplexing, not least because most of them are aware of the degree of differences which separated the Founding Fathers on a host of important issues, which were only thinly papered over in the famous Federalist Papers.

The importance of this development, made possible by the fact that most of the writing available on interpretation was dedicated to Common law and not constitutional or statutory interpretation, is crucial for the understanding of all that follows. It must also be combined with two other developments of relatively recent vintage. The first is that the Supreme Court, especially during the Rehnquist years, has asserted a monopoly on constitutional interpretation or, as one American commentator has put it, '[T]he Rehnquist Court's activism explicitly denies the people any role in determining the ongoing meaning of their Constitution, other than by the grace of the Justices themselves'.[17] The second, accepted only by the originalists, is that when interpreting statutes, the consequences of interpretation are to be disregarded. Thus, whether in dealing with the Constitution or with

[11] Though in modern Europe the terms 'Right' and 'Left' are—happily—losing much of their original appeal (as most parties with real pretensions for power realise that they must occupy the central ground), in America they are still widely used and have thus been retained here but without the use of inverted commas.

[12] 410 US 113, 93 S Ct 705 (1973).

[13] 'The Wages of Crying Wolf', 82 *Yale LJ* 920 (1973).

[14] Many lawyers have, naturally, linked this to civil unrest on American campuses in the 1960s, which began with the liberalising trends of the early 1960s and were then reinforced by the reaction to the Vietnam War.

[15] *A Matter of Interpretation: Federal Courts and the Law* (Princeton University Press 1997); 'The Rule of Law as a Law of Rules', (1989) 56 *U Chi L Rev* 1175; and 'Originalism: The Lesser Evil', (1989) 57 *U Cin L Rev* 849. Some of his underlying theories also come through in 'Assorted Canards of Contemporary Legal Analysis', (1990) 40 *Case W Res L Rev* 581.

[16] See, eg, the views of John Bolton, former US Ambassador to the United Nations: 'Should We Take Global Governance Seriously?', (Fall 2000) vol 1 no 2 *Chicago Journal of International Law* 206 *ff.*

[17] Larry D Kramer, 'The Supreme Court 2000 Term Foreword: We the Court', 115 *Harv L Rev* 4, 130 (2001). In similar terms, Sarah K Harding, 'Comparative reasoning and Judicial Review', 28 *Yale J Int'l L* 409, 449–50 (2003).

federal statutes, Justice Scalia and his followers[18] believe themselves to be interpreting a legal text (enacted at a particular time and place) in terms of the original understanding of that text (the understanding at the time of its enactment) and the understanding within the polity entitled to enact it. For the same reason, these judges refuse to look at the legislative history of statutes. They do look to the legislative history of the Constitution, and their explanation for how that is consistent does not seem very convincing, but they look to constitutional history for evidence of original 'understanding'. They sometimes assert the relevance of the traditions of the American people, but mostly to narrow down a constitutional text, not to expand it. As stated, for the same reasons they also claim to give little weight to the consequences of statutory interpretation; and none at all if the statute is clear. In Scalia's view, federal judges should have no discretion to make law or policy. Though, of course, he is not so naive as to think such discretion can be stamped out, he views its survival as a defect in the system, resulting from the inability of legislators and constitution writers to be sufficiently clear and specific. Federal judges thus do not make law—they interpret law that was enacted, and they interpret it on the basis of original understanding.

Three points flow from this belief.

It is, first, totally alien to prevailing European thought, which has come to accept the law-making power of judges. Secondly, it is alien to the kind of interpretation which English judges have adopted when interpreting Caribbean constitutions containing provisions very similar to those found in the American Constitution (for example, the Eighth Amendment).[19] Finally, it is in this context that one must place the current dislike of the conservative judges of the US Supreme Court towards foreign ideas, even if they are used as a mere source of inspiration and thought, and nothing more. We thus see how this wider understanding of the American Constitution makes it conceptually impossible for foreign law to cast any light on the question of interpretation. And if this happens in the courts, at any rate in matters concerning federal law, then the study of foreign law and comparative methodology in the classroom is also likely to be affected. If neither of these two consequences has really occurred it is because the Supreme Court has, until now, been in practice divided on these issues.

[18] In summer 2005 this meant Chief Justice Rehnquist and Justice Thomas.

[19] A notable difference between the English and American approaches can be found in the area of how constitutions should be interpreted. This is what Lord Bingham of Cornhill had to say on the matter in *Charles Matthews v The State* No 12 of 2004, 2004 WL 1372517 at p 8: 'The task of expounding a constitution is crucially different from that construing a statute. A statute defines present rights and obligations. It is easily enacted and as easily repealed. A constitution, by contrast, is drafted with an eye to the future. Its function is to provide a continuing framework for the legitimate exercise of governmental power and, when joined by a Bill or Charter of Rights, for the unremitting protection of individual rights and liberties. Once enacted, its provisions cannot easily be repealed or amended. It must therefore be capable of growth and development over time to meet new social, political and historical realities often unimagined by its framers. The judiciary is the guardian of the constitution and must, in interpreting its provisions, bear these considerations in mind. Professor Paul Freund expressed the idea aptly when he admonished the American courts "not to read the provisions of the Constitution like a last will and testament lest it become one".' Of course, though one is inclined to admire the Bingham approach more than that of Justice Scalia, this does not mean that it is acceptable to those conservative judges who take the Scalia line. To put it differently, in comparative law one must not assume that a value judgment on a particular interpretative approach also means that it is transferable to a different legal system. Still, the reader must note that Lord Bingham is buttressing his approach on how constitutions should be interpreted by quoting a distinguished Harvard constitutionalist; and this must clearly suggest that such an approach could be adopted in the United States.

4. THE DIVIDED (SUPREME) COURT

The above has been intended to stress a point an observer of foreign law can easily miss. Simply put, it is this. The ability to read a foreign text does not mean that the reader will understand foreign law. This is an error which even high British judges have occasionally committed.[20] It is also a mistake that 'amateur' comparatists not infrequently make, especially when they demand that comparative law be limited to Anglophone countries.[21] Indeed, in one sense, the more learned such a judge is in his own law, the greater the risk that he will 'fill in gaps' in what he does not entirely understand by subconsciously transposing his own solutions and ideas into the foreign landscape. What we stressed above suggests that constitutional law generally requires sensitivity towards politics. Without this, the foreign observer is bound to go astray.

Yet, if beyond this point we also gave the impression that the American interpretative techniques are monolithic, then we have misled the reader. For the reality is that the American Supreme Court is not monolithic and never has been. Its decisions often depend upon shifting alliances between what is, at present, a court consisting of three right wingers, three liberal, and three shifting (but otherwise) conservatively inclined judges. To make matters both more intriguing and more complicated for foreign observers, this composition can (and will soon) change (with long-term effects). For each time an incumbent President appoints justices who reflect his own—right or liberal—point of view, the effects on law and thus society can be as serious as his most important foreign or economic policy decisions, and often more lasting in terms of time. Thus, at the time of writing, President Bush's success in appointing two conservative judges to the bench seems to have resulted in one highly conservative voice (Alito) and one likely conservative voice (in the form of the new Chief Justice John Roberts) altering the old balance. How decisive this shift may prove to be will depend on how adverse (in extent) will be the consequences of President Bush's adventures in the realm of foreign relations. The latest decisions of the US Supreme Court on abortion and positive discrimination suggest that the court is, indeed, moving to the 'right' with Justices Stevens, Breyer and Bader-Ginsburg remaining the only consistent liberal voices.

In the spring of 2005 a recorded[22] and subsequently reprinted[23] debate took place in France between the then first President of the Cour de cassation, M. Guy Canivet, and Justice Steven Breyer of the US Supreme Court. Its significance is such that we have chosen to discuss it in more detail in one of the following Chapters in order to leave our readers with an enduring memory of two senior justices talking of comparative law in a way which comes very close to the various theses advanced here. But if we see in this exchange a clear

[20] See, eg, the criticisms of Lord Cooke in 'An Impossible Distinction', [1991] 107 *LQR*, 46, pp 57 *ff.*

[21] See, eg, Jane Stapleton, 'Benefits of Comparative Tort Reasoning: Lost in Translation', (2007) Journal of Tort Law (Article 6). The error here is in treating foreign scholarly work or decisions as a kind of precedent (which no full-time comparatist has, to our knowledge, ever suggested) and not as a source of ideas or reflection. The same goes when one is invoking foreign law in order to prove how a particular institution, for instance assisted euthanasia, has worked in other systems. Here comparative law is only providing empirical evidence of how a rule has worked.

[22] To access the internet version of this debate see http://www.radiofrance.fr/chaines/franceculture2/emissions/bien_commun/fiche.php? diffusion_id=49499.

[23] See http://www.culturedroit.com/pages/culture-droit-1-le-voisinage-des-cours-supreme-a-l-heure-du-village-mondial-stephen-breyer-guy-canivet.htm.

(albeit indirect) vindication of what we are calling for, it does not mean that we do not also see in it some of the pitfalls of comparative law—the generalisations against which Carbonnier warned[24] or the over-simplifications which Scalia attacked in his dissent in *Roper v Simmons*.[25] Indeed, in our conclusions we express the most severe reservations for the image of American law that Justice Breyer tries to project every time he is in the company of his French hosts.

Espousing the general philosophy of a judge or academic does not mean that we feel obliged to follow him in everything he says or feel constrained in criticising him when, in our view, he says it unconvincingly. One of the few advantages which academic lawyers have over judges and practitioners in today's world is the ability, indeed, *obligation* to remain intellectually independent. This independence includes the ability to see the weaknesses in the presentation of their own preferred views and then try to rectify them. Falling in love with one's own theory is a temptation to which we have all, at some time or another in our careers, succumbed; but a constant attempt must be made to avoid this pitfall. A careful analysis of our text (and the deliberate credit we give to some of our intellectual opponents) must show that we have at least tried to abide by this principle. But why all these comments and observations?

The answer is simple: in his debate with President Canivet, Justice Breyer's presentation of American law and its attitude towards foreign law conveys the impression that it is monolithic, clear, and unambiguously in favour of what he (and we) would like it to be. For better or for worse it is not; and we will later *try*—and the word 'try' is deliberately italicised in order to indicate the tentative nature of our suggestions—to understand/explain this rather inexplicable presentation of American law. Here, therefore, we shall limit our observations to highlighting the divergence of views and stressing some of the advantages that flow from the opposing arguments.

It is thus one of the primary functions of comparatists to warn national lawyers against the danger of thinking that they can understand foreign law simply because they have mastered a foreign language, learned something about foreign law in the course of their own readings, or listened to a great figure from that system pontificate about his law. Nine times out of ten, such presentations, for understandable but sometimes also inexplicable reasons, will only give part of the picture. The understanding and exegesis of foreign law is an art that has to be learned, often by trial and error; and it is, as we have explained in detail elsewhere,[26] best begun by comparing comparable and relatively narrow factual situations. Such 'low-level' comparison gives reassurance to the novice since it makes him realise that the problem he is studying also exists in his own system. Later, this analysis can then be expanded progressively in a way that concentrates on more detailed aspects of the law, then the political system, and ultimately the foreign society itself. The excitement grows as the focus broadens and the whole picture begins to emerge.

What then is the current attitude of the Justices of the US Supreme Court on matters of foreign law? Before attempting to answer this question, let us clarify a few more immediate points.

First, we are not here talking of cases where foreign law is applied because the rules of conflict of laws so require.

[24] Jean Carbonnier, 'A beau menir qui vient de loin' in *Essais sur les lois* (1995), pp 227 *ff*.

[25] 125 S Ct 1183, 1222 *ff* (2005).

[26] *Comparative Law in the Courtroom and the Classroom. The Story of the Last Thirty Five Years* (2003).

Nor, secondly, are we talking of foreign law in the sense of public international law (though even this is currently under attack in the United States, which is showing an open hostility towards customary international law and little respect for international human rights law).

Nor, finally, are we thinking of a set of rules that may be applicable because two or more countries are subject to the decisional law of some supra-national court (for example, the European Court of Justice).

What we are talking about is the quantitatively few but qualitatively important type of cases where national law is silent, dated, or contradictory, and the national judge asks himself whether he might be allowed to seek inspiration from the practice of other sister courts.

Remaining always with the US Supreme Court, the answer to our question is both simple and confusing since its judges rarely speak with one voice. All one should say is that despite our preceding comments, in two of the most controversial and oft-disputed types of cases (the availability of the death sentence and homosexual rights) the liberal wing of the court seems, *at present*, to be winning. Yet, for a variety of reasons, we shall argue (or at least consider the possibility) that the conservative, originalist, textualist view (which we emphatically do *not* share) can be the more consistent, is certainly the most strongly phrased and vivaciously advanced, and—in some respects—could even be regarded as the most stimulating of the two positions one can adopt on such matters. Let us take these comments in turn.

5. CONSISTENCY IN OPPOSING FOREIGN LAW ON THE GROUNDS THAT IT IS IRRELEVANT

Those who oppose the use (in any form) of foreign law are (fairly) consistent in their rejection of its relevance. They have also managed to erect a theory—originalism—which, despite its (many) drawbacks, provides a fairly common platform. On the other hand no such common core or theme unites the opponents of this school, as Scalia has been quick to point out and exploit in his extra-judicial writings. One must acknowledge that much; and do so with admiration since we live in times when opportunism—even judicial opportunism—flourishes.

One must also clarify that it is not only foreign ideas they wish to stop from influencing the interpretation of statutory texts; it is also local ones. For Scalia, the originalist,[27] believes that, whether he is dealing with the Constitution or with federal statutes, he is interpreting a legal text, enacted at a particular time and place. To understand and apply it, all he needs to know is the understanding of the text at the time of its enactment by the polity entitled to enact it.[28] What we in Europe call 'historical interpretation' receives sole attention; and any 'purposive' or 'teleological' interpretation is deliberately ignored. With such a starting

[27] See *A Matter of Interpretation: Federal Courts and the Law* (Princeton University Press 1997); 'The Rule of Law as a Law of Rules', (1989) 56 *U Chi L Rev* 1175; 'Originalism: The Lesser Evil', (1989) 57 *U Cin L Rev* 849; and 'Assorted Canards of Contemporary Legal Analysis', (1990) 40 *Case W Res L Rev* 581.

[28] Though this has, occasionally, allowed him to attempt some fairly bold interpretations of the original understanding of the draftsmen. See, for instance, *Kyllo v United States* 533 US 27 (2001): a thermal control device, checking from the outside premises to detect whether cannabis is grown within, can be treated as violating the unlawful search and seizure clause of the 4th Amendment.

point, the possibility of foreign law casting any light on the enactment in question is excluded—*indeed, such an approach precludes foreign law before one even gets to other reasons which make many American judges hostile towards foreign ideas.* If the law he has to apply is bad or outdated, the change should come from the appropriate legislature. But it is not for the (unelected) judge to impose his moral values on society through legal sophistry aided by selective foreign borrowings. This, at least, is the creed of those who subscribe to this school of thought; and to us it suggests that they are again trying to be as consistent as possible in setting out their theoretical objections to going outside the Constitution when interpreting its provisions.

Scalia's liberal opponents do not deny the fact that they, too, have to interpret the American Constitution; but they do give themselves more freedom as to where to look for inspiration. Thus, in *Printz v US*,[29] Justice Breyer, after citing European practices, added that:

> Of course, we are interpreting our own Constitution, not those of other nations, and there may be relevant political and structural differences between their systems and our own . . . But their experience may nonetheless cast an empirical light on the consequences of different solutions to a common problem—in this case the problem of reconciling central authority with the need to preserve the liberty-enhancing autonomy of a smaller constituent entity.

On this issue, which is the one that concerns us here, Justice O'Connor recently expressed similar views when she stated that

> this Nation's evolving understanding of human dignity certainly is neither wholly isolated from, nor inherently at odds with, the values prevailing in other countries. On the contrary we should not be surprised to find congruence between domestic and international values, especially where the international community has reached clear agreement—expressed in international law or in the domestic laws of individual countries—that a particular form of punishment is inconsistent with fundamental human rights.[30]

Earlier, in *Atkins v Virginia*,[31] Justice Stevens stressed in a note that used evidence of wide-spread foreign practices that although this was

> by no means dispositive, their consistency with the legislative evidence lends further support to our conclusion that there is consensus among those who have addressed the issue.

As a result of such thinking (and evidence), the execution of mentally retarded criminals was seen as being prohibited by the Eighth Amendment. More recently, the same happened in the case of murderers who were under the age of 18 at the time they committed their crimes.

The above citations suggest that a sizeable section of the United States Supreme Court does not see a clear-cut divide between American and international values, certainly in times such as ours when national borders have become porous and notions of justice as well as taste seem increasingly to be cut out of the same cloth. Of course, as already stated, many in the United States (especially liberal academics)[32] do not share this view and insist that on

[29] 521 US 898, 977 (1997).

[30] 125 S Ct 1183, 1215 (2005). This citation is important. For, though the way foreign law was presented to the court and used by it may leave much to be desired, it does show that five out of nine judges were, in principle, not opposed to the idea of looking at foreign law.

[31] 536 US 304, 316 n 21 (2002).

[32] For an excellent collection of essays (limited, however, to public law) see Michael Ignatieff, *American Exceptionalism and Human Rights* (2005).

a whole range of issues (such as, for instance, the death penalty, homosexual rights, or child chastisement) Americans should be willing to engage in dialogue with those who have different ideas to offer.

On closer analysis America is a very diverse country and does not hold monolithic views. This diversity covers the whole spectrum of life, wealth, welfare, and ideas. Naturally, it could not exclude law. Even on the death sentence, for example, a legal/political issue as widely debated and divisive as that of abortion, opinions differ greatly. What we must try to understand is not the different opinions, but the different shades in practice. Thus, though a majority of States have the death sentence on the statute books, nearly a third of them refuse to carry it out.[33] A closer analysis of such statistics does not reveal as clear a national consensus as the American Right believes there is—or is, invariably, suggested by opinion polls. For how else can one explain the fact that the death sentence is formally retained but not carried out? A partial but plausible explanation is a dislike of it (especially in the light of some much publicised errors in convictions) combined with the lack of political courage to abolish the penalty altogether.

Yet even if we are wrong in our hypothesis, namely that the general public is in favour of the death sentence, we feel Arthur Chaskalson, the recently retired President of the South African Constitutional Court, put the matter correctly in the South African death penalty case when he wrote:

> [I]f public opinion were to be decisive there would be no need for constitutional adjudication. The protection of rights could then be left to Parliament, which has a mandate from the public, and is answerable to the public for the way its mandate is exercised, but this would be a return to parliamentary sovereignty, and a retreat from the new legal order established by the 1993 Constitution. By the same token the issue of the constitutionality of capital punishment cannot be referred to a referendum, in which a majority view would prevail over the wishes of any minority. The very reason for establishing the new legal order, and for vesting the power of judicial review of all legislation in the courts, was to protect the rights of minorities and others who cannot protect their rights adequately through the democratic process. Those who are entitled to claim this protection include the social outcasts and marginalised people of our society. It is only if there is willingness to protect the worst and weakest amongst us, that all of us can be secure that our own rights will be protected.[34]

Roper's use of foreign ideas in a 'supplementary' manner is attractive. Yet its full implications still have to be worked out. For it gives no clue when this is permissible and when it is not.[35] Most (but not all) of the foreign material used by the US Supreme Court has been in the context of the death penalty and homosexual rights; and it has been brought into play be relying on the Eighth Amendment that prohibits 'cruel and unusual punishment', a phrase with a special meaning when it was enacted, but which must now be interpreted against the background of 'changing circumstances' or, as the Eighth Amendment jurisprudence calls them, 'evolving standards of decency'.[36]

[33] Thus, at the time of writing, there exist 12 'abolitionist' States, 24 States which recognise the death penalty but rarely practise it, and a further 14 'executing' States. With the exception of Arizona, the other 'executing' States coincide with the so-called 'bible-belt' area of the United States.

[34] 1995 (3) SA 391, para 88 (CC).

[35] See, eg, Justice Scalia's point in *Roper v Simmons* 125 S Ct 1183, 1228: 'To invoke alien law when it agrees with one's own thinking, and ignore it otherwise, is not reasoned decision-making, but sophistry'.

[36] This trend to look at foreign practice to help determine what was meant by 'evolving standards of decency' began with the decision in *Trop v Dulles,* 356 US 86 (1956) and remained unchallenged until *Thompson v Oklahoma* 487 US 815, at 869–70 (1988), decided two years after Justice Scalia joined the Supreme Court. For details see Professor Michelman's elegant contribution to the *Ignatieff Essays* (above note 26), pp 241, especially at pp 245 *ff.*

But can/should this also come into play in instances which do not involve the Eighth Amendment? For instance in cases where 'due process' or 'equality' is involved? This has not happened yet; but it is interesting to note the technique of treating wide, if not open-ended, sentences in statutes as 'entry points' for broader values. So it is tempting to draw an analogy, without taking it too far, to the famous notion of *Drittwirkung*, which entered into German private law through the general clauses of the Civil Code and allowed constitutional values to influence private law disputes.[37] In 'cruel and unusual punishment' terminology one sees something not so different. For broader values were allowed to come in and reshape the content of rules which for decades had fixed meanings.

Likewise, those who have advocated the use of foreign law do not seem to have given clear guidance whether it can be used to enlarge rights (contained in the Constitution) or also restrict them. Up to now, the practice of the Supreme Court has been to use foreign ideas to extend rights—hence the complaints by the American Right. Jurists who tend to oppose the use of foreign law have tended to see this point as an important one, and thus raise the question given at the beginning of this paragraph.[38] Could one, for instance, invoke the German Constitution[39] or the most recent decision of the Strasbourg Court in the Caroline case[40] and argue that privacy should be balanced against free speech and, thus, restrict the famous First Amendment? For us, by parity of reasoning, the same answer—in principle—should apply whether one is using the foreign model as a reason to expand or restrict local rights. For, ultimately, what really matters is the convincing force of the foreign rule and not whether it expands or restricts national law. One can imagine, however, the howls of anguish that would come from a section of American society, especially the press, at this prospect.

Finally, those who advocate the use of foreign law have also failed to address the question in what form this material should be introduced to the (potentially) borrowing court and how best this should be considered by it. We will return to this important objection below.

These 'omissions'—taken as a whole—are seen by those who oppose the use of foreign law as a sign of loose or incomplete thinking on the part of those who favour the open model. The conservatives, on the other hand, enjoy the benefit of a clear and unswerving rule. Or so at least they believe.[41]

6. STRONGLY PHRASED REJECTION OF RELEVANCE OF FOREIGN LAW

The opponents of foreign law have also had an impact through the strong and emotive use of language they have used to express their opposition to it. This may not be particularly appealing to jurists—especially those operating in Europe, accustomed as they are to

[37] The famous Lüth decision of 15 January 1958 of the Constitutional Court explains this most clearly; see BVerfGE 7, 198 (= NJW 1958, 257).

[38] See, eg, Michael D Ramsey, 'International Materials and Domestic Rights: Reflections on Atkins and Lawrence', 98 *Amer J Int'l L* (2004), pp 69 *ff*; David S Law, 'Generic Constitutional Law', 89 *Minn L Rev* (2005) 652, 731 *ff*.

[39] Arts 1 and 2, discussed in detail (in English) in Markesinis and Unberath, *The German Law of Torts, A Comparative Introduction* (4th edn 2002), pp 392 *ff* and 412 *ff*.

[40] ECtHR No 59320/00 of 24 June 2004.

[41] Antonin Scalia, 'Originalism: The Lesser Evil', (1989) 57 *U Cin L Rev* 849 *ff*.

understating these objections and criticisms. But in the currently polarised American political scene, this extreme language has helped galvanise the support of those who share these views. In contemporary America, law feeds on politics and vice versa. Moreover, some judges—for instance Scalia in the United States and Lord Hoffmann in England—have the talent of phrasing headline-catching phrases, which offer them and the cause they favour more space in the newspaper columns than that given to the views of other judges, at least as well qualified and worthy of attention as themselves. This happened with Scalia's lines in *Roper*,[42] which 'grabbed' the headlines of the national press the day after the judgment was delivered.

Here, for instance, is how Justice Scalia opposed the liberalisation of sodomy laws in the recent Texas decision of *Lawrence v Texas*. He said:

> Constitutional entitlements do not spring into existence because some States choose to lessen or eliminate criminal sanctions on certain behaviour. Much less do they spring into existence, as the Court seems to believe, because foreign nations decriminalize conduct . . . *The Court's discussion of these foreign views . . . is therefore meaningless dicta. Dangerous dicta, however, since 'this court . . . should not impose foreign moods, fads or fashions on Americans'*.[43]

It is the italicised end of the quotation that will arrest the attention of the foreign reader. And yet it is the opening statement that holds the key to the Scalia doctrine, gives it coherence, and also earns it its opponents. Paraphrased, it states that contemporary law reform in the American States and, a fortiori, in foreign countries, cannot change the original understanding of the United States Constitution.

And here is how Justice Scalia, opposed to the majority opinion in *Roper*, holds himself up as the true defender of the American way of life:[44]

> Though the views of our own citizens are essentially irrelevant to the Court's decision today, the views of other countries and the so-called international community take center stage.

And further down comes the peroration which, if accepted, will insulate in perpetuity American law from any kind of outside influence:[45]

> I do not believe that approval by 'other nations and peoples' should buttress our commitment to American principles any more than (what should logically follow) disapproval by 'other nations and peoples' should weaken that commitment.

How we speak often says much about how we think. Justice Scalia's words talk volumes of how he perceives the underlying 'values' that are currently shaping the case law of foreign courts, especially the courts in Strasbourg and Luxembourg, which are comparable in standing to his own not only in form but also in achievements.[46] His judgments thus combine—it must be admitted with a measure of admiration—closely knit argument with verbal pyrotechnics of the kind that lend themselves to citation by newspapers, uninterested (as are the majority of their readers) to utilise in a restricted space sophisticated and nuanced legal arguments. The medium—and we must, of course, include here television—thus dictates the form of speech that will travel best. Judges who can master the art of

[42] 125 S Ct 1153 (2005).

[43] A reference to *Foster v Florida*, 537 US 990, (2002) (Thomas, J).

[44] *Roper v Simmons* 125 S Ct 1153 at 1225 (2005).

[45] *Ibid*, at p 1229.

[46] For who can deny the democratic credentials of the German Federal Constitutional Court, which has achieved in law a revolution similar in importance and amplitude to the so-called post-War economic miracle.

combining the two talents—legal reasoning and headline crafting—are the ones who will achieve the greatest notoriety. Naturally, they can be found in all systems where judgments are eponymous, including the English.[47]

Let us, however, return to the substance of the Scalia argument hidden under the dismissive words 'passing fads and fashions'. The values that underlie the judgments he condemns are, in short, ephemeral. But something ephemeral also suggests that it is not only passing but also shallow, not well thought out; and that is why it is transient. Yet, the possibility that these (different) values can equally be strongly held and honestly arrived at does not seem to be allowed by the words the Justice chooses to use. Advocacy here seems to have gained the upper hand over reason, since in crafting this particular phrase, 'effect' is his main aim. While not stooping as low as Bork in the terminology he reserves for his opponents' thinking, one cannot help feeling that Justice Scalia has a rather low view of the inhabitants of the Continent from which he, himself, hails. That Justice Scalia is, indeed, using these words in a pejorative manner can also be seen from his earlier dictum in *Atkins*,[48] where he wrote:

> Equally irrelevant are the practices of the 'world community,' whose notions of justice are (*thankfully*) not always those of our people. (Italics added.)

That 'thankfully' says it all, does it not?

As already suggested, other jurists of the American Right have used even more vivid language to express their dislike of European criticism of American 'insularity'. Thus, Professor Robert Bork has referred[49] to academics who like the present authors argue for an open mind, as socialist, anti-religious, 'faux intellectuals . . . [hoping] to outflank American legislatures by [imposing] liberal views on the United States'. And at pages 24–5 of the same book he described the European reaction to Justice Kennedy's reluctance to cite in *Stanford v Kentucky*[50] foreign law as 'insolent browbeating'. Bork reserves even more scathing remarks for the widely admired work of the recently retired President of the Israeli Supreme Court, the uniquely cultured Aharon Barak.

In our opinion, it would not be entirely unreasonable to suspect that Professor Bork, who after an animated Senate hearing was rejected as President Reagan's nominee as a Justice to the Supreme Court, may have subconsciously allowed personal reasons to shape such vitriolic hyperbole. But the greatest irony must surely be that the judge he defended for siding with the majority in *Stanford v Kentucky* and *refusing* to take into account foreign law—Justice Kennedy—was fated to be the judge who gave the majority decision in the most recent death penalty case of *Roper v Simmons*[51] which *did* indeed invoke foreign law as a supplementary reason for the changed outcome.

This must be more than ironical. For it offers a good example of how the 'time factor' can legitimise the use of foreign law and reverse old practices when there are reliable signs that public mores have changed. And by 'time factor' we refer to another neglected element in

[47] Lord Hoffmann is, for instance, the English (South African in origin) judge who has this double talent. For an example see his judgment in *Jameel (Mohamed) and another v Wall Street Journal Europe Sprl* [2006] 3 WLR 642—discussed in detail in Markesinis and Deakin, *Tort Law* (6th edn 2007 by Angus Johnston, Simon Deakin and Basil Markesinis), ch 21—and how it received top newspaper coverage (*The Times* even going as far as producing a half-page photograph of the learned judge). The more rhetorically restrained and less wide-sweeping opinion of Lord Bingham, the Senior Law Lord, received no mention.

[48] 536 US, 536 US 304 at 347–8 (2002).

[49] *Coercing Virtue: The Worldwide Rule of Judges* (revised edn 2003), pp 2–16.

[50] 492 US 361 (1989).

[51] 125 S Ct 1183 (2005).

comparative studies, namely how the passage of time may alter societies and ideas and thus make change and transplantation possible where, only a few years earlier, it was believed to have been out of the question. One more reason, along with many, to doubt the wisdom of those who see in 'cultures' obstacles to convergence. For cultures and societies, too, can—and do—change and adapt with time, and are influenced by the fashions, manners, tastes and thinking modes of the countries which provide the icons which others try to imitate.

7. THE STIMULATING SIDE OF 'NEGATIVISM'

It would be wrong—certainly misleading—if we allowed our own opposition to the originalist thinking to conceal the fact that not only does it make much political sense to a large percentage of the American population; it is also an excellent foil against which one must test—and refine, whenever it is found wanting—one's own arguments. For however much one may disagree with Justice Scalia, there is no denying his intelligence, his consistency, and the sincerity of his beliefs. The death penalty cases can, again, provide the focal point of our discussion.

Unlike the South African Constitution of 1993/1994, which deliberately left the question of the death penalty to be decided by the newly established Constitutional Court, the American Constitution in several of its provisions makes it clear that it recognises this extreme sanction. Thus, the moderating impact of modern views on this matter has only been felt through the Eighth Amendment and its prohibition of 'cruel and unusual punishment'—a term understood to take into account the 'evolving standards of decency'. It was reliance on this 'escape phrase' that allowed the Supreme Court to overrule in *Atkins v Virginia* its earlier decisions in *Penry v Lynaugh*[52] and proscribe the death sentence in the case of mentally incapacitated persons and, more recently, to overrule in *Roper v Simmons*[53] its earlier decision in *Stanford v Kentucky* and prohibit the carrying out of a death sentence in the case of persons who committed murder while under the age of 18.

Both landmark changes were five to four decisions reflecting the political divisions in the Court and thus the importance of the 'swing votes'. For in *Roper*, Justice Kennedy, delivering the majority opinion, relied (as he did not in *Stanford v Kentucky*) on foreign practice to *bolster* the conclusion reached by himself and his colleagues in the majority on the basis of the 'internal' review of the changing pattern of State practices. He then proceeded to add:

> Our determination that the death penalty is disproportionate punishment for offenders under 18 finds confirmation in the stark reality that the United States is the only country in the world that continues to give official sanction to the juvenile death penalty. This reality does not become controlling, for the task of interpreting the Eighth Amendment remains our responsibility. Yet at least from the time of the Court's decision in *Trop*,[54] the Court has referred to the laws of other countries and to international authorities as instructive for its interpretation of the Eighth Amendment's prohibition of 'cruel and unusual punishments'.

[52] 492 US 302, 109 S Ct 2934.
[53] 2005 WL 464890 (temporary citation).
[54] *Trop v Dulles* 356 US 86, 102–3, 78 S Ct 590 (plurality opinion).

We italicise the word 'bolster' since Justice Kennedy was eager to stress that while

> [T]he opinion of the world community, [*does not control the outcome*], [it] does provide respected and significant confirmation for our conclusions mainly reached on other grounds.

Yet the 'negativist' approach of the originalists has also some advantages, and among them is the condemnation of judges who choose to impose their own views about morality, by-passing the constitutional wording (as originally understood). It is thus permissible to downplay the caveat indicated by the italicised words of Justice Kennedy in order to support the view that the court was here doing more than simply interpreting the law of the United States. This criticism of Justice Kennedy's stance, strongly voiced by the dissenting Scalia,[55] is at the very least arguable since due regard must be had of the fact that the 'shift' in court practice that took place between *Stanford v Kentucky*[56] and *Roper v Simmons*[57] in favour of abolishing the death penalty for juveniles was much lower (namely four States)[58] compared to that which justified the Court in *Atkins v Virginia* to overrule *Penry v Lynaugh*[59] (16 States passing specific statutes since the earlier case was decided). Justice Scalia may thus have been right when pointing out the unreliable basis of the test which now allows the Supreme Court to find (on the basis of arguably slim evidence) that there has been a shift from previous practice. For this now makes it easier for the court to detect a 'shift' in national consensus rather than insist, as it arguably used to do, on an 'overwhelming opposition to a challenged practice'.[60] So there is more than irony, indeed there is a measure of truth when Scalia observes that:[61]

> To invoke alien law when it agrees with one's own thinking, and ignore it otherwise, is not reasoned decision-making, but sophistry.

Though these authors feel that there is, among political and legal circles, a clear worldwide opposition to the death penalty, they also recognise that this may not always and accurately reflect the views of the voter in the street. This means that the accusation that the judge 'importing' such a reform may thus be supplanting his own view for that of the electorate is not one which can be ignored, though one, equally, cannot ignore that legislative reform is not always easy to achieve because of the fudges which current political realities tend to promote. Thus, the final answer on this point must be that the issue here is not one that lends itself to easy answers, and that the originalists, through their persistent opposition towards the use of foreign law, may be rendering comparative law a service in so far as they are alerting jurists of all hues of the need to address these points more cogently.

Merely quoting that most states have abolished the death sentence may thus not, on its own, be enough. For in appropriate circumstances, one may need additional information. For instance, does a state have the death sentence on the statute books but does not enforce it? Does life imprisonment mean, in practice, life imprisonment (as it does in the United States) or does it mean that parole rules can, effectively, make a mockery of the term? And,

[55] 'Though the views of our own citizens are essentially irrelevant to the Court's decision today, the views of other countries and the so-called international community take center stage' (per Justice Scalia, at p 1225).

[56] 492 US 361, 109 S Ct 590.

[57] 125 S Ct 1183 (2002).

[58] Plus one State Supreme Court that had construed the death penalty statute not to apply to the under-18 offenders: *State v Furman*, 122 Wash 2d 440, 458, 858 P2d 1092, 1103 (1993).

[59] 492 US 302, 109 S Ct 2934.

[60] See p 29 (temporary citation).

[61] *Roper v Simmons* 125 S Ct, 1153, 1228 (2005).

finally, does it mean that the death sentence was abolished because that state's citizens abhor it, or because it was an externally imposed condition for that state joining some wider economic or political organisation such as the European Union? An 'abolition' of the latter kind could thus be seen as a political compromise in order to gain a wider political advantage and not one stemming from any belief—let alone conviction—that the imposition of the death sentence should not be allowed to exist.

The Scalia dissent may have offered a further service to comparative law when doubting the 'form' in which the (apparently) universal practice towards juvenile death sentencing was presented. This took the form of amicus briefs, was not discussed or contradicted in open court, and the way the data was collected was never tested in a scientific way. This, of course, does not speak conclusively against the use of evidence of foreign law before a national court, but it does suggest that, for instance, the way in which this was handled by the House of Lords in *Fairchild v Glenhaven*[62] was more convincing. In that case, their Lordships themselves asked counsel for both sides to address them on the attitudes taken by the supreme courts of Continental Europe on the issue there at hand and, when dealing with that information, they, themselves, added that the material had to be used selectively, intelligently, and with caution.[63]

The cautionary remarks made in this sub-section are only intended to alert the reader to another (healthy) warning advanced by those opposing the use of foreign law. But if this warning, once again, criticises the way that foreign law is studied in universities and presented to national courts, it does not imply that if the right methodological approach towards foreign law can be developed, its utility cannot increase in the years to come. We thus conclude by referring the reader to a very detailed consideration of the dangers and difficulties of comparative law which we have attempted elsewhere,[64] and assure him that to most of these worries satisfactory answers seem to be emerging at a pace quicker than ever before in the history of comparative law.

8. WIDER REASONS WHICH MAY HELP THE CURRENT CLIMATE OF INSULARITY SPREAD FURTHER

Though one can criticise the way practising lawyers have tried to introduce foreign law in American constitutional litigation, the real obstacle to the use of such material is this naïve belief that it should have no role to play in the shaping of American law. At the risk of repetition, we also stress again that this 'lack of interest' in foreign ideas must be seen against the wider context of the American political debate about the proper role of judges.

Yet, what (plausibly) applies to constitutional interpretation may, as stated, already be (implausibly) *infecting* interpretation in the area of private law, as well, contradicting the well-established contrary practice to which we alluded at the beginning of this Chapter. The spreading of this 'introversion disease' may be aided and abetted by an 'opposite disease' in the ascendancy at the moment among the governing political neo-conservative elites.

62 [2002] 1 AC 32.

63 On which see Lord Bingham's views in *Fairchild*, [2002] 1 AC 32, at p 66.

64 Sir Basil Markesinis and Dr Jörg Fedtke, The Judge as Comparatist, 80 *Tulane Law Review* No 1, 11–167 (2005).

This is based on the belief that America is 'a city on the hill', not only a paradigm to others but—and this is the most modern twist to this imagery—morally bound to improve others who do not attain its own standards.[65] Those dealing with the current Iraq conundrum, in all its twists and turns, are agonisingly searching for a justification for the disastrously evolving enterprise and seem to have settled on the idea that it is America's mission to install democracy (from the top down) and thus influence the comportment of other Middle Eastern states (among which one finds many a violator of human rights with tacit American support). Regime change has thus acquired among neo-conservatives a legitimacy which would strike many as not only worrying but also as a manifestation of the 'rights' of the most powerful. However rotten the replaced regimes may be (and the United States has since the War supported and still supports quite a few of them if this suited its own interests), their forceful replacement does not augur well for the rule of law.

This kind of approach is thus both unwise and dangerous. Yet, indisputably, there are many politicians, journalists, and even lawyers, who see in the United States an example to the world: the one that first implemented democracy, protected human rights, recognised judicial review, and now re-proclaims the merits of a property-owning nation, with its citizens taking this fate in their own hands. This is to say nothing of its own type of capitalism which, though prone to suffer from greed, is also promoted as the only way of increasing standards of living. It is not the 'model Anglo-Saxon' that the French and other European states which retain a minimum of 'social consciousness' in their political programmes should be worried about; it is the much more 'aggressive' American version. Whether President Sarkozy's reputed admiration for the United States will actually make him imitate the so-called Wall Street variant of 'uncontrolled capitalism' remains to be seen. We would venture the thought that nothing as extreme as that will come to France in the foreseeable future.

In any event, to return to our earlier point, one *may* debate to what extent these American claims are justified and not exaggerated. On the other hand one *must* also question whether America has any right to 'force' others to adopt its values rather than merely rely on the superiority of its ideas and ideals to attract their own adherents—something which, of course, works both ways. But what one *cannot* doubt is the fact that many Americans—especially those who form the ruling elites of today—believe in the superiority of their values. Such beliefs thus form part of the current 'political climate' that we find in this great country; and they are reinforced, in the minds of many Americans, by non-legal arguments such as the contemporary European reservations about America's transformation of public international law to suit its foreign policy and down-play human rights. Reason and sentiment—moral, political, religious, and economic—thus seem to combine with legal concerns to produce an 'unstable' mix the likes of which has rarely been encountered in the history of comparative law and the movement of ideas. Taken together they

[65] The key words coming from John Winthrop's address on the founding of the Massachusetts Bay Colony (and probably derived from Matthew 5:14). The phrase became 'politicised' over the ages, and certainly after the 'Reagan years' when it was often cited and associated with the idea 'we are an example to the world'. But the original wording deserves to be cited (in its original spelling) to show that it was a cautionary message, more religious than political: 'For wee must Consider that wee shall be as a City upon a Hill, the eies of all people are uppon us; soe that if wee shall deale falsely with our God in this worke wee have undertaken and so cause Him to withdrawe His present help from us, wee shall be made a story and a byword through the world, wee shall open the mouthes of enemeis to speake evill of the wayes of god and all professours for Gods sake; wee shall shame the faces of many of God's worthy servants, and cause theire prayers to be turned into Cursses upon us till wee be consumed out of the good land whether wee are going'.

must account for the growing suspicion which a substantial proportion of the American population (including lawyers) nurtures towards contemporary Europe, its values, its law, and its courts. A fear or dislike of foreign values nowadays thus comes with a very inadequate understanding of the 'rest of the world', its sensitivities, its structures, its law, and its achievements. That is why we repeat our earlier conviction that however inept lawyers may have been in trying to interest American courts in foreign law, the main cause of resistance must be sought elsewhere.

This emerging and complex picture of America's self-conscious superiority may thus make it adverse to borrowings and intellectual dialogues even in the areas where once there was give and take, and which the more globalised economic and commercial world we live in today makes even more necessary. Yet here, the movement of ideas on technical matters that are regulated by the kind of rules we are envisaging should be facilitated and not impeded out of abstract notions of principle, which may be relevant to the constitutional group of cases but not this category of disputes.

In making the above suggestion we do not, of course, delude ourselves in believing that it will stop opponents of all forms of foreign dialogue from trying to prevent it even in the case of comparison of rules (and not values). For it does not take much ingenuity but only a minimum amount of disingenuousness to claim that, for instance, even ordinary contract or tort rules can be linked to 'values' held dear by some societies in order to preserve the status quo. Thus, any teacher of contract law in almost every state on the European Continent will be aware of the growing number of rules favouring consumer protection. Almost all—certainly those which strive for greater employment protection—could be declared as incompatible with the American form of capitalism, which seems hell-bent since the 1980s to unpick the New Deal of the 1930s and return closer to the 19th-century ideal of laissez-faire. Those who imagine European (including English) lawyers as being 'socialists', 'anti-religious', or 'faux intellectuals' will certainly be tempted to try this tack.

The same could, likewise, be argued in the domain of tort rules,[66] which in Europe are, admittedly, fashioned against the reality of a safety net provided by a more developed system of social security. The conclusion of this sub-section thus is that the more America becomes anxious to assert its interests globally and export its institutions, the less sensitive it has become to different values if they are incompatible to those held by its ruling elites. The fact that a section of its judges do not seem to share this view does not mean that in the current political climate they are set to get their way. The recent two nominations in the Supreme Court could prove of crucial importance for at least one generation of Americans. Europeans should also take stock. For open-minded lawyers, the possibility—not perhaps evident at present—that the new Chief Justice may turn out to be more moderate than those who nominated him may have hoped, is something that could happen; indeed, it may, one day, be suggested to him by his undoubted intelligence.

[66] A host of tort rules—eg, class action suits, capping of damages, availability of punitives—could fall into this category. For restrictions imposed on any of them would, in Europe, be seen as reflecting tort choices where, in the United States, many would regard them as giving a free hand to enterprises to place profit before social responsibility.

9. COMPARISONS WITH OTHER WORLD COURTS

What is remarkable about the above scene (as well as the French, to which we shall refer in the last section) is that while it has been hardening in the way suggested, the supreme courts of other systems have been moving in the opposite direction. Thus, almost all the major legal systems we have been looking at in the course of working on this topic have made significant strides towards using foreign law as a source of local inspiration. In this category one thus finds some very unlikely bed-fellows: the House of Lords, for long considered (by outsiders) as an enclave of tradition and conservatism; the Canadian Supreme Court, a modern champion of constructive but not slavish engagement with its southern neighbour; the South African Constitutional Court,[67] a newcomer with an enviable record of comparative law in action and, to complete this short list, even the Israeli Supreme Court, which has shown itself able to borrow in matters of human rights from a wide range of cultures even when this led to internal opposition based on strong religious views. The contrast with the United States is thus not only great; it also raises another interesting question, namely which of the two models—the open or the closed—will, in the end, prove more attractive to the new democracies and, in the long run, the most formidable of all emerging powers: China. We have pondered over some of these questions elsewhere;[68] and also review the state of affairs in contemporary Germany and South Africa in two Chapters especially devoted to these important countries. So, in this last section of this Chapter, we shall devote the remaining comments to the situation in France.[69]

10. COMPARISONS WITH FRANCE

(a) General Remarks

The preceding narrative suggests a serious split within American legal circles—judicial and academic—much as Justice Breyer seems to have tried to conceal it in his recent appearances in France. It also shows a rift with the practice of other interesting courts such as those of South Africa, Israel, and Canada which have, by contrast to the American courts, embraced the study of foreign law on a fairly regular basis.[70]

We attributed the above American posture first to the fact that American law has become self-sufficient, indeed inundated, by legal materials and ideas of its own, but also, secondly, because, since the collapse of the Iron Curtain and the Soviet Empire, the United States has felt psychologically and politically confident enough to proclaim its status as the only super-

[67] South African private law has, of course, a different and longer tradition of drawing inspiration both from Roman Dutch law and the common law.

[68] Sir Basil Markesinis and Jörg Fedtke, *Judicial Recourse to Foreign Law: A New Source of Inspiration?* (Routledge-Cavendish 2006).

[69] France will also provide our main focus for the next Chapter, thus enlarging somewhat the observations made in this Chapter.

[70] Interestingly, however, this has not meant that they have always absorbed it into their own system, nor have they seen their own system, as a result of its open-mindedness, being taken over or corrupted by foreign ideas. On this see Chief Justice Brian Dickson's comments in 'Has the Charter Americanised the Canadian Judiciary?', 26 *UBC Law Rev* 195 (1992).

power, not in need of anyone. Such a posture makes it easier to extend its undoubted political and technological superiority to other areas of life, and thus say 'no' even to legal ideas. American 'uniqueness' seems to dictate such hubris.

Not everyone would accept the first (and technical) argument as being decisive. For one can argue that we live in a world where borders are porous and that therefore ideas can and must travel as freely as goods, services and, alas, even terrorism. The exchange of ideas is thus inevitable; it may even be desirable; and it is made necessary in the domain of commercial transactions.

The validity of the second objection is more difficult to evaluate.

For those who belong to this second group of jurists—let us call them the internationalists—the exchange of ideas benefits all. For the possibility of a new solution or a new angle, or new empirical data, can always help a legal system, however rich it may already be. It can help discard solutions which have become dated, fill lacunae which often result from scientific progress found in one country but not in others,[71] and encourage the adoption of those ideas which have been shown to work in practice in other parts of the world.[72] Additionally, in some areas, especially of commercial practice, a certain degree of harmonisation if not even uniformity is something that contemporary market conditions welcome. The same may also be true in certain areas of human rights protection given the growing belief that an increasing number of values are these days cut out of the same cloth and thus cannot be exalted in some systems while totally ignored by others. As always, the synthesis here is a matter of skilful compromise which takes into account the need for greater protection of human rights—which our times demand—but does not totally ignore local conditions and traditions in a way which makes the idea of borrowing or influencing totally utopian. To allow hegemonic sentiments of a political kind to interfere with such a way of reasoning is neither appropriate in intellectual nor advisable in commercial terms.

On which side of this divide does France stand?

It does not require much imagination to see that here, too, the legal position one adopts cannot easily be separated from the local political ideology and formal (mainly university) training. The attitude one adopts towards the problem—if one believes there is a problem—and its right solution will thus also be determined by the educational and formal training the commentator has received. A local lawyer, who knows something about foreign law, is thus not likely to react to this problem as a true comparative lawyer will do. The majority of those who write about 'comparative law' these days seem to fall into this category of national lawyers with an interest in foreign law rather than the true 'mongrel' which the genuine comparative lawyer tends to be.[73] For France, unlike England (and, more so, the United States), never benefited from an influx of émigré comparatists and has been forced to draw on its own sources. Rejuvenation of indigenous comparative talent has, we think, proved difficult.

[71] See Guy Canivet, 'Le juge entre progrès scientifique et mondialisation', *RTDCivc*, 2005, pp 33–46.

[72] See Sanford Levinson, 'Looking Abroad When Interpreting the US Constitution. Some Reflections', (2004) 39 *Texas Int'l L J* 353, at 363–4.

[73] We submit that this distinction has not always received the attention it deserves. For colleagues like Rheinstein, Schlesinger, Fleming, Kahn-Freund, Baade, Reimann, Legrand, and Mattei have the characteristic (advantage?) of having been brought up in different countries, lived in different cultures, received double (if not triple) education, and thus—one could argue—having acquired an additional 'feel' about the foreign system they are interested in. Having studied in more than one country can come a close second; but it still does not give one the insights of true cosmopolites.

Modern comparative studies insist, more than ever, that rules can only be understood within their wider context. But pride in one's culture, coupled with familiarity with a particular kind of training and thinking, can make people lazy, defensive, and even introverted—especially if they see in the 'foreign' a threat to their way of life and *modus operandi*. We are strongly tempted to think that this has been a second reason for 'internal' decline, at any rate if one compares the comparative scene in France with that of contemporary Germany or Italy.

Thus, if some American jurists strike us as 'closed' because, like most of their compatriots, they feel self-sufficient and powerful, French academics give the impression of being 'closed' because they feel beleaguered, defensive, afraid to innovate, and, often, even linguistically ill-equipped for this new challenge. (Indeed, we venture to suggest that French legal academics are as monoglot (at least as far as English is concerned) as their American counterparts are towards French.) Additionally, we submit that they are also handicapped by being obliged to operate within a state-run structure which does not lend itself to innovations and private initiatives. This last point is, we feel, hugely relevant; but we find it difficult to comment on it further, not knowing at the stage of writing to what extent President Sarkozy's attempt to breathe new life into university autonomy is likely to become reality and not get mired down in the usual political compromises that have plagued the reform of state institutions in France. Yet even if these reforms succeed, it will be some time before we see their beneficial effects reflected in the finances and practices of French law faculties.

For us, therefore, by far the greatest problem experienced by modern France may be linked to the fact that there seems to be no agreement as to the kind of society the French, themselves, wish to live in. The same self-doubt seems slowly to be creeping in as to France's position as a player on the international scene. For, at the very least, this is very different—diminished one would say—to what it was even half a century ago. If this is true of the society as a whole, it is bound to affect its attitude towards law, the administration of justice, and, of course, the branch of the law we are interested in: foreign law and comparative methodology. Proclaiming that the French may stand to learn from the experience of others might give them a well-deserved chance also to influence others; but politically, such admissions may not be easily tolerated within the country.

Of course, the problem of self-doubt and internal crisis is not only a French problem. English power has declined on most fronts since the end of the Second World War, the country—in the famous words of Dean Acheson—finding itself in the position of 'having lost an Empire and [still] being in search of a role'. This poignant observation was uttered in the late 1940s but these days has acquired an added dimension, notwithstanding the slogan 'cool Britannia'. For England suffers from a further dilemma which does not affect France—does it belong to Europe or the United States? Or can it really play the role of an honest broker between the two? Though this is primarily a political question, it also has a legal aspect to it; for there is much in contemporary English law which is pulling the country both towards modern European law but also towards its traditional American and Commonwealth anchorages—and it is by no means clear which side will prevail.[74] This is because the judges are, just as much as the politicians, pulled in different directions; and they—the judges—are also weighed down by their legal training which, for linguistic if no

[74] Is English law, for instance, going to go down the American or European path in the areas of free speech and privacy? Here, as elsewhere, the immediate technical answer may be determined by wider commitments assumed within the European context.

other reasons, makes them feel more comfortable in using American and Commonwealth law. As we have noted elsewhere in the book, this is a double-edged sword.

We raise these points not because we feel this is the right place to address them in detail but because we feel convinced that they can help explain the internal doubts that affect the psychological state of a country, its judges, its legislators, and its practitioners. And if all of the above are, in different ways and degrees, racked by doubt (as the English and French undoubtedly are), not only do they tend to be unnecessarily critical if not destructive[75] of their own institutions, but also show mistrust towards those who are doing better.[76]

But to return to France—if such ambivalence exists on the socio-economic front, it is bound to be reflected in its law, as well. During the bicentenary celebrations of the Code civil one of us borrowed an idea from Portalis' famous *Discours préliminaires*, an author and a text one admires more and more as one has the chance to re-read him more attentively. There Portalis asked a question which we put in the affirmative tense: 'un bon Code civil ne pouvait naître au milieu des crises politiques'[77] (a good civil code cannot be born during an ongoing political crisis). Professor Halpérin, in his gem of a book *L'impossible code*, completed the idea with the words 'il fallait une stabilisation pour que s'édifie une legislation durable'[78] (one needs stability before one can pass durable legislation).

The leading author thus had the temerity to suggest in a public lecture delivered at the Court of Cassation[79] a reason of his own, explaining why the Napoleonic Code, despite the many challenges it has faced, and despite the even more numerous amendments, is still (more or less) alive. Such (original) success must surely result from the fact that Bonaparte read correctly the 'mood' of his times and reflected it in his Code. Additionally, through the skilful drafting of his undoubtedly cultured chief draftsman (Portalis), he also gave it the means to adapt in the future and absorb fairly easily changes in society, including internal revolutions and two World Wars.

According to the view we have taken the French of today are not quite sure in what type of society they want (and, just as important, can afford) to live in. A society of social entitlements which are no longer affordable (which most of them understandably want)? A society where the rigid hierarchy and thinking of the Grands Ecoles prevails, determining promotion on the grounds of age or performance at the graduating exams rather than

[75] 'Destructive' sounds like a strong word but anyone who has followed English political life during the last 30 plus years will have noticed the growing ferocity with which all its major institutions are, in common parlance, 'rubbished'—mainly by the press. This applies to the monarchy (the country's pride), the House of Lords, and even its judiciary. We said 'mainly' by the press, for we feel the doubts that this Fourth Estate has persistently instilled in the minds of citizens over the last few years have been unnecessarily extreme and destructive. Yet it is not just the press which has undermined the justice system. Thus, early in 2007, Prime Minister Tony Blair said that '(T)he criminal justice system is *the* [sic] public service *most distant* [sic] from what most reasonable people want' (*The Times*, 16 May 2006, p 6). Such populist statements might just about be understandable (if still open to criticism for their sweeping terms) had they come from a newly elected head of government who was inheriting a bad situation. But the condemnation sounds less than convincing when it comes from an experienced and talented leader who has been in office for over nine years, has been supported by huge parliamentary majorities (effectively allowing him to legislate at will), and one who, additionally, has already passed during this period over 40 'law and order' bills. So how does it help to describe the justice system as a whole in such sweepingly damning terms?

[76] We note in passing, since in this work we are not examining smaller European legal systems such as the Dutch, Greek, Belgian, or Portuguese, that in these countries polyglots are the rule as is the interest in foreign legal systems.

[77] Jean-Etienne-Marie Portalis, *Ecrits et discourse juridiques et politiques* (Press Universitaires d'Aix-Marseille 1988), p 22.

[78] (1992), at p 263.

[79] 'The Enduring (Double) Legacy of the Code Napoléon', (2005) *LQR*, 80 at p 86.

success in real life? A society that is prepared to invest less in technology and research than agriculture? A society which is willing to de-regulate business and commerce more than it now does? A university system that is unable even to contemplate the possibility of enlisting the assistance of the private sector? A university governance that has to go to its Ministry before it can ever authorise refurbishment of one of its buildings? All these questions, and many others of the same kind, remain unanswered, though one report, published by the World Bank in the early 2000s and entitled *Doing Business in 2004. Understanding Regulation*, so damned the French system for being uncongenial for doing business in the country that its shock waves were felt not only by the legal profession but by the entire French intelligentsia—which hastened to condemn it as biased, one-sided, and methodologically flawed.[80] But the essential fundamentals, touched upon by this report and easily discernible by all those involved in the world of French business and finance, are still there. They were only obliquely addressed during the presidential campaign waged in 2007; and they will remain unanswered for as long as the logically compelling responses would mean a loss of votes for any party which promoted them.

The reader will not find answers to these questions in this work. If the French themselves shy away from these issues, foreign academics can do no more than raise them for consideration. And they must be borne in mind because of the important consequences they have for law. These consequences can be found in past action; and will also influence future initiatives.

For as far as the past is concerned, this inability to express a unified and widely held view of what France is today and how it should be governed has allowed the old Code (with all its accumulated sociological prestige) to survive (more or less) in force *faute de mieux*. And the same political ambivalence, if it continues in the future, will affect the law in general, and comparative law in particular—how much it will tag on to German-inspired guidelines, or manage to make its own imprint on the law of the emerging Europe. Some French academics project optimism. A closer analysis of their texts suggests that they are aware of the crisis in fundamentals but do not have the courage to address them openly. The convention that academic discourse must be conducted in low-key terms, as purely scientific debate dictates, means that the rigorous debate that is needed is not taking place. The cracks are merely papered over.

Thus, even those who detect (or would like to detect) a renaissance in comparative studies in France—Professor Fauvarque-Cosson being one in her essay in the Zimmermann/Reimann *Oxford Handbook*—have focused on European (that is, community funded and supported) developments and, on the whole, missed out on what has been happening in the Anglo-Saxon world as well as the way other courts have come to use foreign law.

All of the above aspects have thus remained out of everyone's sight in France, except for occasional and very generalised references. As stated, this may be partly because of language difficulties. Partly, it may also be because the glow of America has been dimmed by the Iraq War and American attitudes towards France. Finally, the fears which the success of streamlined global law firms—English and American—have had in Paris may be causing more real concern than is obvious at first sight, especially since survival in France is seen by many as taking the form of enhanced protectionism rather than increased productivity and compet-

[80] For references see B Fauvarque-Cosson, 'Developments of Comparative Law in France' in Mathias Reimann and Reinhard Zimmermann (eds), *The Oxford Handbook of Comparative Law* (2006), pp 35 *ff*, at p 62 note 101.

itiveness. Few have been those who had the courage to try to address these differences, pacify these fears, and build links between the two systems. Those who have done this have been primarily judges and practitioners, not academics.

How dire, in our view, the position is in France can only really be measured if the comparative literature of that country is compared with that coming out of contemporary Italy. For the younger generation of Italian comparatists have overcome the linguistic obstacles which confronted their predecessors and have also displayed a marked re-orientation of interest towards what is happening in the Anglo-Saxon world.

One reason why the French academics have missed the opportunity to adapt is because the higher educational establishment in France had not—yet?—embraced a modern understanding of the utility of studying in a practical, focused, usable manner foreign law, sometimes showing it to be unsuitable for local conditions and sometimes learning from its successes. Above all, the state educational establishment has not realised that it must cut some slack on the universities and allow them to do their thing. Ministerial 'dirigisme' has, in our view, seriously handicapped French law, certainly comparative law studies in contemporary France.

It is not only the general law that is affected by this indecision with regards to the basics of society. In the subconscious of the French legal mind we think we find traces of the same ideas and worries, and they may explain the ambivalent attitude contemporary French lawyers seem to have towards the study of foreign law. We would greatly hesitate before calling it arrogance (though we think that this adjective could be applied to *some* American jurists). Yet, as we shall note below, at least one French comparative lawyer has described his own colleagues as 'ethnocentric'—a word which to us describes perfectly the collective psychology which is often found during periods of transition, not confidence. Suffice it thus to float the idea that *for opposite reasons*, sections of the American and French legal worlds may be displaying the same 'withdrawal' symptoms, repelling what is foreign, and for different reasons treating it as unacceptable. In this sense, and this sense alone, the French have thus become strange bedfellows with the Americans towards whom they otherwise nourish such ambivalent feelings.

Such attempts to compare national attitudes towards foreign law may be very risky. To begin with they could be too broad; and their formulation requires much material, to be drawn from many disciplines, before it can begin to be credible. What we have done here has been to generalise, albeit on the basis of many discussions with numerous French friends (and not only lawyers). Occasionally this may be permissible if those who make these wide statements are conscious of the dangers they entail but still wish to flag up a point for further discussion. Provocative ideas, provided that they are put forward in good faith, may justify a sequel essay; they may bring about a riposte by a disagreeing author; they may even, one day, attract some kind of official response. All of these reactions could serve a purpose. But here, instead of contemplating any of these possibilities, we must insist that it is our duty to advance such ideas in order to force French colleagues to react and reflect on their state of the law in general and that of comparative law in particular.

We hasten to add that since there are as many prescriptions about comparative law as there are comparatists, the three sub-headings are inter-related to fit into the 'brand' of comparative law outlined above: inter-disciplinary study of the law; focused examination of legal problems; and emphasis on what is of potential practical use. All this, of course, can work if the negativism and destructiveness that underlie the teachings of some French comparatists are cast aside by the academic world as they seem to have been ignored by the country's judiciary. The legal systems of the world are converging, influencing each other, learning from each other—however much this may annoy these (isolated) teachers. Those who believe otherwise should, perhaps, be teaching other subjects. Most certainly, however, they will *not* contribute to the rejuvenation of the study of foreign law in France unless someone is willing to pay for the costs of such instruction *and* there is an audience willing to be so instructed.

All this may sound like a tall order. Yet we feel we can draw some comfort from the fact that the former First President of the Cour de cassation has come very close to expressing similar thoughts in a much admired lecture he gave in London not that long ago.[81] What he has convinced his Court to do in recent years is a testimony to his strong character, his reforming tenacity, and his open-mindedness; it also provides very tangible proof that what we call for in our own system can also work in others.

(b) Issues to be Resolved

So let us complete this series of ideas and criticisms by moving forward to our own concluding observations and recipes under three sub-headings: (i) The general attitude of France towards foreign law and comparative methodology; (ii) who should take the initiative to encourage greater consultation of foreign law?; and (iii) how should this be done?

(i) Comparative Law in France—Its Present State

A foreign observer need not worry too much in expressing a critical view on this topic since his French colleagues publish at regular intervals proceedings of colloquia which review the health of the subject in their own country. Their language is polite, the overall tone one of (forced, we think) optimism, but the picture they describe is not attractive, notwithstanding their cosmetic efforts. Of the many citations we could give, we are content to mention one which comes from a short piece recently published in Dalloz by Professor Olivier Moréteau, the former Director of an Institute of Comparative Law which bears the name of the great Edouard Lambert.[82] Moréteau in fact gave up his post in France and moved to the Law School of Baton Rouge in Louisiana. His reasons are known to himself; but his writings suggest a good measure of exasperation with the general background which prevented him from doing his job properly at home.

Professor Moréteau talks of the French culture being 'très ethonocentriste'. He further suggests that the French jurists 'sont trop rarement équipés pour juger des . . . traveaux [comparatives]'. He finds many of them 'repli sur soi', endowed even by 'une certaine arrogance', and cultivating 'les délices du splendide isolement'. He asserts that '(L)a France est

[81] See 'The Use of Comparative Law Before the French Private Law Courts' in Guy Canivet, Mads Andenas and Duncan Fairgrieve (eds), *Comparative Law Before the Courts* (2004), pp 181, at p 192: '[The] *remnants* of a common legal space revolving around the *splendour* of the French Civil Code undoubtedly formed the background against which legal transplants were performed and comparative methodology made its way through the French courts and legal academy. But, *since this common space was fuelled more by the French empire's political power or prestige and less by the efficiency of the French 'legal product'*, the radiance of the French civil law culture slowly began to *wane* in the twentieth century, *accustoming our national courts to a rather provincial state of mind*'.

[82] 'Ne tirez pas sur le comparatiste', Dalloz 2005, No 7 pp 452 *ff.* Many of Professor Moréteau's criticisms are contradicted (though without any reference to him or his work) by Professor Fauvarque-Cosson in her essay in the *Oxford Handbook.* But in the absence of specific details we cannot evaluate the persuasive value of her arguments.

faible de ce qui fit jadis sa force: le rayonnement de son système juridique', and complements this statement with another: most of the efforts to export French culture tend to be limited to the countries once in the domain of 'francophonie'. Are these not the kinds of accusation levied against Justice Scalia, though one must hasten to add that in his case even his severest critics accept the power of his intellect.

Let us, however, return to Professor Moréteau. His is a seriously damning collection of comments coming from a respected colleague who directed until recently one of the country's leading centres for comparative law. His position means that they must be taken as an accurate as well as serious description of the French 'malaise'. It is not we (the outsiders) who are pointing out some weaknesses in the French system; it is qualified 'insiders' who see things in this way. Our impression, further, is that Professor Moréteau is mainly targeting academics *and bureaucrats linked to education*, not judges. What more can an 'outsider' add?

Only one comment is necessary. In our view our French colleague has damned his own comparative law culture not because he finds no utility in the subject; has an incomplete picture of what is happening in France (as we might be accused of having); or, finally, because there is no young talent available to take up the challenge. He is simply courageous enough to describe openly what he sees—state intervention, lack of financial means, and cosy university groups which ensure the preservation of the status quo but dare not innovate to meet the challenge of our times.

We admire this position and share Professor Moréteau's desire to strengthen the standing of the subject and promote French culture. Goethe, when asked once to condemn the French when they invaded his own country, refused to do so because 'he owed them so much intellectually'. We are happy to follow this example and acknowledge a similar debt to French culture and to many French jurists with whom the leading author in particular has worked with. If we speak plainly, it is because of our ambition to save our subject from the threats it is facing from different quarters. We also wish to play our part in giving European culture a stronger voice; and in this exercise the voice of France is crucial (even though the French comparatists have managed to silence it themselves). Our recipe for improvement is complex and cannot work on its own. It requires to be combined with a raft of other measures, some of which Professor Moréteau identified in his paper and are what we would call typically French.

Before we leave this admittedly critical and pessimistic picture of comparative law in contemporary France, let us (in the interests of fairness) urge our readers to study (not just peruse) the account given by a colleague who professes the opposite view. This is Professor Fauvarque-Cosson; and she believes that there is a 'renaissance' in comparative studies in France.[83] We submit that, if carefully read, her piece supports our thesis and not the upbeat account which she clearly wishes to convey. To prove our point, let us start with some statistical *facts* that emerge from her paper.

First one must note that the Chapter devoted to France, a main if not *the* main progenitor of modern comparative law, amounts to 32 pages (including a one-page table of contents). What can one learn from such a condensed account? More importantly, to whom is it addressed? The historian, the general reader, the practitioner, the judge, or the legislator? In our view, the essay is too short and too descriptive to be targeting practitioners of any

[83] Bénédicte Fauvarque-Cosson, 'Development of Comparative Law in France' in Mathias Reimann and Reinhard Zimmermann (eds), *The Oxford Handbook of Comparative Law* (2006), ch 1.

kind. What about the student—assuming that libraries will be able to buy the book at £120? This is more debatable; but there is a further question that is not easy to answer: 'What will the reader of this piece gain from it?' Since the historical part will, probably, be of little interest to him, and the modern part only contains very general information (which he may already have from other sources), what is the *net value added* by a piece which undoubtedly reflects much reading and presents its material in a calm and balanced manner but hardly in a thought-provoking way? None of this, of course, should be blamed on Madame Fauvarque-Cosson; but it *does* question the utility of large but 'bitty' books of this kind, written by many authors (who inevitably do not share the same views, or methods, or tastes), and which try to cover too much ground in too small a space to do so in a meaningful manner. They can rarely succeed in doing anything more than give a flavour of the subject or how it is faring in a particular country.

Secondly, the reader must note that 20 of the 32 pages are devoted to the 'past'. Of the remaining 10 pages, seven are meant to flesh out the ambitious title *The Renaissance of Comparative Law in France*, while five pages deal with what is described in a sub-heading as the *New Challenges*. These figures alone might tempt a cynic to paraphrase Oscar Wilde when he once wrote that 'he liked a woman with a past and a man with a future'. That, as we said, is one of the problems which countries like France have in confronting (that is, learning) to invest in the future, and not to be nostalgic about the past.

Thirdly, the 31 pages of text are supported by 111 footnotes. In them 36 French authors are cited in approving or neutral terms (the only disapproving reference is to Professor Legrand's well-known position, the mildly phrased text appearing just after note 88). What is, however, most revealing is that the section entitled *Renaissance* cites (cursorily) only four French authors, of whom the one most widely cited is the former First President of the Court of Cassation; and he is a judge! What does that say about the *renaissance*? And who is bringing it about—the real world or the cloisters of the near-by (ruined) monastery of Cluny?

The rest of the literature in this section refers to numerous European projects and initiatives—Lando, von Bar, Trento—in which French jurists may have played a part (Madame Fauvarque-Cosson is, herself, a loyal member of the von Bar team), but all these can hardly be described as *French* projects. A careful reading of these lines will not only confirm our view that it is *Europe* that has stirred French lawyers into a reaction. More importantly, this reaction (divided, as Professor Fauvarque-Cosson honestly admits) seems to be prompted by the sense of historical inevitability rather than conviction. For how else can one interpret her statement 'non-participation in European academic projects is both useless and irresponsible because it will not stop the process of Europeanisation'?[84] Strip this sentence of its cosmetic elegance and what one is left with is something along the lines 'if we do not join the von Bar movement we have little else to do'. How much more courageous (if somewhat intemperately phrased) was Professor Yves Lequette's reply[85] to the von Bar ideas!

In any event, Madame Fauvarque-Cosson's argument can hardly be called a 'legal' one. In our view, in essence it is an argument of realistic politics; and if we are right in this, then the reader must be reminded that gone are the days when something happens in Europe simply because the Brussels bureaucracy wishes it. Madame Cosson should know this, given how her compatriots scuppered in a referendum the much vaunted idea of a European

[84] At p 57.

[85] 'Quelques remarques à propos du projet de code civil européen de M Von Bar', Dalloz, chron 2002, no 8, p 2202.

Constitution. A teacher should tell his students that he or she supports a constitution or civil code because they are good or necessary, not because they are inevitable (which they are not) or because some central bureaucracy has so decreed.

Finally, let us underline the 'cloistered' approach to the subject, that is, the approach which says what academic initiatives are doing about its promotion (we suggest very little of real use)—not to mention (let alone discuss) the use of foreign law in court decisions. Even the tantalising view of the former President of the section du contentieux of the Conseil d'Etat, M. Bruno Genevois, thus only receives a fleeting mention on page 58 instead of being seized up and made the subject of a sub-heading. Such an indifference to case law, such a failure to discuss its content, its innovations and its shortcomings, and spending all 31 pages of the essay on what *academics* say can only come from the pen of a Continental lawyer, trained in the Continental way, and minimally (if at all) sensitive to Anglo-Saxon realities. Thus, the only reference to the 'real' world and how comparative law can affect it is to the legislature.

This is again a typical Continental European reaction for it ignores the growing importance of case law and the growing interaction that is taking place among senior judges. It also fails to give us a hint on how precisely comparative law is influencing legislative work; what kind of material is reaching the legislatures; who prepares it; whether it is subjected to any scrutiny other than an examination by ministerial civil servants; and how able legislators are to understand English drafting techniques or discover the ratio decidendi of the decisions of multi-member supreme courts. These are the kind of focused, detailed, meaningful points which we should be discussing—rather than filling the pages of a book with a descriptive narrative that does little to further the subject we all wish to preserve.

For those of us who feel that comparative law must learn to target an audience and how to interest and instruct it, a mentality and educational change has to take place. How and where does one start? By re-orienting our gaze and asking the next two basic questions.[86]

(ii) Who is Able to Take the Lead in Promoting the Use of Foreign Law in France?

An academic would normally think of fellow academics and assign to them this task. That is what most academics seem to recommend when they speak at French colloquia—and we stress *French* because at international meetings the French presence seems to be weak, at any rate when compared with the German, the Italian and, increasingly, the Spanish. We hope that we will not be considered as being disloyal to our French brethren if we argue that this (revitalising) task is not one that they can perform on their own. For academics no longer are opinion-formers, whether one sees them individually or as a closely knit class[87] (not in France and, probably, not in most European systems either). In France, and as far as comparative law is concerned, lawyers thus seem to fall into one of three groups; and each group has looked upon comparative law in a different way.

The first is still composed of academics (largely) using David's method and attributing to comparative law primarily a mission civilisatrice.[88] Professor Moréteau, without being as

[86] There is a third (purely financial) one but with huge psychological implications for the French: can they somehow find a way to enlist the support of the private sector and confront the growing financial difficulties which they otherwise face?

[87] See Professor Philippe Jestaz and Christoph Jamin, *La Doctrine* (2004).

[88] We say nothing of some notable exceptions like our colleague Mireille Delmas-Marty who, especially in her work on criminal law, has followed the example of the late André Tunc and made a focused use of foreign material when discussing the European perspectives of her chosen subject.

blunt as we are, seems to suggest that this mission has failed; and if we read him correctly, he also implies that it may have let France down. Though we are admirers of French culture and cannot conceive Europe without a strong dose of French ideas, we agree with Professor Moréteau's pessimistic conclusions. This is a sad admission, especially for the leading author, who pleads guilty of praising—in public and repeatedly—the undoubted greatness of Napoleon and de Gaulle.[89]

The second group of French lawyers, mainly interested in the conflict of laws, Community law, or private law rather than comparative law proper, seem to us to be consumed by the desire to 'react' to European (but not French) initiatives. With few exceptions, many of our university colleagues have been anxious to become part of this 'fire storm' lest they be swept away by it. Professor Fauvarque-Cosson seems, as we already noted, to admit this implicitly. In following this path, the flower of the French legal academe has become 'reactive' not 'proactive' in an attempt to salvage what they can of what once used to be a French pre-eminence. The effort to give it a new lease of life has yet to manifest itself (even though some admirable French scholars are considering ways of updating their own civil code).

If our assessment of the French comparative law scene is—even remotely—correct, then what is happening in France is a recipe for marginalisation even though France (along with Germany) was once the motor of Europe. Such a state of affairs can only please those who see the country as part of the 'old Europe' and not those who are devoted to European co-operation. What we said earlier about Professor Fauvarque-Cosson's essay supports, we feel, this critical assessment of the work of the group of comparatists to which she seems to belong. It still leaves us with some difficulty in explaining what we see as a self-imposed subjugation to initiatives like the one of von Bar.

Of course, the current but partial subjugation to Germanic leadership is not a new experience for French academics.[90] After the defeat in the Franco-Prussian War of 1870 a considerable number of French intellectuals attributed in part at least this defeat to the superiority of the German educational system. To what extent this is plausible is too complex an issue to discuss here. But the fact remains that the appearance of the German Civil Code of 1900 seduced the minds of some of the greatest French intellectuals such as Saleilles and Gény. That was understandable at that time given the excellence of German thought; the current subjugation is, however, less easy to comprehend.

For first, the intellectual activity that preceded the creation of the BGB was one of those very rare and most impressive intellectual phenomena in legal and, generally, cultural history. Secondly, the French scholars who recognised the novelty and utility of some of the German ideas were, themselves, great jurists and confident men of letters. And confident scholars are always willing to learn from others and are not afraid of dialogue or even borrowing. The von Bar project does not fall into this category; it owes the attention it attracts mainly to the impression that the European Commission is hell-bent to see something along these lines one day become accepted in the whole of Europe. That, in itself, is not a good reason for adopting it.

Besides, why should the French sacrifice their own legal system and tradition? How (if ever) can one see the English following suit? And what the logical argument could be for the

[89] 'Deux cents ans dans la vie d'un code célèbre. Réflexions historiques et comparatives à propos des projets européens', RTDciv 2004, pp 45 *ff.*

[90] See Olivier Beaud et Patrick Wachsmann (eds), *La Science juridique française et la science juridique allemande de 1870 à 1918* (1997).

Dutch to scrap a Code which it took them over 40 years to draft is anyone's guess. The truth of the matter is that many Europhiles refuse to see in this exercise much more than the kind of example that helps make the Commission—indeed Brussels as a symbol—look so out of touch with what European citizens need or wish. A number of colleagues are, however, still wasting time on such projects and thus allowing French comparative law to slide behind the position traditionally held by Germany and nowadays closely coveted by the Italians. For the jurists of both these countries are not only much more productive in the comparative field (wherever they may happen to be settled); they are also keenly aware that the European impetus is giving them, as German or Italian lawyers, the chance to put the imprint of *their own system* on the law of the emerging Europe.

The third group of lawyers with a contact to foreign law is found in the larger firms—French or multi-national—*and* the courts. On the whole, both types of jurist seem to be neglected in contemporary discussions about comparative law;[91] and yet they are to us the most active in the field if not also the most important. This group must be divided into two sub-groups and examined in turn.

The first is formed by French-based international practitioners who apply foreign law and employ comparative methodology in their daily work. On the whole, we cannot assess the details of their work since we have little evidence of how they do it. But those of us who have some (slight) involvement with international legal practice know that what we say *does* happen since multi-national firms no longer advise their clients on one system but on many, and are thus able to tell them where to go and which countries to avoid! This enviable position they have achieved, despite local opposition, by recruiting young lawyers from many systems, by paying and promoting them on the basis of Anglo-American and not Continental European models, and also by moving them around in a way that makes them acquire not only physical but also—what is more difficult—intellectual mobility and adaptability. We touch upon some of these points in the Chapter devoted to international commercial practice.

To say to these people—as some teachers do not tire of doing—that international co-operation is not working, that the way to combine different legal solutions is not being constantly refined but, on the contrary, that systems are, because of cultural reasons, destined to live for ever apart, or to tell them that they must consult works on sociology or anthropology, will attract not only their mirth but also their neglect. We know, again from varied personal experience, that these practitioners are always on the lookout for useful, practical, functional co-operation with academics that are prepared to plant their feet firmly into the ground and work with them.

Again, however, we see no real will for such a co-operation on the academic side. Indeed, this very real presence of comparative law is ignored completely in Professor Fauvarque-Cosson's piece. To us, her chapter in the *Oxford Handbook* seems to limit the practical utility of comparative law to the legislative process. This is only a partial presentation of reality; and it may well have been determined subconsciously by the university education she has enjoyed in France. In any event, whatever the cause, the final product of her labours is, in our eyes, disappointing.

In France, however, the courts—the second players in this group—have played both a crucial *and* an increasingly open role in the development of comparative law. Thus, our targeting of judges as the main recipients of the message 'knowing how to use foreign ideas

[91] In Professor Fauvarque-Cosson's essay there is hardly a reference to this phenomenon, even though she must know how active they are and what consternation they are causing to the practising profession in her own country.

can be useful' is just as important and just as workable in France as it is in the Common law world. To put it differently, this is the part of the French legal profession which is moving with the times more than any other. We suggest that it may also be more open to academic give and take than is the legislature, which is more easily approached through the medium of the civil service.

This is a crucial conclusion because (a) judges are the ones who fashion law (under the guise of interpretation) more often than the legislator; (b) if the highest courts send out a signal that they are interested in foreign law, the practitioners will have to follow suit; and (c) since the latter cannot do this kind of work on their own they will, in turn, enlist the help of academics.

Each of these groups could thus be persuaded to do what each can do best, and collaborate in the advancement of the law. This would, incidentally, also bring France into the main world picture as a system which has ideas and is willing to trade them in a world in which more and more depends on the exchange of goods as well as ideas. Lawyers of all types who thus look to South Africa, Canada, Israel, or even America for legal ideas will also be forced to take into account what the French courts do, how they do it, and weigh the advantages of one system against those of others. France would become a player in this international game and not a mere onlooker or borrower. Of course, not all French judges or practitioners will welcome the engagement with foreign law if it involves it taking precedence over French law. Were we French administrative law judges, for instance, we would thus see ourselves as being well placed to export French ideas and solutions. But switch to commercial law or arbitration, and then one senses both the fear of Anglo-Saxon law and the need to learn from its practices.

The work of this group—the judiciary—is not only crucial; it is also more accessible in that (unlike the international law firms) it is open to scrutiny since it can be observed by all and even guided to greater perfection. Can we comparatists refocus our gaze on this group (without ignoring the others)? We have yet to read a French comparative piece advocating this in a *detailed* way, so let us see how it might work in practice.

To effect such a switch one needs to begin by accepting that there is a crisis and that the present focus on pure academics and the support of bureaucrats should change. It is neither sufficient to revitalise the role of comparative law nor, on its own, modernise French justice and bring it into line with what is happening elsewhere. One needs to acquire the will to combat the present crisis, even if this means a change in mentality. This means more than just dreaming of a state-run foundation, as various committees (aided and abetted by the Ministry of Education) have done in the past by producing structures which suffer from all the defects which state-run or state-controlled bodies have had in France for years now.

The French academic world does not lack talent. What it lacks is the imagination to seek additional funding from new sources (including the private sector) and the freedom to operate beyond the kind of oppressive, supervisory, restraining role currently performed by the state and extending over the most trivial administrative decisions. To put it differently, it is content in living under the cosy shadow of state supervision even if the price is stagnation, at least as far as comparative law is concerned. It is interesting to see how difficult it is to get out of this kind of framework. For we are told[92] that the never-created but

[92] By Professor Lyon-Caen. As a Special Advisor of the then (Socialist) Minister of Education it is logical to assume that neither the Minister nor his adviser would have been particularly favourable to the idea of a foundation, independent of the Ministry and privately funded. Indeed, such notions, even after eight years of conservative rule, appear vulgar to many French bureaucrats and academics, seen as likely to compromise academic

long-planned and long awaited Foundation for Comparative Law Studies would, again, have been a state-funded and state-controlled organisation.

A monograph or textbook is not the place to include autobiographical information, yet one piece of information must be made more publicly known than it is since it ties in so well with the arguments made above.

Many of the comparative law activities of the Law Faculty of Paris I in which Madame Fauvarque-Cosson operates have been greatly facilitated by a substantial gift engineered in the late 1990s by the leading author after a long talk with the then Chairman of Clifford Chance, Keith Clark, and the then head of the Paris office of the said multi-national firm, Trevor Brown. The first was a practitioner with huge imagination; he could see the world shrinking, could see the benefits for his firm if he exploited this move first so he acted accordingly. This generous gift has provided Paris I with the funds to invite Oxford scholars to teach in Paris in English; consolidate the possibility of French scholars coming to Oxford to teach French law in French; has allowed Paris I to enrich considerably its holdings of books on English and American law; and, finally, to organise the occasional joint conference. The funds were placed by Clifford Chance in a specially created *Association Oxford-Sorbonne*.

Even the name Sorbonne (rather than Paris) calls for a comment. For it was insisted upon by Paris I so that the funds so received could only be used by them and not shared with the sister (and larger) University of Paris II with which Oxford (rightly) also had close links but with which Paris I has been at war for over 10 years now. Would such additional and greatly needed funds have ever reached Paris I without the generosity of the (English) private sector and with the initiative of individuals imbued with the spirit of free enterprise and entrepreneurial activity? What has enabled Paris I to run part of its international programme with England came from an English, not French initiative; and has been kept alive mainly by English and not French money.

This is not the only initiative the Anglo-Saxons have brought to the French legal scene. For without a similar and equally generous gift recently made by the Cornell Law School,[93] would the Cour de cassation have been able to establish in its own building the first and only *Centre for Documentation for American Law*? Such projects need funds from the private sector. Moreover, they call for action, not committee meetings; determination on the part of those who wish to strengthen links between different legal cultures, not endless planning; and imagination of the kind shown by President Guy Canivet, who, when the opportunity presented itself to him from Cornell, immediately gave this wonderful project his invaluable blessing. The whole deal was 'clinched' in less than one week; had it been obliged to receive ministerial sanction, it would never have happened.

The third and last example to make the criticism strike comes clearly. In the spring of 2008 the Institut de France—France's prime centre of learning which includes the famous Académie française—agreed in principle to receive a hugely generous amount from the Alexander Onassis Public Welfare Foundation in order to establish two prizes to be awarded, one to an eminent lawyer and one to a distinguished classicist. The law prize will not be awarded for distinction in a particular branch of the law but for a contribution that demonstrates 'the unifying power of law' in the 21st century.

independence and (worse still) 'smacking' of American practices. Yet both the present authors have worked, taught, and conducted research in American and European institutions, and have come to admire greatly the advantages gained by American law faculties through their ability to raise and manage their own funds. Here, and not only here, Europeans stand much to learn from the American scene.

[93] In March 2007.

What all these events happening in contemporary France have in common are two things. First, they are supporting local law and local institutions by encouraging a more globalised approach to law. Secondly, they have all originated from outside France but have been realised because they found leading Frenchmen to support their realisation. Those who see nothing but obstacles in cross-cultural ventures must feel deeply disappointed by such developments.

So, if French comparatists wish to see their subject flourish, these are the kind of projects they need to invent, encourage, and support, and not waste their time (and public money) trying to create state-run centres for comparative law which take the form of endless talking shops or argue ad nauseam how culture is an insurmountable obstacle to legal co-operation and even gradual harmonisation of law.

That is the first lesson—but there are others which must be learnt. Those who teach the subject will thus also have to appreciate that ideas, like goods, have to fight in the market place; and in this fight their value is often determined by packaging. If the terms we use seem somewhat inappropriate it is because we wish to drive the point across clearly and not hide behind euphemisms. For this, after all, is a true crisis; and what we said about American law earlier on shows that our colleagues across the Atlantic are not in an 'importing' but 'exporting' mood. They more or less expect us to follow their law as they often wish to impose on us their policies. Between friends there is dialogue not coercion. But friends can also teach one another; and the American educational system owes much of its success to the link it has created and continues to cultivate with the private sector. And the private sector responds if the topic is relevant and not of antiquarian value; if the product offered is useful and not a luxury which should be sought elsewhere; and if the method of operating is streamlined and heavily centralised. We have made many critical observations about the American system. Time now to stress some of its many virtues;[94] and one of them is the fact that they have found a way to finance legal training in a way which, in the end, is bound to leave us all in Europe trailing far behind.

(iii) How to Make the Use of Foreign Law More Attractive

We already gave our reasons why we think courts can play a major role in reviving interest in the study of foreign law. More importantly, we think that there are signs that this is happening. The question is to know where to find the signs for it, and then to encourage them to multiply. If academics help the courts, the courts will, indirectly, return the favour. But are we right in singling out this change for further study? We think that we are.

Take, first, the Conseil d'Etat—possibly France's most famous court. We detect a slow but growing interest in foreign law being manifested in the conclusions of the *Commissaire du Gouvernement* in areas such as civil liability, extradition, or civil liberties. In some earlier examples (for instance the arrêt Cames,[95] a case dealing with a compensation claim arising from injuries sustained in a state arsenal), Commissaire Romieu limited his comparative inquiries to Belgian and Luxembourg law.[96] The scope of this work is not wide but

[94] See also Basil Markesinis, 'Understanding American Law by Looking at it Through Foreign Eyes Towards a Wider Theory for the Study and Use of Foreign Law', 81 *Tulane L Rev* No 1, pp 125, 171–2 (2006).

[95] CE 21 June 1895, Cames 509 concl Romieu; D 1896. 3. 65.

[96] In the early days, the giants of French administrative law (such as Laferrière, Duguit, Hauriou and Carré de Malberg), like their counterparts in private law, had a visible interest in German rather than English law, something which must be explicable in part because of the Dicean influence but also because indigenous English administrative law is a product of much more recent times.

its limitation to systems which have some affinity between themselves is understandable. If this interpretation has some truth in it, surely it confirms our repeated theme, namely that borrowing will be attempted if it seems sensible and feasible.

In later cases, for instance in one decision where the question was the extent of the liability of the state for negligent supervision of banks,[97] the range of research was widened considerably to include American, English, and German law. The widening of the scope of the research can be due to many reasons but one would venture the guess that the subject-matter triggered the interest in Anglo-American law. The same happened in what one could describe as the administrative equivalent of the affaire *Perruche*,[98] where Madame Pécresse looked at American and English law.[99] Here there may be an additional reason for the growing confidence of the Conseil d'Etat to look elsewhere for supporting inspiration—the fact that this problem was first addressed by American courts (which also have the widest and most extensive case law on it).

In yet another case, dealing with a request to extradite a person to a state which applies the death sentence, the Commissaire looked at German, Italian, Austrian, Danish, Swiss and English law and practice.[100] The search is, by now, becoming ambitious; and it is a shame that such 'intellectual adventurism' on behalf of this court has not been widely noted abroad. And so we reach the culmination of this process with a fairly recent decision of the Conseil d'Etat where the English High Court[101] is cited in its opinion.[102] We know of no other judgment before this to have cited a court decision and not just legal or academic texts.

The Cour de cassation was always in a different and, for our purposes, more difficult position. Citing authority of any kind other than to the Code which they are meant to be applying deductively, French courts run the risk of a legal challenge (*pourvois*) for annulment. The same goes for the Cour de cassation, thus putting it at a 'structural disadvantage'[103] when it comes to citing any authority. The evidence of what influenced the court to reach its decision thus has/had to be found either in the opinion of the Avocat Général (which is only advisory and does not bind the court) or the *conclusions* of the *juge rapporteur* who usually guides the court towards agreeing to its final decision. These documents, until recently not always made public, invariably focused on internal law for guidance.

It was during the 'reign' of its former First President Guy Canivet that the Cour de cassation began to show an equal appetitite to inform itself about foreign practices. Canivet, recently promoted to the country's Constitutional Council, proved a great reformer of court practices. And in this context he left his colleagues in no doubt of his wish to take into account foreign learning; and despite his very onerous official duties, he also found time to chair the meetings of the Société de Législation Comparée. This same interest persuaded him to find time to attend meetings of the British Institute of Comparative Law and act as

[97] CE 30 Nov 2001 *Ministre de l'Economie, des Finances et de l'Industrie c Kechichian et al, Les Petites Affiches*, 7 February 2002 No 28 concl Seban; discussed by D Fargrieve and K Belloir, 'Liability of the French State for negligent Supervision of Banks', (1999) 10 *European Business Law Review* 17.

[98] Ass Plén 17 Nov 2000, JCP 13 December 2000, no 50, 2293.

[99] CE 14 February 1997 *Centre Hospitalier Regional de Nice*, RFDA 1997, 374, concl Pécresse.

[100] CE 15 October 1993, Mme Aylor, 283 concl Vigourouz; RFDA 1993,1179.

[101] *Abna Ltd v Secretary of State and FSA* (6 October 2003).

[102] CE, no 260768 of 29 October 2003.

[103] See Guy Canivet, 'Le juge entre le progrès scientifique et mondialisation', 33 No 1 RTDCiv (2005), at p 25: 'En France, la Cour de cassation et les autres juridictions sont *structurellement* contraintes, par le style d'écriture traditionnel de l'arrêt à phrase unique et l'impossibilité de l'explication interprétative de la règle, à nc pas se referrer expressément aux droits étrangers dans le corps même de l'arrêt'.

co-editor for one of its most successful volumes.[104] But Guy Canivet, like Aharon Barak and many senior German judges of the German Constitutional Court (including its current President Hans-Jürgen Papier), is not only a judge; he has taught law and has even co-authored an elegant piece on academics as judges[105]—something which can happen in many Continental countries.[106]

With such a background and mentality, his insistence that foreign law be used by his judges was thus not a surprise. The example given by the Conseil d'Etat thus spread to the senior civil and criminal court of France. And the way that foreign law was 'fed' to the Court also betrayed Canivet's extra-curricular preoccupations. For in at least two instances[107] the Court requested the Société de Législation Comparée to prepare notes on the state of foreign law on the issue then before it[108] in order to provide it with ideas and inspiration.[109] And not only did that happen; the Court also insisted (unknowingly addressing one of Justice Scalia's criticisms of comparative methodology in *Roper*) that these documents be circulated in advance to all parties concerned so as to give them the chance to discuss them and express views on their merits.

The examples have since multiplied, and one more recent instance will suffice to prove all of the above. It can be found in the decision of the First Civil Chamber of the Court of cassation in the case of Stéphane Chapin and Bertrand Charpentier.[110] Both these men decided to 'marry' and, despite the opposition of the local Procureur, the Mayor inscribed their 'union' as a 'marriage' in the official records of a small village in the region of the Gironde. The Court of First Instance, acting at the instance of the Procureur of the Republic of Bordeaux, ordered that the marriage be declared void. The competent Court of Appeal, which next heard the case, confirmed this decision on the grounds that according to the Civil Code only marriages between heterosexuals could be so registered. A further appeal to the Court of cassation, inter alia on the grounds that this violated European human rights law, was rejected.

What makes this case interesting for our purposes is the fact that the Cour de cassation asked the Institute of Comparative Law of the University of Lyon to provide an account of how other systems dealt with the issue. It did so because (as the Avocat Général Domingo said early on in his long, detailed, and fascinating report) the matter could not be resolved by means of a simple hermeneutical interpretation of the Code given that the text of the relevant articles was mostly silent and only indirectly gave evidence that marriage was

[104] With Professor Mads Andenas and Dr Duncan Fairgrieve, *Comparative Law before the Courts* (2004). The choice of the co-editors is itself indicative of a keen interest in detailed comparative law since both are among the leading comparatists currently working in Britain and (in the case of Dr Fargrieve) France.

[105] 'Des "Professeurs-Juges" aux "Juges-Professeurs"' in *La Cour de cassation, L'université et le droit, Etudes en l'Honneur de A Ponsard*, Editions du Juris Classeur (2003), pp 115 *ff.* See also his 'La Cour de cassation et la doctrine' in *Propos sur les obligations et quelques autres thèmes fondamentaux du droit. Mélanges offerts à Jean-Luc Aubert*, Dalloz (2005), pp 373 *ff.*

[106] And Commonwealth countries such as Canada. The former Chief Justice Bora Laskin and, more recently, Justice Iaccobucci are good examples of having combined both professions.

[107] In the above-mentioned *Perruche* case and also in Procureur général près la cour d'appel de Metz, Ass plénière 29 June 2001, D 2916. The whole topic is discussed in greater detail by Guy Canivet, 'The Use of Comparative Law Before the French Private Law Courts' in Guy Canivet, Mads Andenas and Duncan Fairgrieve (eds), *Comparative Law Before the Courts* (2004), pp 181, esp pp 187 *ff.*

[108] This is also the standard way by which German courts inform themselves about foreign law.

[109] For more details see Guy Canivet, 'The Use of Comparative Law Before the French Private Law Courts' in Guy Canivet, Mads Andenas and Duncan Fairgrieve (eds), *Comparative Law Before the Courts* (2004), pp 182 *ff.*

[110] Pourvoi no B 05-16.627, Arrêt no 511 FP-P+B+R+1 of 113 March 2007.

conceived as a union between heterosexuals. In such circumstances it was felt that the problem could only be resolved if a wider reflection on the institution of marriage was undertaken against a fairly detailed historical survey and—here is the key as far as we are concerned—the resolution given to this (new) problem by other major legal systems. The court thus considered the laws of a number of American States, England, Denmark, Sweden and Germany (which had solved the problem by means of passing special legislation permitting same-sex partnerships), the laws of the Netherlands, Belgium, and Spain, as well as a decision of the Supreme Court of South Africa, which had allowed a 'fully blown' marriage. The result reached (that France had opted for the first approach and that this was in no way incompatible with the case law of the Court of Human Rights of Strasbourg) is not what concerns us here. What is important for the purposes of this work are four points.

First is the new tendency of the Court of cassation to inform itself about the laws of other systems before deciding a novel or difficult point of national law. The importance of this is particularly felt when the local texts are silent on the point, and the problem (often l e it is new) has been one confronted by other 'major' legal systems of the world. Second way this material is assembled—not under the aegis of 'interested parties' but by speciali and neutral institutions such as well-established centres of foreign and comparative la which are found in most major European systems. This material was then distributed to th parties, who had a chance to comment on it before it was discussed by the Avocat Génér and then the Court itself. Third is the fact that this way of proceeding minimised weight—real or alleged—of difficulties concerning the reliability and up-to-date na the research of the parties as well as the excuse that the judges were not in a positic foreign texts for themselves. This of course does not mean that the research co these institutes is infallible; it does however insulate a court from criticism of ous incompetence, given that these institutions are staffed and equipped by sonnel and (largely) set up and paid by the state to provide precisely this and 'scientific' service. Finally, this kind of very thorough research puts the Fre Court ahead of the German and English highest courts. We feel confident in predic once this practice becomes more widely known and, of course, is refined in its applica n, it will find other imitators in Europe and elsewhere.

Now these are signs of progress. Even though the form in which foreign law was presented has not always been ideal or as thorough as one would have liked it to be, even if the frequency is not yet so overwhelming, even if (understandably) it is limited to the highest levels of the judicial process—the above examples show that such exercises have been undertaken and may well be on their way of becoming routine.

Those law teachers who constantly advocate applying Jacques Derrida's deconstructionist methods to law and argue that modern legal systems cannot cross-fertilise each other should carefully ponder over the implications of this practice. Probably they will not, since academics often fall in love with their theories. Yet if they persist, they will remain voices crying in the wilderness. That, however, is not a way either to teach or influence the future growth of comparative law. In the meantime, this kind of activity, undertaken by judicial officers, is the activity which is breathing new life into comparative law in France.

Let us, however, return to the question how one can improve the use of foreign law by national courts. We put our views forward in the form of six propositions; and we are advancing these ideas for discussion not because we think that they are fully developed but because we think they provide a *different* starting point.

First, as Lord Bingham once put it before having himself recourse to foreign law—mainly French and German—in order to construct his argument,[111]

> [I]f . . . a decision is given in this country which offends one's basic sense of justice, and if consideration of international sources suggests that a different and more acceptable decision would be given in most other jurisdictions, whatever their legal tradition, this must prompt anxious review of the decision in question. In a shrinking world . . . there must be virtue in uniformity of outcome whatever the diversity of approach in reaching that outcome.

This is what the French supreme court is doing in a pioneering manner.

Secondly, though a court is free to consult as many foreign jurisdictions as it deems appropriate (or can by virtue of its resources), it must try to focus on either major jurisdictions whose laws have proved their worth over time and space, and/or consult courts of new countries which have proved creative. We considered this point above, so we need only to refer briefly to it here. Suffice it to say that the effort we are asking the judges to make does not mean that

> development of the law in this country [France] can depend on a head-count of decisions and codes adopted in other countries around the world, often against a background of different rules and traditions.[112]

Once again, judges and legislators (aided by academics) must learn to choose where to seek inspiration and guidance. In the development of the basic principles of European Community law they can find excellent examples of methodology, some due to the talents of early French Advocates General. We feel that this is, broadly, what the Cour de cassation is doing.

Thirdly, great French figures such as Saleilles and Lambert did wonders for French comparative law. But they also left a dark legacy (especially the latter) by encouraging a long tradition which has removed the Common law from its immediate list of interests. Nowadays, of course, law and politics combine, and in the post-referendum climate in France foster the clash between the Anglo-Saxon versus the Gallic ideologies. It would be a great shame if this politically accentuated difference was allowed to impede a stronger legal dialogue between the two systems. Again, the French Supreme Court is branching out on its own and paying particular attention to what is happening in the Anglo-American world.

Fourthly, those presenting the foreign material to the national (potential) borrower must learn the art of 'packaging' it in a way which makes the material usable by the 'importer'. The leading author has dealt with this subject in many of his works over a period of 35 years;[113] and the extent to which it has worked in practice—at any rate in Great Britain—makes one feel that the method deserves at least some attention and, one would hope, further refinement. This means the French should focus their minds not on *droit comparé* but on *Rechtvergleichung*, for the first is a subject that does not exist whereas the second is a methodology which needs more attention. This step remains to be perfected in France but we venture to suggest that if it is still in its infancy it is because French academics persist in dealing with foreign law at a level of generalities, neglecting case law and the need to 'package' it in a way that could be useful to their courts.

[111] *Fairchild v Glenhaven Funeral Services Ltd* [2003] 1 AC 32, 66.

[112] Per Lord Bingham, *ibid* at p 66.

[113] *Foreign Law and Comparative Methodology. A Subject and a Thesis* (1977) and *Always on the Same Path. Essays on Foreign Law and Comparative Methodology* (2001).

Fifthly, 'packaging' requires that the potential borrower is presented with factually equivalent situations, shown what results they produce in practice and what broader consequences they may have on other, related parts of the law, and, where necessary, given the wider background of the foreign system. This is neither easy to do nor instantly achievable in a country with a tradition of borrowing which has been traditionally slanted towards German rather than Anglo-American law and, moreover, has derived its inspiration from books and treatises rather than foreign case law. Yet it is the 'contrast' of the images—Common law/civil law—which is most likely to stimulate the legal mind towards new thinking. This material should also, where possible, be made available to all parties in the judicial or legislative process well in advance, inviting them to consider it and—through the purifying ordeal of adversarial analysis—(hopefully) reveal its value (or lack of it) to those who make decisions. For what matters most in such exercises is not the *specific solution* but the *thinking process behind it.* Guy Canivet has touched on this idea over and over again, which only goes to prove that no French reader of this text should rush to call its prescriptions unworkable in France since one of the country's most eminent judges has made similar recommendations.

Finally, let us not forget that if the French show a focused interest in foreign law they may not only benefit from its experience (particularly on commercial practices) but also acquire the right to ask others to consider their own solutions where historical experience, logic, or common sense makes them worthy of consideration. In our view, the recent innovations of the Cour de cassation will soon come to the attention of other courts and give it a higher profile than it has ever had before outside the world of francophonie.

11. COMPARATIVE POSTSCRIPT

The sketch attempted in this Chapter tries to show that the connection between judicial decision-making on the one hand and politics and ideology on the other often lurks just under the surface of judicial decisions which give the impression to depend on statute or precedent. To a considerable extent, the same idea can be found in the next Chapter where English and French law will be compared on a narrower (but important) topic.

This linking of political ideology and purely legal interpretation does, of course, not figure prominently or openly in most cases. The bulk of case law does, indeed, depend for its outcome on an almost mechanical application of precedent or a deductive application of a statutory provision to the facts before the judge. But in important, new, and controversial areas of public and private law this is not so; and judicial discretion is increasingly shaped by a host of underlying factors, including political ideology and the judge's own background, outlook, and mentality.[114] To argue that this is a new idea would be wrong; to deny that in modern American constitutional law this link has achieved new heights would, however, also deprive us of the chance to draw a number of conclusions.

What is especially fascinating in the contemporary American debate is the degree to which German theorising has been replicated, sometimes in extreme forms. The extremes are not, we think, caused by the fact that American judges and academics are more

[114] See Basil Markesinis, 'Judicial Mentality: Mental Disposition and Outlook as a Factor Impeding recourse to Foreign Law', 80 no 4 *Tulane L Rev* 1325–75 (2006).

conscious of the fact that 'political thinking' tends to affect the canons of statutory interpretation but arguably because of their more polemical language, which is so obvious in the modern American legal discourse; for the latter seems to us to be less inclined to try and hide the political ideology which underlies the dry canons of construction of legal texts. The American eponymous judgment thus brings the political element in a legal dispute more to the fore than is the case in the European context—national or at the level of the two European courts—where niceties smooth the edges, make legal debate more civilised, but also often hide the real battle that is taking place under the surface.

Scepticism to things foreign is another notable feature of contemporary American legal debates. It is, of course, also tied to confidence in things local. Pride is something to be understood and respected, especially when it is warranted. Not surprisingly, it has also be seen as a cardinal sin, especially when it is accompanied by arrogance. In many areas of human endeavour we find both these aspects of 'pride' in contemporary American intellectual life; and we believe that it will only last until the dominance acquired after the collapse of the Soviet Union is lost and the next world rival acquires an equal standing. We do not suppose that this will happen in the near future; and that is why we tried to suggest some more narrow and practical lessons which we can learn from American scepticism towards other cultures and, above all, the values currently adopted and shared by most European courts.

To put it differently, we must take the American objections to legal borrowings seriously, and try and learn from them and not denounce them outright. This does not mean that, for the time being, we have a good chance of influencing the thought of our American colleagues; indeed, the shift to the 'Right', established by the judicial appointments of President Bush, is certain to outlive his own tenure at the White House. Yet the scepticism of American judges towards foreign law and values could teach those of us with more obvious internationalist tendencies to perfect our own methods of finding, analysing and using foreign law in our own courts. In particular, we must try to learn *where* to seek enlightenment, *how* to use foreign material, and explain *why* by doing so we are not endangering the rich diversity of European culture. This does not mean concocting 'synthetic codes' on the basis of the minimum common denominators found in a number of legal systems; nor does it mean leaving such a delicate task to be designed by travelling academics and then enforced by EU officials. But it does mean understanding what unites and what divides us; and learning to what extent the movement of ideas across borders is an advantage, and from what point onwards it becomes an unwelcome imposition. This understanding can come only from real experience, not academic seclusion; and this, essentially, requires political realism and not donnish learning. This, then, is our main message which, in essence, is nothing more than a call for co-operation of all agents who help make and apply law to our daily problems.

The attentive reader will have noticed that we see in comparative law not only a subject to exercise one's analytical talents but also a political tool for promoting one's own culture. The experience in the United States at present seems to us to illustrate the deep agonising this topic is causing to this great friend and ally. However, this period of (legal) indecision, doubt, insularity, and even arrogance which is found in some of this country's lawyers must not be condemned with too much haste since, for different reasons, it may well find parallels on this side of the Atlantic. It must thus be used as an opportunity for reflection and self-examination. Do we, ourselves, do the same? Are we, also, quick to see foreigners in terms of stereotypes and damn their attributes? If we do, we must be condemned as much as we condemn such attitudes in the United States. More importantly, it also offers an opportunity for our Continent to react and re-assert its own credentials. Arrogance must not be met by arrogance; introversion must be answered by open-mindedness; heated debate replaced by calm dialogue, even when one's views are expressed boldly and without too many niceties. The intelligent study and use of foreign law could be one of the weapons at our disposal. And it will be intelligent if it is appreciated that it forms part of what Aristotle considered the supreme science of politics.

7

THE FOCUSED APPROACH IN PUBLIC LAW: A LOOK AT ENGLISH AND FRENCH LAW

1. INTRODUCTION: THE GENERAL AND THE PARTICULAR

This Chapter again deals with public law. The systems compared here are the French and the English. The German position on the main topic under consideration, tortious liability of statutory bodies (mainly public authorities), is addressed separately below.

The material presented here is again an example of the detailed and functional comparison which we advocate throughout this book. The comparison in both these Chapters is thus not one which compares the entire field of administrative law,[1] let alone public law, in different countries. This would require a much larger effort and would be outside the scope of this book.[2] Consistent with our theory of trying to limit comparative law to narrow and definable subjects, our aim here is to look at one type of litigated case and compare both results and reasoning, as well as investigate the factors 'behind the judicial scene' that produce these outcomes in order to see what we can discover about other people's law (as well as ourselves).

The types of cases we have chosen are taken from one area of litigation which overlaps the domains of tort law and administrative law. From the outset they thus raise difficulties of classification, which will be discussed more fully in Chapter Nine. Additionally, these cases—though forming only a small percentage of the total volume of litigated tort/administrative law issues (especially in France)—are important nonetheless. For they will not only enable us to examine how similar factual configurations have been dealt with in most systems. They will also tell us how they have been treated by different courts and, more importantly, help us show that the solutions adopted by national courts may change from time to time in one and the same country. This, among other interesting consequences, means that the compared systems may converge as well diverge, and are not condemned[3] by 'culture' to remain always apart.

Such comparisons, however, can yield further important benefits. For the cases here reviewed will enable us to suggest the kind of *further* research which a jurist faced with divergent court answers may feel compelled to undertake in order to understand better

[1] This is admirably achieved by a scholar who knows not only how to summarise but also how to be original at the same time: John S Bell, 'Comparative Administrative Law' in Matthias Reimann and Reinhard Zimmermann (eds), *The Oxford Handbook of Comparative Law* (2006), pp 1259–86.

[2] This has, to some extent, already been done by others. For Anglo-French comparisons see Duncan Fairgrieve, *State Liability on Tort. A Comparative Law Study* (2003) and Spyros Flogaitis, *Administrative law et droit administrative* (1988) and *La notion de décentralisation en France, en Allemagne et en Italie* (1979). For German/European work see Jürgen Schwartze, *Administrative Law Under European Influence* (1996). Finally, for an Anglo-American approach see Bernard Schwartz and Henry William Rawson Wade, *Legal Control of Government* (1972).

[3] Thus Pierre Legrand in most of his work, notably: 'The Same and the Different' in Legrand and Munday, *Comparative Legal Studies: Traditions and Transitions* (2003), pp 240 *ff* and *Le droit comparée* (1999).

both the foreign law and his own (apparently inevitable) solutions. This 'learning where to look' is already a benefit gained by the outside observer, however experienced he may be in his own system. For it will accustom him to the fact that he must learn early on in his comparative life the art of overcoming the artificial hurdles of classification which history or accident have imposed upon different legal systems. This further and more complex enquiry will then offer our comparatist jurist the chance to evaluate to what extent local cultural or technical rules, lying perhaps outside his chosen area of comparison, intermingle with his subject and help explain the result reached by a particular system.

All of the above not merely helps restate the obvious, namely that we remain keenly aware of the fact that legal rules or judicial decisions can only be understood within the broader context of their society; it will also show that, in our view, these broader 'cultural' factors may change within one and the same system and, as they change, so will its law.

Since here we are talking of public law we must also stress that in this area more than in 'pure' private law the wider political setting has a deeper and more obvious impact on the legal problem before a court. In some respects this may accentuate the differences over the similarities that exist between different legal systems, and make borrowings more problematic. Those who, like us, believe in stressing the often missed similarities must in this area of the law be exceptionally vigilant.

The change of political views and the consequences they can have on litigation (which, on its face, has nothing to do with political struggles) has happened both in France and elsewhere, and systems may thus seem far less different depending on how cultural factors move or change in a globalised setting.

But there may be more than a convergence of solutions. If properly instructed, one may be able to discover similarities in the reasoning, especially in the underlying policy arguments that dictate a particular judgment and, in the end, militate for or against liability. The quotations we give later will also show that the underlying policy arguments can be the same even in two systems which, in the present phase of their development, may appear to be quite different in their philosophies as well as their results. That French law currently favours claimants thus does not mean that the policy arguments for or against liability have disappeared just as they exist in current English law. The current French solutions are thus nothing more than a reflection of a change in French political thinking which more or less foreshadowed the coming of the Mitterrand years.

The above observations not only put the differences between French and English law in a more meaningful perspective than the partisans of 'irreconcilable differences' would like us to believe. They could also be seen to leave open the possibility that, one day, French law might revert to its original more pro-defendant position (for reasons similar to those advanced by English judges) or, conversely, we could see Lord Bingham's views triumph in England, pushing English law closer to the (currently) more socially conscious French rules. Which of these two alternatives occurs is not our concern. What we are interested in pointing out is that either could happen and thus having recourse to wider cultural factors in order to suggest that comparison is difficult and convergence is impossible is not really a convincing position to hold.

In our view, however, the focused approach which we advocate again presents an important benefit. Put simply, it is that the study of a foreign legal system, especially through decisional law rather than through doctrinal writings, has the advantage of putting the novice at ease by creating an initial shield from the often so off-putting conceptualism of foreign systems. For invariably in such studies one is starting the discovery by looking at litigated situations that are the same in most countries.

Teaching and understanding law through cases also offers the inestimable advantage of making the student's experience of the world deepen as his study progresses in sophistication. Of course, the product of such research, initially quite fragmented, can resemble a painting of the pointilliste school. This means that one has to learn to stand somewhat back and slowly take in the whole. The contrast with the world of geometry, architecture, and consistency, which *academic lawyers* so like to construct—forcing them to prepare handouts and subjecting them to the modern teaching assessment exercises that give preference to structure over themes and insights—could not be greater. Yet the comparative juxtaposition of factually similar cases makes one feel at home. For the observer is comparing familiar situations and is not confused by structures, terminology or concepts that are either impossible to translate or, if apparently translatable, misleading. The study of French or German administrative law reveals many such terms which do not yield to an obvious translation or, more troublesome, to a translation which must be slightly mutated to accommodate the circumstances. So the reality (or illusion) of similarity is shattered once we move to concepts, which is how comparative law has often been taught. The comparison of two systems through their concepts is thus—at first instance at least—off-putting. This is because, look if you must, you cannot find the concept, notion, or architecture[4] you are looking for which is so self-evident to your foreign colleague.[5] By contrast, the two systems come much closer when you look at litigated cases and discover that the differences in result are diminished. That neither system functions as purely as it is meant to do is inevitable since the neatness that can exist in the world of ideas is rarely found in the real world of litigation. But discovering this on one's own through detailed research has its particular rewards.

2. A STUDY IN PARALLEL

In accordance with the above methodology, we shall in this sub-section look at one factual variant in two legal systems: the English and the French. Lack of space prevents us from including the German counterparts; though the conclusions that one can draw from this system are, in their essentials, not that different from those applicable to French law.[6] The

[4] By this we mean the systematic arrangement of the subjects. The English tort of nuisance thus appears as part of the French law of property (and related rights), and a search for it in a French tort treatise would produce little of interest to a common lawyer. It is only when one reflects on the generic rubric of *troubles de voisinage* that one realises that what one system sees as rights another can, equally sensibly, examine under the heading of wrongs. History is, of course, responsible for this different optic which does not, however, affect the similarity of litigated cases nor their outcome.

[5] The same is, of course, true if one compares French and English law. The cardinal common law notion of 'duty of care' is thus totally absent from Article 1382 CC though many decades ago Planiol and Savatier came close to recreating it for French law; see Planiol, *Traité élémentaire de droit civil* (11th edn), no 863 and Savatier, *Traité de la reponsabilité civile* (2nd edn 1951), pp 56–134. Examples such as these are particularly important since they show how close the different systems can be, and that if they have come to follow different paths this does not mean that their differences are insurmountable.

[6] The next few sections make use of material contributed by Professor Jean Bernard Auby (and to a lesser extent by the first of the present authors) to a book co-authored with Professor Dagmar Coester-Waltjen and Dr Simon Deakin entitled *Tortious Liability of Statutory Bodies* (1999). In *practical* terms, the most important difference between French and German law is the absence of statistics (eg, details of award levels) in France as compared to the enormous volume of information available in Germany (see our observations on that in Chapter Nine).

aim is to show how one can compare different systems at a level of considerable specificity and then, as one fans out, begin to get a wider picture of the foreign legal system. Here we apply our chosen method to public law. The factual variant we look at deals with claims for negligent exercise of powers vested in social services meant to protect children in danger or with special needs.

X (Minors) v Bedfordshire County Council[7] was one of two 'child-abuse' actions (consolidated and heard together with three other cases not discussed here). It arose in connection with a claim that a local authority negligently and in breach of its statutory obligations failed to exercise its powers to institute care proceedings after it had received serious reports that the claimant/child had been the subject of parental abuse and neglect. The second case—*M (A Minor) v Newham London Borough Council*—was the mirror image of the first. For here the complaint was based on the negligent removal of a child from maternal care on the basis of an unfounded belief that the abuse had taken place by the mother's cohabitee and the conclusion that the mother was unable to protect her child. The cases were tried on a matter of law—that is, on the basis that the facts were assumed to be as pleaded—and the House of Lords held that no action lay against the local authority either for its alleged violation of statute or for the tort of negligence. These may be two of the most important recent cases on this kind of subject because of the trouble Lord Browne-Wilkinson took to elaborate his (policy) reasons that led him to decide the case in favour of the defendant councils.

The comparison with the French equivalents is instructive both in substance and style. For in substantive terms the results are diametrically opposed; and in terms of style the judgments are typical of the way judges formulate their reasons in each system. In France they are laconic; one might be tempted to say that judges are continuing the old Royal style of justice where no reasons were given.[8] In the Common law, by contrast, the judgments are not just more expansive; they may also be more informative of what is really happening in the judge's mind.

But let us return to the factual situation of *Bedfordshire*. In the French equivalent of *X v Bedfordshire*, the social services were held liable because of their negligence in the exercise of the powers vested in them for the purposes of protecting children in danger of family abuse (this administrative duty is called *protection maternelle et infantile*). In *Epoux Quaras*[9] a three-year-old girl had been sent, with the agreement of her parents, to stay with a foster family for three months. The foster family—which was not French—had been selected by an association devoted to childcare. The child was seriously maltreated. Her parents were granted compensation. The *Conseil d'Etat* considered that the administration was at fault for not having verified the reliability of the foster family carefully enough.

Another French case offers a possible comparison with *Newham*.

In *M et Mme Pillon*[10] the *Conseil d'Etat* held that a social service had committed no fault in not warning the authority able to institute care proceedings about the threat posed to the health of children entrusted to the care of a particular family (information collected by the agency pointed to such dangers, and the concern should have been even greater given that the family had refused permission to the social workers to enter their house and talk to the children). It follows from these facts that had fault been found, liability would have ensued.

[7] [1995] 3 WLR 152.

[8] On this see Sir Basil Markesinis, 'French System Builders and English Problem Solvers: Missed and Emerging Opportunities for Convergence of French and English Law', 40 *Texas Intern L J* No 4, 663 (2005).

[9] Conseil d'Etat, 23 septembre 1987, *Recueil des arrêts du Conseil d'Etat*, 290.

[10] Conseil d'Etat, 4 mai 1983, no 22811.

To an English lawyer the facts as given would indicate the presence of fault, but we cannot labour this point too much given that the finding of fault depended on the particular circumstances of each case, and we do not have them before us as the court did.

The outcome of the litigation, however, clearly shows how the controlling device of fault works in practice. But one must also note the dangers that may arise from the fact that such determinations may only be possible *after* litigation has taken place. To an English lawyer this observation will not just be crucial, but also, arguably, a reinforcement for his view to dispose of such disputes without the cost and delays of a full trial. Nevertheless, one must also repeat (perhaps with some degree of surprise) the paucity of French litigated examples—something which must indicate that in *practice* the potential liability rule has not opened the floodgates of litigation. Probably, as in Germany, the acceptance of liability *in principle* means that these conflicts are settled and not litigated. Unlike Germany, however, we do not have empirical evidence about these conflicts (whether settled or litigated), their success rate if the latter occurs, and—above all—the levels of damages which they produce.

In this context, it must be noted that England, too, lacks empirical evidence on these matters and that this may encourage our judges to resolve such disputes largely on the basis of (their own) hunches as to what might happen if liability was accepted in principle—and hence to exclude damages (in our view often the most important remedy) by arguing that deserving claimants have a host of other remedies.[11]

But let us resume our comparison with French law.

The factual examples we have chosen could not be narrower. Yet, as will be shown, the true value of our example lies not so much in the human interest in these actions which, of course, is great. It also lies in the fact that the arguments used in these cases for and against liability are broadly applicable over a wide range of state liability situations. This means two things.

First, we can draw supporting statements from cases dealing with factual permutations of our chosen example. Secondly, it means that if at some stage we reach a point where the systems diverge despite the factual similarity of the instances considered, we have to start looking into other areas of the law for explanations. Which areas these are (for example, procedure, form of trial, measure of damages, or history) does not really matter. What matters is that the search (and the knowledge that comes with it) has now been broadened to include such topics as the law of damages, the law of social security, the law of procedure, and the legal history of each system.

Equally noteworthy is the fact that, equipped with the sense of security acquired by the knowledge that we are dealing with a familiar problem, we feel courageous enough to venture into these others areas of foreign law which, had we tried to tackle them *de nuovo*, we might have found forbidding. It is our submission, therefore, that our proposed methodology draws the researcher into the foreign system rather than allowing different conceptualisms to put him off its study. One might even express the idea differently and say that this way of looking at foreign law 'traps' the wandering mind and prevents it from looking elsewhere; and the more it looks, the more still it will wish to discover. The knowledge of the enquirer, superficial at best to begin with, broadens as it deepens, and the study of foreign law progressively acquires the features of a truly comparative exercise.

[11] This was the position of Lord Browne-Wilkinson in *Bedfordshire* and Lord Steyn in *Elguzouli Duff v Commissioner of Police of the Metropolis.*

One further point needs to be addressed. Is the similarity (or the potential re-emergence of a once existent similarity) affected by the differing judicial styles? In a thoughtful piece, Professor Gerhard Dannemann seems to suggest that we are inconsistent when arguing in favour of similarities or convergence and yet note the differences in judicial styles (as the leading author has done repeatedly).[12] We do not see this inconsistency.

For our method is precisely aimed at showing the similarities that exist between the legal systems *but are concealed by the different apparel.* The quotations we give below from the works of many eminent French experts show that the policy arguments used by the English courts are not unknown in France. Moreover, the practice of the French courts up until the 1960s also shows that their decisions did not differ significantly in their results from those reached by their English counterparts. Yet both these similarities, one still alive and well, would completely escape foreign observers who did not know how to study and research foreign law. Indeed, as we suggest below, some of the points made in this Chapter may not be clearly imprinted even in the French legal minds; and it takes comparatists such as Dr Fairgrieve to bring them out into the open.

The same lesson was made in the two volumes on the German Law of Obligations published by the leading author, the second of which (devoted to the German law of Contract) initially involved Dr Dannemann (as he then was). There, too, the presentation of the material was through decisions which we all knew were stylistically different from the English decisions. There, too, the emphasis was to present German law in a way that made it accessible to a Common law reader. There, too, much effort was made to show how the two contract laws—the English and the German—had many common points and not only differences. And talking of differences, neither Professor Dannemann nor we, nor, indeed, any comparatist worth his salt are unaware of the differences that exist between the various legal systems. It is just that those of us who believe in the emerging Europe and the exchange of ideas have consciously chosen to stress similarities—knowing that everyone up until the 1970s had been talking about the differences. Is this way of analysing legal material wrong? We submit that there is much evidence besides that which we adduce ourselves, and many other authors who venture to suggest otherwise. Nor is the method intellectually dishonest, as Professor Legrand has come close to suggesting. The underlying political philosophy has repeatedly been made clear.[13] And in admitting that we also have political beliefs that shape our legal views, we are no different from such greats of our subject as Ernest Rabel or René David. On the whole it would thus be preferable if our views were approached critically (by all means) but also constructively in the interests of what we regard as the 'common legal venture' (the success of the subject in educational and practical terms) rather than be dismissed as 'tenaciously delusional or stubbornly disingenuous'.[14]

So let us proceed with our experiment. How did the French and English courts deal with our problem?

[12] 'Comparative Law: Study of Similarities or Differences?' in Mathias Reimann and Reinhard Zimmermann (eds), *The Oxford Handbook of Comparative Law* (2006), pp 383, 395.

[13] See Basil Markesinis, *Foreign Law and Comparative Methodology: A Subject and a Thesis* (1997).

[14] Legrand, 'The Same and the Different' in Pierre Legrand and Roderick Munday (eds), *Comparative Legal Studies: Traditions and Transitions* (2003), pp 240 *ff* (at p 247).

3. THE REASONING OF THE COURTS

In the *Bedfordshire* decision the 'technical' (legal) arguments connected with tort liability[15] were limited to the enquiry whether the local authority owed a direct duty of care to the children.[16] Lord Browne-Wilkinson's remarks are brief on two of the usual requirements of liability—foreseeability and proximity—largely because the local authority (wisely) chose not to challenge the fact that they were satisfied in this case. Instead, he asserted (without discussion and, some might argue, not so convincingly) that the requirement of 'fair, just and reasonable' (essentially introduced into our system by the *Peabody*[17] and *Caparo*[18] judgments to provide English judges with an extra ingredient to exclude liability for pure economic loss) also applied to cases involving physical harm to the person.[19] This meant that if the court did not think that it was 'fair, just and reasonable' to discover a duty of care there would be no primary liability.[20]

To decide whether the imposition of liability in this case would be 'fair, just and reasonable', Lord Browne-Wilkinson then switched his gaze towards the policy arguments which, in his view, militated against the presence of any duty. In his Lordship's view these were basically four.[21]

First, imposing liability on the public bodies in question would make bad economic sense. This, of course, is on the assumption that the measure of damages would be great.

Secondly, liability would inhibit the freedom of action of these bodies.

Thirdly, it would be inappropriate for the courts to control elected bodies and tell them how to exercise their discretionary powers.

[15] It would involve too great a digression into English administrative law rules to discuss the local authority's liability for breach of statute. The discussion in the text is thus limited to the tort of negligence.

[16] The question of vicarious liability for the torts of its employees was, initially, left open. It was finally decided in favour of the claimants in *Phelps v Hillingdon London Borough Council* [2000] 3 WLR 776—a decision of the House of Lords which, however, still left open the question whether the local authority could be *primarily* liable.

[17] *Governors of the Peabody Donation Fund v Sir Lindsay Parkinson & Co Ltd* [1985] AC 210, 241C, per Lord Keith. The idea can, however, be traced back to Lord Morris' judgment in the *Dorset Yacht* case in 1970.

[18] *Caparo Industries plc v Dickman* [1990] 2 AC 605.

[19] [1995] 3 WLR 152 at 183. This was, indeed, accepted by the majority in *Marc Rich & Co AG v Bishop Rock Marine Co Ltd* [1996] 1 AC 211—a case involving property damage. Two years later an attempt was made to transport this reasoning to cases of physical injury in *Perret v Collins* [1998] 2 Lloyd's Rep 255 but it was boldly rejected by a unanimous Court of Appeal. Lord Justice Hobhouse (as he then was) had this to say on this crucial issue (at 258): 'What the second and third defendants seek to achieve in this case is to extend decisions upon "economic" loss to cases of personal injury. It represents a fundamental attack upon the principle of tortious liability for negligent conduct, which had caused foreseeable personal injury to others. That such a point should be considered to be even arguable shows how far some of the fundamental principles of the law of negligence have come to be eroded. The arguments advanced in this case [viz that the kind of wider policy considerations used in *Marc Rich* to justify the majority decision should also be used in this case and absolve the defendants from all liability] illustrate the dangers of substituting for clear criteria, criteria which are incapable of precise definition and involve what can only be described as an element of subjective assessment by the Court; such ultimately subjective assessments tend inevitably to lead to uncertainty and anomaly which can be avoided by a more principled approach'.

[20] No-one to our knowledge has discussed fully how the vague words 'fair, just and reasonable'—which are tantamount to an invitation to the judge to act as a legislator—quietly 'slipped' into physical injury cases which traditionally (and unlike pure economic loss) have been regarded as a kind of harm which tends to attract the semi-automatic and sympathetic reaction of the law. This, of course, takes the form of an award of damages.

[21] A more recent case where the traditional policy reasons were re-considered, slightly re-arranged so as to be more relevant to the facts, and approved by most of the judges on the panel was *D v East Berkshire Community Health NHS Trust and others; MAK and another v Dewsbury Health Care NHS Trust and another; RK and another v Oldham NHS Trust and another* [2005] 2 WLR 993.

Finally, the victims in these cases had alternative remedies, which make a tort remedy not only dangerous but also superfluous.[22]

This part of the judgment is the most crucial for present purposes, for the truth of the matter is that these alternative remedies are of varying efficacy.

Thus, some of the newly invented remedies—for instance an ombudsman report—proved most successful in the *Barlow Clowes* affair since it led to the government paying out to the investors who lost their life savings in the order of £16 million. As a result several ombudsmen schemes are currently in operation.[23] In a handful of other cases the non-liability rule could be justified by the existence of *truly* alternative and *effective* remedies. In *Olotu v Home Office*,[24] for instance, the remedy of *habeas corpus* was available to the illegally (over-)detained claimant; and the judgment contains hints that he might, additionally, have grounds for complaint against those who failed to alert him as to his possible remedies. But we submit that these cases are, in numerical terms, very much the exception.

So, how serious are judges when they tell us that a poor, under-privileged, and (probably) uneducated citizen who has found himself unjustly held in custody for over three months (as in the *El Guzouli* case) can bring a successful action for malicious prosecution or misfeasance in public office? It is not just that his social and economic position makes it near impossible for him even to contemplate taking on the governmental apparatus that is responsible for his misery—especially in these days of reduced generosity on the part of the Legal Aid Board; it is also that the torts in question have ingredients that make it very difficult to invoke them with any real chance of success. Finally, the availability of purely administrative law type of remedies (for example, judicial review)—usually favoured by public lawyers—are only in theory attractive. For in practice they hardly achieve any (moral) satisfaction; they promote no deterrent function; and they bring about no compensation whatsoever. The *Barrett* decision in the House of Lords provides some signs that not all of the judges are convinced by the prevailing argumentation which we are criticising. Thus, it is submitted that Lord Hutton was right to go beyond what we are saying and not merely test the effectiveness of the alternative remedy (as we are suggesting) but assert boldly that 'the jurisdiction of the court should not be excluded because of the existence of other measures of complaint'.[25]

What about the French motivation?

In *M et Mme Pillon*[26] the exact nature of the duty that should have made the social service more careful in the placement of children was not specified. On the contrary, in *Epoux Quaras*,[27] the *Conseil d'Etat* referred to certain provisions in the Public Health Code (*Code de la Santé Publique*) which require that social services supervise the health of all children under a certain age. In short, almost the same brevity encountered in the reasoning of the judgments of the *Cour de cassation* is, again, the hallmark of the administrative jurisdiction, especially if its products are compared to the much longer and fuller judgments of the highest English courts. If we stop at this point, therefore, we are forced to concede considerable

[22] A critique of these policy arguments in a comparative context can be found in BS Markesinis, JB Auby, D Coester-Waltjen and SF Deakin, *Tortious Liability of Statutory Bodies. A Comparative and Economic Analysis of Five English Cases* (1999), pp 73 *ff.*

[23] They are described briefly by Peter Cane, *Tort Law and Economic Interests* (20th edn 1996), pp 366 *ff.*

[24] [1997] 1 WLR 328.

[25] *Barrett v Enfield London Borough Council* [1998] 3 WLR 79 (at 114).

[26] Conseil d'Etat, 4 mai 1983, No 22811.

[27] Conseil d' Etat, 23 septembre 1987, *Recueil des arrêts du Conseil d'Etat*, 290.

differences between the systems. But why cannot we probe more deeply? The search for similarities can proceed by consulting additional sources.

4. IN SEARCH OF A *RAPPROCHEMENT*

In one sense what is most remarkable about the comparison of these two systems is not that they (a) nowadays reach different results in these factually equivalent situations but that they (b) choose to motivate their judgments in such a patently different way. The English allusion to policy, with all its attractions and weaknesses (even if it is attempted without empirical evidence to support it[28]), is thus notably absent from the French decisions. Closer examination of the systems, however, reveals that the second assertion—(b)—is only partially correct.

This becomes clear once one moves away from the decisions themselves and starts looking at their supporting official as well as academic literature.[29] Here one finds evidence to support two observations.

First, the English concerns can be found duplicated in France and can even be traced (though more tenuously) to judicial decisions. This, however, is a crucial assertion. For the more one can substantiate this point, the closer one can bring the two systems and challenge the illusion of difference and separateness.

Secondly, further study of these policy arguments also reveals that, at the end of the day, they have fared differently in the two systems. The (final) rejection by French law of the English policy concerns thus leads us to the question why this has happened. Are they 'right'? Are we 'right'? Or are we both 'right' within the context of our respective legal systems? The answer will be found at a different and deeper level of enquiry. And revealing as it does a different socio-political philosophy, this once again leads us to assert a divergence and then gives rise—or at least ought to give rise—to an urge to understand it. The absence of overt discussions, however, again makes the search difficult and any conclusion speculative. But one thing is clear. At this last stage and deeper level of our enquiry we are no longer comparing legal or legalistic arguments but competing philosophies about the role of the state in modern society. We shall deal with this aspect of the problem below. *Here suffice it to note that such core political, moral, or philosophical issues may be incapable of a right answer—let alone a single answer.* Equally, one must note that what works for the specific problem discussed here also works for other legal problems subjected to a similar kind of analysis.

(a) Policy Reasons and Concepts in Decisions Involving the Liability of Public Bodies

As already stated, what most distinguishes Common law judgments from French ones is not just their greater length but also their increasing willingness to confront *openly* the underlying

[28] Though we at least have much respect for Lord Justice Buxton's reaction when, presented by counsel with some policy concerns, he retorted that '[t]here is no evidence to support any of these contentions . . . In my respectful view, the Court should be very cautious before reaching or acting on any conclusions that are not argued before it in the way in which technical issues are usually approached, with the assistance of expert evidence'. See *Perrett v Collins* [1998] 2 Lloyd's Rep 255 (at 276–7).

[29] Whenever it is published. Unfortunately, the conclusions of the *Avocat général* and the *Commissaire du Gouvernement* are not always easily available.

policy issues. This makes the reading of English decisions not only more attractive but also more informative as to what is really happening not only during the secret judicial deliberations but also in the mind of the judge himself. Last but not least, such greater frankness could make the argument of future cases more meaningful as counsel confront openly and with increasing evidence of an inter-disciplinary nature the issues that lie at the core of the dispute, thus addressing the true concerns that judges may have about how to decide the case. Let us look at a specific example taken from a decision that literally shook France when it was handed down.

The emphasis that the causation issue[30] received in the French cases of wrongful life as a result of the *Perruche* decision of 2000[31] is as good an illustration as any. And it contrasts sharply with the parallel American[32] and German[33] judgments, which state quite clearly that they will not allow conceptual debates to interfere with the pursuit of justice.

This (apparent) absence of policy factors in French decisions is even more obvious in the group of cases which deal with the potential liability of public bodies operating under statutory authorisation. Once again, the disputes we have in mind find factual parallels in both countries so by studying them one can see how the two systems have dealt with similar problems.

These cases involve such varied matters as the potential liability of the police for failing to prevent the commission of a crime or the negligent failure of the social security services to remove a sexually abused child from the care of its abusing relatives. Another example of contemporary significance is the possible liability of a school authority for failing to diagnose the learning problems of one of the children in its care and thus failing to provide it with the appropriate kind of training.[34] In all these cases, English and French law reach different outcomes. The English—with some ups and downs—tend to deny liability almost systematically; the French nowadays not only allow it—they also give the impression of taking it for granted.

The difference in results is matched by a difference in motivation of the judgments. Once again, the Anglo-American judgments are replete with allusions to policy reasons justifying their results while their French counterparts resort to a myriad of concepts, some known to English law (for example, causation and contributory negligence) and others unknown (such as *faute lourde* or *égalité devants les charges publics*). Yet the true picture is once again

[30] At is barest the argument is this. The doctor's negligence in failing to diagnose the mother's rubella did not cause the child's impairment but only allowed it to be born. Therefore the doctor should not be liable for anything towards the child. The best reply to this argument, suitable to the way the case was pleaded under French law, has come from Professor Michelle Gobert in 'La Cour de cassation méritait-elle le pilori?', *Les Petites Affiches*, 8 décembre 2000, p 4.

[31] *Assemblée Plénière* of 17 November 2000, published in *La Semaine Juridique*, No 50, 13 décembre 2000, pp 2293 et seq.

[32] *Procanik v Cillo* 478 A 2d 755 (1984) at p 763. 'The philosophical problem of finding that such a defective life is worth less than no life at all has perplexed [many] distinguished members of this Court. We need not become preoccupied, however, with these metaphysical considerations. Our decision to allow the recovery [by the child] of extraordinary medical expenses is not premised on the concept that non-life is preferable to an impaired life, but is predicated on the needs of the living.'

[33] See BGH of 23 October 1951 (BGHZ 3, 261), where the court, after reviewing the various German theories about causation, said: 'The search is for [a] corrective that restricts the scope of the purely logical consequences to produce an equitable result. . . . Only if the courts are conscious of the fact that it is a question here not really of causation but of the fixing of the limits within which the originator of a condition can be equitably be presumed liable for its consequences . . . will the danger of schematisation . . . be avoided and the correct results be guaranteed'.

[34] The leading English decision is *Phelps v Hillingdon London Borough Council* [2000] 3 WLR 776. For a factually parallel German decision see OLG Hamm, 11th Civil Senate, 23 March 1990, 11 U 108/89.

not what appears to the naked eye but what is discovered after painstaking research hidden under the surface of a published decision.

Our general thesis thus remains unaltered even in the area of public law. It is what happens under the surface—what we will later call the 'core' of the problem—that really matters, and it is this that shows whether the systems can converge or are destined to remain divergent *until*[35] the underlying philosophy is re-assessed. The remarkable monograph of Duncan Fairgrieve, referred to at the beginning of this Chapter, has thus shed new light on the issue at hand. It also provides additional supporting evidence for a thesis that we have been promoting for over 30 years. We are grateful to him for allowing us to draw on his material and ideas, and present them here in a crass but nonetheless tantalising form.

Thus, in the factual scenarios here considered, two arguments have, above all, carried weight with English judges when deciding against liability. First is the fear that liability would impose a crushing financial burden on the state, and second is the danger that the threat of legal action would make officials hesitant to act. We could almost call these 'English' arguments since they do not figure in the French judgments. Yet, as stated, both of them can, in fact, be found in France as well, though they must be sought in the interstices of the academic literature and not in the motivation of courts. With regard to the second of these arguments Professor Chapus has, for instance, admitted that

> [A]dministrative authorities might be held back from acting with the speed that is sometimes required for fear of committing a fault and thus being the cause of damages liability. In other words, the risk of too frequent an imposition of liability would translate into a certain reluctance to act.[36]

Likewise, many argued that the easy imposition of liability would seriously deplete the reserves of the public purse. This view has thus been shared by Professors Weil,[37] Hauriou[38] and Touchard[39]—though it has been countered by other, equally eminent experts[40] as an illegitimate consideration which should be ignored by the judge. Yet another group of commentators has claimed that, good or bad, these academic preoccupations have actually influenced judges and thus determined judicial outcomes whether we like this or not. An unpublished (but widely influential) thesis by JC Hélin[41] has thus maintained that

> (I)t is difficult to deny that the financial argument, invoked by the doctrine in order to restrict the ambit of liability, has been taken into account in the case law itself.

Equally fascinating are two other points.

The first is how these policy reasons (against the imposition of liability) have surfaced in the French judgments in legal/conceptual clothes but are not immediately apparent to anyone who does not know what he is looking for. Dr Fairgrieve, for instance, a Common

[35] We stress *until*, for underlying cultural differences do not act as permanent inhibitors for convergence or divergence of legal systems. Cultural habits, fashions, tastes, and pre-dispositions change and, indeed, tend these days towards a considerable degree of uniformity as industrialisation, globalisation, modern communication, and increased travel makes the imitative process easier and quicker.

[36] R Chapus, *Droit Administratif Général*, Vol I (13th edn 1999), p 1463.

[37] *Les Conséquences de l'Annulation de l'Acte Administratif Pour Excès de Pouvoir* (1952), p 255.

[38] Case note on CE 29 May 1903, *Le Berre*, Sirrey 1904.3.121.

[39] The latter even going as far as suggesting that the judge should protect public funds. See 'A propos de la responsabilité pour faute de l'Administration Fiscale', *RDP* 1992, 785 at 806.

[40] Such as Georges Vedel, *Droit Administratif* (2nd edn 1961), p 281. Likewise Clinquennois, 'Essai sur la responsabilité de l'Etat du fait de ses activités de contrôle et de tutelle', *Les Petites Affiches*, No 98, 16 August 1995, 4.

[41] *Faute de Service et Préjudice dans le Contentieux de la Responsabilité pour Illégalité* (1969), p 63.

lawyer by training, applied Common law techniques in analysing his raw French material.[42] And what he has revealed is as remarkable as it is encouraging for all those who have for decades now been arguing that the systems are very similar once you scratch below their surface of juridical reasoning and search for *core* politics (and not just what the English judges call policy reasons).[43] The point must be emphasised over and over again; for decades of prejudice, legal and political, have been erected on the notions of separateness, difference, and ethnicity.

Secondly, what gives Fairgrieve's thesis an extra dimension is the fact that the raw material it uses is widely available in France and yet, in another sense, it is little used by French administrative lawyers and entirely unexploited by French public law comparatists. It thus took a Common lawyer's mind to draw it out and demonstrate its significance, especially for the purposes of comparative methodology. In the long run, this kind of work could, however, encourage French lawyers to apply this method to their own material. And this not only as a way of testing the viability of their answers but also as a way of demonstrating to outside observers the system's richness and sophistication, which can often be concealed behind its blandly phrased judgments.

It is also a good way of starting to make French legal literature and case law more interesting to the wider international public. The leading author has worked for a very long time with different French judges and has absolutely no doubt that the French judiciary, and French politicians as well, would dearly like to see their legal culture receiving more attention abroad. But how can this even begin to happen if one starts with the Legrand premises? These may stimulate inter-academic debates; but by definition they will fail this wider aim of promoting legal exchanges given that they insist on the separateness of legal cultures. At the risk of repetition we must thus again revert to a point made earlier—this debate about how to treat, study, teach and apply foreign law is not only a matter of academic interest; it carries with it deep political implications.

Thus, the requirement that state liability be engaged only if there is a *faute lourde* is, very likely, one of these surreptitiously controlling devices based on the kind of policy reasons that have been openly invoked by English courts.[44] No wonder that those who condemn such defensive attitudes as something of a bygone era seriously doubt whether 'the administrative judge [should be allowed to] prioritise systematically and protect the finances of the state'.[45]

This, it must be noted in passing, is a fascinating approach, for it turns on its head Lord Hoffmann's very same argument used in England to achieve the opposite result, namely to allow the judge to use economic arguments to protect the state.[46] Be that as it may, this

[42] This technique when presented to French students and colleagues has, in the experience of the leading author, fascinated our foreign colleagues since it makes them more keenly aware of points which they have relegated to their subconscious. To the extent that one can generalise from such experience we would say it proves that, for the purposes of comparative law, the best way to present foreign law is not how the foreigners see their own law but how an *outsider* would see and (better?) understand it. The last point then makes further comparison possible.

[43] See, eg, Basil Markesinis and Professor Christian von Bar, *Richterliche Rechtspolitik im Haftungsrecht* (1981).

[44] Indeed, recently Lord Bingham openly suggested that it be used by English courts to distinguish actionable negligence from non-actionable errors. But his argument, supported by comparative references, was not even considered by the other judges of that panel.

[45] Clinquennois, above note 37.

[46] For instance in *Stovin v Wise* [1996] AC 923. One must also bear in mind that the Hoffmann approach can also be found in France. See, eg, the views of Touchard, above note 36.

French use of the notion of *faute lourde* has led other influential commentators to express the hope 'that, in due course, the requirement . . . will cease to be part of the law'.[47]

Yet, once again, whether one adopts or deplores the philosophy that allows judges to act as protectors of state finances, one cannot deny that Professor Deguergue[48] sounds convincing when she argues that

> (A)ll authors agree that the principal function of *faute lourde* is to lighten the liability of public bodies.

And even if the use of this notion—*faute lourde*—were to weaken or be seriously eliminated from some of the areas where it has been used, French law still has ways for essentially re-introducing it in some oblique form in order to keep liability within reasonable bounds. It is thus already accepted that not every minor malpractice such as simple errors constitutes *faute simple*; and that this distinction between *faute simple* and *erreur*, if properly applied, can avert a tidal wave of cases or an obliteration of public finances.[49] One specialist author has thus expressed this thought in the following manner:[50]

> Finally, it is fairly clear in our country that the judicial mind is increasingly uncomfortable with the raising of the threshold of public liability achieved through the notion of administrative gross negligence. Since the protection that this notion accords to public authorities has been judged excessive, it will be up to the judge to decide whether to rely on it or not, without, however, either provoking a tidal wave of litigation or burdening public finances. For in that case the fault/error duo would supplant the ordinary negligence/gross negligence alternative.

In French administrative law this wide-ranging discussion over the ambit and purpose of the notion of *faute lourde* shows, in our view, that the legal concepts in that country are as pliable as their English counterparts, and can be made to bend to judicial views on policy. More importantly, the citations that we have given show that the French authors, themselves, accept this point. In our opinion, it requires only a small step further to accept that, in the light of the above, the concepts should be accorded some but not total respect or reverence. They are, as we keep saying, the tools that formulate judgments but not the reasons for them. This, however, is proving a difficult point to digest, especially for Continental lawyers who are trained in a legal and legalistic manner, and have hitherto been discouraged to look at issues from an inter-disciplinary and policy-oriented perspective. Yet one has to move away from them to see similarities which are clearly there.

The same observations (about policy behind concepts) can, we submit, be made of the notion of causative theories in administrative law. To the extent that this is supportable by evidence, it re-affirms the view that the leading author expressed in the context of the *Perruche* affair—that one should not take legal concepts too seriously.[51]

We thus note—in the context of the problem examined in this Chapter—the frank and illuminating observation of Professor Chapus who, referring to the use of the *théorie de causalité adéquate* in the context of (French) administrative law states that its

> judicial assessment is not mechanical. It is undertaken with a good deal of freedom and is influenced by common sense and subjectivity.[52]

[47] Roger Errera, [1990] *PL* 571.

[48] *Jurisprudence et Doctrine dans l'Elaboration du Droit de la Responsabilité Administrative* (1994), p 638.

[49] This has been admitted even by some *Commissaires du Gouvernement*; see, eg, CE 29 June 1997, RFDA 1998, 87.

[50] Michel Paillet, *Responsabilité Administrative* (1996), para 259 (translation by BS Markesinis).

[51] Basil Markesinis, *Revue trimestrielle de droit civile.*

[52] P Chapus, *Droit Administratif Général, Vol I* (13th edn, 1999), p 1414. Likewise M Deguergue, *Jurisprudence et Doctrine dans l'Elaboration du Droit de la Résponsabilité Administrative* (1994), para 147.

Chapus continues with the observation that this is also the reason why the potentially more expansive theory of *équivalence des conditions* has, on the whole, met with less favour with French administrative courts (and, one could add, German courts as well). Yet other authors have maintained that overall causative theories have received a restrictive application in order to minimise the burden on public finances.[53] Fairgrieve has gone further than to repeat such statements and meticulously collected case law and references that show that 'the test of causation has been used to ward off large liabilities in sensitive areas such as planning, travaux publics, tax and regulatory activities'.[54]

The same protective philosophy can be found in other causative-related devices such an act of a third party or *faute de la victime.* Thus, where it can be proved that third party conduct—some say *faute*—contributed to the injury suffered by the claimants, the administration will be expected to pay only the share of the damage which is due to them[55] (there being nothing equivalent to the English notion of joint and several liability). And where children have contributed to their injury, their damages seem often to be reduced substantially, the apportionment process often (apparently) over-favouring the administration.[56]

(b) A Divergence in Fundamental (Political) Philosophy?

Approaching the case law of different countries in the above way thus leads us to a number of conclusions.

First, legal systems when compared through their decisional law reveal a considerable factual similarity of litigated instances. That should not be a cause for surprise; but stressing it has its advantages. For beginning the comparison by using such material (instead of the *doctrine*), one has the advantage of putting the reader at ease since he feels he is on familiar terrain and not lost in a jungle of legal notions and concepts. This kind of approach has the further advantage of avoiding the enquirer taking sides at an early stage of his learning process on an issue which has deeply divided professional comparatists—does one describe a system as it views itself[57] or does one try to present it from the perspective of the potential receiver or, at the very least, the outside observer? Thirdly, it avoids getting mired in the often extremely abstract discussion of the issue at hand found in foreign (particularly German) textbooks and treatises, which can be so off-putting to anyone other than the most expert observer and stunt at its birth any further enquiry into the other system. On the minus side, however, it must be admitted that the approach advocated by us presents the considerable drawback of requiring the researcher to do much original work before one can find the obvious objects for comparison. By definition, no judge has the time to do that; but that is where academics can be of assistance both to their students as well as to their courts in helping to bridge the gap.

Secondly, the cases we discussed here are among the most controversial and widely discussed tort/administrative law cases in England at the present time. A search of the French case law finds very few equivalents; and if one were to ask a French administrative judge

[53] C Guettier, *La Responsabilité Administrative* (1996), pp 127 *ff.*

[54] Unpublished thesis, p 162 (references omitted).

[55] CE 28 octobre 1977, Commune de Flumet, (1977) Rec 412; CE 14 mai 1986, Commune de Cilaos (1986) Rec 716.

[56] S Rials, *Le Juge Administratif Français et la Technique du Standard* (1980), p 331.

[57] Legrand, 'The Same and the Different' in Pierre Legrand and Roderick Munday, *Comparative Legal Studies: Traditions and Transitions* (2003), pp 240, 289 *ff.*

what he felt about them the answer would be (indeed was): 'What is so special about them?' The result is an apparent paradox: a system that favours claimants is not, in these types of cases, inundated by legal claims and thus sees nothing unorthodox or disturbing about them. On the other hand, the English system, which constantly deploys the notion of duty of care to 'nip all liability in the bud' continues to see cases coming not just before its lower courts but even reaching its highest court. What has acquired almost nightmarish proportions in England and is currently causing huge headaches to the Law Commission is thus a non-problem in France. This reaction can be found in other areas of the law as well;[58] and it must lead any reasonably inquisitive jurist to ask how this can be so.

As far as French law is concerned, our guess is that the level of damages awarded is modest; that this is widely known; and that, as a result, such claims are invariably settled. We shall see, this time with the aid of concrete figures, that this is what largely happens in Germany. If the thesis is supportable—and comparatists who disagree with our method should try and disprove it with detailed work and not by writing general and descriptive pieces about French or German or Italian law—then English lawyers would do well to study the information and ideas contained in Chapter Nine of this book. For this could not only explain the foreign system; it could also guide the future development of the indigenous. A further (related) point is that what we say is neither novel nor unusable in England. For it was predicted by Paul Craig, Professor of *English* Law (not foreign or comparative) at the University of Oxford in a co-authored piece with Duncan Fairgrieve.[59] Secondly, this approach was advocated by the Senior Law Lord in the aforementioned *East Berkshire* case.[60]

Thirdly, when the comparison of the case law of the two systems is pursued beyond the factual configurations of the disputes, the first differences begin to appear and they are at the level of concepts and methods of reasoning. But becoming aware of these differences does not vindicate the position of those who argue that systems cannot really be compared; for all we have really established is that their concepts and notions are different, which is not the same thing as saying that they cannot be understood, compared and even imitated if we go beyond the concepts and find what is really causing the difference. The need for an explanation thus becomes pressing and the researcher is pushed into a different and even deeper level of enquiry that involves him searching for the policy reasons of a particular judicial solution rather than for the verbal devices used to formulate them. This search eventually reveals that the policy arguments are closely linked to wider political debates that dominate one system but can also be found in the other. Indeed, the little that has been cited above suggests a quite remarkable degree of duplication of ideas. French law thus is not unaware of Lord Hoffmann's worries; it just does not treat them as insurmountable or politically determinative.

This is an important point; but important, too, is another one which comes with it. Quite simply it is that this French material is discovered at different levels or in different sources—for example, academic writings (often in inaccessible journals rather than in the main treatises), preparatory papers leading to legislation, and conclusions of advocates general. The one place from which they are missing is the judicial opinions themselves. The art of discovering the equivalent material is thus one which must be mastered but is not easily

[58] Such as liability for pure economic loss and psychiatric injury, both highly restricted in the common law.
[59] Paul Craig and Duncan Fairgrieve, 'Barrett, Negligence and Discretionary Powers', [1999] *PL* 626 *ff.*
[60] [2005] 2 WLR 993.

learnt.[61] When mastered it must be applied by teachers who, with the assistance of numerous specific examples, can then show their students how to surmount such artificial hurdles of legal classification which more often than not are the product of historical accidents and not logic, as well as the language problems associated with a different terminology. Thus, to give but a most obvious and elementary example, the cardinal English notion of duty of care is untranslatable in legal French or German, and its role can only be understood by stating the function it performs in English law—defining the range of interests and relationships which are protected by the law—and then giving the French and German lawyer the techniques that he uses to achieve this very same task. Incidentally, the researcher who has reached this stage can now take a stance towards the difficult issue mentioned above—does one present foreign law as it views itself or as it presents itself from the perspective of the potential borrower? As already stated, adopting the first approach kills all further enquiry into the foreign law—something, one would assume, teachers of comparative law would by definition wish to encourage!

Even more intriguing (and difficult) is the task of tracing the impact that this material has had on the case law of countries such as France which pretend to ignore it. The discovery of conclusive answers is by no means guaranteed and can often only be attempted by talking to the real protagonists of litigation: judges and practitioners. But the pursuit of these aims gives the foreign observer at the very least a deeper and, it is submitted, more satisfying understanding of his own case law as he grapples with the difficulties of the foreign solutions.

It should be clear that the student of foreign law who started with the simple reading of a case but has managed, with the help of his teacher, to reach this far, has already made great strides towards understanding foreign law and is perhaps even beginning to get ideas from it concerning his own system. But there is more to follow.

Fourthly, intelligent questioning of this similar, policy-impregnated material thus leads one to the final and deeper level where one has to confront the core issues. At this level, legal arguments become subservient to political, economic, or moral ones, which now come to the fore. *Inevitably, the key issues that have to be resolved here are not always susceptible to one answer; nor, indeed, are they always capable of receiving a right answer.* Certainly this cannot come from lawyers acting on their own.

We have always felt this to be true of our system and were thus delighted when we came across the same idea expressed by some eminent French colleagues while criticising the over-legalistic dissection to which the important *Perruche*[62] decision was subjected to by

[61] No wonder then that even some knowledgeable teachers of French law express their worries that our approach will involve hard work! See Sophie Boyron, review in (2005) 68 (3) *MLR* 495–6.

[62] The *Perruche* decision of the *Assemblée Plénière* of the *Cour de cassation* of 25 November 2000, dealing with a wrongful birth claim by a seriously handicapped child, is published in *La Semaine Juridique*, No 50, 13 décembre 2000, p 2293. The Plenary Session of the Court of Cassation granted damages to the impaired child but, in the light of a ferocious reaction by the medical and religious organisations as well as organisations representing impaired people, the effect of the decision was overturned by legislation (hurriedly passed through Parliament). The position in Germany has been just as controversial, indeed, in one sense even more complicated due to diverging views between the two sections of the Constitutional Court and the Federal Supreme Court. The position in private law thus seems to have settled in the following way: (i) both parents have a contractual claim for wrongful birth and pregnancy cases; (ii) this entitles them to full maintenance costs (whether the child is healthy or not; if it is not, the measure of damages may be greater to cover the extraordinary medical expenses); and (iii) the mother may additionally claim pain and suffering in cases of wrongful birth that result from complications. In all these actions, the child itself had no claims. For a summary of the current position of German law on this topic see Basil Markesinis and Hannes Unberath, *The German Law of Torts: A Comparative Treatise* (4th edn 2002), p 179.

most French jurists. These three French colleagues were thus, in our view, right when (criticising the excessive emphasis on concepts) they said that[63]

> the jurist cannot make use of the law and claim that it can solve [problems] by itself when, in reality, he can only (and does only) opt for an ontological, logical, or moral stance without being any more qualified than anyone else to do so. *On the other hand, it falls upon him to create the tools and the techniques which make practicable in law the political solution he has decided to adopt.* And that is no mean feat.

The italicised sentence is crucial. And it shows that it is thus at this final and third level that our illustrations from Anglo-French administrative law finally find the reason for the diverging answers. The fear, for instance, of financially crushing deserving defendants (though genuinely entertained by both systems) in France has given way to a broader philosophical consideration. For the purposes pursued in this Chapter this, broadly speaking, had two important consequences.

First, it is worth repeating that this underlying broader philosophy was not always different in France and England. The divergence developed[64] as the French state, in the late 1960s and certainly from about the mid-1970s onwards, was progressively seduced by the idea of equality, socialisation of risks, and social solidarity. Under this newer French philosophy the law tends to admit that when citizens suffer damage of a certain type and size it is the duty of the state to compensate them. This is so even if it is not possible to link them with something which could be called maladministration. This vision explains why, in the recent past, in France (and a number of other countries) several pieces of regulatory legislation were put into place in order to grant people compensation—from the public purse—for damages having sometimes no relation[65] to any administrative action or omission. The 1990 Act for victims of terrorist activities as well as the 1991 Act concerning people affected by transfusions of blood contaminated by the AIDS virus fall under this category.

Secondly, this re-orientation was, primarily, a political one and the law simply followed suit. French judges thus did not see it as being their role, as some English judges have done, to protect public finances against numerous and excessive claims for damages. The size of budgets of the central and local authorities was a political matter; and politics should decide how the money is spent. As for the judges, they had to apply the law on the basis of accepted legal reasoning, and this did not include an obligation to twist it in order to make it over-protective of the financial interests of public budgets. If they were conscious of the need not to allow things to get out of hand, they should do this through the medium of causation, fault, or the measure of damages—that is, accepted legal concepts which they had to define and determine.

The fact that England could do the same was made most clearly in *Phelps v Hillingdon*, particularly at the hearings at First Instance and in the Court of Appeal. Causation could thus raise formidable problems for future claimants, especially since the absence of records and delays in bringing such claims might make it very difficult to substantiate them. But even leaving problems of evidence aside, the hurdles of *Phelps* on causation are formidable. Claimants would have to satisfy the court, first, that if their difficulties had been discovered

[63] Article published in *Le Monde* of 21 December 2000 by Professor de Béchillon, Olivier Cayla and Yan Thomas, directeurs d'études à l'Ecole des hautes études en sciences sociales (translation by BS Markesinis).

[64] While the underlying philosophy and concerns were similar, the legal solutions were likewise closer then than they are today; see P Weil, *Les Consequences de l'Annulation d'un Acte Administratif pour Excès de Pouvoir* (1952), p 255.

[65] Or at least without the need of demonstrating such relation.

in time, the school ought to have taught them in a different way and then, if this had happened, their ultimate educational attainment would have improved. These are not insubstantial hurdles; and overcoming them still leaves open the question of the extent, in financial terms, of the claimant's future loss. The quantum problems are thus also likely to be formidable.

This last point was well made by Garland J at First Instance and Lord Justice Otton at the Court of Appeal hearings in *Phelps*. For even if a duty is recognised and the inadequacy of the educational training received by the plaintiff is proven, it does not mean that his or her claims for lost earnings can be made on the basis that he or she would have grown up to have the earnings of a Bill Gates. As Garland J put it:[66]

> It is quite impossible to make any specific findings as to the plaintiff as she might have been. I have commented that the attempt to do so is to enter deeply into the realm of hypothesis. Clearly, she would be somewhat, perhaps substantially, more literate than she is now. She would probably have greater self-confidence and self-esteem, which would improve her employment prospects. Whether she could ever have become a computer operator I regard as pure speculation.

To put it simply: the failure of the local authority to provide the right educational assistance which, by law, it is obliged to provide to dyslexctics should in most cases be limited to the cost of acquiring such assistance privately. Privately and, one hastens to add, quickly.

If the award is thus modest and, we submit, obviously needed to make up for the negligent omission, why encourage litigation? If it is known that it will come, almost as a matter of course (and that will be the case if it is modest!) who will litigate? Thus, why not say that (barring exceptional circumstances) this is what will be awarded; and any attempt by the local authority to deny responsibility or drag its feet (resulting in litigation—perhaps even deliberately in order to exhaust the weaker claimant) would be penalised with costs.

This, of course, may not be the final answer nor will it be the appropriate reaction to every type of negligent misuse of statutory powers. So, if outside the *Phelps* type of cases we have instances of truly serious harm, requiring higher levels of award,[67] then the statutory bodies that caused it (especially if they caused it through repeated errors[68]) should be made to pay for it. The notion of an administration according to the rule of law means an administration which is accountable for its negligent behaviour, especially if the negligence is repeated over a period of time. In our view it is thus wrong for judges, however well intended they may be, to transform the power to apply the law into an essentially political decision when resolving disputes between individuals. The French have something to teach us here, even if we remain unwilling to follow their overall socially conscious political philosophy.

Once the above 'philosophical stance' is noted—even if not accepted—one can see why French judges are likely to disregard the cost that a liability rule might entail for public authorities. More interestingly, the idea—so obvious in some English judgments—that such resources might be better used in another 'public' context becomes equally irrelevant. In the kind of consumerist vision of public liability which has become predominant in French law since the late 1960s (a vision which is to a large extent shared in Germany), compensating the damages suffered by citizens because of administrative activities can never be

[66] (1997) 96 LGR 1, 26.

[67] We know, for instance, that the imprisonment of wrongfully imprisoned persons comes at a substantial public cost. Should public finances be pleaded as an excuse to not make good such a grave infliction of injustice?

[68] See *Lawrence v Pembrokeshire* [2006] EWHC 1029 (QB)—at the time of writing under appeal.

a wrong use of public money. On the contrary, it may even be seen as the best possible use of resources when it is viewed as serving the principle of equality by avoiding a result that means that people who have randomly been affected by administrative action remain without compensation.

The reader digesting the thoughts in the previous section may accept them as an explanation of the French decisions. But the superficial reader—and for present purposes even educated English lawyers might fall into this category—may precipitously dismiss them as *totally* alien to the role of the state as it has come to be seen in England during the last 20 years. Certainly the views of some judges (such as Lord Hoffmann) and academics (such as Tony Weir) would seem to espouse such a 'conservative' philosophy that is prepared to allow (if not encourage) judges to act primarily with the view of shielding public finances.

Yet something that comes close to the (new) French philosophy can also be found in England when one reads such documents as the First Report of the Select Committee on the Parliamentary Commissioner for Administration[69] or the views of leading judges as Lord Bingham.[70] So, what really matters is not so much to realise that the prevailing political climate is different in France and in England; and even less to exercise the political decision and choose between them. For the jurist, certainly the comparativist, what is much more important is to realise that these views and debates have, despite misleading appearances caused by different concepts and notions, their *exact* equivalents in England and France (and, indeed, Germany and Italy). A no less significant realisation would lie in the fact that the answer to this 'core' question is not one that can be given by lawyers or lawyers acting and thinking on their own. The previously quoted views of Professor de Beschillon[71] and his colleagues thus come back to mind as containing a truth that is equally valid on both sides of the Channel and thus proves how similar we really are.

A not dissimilar kind of attitude would colour the view of a French judge towards the so-called inhibition argument.[72] For though it is not unknown to French public liability, it certainly plays a secondary part. This is so because, apart from its fundamental compensatory function, public liability is also viewed as a way of disciplining the administration. In that role, it complements judicial review by imposing payment of compensation, whereas the former provides for the annulment of illegal decisions. The number of cases where mainly children have been victims of local authority disorganisation, errors, or even repeated negligence are, if not increasing in numbers, certainly making the newspaper and television headlines. Just as disturbing is the fact that in England both the authorities and their servants remain 'unpunished'. Protecting the finances of the administration is one thing; but disciplining it for its negligence (and, one hopes, sending a signal to others to behave better) is another. Our blatant preference for the first 'value' may be starting to wear thin.

Finally, would a French administrative judge refrain from imposing public liability because he thinks that it would mean that he has second-guessed the public body in the exercise of its discretion? This approach, which has found such an appeal in England, would

[69] 'We agree that the priority in expenditure should be the improvement of services. Effective redress is itself a service improvement. It may be unfortunate that funds are spent in compensation. It cannot, however, be right to use such argument against schemes which justly reimburse the complainant for financial loss. The answer is not to avoid compensation but to avoid the original failure of service.' (1994–1995, HC 112, para 70).

[70] '[S]ave in clear cases, it is not for the courts to decide how public money is best spent nor to balance the risk that money will be wasted on litigation against the hope that the possibility of suits may contribute towards the maintenance of the highest standards.'

[71] Above note 51.

[72] Namely that the imposition of civil liability will make civil servants reluctant to act.

hardly strike a French judge as a natural one. The reason is the following. In practice, in a large majority of cases in which the administration is held liable, the fault which has been identified is an illegality. Illegality, in other words, is the most ordinary form of administrative fault. In Chapter Nine we shall see that this is also true of Germany, which begins to make English civil servants or local officials look an unusually weak lot. We refuse to subscribe to this—just as we refuse to subscribe to the view that the award of damages would have this effect. The official in question as much as the judges who have so persistently held this defensive view have been cut off from realities for too long.

This strong relation between fault and illegality has the consequence that the adjudication of administrative liability largely mirrors judicial review of administrative legality. The judges' attitude when faced with questions of discretion is the same in both cases. This means that judges have no reason to think that accepting liability would especially impinge upon administrative discretion: they respect it and review it to the same extent that they would otherwise do when reviewing questions of legality.

5. WIDER CONCLUSIONS

Looking at foreign law the way we have done in this Chapter is both difficult and time-consuming. It takes time to read decisions in order to find factual equivalents that lend themselves to comparison. It takes even more time and effort to ensure that, having delved deeper into the procedural, constitutional, and political peculiarities of each system, you feel confident enough to emphasise their similarities and explain their differences. Finally, it takes Jovian patience to remain faithful to the overall cause of searching for and emphasising similarities in order to facilitate greater European integration without distorting the raw material you have discovered. This is particularly so as one becomes conscious of the difficulties of imparting this expertise upon those who really matter, namely judges and practitioners. For we will not tire of stating that academics, with few exceptions, have both in England and France approached foreign law and comparative methodology in an excessively theoretical and abstract manner,[73] unwittingly making it of little interest in the classroom and of even less use in the courtroom. As we keep saying, the high priests of our subject (and many of their disciples who have been too lazy to try and invent a new methodology appropriate to our times) bear a great responsibility for this sorry state of affairs.

If one perseveres despite the above, one realises that the core issues that confront our European countries are the same even though the answers they receive may be different. The next realisation is that if the answers differ it is not really because of the concepts or even the arguments used on the surface but because of understandable and legitimate divergences at the core. As stated, however, at the core we do not find legal, certainly not legalistic, arguments. On the contrary, we here encounter political, moral, social, and economic issues. Because these issues are of wider import, lawyers alone cannot solve them. Their legal solutions are forced to fall into line with political directives, which can be infinitely

[73] In part this is because it is easier for them to use foreign books as models and, with suitable adaptations and additions, transmit their way of describing the foreign law rather than going into the trouble of devising a way that makes foreign law digestible by a foreign reader but without betraying its essential features or distorting its own solutions.

nuanced in different legal systems.[74] Moreover, and this is just as important, they are not issues that can be described as 'typically' French, German, or English since they appear across borders and thus by their very nature encourage comparison. For the question how much 'protection'—and we use the word in its widest possible sense—can the modern state give to its needy and weak citizens is one which is currently being considered everywhere in Europe, so there is nothing 'English' or 'French' about it. Finally, individual systems—for instance the French—can and have vacillated over what kind of answers are appropriate to these fundamental questions. Thus, as swings and changes have taken place, so have the results of the judicial decisions altered.[75] Perhaps the answer lies somewhere in the middle; but striking the right balance between economic needs and social obligations has never been more difficult to achieve given the current high expectations of democratic entitlements that successive governments of all political colours have generated with the undoubted need to make European economies competitive with the emerging markets of the Far East.

So the real differences between the systems do not lie at the surface where sets of similar facts lead to litigation (call this the 'first circle') but at the core (or what we call the 'third circle'). But what stops us from realising this phenomenon and, where necessary, addressing it in an intelligent way (especially if harmonisation of laws is our aim), is the 'second circle'—where the bulk of our legal disputes take place and where concepts, notions, and legal reasoning reign supreme. Unfortunately, it is here that most jurists have focused most of their energies; and, in keeping with 19th-century ideas of state sovereignty, this has led to a state-based law. This, in turn, has led the same jurists to over-emphasise (undoubted) differences rather than stress equally important similarities, and to stick jealously to the tools that their system has bequeathed them. How right Mark Twain was when he wrote that 'loyalty to petrified opinion never yet broke a chain or freed a human soul'.[76]

But this is not what the 21st century requires given the move towards transnational legal regimes, be they in the human rights area or in the domain of commercial law. This emerging, new, and interdependent world cannot work with a legal science that is too strongly attached to parochial structures or local ways of doing business. It needs broad and flexible legal minds to import what is useful and to export what they, in their own countries, have done best. To do this, one must identify and confront the core issues and realise that they cut across national borders, offering great opportunities for traffic in legal ideas. Describing comparative law in Britain and talking about Frederick Parker Walton, Maurice Amos, Frederic Maurice Goadby, SG Vesey-Fitzgerald, Robert Warden Lee, John Macdonald and JEG de Montmorency means nothing to a contemporary audience, and presents an interest only to those few who might wish to learn something about the history of the subject (or rather lawyers with an interest in foreign laws) in 19th- and early 20th-century Britain. It is

[74] This is yet another reason why the attempt to draft a European Code seems a near impossible task. For it is not sufficient to say that the rules drafted are suitable to a free market economy; one must also ask *which* free market economy: the English, the French, or the German? These nuanced versions of the same basic model may dictate different results, for example in such matters as pre-contractual liability, exemption clauses, employment contracts, or landlord and tenant contracts. Emphasising the growing similarities achieved in our laws—not least by the EU—has never meant ignoring the subtle differences. This combination can be achieved in lectures or comparative law books; but when one is thinking of codification, one must assume also a growing unification in the underlying ways that the European economies and politics work. That still has some way to go!

[75] Thinking of the *concubinage* cases that divided that civil and criminal sections of the *Cour de cassation* throughout the 1950s and 1960s, and how the Cour de cassation changed its stance in the 1970s, readers will understand the point (in addition to discovering another example of how legal concepts—there the notion of *dommage légitime*—were distorted by policy considerations).

[76] Cited by A Ayres, *The Wit and Wisdom of Mark Twain* (1989), p 173.

the mistake (if we may so describe it) that Professor John W Cairns makes in his 43-page account of 'The Development of Comparative Law in Great Britain',[77] which (written by a Scottish legal historian rather than an English comparative lawyer) understandably devotes 35 of its 41 pages to the past—for many the very distant past—but fails to address adequately the contemporary challenges faced by the subject as well as the opportunities it is presented with. Read by the proverbial 'man from Mars', such a chapter would, of course, lead to the conclusion that comparative law in contemporary Britain is in a ghetto. We said it in the first two Chapters of this book and repeat it here—in scholarly terms surveys of this kind may be outstanding; but they do not contribute a single iota to the subject's survival in 21st-century Britain!

The proper understanding of the systems thus require us to reduce the importance of history as well as the second circle (concepts), and find and define the real issues that lurk in the third. In the controversial *Perruche* decision, where the *plenum* of the *Cour de cassation* had to decide whether to give *any* kind of damages in a wrongful life claim, the dominant theme was that of life itself. However affected and diminished, our current thinking cannot accept it as 'damage' or 'harm'. And for as long as this remains true, compensation for 'being born' cannot and will not be sanctioned anywhere in the world. This is true and philosophically tenable, though not as incontrovertible as courts functioning in a politically correct age would like us to believe.[78] At the same time, the same public opinion is not prepared to allow impaired children to suffer because eminent jurists such as Dean Carbonnier once argued that 'life, even if affected by misfortune, is always preferable to nothingness'.[79] As the leading author argued in an article in the *Revue trimestrielle*,[80] the *opinion savante* has no better claim to our loyalty than the *opinion souffrante.* Only academics, it seems to us, can aspire to such levels of intellectual arrogance by associating themselves with such broad pronouncements about 'nothingness' being worse than 'existence'. Shakespeare left the issue open; and before him so did many of the wisest Greek philosophers. So, what *Perruche* did was to make sure—without entering the major philosophical debate—that the affected child had its extra needs taken care of in an adequate way.[81] Provided its damages are not (eventually) duplicated with those already given to the parents by the Court of Appeal which will finally put an end to this protracted litigation, the dignity of the French legal system was will not be affected. We think that this is the true meaning of *the Assemblée Plénière* of 17 November 2000. It is also the interpretation that brings the case—in its ultimate result—in line with American and German law because it looks at the core of the problem and is not distracted by the biased use of concepts. In France this dimension has, in our view, been missed. For most lawyers used the causation debate to block out of sight the fact that the court was trying to take care of the child and, at the same time, remain faithful to the prevailing view that impaired life was not less valuable than a healthy one. Various political lobbies saw to the rest; and the decision was subsequently reversed by legislation. Here

[77] In Mathais Reimann and Reinhard Zimmermann (eds), *The Oxford Handbook of Comparative Law* (2006), pp 131 *ff.*

[78] Writers such Herodotus, Sophocles, Shakespeare, and Nietzsche—to mention but a few—never managed to solve this underlying issue, so how can we expect a judge to do this for us? For fuller references see BS Markesinis in *Revue trimestrielle de droit civil*, 2000.

[79] Quoted by l'Avocat général Sainte-Rose in his conclusions in the *Perruche* case, *La Semaine Juridique*, No 50, 13 décembre 2000, pp 2293 (at p 2307).

[80] 'Réflexions d'un comparatiste anglais sur et à partir de l'arrêt Perruche', *RTD civ* (1) janv-mars 2001, pp 77–102.

[81] M le Conseiller rapporteur Sargos makes this clear, we think, in his report to the Court; see *La Semaine Juridique*, No 50, 13 December 2000, p 2302.

we see echoes—dangerous echoes—of the American 'pro life' debate in its most extreme forms.

The examples of tortious liability of statutory bodies, which have provided the main theme of this part of the book, must be approached in the same way, as the simple juxtaposition of English and French law will only reveal a false picture. For the equation made by French (not English) law between illegality and fault makes French law appear doctrinally different and philosophically pro-claimant in a most extreme manner. Yet this is precisely the kind of opening statement which, though correct in one sense, does great disservice both to French and English lawyers. For, on the grounds that the differences between the two systems are so great, the statement almost inevitably implies that their further comparison is meaningless. It thus takes the works of Fairgrieve and his French counterparts (such as Hélin) to alter the first impression and show how the normative use of a multitude of concepts—such as *faute lourde*, *causalité*, or *faute de la victime*—go a long way towards reducing the differences which on paper seem so glaring. But this is still only the beginning of the kind of enquiry we need in order to make comparative law attractive as a discipline and useful to our courts. For the fact remains that in the eyes of those who have fashioned French administrative law, the economic concerns which troubled their English counterparts were only one part of the equation. What, in a sense, was paramount in their minds was to make a philosophical stand and subordinate economic expediency to it. This stand was founded on the ideas of equality, risk-socialisation, and social solidarity—activities which benefit us all must also spread their costs among us all. Though we know that in France (as everywhere) fashions change, one suspects that this edifice could become unstable only if the level of damages seriously endangered the financial viability of the 'deserving pockets' that meet these bills. Our theory, however, works only on the basis of an *unproven* assumption that in this type of case[82]—unlike those involving medical malpractice—the level of damages awarded by French administrative courts is much lower than those that might be reached by English courts should they ever become sympathetic to these claims. We stress, however, *unproven* (as far as French law is concerned). For, as we shall see in Chapter Nine, this (as yet unquantified) moderation of French law, coupled with the more concrete data that one can collect from Germany, might hold out some lessons for English law as it contemplates a more liberal stance in its post-*Barett* and *Phelps* phases. In one sentence this is: compensate but do not go overboard! Certainly, a number of dicta from *Phelps* could be collected to suggest that such a development of the law of damages might not be unwelcome to their Lordships—provided that sufficient empirical evidence to support this conclusion is found in German law.[83]

Yet French law might make an even more important contribution to our legal theory if its underlying philosophy were ever to be adopted by our judges. For some such idea as that of social solidarity could well provide the underlying theme that could bring together the patchwork of remedies—given by ombudsmen, criminal injuries compensation boards, or the Common law—that are slowly being crafted in the penumbra of public law proper in our country.

Of course, such a suggestion runs counter to Common law incrementalism, especially the English variant, and the system's aversion to fashioning wide and unifying principles. Yet is this not what happened to our private law of unjustified enrichment thanks to the

[82] Such as *Bedfordshire*, *Barrett* or *Phelps*.

[83] Though how, for instance, a dyslexic child should be compensated for not having been given a proper education remains to be worked out.

combined tenacity of judge and jurist? And if it happened in one part of the law, and happened in the short space of 25 years or so, why cannot it also happen in the troublesome area where public law and tort overlap with such confusion?

In any event, the main concern of this Chapter has not been to theorise on the borderline of tort and administrative law but to promote a better way of bringing together the different legal systems. We have thus tried to apply the approach we sketched here to the entire area of the law of obligations and, most recently, to expand it to include some areas of human rights. It is our belief, but not yet supported by adequate personal research, that this methodology can be applied successfully across the various areas of the law and across national borders. And if it can, it will (we think) suggest that despite formidable differences, the similarities that exist among contemporary European systems are growing by the day. More importantly, the similarities are growing not because Community legislation, model laws, or international treaties are regulating more and more aspects of our life but because growing urbanisation, industrialisation, inter-state commerce and travel are attenuating local differences of behaviour and thought, and are assimilating human tastes, attitudes and values. In short they are affecting the core or third circle; and this, sooner or later, will force our lawyers to make their reasoning more open, more susceptible to inter-disciplinary data, and more user-friendly. Such an approach will not only facilitate greater mutual understanding; it will also ensure that good ideas, be they English or French, will travel faster and further. And the true comparatist can ask for nothing more.

8

ANOTHER LESSON ON PACKAGING: THE GREY ZONE WHERE TORT LAW OVERLAPS WITH ADMINISTRATIVE LAW[1]

1. INTRODUCTORY OBSERVATIONS

The liability of statutory bodies, largely but not exclusively local authorities of different kinds, for their negligent conduct has been a controversial topic in English law. It has moved from a position of wide-ranging immunities,[2] to statutory liberalisation,[3] to further liberalisation through decisional law,[4] to a more closely fought battle in the courts between those whom we describe as 'traditionalists or activist conservatives'[5] and 'pragmatic modernisers'.[6] At the time of writing, the first group has, again, gained the upper hand, retaining English law close to its historical origins and, arguably, thus refusing to allow this area to keep in touch with modern times and demands.[7] The schools of thought opposing change, however, do not monopolise the legal scene. For we also encounter some Law Lords who give the appearance at least of sitting on the fence, conscious of the fact that the issues before them are not as simple as the 'traditionalists' would like us to believe,[8] while other

[1] Versions of this Chapter have appeared in the European Business Law Review and Public Law. We are grateful to Professor Mads Andenas of the University of Leicester and Mr Martin Matthews of University College, Oxford for their useful comments. The views expressed here are, of course, our own.

[2] Eg, by Crown immunities and the Public Authorities Protection Act of 1893.

[3] Crown Proceedings Act 1947; Law Reform (Limitation of Action etc) Act 1954.

[4] *Anns v Merton London Borough Council* [1978] AC 728.

[5] See *Stovin v Wise* [1996] 3 WLR 388, 411 per Lord Hoffmann, who has consistently adhered to his firmly phrased principle—'(T)he trend of authorities has been to discourage the assumptions that anyone who suffers loss is prima facie entitled to compensation from a person . . . whose act or omission can be said to have caused it. The default position is that he is not'. Lord Hoffmann has taken equally narrow positions in other fields of law, for instance in restricting minority shareholder remedies (see *Re Saul D Harrisson & Sons plc* [1995] 1 BCLC 14 and *O'Neill v Phillips* [1999] 1 WLR 1092, which have been met with legislative approval) and tort remedies for breach of EU competition law (see *Inntrepreneur Pub Co (CPC) and others v Crehan* [2006] UKHL 38). Likewise, he has refused to grant any new remedies in privacy-related cases such as *Wainwright v Home Office* [2003] UKHL 53, 16 October 2003, displaying a remarkable consistency towards civil law remedies. The latter judgment was recently overruled by the European Court on Human Rights in *Wainwright v The United Kingdom*, Application no 12350/04 of 26 September 2006.

[6] Thus see Sir Thomas Bingham (as he then was) in *M v Newham London Borough Council* and *X v Bedfordshire County Council* [1994] 2 WLR 55 at p 532: 'If [the child/claimant] can make good her complaints (a vital condition, which I forebear constantly to repeat), it would require very potent considerations of public policy, which do not in my view exist here, to override the rule of public policy which has first claim on the loyalty of the law: that wrongs should be remedied.'

[7] Or, for that matter, holding this area back from following the general development of tort or administrative law.

[8] Thus Lord Nicholls of Birkenhead (speaking for the minority) in *Stovin v Wise* [1996] AC 923 and (speaking for the majority) in *Phelps v Hillingdon CC* [2001] 2 AC 619, 667: '"Never" is an unattractive absolute in this context' (referring to the notion of duty of care). This bold statement disappeared without explanation from his radar screen in *East Berkshire.*

judges in the Court of Appeal, through interpretations that skilfully depart from what a 'traditionalist' approach dictates, seem to indicate a certain unhappiness with the rigid adherence to the non-liability rule.[9]

The battle between these two schools of thought, most recently repeated in the *Gorringe*[10] and *East Berkshire*[11] cases, can be waged at different levels.

It can, first, be philosophical—should, as a matter of *principle*, the state, local authorities, or other statutory bodies pay damages for their negligent and damaging conduct or not? The polar positions of Lord Bingham and Lord Hoffmann have been mentioned in the notes above for the additional reason that they show that the German material discussed in this article can, if the deciding judge has an open mind, be fitted into the English framework or, alternatively, stopped in its tracks if the judge in question enjoys the (wrong) kind of self-assurance that is often found among introverted spirits. To put it more neutrally, the utility of foreign material is not inhibited because precedent precludes its use, or excluded by the general structure of the (potentially) receiving system, but is, to a large extent, determined by judicial mentality and outlook, as the diverging Bingham/Hoffmann positions suggest.[12]

This position of principle—liability or immunity of public authorities—can, itself, be the result of different factors.

History is one. In the context of the common law judges have invariably favoured a conservative stance since various reasons—lack of manpower being one—for a long time prevented the Royal Courts from realising their ambition to enhance their jurisdiction.

Pragmatism, misplaced we would argue, has been another; and this, as well, has over the last 10 years or so taken many forms.[13] The most recent manifestation of this attitude is summarised in the following quotation from the judgment of Lord Brown of Eaton-Under-Heywood, who gives two of the concerns most *en vogue* these days. He said:[14]

> There is always a temptation to say in all these cases that no one, whether a doctor concerned with possible child abuse, a witness, or a prosecutor, will ever in fact be held liable unless he has conducted himself manifestly unreasonably; it is unnecessary, therefore, to deny a duty of care, better rather to focus on the appropriate standard by which to judge whether it is breached. That, however, is to overlook two fundamental considerations: first, the insidious effect that his awareness of the proposed duty would have upon the mind and conduct of the doctor (subtly tending to the suppression of doubts and instincts which in the child's interests ought rather to be encouraged),

[9] We would place in this category the most recent decision of the Court of Appeal in *Department for Transport, Environment & The Regions v Mott MacDonald Ltd and others* [2006] EWCA Civ 1089.

[10] [2004] 1 WLR 1057.

[11] *D v East Berkshire Community Health NHS Trust and others; MAK and another v Dewsbury Healthcare NHS Trust and another; RK and another v Oldham NHS Trust and another* [2005] 2 WLR 993.

[12] Lord Bingham recently returned to expressing his regret for the absence of any comparative material from Counsel's list of authorities in *HM's Commissioners of Customs and Excise v Barclays Bank plc* [2004] EWCA Cov 1555 at 50, a regret noticeably absent from Lord Hoffmann's opinion in the same case. This entire topic, more studied by American scholars working in the field of public law than in England, was addressed in Basil Markesinis and Jörg Fedtke, *Judicial Recourse to Foreign Law: A New Source of Inspiration?* (2006) where one can also find responses by former Justice Laurie Ackerman (Constitutional Court, South Africa), President Aharon Barak (Supreme Court, Israel), Justice Brun-Otto Bryde (Federal Constitutional Court, Germany), Sir Sidney Kentridge, Vice President Christos Rozakis (European Court of Human Rights) and Judge Konrad Schiemann (European Court of Justice).

[13] For instance, claimants have alternative remedies for redress that would cause less disruption to public administration; see *Elguzouli-Daff v Commissioner of Police of the Metropolis* [1995] QB 335, at 346 *ff.*

[14] [2005] 2 WLR 993, § 137.

and second, a consideration inevitably bound up with the first, *the need to protect him against the risk of costly and vexing litigation, by no means invariably soundly based.*[15]

This intellectual battle can, secondly, be engaged in a more legal way, namely by asking whether this is an issue that should be decided by the legislator or whether the courts can themselves set the contours of liability. Over the last 20 years or so, the Lords have on a number of important tort crossroads felt more inclined to leave the resolution of the problem before them to the legislator rather than to deal with it themselves;[16] and this trend, also encountered in the United States, has led a well-known jurist and now judge—Guido Calabresi—to discuss the phenomenon in an interesting and appropriately entitled monograph.[17] The battle can also be conducted by 'playing around' with the usual tort tools—for example, duty and causation—which, however, represent nothing more than the verbal devices used to formulate a judgment but rarely (if ever) explain it.[18]

In the typical kind of cases that concern us here, however, the English courts have adopted what is, essentially, a double-angled approach, distinguishing between a Common law duty to pay compensation to a particular claimant and one which stems from the breach of the relevant statute. In the 'highway' cases[19] the first has been (too easily) denied—often with the agreement of counsel for the claimant[20]—on historical grounds, even where physical injuries are involved and the usual 'policy' reasons for denying a duty of care do not play a large role.[21] The battle has thus shifted to whether the statute in question creates or excludes a private remedy. This is a notoriously ambiguous area which allows both sides to 'win' by artfully presenting their 'policy' preferences under the guise of statutory interpretation and sophisticated consideration of precedent or, which is even less satisfactory, in a brief and peremptory manner.[22] It can also lull all but the most alert reader into forgetting that, in the words of Lord Denning, the dividing line in discovering Parliament's intention to grant a civil remedy or not is 'so blurred and ill-defined that you might as well toss a coin to decide it'.[23]

This basing of liability under two possible headings and treating them as separate can trace its rationale to history; but it could also be seen as an ingenious way of fending off liability. For liability in negligence can be cut off easily by relying on the traditional dislike of the Common law to find liability for omissions, while the possibility of basing such liability on the relevant statute opens a Pandora's Box which able judges and practitioners can exploit to justify a decision they have already reached on other grounds: no liability. If the

[15] At 1037 (references omitted, emphasis added).

[16] Thus see Lord Bridge's views in *D & F Estate Ltd v Church Commissioners for England* [1981] 1 AC 177, 210. Providing a remedy for privacy violations is another example where judges have hesitated to act.

[17] *A Common Law in an Age of Statutes* (1985).

[18] The idea (if not the exact phrasing) comes from the late Professor John Fleming, one of the finest tort lawyers of our times; see JG Fleming, 'Remoteness and Duty: The Control Devices in Liability for Negligence', (1953) 31 *Can Bar Rev* 471 at 497 *f*.

[19] Such as *Gorringe v Calderdale Metropolitan Borough Council* [2004] 1 WLR 1057 and, of course, the earlier *Stovin* decision.

[20] See *Gorringe v Calderdale Metropolitan Borough Council* [2004] 1 WLR 1057 at para 17.

[21] The way the 'fair, just and reasonable' test originally added to the armoury employed to deny liability was first devised for economic loss cases, notably in *Caparo Industries plc v Dickman* [1990] 2 AC 605, where the House of Lords' decision is a classic example of judicial activism. The way in which it spread from there to infect physical injury cases is a legal mystery (awaiting careful examination) though it is also a tribute to the determination of conservative judges to employ every conceivable weapon at their disposal to cut down tortious liability.

[22] See, eg, Lord Steyn in *Lavis v Kent County Council* (1992) 90 LGR 416, 418, a position adopted equally briefly by Lord Hoffmann in *Gorringe v Calderdale Metropolitan Borough Council* [2004] 1 WLR 1057 at para 16.

[23] *In Re Island Records* [1978] Ch 122, 135.

splitting of the possible headings of liability is not, it is submitted, rationally convincing (since in both cases the basis of the complaint is the claimants' harm caused by the defendant's negligence), it is too well entrenched in English law to challenge it outright. At present, the most that seems to be contemplated by the Law Commission is the making of monetary remedies available for breaches in public law. Though these tentative moves are being opposed by traditionalists, the pressure to do something about this subject is also growing, if only in order to co-ordinate more effectively the range of possible remedies made available to litigating parties by both national and European law.

The ideas found in the previous paragraph lead us to another observation which must be borne in mind by anyone who would like to see the current English rule softened. Simply put, it is this.

Structure, system, and internal consistency are attributes highly valued by German lawyers; and their Civil Code—the *Bürgerliches Gesetzbuch*—has adopted them to perfection. Every German lawyer is thus taught from the outset of his career how the various parts of the Code interlink, so that tinkering with one could seriously affect the working of others. The Common law is not known for such attachment to symmetry, consistency, and logic.[24] Yet, notwithstanding the general truth of this statement, the fact is that its rules are more closely interlinked than most of its lawyers might openly admit. Thus, to offer but one illustration, its refusal to recognise a legal obligation to act in favour of another person is matched by the ignorance of the notion of *negotiorum gestio* (though both these statements must be taken with a pinch of salt and have, indeed, been watered down in other Common law jurisdictions such as that of the United States, which are less hamstrung by the weight of tradition).

In a general sense, however, our statement is, we believe, of great practical significance for the subject of this article. For the preference for immunity of negligent statutory bodies is often not only connected to the mysteries of statutory interpretation; it can also be linked to other tort law rules of the Common law equally negative and absolute as that concerning negligent omissions—such as the rule that there is no liability in tort for negligently inflicted pure economic loss as well as negligently inflicted psychiatric injury. And, as if all this were not enough, private and public law can, as already hinted, get intertwined with the tort aspect of these cases, causing confusion to outsiders—such as the judges sitting in the European Court of Human Rights in Strasbourg dealing with English—but also giving native lawyers endless opportunities to exploit differing judicial statements and avoid imposing liability.

But why such hostility towards the liability rule? When one reads the facts of cases such as *X (Minors) v Bedfordshire CC*,[25] *Osman v Ferguson*,[26] or *W v Essex CC*,[27] to give but a few well-known examples, one not only feels human revulsion at the way the claimants were treated but is also left in no doubt that some official was seriously negligent. The horror over the facts is surpassed only by the realisation that, in the end, both the immediate 'wrongdoer' as well as his employing council 'got off' lightly or even completely. To a non-lawyer, such results make no sense. The lawyers who defend them—to the extent that they accept

[24] See, inter alia, the views of Lord Lloyd of Hampstead in 'Reason and Logic in the Common Law', 62 *LQR* [1948] 468 *ff.* Justice Holmes' classic statement that '[T]he life of the law has not been logic: it has been experience' also points in the same direction; see *The Common Law* (1991), at p 1.

[25] [1995] 2 AC 633.

[26] [1993] 4 All ER 344.

[27] [2001] 2 AC 592.

that they do not live in a juristic vacuum—must therefore come up with the real reasons that lie behind their legally or legalistically phrased judgments. Not to do so leaves the gap that separates them and the general public as deep as it can get.

In our view the *determinant* factors behind such attitudes which offend so deeply the ordinary sense of justice are 'economic' arguments or, rather, a cluster of economic concerns about the effects of discovering a duty and thus, possibly, imposing liability. Lord Hoffmann has been among those who have on many occasions and in many guises articulated these fears;[28] and they are based on two beliefs or, rather, assumptions: liability would have ruinous economic results and would flood our over-worked and inadequately staffed courts with too many claims.

This is the aspect of our problem on which we will focus our main attention; it also represents the lowest analytical level of abstraction, especially if compared with what we called the 'philosophical' and 'purely legal' ways of handling these problems. The question we ask and try to answer is thus whether these economic fears could be exaggerated. Most lawyers and judges who believe in them would, if pressed, probably accept that we do not know this for certain for lack of empirical evidence to guide us either way.[29] With the assistance of foreign empirical evidence we will thus try to (a) calm these fears by suggesting that they are unsubstantiated; and (b) argue that if the foreign material is packaged properly, it can and should be used by English courts in weighing the validity of arguments against civil liability advanced on earlier occasions.

The invocation of foreign law as a way of assuaging local concerns about the consequences of a change in the rule should not, however, cause any 'panic' to national lawyers. *For what these figures will show is what has already been intuitively predicted by the Professor of English Law at the University of Oxford, namely that the shift from 'duty' to 'breach' would not necessarily have the feared consequences.*[30] Recourse to foreign experience has, with caution, also been championed by a number of our most senior judges, such as Lord Bingham (who is also on record as saying that he is not frightened by such a switch from duty to breach).[31] So the exclusion of this carefully assembled empirical evidence supporting the position of eminent English lawyers should not be attempted before it has been carefully considered and rejected on the basis of reasoned argument, not hunches. Anything less would, it is submitted, be more than 'introverted'—it would be blinkered and distinctly un-intellectual (if not un-judicial).

A second reason why lawyers who are content with the status quo should not be worried by the proposals presented here is because we intend to use our empirical information to challenge only their (unsubstantiated) fears on the consequences of liability being imposed for physical harm caused by negligent local authorities. We are thus not challenging the whole range of Common law rules interrelated with our main subject (such as the rule about economic loss or the non-liability rule about emotional distress). We contend, therefore, that the immunity rule of statutory bodies can be expanded without, at present, interfering with other immunity rules (which does not mean that they are justified!).

Equally important is, thirdly, the fact that what we wish to begin demonstrating is that a possible revision of the rules will *not* trigger an uncontrollable state of affairs on the national

[28] Most recently in *Sutradhar v Natural Environment Research Council* [2006] UKHL 33 at 42. See also *Gorringe v Calderdale Metropolitan Borough Council* [2004] 1 WLR 1057 at § 33 and *Stovin v Wise* [1996] AC 923.

[29] According to Professor Harlow, *State Liability—Tort Law and Beyond* (2004), studies of this kind are 'uncommon, inconclusive and sometimes unreliable, and such information as we do possess is fragmentary'.

[30] Paul Craig and Duncan Fairgrieve, 'Barrett, Negligence and Discretionary Powers', [1999] *PL* 626 *ff.*

legal scene (for example, opening of floodgates or the financial ruin of local authorities). On the contrary, it is hoped that our views will start a transnational dialogue on this important topic, which will bring to the attention of English practitioners new information, new arguments, and a renewed desire to attempt an empirical approach to the problem before us and which, we feel, is overdue. At the risk of excessive repetition, we repeat our conviction that to deny *a priori* the consideration of such a limited but well-documented agenda would be something no true scholar nor open-minded judge would really wish to do. If we are right in this belief, what follows will help expose the real arguments to the market of legal ideas, letting it then determine their respective value on the grounds of merit rather than mere superior authority.

The main thesis of this Chapter is thus presented in section 6 below. But since the German system is not widely known, we include in section 4 a short description of its basic rules and then look briefly at some of its recent case law in section 5. We will end with some concluding thoughts, contained in section 7. They will focus both on the substantive issue of our research as well as the methodological problems one encounters when attempting serious and detailed comparative work, points which must be stressed given that some academic colleagues deny the utility of comparative law in principle while others would wish us to draw conclusions from elegant but aphoristic statements. Before moving to these topics, however, we complete our introductory points with some comments on how our preliminary observations have played out in the English 'highway' cases. For reasons which will soon become obvious, we do this in two separate sections.

2. THE NON-LIABILITY RULE FOR OMISSIONS IN THE 'HIGHWAY' CASES

When a legal rule appears strange to modern eyes or different to that found in most other legal systems, the temptation to question its continued survival must be great.[32] Those who are intellectually less daring might instead try to discover the reasons for its birth and treat them as immutable. In American constitutional law this is referred to as 'originalism'; and it has been associated with judges who belong to the extreme Right. The movement has no parallel in the UK. Yet in *Gorringe*,[33] Lord Hoffmann came close to treating history as *a* decisive reason for the highway cases. History, however, cannot determine the present, even less the future, especially in a rapidly changing world. If a rule is to survive, it may call for a new justification; and if none of real value can be found, it will atrophy. The current highway cases find their rationale in two such rules.

[31] *D v East Berkshire Community Health NHS Trust and others*, [2005] 2 WLR 993 at para 49 (per Lord Bingham): 'I would for my part regard that shift as welcome, since the concept of duty has proved itself a somewhat blunt instrument [...].' The efficacy of the 'serious fault' device, the French *faute lourde* apparently favoured by Lord Bingham, was not even considered by the other judges in *East Berkshire*. Yet Andenas and Fairgrieve (in 'Misfeasance in Public Office, Governmental Liability, and European Influences', 51 *ICLQ* 2002, 757 *ff*) show on the basis of a detailed examination of French case law how well it has worked there in practice (at 770). The same can be said of the use of the causation device. One can try to ignore these facts by saying that the shift from duty to the other, above-mentioned devices would entail full-blown litigation. But the point of the French statistical evidence is precisely that if the devices are taken seriously by the courts, litigants get the message and do not chance litigation lightly, even in France where the costs are nowhere near as prohibitive as they are in England.

[32] So at least thought Lord Bingham in *Fairchild v Glenhaven Funeral Services Ltd* [2002] 3 WLR 89.

[33] *Gorringe v Calderdale Metropolitan Borough Council* [2004] 1 WLR 1057.

The first, as Lord Hoffmann described it briefly in his *Gorringe*[34] judgment, is the impecuniosity of the parishioners who had to maintain the highways. The second is the traditional rule of no tort liability for omissions. This, too, has a lack of (human) resources rationale. For in its formative stage the Common law did not have the time nor the resources to deal with people who were not 'good'; it could/would only interfere if they had been 'bad'.[35] The misfeasance/non-feasance dichotomy had been born, creating yet another Common law peculiarity.

From the middle of the 19th century onwards, in an era in which private selfishness was elevated to a public virtue, the omissions rule was also to find a new, supporting rationale: the less the state and its various emanations did, the better. This philosophy, which reached its most extreme forms in Victorian England and, in our times, during the Reagan/Thatcher decade of the 1980s, is also echoed early on in Lord Hoffmann's judgment in *Gorringe*.[36] Slender resources enter the calculation, albeit in a different form.

How the Common law survived in the statutes that put in written form its old content is, to some extent, an illustration of how habit, judicial conservatism, and brief and conclusionary judgments can help continue an existing state of affairs. But this process of deciding had much to commend it to judges (a) reluctant to re-think legal issues; (b) (understandably) worried about continued limitations of their resources; or, more generally, (c) ascribing some merit to legal statism. If to these factors one adds two more, one can understand judicial reluctance to disturb the legal rules which judges learned in their youth. These are, first, the fact that they are not particularly well-trained to undertake interdisciplinary examination of the problems before them and are thus slow even to consider this possibility; and, second, even if they wished to do this, they were hampered in this task by the total absence of empirical data to support or question their preferred options.

The problem is that for a long time the highway cases did not demand any of the above-mentioned deeper thinking. All they required was to consider the continued validity of the argument concerning limited resources. We do this in the next section; and in the main part of this Chapter (section 6) we try to show how other systems have avoided the very same risk, suggesting (there and in section 7) that these ideas are transplantable into our system. The other thing the highway cases required was belief in the idea that the old Common law could be treated as having survived within the modern statutory regime.

The argument that these statutes were 'consolidating' statutes, thus not allowing extension of the old law,[37] may have been arguable for 19th-century legislation such as the Highways Acts 1835 and 1865 but, *in substance*, was far less convincing in the case of statutes passed during the last quarter of the 20th century. We find some clues that this may be so in those cases where modern courts have limited the right to maintenance to the 'surface' of the highway.[38] This made perfect sense in the 18th and 19th centuries where highways (roads or paths would be a more accurate description) were simply covered surfaces (or, originally, simple mud tracks) and not modern and complex cement and tar structures, frequently concealing beneath them cables, sewers, or gas pipes. The idea that old notions of what maintenance means could continue to be valid under modern conditions of design and construction must have weakened with the passage of time. But the courts held out.

[34] *Ibid* at § 12.
[35] And, again, 'bad' only in certain ways (eg, disturbing the King's peace or obstructing his highways).
[36] [2004] 1 WLR 1057, §§ 12, 33.
[37] Thus see Lord Denning in *Haydon v Kent County Council* [1978] QB 343, 355.
[38] *Ibid* at p 356G.

The case of *Department for Transport, Environment & The Regions*,[39] discussed below, brings out the point we are making clearly, for there the cause of the problem emanated below the surface of the road. We welcome not only the result reached by the Court of Appeal but also admire the careful way the judgment of Lord Justice Carnwath was drafted (presumably, we speculate, to make it appeal-proof). So, returning to the general question of the proper ambit of the Highways Acts, we are inclined to paraphrase Lord Hoffmann from another type of case,[40] and argue that the remedies accorded by a statute should be 'ambulatory . . . fashioned according to the law as it sta[nds] from time to time' and should not be frozen in time because an enactment (consolidating very old case law) is called a 'consolidating Act'.

So we come to the meaning of keeping the highway 'in such good repair as renders it reasonably passable for the ordinary traffic of the neighbourhood at all seasons of the year'[41] which, as stated, by means of various statues (starting in the early to mid-1800s and culminating in s 41 of the Highways Act 1980) place a highway authority 'under a duty . . . to maintain the highway'. But the protection given to the public, even for physical injuries resulting from the negligence of the highway authorities, remains incomplete; and such protection as is available has come in a tortured and slow manner.[42]

Other difficulties also had (and have) to be surmounted.

Given the fact that in those early times the interrelationships of public and private law duties had not been studied in the way they nowadays are, and given also that the tort of negligence was not in existence (or remained for at least the first half of the 20th century in an embryonic state), it is not surprising to find that breach of these duties was, originally, only enforceable by means of a prosecution or indictment. It was not until the Highways Act 1961 that such a right was given to an injured individual by the failure to 'maintain the highway', though this was by no means absolute but depended on the circumstances of the case.[43] But even this (small but significant) extension only applied to the failure to 'maintain'; and what was included in this word remained in doubt, the duty to remove ice from a road being excluded as late as 2000.[44] This typical form of omission, widely penalised—to our knowledge—by all Continental European systems, was thus not made actionable until the legislator imposed such liability by virtue of s 111 of the Railways and Transport Safety Act 2003, thus filling another gap in our law. But one more, the most obvious, remains to be filled: the extension of the word 'maintenance' to include omissions that make the highway dangerous and likely to lead to physical injury of its users. Nowadays, painting on the surface of the road a 'slow down' sign does not seem so difficult to include under the phrase 'maintaining the highway'. But it is impossible if one is wedded to what maintenance must have meant 100 years or more ago.

Legally speaking, the two devices used to keep the tort and public law remedy interlinked were two.

[39] [2006] EWCA Civ 1089.

[40] *O'Rourke v Camden London Borough Council* [1998] AC 188, 195.

[41] *Burnside v Emerson* [1968] 1 WLR 1490, 1497 (per Diplock LJ). It is submitted that the words 'reasonably passable' and 'all seasons of the year' give away the scope of the imposed duty reflecting, as it does, old conditions and expectations of travel.

[42] Continental European lawyers who are (incorrectly) taught to believe that flexibility and adaptability are two of the major virtues of the common law case system can pause and draw breath at this very late removal of a lacuna in our law.

[43] *Haydon v Kent County Council* [1978] QB 343.

[44] *Goodes v East Sussex County Council* [2000] 1 WLR 1356.

First, it was held that there is no independent cause of action under the tort of negligence and, secondly, the relevant statutes did not, if 'properly' interpreted, give birth to such an action. But this is, in our view, a legal façade. Only in later times was the possibility of a tort remedy considered possible, and that was in the rare cases that it could be shown that the local authority had acted 'wholly unreasonably' (in the administrative law sense of the term) in not exercising its powers to maintain.[45] The real explanation lies in the combined effect of the cumulative reasons given earlier when explaining judicial timidity (lack of resources being the most important).

Before looking at an important case that, we feel, lends some support to our assertions, a warning of general import must be inserted.

Law students who from an early age are not taught to take with a pinch of salt the meaning of the expression 'with due respect' should understand that this excessive politeness may deprive them of the ability to realise that it is not in the interests of their training to treat judicial pronouncements with reverence. On the contrary, they must be encouraged to learn more about particular judges, their legal and political ideology, their mentality, outlook, and training, and see their judgments as reflecting all these factors[46] as much as embodying the observance of precedent and the following of the wording of statutory law.

Judges may, of course, consciously or unconsciously conceal these factors in felicitously phrased opinions, but it is submitted that they are always there. Moreover, a senior judge, like the academic, can easily make his own views sound as if they enjoy wider support than they do, for instance by a) citing judgments which go his way but are less clear than he suggests or are phrased in a conclusionary manner; b) citing lower courts agreeing with his view (as if they really had any option not to do so) or, if there was a divergence of views between, say, different justices of the Court of Appeal, relying (without or with little reason) on the one who agreed with his own views; c) citing earlier decisions (his own or of his colleagues) which are *not* really in *pare materiae* with the point currently before him; and/or, finally, d) reflecting in the tone of the judgment advocacy rather than decision.

In many of his recent tort decisions, the highway cases included, Lord Hoffmann would appear to be employing his formidable talents to do all four of these things. Not everyone, himself included, will accept such an interpretation. Yet we argue that it is plausible. Let us look at *Gorringe* as an illustration of how compelling such techniques may appear to be—until, that is, they are subjected to closer scrutiny when doubts begin to emerge.

(a) Unclear Judgments or Conclusionary Justifications

In *Gorringe* Lord Hoffmann argued that[47]

> The new private law duty was however limited to the obligation which had previously rested upon the inhabitants at large, namely, to put and keep the highway on repair. As Lord Denning explained in *Haydon v Kent Country Council* [reference omitted] that remains the meaning of 'maintain the highway' in section 41 of the 1980 Act today. In *Goodes v East Sussex County Council* [reference

[45] *Larner v Solihull Metropolitan Borough Council* [2001] RTR 469 PIQR at 475 (per Lord Woolf LCJ). Lord Woolf's approach, influenced by the dissenting judgment of Lord Nicholls in *Stovin v Wise*, was criticised as incompatible with his own (majority) judgment in that same case, and was again criticised in *Gorringe*, at para 32.

[46] On this see Chapter 5 of Basil Markesinis and Jörg Fedtke, *Judicial Recourse to Foreign Law: A New Source of Inspiration?* (2006).

[47] [2004] 1 WLR 1057, § 14.

> omitted] the House of Lords decided that the duty therefore did not require the highway authority to remove ice or snow from the road.

This statement is accurate but not, it seems to us, complete. It thus (i) says nothing of the fact that Lord Denning in *Hayden* was in the dissent; (ii) fails to mention that the two other judges (including Sir Reginald Goff LJ) took a different view as to the meaning of the term 'maintain'; (iii) fails to alert the reader to the fact that even if one construes 'maintain' in a broader sense, one can still avoid the imposition of liability (as was done by Goff LJ); (iv) does not mention the fact that the subsequent approval of the Denning ruling came from the House of Lords, *Lord Hoffmann being the person writing the opinion of the majority*; (v) fails to mention another Denning judgment—*Burnside v Emerson*[48]—which was less restrictive that *Hayden*; and (vi) also fails to comment, even in passing, on the speed with which the (normally slow moving) legislator acted to reverse the effect of *Goodes*. Finally, though for this Lord Hoffmann cannot be blamed, we must (vii) note the continued vitality of *Burnside*, which most recently enabled the Court of Appeal to hold a highway authority liable for an accident that happened because water accumulated on the surface of a road leading to a traffic accident.

These 'omissions'—or so we see them—in Hoffmann's judgment may well be caused by his intention to keep his text lean and muscular. They can equally be explained by saying that he assumes that his serious and professional readers will know the missing points we have supplied. Yet will they?

One of us has over the years addressed practising barristers and solicitors on many occasions; and though he has come to admire their advocacy talents and experience, he would argue that they are not always as keen as they should be in appreciating the psychological effect that a skilfully drafted or truncated judgment can have on a reader. Cardozo, for instance, was known (and admired) for his ability to present the facts in such a manner as would make his conclusion easier to justify.[49]

If the last point is not one frequently made in England it may be because the kind of literature that examines judicial psychology, outlook, and disposition, has not yet seen the light of day here. But the point is not only made in the United States; it has also been stressed by the former President of the German Constitutional Court, Professor Jutta Limbach, who was also quick to make it clear that none of these factors amounted to bias (a point to which we, too, naturally subscribe). Since Lord Hoffmann is also the Honorary President of the British-German Jurists' Association, he may be interested to read the views of an equally senior justice on this important but neglected aspect of judicial decision-making. President Limbach, speaking in 1996 at the Humboldt University of Berlin, thus said:[50]

> If formally approached, it is of course the duty of the *Bundesverfassungsgericht* to answer authoritatively the question whether a certain provision is constitutional. The Court must, however, be aware of the fact that the answer to this question is the result of highly complex considerations involving a balancing of interests and values. There is no absolutely correct decision; at least such a decision cannot be achieved by us on this earth. The dissenting opinions of judges are, in many cases, proof of this fact. Conflicting views between judges do not materialise from thin air. *In addition to different historical and cultural perspectives which play a role, judges also have diverging*

[48] [1968] 1 WLR 1490.

[49] See Judge Posner in *Cardozo. A Study in Reputation* (1990), pp 33–57. A more focused example is given by the late professor Karl Llewellyn in 'A Lecture on Appellate Advocacy', 29 *U Chi L Rev* 627, 637 (1962), commenting on another of Cardozo's famous judgments, *Wood v Lucy, Lady Duff-Gordon*, 118 NE 214 (NY 1917).

[50] *Das Bundesverfassungsgericht als politischer Machtfaktor* (1996). The emphasis is ours.

> *opinions concerning social values. We know that individuals have an a priori understanding of certain issues which more or less affects the legal solutions they opt for. This has nothing to do with prejudice or bias. We are all determined by certain basic views which are independent of the process of applying the law and which are formed by intuition rather than by rational analysis. This is a mixture of moral, legal, philosophical, and political convictions, and it includes an individual's understanding of the world that we live in.*

(b) Citing Lower Courts which are in Agreement

Selectively stressing lower courts (or judicial opinions) agreeing with one's view (in any hierarchical system) without explaining why they are preferable to other decisions of courts of similar standing makes such citation techniques less weighty. Subliminally, however, this way of using decisions tends to generate the impression that one's views have gained acceptance on a wider level than might be the case. Thus, in *Gorringe* Lord Hoffmann wrote:[51]

> *Stovin v Wise* was applied in *Capital & Counties plc v Hampshire County Council*[52] to fire authorities, which have a general public law duty to make provision for efficient fire-fighting services . . . The Court of Appeal held, in my view correctly, that this did not create a common law duty.

The statement is then followed by a quotation from Lord Justice Stuart-Smith's judgment to the effect that 'if, therefore, they [that is, the fire brigade] fail to turn up, or fail to turn up in time, because they have carelessly misunderstood the message, got lost on the way or run into a tree, they are not liable'.

This rider was, as already indicated, made in order to express his preference for Lord Justice Stuart-Smith's view over that of Lord Woolf in *Larner v Solihull Metropolitan Borough Council*[53] (which, following the dissent in *Stovin*, thought that in exceptional circumstances such a duty might fall on the defendant authority).

The way that Lord Woolf's reliance on the dissent in *Stovin* is dismissed is interesting. For though Lord Hoffmann is entitled to do this on the grounds that it is inconsistent with the decision of the majority of the House of Lords in *Stovin*, the inconsistency may have been generated by some 'ill-advised speculation' of his own in *Stovin*. 'I have sinned' is always an admission that tends to get sympathy for the sinner, even if it is made in a rather off-the-cuff manner; but choosing to place more weight on Lord Justice Stuart-Smith's view of the *Stovin* ruling is, to say the least, questionable given that the learned justice's views on the matter are so obviously inclined in favour of the non-liability rule that they have even led him to try and defy the House of Lords' ruling and left him reprimanded twice by them. How else can Lord Hoffmann's preference for them be justified than by the assumption that he likes these views because they reflect his own outlook?

Is this too harsh a statement? Maybe; and if it is understood in this way we deeply regret it. Yet look how he goes further into the *Gorringe* case with the Court of Appeal's judgment in *Larner*:

> The simple facts which I have summarised at the beginning of this speech seem to have disappeared from view in the enthusiasm for a hostile judicial inquiry into the council's administration. If section 39 continues to provoke investigations of this nature, much of the road safety budget will be consumed in the cost of litigation.

51 [2004] 1 WLR 1057, § 32.
52 [1997] QB 1004.
53 [2001] RTR 469 at 475.

This last sentence is the giveaway line of what lies behind this repeated use of the duty of care concept: the fear of unlimited litigation, high damages, and misuse of public funds. He fears and/or dislikes this eventuality so much that he tries to avoid it at all costs. The question, however, remains: is it really up to the judge to ensure the protection of the public purse? And can such well-intended (though, for us, misconceived) interference be allowed by the amorphous phrase 'fair, just and reasonable' or the search of the elusive legislative intent? And are these fears justified by the experience of other countries which might contain transplantable elements? It is with this last point that we are mainly concerned here. But before we come to this crucial question, one more criticism must be made about the way Lord Hoffmann uses authority to bolster his philosophical position on the matter.

(c) Welfare Law Legislation

In *Gorringe* Lord Hoffmann invoked (his own) judgment in *O'Rourke v Camden London Borough Council* where, referring to the homeless persons legislation which was relevant in that litigation, he said:[54]

> The . . . Act is a *scheme of social welfare*, intended to confer benefits at the public expense on grounds of public policy. *Public money is spent on housing the homeless not merely for the private benefit of people who find themselves homeless but on grounds of general public interest: because, for example, proper housing means that people will be less likely to suffer illness, turn to crime, or require the attention of other social services.* The expenditure interacts with expenditure on other public services such as education, the National Health Service and even the police. It is not simply a private matter between the claimant and the housing authority.

Lord Hoffmann relied on a second broad reason for denying a monetary remedy. For, he argued, the existence of a duty to provide accommodation depended 'upon a good deal of judgment on the part of the housing authority'.[55] This made judicial review a more appropriate remedy, even though one must never forget that this remedy is more effective in ensuring *future* compliance than providing redress of injury *already sustained* by the claimant. Indeed, we think it is considerations such as these which, inter alia, have led an important group of jurists to advocate the need for a general right of compensation for loss resulting from unlawful government activities.[56]

We have italicised the words 'scheme of social welfare' because it is, generally, true to say that social welfare legislation or, in Germany, programmatic declarations found in the Constitution and proclaiming that the Federal Republic adopts the so-called *Sozialstaatsprinzip* are, in most cases, unable to be relied upon by the courts to provide a basis for actionable private law rights, certainly monetary awards. The reason is not difficult to grasp. For though commendable aspirations in any society, the notions covered by the principle and associated with social and welfare justice, fairness, and equality may be too expensive to be turned into actionable private law rights. Claimants are thus restricted to the more limited scope of protection offered by specific rules of social security legislation resembling our order of *mandamus*.

[54] [1998] AC 188, 193.
[55] [1998] AC 188, at p 194.
[56] See, eg, the All Souls Committee of 1988 Report: Administrative Justice—Some Necessary Reforms (1988), Chapter 11.

The above, however, represents (for both systems) only the starting point. For 'social welfare legislation' can be of different kinds, and we feel the words of Romer LJ cannot be bettered when he said[57] that it is of

> cardinal importance, in considering whether a civil suit lies for breach of statutory duty, to see whether, on a broad view, that duty has been imposed for the general welfare on the one hand or in the interests of individuals or a defined or definable class of the public on the other.

Now this dictum could be used to support both our starting point and Lord Hoffmann's concluding one cited above and placed in italics in the quoted part of his opinion in *O'Rourke*. But Hoffmann's approach is, in fact, not tenable. Lord Justice Carnwath has put this objection well, so we content ourselves in citing his clear argument. Writing extra-judicially he thus observed:[58]

> The question is not answered by the observation that money spent on housing the homeless also achieves a public benefit, in that those housed are less likely thereby to require attention from health or other welfare services. That could equally be said of safety-at-work legislation, which nonetheless gives rise to private rights of action. There is perhaps an even closer analogy with the Health Service itself. A health authority, whose doctor fails to admit a patient to hospital because of a negligent diagnosis . . . will not escape liability merely because they are part of a public welfare service. Why should a housing authority be in a better position, if its officer leaves an applicant on the streets as a result of a perverse failure to accept him as 'homeless' or in 'priority need'?

The reason why we cite Lord Justice Carnwath's piece is not only to keep reminding our readers that Lord Hoffmann's views arguably prevail by reason of the superior authority of the House of Lords rather than the intrinsic persuasiveness of their internal reasoning, but also because Lord Justice Carnwath's analysis seems to us to be more convincing on the second of Hoffmann's arguments in *O'Rourke*: deciding in favour of such applicants involves 'a good deal of judgment on the part of the housing authority' and this should only be questioned by means of judicial review but should not be exposed to an action for damages.

We take this view since, again, we see his meticulous discussion in the aforementioned article in *Public Law* to come closer to a judicial (and, we would add, judicious) consideration of the Housing Acts, its history, and its case law precedents than Lord Hoffmann's opinion in *O'Rourke* which, in our considered view, seems more like advocacy for a position which he, no doubt, honestly sees as right—as we, equally honestly, find to be wrong. So, this again, is how the learned Lord Justice put his objections:[59]

> As to the second 'contra-indication', the reference to the need for 'a good deal of judgment' is curiously imprecise. The questions for the authority are largely ones of fact: Is the applicant homeless? Does he have dependent children? and so on. There is, it is true, an element of value judgment in deciding, for example, whether he is 'vulnerable' by reason of disability; but the issues are narrowly confined by the statutory definitions.

The reason why we find this argument convincing is because the deciding process in such cases has, since the coming into force of the Housing (Homeless Persons) Act 1977, involved two phases: the making of reasonable enquiries which, if the authority has 'reason to believe' that they might meet the statutory requirements, place them under an 'interim duty' to provide the homeless person with housing—a duty which then becomes

[57] *Solomons v Certzenstein* [1954] 2 QB 243, at p 265.
[58] 'The Thornton Heresy Exposed: Financial Remedies for Breach of Public Duties', *PL* 1998, 407 at p 415.
[59] *PL*, 1998, 405 at p 415.

unqualified if, on completion of the enquiries, the authority is satisfied that the homeless person has met the statutory demands.

The excursus into *O'Rourke* must thus be seen both as a dubious or, at the very least, controversial precedent to be used as an additional stepping stone in reaching the *Gorringe* result, but also as another superb example—for those who share the view that tort law should be excluded from these kind of cases—of advocacy leading our law to this—for us—unfortunate end.

(d) A Missed Point?

From the time of Roman law we know that lawyers were aware of a way to impose liability for omissions. The collection of Roman and Mosaic law gives us the example of a man who was asked to watch over a fire. He fell asleep and the fire spread and caused more damage. He was held liable.[60] The decision suggests that in many cases an omission can be seen as a bad act and escapes the misfeasance/non-feasance dichotomy. This could have worked in *Gorringe*, for we are told that the road where the accident occurred did carry such a 'slow down' sign before its most recent resurface. That suggests that the highway authority was aware of the dangers and had tried to warn users, especially those unfamiliar with the peculiarities of that stretch of road. The cost of re-painting such a notice would have been tiny compared to the cost of tort liability (borne by the local community) or the health service (again borne largely by local funds going to the local hospital). A cost-benefit analysis would/should have led to this precautionary measure being taken. But it was not; and its omission was not even considered—swallowed up as it were by the neo-conservative argument that people should look after themselves. We know, however, that they do not; and, as indicated, the local authority in that case must have carried a large part of Ms Gorringe's medical bill and will in the future continue to carry many such bills because Lord Hoffmann sent it a signal that it need not do anything about the problem.

3. FURTHER DOUBTS ABOUT LORD HOFFMANN'S REASONING IN *GORRINGE*

Any reader who allows himself to see these sections, indeed the entire Chapter, as an anti-Hoffmann polemic will be seriously mistaken, for as is made clear throughout the narrative we yield to no one in our admiration for this judge's learning and legal ingenuity. But our text has not refrained from externalising a serious intellectual disagreement on some difficult and controversial matters which invite and, indeed, have received divergent reactions from the entire legal community.

Our diverging views are not only strongly held; they also refer to an important issue of principle: the continued role of tort law in relation to duties of public authorities at a time of streamlined judicial review procedures. We have no doubt that in this context Lord Hoffmann is playing a key role in 'eliminating' tort, here and elsewhere, as an appropriate system for legal redress for harm negligently caused; and though he often manages to carry

[60] Coll 12, 7, 7.

with him his colleagues in the Lords, his views do not command, as he sometimes implies, universal approval among academics and, more importantly, among his fellow judges. Our citations and footnotes must attest to this already.

These points must be brought out into the open not only because we disagree with the results they lead to but also with the techniques used by the learned Law Lord to sway other lawyers to his point of view. The material presented and arguments made in this Chapter are meant to show anyone who is still open-minded on these issues that there exists an alternative position to that advocated by Lord Hoffmann. If, in the process of presenting this alternative, we have erred either in substance or style of presentation, we stand by to be corrected in order to return to the battle with refined arguments. The economic rationale of Lord Hoffmann's positions, relating to externalities, defensive practices, insurance, and the 'defendant of last resort' argument, was already discussed and rejected elsewhere.[61] In this section we will thus focus on the human rights dimension before we move on to the presentation of German law.

English law has traditionally shown little interest in the inter-disciplinary, even having neglected to combine the study of different branches of the law which may affect one and the same issue.[62] Law and economics, for instance, is not a method of understanding law in England as it has been in the United States. Linking tort law with constitutional law or human rights considerations has also been rare. The ability to criticise local authorities, for instance, was for a very long time treated as a pure question of defamation law; and it was not until the Court of Appeal judgment in *Derbyshire* that the impact of the European Convention on Human Rights was considered. Interestingly, the House of Lords, while agreeing with the result reached by the Court of Appeal, chose (more mundanely) to discover that the Common law after all also thought in analogous ways.

But the human rights dimension was yet to make itself felt in a big way. Not surprisingly, in a lecture delivered in 1988, Lord Hoffmann positioned himself on the conservative (small or large C?) side by drawing attention to the dangers of accepting too readily an international view of human rights law.[63] In

> a confident democracy [we should assert, he claimed] our own hierarchy of moral values, our own culturally determined sense of what is fair and unfair; and not allow them to be submerged under a pan-European jurisprudence of Human Rights.

This is a confident piece of advocacy with rhetorical overtones; but on the basis of what evidence can he speak for '*our own* hierarchy of moral values'? For his own 'set of values' do not seem to be the same as Lord Bingham's or other judges'. Is his conception of our 'moral values' more English than Lord Bingham's? Or does his position in the House of Lords give to his evaluation of 'what is far and unfair'—for instance in the matter of overruling

[61] See BS Markesinis, JV Auby, D Coester-Waltjen and SF Deakin, *Tortious Liability of Statutory Bodies. A Comparative and Economic Analysis of Five English Cases* (1999), pp 76 *ff.*

[62] An example which is relevant to our theme—the Europeanisation of national law—can be found in the law of defamation, developed for years as if it were in no way affected by human rights law, especially the European Convention on Human Rights. The Court of Appeal in *Derbyshire Council v Times Newspapers Ltd* [1992] 1 QB 770 was the first to stress the importance of the European Convention on defamation law, bypassing to a large extent the very technical arguments advanced by the legal experts—eg Carter Ruck, *Libel and Slander*, 4th edn (1992), 73—who were trying to predict the future of *Bognor Regis UDC v Campion* [1972] 2 QB 169. The House of Lords approved the result but chose, as it has since tried to do again, to find the answer in the common law. But if the common law was as effective as some have claimed, why was it also often found by Strasbourg to be deficient, especially outside the area of free speech?

[63] 'Human Rights and the House of Lords', (1999) 62 MLR 159.

Thornton v Kirklees DC—a more English colour than, say, that of Lord Justice Carnwath's contrary evaluation? And is Lord Hoffman that confident that his desire to avoid us being 'submerged under a pan-European jurisprudence of Human Rights' will not, in the long run, follow our earlier unsuccessful resistance to the other great corpus of European law which is flowing up our estuaries but emanates from the nearby city of Luxembourg? Talking extra-judicially, the learned Law Lord is, of course, free to argue anything he wishes. In this context, however, his views about the separateness of 'our values', though deserving full attention, will ultimately be proved right or wrong by the political and not the judicial process.

The English system was put to the test when Strasbourg handed down its decision in *Osman v UK.*[64] It caused a shock not only because it was seen as a European intervention in the law of this country but also because it showed how this European court, composed—some noted—in many cases not by 'proper' judges but retired politicians, had misunderstood our law and our love affair with the notion of duty of care. In the rush to condemn the decision, little notice was paid to the fact that the English judge in that court had concurred with the result. More importantly, little was said of the fact that during the preceding years, under the tutelage of (literally) a handful of judges at the Court of Appeal and the House of Lords, the extensive use of the notion of duty of care had led to the creation of extensive immunities covering, for example, the police, the public prosecution service, social services, the fire brigade, or the lifeboat service. Strasbourg took the view that preventing the case being heard at such an early stage of the proceedings was incompatible with Article 6(1) of the Convention; and after a 'skilful campaign' conducted by the British legal establishment it was 'forced'—we feel that 'persuaded' is too weak a word—to backtrack. English judges and academics consumed by the fear of an explosion in litigation could once again breathe freely. But the comfort was illusionary, for the clock cannot be set back. Ours is a 'rights society', first feebly proclaimed by the Citizen's Charters created by the Major Government and then more boldly confirmed by the Human Rights Act 1998. Many welcomed this Act, advocated for decades by Lord Lester of Herne Hill and skilfully steered through Parliament by the then Lord Chancellor Lord Irvine of Lairg. Though, subsequently, many (invariably Conservative) supporters have blamed it—often quite wrongly[65]—for many of our current ills, the ideas behind the Act are here to stay even if parts of it (as well as our continued adherence to the Convention) were ever to fall victim to political calculations to pacify public hysteria whipped up by the tabloid press.

This is too big an issue to be discussed here.[66] Yet we cannot but note the astuteness of Lord Bingham in alluding to this background factor in his dissenting judgment in *East Berkshire.* More importantly, he predicted that if the Common law refused to evolve, Strasbourg might strike again. He thus said that[67]

> the question does arise whether the law of tort should evolve, analogically and incrementally, so as to fashion appropriate remedies to contemporary problems or whether it should remain essentially

[64] *Osman v United Kingdom* (1998) 29 EHRR 245.

[65] For instance attributing the early release of criminals from their prison sentences to the Human Rights Act 1998 or blaming it for the inability to extradite suspected foreign terrorists to countries which practise torture or accept the death sentence.

[66] See, eg, Lord Justice Carnwath's articles 'Welfare Services—Liabilities in Tort After the Human Rights Act', *PL* 2001, 21–219 and 'Welfare Services—Liabilities in Tort after the Human Rights Act. A Postscript', *PL* 2001, 475–9.

[67] *D v East Berkshire Community Health NHS Trust and others; MAK and another v Dewsbury Healthcare NHS Trust and another; RK and another v Oldham NHS Trust and another,* [2005] 2 WLR 993 at para 50.

static, making only such changes as are forced upon it, leaving difficult and, in human terms, very important problems to be swept up by the Convention. I prefer evolution.

Less than a year later, Strasbourg in fact returned to the fray in the case of *Keegan v The United Kingdom*.[68] The Fourth Section of the Court held that such an action should be possible under Article 13 of the Convention if local law denied it.

The dispute arose as a result of a botched investigation of the Liverpool police which broke early one morning into the claimant's home believing it to be the home of a known and dangerous criminal. Strasbourg took the view that the facts of the case amounted to a violation of Article 8 of the Convention. They also took the view that Article 13 of the Convention required that a remedy be given in domestic law if the grievance in question could be regarded as 'arguable' in terms of the Convention. Naturally, the Court admitted that this did not amount to a guarantee that a remedy would be given since under the Contracting State's laws an effective remedy should only be provided in principle. English law, however, did not allow such a remedy to be considered unless the police had acted with malice, which they had not. The absence of a remedy for negligence, however, denied the courts the chance to examine the proportionality and reasonableness of the police activity, the national law setting in such cases the balance in favour of protecting the police. Damages were thus accorded to the claimants, the amount being fixed at levels higher than those which the defendants thought justifiable.

The facts of the case make it clear that it is not—yet—as threatening as *Osman*. But it does have the potential of growing further and justifying, if a case with appropriate facts came before the Court, for Strasbourg to question the continued reluctance to hold the police and other statutory bodies liable for negligently caused harm. It also illustrates the importance of this new tort/human rights linkage which will, sooner or later, be resolved from abroad if the local courts persist in their refusal to adapt English law to the demands of its present-day environment. So the question which must be asked is whether they can persist for much longer in denying the European[69] realities?

The most recent batch of decisions,[70] dealing with alleged child abuse leading to the separation from their parents, seem to be trapped by the *East Berkshire*[71] ruling and the unusual decision of the judges forming the majority to stress that they decided the case the way they did not only because of the reasons they themselves gave in the opinion but also for the reasons given by each of the others who formed the majority.[72] Security in numbers

[68] Application no 28867/03.

[69] Law emanating from Luxembourg is, of course, now part of own legal system, so its existence cannot be denied nor its influence on our law (and, just as importantly, on the way our judges interpret law) belittled. But Strasbourg law, it is often argued, is less binding in its detail since the Convention, to which we signed up almost half a century ago, only sets out 'minimal' obligations and allows much room for variation in detail. Yet how realistic such an analysis is, given the existence of a central court charged with the creation of a uniform interpretation of the articles of the Convention, and given also its widening jurisdiction, is open to much debate.

[70] *Lawrence v Pembrokeshire* [2006] EWHC 1029 (QB) and *AD and OH (a child: by AD his litigation friend) v Bury Metropolitan Borough Council* [2006] EWCA Civ 1.

[71] *D v East Berkshire Community Health NHS Trust and others; MAK and another v Dewsbury Healthcare NHS Trust and another; RK and another v Oldham NHS Trust and another*, [2005] 2 WLR 993.

[72] Principal among them was the argument that the local authority's duty to the child was not coterminous to that owed to the parents. German courts, by contrast, though acknowledging the duty of public authorities to protect the interests of the child, at the same time stress the rights of the parents and the high interest of both parents and children to an undisturbed family life; see, eg, the reasoning in BGH NJW 2005, 68 *ff*. Indeed, the German Civil Code itself calls for strict adherence to the principle of proportionality in all decisions concerning the welfare of children, including—as ultima ratio—separation of children from their parents (§ 1666a BGB). For a recent case of the Federal Constitutional Court see BVerfGE 1 BvR 605/02 of 21 June 2002 (ruling in favour of the parents).

one might be tempted to call this; yet this is hardly sufficient to protect them from the 'brooding omnipresence of European law'—to use in a different context Justice Holmes' well-known metaphor[73]—from which this country will never escape unless it has the courage to opt out (*and, actually, commits the folly of moving further away*) from the centre of European decision-making.

What is striking about these two decisions is not the unnecessarily long regurgitation of the dicta from the majority in *East Berkshire* but the minimal lack of attention to two elements of these cases: first the fact that the local authorities and their officials were guilty of *repeated and gross violations* of their duties. These could/should have prompted the lower judges to consider, or at least to reflect on, Lord Bingham's safety-valve device of contemplating the imposition of liability only in cases of serious fault along the lines of the French notion of *faute lourde.*

For even if some judges dislike the idea of borrowing from foreign systems and even if it could be said that our law does not know as a term of art the notion of 'gross' negligence, can our judges ignore the fact that in this case they were faced not with a comedy but a catalogue of errors? Can they overlook the fact that the ombudsman found maladministration not on one but on various counts?[74] And should they disguise their deep-rooted suspicion of tort liability by pretending that the interests of the child meant that they should 'single-mindedly'[75] ignore the interests of the parents? For even if this were convincing in all cases, is it not true to accept that the interests of the child are not simple and easily defined interests but interests endowed with multiple facets, at least one of which is coterminous with that of its parents, namely the interest to keep the family unit together?

This is nothing more or less than the interest envisaged in Article 8 of the Convention; and its violation should lead to the award of damages especially if the errors kept happening with hair-raising regularity. Surely, in such cases the public interest is not solely and always on the side of shielding local authorities from the economic consequences of their shoddy behaviour; it also encompasses the need to send out a signal to them that mistakes are one thing but repeated negligence quite another (intolerable) form of behaviour.

Secondly, let us retain this optic of looking at what happened in this case and not fall into the trap of describing the parental claim as one arising out of emotional or psychiatric distress. For such an analysis would not only be wrong; it would also lead conservative judges to invoke the messy state of the law of nervous shock in order to come back to their favourite starting point: immunity!

Let us instead recognise that we are here dealing with a new situation of human rights torts where the monetary compensation awarded is a sign that society values a certain state of affairs—here family life, including family union—and expresses its disapproval *especially* when it has been disturbed by its own agents. After all, English tort law is not a stranger to moving into action even in the absence of any quantifiable damage, if what it is really doing is helping to vindicate a right—like, for instance, the human freedom of locomotion in the case of false imprisonment or reputation in the case of libel—from being violated in an unwarranted manner. Again, the most recent Strasbourg case law would favour, we think,

[73] *Southern Pacific Co v Jensen*, 244 US 205, 222 (1917).

[74] Summarised in § 16 of *Lawrence v Pembrokeshire* [2006] EWHC 1029 (QB).

[75] These words appear repeatedly in Mr Justice Field's judgment in *Lawrence.* For the reasons given in the text we find them unfortunate.

such an approach; and it is, itself,[76] suggesting the award of damages which we would find both reasonable and by no means excessive or even ruinous.

Strasbourg is already thinking along these lines. As long ago as 1988 a mother was separated from her child which was made a ward of court in order to protect it against the alleged violence of the mother's partner. When the mother's conditions improved she applied to re-establish access with the child which, in the meantime, had been put up for adoption by the council. The local council's delay in producing the relevant documentation that would determine the mother's right of access was described as 'deplorable' by the English judge hearing the case; but the child ended up being adopted and the mother being denied access to it. Since, in effect, there was no other real remedy left to the mother, she began proceedings in Strasbourg complaining that the delay in determining her right of access to her child amounted to a violation of Articles 6 and 8 of the Convention. She won on both grounds.

The case presented many novel points, and they are still with us today.

First, awards against delays in court proceedings cannot be made according to section 9 of the Human Rights Act 1998. But the delays of a local authority can result in it being landed with monetary consequences.

Secondly, the Strasbourg court has since sent out signals that it is not likely to succumb to the tempting voices which convinced it to back-track from *Osman*[77] and set the level of damages at demeaningly low levels. On the contrary, they are determined to send just about the right signal to local authorities that sloppy behaviour will simply not be tolerated. The *Keegan* case shows that they are sticking to their guns or, rather, their own figures—not too high but neither too low to be meaningless.

Thirdly, it is clear that whatever the nature of this remedy, it resembles more what Lester and Pannick describe as a 'new public law tort of acting in breach of the victim's rights'[78] and this, as already stated in the previous paragraph, can only mean that the foundations are being laid for evading other restrictive rules of English tort law such as the rule of nervous shock.

The human rights dimension of these cases is thus crucial, indeed innovative, for all sorts of reasons. For, first, not only does it suggest that the system of remedies developing in human rights legislation is different and not easily reconcilable to those found in domestic law; it also shows that judges in Strasbourg are likely to continue their own development of the law, and in doing this they may not be able to provide English law with the more fine-tuned approach that our courts could adopt were they freed from the conservative tendencies of the House of Lords.

Secondly, our courts do little justice to the subject or to their own ingenuity by sweeping the intelligent discussion of these issues under the carpet of such meaningless notions as 'fair, just and reasonable' or denying access to justice on the basis of hunches—rather than actual empirical evidence—as to the consequences which successful actions might entail. If they fear floodgates, let them give us their figures as we have given them ours. Arguments of this kind are, in the end, resolved by reason, not authority.

In the light of the above one can only hope that they will have the sagacity to adapt their law pragmatically and in a controlled manner in order to fend off the risk of being faced with a more heavy-handed reaction from Strasbourg. Lord Bingham would favour such a

[76] As the *Keegan* case suggests.

[77] *Z v UK* and *TP and KM v UK*, Applications 29392/95 and 28945/95. See Lord Justice Arden's concurring opinion suggesting an award in line with those recommended by the guidelines of the Judicial Studies Board.

[78] 'The Impact of the Human Rights Act on Private Law: The Knight's Move,' (2000) 116 LQR 380, at 382.

hope; Lord Hoffmann is likely to remain resolutely attached to his own position, no doubt anticipating that he will be able to divert or evade that troublesome issue: Europe. In our view he is unlikely to succeed, for Europe is the defining issue of our times. But should he get his way temporarily, we would venture to guess that his victory will not last longer than his own hold to judicial office. But since it is always dangerous to prophesy the future, let us leave matters at that.

4. THE STRUCTURAL APPROACH TO THE BREACH OF STATUTORY DUTIES AND ITS JUSTIFICATION IN GERMANY

Time now to turn our attention to German law and explore how, if at all, we may be able to learn from its experience on this matter. A closer look at the legal approach in Germany—a system which initially addressed the tortious liability of public servants over a century ago—is thereby necessary before we concentrate on the empirical material. Of the many different causes of action which are summarised under the heading 'state liability' (*Staatshaftung*) and include, inter alia, legal expropriation, we will limit ourselves to the breach of official duties (*Amtspflichtverletzung*).[79]

The German Civil Code established the personal delictual liability of public officials in 1900 by stating as a general principle that officials who wilfully or negligently commit a breach of a duty incumbent upon them and owed to a third party (*drittbezogene Amtspflicht*) shall compensate that third party for any damage arising from the breach.[80] The Code does protect individual officials to some extent by excluding, inter alia, their obligation to compensate in cases of less severe infringements of their duties (so-called 'leichte Fahrlässigkeit' or 'simple negligence') if the injured party can obtain compensation elsewhere, but it was left to the constituent states of the German Empire and—later—the Weimar Constitution of 1919 to introduce a general rule which channelled this personal liability of public officials to the relevant public authority.[81]

The German Constitution of 1949 chose to confirm this fundamental change in the operation of § 839 BGB. According to Article 34 of the German Constitution,[82] liability rests first and foremost with the state or public authority that employs a person who violates an official duty vis-a-vis a third party, and recourse is only allowed against the individual officer in question if he acted intentionally or with a particularly high degree of negligence. If the requirements for § 839 BGB and Article 34 BL are met, the state thus assumes responsibility for the tort committed by the official, and the tortfeasor—despite the wording of the Civil Code—will not be a party to the action.[83]

At its core, this structure still reflects the 19th-century notion of a personal liability of public officials, but is strongly tempered by modern considerations of a state which should accept responsibility for the negligent wrongs committed by its servants. The constitutional

[79] For a brief overview (in German) of the various causes of action see F Ossenbühl, *Staatshaftungsrecht* (5th edn 1998), pp 1/2.

[80] § 839(1) BGB. This provision was modelled along the lines of Prussian and Saxon law; see PrALR II. Teil 10. Titel §§ 88–91 (for Prussia) and § 1507 SächsBGB (for Saxony).

[81] Article 131 of the Constitution of Weimar (Weimarer Reichsverfassung, WRV). For more details see F Ossenbühl, above note 79, pp 7–9.

[82] *Grundgesetz* (Basic Law, BL).

[83] H Jarass and B Pieroth, *Grundgesetz für die Bundesrepublik Deutschland* (6th edn 2002), Art 34 at no 23.

solution adopted in 1919—and later transferred to the Basic Law—thereby finds its justification, first, in the desire to avoid overly defensive attitudes of public officials, especially when confronted with emergency situations which require an immediate response, and, secondly, an overall duty of the state to offer protection to individuals who perform public functions on its behalf (a consideration which is equally important in the area of German labour law today). An additional reason lies in the fact that the state is thought to be a more solvent debtor than the individual public employee.[84]

At a deeper—constitutional—level, governmental liability is justified by the rule of law. The executive is bound by the law,[85] and citizens adversely affected by unlawful activities of the state have a constitutional right to judicial review.[86] The duty of the state to provide compensation is viewed as a third element in this network of constitutional protection; the obligation to compensate damage caused in the exercise of special public law powers is thereby often regarded as part and parcel of the considerable powers that public bodies may exercise vis-a-vis the citizen.

It is important to point out that the combination of rules found in the Civil Code and the Basic Law only creates a very basic legal framework of protection and requires more specific rules and guidelines in order to become fully operational in practice. One reason for this is the catch-all character of these provisions which are, in principle, applicable to any type of state activity. This is where the courts have taken over, producing, over the decades, both a rich and complicated case law covering most aspects of public administration.[87]

Equally diverse are the official duties which, if violated, can merit compensation.[88] The courts have also expanded the scope of state liability by reducing in certain instances the impact of the fault requirement found in § 839 BGB[89] and by adopting a fairly restrictive approach to the interpretation of the statutory privileges contained in that provision. Over the years, German public authorities have thus been less and less able to invoke successfully the limitations placed on the liability of the individual official by the Civil Code, though some pockets of protection continue to exist.[90]

[84] See F Ossenbühl, above note 79, pp 9/10; BGHZ 69, 128 (at p 124).

[85] Article 20(3) BL.

[86] Article 19(4) BL.

[87] Involving, inter alia, medical malpractice, law enforcement by public prosecutors, general police activity, decisions of health and safety authorities, building and planning law, duties of care concerning the safety of publicly accessible roads, waterways or harbours, activities of the military, data protection, warning statements concerning defective products, social security, and the participation of state employees in public traffic. For a dense summary of the duties of care owed to citizens in various contexts see A Kunschert in *Geigel, Der Haftpflichtprozess* (23rd edn 2001), pp 582–96, and H Sprau in *Palandt, Bürgerliches Gesetzbuch* (65th edn 2006), § 839 at nos 91–175.

[88] Starting with the most basic obligation to act lawfully, German courts have developed a dense framework of responsibilities such as the duty not to act ultra vires, to adhere to the established administrative procedures in a given area, to exercise discretion (*Ermessen*) according to the principles of administrative law, to act in accordance with the idea of proportionality, to take decisions in due course, to provide the citizen with correct information, to act in a way which is consistent with previous administrative practice (both in general and the specific case) and, finally, the duty to counteract any illegal measures previously taken by a public authority in a particular situation. A good English introduction to the main principles of German administrative law is provided by M Singh, *German Administrative Law in a Common Law Perspective* (2nd edn 2001). References to German case law are listed, inter alia, by H Sprau in *Palandt, Bürgerliches Gesetzbuch* (67th edn 2008), § 839 at nos 31–42.

[89] Local building/planning authorities (*Baubehörden*) were particularly affected; cases include harm caused by illegal building permits and the planning of living areas on contaminated ground. See Infratest Burke Rechtsforschung, *Zur Reform des Staatshaftungsrechts* (1999). This survey was conducted with the academic guidance of Professor Hans-Jürgen Papier (today President of the Federal Constitutional Court).

[90] Eg, in case ambulance or police vehicles invoke special rights of way under § 35 *Straßenverkehrsordnung* (Road Traffic Ordinance) or if public authorities act to avert immediate dangers to the public (*polizeiliche Gefahrenabwehr*).

This brief assessment of German law dealing with the delictual liability of public bodies thus indicates two things. On the one hand, the courts have exercised an unusually high influence in shaping the development in this area of tort law[91] and, more importantly have shown a tendency to expand gradually the liability of public authorities. On the other hand, these developments have not led to any serious discussions about the role of judges influencing how public funds are used. This could be due to the fairly limited overall impact which these cases have actually had on German administrative practice.

A *theoretical* explanation for the acceptance of this judicial influence on public spending can again be found on the constitutional level. Article 34 BL is not only a 'technical' provision which redirects the claim of the citizen against the individual public official to the responsible public authority; this article also contains a fundamental constitutional choice (similar to that expressed by Lord Bingham in *Bedfordshire*[92]) that—in principle—wrongs committed by the state should lead to compensation. This decision—in conjunction with the rule of law—seems to offer a powerful legal basis for the position taken by German law. Thus, in Germany, apart from very few exceptions, budgetary constraints have not been raised as an argument to undermine the principle that 'wrongs should be remedied'. Courts have been willing to enforce it, regardless of the potentially negative effects which their decisions might have on the financial position of public authorities, though (as we shall see) there have not been any such negative effects.

Interesting exceptions, however, do exist. A recent example is the degree (not duty!) of care required by public authorities in the maintenance of roads in the Eastern parts of the country following German reunification. In dealing with claims of motorists who had suffered accidents due to the poor condition of roads and highways in the area of the former German Democratic Republic, courts were for some time willing to accept a lower level of safety in the light of the financial and administrative burdens caused by years of neglect at the hands of the former regime.[93] This standard was subsequently raised to Western levels as the responsible public authorities were expected to have improved the quality of roads and highways over time.[94]

Of wider importance is a second exception concerning the compensation of damage caused by unconstitutional statutes enacted by the German legislator. In a line of cases reaching back to 1987 (and in contrast to the position taken by the European Court of Justice when it comes to legislative compliance of the Member States with Community law), the Federal Supreme Court has rejected claims of victims with a view to, inter alia, the budgetary prerogative of Parliament.[95] But these examples are, as stated, exceptions to the rule that German courts will not usually consider the economic consequences of their judgments for the public purse. In this, of course, they seem to share the view also prevalent in France.

The above must, however, be qualified by admitting that the German legislator has recently lost his appetite in further expansion of state liability. An ambitious reform of the

[91] A feature noted by many German writers. Thus, see F Ossenbühl, above note 79, p 3—'Staatshaftungsrecht ist . . . case law'—and C Stein, P Itzel and K Schwall, *Praxishandbuch des Amts- und Staatshaftungsrechts* (2005), p 3 ('richterrechtlich geprägt').

[92] [1995] 2 AC 633.

[93] See KrG Potsdam VersR 1993, 1501 *ff* and KG Berlin VersR 1993, 1371 *ff*.

[94] See OLG Brandenburg VersR 2001, 1259 *ff*, OLG Dresden VersR 2001, 1260 *ff* and OLG Brandenburg VersR 2002, 504 *ff*.

[95] *Haushaltsprärogative des Parlaments*; see BGHZ 100, 136 (at pp 145 *ff*), BGHZ 102, 350 (at pp 358 *ff*) and BGH VersR 1988, 1046 *ff*.

law, triggered by academic debates in 1968[96] and launched more than a decade later,[97] was aimed at a simplification of the rules and, more importantly, at providing a higher level of protection for the citizen. The fate of this reform project is interesting for the purposes of our account, and worth elaborating in more detail.

The State Liability Act of 1981[98] was declared unconstitutional due to a lack of federal legislative competence.[99] When this competence was eventually introduced—through an amendment of the Basic Law in the context of a limited revision of the Constitution following German reunification[100]—the resulting opportunities were not pursued with much enthusiasm. Interestingly, German reunification also saw the survival of a stricter form of state liability in some parts of the former German Democratic Republic, where the State Liability Act of 1969[101] continues to be in force—albeit with some modifications—as regional legislation.[102] Thus, though the language of the Unification Treaty expresses strong political support in favour of a more coherent and protective solution for the country as a whole,[103] in practice this did not translate into any substantive changes of the law.

There are indications that financial concerns, especially regarding the introduction of a direct and strict liability for wrongs committed by public authorities, lie at the heart of this legislative restraint. A comprehensive analysis of the financial implications of such an approach for public budgets on all three administrative tiers of the system was initiated by the Federal Ministry of Justice and completed in 1999,[104] but successive governments have thus far refrained from taking the project forward. In a written response to questions raised in Parliament by members of the Liberal Party in October 2004, the former Government of Chancellor Schröder again acknowledged that a more coherent and *generous* system of state liability (based on a primary obligation of public authorities to compensate damage) remained a desirable political aim.[105] The additional estimated annual costs of over £340 million, however, seem to have moved this item to the lower end of the political agenda, where it is highly likely to stay for the foreseeable future.

This brief exposition of some German developments indicates that financial constraints have prevented the *legislator* from introducing stricter forms of liability for wrongs committed by public officials in the exercise of their duties. These pressures, however, have not, as a rule, prevented the *courts* from continuing to develop the law incrementally and increasing, in many cases, the potential liability of the state. On the other hand, judges have made

[96] See the deliberations of the 47th Deutscher Juristentag, vol II (1968), L 145.

[97] For more information on the reform discussions of the 1970s see E Klein/A Krekel in Soergel, *Kommentar zum Bürgerlichen Gesetzbuch* (13th edn 2005), Band 12, Anh § 839 at nos 20–22.

[98] *Staatshaftungsgesetz* of 26 June 1981, BGBl I, 553 *ff.*

[99] BVerfGE 61, 149 *ff.* For a readable (German) account of this decision see T Linke, 'BVerfGE 61, 149—Staatshaftungsgesetz. Das Ende einer Reform: Bundesstaatlichkeit gegen Rechtsstaatlichkeit?,' in J Menzel (ed), *Verfassungsrechtsprechung* (2000), pp 332 *ff.*

[100] Article 74(1) no 25 BL; Gesetz zur Änderung des Grundgesetzes of 27 October 1994, BGBl I, p 3146. For an account of the reform discussions leading up to this amendment see E Klein and M Breuer in Soergel, *Kommentar zum Bürgerlichen Gesetzbuch* (13th edn 2005), Band 12, Anh § 839 at nos 26–32.

[101] Gesetz über die Regelung der Staatshaftung in der Deutschen Demokratischen Republik of 12 May 1969, GBl I, 34 *ff.*

[102] See Art 9(1), (2) in conjunction with Schedule II, Chapter III, Part B: Bürgerliches Recht, Subsection III, no 1 of the German Unification Treaty (*Einigungsvertrag*) of 31 August 1990, BGBl II, 889 *ff.*

[103] See Unterrichtung der Bundesregierung zum Einigungsvertrag, BT-Dr 11/7817, p 63.

[104] Infratest Burke Rechtsforschung, *Zur Reform des Staatshaftungsrechts. Rechtstatsächliche Untersuchungen zum Geschäftsanfall in Staatshaftungssachen bei Bund, Ländern und Kommunen* (Munich 1999).

[105] Antwort der Bundesregierung auf die Kleine Anfrage der Abgeordneten Rainer Funke, Daniel Bahr (Münster), Rainer Brüderle, weiterer Abgeordneter und der Fraktion der FDP—Drucksache 15/3859—of 20 October 2004, BT-Dr 15/3952.

it quite clear that they cannot be expected to provide a financial remedy for each and every wrong, and the political statements referred to above do not convey the image of an overly generous system of governmental liability.

5. RECENT GERMAN CASE LAW

Some recent cases involving social services (monitoring of foster-children), highway authorities (safety of roads), and prisons (living conditions of prisoners) may serve to illustrate the German position, especially because of their factual affinity with analogous English decisions already discussed above.

(a) Social Services

The first decision resembles the *Bedfordshire* facts.

The claimant was born outside legal wedlock and, in 1990, put under the full-time care of a married couple with the consent of his natural mother. The fostering couple had three children of its own and was later given custody of two further foster-children. Three years later, the whole family moved from Bavaria to the neighbouring state of Baden-Württemberg. In accordance with administrative procedures, the local Bavarian social authority informed its counterpart in Baden-Württemberg (the defendant in this case) of the move, and requested that it take over the monitoring of the three foster-children. The defendant, however, refused to comply, arguing that it was uncertain whether the plaintiff would remain with the family on a permanent basis since his natural mother had by then refused to extend her consent to the foster arrangements. In these circumstances, the defendant felt that responsibility for the claimant rested with the Bavarian authorities despite the family's physical move to its own territory. The unfortunate dispute between the two authorities continued for a number of years until, in April 1997, a meeting was arranged between all parties concerned. After this meeting, in which the existing care arrangements were reviewed and confirmed, the defendant agreed to take on the case. A social worker from Bavaria conducted a final monitoring visit on the very same day, and filed a closing report with the defendant.

Seven months later, the youngest of the three foster-children died of malnutrition, and both the plaintiff and the other remaining foster-child were found severely undernourished. The foster-parents were subsequently sentenced to life imprisonment for murder. The criminal investigation into the events thereby established that they had treated their own children well, but had severely neglected all three foster-children.

When confronted with the claim for compensation, the courts on all levels[106] held that the responsible social workers had violated statutory duties of the defendant/child which prescribed that the social authority should have assumed responsibility for monitoring the foster-family on arrival at their new home.[107] Regular visits both on occasion of the move and, later, on a regular basis would have been necessary in order to establish a relationship of trust between the monitoring social workers and the claimant, and to assess the financial

[106] OLG Stuttgart, NJW 2003, 3419 *ff*; BGH NJW 2005, 68 *ff*.

[107] § 86 of the Federal Social Security Code (Sozialgesetzbuch Teil VIII).

needs of the child. An interview with the claimant would thereby have revealed the increasingly inadequate care given to the child as early as September 1994 (a year after the move). These statutory duties were not dependent on any formal agreement between the two social agencies and were left unaffected by the visit of the Bavarian colleague conducted in April 1997. The claimant was awarded £17,000 as compensation for pain and suffering.

It is interesting to see how anxious the *Bundesgerichtshof* was in striking a careful balance in this case between excessive monitoring of families with foster-children (which would be detrimental to the development of a normal family life) and adequate safeguards concerning the well-being of minors, especially if substantial changes in a family's living circumstances or routine became apparent. The BGH thus emphasised the importance of a flexible degree of supervision which should be more intensive at the outset and gradually recede into the background as the relationship between foster-parents and a child placed into their care develops. This translates into a correspondingly higher standard of care at the beginning (with a higher chance of claims to succeed against social authorities if referring to events which have taken place during this phase), and a decreasing standard of care towards the end (with the chances of victims declining in parallel). The decision thus displays quite a nuanced approach when it comes to balancing the public interest in safeguarding the well-being of foster-children with the constitutionally protected interest of foster-parents to develop and sustain, as far as possible, a normal family life. The duty of care owed to the claimant was thereby never questioned, though the Court *did* spend considerable time in establishing whether it had actually been breached by the defendant authority.

The contrast between the German decision and both *Bedfordshire* and *East Berkshire* is quite striking. As explained above, English judges have over the past years sought refuge behind the argument that it is not 'fair, just and reasonable' to find a Common law duty of care for breach of many statutory obligations, and have done so by invoking a variety of policy considerations and constitutional justifications. Lord Bingham when reviewing in *East Berkshire* the whole range of reasons which initially led to the rejection of the children's claims in *Bedfordshire* thus identified six such considerations. They were:[108]

First, that accepting a duty of care would cut across the whole statutory and interdisciplinary system for protecting children at risk, and raise almost impossible problems of ascertaining and allocating responsibility between the various authorities involved in the process.

Second, that the task of a local authority and its servants in dealing with children at risk is extraordinarily delicate and that there was a difficult line to tread between taking action too soon and not taking it soon enough.

Third, that local authorities might adopt a too cautious and defensive approach to their duties.

Fourth, the risk of serious conflicts between social workers and parents, which could put at risk the joint effort often required between the parties in these cases.

Fifth, the availability of alternative remedies.

And finally, sixth, the general principle 'that the law should develop novel categories of negligence incrementally and by analogy with established categories, rather than by a massive extension of a prima facie duty of care restrained only by indefinable "considerations

[108] [2005] 2 WLR 993, at §§ 24 *ff.* The force of some of these factors has, since *Bedfordshire* was decided, been seriously challenged by the courts.

which ought to negative, or to reduce or limit the scope of the duty or the class of person to whom it is owed"'.[109]

Some of these policy considerations also feature in the German case, but are approached differently. The case thus focuses precisely on the question which of the authorities involved *was* responsible, and addresses the difficult task social workers face when intervening in family affairs by developing a sliding scale of monitoring duties—more intensive at the beginning and less intrusive as the family starts to function normally.[110]

This approach involves a complex set of interests which require balancing: those of the foster-child, which needs the protection of the state; those of the parents, who will—in the great majority of cases—wish to develop a 'normal' family life; and those of society, which must prevent child abuse. Public authorities thereby owe a duty of care not only to the children, but also to parents, and must exercise their powers only to the extent that is absolutely necessary in the specific circumstances. This marks another potential difference with English law.

These nuances of the German judgment deserve to be studied in England, especially since its entire approach, here as in other such cases, is casuistic and thus easily usable by Common lawyers.

One last point might deserve special mention. The mother in the German case had no claim because she (along with the father) were the tortfeasors; but English cases have shown that where a foster-child has been abused by another member of the family (for example, another child in the care of the same parents), the mother's right for nervous shock will have difficulty in succeeding. Such a situation could not arise in German law, partly because it does not experience the difficulties our own tort law system has with compensation of nervous shock but also because the position of the parents is identical (in constitutional and legislative terms) with that of the abused child.[111]

(b) Highway Authorities

Another line of recent cases comes close to the facts considered by the House of Lords in *Stovin v Wise*. As discussed above, Lord Hoffmann thus argued in *Stovin*[112] that 'the creation of a duty of care upon a highway authority would inevitably expose the authority's budgetary decisions to judicial inquiry', which would, in turn, 'distort the priorities of local authorities'.[113]

By contrast, *German* highway authorities were recently told by a number of higher courts across the country to check the safety of trees alongside public roads twice a year (instead of only once) in order to meet the duty of care (*Verkehrssicherungspflicht*) owed to drivers.[114] The existence of such a duty was, once again, not questioned in principle; the courts, however, made a special effort to set out guidelines that would help define what would constitute a breach.

[109] Brennan J in *Sutherland Shire Council v Heyman* (1985) 157 CLR 424, 481.

[110] For further details on the approach of German courts in other cases see BS Markesinis, J-B Auby, D Coester-Waltjen and SF Deakin, above note 61.

[111] For details on the constitutional protection of parent's rights see, eg, Dagmar Coester-Waltjen in Ingo von Münch and Philip Kunig (eds), *Grundgesetz-Kommentar*, Band 1 (5th edn 2000), Art 6 at nos 57 *ff*.

[112] [1996] 3 WLR 388.

[113] At 419.

[114] OLG Düsseldorf VersR 1992, 467 *ff* and VersR 1997, 463 *ff*; OLG Brandenburg OLGR 2002, 411 *ff*; OLG Hamm VersR 2003, 1452 *ff*. BGH VersR 2004, 877 *ff*; H-J Hötzel, 'Verkehrssicherungspflicht für Bäume—Zehn Jahre Rechtsprechung zum Visual Tree Assessment', VersR 2004, 28 *ff*.

These cases provide a good practical example of the differences between the two systems as they show quite clearly the financial effect of court decisions on public budgets. Consider, for example, the City/State of Hamburg, which has an estimated 245,000 trees situated along its public roads and highways. At an annual cost of over £27,000 per 10,000 maintenance checks,[115] the requirement of a second inspection would land the municipality with an additional bill of roughly £650,000.

On the other hand, the authority might decide simply *not* to comply with this higher standard of 'double inspection' and choose, instead, to accept the risk of having to pay out damages to injured victims. Economically, this is a viable alternative policy since the risk of liability is, in most cases, fairly low (and the local authority has the means to estimate this). A recent decision of the BGH on this point, dealing with a car damaged by a falling tree branch, thus obliged the 'negligent' local authority to pay £700 as damages.[116]

This option not to comply with the requirement of a second inspection is, furthermore, a tempting one since liability in such cases does not follow automatically but will depend upon it being shown that the local authority was actually at fault. Thus take, for instance, a car accident caused by a dangerous pot hole. What will German courts ask if there were an accident and they needed to establish whether the highway authority in question was in breach of its duties, which, as stated, do exist as a matter of law? Judges will determine what could reasonably have been required to avert the danger in the circumstances. Repairing the road is obviously one answer; but it will probably also be the most costly one as far as the local authority is concerned. Alternatively, it might be held that the municipality could have set up warning signs or introduced speed controls, which are both cheaper options than that of repairing the pothole. Closing the road altogether might be another, though it would be rejected if it were thought as an excessively radical solution.

Pursuing such casuistry serves no purpose other than to show that, ultimately, these are issues of proportionality. Depending on what was required in the light of the danger, the authority will have either failed or succeeded in meeting the necessary standard of care. The recognition of duty in law thus does not necessarily mean that liability ensues in most cases. Nor, as the case law shows, is the level of damages crippling. This means that in practice the prescribed extra inspection may not take place, local authorities opting instead for carrying the cost of those cases in which they are actually found to be liable. The system works in practice because it is not as prohibitively expensive as it might appear at first sight. Nor does it mean that all these hypotheticals have to be litigated since the existing and rich statistical information means that there is a basis for out of court and, in practice, rapid settlements. The prediction by Professor Craig and Dr Fairgrieve that something like this would also happen in England if there was a shift from duty to breach seems to be empirically confirmed by German practice.

(c) Prisons

A third example shows, however, that German courts will not always grant monetary compensation as a remedy—even when it comes to the most sacred of rights under the German constitution, namely human dignity.

[115] See H Baumgarten, 'Baumkontrolle in Städten und Gemeinden', in D Dujesiefken and P Kockerbeck (eds), *Jahrbuch der Baumpflege* (2004), p 171.

[116] BGH III ZR 225/03 of 4 March 2004.

The living conditions in German prisons have received some public attention over the past years in the wake of two decisions of the Federal Constitutional Court[117] and, subsequently, several judgments of lower courts on the matter.[118] The *Bundesgerichtshof* recently approached the problem by emphasising that public authorities cannot be allowed to invoke, per se, limited resources in their attempt to avoid liability when human rights are at stake. It then went on to show that casuistry and proportionality influence the outcome; and these in turn also affect the number of claims that are entertained by victims. The facts of the case were as follows.

The claimant, serving a sentence in a Bavarian prison, was temporarily moved to a different facility. In transit, he was held for two days together with four fellow prisoners in a cell measuring $16m^2$. Furnished with a double bunk, three single beds, five chairs, two tables, and two cupboards, this cell also featured a washbasin and toilet, both cordoned off only by a simple screen. Prisoners were permitted to leave the cell for one hour per day. The *Landgericht* Hannover, on application of the claimant, found these prison conditions to be a violation of human dignity as protected by Article 1(1) BL. In a separate action, the claimant subsequently demanded compensation from the State of Lower Saxony (the defendant in this case) and was awarded £140.[119] On appeal, the *Oberlandesgericht* Celle confirmed the findings but nevertheless rejected the claim in full[120]—a decision which was subsequently upheld by the *Bundesgerichtshof.*[121]

A duty of care (*Amtspflicht*) to provide prisoners with adequate living conditions no doubt exists under German law. It is worth mentioning that the BGH was at pains to point out that even temporary bottlenecks caused by unusually high numbers of incoming prisoners in a particular facility do not relieve the public authorities from their statutory obligations, and have no effect on the illegality of prison conditions as established in this case. Prison authorities are obliged to anticipate such difficulties and to organise their facilities appropriately; any failure to do so (so-called *Organisationsverschulden*) will put the state at fault.

At the same time, however, the Court curbed the economic consequences of this ruling by limiting compensation in money to the more serious kind of instances. Compensation was thus not required here since the plaintiff was held in the cell for only a fairly short period of time. This very limited infringement did not, on balance, call for a payment to either compensate him for any non-pecuniary loss or to provide satisfaction for the violation of his rights. Alternative remedies open to prisoners (and successfully invoked in this case) can, furthermore, provide protection and—by way of a formal legal ruling against the state—a sufficient degree of satisfaction. The BGH indicated, however, that financial compensation could be an appropriate response in different circumstances. This would depend on the duration of the confinement, any lasting physical or psychological consequences of the treatment, the gender, age, and physical condition of the victim, and the existence of any malicious intent on the side of prison personnel.

Once again, this shows how German courts approach these cases. This does not mean denying in an outright manner the existence of a duty of care, but searching for the appro-

[117] BVerfG, NJW 2002, 2699 *ff* and NJW 2002, 2700 *ff.*

[118] See, eg, OLG Celle, NJW 2003, 2463 *ff*; OLG Frankfurt a.M., NJW 2003, 2844 *ff*; LG Karlsruhe, StV 2004, 550 *ff*; OLG Naumburg, NJW 2005, 514 *ff.*

[119] LG Hannover, StV 2003, 568 *ff.*

[120] OLG Celle, NJW-RR 2004, 380 *ff.*

[121] BGH NJW 2005, 58 *ff.*

priate balance between the interests of the state and those of the individual affected by the actions of public authorities. The answer is to be found in the area of breach, fault, or on the level of damages. In Germany, the various claimants in *East Berkshire* might thus have very well received different answers from one and the same court, depending on the particular circumstances of their respective case. The fact that a claim involving £140—the price of a dinner for two in any better London restaurant—could reach the highest German civil court in the first place is thereby both the result of substantially lower litigation costs *and* a fundamentally different philosophy when it comes to the balance between the interests of the individual and those of society at large. This, of course, still leaves unanswered the question whether this way of resolving disputes necessarily involves litigation, with all the ensuing consequences of cost, delay and so on. We shall return to this issue in greater detail below.

6. THE ECONOMICAL CONSEQUENCES OF 'STATE LIABILITY' (*STAATSHAFTUNG*) IN GERMANY

How, then, has the German approach, outlined above, fared in economical terms? We will try to provide some details, especially with regard to the overall amount of compensation paid out to the victims of wrongful state activities by German public authorities on all three levels of government and the number of cases which reach the courts each year. The figures we present include claims against a) all federal authorities, b) state and municipal authorities in what used to be West Germany (partly on the basis of representative samples), and c) the city-state of Berlin. The data thus covers roughly 80 per cent of the German population after reunification. It stems from two comprehensive surveys conducted on behalf of the German Federal Ministry of Justice from 1974 to 1977[122] and, more recently, 1993 to 1995.[123] On both occasions, the Ministry aimed to establish the financial burdens resulting from the liability of public authorities on all three levels of German government in order to evaluate the feasibility of reforms in this area of the law. It is thereby interesting that the avowed aim of both initiatives was to *increase* not *limit* the level of protection for citizens suffering damage through the activities of public authorities. For the purpose was to replace, inter alia, the current German system of indirect liability for the breach of a statutory duty (channelled away from the *personally* liable official to the public body in question) with a direct, and in most cases fairly strict, statutory responsibility of the Federation, the states, or the municipalities. Indeed, a federal statute to that effect was enacted in 1981[124] but, subsequently, declared void by the Federal Constitutional Court due to a lack of federal legislative competence.[125] Two further initiatives launched by Bavaria (in 1989) and Hamburg (in 1990)[126] fell victim to political disputes; and other legislative reforms have failed to materialise despite a subsequent amendment of the Basic Law, which eventually created a federal competence for state liability in 1994.[127] Currently, the issue is not on the

[122] Bundesministerium der Justiz (ed), *Zur Reform des Staatshaftungsrechts* (1977).
[123] Infratest Burke Rechtsforschung, above note 104.
[124] Above note 122.
[125] BVerfGE 61, 149 *ff*.
[126] BR-Drucksache 644/89 and BR-Drucksache 632/90. Both initiatives were triggered by the wish to establish common ground with the more protective regime of the former German Democratic Republic.
[127] BGBl I, 3146.

legislative agenda—possibly due to the change in political priorities following the snap elections in September 2005 and, more importantly, the difficult economic situation faced by the country over the past decade. That is *not* to say, however, that developments have come to a standstill. On the contrary, as will become obvious in the course of this analysis, governmental liability in Germany is, much more than other parts of the law, strongly influenced by court decisions, and a number of important judgments concerning the interpretation and application of § 839 BGB (the relevant provision in our context) have over the past two decades introduced substantial changes in *favour* of victims suffering from wrongs committed by public officials.[128]

A separate study conducted for the area of the former German Democratic Republic (East Germany) is not included in our analysis because of the different legal approach to governmental liability that applies there. In legal and statistical terms the re-unification process is not yet complete and thus precludes our extending the figures to the entire country.

A final comment on the availability (or rather lack) of similar statistics in the United Kingdom must be made before we focus on Germany. If financial arguments concerning the burdens of governmental liability *are* important for English tort law, it is surprising that the *empirical basis* on which wide-ranging decisions concerning the liability of public bodies are made is, on the whole, so thin. This was the case in 1893, it seems, when the Public Authorities Protection Act was passed by Parliament without any evidence put before the House that local authorities were subject to a particularly high risk of being sued at the time, or that the financial consequences of single cases were overly burdensome.[129] More worrying, however, is the fact that a century later experts on the subject *still* identify a dearth of empirical data concerning the amount of cases brought against public authorities, the overall financial impact of governmental liability on public budgets, and the effects which higher or lower standards of liability would have on the delivery of public services.[130] The Public Law Team of the Law Commission thus stated as recently as October 2004 that 'research into the effects of extending or restricting liability would be a key element in the development of an acceptable framework of public law liability'.[131]

In the light of this assessment it is surprising (and very worrying) that some academic colleagues still defend the invocation by leading judges of economic intuition in order to limit liability: '[T]he problem,' writes Professor Jane Stapleton,[132] is easily 'cured' and judicial reasoning 'put . . . on a sound basis' by 'expressing . . . concern in terms of *risk* that these socio-economic consequences *might* flow from a finding of liability.' A judge, according to this view, 'might well assess that risk (we stress: *based on little more than intuition!*) as one that weighs heavily against the imposition of liability' if he 'thinks there is

[128] The courts have thus developed a more objective approach in determining whether the public official was at fault, and have in traffic accident cases restricted the application of § 839 (1) sentence 2 BGB, which allows the state to escape liability if the victim is able to find compensation elsewhere.

[129] See Tony Weir, 'Governmental Liability,' [1989] Public Law 40 at 48.

[130] Cherie Booth and David Squires, *The Negligence Liability of Public Authorities* (2006), p 227 note a 'general lack of evidence available on the consequences [of imposing a duty of care on public authorities]'. According to Carol Harlow, *State Liability—Tort Law and Beyond* (2004), studies of this kind are 'uncommon, inconclusive and sometimes unreliable, and such information as we do possess is fragmentary'. See also BS Markesinis/J-B Auby/D Coester-Waltjen/S Deakin, above note 61, p 117: 'expensive and rarely done'.

[131] Public Law Team/Law Commission, *Monetary Remedies in Public Law. A Discussion Paper* (11 October 2004), at no 7.12.

[132] Jane Stapleton, 'Benefits of Comparative Tort Reasoning: Lost in Translation', (2007) *Journal of Tort Law*, vol 1, Issue 3, at p 11 of the online version at www.bepress.com/jtl/vol1/iss3/art6.

even a *mere chance* that doctors or public authorities might indulge in wasteful defensive measures'. We would be very reluctant to explain these academic hermeneutics to the deserving victims of wrongs committed by public authorities—especially if there is *evidence* elsewhere that the 'risk' of wasteful (rather than appropriate!) defensive measures is in fact very low.

That empirical studies on the matter are so hard to come by is, beside the cost of such exercises, due to a number of interrelated factors which we will not explore further here.[133] The task, however, cannot be avoided. Without a more refined understanding of how tort law affects public budgets, legislators will be reluctant to even contemplate the introduction of monetary remedies in judicial review proceedings (especially in financially difficult times)—as will the courts be when thinking about the merits or drawbacks of moving from duty of care to breach as the crucial 'gatekeeper' in the assessment of tortious claims against public authorities. We need to leave the quicksand of speculation and reach the firmer grounds of an informed impact assessment in this area of the law, even if this involves using only a single system as a starting point.

(a) How Successful are Plaintiffs and how much Compensation is Paid by Public Bodies?

A first important point to note is the low success rate of individuals claiming to have suffered damage through administrative activities in Germany. This follows from the ratio between demands raised against public authorities and the amount of compensation eventually paid at the end of disputes (whether in or out of court). On average, only 28.2 per cent of all demands were successful. Thus, despite the fact that the total amount of damages demanded from public authorities (at the outset of the complaint) in 1993, 1994 and 1995 was roughly of the order of £380 million per annum (at prices of that period), the total cost of state liability between 1993 and 1995 only averaged at £107 million per annum in West Germany and Berlin. All figures presented here are thereby based on the official exchange rate between the German and British currencies on the first trading day in each of these years.[134]

[133] In some areas, situations potentially attracting the liability of public authorities (even under a 'generous' approach) might never materialise; alternatively, they can arise quite unexpectedly. This occurred after the ECJ developed Member State liability for breach of Community law. Potential tortfeasors in this area are as varied as the functions performed by the modern state; and detailed information concerning the costs of wrongful administrative activities is not often systematically recorded despite (or perhaps because of) the excessive amounts of paperwork compiled by public authorities. Financial risks can also increase as when the public sector takes on additional regulatory responsibilities or, conversely, decrease as a consequence of the new trend to privatise many public functions. New administrative techniques, such as e-government and the increasing reliance on modern information technology, can create additional potential for mistakes, particularly in the first years following their introduction, and it is often difficult to foresee their effect on the volume of delictual claims brought against public authorities each year. Liability can arise on different levels of an administrative system, depending on where certain functions are performed or public services delivered. Finally, governmental liability, situated on the public–private law divide, brings together both notions of (private) tortious liability and (public) administrative law, making it often difficult to predict the likely outcome of litigation. For a detailed description of the practical difficulties see Infratest Burke Rechtsforschung, above note 104, *Bericht*, pp 2–18.

[134] Deutsche Mark (DM) 2.459 to £1 on 1 January 1993; DM 2.571 to £1 on 1 January 1994; and DM 2.431 to £1 on 1 January 1995. The average exchange rate in these years was thus DM 2.487 to £1.

Table 8.1: Demands raised, demands rejected, and payments made by public authorities in state liability cases arising on all levels of government (excluding the former GDR) between 1993 and 1995

Year	Demands raised (£)	Demands rejected (£)	Compensation paid (£)
1993	279,105,733	174,401,789	104,703,944
1994	405,069,233	315,856,087	89,213,146
1995	453,182,229	325,976,141	127,206,088
Ø	379,119,064	272,078,005	107,041,059

(b) The Overall Amount of Compensation Paid out by German Public Authorities Each Year

£107 million is a considerable annual burden for public budgets in any country, even if the earlier of the two German studies discussed here estimated the overall share of state liability (including all causes of action and not only breaches of official duties) at a modest 0.015 per cent of the total public budget at the time.[135] A number of substantial downward adjustments are, however, necessary if our aim is to compare the effect of different approaches to governmental liability on both sides of the Channel. These include, first, the deduction of compensation paid under the heading 'state liability' in Germany which would *equally* attract liability under English law, albeit in a different guise or under a different heading.

Thus, exact German figures can be given for four types of claims: damage caused by foreign NATO troops, traffic accidents, medical liability, and liability under Community law. Compensation paid in these areas will have to be factored *out* of our overall figure of £107 million, though the remaining amount will still not represent an exact counterpart of what English law would regard as typical liability for breach, for it will still include a number of other claims which equally attract liability in the United Kingdom but would be examined there under different headings. The remaining annual burden will then have to be reduced in proportion to the differences that exist between both countries in terms of population size.

(i) Compensation on the Basis of the NATO Statute

Compensation payments by the Federation in Germany include demands resulting from damage caused by NATO troops in normal traffic accidents and military operations (for example, tanks exercising in the countryside and destroying forests or crops). These payments are regulated on the basis of the NATO Statute, which requires the host country to come up for 25 per cent of the damage and is equally applicable in the United Kingdom. In Germany, the fairly high number of NATO personnel resulted in an annual burden of roughly £4.6 million between 1993 and 1995.[136] So this amount will have be taken away from our annual base of, roughly, £107 million.

*(ii) Public Traffic (*Verkehrsteilnahme*)*

A far larger group of cases found at all levels of government each year involves harm caused by officials and employees while driving in the exercise of regular official duties (rather than emergency services, for which special rules apply). This type of activity, likewise, attracts lia-

[135] Bundesministerium der Justiz, *Zur Reform des Staatshaftungsrechts* (1977), pp 5, 71.

[136] This amounts to roughly 27 per cent of the annual overall amount of compensation paid on the federal level. Roughly 50 per cent of all claims made against the Federation in these years fell into this category. The number of cases is, however, declining due to the gradual decline of foreign troops in Germany.

bility (in negligence) in the United Kingdom but it would not be brought under the heading of breach of statutory duty. There is, however, a further difference between Germany and England. The stricter rules for damage caused by motorists (whether public or private) in most Continental systems tend to put German public authorities at a disadvantage when compared to their English counterparts. Roughly 80 per cent of all demands resulting from traffic accidents involving public officials are thus met in or out of court by public authorities of some kind. These claims represent a substantial share of the overall amount paid to the victims of wrongful state activity each year. Between 1993 and 1995, 22 per cent of all claims against the Federation, 35 per cent of all claims against state authorities, and 34 per cent of all claims against municipalities thus fell into this category. The total annual costs of these payments averaged at £43.9 million.

(iii) Medical Liability

A third important area of civil liability arises in the context of medical accidents. Compensation paid for personal injury caused by the National Health Service would not normally be regarded as a case of governmental liability in the United Kingdom although these costs are, in fact, largely covered by the public purse. In Germany, by contrast, cases arising from medical malpractice in hospitals and clinics run by the states or municipalities fall into the category of 'state liability' and are thus included in our initial overall figure of £107 million. In more recent years, privatisation of the medical sector (increasingly popular in Germany for general economical reasons) has reduced substantially the percentage of payments made under this heading. This also means that these same cases will now be more often dealt with under the general rules of tort law (and the actions directed against private legal entities) rather than § 839 BGB and Article 34 BL. This was not the case, however, in the mid-1990s when approximately £8.7 million was paid by public authorities each year to patients who had suffered harm through medical treatment in publicly run hospitals and clinics. This figure thus did not include (nor does it include today) claims made against private providers of medical services which, as stated, are in the ascendancy.

(iv) Compensation on the Basis of Community Law

Finally, from our above-mentioned annual total we have to deduct compensation payments made by German public authorities due to the infringement of EU obligations, again equally actionable in the United Kingdom under the common rules of Community law. Payments made under the heading 'legislative wrongs' on the federal level thereby amounted to approximately £3.4 million per year.

Table 8.2: Deductions from the overall amount paid by German public authorities (1993–1995)

Average overall annual compensation paid out (£)	107,000,000
. . . of which compensation paid on the basis of NATO obligations (£)	4,600,000
. . . of which compensation paid for traffic accidents (£)	43,900,000
. . . of which compensation paid for medical malpractice (£)	8,700,000
. . . of which compensation paid for infringements of Community law (£)	3,400,000
	46,400,000

(v) Other Factors

While our initial overall annual figure of £107 million must thus be reduced to roughly £46.5 million if we attempt to assess the possible financial impact of the German approach to governmental liability in the United Kingdom, a number of additional factors need to be taken into account, and these will lead to a further reduction of the total bill. In this context, a crucial point is the definition of recoverable damage.

Pure economic loss can be recovered under § 839 BGB and accounts for a fair share of the compensation paid by German public authorities, particularly in cases involving building permits and planning law, commercial interests affected by regulation, or negligent misstatements made by regulatory authorities. These would include situations such as *Anns* and other cases dealing with negligent certifications by public officials. English common law, by contrast, is much more restrictive in this respect, and would not normally allow recovery.

More importantly, however, our remaining overall figure represents payments for damage caused by German public authorities in a range of very different situations. The German concept of *Staatshaftung* is, as indicated above, extremely wide and includes not only the breach of statutory duties exercised by or on behalf of any public authority (*Amtspflichtverletzung*) but also a number of additional causes of action such as—legal—expropriation (*Enteignung*) and—again legal—exceptional individual sacrifices for the common good (*Aufopferung*). The latter involves, for example, the compensation of victims of health and safety measures such as the culling of livestock or compulsory vaccinations to prevent the spreading of highly contagious diseases such as bird flu. Private law actions against public authorities based on the general rules of tort law were also included in the 1993/1995 study. These points, which we cannot individualise and quantify here, cannot, however, be overlooked in the overall assessment. In practice, therefore, if one wishes to attempt to compare like with like, one would have to make a further *downwards* adjustment of the German annual costs of governmental liability in the UK context.

Other factors, addressed to some extent in the further course of this analysis, are the different levels of damages and legal costs in both countries. On balance, these seem to be higher in the United Kingdom, which could in turn require an *upwards* adjustment of our assessment.[137] Inflation and a trend towards an increasing amount of litigation in general (discernible in both countries over the past decade) will also have to be taken into account when analysing these figures today. Again, these are elements which cannot be introduced in our discussion with any degree of reliability, though we mention them so as to make our reader fully conscious of the subtle differences between the two legal systems and, incidentally, remain true to our call that comparative methodology should aim to compare not just rules but also how they are understood and operate within their own environment.

Apart from all of these factors, our analysis requires one final *downward* adjustment of roughly 13 per cent due to the different size of the German and UK populations.[138] The

[137] On the other hand, higher costs are also a disincentive to litigation; and would be a truly serious one if litigants and their advisors believed that the courts would use strictly fault and causation as the devices that would keep liability under control. The rich experience in France, studied by a common lawyer who has made this one of his specialised subjects, shows how well this has worked. Thus, see M Andenas and D Fairgrieve, 'Misfeasance in Public Office, Governmental Liability, and European Influences', 51 *ICLQ* 2002, 757 *ff.*

[138] The German figures determined for this period represent demands arising from a population of roughly 69 million citizens (disregarding the fact that payments made by federal authorities, included in this analysis, represent the *whole* German population—ie over 80 million inhabitants). The United Kingdom in 2002 had a population of roughly 60 million.

overall amount of compensation paid in governmental liability cases under the seemingly 'more generous' German rules is thus not likely to have exceeded £40 million per annum between 1993 and 1995 once the figures are adjusted to the English scenario. It was probably less.

(c) A Closer Look at the Claims Made against Public Authorities and Subsequent Litigation

An analysis of the burden which the German approach to governmental liability places on public bodies and the court system must take into account the overall number of claims initially made against public authorities, the percentage of these claims which actually reach the courts, the length of legal proceedings in this area of the law, and the reasons why claimants fail both in and outside a court of law. Finally, we will also try to shed some light on the average level of damages in Germany.

(i) The Number of Claims, the Average Single Demand, and the Average Single Payment

The starting point of our analysis is threefold. First, we will look at the total number of demands initially raised against German public authorities on all levels of government. The second step will focus on the average single demand for compensation. Finally, we must look at the average single amount eventually paid out on the basis of these demands.

Table 8.3 below shows that the total number of demands filed with public authorities on all levels of government between 1993 and 1995 averaged at about 113,000 per year. The average single demand amounted to £3,390. Single payments eventually made by public authorities were, however, substantially lower, the average claimant only receiving £951. A substantial number of claimants—between 18 per cent on the federal level and 37 per cent on the municipal level—did not receive any payment at all (see Table 8.7 below). Large claims were obviously more often rejected or reduced than smaller ones.

Table 8.3: Demands filed with German public authorities (1993–1995)

Year	Total number of claims	Average demand (£)	Average payment (£)
1993	119,167	2,342	878
1994	110,927	3,651	804
1995	108,449	4,178	1,172
Ø	112,847	3,390	951

The pattern of these demands is somewhat different at the three levels of government. Germany is a federal system in which the bulk of public administration is performed on the lowest tier. The Federation and the states thus attract a small percentage of the complaints simply because federal and state authorities which provide services (or otherwise interact directly with the citizen) exist only to a limited degree. As shown in Tables 8.4–8.6, by far the largest number of claims was brought against municipalities, which also have to bear the largest financial burden due to payments actually made to successful victims. Interestingly, substantial differences in the amounts *demanded* (ranging, on average, from roughly £2,000 on the federal level to more than £6,000 on the state level) did not translate into large differences when it came to *payments* (ranging, on average, from £850 on the federal level to £1,000 on the state level).

Not reflected in these statistics are the large differences which exist between single demands. While cases of only a few hundred pounds resulting from traffic accidents make up a considerable percentage of the total annual burden of governmental liability in Germany, single demands of more than £40,000 are not unusual. This includes compensation for pain and suffering under § 823 BGB. Some larger cases at the federal level involved even higher demands, sometimes in the order of £1 million, with the highest single amount of £15.5 million recorded in 1994. Estimates indicate that below 2 per cent of all cases involve large amounts (so-called *Großschadensereignisse*), but that these can add up to a considerable share of the overall amount of compensation paid out to victims.[139]

Table 8.4: Demands filed with federal authorities (1993–1995)

Year	Total number of claims	Average demand (£)	Average payment (£)
1993	29,046	1,237	638
1994	19,118	2,723	859
1995	15,855	2,078	1,073
Ø	21,339	2,012	856.66

Table 8.5: Demands filed with state authorities (1993–1995)

Year	Total number of claims	Average demand (£)	Average payment (£)
1993	17,564	3,857	893
1994	18,356	5,808	862
1995	19,094	9,465	1,249
Ø	18,338	6,376	1,001

Table 8.6: Demands filed with municipal authorities (1993–1995)

Year	Total number of claims	Average demand (£)	Average payment (£)
1993	72,557	2,417	970
1994	73,453	3,354	775
1995	73,500	3,258	1,174
Ø	73,170	3,009	973

[139] Eg, 25 per cent on the municipal level; see Infratest Burke Rechtsforschung, above note 104, *Bericht*, p. 32.

Table 8.7: Average number of annual demands which did not result in *any* payment (1993–1995)

Level of government	Average number of annual demands which did not result in any payment by public authorities	Percentage of all annual demands
Federation	3,950	18.51
States	5,433	29.62
Municipalities	26,756	36.56

The fairly high number of demands brought against German public authorities each year must again be reduced by those which could equally arise in the United Kingdom. Exact figures exist for the same four categories already discussed above.

Table 8.8: Average number of annual demands arising from NATO operations, traffic accidents, medical liability, and legislative wrongs in the context of Community law in Germany each year (1993–1995)

Area	Federation	States	Municipalities
NATO Statute	12,137	–	–
Traffic accidents	4,727	6,403	24,600
Medical claims	172	833	3,842
Community law	2,053	3	1
Total	19,089	7,239	28,443

Between 1993 and 1995, more than 54,700 demands raised against German public authorities at all three levels of government were thus based on the NATO Statute, traffic accident rules, alleged medical malpractice, and legislative wrongs in the context of Community law each year. Assuming that such cases would equally give rise to liability of public bodies in the United Kingdom, this substantially reduces the difference between both systems when it comes to the administrative workload caused by the victims of wrongs committed by public bodies. The remaining figure of roughly 60,000 demands per year will thereby again require a final downward adjustment by roughly 13 per cent due to the differences in population size, and will include a number of situations in which English public authorities might equally be approached by citizens.

(ii) Cases which Reach the Courts

More important for our analysis are the number of demands which are not resolved outside the courtroom but end with litigation. As shown in Table 8.9, the overall number of claims is fairly low in Germany (below 5,000 lawsuits per year against all levels of the administrative system between 1993 and 1995). This indicates that German public authorities have in practice developed effective strategies to settle disputes out of court, and that only the more desperate plaintiffs or those faced with atypical situations actually proceed with litigation.[140] The availability of statistics for amounts paid in comparable cases and the relatively low levels of compensation also means that an 'offer and compromise' can easily be made, putting to an

[140] The latter point is raised by Infratest Burke Rechtsforschung, above note 104, *Bericht*, p 10 *f*.

early conclusion most demands which could otherwise develop into fully blown disputes. This conclusion thus lends support to the prediction made in England by Professor Paul Craig and Dr Duncan Fairgrieve that the adoption of a liability rule in English law would soon lead to a body of precedent which would allow for settlements of most claims out of court.

The German position, however, does come at a price. This is the fact that most local authorities employ fairly large departments of in-house lawyers and paralegal personnel that processes (amongst countless other legal matters) the demands made against them. We have not even tried to put a price tag on this given the infinite regional variations and the need to compare in a similar manner the position in England before pronouncing conclusively on this point.

Table 8.9: Litigated cases on all levels of the German system involving governmental liability (1993–1995)

Level	Total number of claims per year (Ø)	Litigated cases per year (Ø)	%
Federation	21,339	640	3
States	18,338	1,100	6
Municipalities	73,170	2,933	4

Differences in population size, the deterrent effect of higher litigation costs in the United Kingdom, and, possibly, the greater 'litigiousness' of German citizens, would thereby seem to call for a *downward* adjustment of these figures in the English context. It seems, furthermore, that a substantial proportion of the litigated cases fall into categories which would also reach the courts in this country. The figures for 1974–1977 thus indicate that 50 per cent of all litigated cases involving 'state liability' were traffic accident cases; another 2 per cent involved medical liability. Cases concerned with *Staatshaftung im engeren Sinne* and *Verkehrssicherungspflichten* (areas which would involve, inter alia, the violation of statutory duties of care in the United Kingdom) made up roughly 48 per cent of the caseload, with lawsuits filed against the postal service forming the lion's share (20.5 per cent).[141]

Table 8.10: Annual share of different claims in the overall amount of litigated cases (1974–1977)

Area	Annual share of payments (in %)	Annual share of claims (%)	Annual share of litigated cases (%)
Traffic accidents	73.4	26	50
Staatshaftung i.e.S. (20.5 postal service)	23.5	71.3	30
Verkehrssicherungspflicht	2.7	2.1	18
Medical liability	0.5	0.1	2

It should be borne in mind, however, that the court system and the numbers of full time judges are substantially larger in Germany than in England, and that it deals with a much

[141] Bundesministerium der Justiz, *Zur Reform des Staatshaftungsrechts*, above note 135, pp 46 *ff.*

higher overall number of cases each year. Figures recently published by the Federal Ministry of Justice thus show that German private law courts of first instance (*Amtsgerichte* and *Landgerichte*) had to deal with more than 1.9 million new cases in 2003. Cases on appeal (*Landgerichte, Oberlandesgerichte* and *Bundesgerichtshof*) amounted to over 133,000 cases that year. Administrative courts, responsible for a considerable share of the cases involving *Staatshaftung* (most actions outside § 839 BGB, Article 34 BL are decided here), dealt with nearly 212,000 new cases in 2003. Interestingly, the combined costs of the court system and the prison service nevertheless amount to less than 1 per cent of Germany's annual public expenditure on all levels of the system.[142] In the light of these overall statistics, the annual burden of litigated cases involving governmental liability in Germany is very low indeed.

Table 8.11: Overall workload of German private and administrative courts in 2003

Court level	First instance cases in 2003	Appeals in 2003
Bundesgerichtshof[143]		5,890
Oberlandesgerichte		56,793
Landgerichte	426,829	70,742
Amtsgerichte	1,500,905	
Bundesverwaltungsgericht		2,219
Oberverwaltungsgerichte	1,128	23,727
Verwaltungsgerichte	210,673	
Total	2,139,535	159,371

(iii) Chances of Success in Court and Reasons for Failure

Despite the theoretically favourable approach that German judges have taken towards the claims of victims suffering from wrongs committed by public authorities over the past decades, the chances of a plaintiff actually succeeding in a German courtroom are fairly slim. As indicated above, both empirical studies show that roughly 70 per cent of all demands raised against public authorities are rejected completely while another 20 per cent of the claimants see their initial claims reduced by the courts.[144]

It is not at all easy to pinpoint the reasons for this state of affairs. Supporters of a comprehensive legislative reform of the German system argue that the low success rate is to a large extent caused by the inherently complex structure of the law,[145] and the fairly high number of state liability cases which go on appeal to the *Bundesgerichtshof* each year certainly emphasises this unfortunate and outdated state of affairs. The fact that cases involving the breach of statutory duties (*Amtshaftung*) are, for historical reasons, assigned to the ordinary courts rather than the highly specialised administrative courts may also contribute to the difficulties experienced by plaintiffs in this area of the law. Different answers concerning particular questions of public law are thus sometimes given by administrative

[142] See S Leutheusser-Schnarrenberger, 'Wege zur Justizentlastung', NJW 1995, 2441 at p 2442; Schäfer, DRiZ 1995, 461 at p 462; R Krumsiek, 'Kosten der Justiz', ZRP 1995, 173; S Weth, 'Die Justiz—ein ungeliebtes Kind', NJW 1996, 2467 *ff.*

[143] Including family matters.

[144] Bundesministerium der Justiz, *Zur Reform des Staatshaftungsrechts*, above note 135, pp 161, 197; Infratest Burke Rechtsforschung, above note 104, Tables B 4.1, L 4.1 and K 4.

[145] F Ossenbühl, *Staatshaftungsrecht* (5th edn 1998), p 6; Tremml/Karger, *Der Amtshaftungsprozess* (2nd edn 2004), p 1.

courts (in the context of the initial public law dispute concerning, for example, the legality of a building permit) and ordinary courts (when dealing with the liability 'fallout' of the very same case at a later stage). These inconsistencies have led to increasing criticism and calls to allocate all state liability cases to the administrative courts, particularly because the initial reason for giving ordinary courts a say in these matters—suspicions that administrative courts might be 'too close' to public administrations and thus take a too favourable view of their interests—has long since fallen away.

More specifically, statistics indicate that a large number of plaintiffs fail to establish the *objective* requirements of state liability claims,[146] followed (where necessary) by the failure to prove that the particular official in question—or, alternatively, the whole organisation—was at fault. The figures given for 1974–1977 thereby suggest that *public authorities* tend to reject demands by arguing that they were not at fault (which is often the most straightforward course to pursue), while *courts*, conducting a systematic analysis of the case at hand, focus more on the objective requirements of a claim (duty, breach) and deal with the question of fault only once these have been established. By contrast, alternative forms of 'satisfaction' for the plaintiff (of the kind often invoked by English courts in order to deny a claim for damages) play a far less important role in practice.

Table 8.12: Reasons for failure (1974–1977)[147]

Reason		Failure rate as percentage of the overall amount claimed from public bodies	Failure rate as percentage of litigated cases
Fault	*Staatshaftung i.e.S.*	45.5	10.4
	Verkehrssicherungspflichten	66.1	6.9
Alternative compensation		1	5.6

These trends were to some extent confirmed by the 1993–1995 study. Most claims for breach of statutory duties (*Amtshaftung*) which were rejected *in full* thus failed on the objective level (no statutory duty or—if duty—no breach).

Table 8.13: Reasons for the full rejection of claims based on Amtshaftung (1993–1995)

Reason[148]	Federal level (%)	State level (%)	Municipal level (%)
No statutory duty or breach	66.8	61.5	59.4
Causation	10.6	4.7	4.1
Fault	15.6	19.1	28.4
Contributory negligence	4.6	5.7	10.0
Alternative remedy	1.4	6.9	6.6
Extent of damage unclear	9.6	3.4	1.8

[146] These include, in cases involving the breach of statutory duties, an act or omission attributable to a public body in the context of its official responsibilities, the breach of a statutory duty of care owed to a third party in that particular context, and, finally, a causal link between breach and the harm caused by the victim.

[147] Bundesministerium der Justiz, *Zur Reform des Staatshaftungsrechts*, above note 135, p 46 *ff.*

[148] Some claims were rejected for more than one reason.

The most important factors which led to a *partial* rejection of claims for breach of statutory duties were, by contrast, insufficient proof of the alleged amount of harm and contributory negligence.[149]

Table 8.14: Reasons for a partial rejection of claims based on Amtshaftung (1993–1995)

Reason[150]	Federal level (%)	State level (%)	Municipal level (%)
No statutory duty or breach	2.4	6.6	19.6
Causation	4.8	14.9	11.1
Fault	4.8	9.1	12.4
Contributory negligence	14.9	22.3	40.7
Alternative remedy	0.6	3.3	2.5
Damage lower than claimed	47.0	36.4	23.5
Extent of damage unclear	19.0	4.1	3.7

Interestingly, claimants seeking compensation on the basis of the general rules of tort law (in most cases for an alleged violation of *Verkehrssicherungspflichten*) usually failed to prove fault. On average, 57.9 per cent of the claims against public authorities on all levels of the system which were rejected *in full* failed on that point.[151]

Table 8.15: Reasons for the full rejection of claims based on general tort law (1993–1995)

Reason	Federal level (%)	State level (%)	Municipal level (%)
Fault	61.5	47.4	64.8
Contributory negligence	7.7	5.3	9.6
Causation	11.5	2.6	16.0
Extent of damage unclear	3.8	5.3	0.8
Wrongfulness	7.7	31.6	8.8

Partial rejections in this area were again based predominantly on a failure to prove the alleged extent of damage suffered or contributory negligence.

Table 8.16: Reasons for a partial rejection of claims based on general tort law (1993–1995)

Reason	Federal level (%)	State level (%)	Municipal level (%)
Fault	7.3	–	10.3
Contributory negligence	14.6	23.1	27.6
Causation	2.4	7.7	3.4
Damage lower than claimed	63.4	61.5	31.0
Extent of damage unclear	14.6	7.7	6.9
Wrongfulness	–	–	3.4

[149] Infratest Burke Rechtsforschung, above note 104, *Bericht*, p 68.
[150] Some claims were rejected for more than one reason.
[151] Infratest Burke Rechtsforschung, above note 104, *Bericht*, p 67.

7. SOME TENTATIVE CONCLUSIONS

There is an important reason for undertaking this survey that goes beyond the academic desire to read, understand, and then transmit further acquired knowledge. In this case we were attracted by the importance and inordinate[152] complexity of the subject as well as its capacity to 'profit' from foreign experiences. Moreover, despite repeated attempts of British conservative judges (aided and abetted by timid academics) to eliminate liability completely, the problem is still with us. All this can only go to prove that the restrictive attitude—pursued with such consistency by judges like Lord Hoffmann and, in days gone by, Lord Justice Stuart-Smith—is not working as desired. The law reports have not yet run dry of new material; nor will they.

Why, one may ask, is this happening? There is some, we would suggest sufficient, evidence to suggest that judges at lower instances do not like this approach and thus try to 'dodge' the restrictive pronouncements of their most conservative colleagues.[153] Additionally, societal needs and expectations keep producing the kind of pressures that inevitably lead to more expectations which, if not properly handled, can lead to litigation.[154] These expectations, though they can be manipulated, faked or exaggerated, are also often justified given the inadequacy of the existing administrative remedies, especially in order to redress harm done and not just prevent future harm. Judges, however talented, can only delay the impetus of such pressures from finding their answer in a legal system; but they cannot stifle them completely. Of course, both these reasons may also combine in a way that explains why the dispute over monetary remedies in public law is not dying easily. The Law Commission's Discussion Paper of 11 October 2004 also gave the impression that its draftsmen were desirous of a change in the direction at least of simplification of the law if not greater monetary generosity towards deserving victims. If they stick to their guns, they will be fulfilling some of the hopes expressed by the All Souls Committee of Justice that addressed some of these issues though, undoubtedly, also disappointing some conservative academics.

We predict that the problem and the pressures will persist for the additional reason given by Lord Bingham in his dissent in *East Berkshire*, namely the potential of turning these cases into human rights cases and invoking the help of Strasbourg. Indeed, our tort law is not just

[152] Whether this is 'necessary' or 'unnecessary' and how this is defined we leave to academics more interested in pure theory than we are. But the matter is explored in the elegant piece of Mr Roderick Bagshaw, 'Monetary remedies in public law—misdiagnosis and misdescription', 26 *Legal Studies* (2006) 4 *ff*, esp at 11 *ff*.

[153] We see *Department for Transport, Environment & The Regions v Mott MacDonald Ltd and others* [2006] EWCA Civ 1089 in that light.

[154] It is too easy to dismiss this trend under the pejorative terms of 'litigation explosion' or 'compensation culture'—not only because more administration inevitably means more maladministration and this, in turn, must call for *efficient* remedies (beyond those once provided by public law) but also because social benefits and support of all kinds are decreasing, leaving more and more poor victims of accidents inadequately cared for. In this context it might not be a bad idea to recall that the expansion of American tort law (between the 1950s and 1970s) was prompted by (a) the inadequacy of tort rules to provide, at the end, remedies to many deserving plaintiffs but also (b) the near-complete absence of an efficient social security system. Britain has by no means yet reached that stage of affairs; but current economic thinking foreshadows more cuts. The difficulties this likely development will lead to cannot be underestimated; and it is small comfort to argue that politicians as well as lawyers will have to grapple with them as well. Incidentally, we italicised above the word 'efficient' remedies since we feel that English courts should be given discretionary powers to award monetary compensation and, indeed, are encouraged by the fact that other important figures of the public law scene agree. Thus see, inter alia, Carol Harlow, *State Liability—Tort Law and Beyond* (2004), p 116, and Lord Woolf, *Protection of the Public—A New Challenge* (1990), p 57.

under pressure from Strasbourg but also Luxembourg since the liability of public authorities of all kinds[155] is, nowadays, under the parallel pressures of the European Union and the internal market of disfranchised claimants. This will, undoubtedly, cause more consternation among Conservatives (this time the word should, arguably, be spelt with a capital C!); and it might even tempt a government looking to catch the headlines to 'withdraw' in some kind of way from the Convention (and try to cause difficulties to the functioning of the EU) in an attempt to re-negotiate the reach of all these 'intruding' rules and regulations.

These may be apocalyptic predictions though, one must sadly add, anything is possible when politics contaminate law. In the meantime, however, differing justifications to prevent erosion of the restrictive status quo which favours all kinds of public bodies will continue; and it will be based on the use of meaningless notions such as 'fair, just and reasonable' or 'incrementalism', while the self-consciously fictitious searches for the elusive legislative intent will continue to appear in print, essentially hiding the temperament and outlook of the deciding judge. If we are going to live with this way of deciding cases we may begin by acknowledging the near futility of these conceptual techniques.

We could have done this; we could have even drawn some comfort from the fact that recently even the House of Lords has begun questioning the near-sacred status attributed to these concepts, which some of us have been criticising for some time now.[156] From our perspective, however, it seemed more worthwhile to address the real problem that lies beneath most of these cases, and show how dialogue with foreign systems might be of use. Rather than continue on the path of 'denial' and barren conceptualism, we have tried to focus on the main concern: limited resources. Much new evidence about the possible economic consequences of a 'liability' rule has thus been provided here for the first time in the English speaking world.

At the same time, naked figures cannot provide the final answer; they must be properly analysed and shown to have worked in the context of a real, existing system, not just in the academic laboratory. We have thus tried to help this debate by looking at the German figures and presenting them in the context of that country's legal system while attempting to do two different things: (a) provide empirical information for our practitioners and judges; and (b) continue our efforts to devise a way of presenting foreign law to national courts in order to make its use easier and more profitable. In many respects the second aim is as important as the first, since those who oppose the use of foreign law invariably try to do so by invoking imaginary rather than real obstacles.

Readers unaccustomed to empirical surveys may instinctively and immediately object to this approach. The opening salvo could be 'why German law and not another system?' Alternatively, they can ask whether the lessons from one system alone can be of any real

[155] We refer here to financial regulators, already the subject of an evolving series of EU Directives which have as their primary aim the protection of depositors. These, too, have created a parallel system of remedies for banking supervision which is not as timid as the ones accorded by English tort law and internal Statements of Principle issued by the Financial Authority, which in 1998 took over many of the Bank of England's regulatory functions. The latest of these, issued in 1998, aims primarily at the solidity of the financial institutions and the financial market, and thus differs in its aims from the European Directives which aim at shareholder protection. The complex interrelationship is elegantly and convincingly explained (and criticised) by Mads Andenas and Duncan Fairgrieve in 'Misfeasance in Public Office, Governmental Liability, and European Influences', 51 *ICLQ* (2002), pp 757–80.

[156] It is thus encouraging to see that their Lordships have finally begun moving in the direction advocated by some of us for years now by downgrading the importance of these terms which, in past decisions, gave to numerous readers the impression that the conclusion reached through their use was purely legal and inevitable whereas they were neither. On this see the doubts expressed in *HM's Commissioners of Customs and Excise v Barclays Bank plc* [2004] EWCA Civ 1555.

value to a potential borrower. The ability of those who fear (or cannot themselves carry out proper) comparative studies to invoke (or invent) reasons for not undertaking them at all is limitless. Let us look at these two possible objections in turn.

Starting with the second question first, we note that comparative law is meant to give the user of the method ideas and *not* binding precedents. The acquisition of ideas does not depend on a head count of legal systems;[157] a single one can be enough, provided it is an advanced system, with a roughly comparable socio-economic environment, and offers reasonable accessibility to its sources and experience. That is why we believe that the need to look at all systems (which is practically impossible) or even to include in one's purview 'lesser' systems is not a real need but an excuse for inaction.

'Why Germany?' is easier to answer. This is because it is the only system we know of which has already gone down the path of empirical and inter-disciplinary research on the subject and has done so with the thoroughness that so often characterises the citizens of that country. Unlike English lawyers, who lack the kind of raw information given in this article, the Germans have masses of it. The challenge is to analyse it, to make it usable by practitioners in the UK, and (more fundamentally) to understand that important questions in the area of tort law require at least an attempt to *verify* basic factual assumptions rather than continue to decide cases on the basis of judicial hunches. We have openly acknowledged that the German statistics do not provide all the answers—but at least the system has (twice in the last 30 years!) invested considerable resources in trying to come closer to the heart of the matter.

This is the kind of work that only academics can do following a model of comparative methodology that helps package the foreign information for national use.[158] But that is where the academic contribution stops. The next step is for practitioners to acquaint themselves with such material and then test its value—not conclusiveness—in the forensic context of a real court dispute. The final and decisive step is for the judge to be persuaded to consider it and either accept it or—just as useful—give his reasons why he finds this material unconvincing (so that the approach can again be tested in subsequent papers and conferences bringing together academics and practitioners). If he does, the process can start afresh, refining the method and, one hopes, improving the reliability of the information given to the courts as final arbiters of such matters. At the very least, this approach shows that the three actors in shaping the law through judicial decisions can help do this better if they co-operate rather than if they work in isolation.

In that sense, this Chapter must be seen as part of the wider debate about the possibility of national lawyers obtaining ideas from abroad and—in the light of the information thus acquired—revising, adapting, or, conversely, reconfirming their preference for their own solutions. For the study of foreign law can make the national lawyer feel both humble and proud; and this is one of the inestimable services that comparative methodology can offer to the national legal curriculum.

Yet this enterprise is fraught with difficulties; and the first is to avoid the kind of overly simplifying 'throwaways' which some comparatists tend to adopt in an attempt to damn the budding efforts of our courts. Take for instance Tony Weir's claim that in *Fairchild v Glenhaven*[159] the House of Lords attempted

[157] *McFarlane v Teesside Health Board* [2000] 2 AC 59 at 81 (per Lord Steyn).

[158] The first of us has discussed this issue in *Foreign Law in the Courtroom and the Classroom. The Story of the Last Thirty Five Years* (2003).

[159] [2002] 3 WLR 89.

> [A] superficial . . . tour d'horizon, omitting [in its judgment] the salient fact that in almost none of the jurisdictions glanced at would the claimants . . . have succeeded.[160]

No amount of style and learning—and the opening lines of this case-note referring to the Iliad possess both these features, for which its author is justly admired—can excuse the imprecise picture that it conveys about (a) foreign law and (b) the quality of their Lordships efforts. The five line throwaway is highly problematic, and here is why.

First and foremost, the House of Lords used the foreign material in the context of possible multiple tortfeasors enquiring as to the ability of the 'but for' test to produce a just result. This was the main conceptual point that had to be decided; and this is also the point that attracts most of Mr Weir's attention. We submit that the useful and detailed information their Lordships supplied on this point on foreign law is impeccable. It has thus made history by citing a famous German practitioner's commentary (*Palandt*) and even the 'motive' of the BGB both in German and English—proof (if any was needed) that the language barrier identified by some colleagues as an insurmountable hurdle for what they call 'mono-linguists'[161] can indeed be overcome.

Criticising their Lordships for not looking *at other aspects of foreign law as well* is another matter, and it should have been carefully distinguished from the criticism that the Court's look at foreign law was nothing more than a 'glance' or 'superficial'. Mr Weir's phrase that in 'almost none of the jurisdictions glanced at would the claimants in *Fairchild* have succeeded' is such a *further point* which the House of Lords did not choose to investigate. Perhaps they should have. But if they had, they would have discovered a situation different to that implied by Mr Weir.

That is the second reason why his throwaway statement is worrying. A more thorough study would have shown that in some systems, including Spain, Italy, the Czech Republic, Hungary and Turkey, the possibility of a tort action is or has become available in the *Fairchild* scenario. Employers' liability thus ended in the Netherlands in 1967 when the traditional workers' compensation insurance was integrated into the general health and pension insurance systems, which does allow asbestos victims to be compensated under tort law. Similarly, asbestos cases are since 1997 subject not only to social law but also tort law in France following decisions of the Cour d'Appel of Dijon of 18 December 1997 (involving the company Eternit) and the social law division of the Cour de cassation of 28 February 2002[162] (ruling for the first time on the question of asbestos, a case again involving Eternit and various other companies linked to asbestos multinationals).

Until the late 1990s, liability of French employers under the general rules of tort law (supplementing the standard coverage by workers' compensation) was limited to narrowly defined exceptions ('faute inexcusable'), which covered less than 0.05 per cent of all occupational accidents and diseases. Both cases radically expanded the concept of 'faute inexcusable' and established a form of safety guarantee of employers, reversing the old rule/exception relationship between (limited) social law liability and (unlimited) tort liability. Employers, so runs the argument of the courts, could simply not have been unaware of the dangers of asbestos (a point fully corroborated by the American history on asbestos

[160] 'Making it More Likely *v* Making it Happen', 61 [2002] *CLJ*, pp 519 *ff* (at 520).

[161] Jane Stapleton, 'Benefits of Comparative Tort Reasoning: Lost in Translation,' Journal of Tort Law, Vol. 1 (2006), p 33 *ff*.

[162] *Société Eternit industries contre M-L X et CPAM de Valenciennes*, Les Petites Affiches, no 62, 27 mars 2002, pp 15–19.

litigation). Liability insurers today thus view employers' liability as the biggest subclass of general liability in France (in terms of both premium volume and claims potential).[163]

Thirdly, careful analysis of the German situation would have revealed that in this system the replacement of tort law by the workers' compensation scheme (*Gesetzliche Unfallversicherung*) is suspended whenever the employer is guilty of intent, recklessness or gross negligence—*the latter in German decisions often being found in cases which we would call 'negligence' in the absence of the notion of 'gross' negligence.*

Fourthly, Mr Weir could have told his readers that in the United States state law often allows employers to stay outside workers' compensation schemes and, where this happens, tort law remains applicable. Students of the American system should also take into account the bad side-effects that the workers' compensation schemes have had in practice, namely to drive claimants' lawyers to find new additional defendants. Product liability litigation was thus often fed by and grew as a result of the difficulties that workers' compensations schemes caused to plaintiffs.

Finally, had Mr Weir spent more time looking at the *levels* of compensation provided under the schemes in the various European legal systems, he would have seen how *distinctly* inferior they are to what can be obtained through general tort law. This is true for both Germany and France (where a finding of 'faute inexcusable' can more than double the amount of compensation awarded to asbestos victims by the workers' compensation scheme).[164]

All these important points are 'lost' in abbreviated statements; and that 'loss' is neither mitigated nor, in this case, excused by the carefully qualifying words 'in almost none'. Worse still, they feed the insular attitudes of national lawyers and make them distrust the undoubted benefits that the study of foreign ideas can bring in its wake. We thus believe most strongly that condensed statements of this kind may produce a rhetorical effect but that they rarely lead to an adequate understanding of foreign law.

To the best of our ability, we tried to give as detailed and as thorough a picture of the foreign law as we could with the view of not only helping practitioners digest the German lessons (such as they are) but also assisting academics to appreciate how comparative law should be done.

Though we believe that the comparison we have attempted has been illuminating and constructive, we also readily confess that it has not been easy. We believe that those who understand what comparative law is all about will appreciate this confession and the efforts we have made to develop and refine a workable methodology. The result may not be perfect; few human endeavours are. But it is specific, detailed, and open-minded, which may be more than attractive throw-away lines designed for effect.

The presentation of our material has thus been accompanied by explanations of how we have assembled and presented our material, and also caveats as to how it can best be used. We have been honest with our readers in mentioning the problems we have faced and the uncertainties still left to be cleared. Such honesty may, of course, lead those who espouse the opposite philosophical view to seize upon the difficulties and uncertainties associated with such exercises and over-simplify (or even distort) both our message and data. The latest 'fad', we are told, is for some to argue that comparative law can never work if it involved

[163] On this see Munich Re Group, *2nd, 6th and 7th International Liability Forum* (1999, 2002 and 2003 respectively).

[164] For a comparative survey of the relationship between general tort liability and social security systems see U Magnus (ed), *The Impact of Social Security Law on Tort Law* (2003).

comparing systems that have different languages. How can such 'fads' co-exist with the opposite 'fad' which encourages us to extend the study of foreign law to 'primitive' systems? God only knows.

Throughout this Chapter we have therefore warned our reader of the difficulties and dangers one encounters particularly on the borderline between empirical and legal research. Analysing the economic consequences of tortious liability thus proved a complex exercise, and our task was made more difficult by at least four factors beyond overcoming the time factor needed to assemble this raw evidence.

Thus, first, we tried to glean some insight into the effects of different approaches to governmental liability in England on the basis of statistical material which was accumulated in another system (the German) operating under a set of different legal rules (not necessarily in the area of tortious liability but more so in the context of administrative and constitutional law) and, perhaps more importantly, characterised by differences in day-to-day attitudes.[165] Yet one must not over-state this 'difference'; for the German starting point is, essentially, the Bingham position. The latter may not yet be the accepted rule in English law (and may even be despised by some academics, indigenous or not); but it does show that there is nothing essentially alien in German thinking so as to make its transplantation impossible. Not surprisingly, therefore, this shift from duty to breach is not without high-powered judicial or academic support even in the UK.

Secondly, the existing figures involve an inevitable degree of uncertainty due to the effects of inflation and the different costs of litigation in both systems. We explained this to our readers and also suggested ways in which these differences could be put into a proper perspective. The cost of litigation in England is, incidentally, a source of considerable concern to anyone who wishes to see an effective and affordable system of resolving civil disputes. But this is too big an issue to be addressed here. *What can be reported is that in Germany, and despite the fact that litigation costs are substantially lower than they are in this country, the courts have not been flooded by claims.* The assumption that other methods of keeping matters under control do exist even in those systems which ignore the sweeping notion of duty of care is proved correct.

Thirdly, different countries will have different overall levels of administrative activity with the potential for liability, and these will again vary over time. As indicated above, the state can thus take on new public functions, or privatise others, and these developments will have a direct impact on governmental liability. This is happening in Germany in the area of medical malpractice law with the result that much litigation is being switched into what we would call 'ordinary' tort headings. This means that the figures for liability of statutory bodies may well go down further.

The negative effect of state liability on public budgets is, finally, effectively cushioned by insurance. Both the Federation and the states in Germany tend to make provisions for potential liability payments directly in their respective annual budgets, but municipalities (which bear the largest burden of governmental liability) usually seek some form of mutual insurance coverage.[166] These special insurance systems spread the loss caused by tortious acts attributed to local authorities, and thus reduce substantially the financial risk for single municipalities.[167] The costs are also kept down by the low level of awards.

[165] For instance the German willingness to pursue small demands or to accept fairly low judicial awards.

[166] So-called *kommunale Schadensversicherung*; see Infratest Burke Rechtsforschung, above note 104, *Bericht*, p 42.

[167] C Rothermund, *Haftungsrecht in der kommunalen Praxis* (3rd edn 2004), p 427.

Similar systems are known in the UK. During the greater part of the 20th century, Municipal Mutual thus provided insurance coverage for most local authorities. In the early 1990s the company ran into financial difficulties and ceased trading in 1992 following a risky internationalisation and diversification of its activities. Heavy reliance on commercial property contributed to its fall when the market crashed in the late 1980s and early 1990s. Other companies such as Zurich Municipal have since filled the gap. A new scheme involving the 32 Greater London boroughs, led by Croydon, became operational in 2007. It writes material damage property covers, including business interruption, and also insures general liability, employers' liability, automobile liability, and risks arising from terrorism. It seems that the boroughs have thus far spent close to £40 million per annum on insurance premiums under these various headings, a figure which the mutual is expected to reduce significantly. The amount spent on insurance is thereby certainly an indication of the risks involved in governmental activities, especially on the local level, but a more thorough investigation is again needed in order to discern the overall effect which a switch from duty of care to breach as a gatekeeper in negligence claims would have. It should also be noted that headings such as automobile liability are part of such schemes, areas which absorb considerable resources but are not directly linked (as in Germany) to the types of governmental liability that we have been discussing here.

Finally, we mentioned—but believe overcame to a considerable degree—the difficulties that are associated with classification and terminology. We noted, for example, how instances of liability covered under ordinary tort rules in England would appear under the various headings of state or local authority liability in Germany. Overcoming artificial hurdles of classification is an art which comparative lawyers must master, for once learnt it can help put matters in their proper perspective. Only when this task has been accomplished can proper comparisons be attempted.

These difficulties being acknowledged, the German experience presented above supports at least five important points, namely:

(1) As the prison case suggests, it is possible to win a case in Germany but not be awarded damages. Other instances could be provided.
(2) The overall amount of compensation paid to the victims of governmental activities is surprisingly low, though this does not mean that in cases involving serious *physical* injuries the figures may not spike upwards.
(3) The number of 'state liability' actions which reach the courts, especially if taken as part of the whole volume of tort litigation, is also small. It is difficult to see why things would be different in the United Kingdom where litigation costs are so high.
(4) Though individual awards are usually modest, unusual cases involving physical injury can produce amounts comparable to those found in English law.[168]
(5) Finally, duties of care are also rejected in German courtrooms, but proof of a breach of accepted duties, fault, and proof of damage are the more important controlling devices, both in administrative practice and (if there is subsequent litigation) in the courts. This must be read in conjunction with point (3) above.

The last aspect is worth emphasis.

The approach to the breach of statutory duties is, in theory, fundamentally different from that in England. Public bodies are, *a priori*, deemed capable of owing duties of care to the

[168] For cases involving physical injury see BS Markesinis, M Coester, G Alpa and A Ullstein, *Compensation for Personal Injury in England, Germany and Italy* (2005).

citizen when exercising their official functions. Switching from duty to breach does not, however, mean that every duty found on the statute books or in administrative rules has the purpose of protecting individuals. Nor does it mean that a claimant invoking it will succeed, for most actions founder on this (and other) rocks. This is an important observation, for it supports empirically views expressed in England both by judges and academics that a change in our law need not have disastrous consequences.

English law, by contrast, starts with the basic presumption that there is no liability unless expressly acknowledged by the legislator or accepted under a common law duty of care, which potential victims are often hard-pressed to establish. This can lead to the rejection of individual cases which do deserve to win (with or without a reasonable award) on the basis of the particular circumstances simply because they belong to a larger group of situations for which duties of care are generally not accepted.

There is a lesson in this.

German claimants, if lucky, will go home with modest amounts but happy that as citizens they have helped externalise state disapproval of illegality while also obtaining some public acknowledgement that they have been wrongfully harmed. In England, by contrast, liability tends to be quite extensive if imposed. This may be particularly pleasing to the rare winners of this particular type of forensic lottery. But it may also be the reason why so many other deserving victims are left with the profound disappointment of not even being allowed to test their claim in court, all in the name of administrative convenience.

How should those who find this idea haunting react to it?

Not a bad way would be by beginning to realise that the genius of the Common law is not to be found in academic work which dryly describes what cases have decided; nor is it to be discovered in the advocate's advice that constantly sees in the existing case law limits that cannot be breached; nor, finally, is it exemplified by a judge who uses his heavyweight authority to hedge off the kind of change in the law that is now and then needed in order to let it keep up with changing societal expectations and altering tastes and values.

What such an observer should realise is that what all these types of lawyers have in common is that they represent the statism of conservatism, not the genius of those who know how to usher in *controlled* change at the right time. But it is the latter kind that created *Donoghue v Stevenson*,[169] *High Trees*,[170] *Hedley Byrne & Co Ltd v Heller*,[171] and *Ridge v Baldwin*.[172] It is the latter kind of jurist who could see, as was necessary, what the bulk of their contemporaries could not even imagine. And more relevant to our present aims, it is the latter kind of jurist who might find arguments in empirical evidence coming from comparable legal systems and use them to set the new limits of our own law. By being willing to consider these possibilities, as Lord Bingham has clearly been, they demonstrate that there is no fundamental block to drawing inspiration from abroad. The only obstacle is personal outlook or mentality concealed behind an artful discussion of precedents or the invocation of unproved fears. This may change once those who have resisted drawing inspiration from other systems are persuaded to look (and question) this evidence or, alternatively, finally retire from the judicial scene.

So let us re-capitulate a long and multi-faceted Chapter which revolves around three themes.

[169] [1932] AC 562.
[170] *London Property Trust Ltd v High Trees House Ltd* [1947] KB 130.
[171] [1964] AC 465.
[172] [1964] AC 40.

First, we believe much of the current conservative attitude of our judges is, in part, due to a lack of empirical evidence showing that the current use of the notion of duty of care is unusually blunt and *can* be replaced with a system that a) has worked elsewhere, and b) is importable to this country (*as the writings of very senior British judges and academics clearly show*). What is lacking is the will to re-think some of these problems in the context of a world very different from that which judges first had to face up to and attempt to regulate. Alternatively, one might be tempted to blame these attitudes to the kind of stubbornness that may accompany the realisation that judicial attitudes go in cycles, favouring in alternating phases expansion and restriction of liability and thus depriving the proponents of 'restrictive' theories of the chance to make a lasting imprint on the law. The highway cases fall precisely into this category. To try to stem attempts to learn from other systems either on the basis of generalisations made by intelligent comparatists or by uninformed national lawyers invoking objections which can be answered in an informed dialogue, amounts to nothing else than an intellectually reprehensible way of standing in the way of a genuine exchange of ideas. The same is true for those who try to ignore this material through (cowardly) silence.

Secondly, to the extent that this piece is read by law students and young practitioners, our aim is to urge them not to confuse respect for age, intelligence, and authority with judicial infallibility. We cannot better Justice Jackson's understated but highly relevant words in the second flag-salute case[173] when he said that

> whenever decisions of one court are reviewed by another, a percentage of them are reversed. That reflects a *difference in outlook normally found between personnel comprising different courts* . . . We are not final because we are infallible, but we are infallible only because we are final.

It is thus arguable, if not likely on the balance of probabilities, to say that some of the conservative judgments of our House of Lords are as much the products of personal 'outlook' of its personnel as the products of strictly legal reasoning that inexorably leads to one *and only one* conclusion. To treat these opinions as unchallengeable or as 'correct' would be of doubtful wisdom. For there are simply too many examples from recent case law that show that the Hoffmann philosophy, though consistently and persistently expounded by the judge, is not widely shared by his colleagues. And even if it (temporarily?) represented the prevailing view it thus does so by virtue of his high office rather than because of overpowering rational strength.

To the extent that this observation seems reasonable to readers it must also be treated as important. For it is one thing for an academic to try to push his theories to their limits and quite another for a judge to give the impression that he is doing the same. For the judge must decide according to the law and not give—or, just as important, appear to give—his philosophical preferences (however legitimate) judicial clothing. The result we are dealing with in this Chapter demonstrates how wrong this can go. Tort liability of public authorities has been held back in a period where tort law has expanded, and judicial review even more so. European human rights law and EU law are thus treated as foreign implants whose contaminating effect must be limited as effectively as possible. Consistent with this attitude, the assistance that the laws of other European countries can offer is thus systematically ignored. Instead, the existing orthodoxy, maintaining the field in a state of arrested development, makes use of economic theory as supporting unwanted consequences (or the risk

[173] *West Virginia State Board of Education v Barnette*, 319 US 624, 641 (1943).

of such consequences) without considering and refuting opposite economic arguments. The force of this argument is thus not tested against competing views—economic or doctrinal—but only buttressed by repeated references to a judge's own earlier opinions or the opinions of like-minded colleagues. Of course, we accept (as all students of the law would do) the possibility that we may have misunderstood what those we disagree with may have been doing. But having studied their views, compared them with those of their other colleagues, and weighed the force of competing arguments, we feel obliged as scholars to voice the concerns that we have.

Thirdly, we remind ourselves as well as the interested reader that this Chapter is as much about methodology as it is about substance. If one believes that dialogue brings illumination, one is bound to trust in the enriching effect of a dialogue with those who see things and do things in a different way. To do this work properly one has to find a way to bridge the gaps that differences in languages, notions, and legal history have created over the years. The process of perfecting this art is slow and painful. But it is not helpful if those who profess an interest in foreign and comparative law restrict their talents to the tasks of a translator or perpetual critic—or, indeed, if they choose to restrict themselves to the confines of a limited set of legal systems which are bound together by a common language. If they call themselves 'comparatists', they must believe enough in their subject in order to try and show how people can gain by comparing ideas and techniques, and by transcending the difficulties that a comparison of different cultures—and hence, usually, languages. We neither ask nor expect more. Spending their time *denouncing* the utility of foreign law and *criticising* particular decisions for the way they have used foreign law with statements that amuse because of their style but are meaningless due to the tone in which they are delivered, does little justice to either their subject or their learning. Indeed, it amounts to little more than a waste of rare and impressive talent. For it is within the power of everyone to be destructive but only the privilege of visionaries to build. The choice is there to be made by all concerned.

8. POSTSCRIPT

In the preceding pages we stated how and why the law can change. In this postscript we wish to add the gut feeling that the tide may be slowly turning and this despite the attempts of influential members of the English judiciary to keep it at bay. A case reported in September 2007 offers the most recent indication that some public authorities at least are beginning to feel the need to bow to the inevitable.

It concerned a 39-year-old woman and her two siblings who were awarded a total of £100,000 in an out-of-court settlement with Hackney council in east London. The council had failed to remove the children from their home, where they had suffered sexual abuse, were beaten, and often deprived of food.[174] The following passage of the article is worth quoting, for it shows that forces greater than the traditional restrictive view of conservative judges are at work here:

> No court has yet awarded damages against a local authority for failing to take children into care. In 1995 five law lords ruled that five children who suffered 'horrific abuse' before they were eventually

[174] *The Guardian* (London) of 17 September 2007, p 15.

> removed from their parents could not sue their local council. The judges ruled that councils owed no duty of care to those affected by the way they carried out their childcare functions. Lawyers say the law has moved on in the wake of the Human Rights Act, which places public authorities under a duty to protect individuals from inhuman and degrading treatment. *They point to cases like that of Ms Routledge [the 39-year-old woman] where councils have paid compensation even though there is no binding precedent obliging them to pay.* [Our emphasis.]

It would be a worthwhile exercise to establish the extent of the trend indicated in the italicised section of the quotation. German experience suggests that it will not create a flood of claims but it may be doing justice. Should we not be comparing details first rather than condemning the utility of foreign law in an outright manner?

9

FOREIGN LAW INSPIRING NATIONAL LAW: LESSONS FROM *GREATOREX V GREATOREX*

1. INTRODUCTION

Here we are not talking of recourse to foreign law because the parties chose it or because it has to be applied because it is so decreed by the rules of private international law. Nor are we referring to the law coming from such courts as that of Strasbourg or Luxembourg—not least because, nowadays, this cannot be properly called 'foreign' law. This is, of course, true of the whole of this book. But in this Chapter our points come out in an exceptionally clear manner since they emerge in the context of a real case. For in *Greatorex* we are focusing only on the voluntary use by judge or counsel of foreign law and foreign legal ideas as a means of shaping national law when this is contradictory, in need of reform, or (as in this case) lacking a direct authority. The number of instances in which this kind of borrowing may happen must, of necessity, be limited, though in intellectual terms, such conscious transplants or (at a lower level) judicial dialogue between judges from different cultures must always be exciting to observe. Yet in a shrinking world in which increased movement of people and ideas is making the approximation of tastes, habits, practices, and even the convergence of law more and more pronounced, this phenomenon can only increase in significance—not decrease.

For a long time the leading author has tried to encourage this trend of planned judicial borrowings.[1] An open mind must, surely, be a pre-requisite for any academic; and an ability to borrow ideas (if not solutions—'ready-made' so to speak) must also be attractive to practitioners when faced with novel issues, provided that they are 'packaged' in a way that is attractive to them. The problem is that foreign law is unlikely to come in a simple form, attractively prepared; and language is by no means the only or even major problem in such attempts to be inspired by a foreign idea if not transplant the actual solution. That is how one was led to the idea of advocating a more co-ordinated use of the different talents that judges, practitioners, and academics bring to the process of creating and interpreting law.[2]

Teaching foreign law and trying to develop a workable theory of comparative methodology has its ups and downs. Many of the difficulties are, we think, linked to the attitude adopted by our fellow-comparatists who have tried to shape wider theories about legal transplants or their impossibility. Certainly, French comparatists have opted for wide-sweeping surveys, covering much ground but in insufficient detail to make their work directly usable by judges, legislators and practitioners. This, one might dare to generalise

[1] See Basil Markesinis, *Foreign Law and Comparative Methodology: A Subject and a Thesis* (1997) and *Always on the Same Path, Essays on Foreign Law and Comparative Methodology* (2001).

[2] A beautifully phrased but not entirely convincing formulation can be found in Sir Robert Megarry's judgment in *Cordell v Second Clanfield Properties* [1969] 2 Ch 9, 16 *ff*.

and suggest, is a feature of the French writing style as a whole which can contribute to its literary appeal and fame, but makes its practical utility more debatable.

Speaking more generally, but focusing on the contemporary scene, we admit that great names have made interesting and useful contributions to this debate about the movement of ideas or legal transplants.

Alan Watson is the one whose work on *Legal Transplants*[3] created the term and sparked off this debate. His work is a seminal piece for those interested in the transfer of ideas; and he brought to bear on the subject his linguistic abilities, his knowledge of history, and his understanding of many cultures.

At the antipodes stands Pierre Legrand, who has flourished amidst the controversy he has skilfully generated around his uncompromisingly 'negative' theories. His temperament must be as aggressive as his expression; his conviction in his beliefs unshakable as it is admirable; and his willingness to remain 'a loner' has paid off, attracting attention—as the statistics shown in Chapter Three show. But despite years of crusading, 'attention' has not translated into 'support' and he is still swimming against the growing current of reality that suggests increased contacts, broadened dialogue, and enhanced convergence (albeit often in a piece-meal manner).

Reinhard Zimmerman is the last we must mention in this short list. He brings with him the thoroughness of the German scholar, the breadth of knowledge of a truly cultured (not just educated) man, and the messianic determination to 'save' Roman law from oblivion. This last passion he shares with the late Peter Birks, even though in Zimmermann's work and personal relations it is pursued with a greater degree of tact and diplomacy.

Where do we fit in?

In the transplant/borrowing camp, without any doubt. But our approach has deliberately steered clear from such grand schemes and theorising. It has been pragmatic and judge- and practitioner-oriented rather than tried to capture the imagination of fellow academics whom, even when we admire, we regard as relatively minor players in this larger 'end game' we are interested in. This is only partly because we are working in a Common law environment where the judge is, as was once said, the 'senior partner in the law-creating process'. For both of us had a civilian training and thus have been exposed to civilian methodology as well as the civilian tendency to treat case law as the supporting material that bolsters the learned professor's theories rather than rely on it as a prime source of law. Indeed, the Common law readers may be surprised to read that the average German professor regards himself as standing—socially and intellectually—above most judges (and some might even include in this definition judges of their national supreme court!).

Not surprisingly, we do not share these views. We also believe that the Common law emphasis on decisions and its undoubtedly superior ability to discuss, refine, redefine, and reconcile conflicting cases represents one of its great strengths, both in the classroom and the courtroom. The pragmatic nature of English law is also a feature we admire and would like it to figure more prominently in the civilian classroom and courtroom, along with a greater willingness to discuss more openly the policy issues which lie hidden behind the concepts, notions and words used by judges the world over. So ours is an approach which focuses on 'small areas' of the law and looks at them pragmatically and with a 'give and take'

[3] Legal Transplants: An Approach to Comparative Law (1974). As one would expect, Pierre Legrand disagreed in 'The Impossibility of "Legal Transplants"', (1997) 4 *Maastricht Journal of European and Comparative Law*, 111 *ff.*

frame of mind, which means that we hold no brief for arguing the Common law or the civilian position.

Our methodology has also been shaped by the visible decline experienced by the subject in the classroom. We have not hidden the fact that we blame Roman law for this phenomenon. And the interests of other comparatists in subjects such as Hindu or Sanskrit laws is something which ties in partly with the old colonial past of England and, equally, with the eccentric character of the true Englishman (always attracted by exotica). But this has been good for 'inventiveness' and less good in making it work for the inventor! The result of all this has not been good for comparative law; it certainly has not prepared it for the challenges and, perhaps more importantly, the *opportunities* that it can offer to all those who wish to use it in the 21st century. Our claim, absolutely phrased, may meet with little sympathy among academics who, despite often proclaiming allegiance to leftist ideas and causes, are really very conservative in mentality.

But what we describe and admire has happened, and has been adopted by international law firms and the business world that operates in our modern globalised environment. Our aim is thus to persuade judges and practitioners to become more interested in foreign law with a view to testing their own ideas, acquiring new ones, updating old ones, and providing similar answers to problems which appear in many countries with similar socio-economic cultures—especially if this is helpful to trade and commerce. The aims and methods we approve of are thus essentially practical.

In a world of unlimited resources there should be complete freedom for academics to pursue other interests, develop other subjects, and pursue different aims. But we do not live in a world of unlimited resources, so choices have to be made. These choices will be made on the basis of practicality, availability, intellectual superiority, and other similar factors. All this will become obvious in the contents of this Chapter, which may well be, along with Chapter Eight, the most 'legal' and 'technical' of the 11 in this book.

The approach we have been advocating seems to have found an excellent practical illustration in the judgment of the High Court in *Greatorex v Greatorex*.[4] It is not the only one that can be found among the English decisions which have used foreign law; but it does provide the clearest example of a transplant of ideas and of how this became possible.

The facts of the case were relatively simple. A young man (whom, as note 9 below explains, we shall henceforth call D2) was injured in an accident caused by his own grossly negligent driving. P, his father, a professional fire officer stationed nearby, suffered serious post-traumatic stress disorder as a result of attending his unconscious son at the scene of the accident. The question was whether the father could claim damages for his harm from the driver/injured son or, since he was uninsured, from the Motor Insurers' Bureau (MIB), which stepped into the gap and became the second defendant in the action. In his judgment for the defendants Mr Justice Cazalet made bold use of foreign law. Yet thus far his judgment has been the subject of only one case note[5]; and from a comparative point of view, it has not received anywhere near the attention given to Lord Goff's opinion in *White v Jones*.[6] Why this is so can, for the time being, be left open to speculation. But without any disrespect to Mr Justice Cazalet it might be legitimate to ponder whether in law (as in many other activities) the importance attached to a pronouncement can depend more on the

[4] [2000] 1 WLR 1976.

[5] Peter Handford, 'Psychiatric Damage Where the Defendant is the Immediate Victim', 117 [2001] *LQR* 397, comparing the result with the more generous Australian law.

[6] [1995] 2 AC 207, 252 *ff.*

high status and profile of its maker than on its own intrinsic value. This is unfortunate, for it means that valuable ideas may be ignored until they are uttered by a person of high visibility or are considered or adopted by an appellate court.

Whatever the answer to this wider question, the fact remains that in terms of comparative law and methodology Mr Justice Cazalet's judgment is, in some respects, more significant than Lord Goff's obiter dicta in *White v Jones*. For, unlike *White*—where foreign law *embellished* an opinion of a high-profile judge but did not influence it *directly*[7]—in *Greatorex* foreign law formed an important part of the argument of both counsels' submissions as well as the decision of the judge. The outcome is as interesting as the way it came about. For this decision can be seen as the result of a de facto collaboration between the three sides of the legal profession.

The discussion that follows will thus be undertaken under four headings: 2) the German model; 3) its application to the English case; 4) unresolved questions; and 5) further ideas from America. The four sub-headings or themes will then be brought together in the form of some tentative conclusions of wider import, where some observations about translating foreign texts will also be found.

2. THE GERMAN MODEL

The case that figured prominently in *Greatorex* was the decision of the German Federal Supreme Court of 11 May 1971.[8] The facts of the case were simple. On 6 March 1965 the claimant's husband (henceforth referred to as D2[9]) was fatally injured in a collision with the defendant's vehicle caused partly by his fault and partly by that of the defendant. (Henceforth we shall refer to this 'primary' defendant as D1.) The claimant in this case (henceforth P) was the wife of D2 (the primary victim of the accident). In her suit against the tortfeasor, she claimed damages for the injury to her health, which she suffered when *told*[10] of the death of D2. The *Landgericht* allowed the claim in full, the *Oberlandesgericht* in part. P appealed to the Federal Supreme Court. The judgments below were vacated, and the case remanded to the *Oberlandesgericht*.

[7] For doubts about the practical utility of the foreign law references in Lord Goff's judgment see Lord Rodger of Earlsferry, 'Savigny in the Strand' in *The Maurice Kelly Memorial Lecture 1995*, esp at pp 24–25; Neil Duxbury, *Jurists and Judges* (2001), p 107.

[8] BGHZ 56, 163 = NJW 1971, 1883 = VersR 1971, 905, 1140, taken from the third edition of Markesinis, *The German Law of Torts: A Comparative Introduction* (1994) (translation by Tony Weir). The German decision is still the subject of controversy not so much for its result but for the way it chose to justify it. Its status as 'good law' has also been thrown into doubt after the decision of the Federal Supreme Court of 1 March 1988 (BGHZ 103, 338). For a summary of the academic views see Staudinger/Hager, *Kommentar zum BGB, Unerlaubte Handlungen*, B39.

[9] D2 is the primary victim of the accident; but because he may, through his own negligence, also have contributed to his injury and the loss of P (the secondary victim), he may be sued by the main tortfeasor (D1) for a contribution or an indemnity. In Germany, D2 can also be referred to as the 'privileged' defendant, for he may benefit from an exemption clause arising from his relations with the claimant enjoying an immunity *ex lege* because of his family relationship with P. As we shall note later, one of the questions that can arise in such cases is whether D2's 'immunity' from action by P can also protect him against an action brought by D1—the joint tortfeasor.

[10] In principle, German law allows recovery for 'distant' psychiatric injury. In practice such claims are kept under control by judges rigorously checking their standard requirement that the shock be an 'appropriate and understandable consequence' of the accident that befell the primary victim. In practice a close relationship (*Schicksalsgemeinschaft*) between the claimant's shock and the primary victim is of paramount importance.

The case involved a claim for what we now call psychiatric damage in England.[11] It also touched upon some of the usual questions that English law, too, has encountered in this area and, it seems, is unable to solve through the courts.[12] How German law handled the shock aspect of the claim is not the subject of discussion in this Chapter since the matter has been discussed in detail elsewhere.[13] But the second part of the German case addressed the question of D2's contributory negligence and how this would/should affect P's claim. The German court's approach need only be reported in its bare essentials and to the extent that it bears on what is the main theme of this Chapter.

Understandably, D1's contention was that P's claim should be reduced to take into account D2's contributory fault. One way to do this was to attempt to rely upon § 846 BGB, which states that

> If, *in the cases provided by §§ 844, 845*, some fault of the injured party had contributed to cause the damage which the third party has sustained, the provision of § 254 BGB [about contributory negligence] applies to the claim of the third party.

The problem with such an approach, however, lies in the italicised section of this paragraph, which refers to what is, in essence, the German equivalent to our Fatal Accident Acts as amended in 1982. In fact, § 846 BGB provides precisely the same kind of answer that we accept in fatal accidents claims: the deceased's negligence affects the claims of the dependants. But in this case, so far as the wife's claim for psychiatric injury was concerned, it was *not* a fatal accidents claim but a direct personal claim based on § 823 I BGB. This was a crucial twist. The German court thus took the view—rightly it is suggested—that the application of § 846 BGB was not available, even for an analogical extension.

With the wife claiming not as dependant but in her own right for psychiatric damage as injury to her health under § 823 I BGB, D1's attempt to mitigate the extent of his liability seemed rather optimistic. For if P's claim was original and not derivative—terms hinted at by the German decision but (as we shall note later) excessively relied upon by American cases—her demand that her damages remain undiminished by her husband's negligence looked unshakeable. Yet the German court, invoking the catch-all clause of good faith contained in the celebrated § 242 BGB, decided to reduce her damages in proportion to D2's fault. Thus, for our purposes, the relevant part of the judgment reads as follows:

> Here the accident to her husband was only able to cause the harm supposedly suffered by the claimant because as a result of their close personal relationship his tragedy became hers. One cannot imagine a person suffering in this manner on hearing a fatal accident to a total stranger; indeed, if it happened, it would be so unusual that one would decline to impute it to the defendant on the ground that it was unforeseeable. But the critical reason of the claimant's suffering this injury to her health was her close personal relationship to her husband and it was thus only fair that her claim should be affected by his fault in contributing to the accident.

[11] *Attia v British Gas plc* [1988] QB 304, 317 *per* Bingham LJ (as he then was).

[12] This at least seems to be the view of Lord Steyn, who argued that the subject might have now passed the stage of redemption by the courts and needs legislative intervention (see his opinion in *Frost v Chief Constable of South Yorkshire Police* [1999] 2 AC 455, 500). It is submitted that *W v Essex County Council* [2001] 2 AC 592 has compounded the uncertainty.

[13] Markesinis, *The German Law of Torts: A Comparative Treatise*, 4th edn by Basil Markesinis and Hannes Unberath (2002), pp 45 *ff.* Note, however, that this was a case of 'distant shock' which would thus not be compensated by English and (most) American courts.

This reasoning was further reinforced by (what we would call) an obiter dictum that was to prove crucial in *Greatorex* litigation.[14] For the German court added that:

> If the husband's death had been solely attributable to his failure to take care of himself, the claimant would have had no claim whatever for compensation for the consequent injury to her. A person is under no legal duty, whatever the moral position may be, to look after his own life and limb simply in order to save the dependants from the likely psychical effects on them if he is killed or maimed. To impose such a legal duty, except in very peculiar cases, for instance wherever a person commits suicide in a deliberately shocking manner, would be to restrict a person's self-determination in a manner inconsistent with our legal system.

To the above rule the only exception that *some* authors[15] are prepared to make is in the context of suicide. Suicide may provoke rescue, especially in a system where the duty to rescue others is recognised by law.[16] Thus they have argued that a person wishing to commit suicide may be under a duty to carry it out in a way which does not 'provoke' any rescue by third parties; otherwise he *may* be liable for any damage suffered. But the point does not appear to have been settled by the courts, and the above amounts to little more than an academic speculation.[17]

3. THE APPLICATION OF THE GERMAN IDEAS TO *GREATOREX*

Prior to *Greatorex* Common law courts do not appear to have faced squarely the problem of contributory negligence *in the context of nervous shock*—at any rate not in England, though in his judgment Cazalet J did allude to some inconclusive Commonwealth authority.[18] In the context of nervous shock, the picture in the United States may not be much clearer, though *Dillon v Legg* contains some seemingly confused views on the subject.[19] However, the same point about contributory negligence has also arisen in 'rescue' cases,

[14] In such factual situations the court can normally rely on § 1359 BGB to bar any action by the wife against her husband (or, in this case, his estate). This is because § 1359 states that one spouse is liable to the other only if he (or she) failed to attain 'the degree of care which they are accustomed to exercise in their own affairs'. So the sued spouse can avoid liability if he can show that in his own affairs he would have displayed a lower standard of care than that required by ordinary negligence. A similar rule can be found in § 1664 1 BGB dealing with the parent/child relations. The rationale of both provisions is to avoid legal disputes between persons who are in such close family relationships, and in many respects draws on the policy reasons which were also touched upon by Cazalet J in *Greatorex*. The immunity rule just described does not, however, apply where D2's fault amounts to gross negligence. Another limitation is that the rule is not applicable in car accident cases.

[15] See Medicus, *Schuldrecht, Besonderer Teil* (9th edn 1999), p 302.

[16] So long as the rescue can be rendered without any danger to the rescuer: § 323c StGB.

[17] Presumably, the same argument could be advanced in other systems (such as the French) which also recognise affirmative duties of rescue. The Scottish case of *A v B's Trustees* (1906) 13 SLT 830 allowed a claim in very similar circumstances but has been generally seen to be based on breach of contract; see Lord Johnston's words at p 831, apparently thus interpreted by Lord Porter in *Bourhill v Young* [1943] AC 92 at p 120. In *Reg v Criminal Injuries Compensation Board, ex parte Webb* [1986] QB 184, 196, Watkins LJ also appeared to take the view that a 'person attempting to commit suicide may well be in breach of a duty of care owed to [others]'. But the observation was obiter; and in *Greatorex* Cazalet J brushed the point aside as irrelevant on the facts before him. An American case has, however, held that a mentally distressed man who tried to commit suicide in his garage is under a duty towards his son who came to his rescue and was *physically* injured: *Talbert v Talbert* 199 NYS 2d 212 (1960).

[18] In English law, the most interesting obiter dicta come from Lord Oliver's opinion in *Alcock v Chief Constable of South Yorkshire Police* [1992] 1 AC 310, 418.

[19] 441 P 2d 912 (1968). The majority in *Dillon* (at p 916) asked the question whether the contributory negligence of the victim *and* the claimant should affect their claims whereas the minority (at p 928) discussed whether the deceased child's negligence can affect the living claimant's claims.

and in those US States which recognise actions for 'loss of consortium or companionship' or loss of 'parental or children's companionship'.[20] In all these triangular situations the same range of legal suits is possible and the abbreviations adopted here (P, D1, D2) are equally appropriate. The lessons that can be drawn from the many consortium cases are not insignificant, and we shall return to them later on, especially in the light of the paucity of the existing English material and the complexity of the German.

Since all negligence reasoning starts with a discussion of the notion of duty of care, *Greatorex* naturally had to grapple with the question whether a victim of self-inflicted injuries owes a duty of care to a third party not to cause him psychiatric injury. Cazalet J acknowledged that there was no binding authority on the question of duty. For guidance he was thus directed to German law, among other systems, and his conclusion was undoubtedly influenced by the decision of the German Federal Supreme Court of 11 May 1971 (cited to him by counsel for the MIB, which had been joined as second defendants since D2 was not insured while driving the car). It will be recalled that to the question now asked by Cazalet J, the BGH had given a negative reply. In the opinion of the BGH the imposition of such a duty would under normal circumstances unduly restrict the person's (D2's) right to self-determination.

Cazalet J expressly followed the reasoning of the BGH and regarded the argument derived from the right to self-determination as enunciated in the German case as 'powerful'.[21] Matters would be different where, by harming himself, D2 causes damage other than nervous shock to another person. It would thus seem that in German[22] as well as Scottish[23] and possibly English law, the ethical duty not to harm oneself becomes a legal duty as soon as the self-harming activity also causes *physical* harm to another person. From this perspective D2's immunity from liability for nervous shock (suffered by others) constitutes an exception. In other words, D2's right to self-determination prevails only if we regard this injury as special. Cazalet J's constant reference to 'policy' lends credence to this view and illustrates, once again, our legal system's difficulty to cope with the ramification of nervous shock and emotional injuries.

4. UNRESOLVED QUESTIONS

In the German decision one of the issues that had to be decided by the court was whether the contributory negligence of D2 could be imputed to P and her claim for damages against D1 accordingly reduced. At this stage it is helpful to reconsider the argument in favour of imputing D2's contributory negligence to P in the light of Cazalet's J analysis of the 'primary victim's' (ie D2's) limited or non-existent liability to others for causing harm to him. For the two issues are interrelated.

[20] In Germany, we have noted that the rescue variant has been considered in the context of suicide. Since loss of consortium claims are not known in German law, the most litigated type of American case finds no parallel there.

[21] See also the Law Commission's report on *Liability for Psychiatric Illness* (1998), Law Com No 249, paras 5.34–5.44.

[22] Similarly, in BGH ZIP 1990, 1485 the court held that as a general rule a lessor did not owe a contractual duty to the lessee not to commit suicide, and as a result the estate was not answerable for the termination of the lease. To impose such a duty would have amounted to an unjustifiable intrusion upon the right to self-determination of the lessor.

[23] See *A v B's Trustees* (1906) 13 SLT 830.

If, generally speaking, a person (D2) does not owe to others (P) a duty of care not to harm himself, then it would appear to be fair that, if a third person (D1) causes physical injury to D2, then D2 should bear his, the primary victim's, causal contribution to the accident. As in America so in Germany, this problem has occurred also in other contexts of adjustment among multiple 'debtors' and the BGH has (not always consistently) applied similar considerations.[24] Because of special circumstances, characteristic of the relationship between D2 and P, P does not have a cause of action against D2 (all other conditions of liability being fulfilled). In the nervous shock case this is because such a cause of action would be contrary to D2's right to self-determination.[25] The result is that D2 is no longer seen as a *Mitschuldner* (joint debtor) with D1 since he is immune to any action by P. This immunity (or privilege) enjoyed by D2 by virtue of his relationship with P 'distorts' the normal rules which apply to the internal relationship between joint tortfeasors and which in German law largely follows the English pattern.[26] The Germans thus refer to this problem as *gestörter Gesamtschuldnerausgleich*, a term that could be rendered into English as 'disturbed internal settlement between joint debtors'.

The composite word is typically Germanic; but its emphasis on 'distortion' and the 'internal adjustment that has to take place between two (possible) debtors' clarifies what it is trying to address. The 'distortion' of the internal relationship between the possible two joint debtors (D1 and D2) because of the rules that govern the relationship between D2 and P can, in terms of contribution rules, be addressed in one of three ways. First, we could say that P can sue D1, and D1 can then claim contribution from D2. Alternatively, we can take the view that P can sue D1 for all his loss but D1 cannot claim anything back from D2 because of his privileged position. (That is why D2 is, in German law, often referred as the 'privileged' debtor.) Finally we could adopt an altogether different rule, namely say that P can sue D1 but only for his share of P's loss.

We see this unfolding in our case as P is forced to sue D1. If D1 could subsequently claim contribution from the primary victim (D2) then, *in the end*, D2 would be held liable for his causal contribution to the accident.[27] But this result of holding D2 liable was, as we saw in the German judgment, seen to be undesirable (because of D2's right to self-determination). So this avenue seems to be blocked. Therefore, it is held that D1 cannot claim contribution from D2 even if the latter was primarily responsible for the accident.[28] This result may follow logically the reasoning just expounded. Nonetheless, many would regard it as unsatisfactory. For it does not seem fair in such circumstances to impose full liability on D1, especially if his contribution to the harm was in terms of causation and fault very low and that of D2 very high.[29] So in such circumstances why should D1 (rather than P) bear D2's causal contribution to the accident? After all, it is because of special circumstances arising out of the relationship between D2 and P that D2 cannot be made liable for causing nervous shock.

It is therefore plausible to argue that the rationale of § 846 BGB should also be applied to claims of secondary victims (those we have here called 'P') in respect of nervous shock, and to reduce accordingly P's claim against D1. This implies that where D2 is solely answerable for the accident, P cannot recover at all. We are thus back to our point of departure! Given

[24] Thus see BGH JR 1989, 60 and cf BGHZ 12, 213.

[25] Approximately the same considerations apply easily if we replace the legal immunity with an exclusion clause contained in a contract between D2 and P.

[26] See § 421 BGB.

[27] Albeit the risk of insolvency of the primary victim (D2) would be transferred from P to D1.

[28] Cf *Alcock v Chief Constable of South Yorkshire Police* [1992] 1 AC 310, 418 *per* Lord Oliver.

[29] The point made by Lord Oliver (above) but rejected (obiter) by Cazalet J in *Greatorex*.

the unusual facts of *Greatorex* (for D2, the primary victim, was solely responsible for his injury) the point did not have to be resolved. But it could arise in other contexts where the personal autonomy argument is not at play. That is where the German ideas, complex though they are, could once again serve as a source of inspiration.

So what will happen where the reason why D2 is not liable to P is a family immunity rule such as that found in §§ 1359 or 1664 I BGB, which applies to all cases other than motor car accidents? D1's liability towards P is not in doubt. But will he then be able to claim a contribution from D2? Or will D2's immunity, which protects him from actions by P, also shield him from a contribution claim brought by D1? To this last question the German Federal Court some 14 years ago gave a positive reply,[30] reversing earlier case law[31] and leaving German academic opinion reeling with the unfairness of a result which means that D1 has to carry the full loss. This solution is even more confusing if one bears in mind that German courts take a different view if the reason of the immunity given to D2 is the result of a *contractual* exemption clause that regulates his relationship with P. For here the courts allow P to claim his full loss from D1 and then allow the latter to claim a contribution from D2 as a result of an analogical application of § 426 BGB. To this variety of answers we must add one more: German academics, almost in their entirety, prefer a liability rule that limits D1's liability to the amount of the loss due to his fault and avoids all further actions. But in English Common law terms such a solution would be contrary to the rule which renders each joint tortfeasor liable for the entire harm of the claimant.[32]

This last-mentioned position does not seem to be the one currently taken by most American courts. The loss of consortium claims, frequently litigated in the United States, suggests another approach very similar to that preferred by German *academics* (but not German courts). The current tendency in the United States thus seems to treat the claims of P (usually the wife) against D1 as being 'independent' but to reduce them to take into account the contributory negligence of the physically injured spouse (D2).[33] Since familial immunities—wherever they are recognised—mean that P cannot sue D2 for his share, and since the American courts have now in their majority come to accept that the action against D1 is limited to his share of the loss, contribution claims between D1 and D2 do not appear to be prevalent.[34] In practice this means that the usual rules of joint tortfeasors (which

30 BGH 1 March 1988, BGHZ 103, 338, 346 *ff*; *Palandt, Bürgerliches Gesetzbuch* (60th edn 2001), no 426.

31 BGH 27 June 1961, BGHZ 35, 317, 323–24 (though this earlier case law may still apply to other factual instances).

32 This may be the reason why in the context of psychiatric injury the Law Commission took a somewhat negative position; see the report on *Liability for Psychiatric Illness* (1998), Law Com No 249, para 5.39. The Commission does not appear to have considered the various alternatives canvassed in Germany on this point.

33 See *Blagg v Illinois FWD Truck and Equipment Company* 572 NE 2d, 920 (1991), with references at p 925; *Feltch v General Rental Co*, 383 Mass 603, 421 NE 2d 67 (1981), reviewing the contradictory American case law; and *Handeland v Brown*, 216 NW 2d 574 (Iowa 1974), where the conflicting views of the majority and the dissent repay careful reading and reveal that many of the problems in American law may be linked to the differing views adopted towards contributory and comparative negligence. Imputed contributory negligence is discussed in detail in Gregory/Kalven/Epstein, pp 716 *ff* (esp pp 730 *ff*) and Harper/Fleming/James Jr/Gray, vol II, chs 8.8 and 8.9. For England see *Mallett v Dunn* [1949] 2 KB 180.

34 Like all such statements about American law this too has to be qualified by mentioning the fact that decisions do exist suggesting that the claimant (main defendant) can sue the primary victim for his share of the claimant's harm. See, eg, *American Motorcycle Assn v Superior Court* 20 Cal 3r 578, 591, 578 P 2d 899 (1978) and *Lantis v Condon* 95 Cal App 3r 152, 157 Cal Rptr 22 (1979). The *Lantis* facts, with the primary victim being 80 per cent responsible for his injuries, illustrate the need to shield the tortfeasor from the risk of carrying the entire loss. But as stated in the text, the solution of sharing the cost with the primary victim may not be the best since it essentially defeats any immunity that the law (or contract) may have given him towards the secondary victim. For an American case that makes precisely this point see *Feltch v General Rental Co* 421 NE 2d 67, 92 (Mass 1981).

entail that each of them is liable for the full amount of the claimant's loss) are never brought into play—a condition which would probably not be condoned by English law.

5. THE AMERICAN DIMENSION

The American dimension is interesting for a number of reasons.

We already noted the paucity of the English material. This means that if we need guidance from within the Common law we must turn to the law in the United States, well known for its richness. Strangely, the richness is there, though not in the context of nervous shock claims such as the one we have been considering here. Nor, indeed, do we find much guidance within the context of rescue situations where the same issues may again arise (rescuer/P in our example sues tortfeasor/D1, whose fault caused rescuee's/D2's injuries—can the rescuee's fault be put forward to reduce the damages due to the rescuer?). But the number of decisions found in consortium litigation is so numerous that more than guidance can be found from the study of their many pages. More precisely, what can be found are two things.

First is the lesson mentioned above, namely that D1 pays but pays only for his contribution to the claimant's loss. As stated, this is different from making him liable for everything and then leaving him to assume the risk of obtaining a contribution from D—the other cause of the P's loss. The American solution is thus not just different from the one adopted by German courts; it is also quite close to that advocated by German academics. Clearly, future English courts have a choice; and it is important to know the pros and cons of each alternative. Once again, we will gain if we look abroad for arguments on points which we have not yet fully addressed. And they should be that much easier to evaluate now that we have tried to set the *Greatorex* discussion against a wider canvass. Bit by bit the pieces of the puzzle fall into place.

But the American cases also hold a further lesson for the foreign observer. Quite simply, they illustrate that the law is a seamless web—a point which is crucial to grasp since it accustoms lawyers (especially comparatists) to seek the explanation of an 'unusual' rule in one part of the law and the accepted principles in another. German tort law and restitution are prime areas of private law which display this need to link different parts of the Code in order to understand a particular solution and then compare it profitably with the equivalent foreign rule.

Thus, in the United States the answer given to our question is to a large extent determined by the rules that are found in other parts of the law of torts. In our scenario what type of rule any particular State adopts towards (a) contributory negligence; (b) joint tortfeasors; and (c) family immunities will influence the solution adopted. The realisation that the law is a seamless web is a valuable one for both the student and the practitioner. The difficulties the coincidence of these rules gives rise to, however, also provide a salutary warning about the dangers of comparative law.

Take the well-known case of *Handeland v Brown*,[35] a decision of the Supreme Court of Iowa dated 27 March 1974. The *main* action involved the loss of consortium claims brought by the father (P) of a young motorcyclist (D2) injured in a traffic accident as a result of a

[35] 216 NW 2d 574 (1974).

collision with a vehicle (D1) at a road intersection. The jury entered a verdict for D1, rejecting the young man's (D2's) claim because of his own negligence. The claimant's father requested an instruction to the effect that his son's negligence could not be imputed to him, but the jury again found for D1. P's appeal to the Supreme Court of Iowa was thus concerned only with this claim. The appeal was successful.

What strikes the reader of this decision is how focused the majority judgment was in its attempts to reject the argument that the father's action was derivative. Like other courts before it, the Iowa court was keen to show that 'the gist of the parental action . . . is a wrong done to the parent in consequence of injury to his child by the actionable negligence of another'.[36] The result was that the damages claimable would not/should not be reduced to take into account D2's fault. An interesting dissent questioned this view to the extent that it would allow the parent of a child injured largely by its own fault to claim full damages from the tortfeasor whose fault had, say, contributed only 10% to the child's harm. It is only here, in a mere three lines,[37] that we find any reference to the contributory negligence rule as a possible reason for this construction. But this sentence, almost a throwaway line, made the leading author and his American students review the judgment and the law in Iowa at the time of the *Handeland* decision. And the prevailing rule then was the old rule of contributory negligence. If that had been applied without further thought in *Handeland*, the court would have been compelled to reject the father's claim as being contaminated by his son's fault.

Seen in this light, the decision is thus not really about whether the parents' claim is independent (which it is) or derivative but how one can ensure that it is not defeated by the child's fault and the old rule about contributory negligence. The problem with such an interpretation, however, is that (a) though it is arguably the true reason for the judgment, it finds few clues in the majority opinion to support it, and (b) if few students or practitioners—at any rate foreigners—notice this, much effort will indeed be diverted towards arguing whether the claim is independent or derivative. This is an arid attempt to define an essentially meaningless term. Yet the size of the American literature and the pages found in American decisional law on this subject[38] suggest that even American lawyers have fallen into this trap and carried out the definitional debate.

Another case that had proceeded in precisely the same manner was *Rollins v General American Transportation Corp.*[39] There, too, the court was confronted by two actions: one by a physically injured man (D2), who had contributed through his negligence to his hurt; and the other a consortium claim by his spouse (P). Both were rejected because of the fault of D2. In that case, too, the discussion centred on the independent or derivative nature of the spouse's claim, saying little of the real issue that must have worried the court. The reasoning was yet again essentially adopted in *Plocar v Dunkin Donuts of America Inc*,[40] another loss of consortium case.

[36] *Ibid* at p 578.

[37] 'Such a result seems unjust. Application of comparative negligence would most adequately rectify the injustice, but we do not have comparative negligence *in such cases*.' We have italicised the last few words of the quotation because to a foreign reader they seem to be confusing insofar as they imply that in the early 1970s Iowa knew the rule of comparative negligence *in other types of cases*. So far as we know, this was not the case.

[38] Conveniently collected in ALR 4th, vol 25. Michael DiSabatino, the author of the annotation, thus remarks on p 9 that '(T)he reason *most often advanced* for denying a spouse or parent recovery for loss of consortium where the physically injured spouse or child has been contributorily negligent is that the consortium action is derived from the physically injured spouse or child's cause of action' (italics supplied). The ALR annotation is up to date to September 2000.

[39] 46 Ill App 2d 266, 197 NE 2d 68 (1964).

[40] 103 Ill App 3rd 740, 748, 431 NE 2d 1175.

By now, however, Illinois (as most States in the late 1970s and 1980s) was moving towards the comparative negligence rule.[41] Our cases missed the significance of the shift, perhaps because the consortium rule had never been openly linked to contributory negligence but, instead, been obscured by the debate over the independent or derivative nature of the claim. Then, 10 years later, came *Blagg v Illinois FWD Truck and Equipment Company*[42]; and the court had to revisit the consortium rule. Happily it did; and did so in an open way when it said:

> The aforementioned cases [*Rollins* and *Plocar*] . . . were decided prior to Alvis and thus were based on contributory negligence principles. Today the absolute bar to recovery for loss of consortium that formerly existed must be reviewed under comparative negligence principles.

The result of the change, however, was obvious; and in line with the bulk of American States[43] where

> the loss of consortium award [is] reduced by the comparative negligence of the physically injured spouse.

To re-assert what had thus far been kept (almost) under wraps, the court concluded with the statement:

> The *Alvis* decision, and the advent of comparative negligence principles, has subsequently reduced the harsh effects of contributory negligence by the physically injured spouse, as the loss-of-consortium plaintiff is no longer barred from recovery.[44]

The discussion about independent or derivative claims is thus now for all intents and purposes dépassé. So, if this were the only lesson to be derived from these American decisions, it would be of limited value. On the educational front, its interest would lie in the need to remind students (and sometimes practitioners) that the answer in one part of the law (consortium claims) is determined by the position adopted in another (joint tortfeasors rules). On the practical front, however, the lesson derived from these decisions remains valid if definitively unresolved. And it consists in the decision to de facto set aside the rules about joint tortfeasors and, as already stated, reduce P's entitlement against D1 *by the comparative negligence of D2*.[45] To English (and Continental European) eyes this may look like a replacement of the 'full liability' that applies to joint tortfeasors by a 'proportionality rule'. But, given that in this case there is a special relationship between claimant and primary victim, the departure from the rule may be justified.[46]

[41] *Alvis v Ribar* 85 Ill 2d 1, 421 NE 2d 886 (1981).

[42] 143 Ill 2d 188, 572 NE 2d 920 (1991).

[43] Collected by the court at p 925.

[44] *Ibid* at p 926. A similar statement, significantly tucked away in a footnote, can be found in the judgment of the Supreme Court of Colorado in *Lee v Colorado Department of Health* 718 P 2d 221, 231, text and note 8 (Colo 1986).

[45] See *Eggert v Working* 599 P 2d 1389 (Alaska 1979); *Turnbow v Wasden* 608 F Supp 237 (D Nev 1985); *Lee v Colorado Department of Health* 718 P 2d 221 (Colo 1986); *Quadrone v Pasco Petroleum Co* 156 Ariz 415, 752 P 2d 504 (1988); and *Blagg v Illinois FWD Truck and Equipment Company* 572 NE 2d 920 (Ill 1991).

[46] The shift from the full liability to a 'proportional liability' rule was considered and rejected by the Law Commission in a paper it presented in 1966 for the DTI entitled *Feasibility Investigation of Joint and Several Liability*.

6. SOME TENTATIVE CONCLUSIONS

Some academics in the UK—notably Sir Roy Goode—have preached all their lives the case for a closer co-operation between judges, practitioners, and academics. We have been converted to this creed from the outset of our respective careers, and have since tried to apply it to the study and comparison of legal systems. How well it can work can be seen by *Greatorex*; and this for a number of reasons. Here are eight.

First, German law influenced the English decision because a practitioner—counsel for the MIB—used its ideas to construct his own argument before the English court. The practitioner was, in turn, able to access and evaluate positively this foreign material because it was made available to him by an academic lawyer in a form that was useable on this side of the Channel. This, incidentally, may also explain why German (instead of French or Italian law) served as a model here, for no French or Italian material on the subject is (so far as we know) available in English. The experience of neither of these systems could thus be used as a source of ideas. This is no mean point to stress over and over again, especially in order to rebut the predilection of some of our colleagues to advise the use of laws coming from 'radically different cultures'. If French law has not addressed this issue in the detail that German law has, can anyone be serious in suggesting to lawyers, especially practising lawyers, to seek their inspiration and guidance from less well known or developed systems? If the word 'academic' has a pejorative connation, this is precisely the kind of situation to which it could apply.

Secondly, German law became attractive to the English practitioners and the judge because it was served to these 'consumers' in an easily digestible way. For the material came in the form of a judicial decision which had facts that bore considerable resemblance to those of the English litigation and thus cried out for comparison to all but the most narrow-minded. Luck determines the outcome of every human enterprise; and as luck would have it, the protagonists in the *Greatorex* case were willing to take ideas irrespective of their national origin. But there is no denying the fact that another counsel or another judge might not have been so diligent in his research or open-minded towards foreign products. The influence that judicial mentality and outlook can have on the outcome of litigation (including, of course, the use or non-use of foreign law) is attracting growing interest in the United States but is still terra incognita in England.[47]

Thirdly, in *Greatorex* luck favoured the comparatist in yet another way. The inspiration or transplantation of foreign thinking was not hindered by one of those Germanic terms that are untranslatable and thus so off-putting to those unaccustomed to the demands that the Germanic culture makes on the intellect of the potential borrower![48] To be sure, as the theory of 'transferred loss' shows (in German: *Schadensverlagerung*), even such notions, provided that they are intrinsically valuable, can penetrate a foreign legal system. Some help from academic quarters can, again, help overcome problems associated with their abstract nature. If another illustration is needed, think of *Drittwirkung*. Ten years ago there was

[47] See Sir Basil Markesinis, 'Judicial Mentality: Mental Disposition or Outlook as a Factor Impeding Recourse to Foreign Law', 89 *Tulane L Rev* No 4, pp 1325–75 (2006).

[48] The leading author has recently argued that German jurists must make an effort to make their rich ideas more exportable if they wish to compete successfully on the international market of ideas and cultural influence; see Sir Basil Markesinis, *Festschrift Canaris* (2007).

hardly an English lawyer who was alive to the problem, let alone the concept. Now, the literature it is generating is almost excessive.

But let us return to the German decision. There the Federal Court had refused to hold that a person was under a duty not to injure or kill himself since such a duty would infringe his autonomy.[49] Such language could easily slide into the English legal reasoning as it began its search for a duty of care as a basis for a tortious obligation to make amends. Indeed, reading *Greatorex* one is left with the feeling that it did so without any jarring—linguistic or conceptual. This is an immensely significant observation for anyone translating foreign legal documents and then hoping to use them in court.

Yet, fourthly, the English court looked only at one side of German law; indeed, it could not have done more since counsel drew the judge's attention to the German decision but nothing else. The English court was thus not made aware that the German result might, in some instances, have also been reached by utilising the immunity conferred by § 1359 BGB.[50] This alludes to the policy reasons, which also weighed heavily in Cazalet J's mind (family relationships) and militate against allowing a legal action. Why did the German court refuse to go down that path?

We can only speculate; but at least three reasons spring to the mind of an outside observer. First, as already stated, §1359 BGB does not apply to car accident cases for the reasons that we know from our law as well. Secondly, the accident in the 1971 nervous shock case was caused by D2's 'gross' negligence and this would have defeated the immunity given by § 1359 BGB. Finally, the court might have wished to create in such cases an immunity that went beyond the family relationships covered by § 1359 BGB. If it did, the result would be that facts such as those encountered in the Australian case *FAI General Insurance Co Ltd v Lucre*[51] would receive the same answer: no duty and hence no liability.

Since *Greatorex* followed the (wider)reasoning, does the same result now hold true for English law? Would a claim by P, who was unrelated to D2, likewise fail? On the other hand, would the outcome be affected by the fact that Cazalet's policy points would be inapplicable to our hypothetical? *Greatorex*, as we keep saying, has left a number of points open, even though it has done a good job in alerting us to new ways of looking at them. If the Germans have discovered too many (subtly different) ways of solving this problem, we, in England, have not even addressed it!

Fifthly, all of the above could not have been undertaken, and the chances of the German ideas influencing the case would have been slim, had the attempt at legal borrowing gone through Codes or academic writings. For even the briefest consultation of the German treatises reveals the discussion in Germany to be theoretical and conceptual in the extreme.[52]

[49] It will be remembered from note 14 above that § 1359 BGB could, in some instances, have served as another way of ensuring the immunity of D2 towards P (this immunity being based on the policy reasons appropriate to the D2/P relationship). These reasons figured in Cazalet J's decision—but not in the German judgment, which chose to justify the non-liability rule by reference to human autonomy. One (further) consequence of this justification is that it ensures that the non-liability rule applies even where there is no family relationship between D2 and P. This is exactly what happened in the Australian case of *FAI General Insurance Co v Lucre* [2000] NSWCA 346; and the verdict there was for the claimant.

[50] There is a problem, however, with the immunity rule contained in § 1359 BGB—its application depends on the status of marriage and not the closeness of the relationship between P and D2.

[51] [2000] NSWCA 346 (decision of 29 November 2000). There, the car accident between D1 and D2 was, again, entirely due to D2's fault. In this case, however, there was no family or other relationship between P and D2; P's claim for his post-traumatic stress disorder succeeded.

[52] Eg Larenz, *Lehrbuch des Schuldrechts I* (13th edn 1982), § 37; Thiele, 'Gesamtschuld und Gesamtschuldnerausgleich', *JuS* 1968, 149; Medicus, 'Haftungsbefreiung und Gesamtschuldnerausgleich', *JZ* 1967, 398; and Medicus, *Schuldrecht I, Allgemeiner Teil* (10th edn 1998), Rn 793.

Had English counsel chosen that course, he would have found it bewildering both to himself and to the court. The fact that parts of German law were still left unused and unexplored does not matter. Further research may produce even more fruits next time around.

Sixthly, what about using the German decisions as a springboard for further study—a method which we have repeatedly described in this book? Yet, even this can only work if the German text is rendered with some sensibility towards the understanding abilities of a foreign audience. When the first of us called for a 'skilful (but well-meaning) manipulation'[53] of a text in order to reveal the hidden similarities, the statement brought howls of anguish from the usual quarters.[54] Maybe the word 'manipulation' (with its pejorative connotations) was not a fortunate choice since it gave opponents of the theory the chance to pounce. But the substance of what the first of us wrote almost 10 years ago remains, we think, valid when it comes to legal translations. For if they are literal, rendered word for word without a conscious attempt to make the substance of the text intelligible and (perhaps) usable, they will fail in law even if they get high marks for accuracy. Those who have studied—not just read—the translation work of Tony Weir will have noticed how much emphasis is placed on the flow of his rendering of the very rigid original German texts even if at times this means sacrificing absolute literary accuracy.[55]

Seventhly, the above would not, of course, preclude recourse to American law as an alternative source of inspiration. But here, again, without appropriate academic preparation, the American material might reveal only part of the picture and thus make suitable inspiration dubious. The dangers are two. For the civilian lawyer, the difference of comparative and contributory negligence would be entirely missed, while the English lawyer, confident that he is reading a language he can understand, might let his guard down and assume that contributory negligence in America has the same meaning as it has in his own country. The hint that our highest courts cannot understand American law without the occasional assistance of academics could be seen as disrespectful towards them. Yet, if anyone thinks so, he must be reminded how the House of Lords in *Murphy*[56] 'misunderstood' the law in the United States and treated a decision of the US Supreme Court resolving a dispute between two circuits as representing the law of torts in America. It was thus a cosmopolitan judge[57] who pointed this out in no uncertain terms in an academic article; and as fate would have it, he was later to join their lordships as a judge.

The lesson of all of this is that the fact that foreign legal material is accessible to us in linguistic terms does not mean that it can be transplanted into our system without thought, caution, and preparation. In our view we are on the verge of forgetting this warning if we go on looking at the theology of the First Amendment in an uncritical manner. But that is for another day!

[53] Basil S Markesinis, 'Why a Code is Not the Best Way to Advance the Cause of European Legal Unity', (1997) 5 *European Review of Private Law*, 519 *ff.*

[54] See Gerhard Dannemann, 'Similarities and Differences' in *The Oxford Handbook of Comparative Law* (2006), p 395 and note 59 (citing Legrand).

[55] BGH of 1 March 1988 (BGHZ 103, 338)—a key case on the legal points discussed in the text above—shows the problems of translating a decision into English which deals with a complex legal point familiar only to German lawyers. We submit that a common lawyer would have great difficulty in following what is being said if he relied only on a translation and was left unaided by the kind of supporting text found in this Chapter. Is the task of such translation difficult? From a translator's point of view, we would say that it is near impossible. But the effort of understanding the point discussed in this case is worth the trouble since it not only shows the degree of sophistication of German legal thought but may also one day help an English court decide what *Greatorex* left undecided.

[56] [1991] 1 AC 398.

[57] Sir Robin (now Lord) Cooke in his 'An Impossible Distinction', (1991) 107 LQR 46 *ff.*

The final point places the case against the wider contemporary discussions about comparative law. Its literature is growing; and Europe, one way or another, is the greatest stimulus. Directives, case law from Luxembourg and Strasbourg, private initiatives to formulate general principles (or 'soft law' as it is sometimes called)—we have it all these days. And yet at the lowest level of a single case that could arise in any country of the so-called 'western' world, we find an illustration which shows how types of reasoning can travel easily if they are packaged in user-friendly ways to those that matter and solve practical problems. That our packaging is creative does not mean that it misrepresents the foreign law. On the contrary, it increases the chances of it having a radiant effect beyond its own system.

Our example also shows that some systems have studied the underlying issues more deeply than others. In this instance, the Germans were ahead of the English (though their thought processes are highly complex). On a different matter, for instance a problem of commercial law such as securitisation, English law might be seen to be more flexible than, say, its French counterpart. The borrowing at specific, pragmatic levels might not have the allure that comes with grand theories; but *Greatorex* suggests that the methodology here advocated not only works: it works well enough to offer an efficient springboard for the further study and understanding of foreign law. And at this stage the endeavour is not only a practical one; it also acquires a worthwhile intellectual component. Those who think that a cosmopolitan approach to law is bound to lack in depth are, we believe, proved to be utterly wrong by this case study. And so are those who fear that 'functional specificity' sacrifices wider cultural studies to the altar of a narrow fact-based problem. For this approach does *not* hinder such wider studies; it simply allows the expositor to bring them in bit by bit as the research fans out to encompass other things. Our studies on privacy and the wider right of personality have shown how this can be done.[58]

Finally, has the work started by *Greatorex* come to a conclusion? We have already alluded to the fact that the point seems to be open if in the next case P and D2 are not related. German academics also seem to be divided as to ambit of the 1988[59] decision which decided the contribution claim between tortfeasors and held that D1 had to carry all the cost to P.[60] The successful completion of the work started by Cazalet J might, once again, be aided by the proper consideration of foreign law. This is the eighth and last point that emerges from *Greatorex*. For though the case made a good start in addressing the complex kind of legal problems that arise in these triangular situations, it did not completely finish the job it started.

The tail end of the judgment—where the extent of liability of the potential defendant is considered—is thus notably hurried, and the only legitimate and convincing explanation one can offer for this is that the resolution of this problem was not necessary to the facts of *Greatorex*. Future courts will thus have to consider whether the same rules apply to cases where D2 is, for other reasons, immune to an action from the secondary victim or, alternatively, protected by an exemption clause.[61] More importantly, our courts will also have to mull over the question whether it is better to allow P to sue D1 for all the loss (and then

[58] See, eg, chs 7, 8 and 11 in BS Markesinis, *Always on the Same Path. Essays on Foreign Law and Comparative Methodology*, vol 2 (2001).

[59] BGHZ 103, 338.

[60] Contrary to the early decision of BGHZ 35, 317 which had allowed D1 to claim a contribution against D2. It must be remembered that BGHZ 56, 163 (the 1971 nervous shock case that guided the English decision) was decided against the background of BGHZ 35, 317 (handed down in 1961).

[61] Which was not the case in *Greatorex* but was considered by the German Federal Court in BGHZ 12, 213 (= NJW 1972, 942).

leave it to D1 to obtain contribution from D2 if he can) or only obtain from D1 the amount which is due to his share of the blame. These writers' preference is for the second option, which is also favoured by German academe and many of the more recent American decisions (ie 'proportional liability'). But the study of German and American law also suggests that there are other solutions (though the theoretical merits of each option seem to have been studied only by German academics).

In the light of the above, the English practitioner can only benefit from dwelling further on foreign, especially German, law. And if this time the dip is into complex German theory and not just case law, it can at least be done with greater confidence since *Greatorex* has successfully broken new ground in the area of comparative law in English courts. To put it differently and in wider terms, the comparative approach to common problems rarely (if ever) runs out of interesting variations, disproving the narrow-minded conviction of many national lawyers that theirs is the only way of doing things. But if one translated case can give rise to so much thought, imagine what could happen if the other 150 decisions found in the same book that provided the German translation for *Greatorex* were subjected to the same kind of scrutiny in search for new ideas and directions. The authors of this book, if no one else, must surely be allowed the hope that this may happen.

10

COMPARATIVE LAW IN COMMERCIAL PRACTICE

1. COMMERCIAL INTERESTS IN A GLOBALISED ENVIRONMENT

Driving out to the airport from the centre of Cairo one encounters a giant mural depicting David Beckham, the English football icon. The image promotes one of the many products that sports companies with a worldwide distribution network hope to sell not only to fans in England, Spain or the United States (where Beckham is now earning his money playing 'soccer') but also to supporters living up and down the banks of the river Nile. Further down the road, an advertisement of Crédit Agricole invites one to join the bank's host of French customers, perhaps by taking out a loan and using the money to reclaim a few more precious metres of farmland from the desert. The taxi could be a Mercedes. The Egyptian driver may be wearing Ray-Ban sunglasses and checking the departure times on a Nokia mobile. You are enjoying a Coca-Cola. All of this sounds rather familiar despite the exotic setting, and the ingredients of this international commercial cocktail are indeed not likely to be very different whichever airport one happens to be using. Upon arrival at one's destination, be it London, New York or Singapore, one is likely to see the same sports products on display, the same banks promoting their financial services, and the same types of car on the street. Needless to say Coca-Cola is omnipresent—it being reported that a vending machine had also once been found in the Gobi desert!

In this day and age, the global marketplace described above is, in itself, hardly worth a comment—indeed, goods and services have been traded and offered across ever-increasing distances for such a long time that travellers are today used to encounter the same products regardless of their whereabouts. With companies such as Starbucks opening more than 500 new outlets in all parts of the world every year, it is by now actually more surprising if a certain item (be it coffee, a newspaper, an internet search engine, or a particular credit arrangement) were *not* available at practically any given location on this planet.[1]

There is, however, more to globalisation than meets the eye. Besides creating new commercial opportunities, the global marketplace has also brought new challenges—for governments hoping to secure employment for their citizens or save national industries from being swallowed up by foreign (and often publicly funded) competitors; for public authorities wishing to protect the health and safety of local consumers against hazards caused by substandard imports; for international law firms offering advice in cross-border commercial transactions[2]; or for national judges increasingly confronted with disputes of an international nature.

[1] Coca-Cola (established in 1886) thus entered the Chinese market as early as 1927, and currently records huge growth rates not only in Egypt but also in Pakistan, China and Russia. See *The Times*, London, 18 July 2007, p 45.

[2] With an estimated value of $1.38 trillion in Europe in the first six months of 2007, mergers and acquisitions, in particular, continue to require a huge amount of cross-border legal expertise; see *International Herald Tribune*—London edition—of 25 July 2007, pp 9, 11. This has provided a strong incentive for Anglo-American law firms to forge alliances with continental European counterparts.

Globalisation has also created new opportunities and challenges for comparative law. We have in this book frequently emphasised the triangular relationship between the judge, the practising lawyer, and the academic, and have tried to define and develop our subject through a highly practical lens. This Chapter will add to our cast of players two further characters: the 'in-house comparatist' in large national companies or multinational enterprises,[3] who—when providing legal support for his colleagues in research and development, production, or distribution—is often confronted with cross-border issues, and his non-litigating, consulting counterpart in legal practice.

Focusing on these players seems to us a worthwhile task. While the odd reference to foreign jurisdictions in court judgments can attract wider attention,[4] in-house lawyers and practitioners performing a purely transactional role are only rarely found in the limelight. Theirs is a backstage role, though no less important for that. And the limited academic attention given to this kind of lawyer is in stark contrast to the practical importance of their work; for the worldwide use of foreign law by in-house legal counsel and external legal advisers must add up to countless daily engagements with foreign law which may or may not, in the end, be obvious in the final 'product'. A large fraction of law students graduating from most universities will be employed by companies with an increasingly international portfolio of activities. The in-house lawyers of Red Bull at the company's headquarters in Austria thus handle and coordinate its extensive trademark matters in roughly 200 jurisdictions worldwide; and internet providers (such as Google or Yahoo! Inc) likewise employ several hundred full-time lawyers in each of their legal departments across the globe to deal with problems that present an international aspect (*in addition* to the external advice sought from international law firms in every major country these search engines operate in). Needless to say, the litigation department is only one of many practice groups in larger law firms, and the majority of clients seek and receive legal advice on matters that are preferably resolved outside the courtroom. Detailed empirical data, if ever compiled, would no doubt confirm that these two groups of lawyers, working across all major sectors of the economy—including mergers and acquisitions, banking, insurance, the internet, or the shipping and airline industries (to name but a few)—come into direct contact with foreign law on a very regular basis. How they deal with this challenge is one of the *untold* stories of a subject with a growing importance.

That said, a distinction should be drawn between the use of *foreign law* and *comparative methodology*, for we are here predominantly concerned with the latter. Do in-house lawyers and their outside legal counsel thus really work *comparatively*? Or is their contact with foreign jurisdictions 'compartmentalised' in the sense that each national market is kept insulated from other countries a particular company might engage in? While questions involving purely foreign law will inevitably arise in the legal departments of most large enterprises and legal consultancies, we can identify at least three areas which also generate an increasing demand for *comparative* experience in commercial legal practice.

[3] Here understood in a broad sense as entities which are able to locate productive facilities and trade across national borders, thereby using their know-how in foreign markets to exploit varying local conditions to their best advantage. For a full discussion of the term see Peter T Muchlinski, *Multinational Enterprises and the Law* (2nd edn 2007), pp 3 *ff*.

[4] See, eg, Austen L Parrish, 'Storm in a Teacup: The US Supreme Court's Use of Foreign Law', [2007] 2 *Illinois Law Review* 637 *ff* on the discussions about the occasional use of comparative law by the US Supreme Court.

(a) Standardisation

There is, first, the simple fact that a given product—be it a commodity or service—is most profitable if it can be designed on a 'one size fits all' basis. Ideally, manufacturers produce goods which can be sold across the globe; a single contract template is designed to cover transactions wherever the customer of a company is located; and one entry into Google produces the same listings wherever the search engine is accessed by a user. This may still be possible in many cases (the Ray-Ban sunglasses in the above scenario might actually qualify), but for an increasing number of products and services, specific national rules will require more or less extensive modifications depending on the geographical target area. Many examples where national laws need to be taken into account in the development or marketing departments of companies with an international reach quickly come to mind—local differences in consumer protection law will require different labelling, with different levels of information about the ingredients, health hazards, or the appropriate use of particular products[5]; local health and safety or environmental standards will necessitate changes to many technical items ranging from toasters to mobile phones, cars or computers; different data protection laws will allow or limit the use of personal information acquired in the course of business transactions[6]; different laws concerning the protection of minors, online gambling, free speech, or intellectual property will force internet providers to insulate restrictive markets from the more liberal regimes[7]; religious rules will require

[5] See, eg, the difficulties that cigarette producers are facing with regulatory measures in the United States and Europe. The tightening regulatory environment in the United States, where the US Food and Drug Administration is expected to take regulatory control of the tobacco industry, was thus one of the reasons for Altira Group, the world's largest cigarette producer, to break up into Philip Morris USA and Philip Morris International; see *The Times*—London—of 30 August 2007, p 47.

[6] The United States and the European Union have for some time now been engaged in battles over air passenger information, scrutiny of international financial transactions, and forced corporate disclosures to US regulators and courts. While serious conflicts were resolved by a series of ad hoc agreements and compromises, data protection and competition law will inevitably lead to further confrontation between the two systems. This has led to calls for a global privacy standard.

[7] In recent years, a number of major United States internet service providers like Yahoo!, America On-Line and CompuServe have thus faced civil or criminal proceedings initiated in the European courts. These proceedings related to questionable content, especially racist or pornographic material they hosted or gave access to and which is lawful in the United States, but contravenes the laws of another country in which it is equally accessible: *Yahoo! v Licra* concerned a civil lawsuit filed against Yahoo! Inc in 2000 by two French civil liberties groups on the basis that Nazi memorabilia was being sold by third parties on Yahoo's US auction site. The French court issued a judgment that ordered Yahoo to 'render impossible' access by persons in France to Nazi-related content on servers located in the United States. The justification for asserting the application of French law was that Yahoo's auction site was accessible in France and therefore had its effect there. Yahoo! did not appeal the French court's decision but sought a declaration of the Federal California court, which granted a declaration that the French judgment could not be enforced within the US as such enforcement would contravene the free speech provisions of the First Amendment of the United States constitution (*Yahoo! Inc v La Ligue Contra Le Racisme et L'Antisemitisme*). The French civil liberties groups, supported by a friend-of-the-court brief (*Amicus curiae Yahoo!*) by industry and public interest organisations, appealed the decision to the 9th Circuit US Court of Appeal, which reversed the lower court's ruling. To avoid further litigation Yahoo! Inc banned the sale of Nazi-related materials on all its auction sites (including the US website). However, this did not prevent the former CEO of Yahoo!, Tim Koogle, from being arrested in France and facing charges of justifying war crimes before a criminal court in Paris, which were later dismissed. In *AG v CompuServe*, the German subsidiary of CompuServe provided its German subscribers with access to newsgroups of a paedophile nature which were hosted by the CompuServe Inc in the United States. Following a police investigation in Germany, the German authorities ordered CompuServe Germany to block access for German users to 282 newsgroups. Access to these newsgroups was initially blocked by CompuServe Inc worldwide (not just for German users), which led to widespread protests that German standards of morality were being 'imposed'. As a result CompuServe Inc restored access to most of the newsgroups as it did not regard them as being illegal under US law. Following this, the German prosecutor brought charges against the CEO of CompuServe Germany, Felix Somm, for facilitating access to violent, child and animal pornography, thus contravening the

banks to adapt their western business models to the predominant customs in other parts of the world (and, due to the increasing immigration of potential customers, also in Europe and the United States[8]); and in the area of contract law, terms and conditions or penalty clauses will have to be adapted to the particular mandatory rules found in the systems a company might wish to conduct its business in. With the emergence of more sophisticated production techniques, combined with equally developed methods for the analysis of foodstuffs, even agricultural products will today require careful legal consideration if they are to be marketed outside their country of origin. Genetically modified crops are thus still anathema in most European societies while increasingly common in the United States[9]; and the world's largest food exporter, China, has recently run into serious difficulties not only with the health and safety standards of toothpaste, children's toys, vinyl baby bibs, computer and mobile phone batteries, car tyres, and medical products, but also with the level of pesticide residue and other chemicals discovered in meat and fish products by health authorities in the United States and the European Union.[10] Needless to repeat again, different standards apply in the US and in many of the EU's 27 Member States.

What emerges, then, is the image of a shrinking world in which means of transport and communication are able to cover great distances in short periods of time *but in which national laws continue to pose substantial—and at times even increasing—obstacles to many commercial activities.* A century ago, the challenge of bringing tea from China or wool from Australia to European markets was thus a logistical one, and sailing vessels like the famous *Cutty Sark* provided the decisive competitive edge. Today, the same products can be brought to London, Paris or Berlin with great physical ease, but they will only reach the shops if produced, packaged and labelled according to national and European consumer protection standards. These standards—and the legal risks involved if things go wrong—require careful consideration and can substantially reduce the attraction which our 'globalised' world holds for many companies.[11] This applies to both sides of the equator, as a

German Act on Dissemination of Publications Morally Harmful to Youths. In 1998, the Amtsgericht Munich convicted Mr Somm to two years of a suspended prison sentence with three years probation, and fined him DM 100,000—a ruling which was reversed a year later but left internet companies wary of cross-jurisdictional issues.

[8] Professor Patrick Glenn thus mentions the US law firm of King & Spalding, which in 1994 created an Islamic finance and investment practice group in order to meet the standards set by Shari'a (see H Patrick Glenn, 'Comparative Law and Legal Practice: On Removing the Borders' (2001) 75 *Tulane L Rev* 977 at 991. In the United Kingdom, too, Islamic law is increasingly influential in the finance sector. The UK Treasury thus estimates that Islamic assets top £125 billion worldwide, and has recently announced a review of all types of government-sponsored savings products in order to make them accessible to those who adhere to Shari'a; see *The Times*—London—of 23 April 2007, p 26 and, more generally, the *Times* Islamic Banking Focus Report of 26 April 2006. Inheritance law is another area where knowledge of both UK taxation rules and Islamic law is of importance in order to provide Shari'a-compliant financial and legal advice. For information on the introduction of an immediate inheritance tax and its effect on the estates of Muslims in the UK see *The Sunday Times*—London—of 7 May 2006, p 10.

[9] The second of the authors was recently involved in a comparative study for the European Commission on the regulation of genetically modified organisms (GMOs) across the 27 Member States of the European Union. Currently, only 1 per cent of the world's genetically modified food is grown in Europe while 55 per cent of the world's acreage in genetically modified crops is located in the United States (where no distinction is made between modified and traditional varieties). The restrictive stance of the EU, which had banned genetically modified crops and food between 1998 and 2004, has led to considerable tension with the United States. The World Trade Organisation (WTO) ruled in 2006 that the EU ban was tantamount to an illegal trade barrier. Seventy per cent of all Germans, however, say that they do not want GMOs in their food. This is commercially relevant since modified foodstuffs must be clearly labelled. A number of European countries, including Ireland, have announced that they wish to stay GM-free.

[10] See, eg, *International Herald Tribune*—London edition—of 9 July 2007, pp 1 and 5/6; 11 July 2007, pp 1 and 8.

[11] See, eg, the information given to UK exporters by UK Trade & Investment (a Government organisation set up to support UK companies on overseas business) on product liability in the United States: 'Product liability is

competition law dispute recently triggered by the Australian Competition and Consumer Commission involving search results provided by Google shows.[12] New internet technologies worth billions of US dollars have thus found *approval* by regulators in the United States and Europe but are *challenged* in other legal systems, or (as in the case of western internet technology in China) face substantial moral criticism 'back home' in terms of data protection and human rights standards if adapted to the legal and political circumstances prevailing in other markets.[13]

In this highly lucrative but equally complex game, the in-house lawyer and his outside legal consultant have to find the legal approach which will allow the product (be it a model contract, a commodity, or a search engine) to pass muster in a maximum number of systems—a puzzle which they can only hope to solve with the help of a comparative approach to law.

(b) Forum Shopping

A second area which requires not only knowledge of foreign law but also comparative experience is traditionally called 'forum shopping'—a term indicating a search for the most

an issue that often causes great concern to British exporters to the United States. Since it can expose manufacturers, sellers, product designers or even licensers of technology to legal action, it is an area that exporters need to understand and protect themselves against. However, the good news is that there are effective steps that can be taken to reduce a company's exposure to product liability lawsuits. These steps involve an investment of time and money but can protect a business against future claims several times greater. It should be borne in mind that these costs fall equally upon all manufacturers, domestic and foreign, and therefore need to be seen as an in-built part of the cost of doing business in the market. The fact that there are over 7,000 UK companies successfully exporting to the US is evidence that these problems can be overcome and that the rewards in the world's largest single marketplace are well worth the effort.' See UK Trade & Investment, *US Product Liability Law* (2000), p 3.

[12] See *The Times*—London—of 13 July 2007, p 9.

[13] Yahoo! Inc is thus under considerable public pressure and congressional scrutiny for having provided Chinese authorities with details leading to the arrest and imprisonment of Shi Tao, a journalist who had used a Yahoo! e-mail account to send information concerning the Propaganda Department to a US-based organisation. The Chinese authorities identified the account and requested Yahoo! to disclose its holder. The company complied, apparently without knowledge concerning the background of the investigation. The House Committee on Foreign Affairs is expected to open a formal investigation into the matter (see *International Herald Tribune*—London edn—of 16 August 2007, p 13). The Congressional Testimony of Jack Krummholtz (Associate General Counsel and Managing Director, Federal Government Affairs, Microsoft Corporation) is revealing here: '[T]he Internet raises issues that often justify government attention, especially on matters of individual privacy, law enforcement, and national security. *On some of these issues, governments around the world have made differing judgments about the legal standards and policy trade-offs appropriate to their own cultures and national circumstances—in many cases issuing regulations or codes of conduct that define limits on permissible content and prescribe procedures for identifying authorship.* While the exercise of governmental responsibilities is usually well-intentioned and limited, it is critically important for the future of the Internet—and thereby for the future of the global community and economy as a whole—that all governments address these issues with deliberation and restraint. Legal and regulatory steps should be taken only with the utmost attention to their wider consequences—*including the impact on individuals, enterprises and societies far beyond the borders of the initiating countries.* International meetings and bilateral consultations may increasingly help to promote the consistency of national actions and to maximise the openness, security and reliability of the Internet platform. Indeed, the greatest influence over time on national policies affecting the Internet, including those of the Chinese Government, is likely to come from a combination of bilateral and multilateral processes of consultation and consensus-building. *But the global consultative process is only just beginning to unfold* [. . .] *Microsoft will continually review the overall value of our services in any particular country and the conditions created by government policies and practices. If we conclude that those practices undercut or completely compromise the value to customers of our services in that jurisdiction, we will consider withdrawing those services until such conditions improve.*' See Congressional Testimony, 'The Internet in China: A Tool for Freedom or Suppression?', House of Representatives, Committee on International Relations, Joint Hearing of the *Subcommittee on Africa, Global Human Rights & International Operations* and the *Subcommittee on Asia and the Pacific* of 15 February 2006 (emphasis added). The World Organisation for Human Rights has announced to sue Yahoo! on behalf of Chinese pro-democracy campaigners (see *The Guardian*—London—of 30 August 2007, p 3).

favourable legal location, often by plaintiffs and defendants in cases hinging on tort law. Though cast in a private international law guise, many questions arising here actually involve the *comparison* of (potential) outcomes in two or more legal systems, and are typically decided on very narrow points of law.[14] For many years, the United States were thus a favoured destination for foreign claimants in cases involving American-made products or industrial activities which have caused injury abroad; low legal costs based on the contingency fee system, the advantages of pre-trial discovery, the use of juries, and potentially higher damages often make the country's legal system seem more attractive than a foreigner's own.[15] Access to the jurisdiction was strongly reduced in the 1980s,[16] and courts are now reluctant to hear claims where victims have access to an appropriate foreign forum. The relevant public and private interests affected by this decision will,[17] however, still be taken into consideration in determining whether to dismiss a case or not,[18] and this will again involve some measure of comparison.[19] Both authors, active in the area of comparative tort law, have thus over the years been approached by plaintiffs and (typically corporate) defendants requiring a comparative analysis of the respective national rules involved in a case—the first group seeking access to American courts, and the latter trying to avoid them.[20]

While this first type of forum shopping (involving a search for the best place to litigate) will be conducted mostly by practitioners in international law firms, in-house lawyers perform quite a similar task in determining, for example, where to establish a firm's headquarters, set up production lines, market a company's goods, or dispose of its production waste. Today's world is thus not only a global *marketplace* but also an increasingly global *production site*—with research and development, raw production, end assembly, packaging, administration, marketing, and accounting *of one and the same company* often spread across a number of different countries depending on their particular local advantages.[21] Needless to say that the best combination of locations is again determined (in advance) not only by extra-legal factors such as access to raw materials, logistics, and wage levels, but also legal considerations resulting from the *comparison* of, inter alia, contract and tort law, company law, environmental standards, labour law, rules on accounting, levels of taxation, or the legal protection given to foreign investments. Even bankruptcy law is today a lively field for comparative work, with global 'court-shopping' leading to the relocation of company head-

[14] For a comprehensive discussion see, eg, Adrian Briggs, *Agreements on Jurisdiction and Choice of Law* (2008).

[15] See, eg, Russell J Weintraub, 'International Litigation and Forum Non Conveniens', 29 *Tex Int'l LJ* 322 (1997); D Robertson, 'The Federal Doctrine of Non Conveniens', Tex *Int'l LJ* 353 (1994) and 'Forum non conveniens in America and England: A Rather Fantastic Fiction', (1987) 103 *LQR* 398. Even the conservative German system is now considering a relaxation of its rigid fee system following a judgment of the Federal Constitutional Court, which recently declared unconstitutional the blanket ban of contingency fees as established by federal law; see BVerfG, 1 BvR 2576/04 of 12 December 2006. Not surprisingly, American experience played a role in the court's reasoning (see nos 72, 91 and 107 of the judgment).

[16] See *Piper Aircraft v Reyno* 454 US 235 (1981).

[17] In particular human rights infringements, which may fall under the special regimes, established by the Alien Tort Claims Act 1789 or the Torture Victim Prevention Act 1991.

[18] See, eg, *Gulf Oil v Gilbert* 330 US 501 (1947).

[19] For similar developments in the United Kingdom see *Smith Kline & French v Bloch* [1983] 2 All ER 72 (CA) and *SNI Aerospatiale v Lee Kui Jak* [1987] 3 All ER 510 (PC).

[20] The Union Carbide accident in India, which led to prolonged litigation, is one example of the type of scenario that we have in mind here. Modern class action cases are another.

[21] Examples from the European automobile industry include Aston Martin, Vauxhall, Daimler Chrysler, Volkswagen and Audi, all of which have shifted substantial parts of their production to eastern European, African and Asian locations. The operational headquarters of Yahoo's European activities are located in the UK while the financial administration is based in the Republic of Ireland.

quarters in order to pursue restructuring programmes which may be permissible under the rules of one country but prohibited by another.[22] In all of the above, the legal feasibility work that precedes the commercial decision does not only require the consideration of the legal regimes of more than one system; it also calls for the examination of the impact that the EU and other international regimes may have on national law. In short, it has become, more than ever, truly comparative in nature. The aim here is to find the best economic conditions for a particular activity, which includes a legal environment that will offer the best protection against being sued. Legal certainty, access to a functional court system, and—more generally—the stability of a legal order are thus also important (if not decisive) considerations.[23]

Choice of law decisions and international arbitration clauses are two special types of contractual forum shopping which deserve separate emphasis due to their enormous contemporary importance. Agreements which place the contractual relationships of the parties under a particular national law of their choice are today standard business practice in companies with a worldwide reach, and international arbitration has emerged as 'the accepted method for resolving international business disputes'[24] in order to avoid slow, unpredictable and/or expensive state court systems. Both mechanisms require the parties to make informed choices concerning the law which regulates a particular business relationship and—should this become necessary—the process of dispute resolution (ie national litigation or international arbitration). While the respective bargaining power of the parties will inevitably influence their preferred course of action, a careful legal comparison of the available alternatives is essential in both cases. Comparative work may later also influence the outcome of disputes, as 'arbitrators from different traditions bring their knowledge to bear on the dispute resolution process'.[25] The same is true if disputes are resolved through recourse to 'general principles of law', an open clause which will in turn require some degree of comparative assessment by arbitrators in order to determine its content in a particular context.[26]

(c) Internal Regulation

A third—perhaps less obvious—area for comparative work arises not from the interaction between commercial entities and the *outside* world as represented by regulators, commercial partners, or consumers (a common characteristic of our first two examples) but rather from the *internal* structure of multinational enterprises. The same considerations which militate for the worldwide use of a single contractual template or marketing of identical products across national borders thus also apply when it comes to the internal organisation of companies with a worldwide infrastructure.

[22] See *International Herald Tribune*—London edition—of 18 July 2007, p 12.

[23] Peter T Muchlinski, above note 3, pp 39/40.

[24] Yves Dezalay and Bryant G Garth, Dealing in Virtue: International Commercial Arbitration and the Construction of a Transnational Legal Order (1996), p 6; see also Stefan M Kröll, 'Arbitration', in Jan M Smits (ed), *Elgar Encyclopedia of Comparative Law* (2006), p 80: 'In particular for international commercial transactions today dispute resolution by arbitration is the rule and not the exception.' Estimates indicate that 90 per cent of all international contracts today contain arbitration clauses; see Gerard J Meyer, 'International Commercial Arbitration', in Marielle Kopenol-Laforce et al (eds), *International Contracts: Aspects of Jurisdiction, Arbitration and Private International Law* (1996), p 86.

[25] H Patrick Glenn, above note 6, p 998.

[26] *Ibid*, p 999.

While 'multinational enterprises' do not exist in positive law, they are today an economic and political reality. In practice, they will often attempt to develop a homogeneous set of rules which regulate internal procedures, codes of conduct, and terms of employment (including promotions, company health and pension schemes, paid leave, part-time work, or employee share options) *regardless* of the geographical location of a particular subsidiary.[27]

National law will, however, set limits to this corpus of internal regulation, and it is again the task of comparative lawyers to identify how far harmonisation can go, and where different countries will require separate (local) approaches. The Sarbanes-Oxley Act,[28] introduced in the United States following financial scandals such as the collapse of Enron, has thus required substantial adjustments to the internal control and auditing procedures of US companies which are not always in line with the requirements established by single European countries or the European Union.[29] More importantly, Sarbanes-Oxley has also extended national regulatory jurisdiction to *foreign* auditors when these act for companies listed in the United States, and requires subsidiaries *not* based in the country to comply with US monitoring, accounting, and auditing standards. In a globalised world, multinational enterprises operating in different markets cannot ignore these extraterritorial effects of national or regional law, and will often have to develop internal procedures which comply with the regulatory framework of more than one jurisdiction—a challenge which cannot be mastered without the help of comparative methodology. It is thereby quite irrelevant which of the various systems a particular company may be operating in is the more restrictive (indeed, American accounting procedures might often even be *less* onerous in substance than their European counterparts); the existence of different sets of compulsory rules are *in themselves* a real hurdle which needs to be overcome in practice.

The three areas set out above thus indicate that in-house lawyers are not only confronted with *foreign* law but are also forced to work *comparatively* in order to find appropriate legal responses to the increasingly complex challenges arising from today's global economy in a number of commercially highly relevant cases.

This, however, is not the whole story, for if we wish to assess the importance of comparative law in contemporary commercial practice we must also take into account a number of factors which have, over the past decades, led to the *harmonisation* of law across national boundaries—again predominantly in areas closely linked to commerce. The combined effects of national regulation and the ability of companies with an international reach to engage in worldwide forum shopping (the two most important factors which have led to an increasing importance of comparative law in commercial practice) must thus be balanced against the impact of what is often called 'uniform law' and which, on the face of it, tends to reduce the need for comparative expertise. Outside the realm of formal law, international business practice is an equally powerful—if not even stronger—force which has led to very similar approaches to the same commercial questions regardless of their local social and cultural contexts, which are often very different.

[27] Peter T Muchlinski, above note 3, p 113; Gunter Teubner, '"Global Bukowina": Legal Pluralism in the World Society' in Gunter Teubner (ed), *Global Law Without a State* (1997), p 3.

[28] *Public Law* 107–204 (HR 3763), 107th Congress, Second Session (30 July 2002).

[29] See Peter T Muchlinski, above note 3, pp 351–3.

2. UNIFORM LAW AND COMPARATIVE METHODOLOGY

While globalisation has turned comparative methodology into an 'indispensable aid to international forms of legal practice'[30] as conducted by the in-house legal departments of companies with cross-border activities, international arbitrators, and an increasing number of transnational law firms, we could, arguably, be looking at a fleeting phenomenon which will in due course be reduced to a mere blip on the screen by the emergence of a growing corpus of uniform law and business practices in an increasing number of areas. How, then, have various factors—ranging from the harmonisation of law to the emergence of regional legal systems such as that of the European Union—affected commercial practice? We feel that the positive effect of these developments has been a rather limited one.

(a) Unification

Looking, first, at the unification of law, it is important to acknowledge that much has been achieved since this aim was identified as one of the core functions of comparative law at the *Congrès international de droit comparé* held in Paris in 1900.[31] A great number of very specific international legal instruments have emerged over the decades both at regional and global levels, the vast majority of which were driven by business interests. This is not the place to compile a list of international treaties and conventions covering subject matters as diverse as air travel, sea transport, copyright and trademark issues, or patent rights[32]; the exercise would be tedious, and reveal little about the true effect of uniform law in commercial practice. Instead we wish to focus the attention of the reader on a single item, the United Nations Convention on Contracts for the International Sale of Goods (CISG), which was developed by the United Nations Commission on International Trade Law (UNCITRAL) between 1968 and 1980, and has by now been adopted by 70 countries across the globe.[33]

Covering an increasing number of international commercial transactions, the CISG has been called 'one of the success stories'[34] in the international unification of private law. It applies to sales contracts for moveable goods between parties located in different contracting states[35] or when rules of private international law point to the local law of a signatory to

[30] H Patrick Glenn, 'Aims of comparative law', in Jan M Smits, above note 21, p 62.

[31] See Lambert, Procès-verbaux des séances et documents, Congrès international de droit comparé (1900): 'Comparative law must resolve the accidental and divisive differences in the laws of peoples at similar stages of cultural and economic development, and reduce the number of divergencies in law, attributable not to the political, moral or social qualities of the different nations but to historical accident or to temporary or contingent circumstances'.

[32] For an overview see Ulrich Drobnig, 'General Principles of European Contract Law' in Petar Sarcevic and Paul Volken (eds), *International Sale of Goods: Dubrovnik Lectures* (1986), pp 305–08.

[33] Ranging from Lesotho (the first to ratify CISG) and Paraguay (the latest newcomer) to many industrialised nations such as Germany, China, Canada, France, Italy and the United States. The United Kingdom is not a signatory. On this see Sally Moss, 'Why the United Kingdom Has Not Ratified the CISG', 25 *Journal of Law and Commerce* (2005–2006) 483–5 and Angele Forte, 'The United Nations Convention on Contracts for the International Sale of Goods: Reason or Unreason in the United Kingdom', 26 Baltimore Law Review (1997) 51–66.

[34] Peter Huber, 'Some introductory remarks on the CISG', Internationales Handelsrecht 6/2006, p 227. See also Peter Schlechtriem, 'Preface' in Peter Schlechtriem and Ingeborg Schwenzer (eds), *Commentary on the UN Convention on the International Sale of Goods (CISG)* (2nd edn 2005), p v, who describes the CISG as 'the most successful attempt to unify an important part of the many and various rules of the law of international commerce'.

[35] Article 1(1) lit (a) CISG.

the Convention.[36] In essence, it provides rules for the formation of a sales contract and specifies the obligations of buyer and seller, including their respective remedies for breach of contract.

The main difficulty in the application of the instrument, however, lies in its interpretation. Article 7(1) CISG stresses the international character of the Convention, the need to promote uniformity in its application (an ambitious but necessary aim if the notion of a common set of rules for international transactions between partners located in so many countries is to work!), and the importance of good faith as a guiding principle in international trade. It is the first two elements of this provision which are of particular interest to us here.

The idea underlying CISG is that of an 'autonomous' instrument which is independent of the legal notions and terminology found in the contracting states. As in the law of the European Union, terms and phrases used in the various translations of the Convention may thus not mean the same thing as identical terms and phrases used in a particular local legal order. Crucially, however, the system lacks a central forum which could develop an authoritative corpus of law (as does the European Court of Justice within the EU), and therefore depends on the promotion of uniformity through national courts in an increasing number of legal systems.

The risk of divergence is substantial. Professor Peter Huber, a German commentator on the CISG, acknowledges the gap between the *theory* of uniformity and the *reality* of differing interpretations of the same document, which must inevitably arise in such a 'decentralised' system:

> The ideal would be a situation where every court or tribunal that has to apply the CISG would interpret its provisions in exactly the same way and with the same results. In practice, of course, this aim is hard to realize, in particular because there is no supranational court having the power to decide with binding effect on the correct interpretation of the Convention. The courts should, however, try to take into account foreign case law (and academic writing) as persuasive authority when interpreting the CISG.[37]

He is, however, anxious to stress the abundance of sources which provide material on the Convention, both in the form of web-based case collections and academic commentaries. Professor Huber thus continues:

> In the light of the principles of autonomous and internationally-orientated interpretation it may seem at first sight rather complicated to work with the Convention. On the other hand, this task is made easier by an extremely well developed system of databases and academic literature structuring the masses of material.[38]

We are far less confident here. Electronic resources have indeed improved access to international case law,[39] but the mindset of judges trained in their own legal system and judicial time constraints seems to set severe limitations on the development of a truly uniform legal practice. More importantly, discussions about particular aspects of the CISG—both in judicial and academic circles—are in most cases limited to the *local* legal discourse and rarely transcend the linguistic and conceptual barriers set by tried and trusted national legal systems and traditions.

[36] Article 1(1) lit (b) CISG.
[37] Peter Huber, above note 31, p 228.
[38] *Ibid.*
[39] See, eg, the CISG website of PACE Law School at http://cisgw3.law.pace.edu.

In a recent article on the difficulties of uniform law in commercial practice, Dr Thomas Simons, a German practitioner and one of the editors of *The European Legal Forum*, a publication which informs regularly on developments in the various areas of the European ius commune, thus identifies 'barriers of language and legal concepts, and the material difficulties of access to the case law produced in other jurisdictions' as the main reasons why decisions handed down by foreign courts are 'usually ignored' *even when they concern uniform law*.[40] And while online information systems developed by various academic and commercial providers are likely to improve in the future, further practical difficulties inevitably result from the fact that many everyday cross-border disputes require the combined application of several international legal instruments. This makes it 'all but realistic to expect a practitioner or judge to prepare his or her case based on research undertaken in three or more databases, conforming to different search methods and obtaining cases prepared under different concepts'.[41] The idea of uniform law will therefore often take a back seat in day-to-day commercial legal practice.

Under these circumstances, comparative methodology remains an essential tool both for practitioners in law firms and in-house legal counsel *even* when their work falls within the ambit of supposedly 'uniform' law. In the foreseeable future only a careful analysis of the jurisdictions bound together by one or more international legal instruments will prevent unpleasant surprises once a particular cross-border transaction reaches a national courtroom,[42] and opting out of uniform law[43] in favour of well-established national rules is more often than not still the preferred course of action—particularly by companies based in the United States.

Finally, mention should be made of the fact that the CISG has not been ratified by a number of important countries such as the United Kingdom, India, and many nations in Central and South America, Africa, and Asia. Other countries have ratified the Convention, but only subject to specific reservations. The unifying effect of the CISG must thus be taken with a strong pinch of salt.

(b) The European Union as a Special Case of Regional Unification

Arguably, the degree of unification is much higher in a regional system of legal co-operation as represented by the European Union—the crucial difference thereby being the existence of a central forum (the European Court of Justice) capable of giving and enforcing authoritative interpretations of common rules as enacted by the European legislator. American in-house lawyers thus often expect a single European answer to most legal problems which might arise in commercial practice, and are then surprised (and often annoyed!) when confronted not only by a European 'directive' but also 27 potentially different (if not conflicting) national laws covering the very same subject matter. And even where 'regulations' have created a more coherent body of uniform law, national *translations*

[40] Thomas Simons, 'European and International Uniform Law', The European Legal Forum 1/2-2007, p I-4.

[41] *Ibid*, p I.5 *f*.

[42] For a detailed analysis of three German cases see, eg, Harry M Flechtner, 'Conformity of Goods, Third Party Claims, and Buyer's Notice of Breach under the United Nations Sales Convention ("CISG"), with Comments on the "Mussels Case", the "Stolen Automobile Case", and the "Ugandan Used Shoes Case"', University of Pittsburgh School of Law Working Paper Series, Working Paper 64 (available at http://law.bepress.com/pittlwps/papers/art64).

[43] Article 6 CISG.

of the same instrument—all of them equally authoritative—and (in the absence of a US-style system of 'federal' courts which reach down to the Member State level) *interpretations* of these translations by *national* courts (all in their respective languages!) render the concept of 'uniform' European law a relative one.

In view of the immense number of cases involving Community law it must be noted that the crucial judicial link between the Member States and the Community, the preliminary reference procedure (which allows national courts and tribunals to approach the European Court of Justice for guidance on the interpretation of Community law[44]) can only achieve a limited amount of consistency in the daily application of these supposedly 'common' rules. Needless to say that commercial practice will in any case strive to avoid litigation in the first place, not least because of the delays which are today a common problem of nearly all national court systems—and which are, on average, increased by another two years if a local court actually chooses to make a reference to the ECJ.

In political and cultural terms, this aspect of today's European Union is—in our view—highly desirable, for it provides a maximum amount of local flexibility within a community of now 27 very different national legal traditions. From a *practical* perspective, however, the difference between dealing, on the one hand, with a certain number of completely autonomous legal systems and, on the other, a selection of EU Member States is often fairly marginal. The factors identified under the previous heading (language barriers, different legal concepts and traditions, and the purely technical difficulties of accessing court decisions and legal material from other jurisdictions) are again relevant here—as is the absence of a *truly* European judicial and academic dialogue on questions of common law.

Cross-references to the decisions of other Member State courts (*not* the European Court of Justice) which could indicate the existence of a meaningful 'horizontal' judicial dialogue are thus still a fairly rare occurrence,[45] and the leading academic treatises on particular aspects of institutional or substantive Community law will not regularly cite or discuss in any detail the views of colleagues researching the same topics and publishing their work in other Member States. Unless a particular question has in fact been decided by the European Court of Justice, comparative methodology will therefore (again) retain its importance as a key to the solution of many cross-border problems both for commercial legal practice *within* the borders of the European Union and international transactions between parties based within the Community and their partners from outside. Whenever the Community lacks the necessary legislative competence to enact common rules (as, for example, in most areas of contract and tort law), international commercial practice will be confronted with the usual plethora of national legal rules anyway.

(c) Harmonisation

A third trend which could arguably reduce the importance of comparative law in commercial practice is the worldwide *harmonisation* of common legal approaches short of systematic *unification*. Three elements seem to us of importance here—first, lex mercatoria as an informal and potentially universal system of business practices; second, the development of

[44] Article 234 of the EC Treaty.

[45] For a detailed comparative analysis on the use of comparative law by judges in the United States, Europe and South Africa see Sir Basil Markesinis and Jörg Fedtke, *Judicial Recourse to Foreign Law* (2006); on the use of comparative law by the European Court of Justice see Markku Kiikeri, *Comparative Legal Reasoning and European Law* (2001).

general principles of international contract and trade law; and third, the un-coordinated adoption of identical or very similar concepts by a growing number of national legal systems in the form of a natural convergence of legal approaches. Let us look at each of these elements in turn.

Discussions concerning the regulatory potential of lex mercatoria go back a number of decades. On occasion of the *London Colloquium on the New Sources of the Law of International Trade* held at King's College in 1962, Clive Schmitthoff thus noted that

> (T)he evolution of an autonomous law of international trade, founded on universally accepted standards of business conduct, would be one of the most important developments of legal science in our time. It would constitute a common platform for commercial lawyers from all countries, those of planned and free market economy, those from civil law and common law, and those of fully developed and developing economies, which would enable them to co-operate in the perfection of the legal mechanism of international trade.[46]

Various factors, including the end of the Cold War, European integration, a steep rise in the number of multinational enterprises, the rapid development of global communication technology, the growing importance of alternative dispute resolution mechanisms, and, more generally, the increasing erosion of national legal boundaries, have since then certainly improved the prospects for the emergence of transnational business law[47]—if not in the form of a coherent corpus of autonomous rules and practices as envisaged by Schmitthoff, then possibly as 'separate sets of transnational commercial law for specialised areas of international business and trade'.[48] Possible candidates for the development of such sub-systems include maritime practice, the international oil industry, information technology, the construction industry, the insurance sector, and international finance and securitisation.

But is this trend really likely to displace the *regulatory power* of national legal orders (as described at the outset of this Chapter) or provide an adequate foundation for international commercial transactions on a larger scale? Practitioners, particularly from the Common law world, seem to be sceptical. A survey conducted among 23 lawyers from 10 countries in the mid-1990s by Professor Barton S Selden, a private practitioner from San Francisco and Adjunct Professor at the Golden Gate University School of Law, did not show lex mercatoria to be a viable basis for contractual relationships,[49] and results of a separate (and much broader) project by the Centre for Transnational Law at the University of Münster in Germany were inconclusive at best.[50] According to the latter study, 'transnational law is being used in international legal practice'[51] but the statistical data given does not indicate that concepts such as 'transnational principles of law', 'general principles of law', 'lex mercatoria', the UNIDROIT Principles of International Commercial Contracts, the Lando Principles of European Contract Law or the Draft Common Frame of Reference (DCFR)

[46] Clive Schmitthoff, 'Introduction' in Clive Schmitthoff (ed), *The Sources of the Law of International Trade* (1964), p 5.

[47] See Klaus Peter Berger, 'The New Law Merchant and the Global Marketplace—A 21st Century View of Transnational Commercial Law' in Klaus Peter Berger, *The Practice of Transnational Law* (2000), pp 14 *ff.*

[48] *Ibid* p 21.

[49] Barton S Selden, 'Lex Mercatoria in European and US Trade Practice: Time to Take a Closer Look', 2 Annual Survey of International and Comparative Law 1995, 111 *ff.*

[50] Klaus Peter Berger, Holger Dubberstein, Sascha Lehmann and Viktoria Petzold, 'The CENTRAL Enquiry on the Use of Transnational Law in International Contract Law and Arbitration—Background, Procedure and Selected Results' in Klaus Peter Berger, above note 44, pp 91 *ff.*

[51] *Ibid* at p 112.

will render codified national law obsolete in the foreseeable future when it comes to the negotiation and drafting of contracts or international arbitration.[52] A 'creeping codification'[53] of transnational law may thus in fact be taking place, in particular through the work of UNIDROIT and academic study groups such as those of Professors Ole Lando, Christian von Bar, or Professor Helmut Koziol;[54] but not only does comparative law provide the basis for these academic endeavours, themselves; in the light of the very limited *practical* impact of these 'restatements' of general legal principles, the method will also remain an indispensable tool for anyone confronted with foreign jurisdictions in commercial legal practice.

A related phenomenon is the unsystematic harmonisation of law which takes place through the adoption of the same—or at least very similar—rules and concepts by autonomous national legal systems across the globe. Transplants of legal solutions are thus probably 'the most common form of legal change'[55] today—notably in commercially relevant areas, and often as a response to successful foreign business practices which have penetrated a particular national market. This is not the place to conduct an extensive comparative survey of specific areas of commercial or company law—two examples will suffice to make our point.

The first is taken from German private law and involves three highly relevant American business models which first appeared in local commercial practice in the 1970s and have since then developed into established contractual templates: leasing, franchising and factoring. Stopping short of formally incorporating these concepts into their Civil Code of 1900, Germans use the English terms *without* translation in academic writing and court decisions,[56] and have by now successfully transplanted the underlying ideas to their own legal order.

A second (and, given the close commercial and political ties between the United States and Germany, an even more surprising but little studied) phenomenon is the effect that globalisation has had on commercial law in Middle Eastern countries. Referring to court decisions from Algeria, Tunisia, Lybia, Syria, Bahrain, Kuwait, Jordan, the United Arab Emirates, and Iraq, Professor Chibli Mallat of the University of Utah thus notes that

> (W)hether from an institutional and technical perspective, or whether in the language proper, Middle Eastern commercial law as found in legislation or court cases reads both for practitioners and scholars as a direct transposition of European law. The long-standing tradition of a civilization closely associated with trade seems irrelevant for the present commercial law of this area . . . Variations will naturally occur in matters of detail, but the language is one which reads as a straight

[52] Klaus Peter Berger, Holger Dubberstein, Sascha Lehmann and Viktoria Petzold, 'The CENTRAL Enquiry on the Use of Transnational Law in International Contract Law and Arbitration—Background, Procedure and Selected Results' in Klaus Peter Berger, at pp 152 *ff*. The question 'are you aware of any cases occurring in your practice in which the parties have referred to transnational law during the negotiation of an international contract, in the text of the contract or in the choice-of-law clause, [or] in international arbitration proceedings?' was answered in the positive ['yes—one or several] by 32 per cent of the respondents for contract negotiations, 32 per cent for contract drafting, and 42 per cent for arbitration. On the difficulties of assessing the content of lex mercatoria for the purposes of contractual relationships see also Guiditta Cordero Moss, 'International Contracts between Common Law and Civil Law: Is Non-state Law to Be Preferred? The Difficulty of Interpreting Legal Standards such as Good Faith', *Global Jurist* Vol 7: Iss 1 (Advances), Article 3, pp 24/25.

[53] Klaus Peter Berger, *The Creeping Codification of the Lex Mercatoria* (1999).

[54] For general background information on the UNIDROIT Principles of International Commercial Contracts and the Principles of European Contract Law see Ole Lando, 'Comparative Law and Lawmaking', (2001) 75 *Tulane L Rev* 1015 *ff*.

[55] Alan Watson, *Legal Origins and Legal Change* (1991), p 73.

[56] See, eg, Hans Brox and Wolf-Dietrich Walker, *Besonderes Schuldrecht* (25th edn 2000), pp *83ff* and 139 *ff*; Volker Emmerich, *BGB-Schulrecht Besonderer Teil* (10th edn 2003), pp 101 *ff*.

> translation from a Western commercial code. Plagiarism—or borrowing—runs through the whole gamut of the field of commercial law, from the objective quality of merchant to the mechanisms of bankruptcy, and typically includes technical rules on commercial papers, transport liability, and company law. The local commercial statutes, and the courts which apply them, adopt terminology and categories which are taken straight from Western practice. The executive, acting as legislator, will also ratify and incorporate Western-made international conventions in which Middle Eastern input is negligible, if not nil. The style of commercial law in the region is decisively Western.[57]

As noted elsewhere,[58] borrowing a particular legal idea does not, however, mean that the system on the receiving end need to follow the model in each and every detail, or emulate further developments that occur in the 'parent system' once the initial transplant has taken place.[59] Constitutional provisions of German origin—at times *verbatim* translations of the Basic Law—have thus been interpreted very differently by courts in South Africa,[60] and we would *not* recommend a US practitioner or in-house counsel to rely solely on their American experience with leasing, franchising or factoring when confronted with similar business arrangements in Germany more than three decades after these concepts first appeared there and local courts and academics set to work at incorporating them into the distinct structures of their own legal system.[61] Islamic banking—as already emphasised earlier in this Chapter, a fairly recent[62] but extremely dynamic[63] phenomenon (not only in Arab institutions but also with companies such as Goldman Sachs and HSBC)—shows that Middle Eastern commercial law, too, has retained some of its originality despite the ultimate dominance of Western concepts. Other examples such as arbitration confirm that foreigners need to be wary of superficial similarities between the local laws and customs of the region and their own systems.[64]

The globalisation of commerce has thus certainly resulted in the spread of very similar approaches both in business and in law, but local factors such as the prevailing legal tradition or religious beliefs will inevitably have an impact on the way the details of such 'harmonised' concepts eventually play out in practice. Comparative methodology again provides the tool which is best able to detect these nuances.

3. SOME SELECTED EXAMPLES

Having argued, first, that commercial legal practice requires not only considerable knowledge of *foreign* law but also a fair amount of *comparative* expertise and, second, that neither the partial unification of law nor less far-reaching efforts at harmonisation will, in the near future, substantially diminish the practical importance of our subject, it is now time to take a closer look at a few selected examples. They are again taken from the areas identified above—standardisation, forum shopping, and internal regulation.

[57] Chibli Mallat, *Introduction to Middle Eastern Law* (2007), pp 300 and 308.

[58] Sir Basil Markesinis and Jörg Fedtke, above note 42, pp 91 *ff.*

[59] Generally on legal transplants see Jörg Fedtke, 'Legal Transplants' in Jan M Smits (ed), above note 21, pp 434 *ff.*

[60] *Ibid.*

[61] For a survey of recent developments in German leasing law see Jan Weber, 'Die Entwicklung des Leasingsrechts von Mitte 2005 bis Mitte 2007', NJW 2007, 2525 *ff.*

[62] See Chibli Mallet, above note 54, p 345.

[63] See *International Herald Tribune*—London edition—of 9 August 2007, pp 1 and 12.

[64] On arbitration in Middle Eastern commercial law see Chibli Mallet, above note 54, pp 345 *ff.*

(a) Standardisation and the Local Pitfalls of the 'World Wide' Web

In an ideal commercial world, multinational enterprises would no doubt use the same contractual templates—drafted in *one* language and including *identical* choice of law clauses and other terms and conditions—for their business transactions in every country they operate in. Local market forces, language barriers, cultural differences and mandatory local law, however, limit the ability even of market leaders to enforce standardised contracts across their whole range of international business relationships. Internet giants such as Google and Yahoo! Inc thus negotiate and draft most contracts in the *local* legal language, under *local* law, and with reference to *local* terms and conditions.

Companies operating in other markets have achieved a higher degree of harmonisation. The pharmaceutical industry, for example, seems to have standardised most contracts with suppliers and distributors, adapting as little as 20 per cent of the relevant terms and conditions to local factors.[65] Companies with a global reach will, however, always face a complex legal evaluation when launching new products, and must be prepared to adjust standard contract terms according to local conditions.

Much will obviously depend on the specific area of the law involved. Providers of internet services offer a particularly interesting example due to the combination of an inherently 'global' commercial environment and very different national approaches to intellectual property rights and data protection.[66]

The latter area is of interest to us here. As is well known, search engines operate a fleet of powerful data centres which hold vast amounts of personal user data ranging from the contents of e-mails to credit card details and website traffic information. Internet-fed identification programmes (or 'cookies'[67]) identify users on occasion of subsequent visits, and thus allow companies to monitor online behaviour and content preferences unless users decide to 'opt out' by adjusting the settings of their web browsers (though this may, of course, affect their ability to view certain pages or utilise particular online services). Registration with an internet company such as Google or Yahoo! Inc will provide further personal data such as the name, e-mail address, birth date, gender, marital status, postcode, occupation, industry, or personal interests. Some financial products and services might also require customers to disclose their social security number and information about their assets. With up to 30 million users accessing the largest providers every month, this information is of considerable commercial value to advertisers.[68]

In a race to develop ever more precise strategies to target consumers, all major search engines are currently trying to link the knowledge they have about their users with advertisements to which these are most likely to respond positively. The ability to tailor advertis-

[65] See Peter Muchlinski, above note 3, pp 136 *ff*.

[66] See, eg, the following comments made by senior Microsoft personnel in Europe in October 2002: 'For example, Europe really took the worldwide lead in the issue of data privacy protection. Our participation in the European Unions Safe Harbour Agreement is an example of our listening and responding to European concerns. And because of our belief in the protections it affords, we have made it the bedrock of our policies and voluntarily subjected all of our data, worldwide, to the Safe Harbour guidelines. *At the same time, there are issues on which European views vary from country to country, such as how to safeguard data that may be used for purposes other than those for which it was legitimately collected*' (Caspar Bowden, Chief Privacy Advisor, EMEA—emphasis added). '[W]hile many Trustworthy Computing issues are global in scope, its also true that regions like Europe have some concerns that are distinct from those of the US and that even within Europe, there are multiple takes on some issues' (Craig Mundie, Senior Vice President and Chief Technology Officer). The full text is available at: www.microsoft.com/presspass/features/2002/Oct02/10-08trustworthy.mspx.

[67] Small data files that are downloaded automatically to computers when websites are accessed.

[68] The value of Google's online advertising in the United Kingdom alone is estimated at £2bn in 2006.

ing to individuals (so-called 'behavioral targeting' or 'one-to-one marketing') ideally creates a triangular co-operation between the search engine, advertisers, and retailers which currently offer the goods or services in question. The advertiser thereby provides the visual components of the display (logos, texts and images), the retailer offers information about particular products held in stock, and the search engine then presents the combined package to selected users, based on the personal information that has been accumulated over time. When accessing a search engine, users would then see advertisements for specific products or services that might be of interest to them, personally, either associated with their current search item or without such a connection.

An even more sophisticated approach could further enhance the marketing value of personal profiles. By utilising the unique IP-address of the computer, search engines could identify the potential location of the user (unless a laptop is used to access the web elsewhere) and provide advertisements which are specifically linked to the geographical region or, conversely, avoid displaying campaigns which are only relevant to other parts of the world. Retailers situated 'around the corner' would then appear on screen while those offering the same goods or services at distant locations would be suppressed (so-called 'geo-targeting').

The easiest and most profitable way of marketing new products of the kind just described is a global launch. But while the world is shrinking in technical and commercial terms, national law still poses considerable hurdles to the 'world wide' web. Legal problems include the amount of time that cookies may be 'planted' on computers (and the information that must be provided to users in this regard), the nature of IP addresses, and—more generally—the retention of all kinds of personal data by internet service providers.

Data protection authorities across the globe have thus for some time now been worried about the ability of search engines to compile individual profiles of their users with the help of cookies. In response to these privacy concerns, Google has recently pledged to reduce the 'life span' of these devices from more than 30 years to 24 months following a user's access of a particular website. An update will take place, however, with every consecutive visit, triggering a fresh two-year installation period.[69] Other service providers are contemplating similar solutions.

Whether this move is sufficient to pre-empt regulatory intervention is, however, not yet clear. In Europe, the EU Directive on Privacy and Electronic Communications,[70] enacted in 2002, took a 'hands-off' approach to the issue by allowing storage of and access to cookies 'on condition that the subscriber or user is provided with clear and comprehensive information . . . about the purposes of the processing and is offered the right to refuse such processing by the data controller'.[71] This does not apply to cases where a technical storage of or access to cookies is necessary to facilitate the transmission of information, or where a service explicitly requested by the user is provided (eg, an online shopping basket). Directives are, however, addressed to the Member States, and national lawgivers across the continent have exercised some degree of discretion when implementing this particular piece of European framework legislation. The specific requirements which must be met when informing users about cookies and other data protection issues thus vary quite considerably from country to country, and national rules concerning the storage of cookies

[69] See *The Times*—London—of 24 May 2007, p 63.

[70] Directive 2002/58/EC of the European Parliament and of the Council concerning the processing of personal data and the protection of privacy in the electronic communications sector (Directive on privacy and electronic communications) of 12 July 2002, *Official Journal*, L 201/37 of 31 July 2002.

[71] See Recital 25 and Art 5(3) Directive 2002/58/EC.

(not addressed by the Directive) might also emerge in the future. Needless to say that other legal systems outside the European Union again have their own data protection laws, which may or may not be compatible with European standards. In preparation of a worldwide launch, internet products developed and driven mainly by US-based service providers such as Google, Yahoo! Inc or MSN (Microsoft) thus require careful scrutiny as to their compatibility with the local laws in other important markets. Under these conditions, a 'one size fits all' solution is still the exception.

IP addresses pose similar challenges. Received and automatically held on the server logs of search engines, the issue here is whether these computer IDs represent *personal* data at all—making them subject to local data protection law—or whether they are merely *technical processing information* which is not directly linked to an individual human being. The answer to this question will for example determine whether smaller, local search engines or internet portals may forward the IP addresses of their own customers to the larger market leaders who operate on an international level and have the technical capacity to develop products such as 'geo-targeting' strategies. If the data is regarded as purely technical information (as, for example, in the United States, the United Kingdom, and France), data protection is not an issue. If, however, the addresses are seen as personal information (which seems to be the case in Germany and Japan), data protection laws, which also cover the transfer of information between companies (both within national borders and in cross-border relationships), become highly relevant.

How do companies respond to these legal difficulties? Though technically possible, country-by-country 'zoning' of the web according to local data protection regimes would be very costly for global service providers working with centrally organised servers. The problem for in-house lawyers, under pressure from their business departments to sign off potentially lucrative products, is thus to develop worldwide solutions. This requires not only an intimate knowledge of the technological side of new internet tools but also the ability to conduct extensive comparative inquiries into the legality of such products in the most relevant markets and the feasibility of contractual variations which might become necessary in order to address any local legal difficulties.

(b) Forum Shopping

As discussed above, forum shopping comes in many shapes and sizes. The first two examples we wish to highlight here both fall into the area of company law and involve fairly recent developments in Germany. Our third example concerns the more general trend of outsourcing parts of a company's activities.

(i) Private Limited Companies

Following three key decisions of the European Court of Justice in the area of company law,[72] an increasing number of German entrepreneurs have over the past years turned away

[72] ECJ Cases C-212/97 of 9 March 1999 (Centros), C-208/00 of 5 November 2002 (Überseering) and C-167/01 of 30 September 2003 (Inspire Art). For Germany see the leading case BGH Case VII ZR 370/98 of 13 March 2003 (Juristische Rundschau 2003, 412 *ff*) concerning a Dutch company with operational headquarters in Germany; Kilian Baelz and Teresa Baldwin, 'The End of the Real Seat Theory (Sitztheorie): the European Court of Justice in Ueberseering of 5 November 2002 and its Impact of German and European Company Law', 3 German Law Journal No 12, available online at http://www.germanlawjournal.com/article.php?id=214; Christian Kersting and Clemens Philipp Schindler, 'The ECJ's Inspire Art Decision of 30 September 2003 and its Effects on Practice', 4 *German Law Journal* No 12, pp 1277 *ff*.

from the traditional German private limited company, the so-called *Gesellschaft mit beschränkter Haftung* (GmbH), and have founded an English private limited company (Ltd) instead. Estimates indicate that 12,000 such companies were created in 2005, as opposed to 80,000 under the traditional German regime in the same year.[73] More recently, the trend has accelerated; today one out of four new private limited companies which take up operations in Germany was created under English law.[74] Their total number is currently estimated at between 30,000 and 50,000.

A comparably simple and speedy registration procedure, lower costs, and lower thresholds in regard to the required nominal capital are the key factors for this remarkable development. In the United Kingdom, private limited companies can be 'born' in as little as 24 hours at a cost of a few hundred euros, and require no more than a single symbolic pound of capital. Founding a German GmbH is, by contrast, a far more onerous procedure that takes up to six months to complete (including a complex interregnum, the so-called 'vor-GmbH'), costs up to €2,000 in administrative and legal fees, and requires a founding capital of at least €25,000 (of which a minimum of €12,500 must be paid into a secure account prior to registration). The differences are reflected in the types of 'German' companies which have avoided these limitations by registering in the United Kingdom; the vast majority are start-ups, most of them with fewer than 10 employees, and will usually engage in the provision of some service as opposed to trade-related activities or the production of goods.

The advantages of the English model, however, do come at a price. While German employees of English limited companies and their customers will rarely regard a 'Ltd' as in any way inferior to a 'GmbH', local suppliers and banks tend to have less confidence in companies founded under English law. The reasons are varied, and certainly include a certain degree of unease towards things unknown. Employees have little to fear, of course, for German labour law applies both to GmbHs and English private limited companies operating in Germany. And customers of service providers—which most German 'English' private limited companies tend to be—will generally not be too concerned about the financial credentials of their business partners. For suppliers and banks, however, the stronger financial security provided by a *Gesellschaft mit beschränkter Haftung* can make a difference.[75]

More important in our context is the fact that English private limited companies conducting business in Germany are subject to a cocktail of UK and German law, which creates considerable difficulties in legal practice. English law will thus regulate the registration of the company and the internal relationship between its officers and shareholders, and require the submission of annual reports and returns. According to a decision of the Bundesgerichtshof, English company law will also determine the liability for a company's debts even if the centre of its activities lies in Germany.[76] But despite its registration in the United Kingdom, German law will regulate most other aspects of a company with operational headquarters or substantial business activities within German territory, including accounting, taxation and employment issues. While this mix can be difficult

[73] According to a study conducted by the Saïd Business School, University of Oxford.

[74] According to statistics of the Statistisches Bundesamt in Germany.

[75] For more information on the basis of a study conducted by the Deutsches Institut für kleine und mittlere Unternehmen eV see Jörn-Axel Meyer and René Schleus (eds), *Erfahrungen mit der Limited—Tagungsreader* (2006).

[76] Case II ZR 5/03 of 14 March 2005.

enough for many entrepreneurs and in-house lawyers, important areas lie on the borderline between the two legal systems. These include the (compulsory) registration of business activities with the appropriate German regional chamber of commerce or details of insolvency law, including the application of German tort law with respect to individual company officers.

Here, comparative methodology becomes an essential tool. Both the initial decision whether to opt for an English private limited company or a German *Gesellschaft mit beschränkter Haftung* and subsequent questions regarding the compatibility of English legal standards with mandatory German law will require a thorough analysis and comparison of both systems (and not just of their bare concepts). Matters will, in fact, become even more complicated with the advent of a company law reform in Germany,[77] which attempts to make the GmbH more competitive in comparison to its English rival[78] and may require a re-evaluation of conventional wisdom. Other European systems such as France and Italy have reformed their own company laws only recently and may now also offer viable alternatives.[79] Interestingly, it is again commercial legal *practice* in a globalised environment (in this case the European Union) which has prompted national *legislators* to review the foundations of their revered institutions (which in the case of the German *Gesellschaft mit beschränkter Haftung* date back to 1892).

The above suggests an interesting competition (if not battle) of legal cultures actively taking place and prompted by the demands of economic competitiveness. This struggle, though economic in its origin, is largely externalised in legal ways, and understanding these requires approaching foreign law in the very specific, functional manner we have been suggesting in other parts of this book.

(ii) Cross-Border Insolvency Strategies

Closely related to our first example is cross-border 'insolvency court-shopping', which can occur if companies run into life-threatening financial difficulties.

Insolvency laws across the Member States of the European Union are still very different, and German companies like the Deutsche Nickel Group[80] and Schefenacker[81] have recently relocated their company headquarters to the United Kingdom and created British corporations and subsidiaries to replace their German entities. One of the main differences between the legal regimes is the degree of influence that minority bondholders can exert over the future of a company. Liquidation was thus avoided in both cases with the help of debt-for-equity swaps, which effectively turn bondholders into shareholders. While German law will require a 95 per cent majority for the move (which was not achieved in either case), the same could be done under English law with a majority of only 75 per cent. Another difference concerns the management of a company under insolvency rules. English law will allow

[77] See Bundesregierung, Entwurf eines Gesetzes zur Modernisierung des GmbH-Rechts und zur Bekämpfung von Missbräuchen (MoMiG) of 23 May 2007, BR-Drucksache 354/07.

[78] See Antwort der Bundesregierung auf die Kleine Anfrage der Abgeordneten Otto Fricke, Dr Max Stadler, Jens Ackermann, weiterer Abgeordneter und der Fraktion der FDP (BT-Drucksache 16/134) of 16 December 2005, BT-Drucksache 16/283.

[79] For a more detailed assessment see, eg, Eva-Maria Kieninger, 'The Legal Framework of Regulatory Competition Based on Company Mobility: EU and US Compared', 6 *German Law Journal* No 4, pp 741 *ff*.

[80] Manufacturer of a wide range of nickel products.

[81] Currently the world's largest producer of rear vision systems, vehicle lighting, and automobile sound systems.

officers to continue to run the company after filing for insolvency while German law requires the appointment of an external administrator. Where the competence of management is not in doubt (as was the case with both Deutsche Nickel and Schefenacker), English law will again offer the more flexible solution.

EU law also has a role to play in these cases. A Council regulation limits insolvency filings to the country in which a debtor's 'centre of interests' is located, and can therefore pose an insurmountable obstacle to this kind of forum shopping.[82] The effect of the rule may diminish in the future as commercial legal practice has (again) initiated a wave of reforms across Europe. This might lead to a convergence of insolvency regimes within the Union, and reduce the scope for cross-border insolvency strategies.[83] Entrepreneurial lawyers who 'want to market their [national] product'[84] are, however, likely to discover yet other differences between the systems and, by exploiting the commercial value of particular local rules, secure the future of comparative law as an applied discipline.

(iii) Outsourcing

Our third and last example under this sub-heading concerns international outsourcing strategies, which will in most cases involve a simple reallocation of activities from within a company to one or more external providers but can also come in the guise of highly complex production networks characterised by a close interaction of numerous specialised firms working towards a common goal. A business strategy honed to perfection in Japan, where the automobile industry pioneered 'just in time' stock ordering in the late 1980s, outsourcing is today becoming increasingly important in a large number of industries, and has spread from the manufacturing sector to service providers as modern electronic communication and information technologies permit the desegregation of activities across ever greater distances.[85]

Affordable IT in particular has led to the outsourcing of services to firms based in other countries, which in turn has increased the need for a careful legal assessment of, inter alia, data protection issues. India is thus developing into a hub for call centres, accounting departments, and a host of other services which do not require physical interaction with other parts of a company or its local customers. Most English readers will have experienced calling a national telephone number in order to sort out some problem with a technical device or utility bill—only to be connected to some remote destination near Hyderabad or Bangalore rather than the company's headquarters in Kent or Surrey. A global IT infrastructure which involves the use of customer data in different jurisdictions will, however, need to take account of the various local data protection regimes—a task made particularly onerous whenever cross-border data transfers occur. Depending on the circumstances of

[82] Article 3(1) Council Regulation (EC) No 1346/2000 of 29 May 2000 on insolvency proceedings, Official Journal L 160, 30/06/2000, pp 1–3. Interestingly, and in line with our earlier observations, enactment of this regulation has not yet resulted in a uniform approach to the problem of cross-border insolvencies. On this aspect see Bob Wessels, 'The European Insolvency Regulation: It's First Year in Dutch Court Cases' (International Insolvency Institute, Third Annual International Insolvency Conference, Fordham University School of Law 2003): 'It is quite easy to demonstrate . . . that a possible idea that "Europe" now has a full-fledged domain of community insolvency law is far beyond reality. It is remarkable to see that every individual EU Member State here follows its own course, without giving any evidence of even sharing draft work products or of mutual alignment or consultation'.

[83] For French law see Hervé Guenassia, 'Overview of the new French Insolvency Law', International In-house Counsel Journal, vol 1 no 1 (June 2007), pp 50 *ff.*

[84] Professor Christoph Paulus (Humboldt University Berlin), quoted by the *International Herald Tribune*—London edition—of 18 July 2007, p 12.

[85] See Peter T Muchlinski, above note 3, pp 48 *f.*

the case, outsourcing may also require a comparative approach in other field such as taxation, choice of law decisions, or questions of contractual and non-contractual liability.[86]

(c) Internal Regulation: Sarbanes-Oxley

Our final example concerns corporate governance. As indicated above, much has changed in this field since corporate improprieties involving companies like Enron, Adelphia, Tyco or ImClone triggered a stream of regulatory intervention by legislators across the globe. The common thrust of these new rules—despite many differences in detail—can be summarised under two headings: first, the improvement of internal controls and auditing and, second, the promotion of a culture that encourages ethical behaviour and compliance with the law. Differences in approach nevertheless complicate matters. First, in America the sanctions tend to be criminal rather than civil, targeting 'bad' directors but leaving victims uncompensated; secondly, the regimes differ by imposing different insurable maxima in the event of liability; and thirdly, how these liability laws work out in practice depends on procedural devices found in the different systems—eg, the presence or absence of class actions, punitive damages, or reliance on juries.

All of the above represent intriguing facets of the problem but here we shall focus on one important difference between the approaches pursued on both sides of the Atlantic. The Sarbanes-Oxley Act, which came into force in the United States in 2002, takes a decidedly *extraterritorial* stance in that parts of it apply not only to US-based companies but also to *foreign* accounting firms they might choose to employ[87] and—more importantly—subsidiaries based *outside* the country. A similar approach is noticeable in those parts of American antitrust regulation which deal with transactions that might have a significant effect on the national securities market or international investments in 'unfriendly' countries such as Cuba, Iran or Libya.[88] The European Union and most domestic European systems, by contrast, tend to limit the effect of their respective regulatory frameworks to their own territories, and are wary of the 'expansionist' approach taken by the United States.[89]

The wide ambit of Sarbanes-Oxley can create considerable difficulties for foreign subsidiaries of US-based companies, which are often caught in between the regulatory grip that the United States exercises over their parent companies, on the one hand, and the jurisdiction of their host countries, on the other. The same is true for European multinationals publicly listed in the US.

There are, for one, possible tensions between the requirements of the Act and mandatory foreign law. As we shall see below, labour law and data protection in particular require careful consideration as to the compatibility of American approaches with local legal standards.

[86] See P Graham, 'Structuring and Negotiating Global Supply/Outsourcing Deals', *International In-house Counsel Journal*, vol 1(1), June 2007, pp 60–73.

[87] Section 106.

[88] For Cuba see the Cuba Liberty and Democratic Solidarity (Libertad) Act (Helms Burton Act) US Public Law 104–114 of 12 March 1996, 35 ILM 357 (1996); for Iran and Libya see the Iran and Libya Sanctions Act US Public Law 104–172 of 5 August 1996, 35 ILM 1273 (1996).

[89] See European Union Press Release IP/03/571 of 24 April 2003: 'The European Commission fully shares the goal of having effective audit systems in place in order to prevent accounting irregularities and restore investor confidence in the securities market. However, this should be done on the basis of internationally acceptable solutions, *including mutual recognition of equivalent systems of oversight*' (Internal Market and Taxation Commissioner Frits Bolkenstein, emphasis added).

A second, related issue is the fact that multinational enterprises have to implement *world-wide* codes of conduct in order to meet the requirements of Sarbanes-Oxley's internal control rules.[90] These codes promote compliance with all relevant law, and include reporting systems to ensure their effective implementation; ideally, they can thus help detect and/or prevent criminal or other improper activity, avoid the loss of business, and act as a shield to personal liability for the directors of a company.[91] Issues typically covered include conflicts of interest, the acceptance of gifts by employees, bribery and corruption, questions of competition law, anti-discrimination strategies, data protection protocols, accounting guidelines, environmental principles, and human rights considerations. Often, they will also provide mechanisms through which employees can anonymously flag concerns in case they become aware of unlawful activities by other members of staff ('whistle-blowing hotlines'). The requirements of Sarbanes-Oxley aside, the value of worldwide harmonised internal procedures and policies is also quite evident given the complexity of multinational enterprises. Sarbanes-Oxley has, moreover, tripled the annual costs for compliance and governance work in American public companies since 2001, and triggered a drive for internal efficiency.[92] Different local mandatory laws, however, often stand in the way of harmonised and therefore more cost-effective internal procedures. In-house lawyers or outside legal counsel are thus under considerable pressure to provide common solutions for the whole group if US-listed multinationals are active outside the country.

Bridging the gap between US standards and foreign law is often difficult. Challenges arise less from the inevitable tensions between different corporate governance regimes than from adjacent areas such as labour law and data protection. German employees, for example, are by law heavily involved in the management of larger companies, in particular when it comes to decisions which have an impact on their general working environment.[93] Confronted with American codes of conduct imposed on German subsidiaries, courts have ruled that a number of provisions (eg, rules on the acceptance of gifts or whistle-blowing hotlines) are subject to these special co-decision procedures set out by German labour law.[94] This makes them more difficult to enact, and has in many cases led to their invalidation—in part[95] or completely[96]—due to the infringement of mandatory co-decision requirements. Problems can also arise with a view to the rights of individual employees. While whistle-blowing hotlines are thus generally acceptable in order to protect the interests of the company and society at large,[97] it would seem that employees cannot be placed under an *obligation* to flag activities of co-workers since no corresponding legal duty to report crimes or other forms of wrongdoing exists under German law.

[90] See section 301 Sarbanes-Oxley Act, section 10A(4) Securities Exchange Act 1934, and the New York Stock Exchange Corporate Governance Rules.

[91] Gary M Brown, 'Changing Models in Corporate Governance—Implications of the US Sarbanes-Oxley Act' in Klaus J Hopt, Eddy Wymeersch, Hideki Kanda and Harald Baum (eds), *Corporate Governance in Context* (2005), p 160.

[92] *International Herald Tribune*—London edition—of 3 August 2007, p 11.

[93] So-called 'Arbeitnehmermitbestimmung'.

[94] See § 87 Betriebsverfassungsgesetz.

[95] Bundesarbeitsgericht, Case 1 ABR 32/01 of 28 May 2002, Neue Zeitschrift für Arbeitsrecht 2003, 166 *ff*; Arbeitsgericht Wuppertal, Case 5 BV 20/05 of 15 June 2005 (Wal-Mart), Neue Zeitschrift für Arbeitsrecht (Rechtsprechungs-Report) 2005, 476 *ff*; Arbeitsgericht Offenbach, Case 3 BV 44/04.

[96] Hessisches Landesarbeitsgericht, Case 5 TaBV 31/06 of 18 January 2007 (for the German text see http://web2.justiz.hessen.de/migration/rechtsp.nsf/4dd04a17de79c763c1257249004a7703/14805b921acee011c12572b100305e6d?OpenDocument). Whether single provisions which require co-decision make the entire code of conduct subject to these special procedures will have to be decided by the Federal Labour Court.

[97] Bundesarbeitsgericht, Case 2 AZR 235/02 of 3 July 2003, Neue Zeitschrift für Arbeitsrecht 2004, 427 *ff*.

Data protection is a further potential source of conflict between American law and European approaches. The French *Commission nationale de l'informatique et des libertés* (CNIL) thus invalidated the whistle-blowing procedures set out in the codes of conduct of McDonald's France and CEAC/Exide[98] on the basis that allegations made anonymously could be disproportionately difficult for the affected employees to disprove. The Commission identified a serious risk that the codes in question could violate the human rights of employees as safeguarded under the French Constitution.[99]

German law could pose similar hurdles depending on the type of personal information which is to be passed on by the whistleblower. Knowledge concerning the violation of accounting procedures would thus seem to be covered by the legitimate interests of the employer to abide by his own legal obligations, while information about personal relationships between employees (which were banned by Wal-Mart) may not be subject to whistleblowing procedures as this would infringe the human dignity and personality rights of employees as set out in Articles 1 and 2 of the German Basic Law.[100]

Other difficulties arise if subsidiaries wish to transfer information involving personal data to their parent companies in the United States. As already pointed out above, the European Union regards US law as substandard in terms of data protection levels. Since parent companies and subsidiaries are regarded as *separate* entities when it comes to the exchange of personal data in Europe, US-based parent companies will have to guarantee European standards of data protection for any personal information which is reported back from their European subsidiaries for any purpose, including compliance with Sarbanes-Oxley. The European Commission has issued guidelines which set out the requirements for such agreements.[101] Alternatively, companies can participate in the so-called 'safe harbour' procedure which was negotiated between the US Department of Trade and the EU.[102]

The difficulties with Sarbanes-Oxley compliance that US-based public companies encounter when operating in European countries was cause for significant concern in business circles. The European Commission responded in early 2006 with an opinion paper, which provided further guidance on the conflict between European data protection requirements as set out in the EU Data Protection Directive[103] and whistle-blowing hotlines as required by the Act.[104] The paper, an attempt to co-ordinate the approach taken by courts and regulatory authorities in France, Germany, and other EU Member States, is an example of the patchiness of Community law described above. It has addressed at least part of these issues, but in-house lawyers and their outside legal counsel continue to grapple with the interpretation of the Directive and national data protection laws on a daily basis. Complex balance-of-interest issues arise, and the formulation and implementation of

[98] Compagnie Européenne d'Accumulateurs, a subsidiary of Exide Technologies, the world's largest industrial and transportation battery producer and recycler.

[99] See CNIL Délibération No 2005-110, May 26, 2005 (McDonalds) and Délibération No 2005-111, May 26, 2005 (CEAC/Exide Technologies).

[100] Landesarbeitsgericht Düsseldorf, Case 10 TaBV 46/05 of 14 November 2005. On 'whistleblowing' and data protection in Germany see Zimmermann, RDV 2006, 242 *ff*; Schmidl, DuD 2006, 353 *ff*; Meyer, NJW 2006, 3605 *ff*; Düsseldorfer Kreis, Arbeitsbericht 'Whistleblowing hotlines: Firmeninterne Warnsysteme und Beschäftigtendatenschutz' (available in German at http://www.datenschutz-hamburg.de).

[101] Regulation 95/46/EG, Official Journal 2001, L 181/19.

[102] See the 'safe harbour' website of the US Department of Commerce at www.export.gov/safeharbor.

[103] Directive 95/46/EC.

[104] Working Paper 117 on the application of EC data protection rules to internal whistle-blowing schemes in the fields of accounting, internal accounting controls, auditing matters, fight against bribery, banking and financial crime of February 2006.

EU-compatible codes of conduct remains a legal minefield. Mapping out appropriate strategies with respect to particular types of personal information—including individual access of company officers to personal data, the confidentiality and/or anonymity of reports, the areas covered by whistle-blowing schemes, disclosure of background information about such schemes and individual rights to a company's employees (and, most importantly, to incriminated individuals), the technical security of processing operations, and the transfer of information to third countries—requires substantial experience, often in a large number of jurisdictions. Many multinational enterprises have responded to this challenge by employing specially trained 'compliance' lawyers. Their task, often an assessment of the financial risks which could materialise from the infringement of either American or foreign law, is a highly comparative one. It is, finally, made even more demanding by the fair amount of uncertainty surrounding the exact reach of American legislation.[105]

Many of the above issues are currently under review on both sides of the Atlantic, and the future of the Sarbanes-Oxley Act is therefore hard to predict. One thing, however, should have become clear, whatever the outcome of these discussions—international commercial practice is highly dependent on precise information about the differences between a large variety of legal systems, and lawyers trained in comparative methodology hold the thread to navigate what is often nothing short of King Minos' labyrinth.

4. LESSONS FOR COMPARATIVE LAW AS A DISCIPLINE

In the years to come, courtrooms are likely to see more judges requesting (or at least willing to contemplate) information on foreign approaches to the domestic issues under consideration in particular cases. Classrooms should consequently prepare future generations of litigation lawyers for legal battles which—we predict—will increasingly provide opportunities for comparative arguments to shine. But the world is far larger than courtrooms and classrooms combined, and the examples set out above show that the need for a very practical form of comparative law is already long upon us. In this Chapter we have tried to provide at least a glimpse of the complex difficulties that in-house lawyers and outside legal counsel already face in a globalised world, and emphasised how important a tool comparative methodology is for contemporary commercial legal practice. States are increasingly willing to collaborate in many areas but the true global players today are companies which operate on an international level. They are driven by economic considerations, which include the value of standardised products, choice of the most convenient legal forum, and the importance of both efficient and cost-effective forms of internal organisation. Comparative legal work is a part of each.

What, then, are the lessons for the subject? There are, we think, at least four.

[105] Section 806 of the Sarbanes-Oxley Act thus provides protection for employees who use whistle-blowing procedures to raise alarm inside a company. In Carnero, a case involving an employee of an Argentine subsidiary of Boston Scientific who was dismissed after reporting alleged cases of accounting fraud to his superiors in the United States, the First Circuit Court of Appeals decided in 2006 that these protections do not apply to foreign employees, and dismissed the claim for reinstatement. See Ruben *Carnero v Boston Scientific Corporation* 433 F 3d 1 (1st Cir, January 5 2006).

First, the need for lawyers with an international outlook might be far larger than currently appreciated. The increasing use of comparative law in courtrooms, though certainly an important indicator, by no means reflects the full extent of comparative work currently conducted in commercial practice. It is, in fact, barely the proverbial tip of the iceberg. Large enterprises across the globe are looking for lawyers with dual or even multiple legal and linguistic qualifications, and even small and mid-sized companies seeking to take full advantage of regional or global markets may from time to time require the advice of lawyers with a grounding in other legal systems (and, which is important for those interested, are prepared to pay very well for such qualifications). Often, this will not just involve the knowledge of foreign law but rather a *comparative* evaluation of commercial risks and opportunities. The meetings of legal departments in multinational enterprises such as Yahoo! Inc—often conducted in weekly conference calls, with in-house lawyers from across the globe attending via video links—can thus at times develop into exercises in applied comparative law. The legal implications of new products are discussed on a regular basis, national approaches are compared, and practical solutions are often transferred from one system to another with the help of colleagues sitting around the table. The increasing need of companies with a global reach to recruit personnel with this type of profile has also had an impact on large law firms, who are equally pressed to offer the kind of cross-border legal assistance required in today's global marketplace.

The second powerful message for comparative law becomes clear when we recall some of the areas briefly touched upon in this Chapter—data protection, health and safety standards, genetical engineering, banking, accounting, compliance issues, company law, insolvency, and many others. Comparative work in commercial practice is *highly specific*—there is simply no time to be wasted on general philosophical, sociological or anthropological reflexions, and the closer a legal source (be it a journal article, a book, or a website) 'homes in' on the problem at hand, the more likely it will be used and affect human behaviour. Asking in-house lawyers the ultimate question ('does academic research provide you with the kind of resources you need for your daily work?') will, however, more often than not be answered in the negative. Colleagues attending a European or global legal telephone or video conference know that Roman law existed; the Germans among them will have heard of Konrad Zweigert and Hein Kötz, as will the French of René David and the Italians of Rodolfo Sacco; and some of them may at some point in their legal education even have read the general introductions to comparative law penned by these eminent authors. But will these books be found in the offices of in-house lawyers in multinational pharmaceutical companies or internet service providers? Will they play a role when dealing with the intricate problems created by today's increasingly complex regulatory frameworks such as the American Sarbanes-Oxley Act? And do they have an impact on choice of law considerations or international arbitration clauses? Hardly.

This tough assessment does not make the work of these comparatists obsolete. General introductions will serve to get students interested in the subject and can provide background knowledge for practitioners who work in an international legal environment. But they will most certainly *not* be a regular point of reference in the day-to-day work of in-house lawyers and outside legal counsel confronted with the kind of problems outlined in this Chapter. Indeed, one might go further and argue that they will not even provide the starting point of their thinking process. What is surprising—dare we say inexcusable—is that academics of the comparative or general variety refuse to acknowledge this reality, and instead attempt to downplay the importance of practical comparative law. Ignorance of what is happening in the real world may be a reason for the positions they adopt; but we seriously doubt that it is a plausible defence for not seeing the inevitable.

A third observation, which also features in other parts of this book, is that commercial legal practice is strongly driven by Western concepts of law. This certainly reflects the fact that some legal systems are more 'mature' than others, and have thought about particular problems relevant to our modern ways of life for a longer period of time. 'Uniform' approaches (such as the United Nations Convention on Contracts for the International Sale of Goods) are thus more often than not 'restatements' of continental European or Anglo-American law, to which other systems such as Islamic law or indigenous African law have contributed next to nothing. To argue otherwise would be to bend one's logic to fit contemporary political fads, not to reality.

An equally important explanation lies in the way commercial practice influences developments in key areas of the law. Multinational enterprises based in the United States and Europe operate in practically every corner of the world and tend to bring their own commercial and legal approaches with them. This is hardly likely to change in the future, and will make the legal systems home to such 'multinationals' more relevant than other legal cultures around the world. At least in terms of commercial legal practice, comparatists are thus well advised to focus on the major legal systems if they wish to secure the future of their subject as an academic discipline. Certainly, those who wish to practise (in one form or another) in a our globalised economy cannot afford to do otherwise.

On a more general level, finally, we predict that comparative methodology (and not just knowledge of foreign law) will have an important role to play for many years to come. Unification or harmonisation of the law on a regional and global level has increased substantially over the last century, but so has national regulatory intervention in areas relevant to commercial legal practice. Consumer protection (in ever so many forms), environmental law, internal auditing standards, compliance procedures, and data protection, are again good examples where multinational enterprises are in the future likely to face a more fragmented rather than a more uniform legal world. The economic pressure to sell the same product across the globe—be it a credit arrangement, 'geo-targeted' internet advertisement, or a bottle of Coke—will, however, remain. With it the need for comparative law, as defined in this book, will grow.

11

REFLECTING ON THE FUTURE: THE SUBJECT AND ITS TEACHERS

1. OPENING REMARKS

(a) Speaking One's Mind

Restrained language has always been considered one of the hallmarks of true scholarship. It facilitates exchange of ideas by fostering mutual respect. It removes passion from the written text or the speech and allows logic to reign supreme. It is also a feature of a legal style which, these days, is being modified if not occasionally neglected. Certainly, reading the legal texts of older British legal scholars, one cannot help but appreciate the muscular tone of their writing, admire their self-confident ability to restrain their footnotes to a minimum (which neither of us, belonging as we do to the Euro-Germanic tradition, can or wish to do) and envy the elegance of their language, which contrasts so profoundly with the use of the neologisms which disfigure the texts of contemporary writers. The main question, however, is whether there are reasons why 'modifications' of this traditional approach may be desirable and not just inevitable given the general decline in legal writing that accompanies our technological era, where 'bullet-form' presentations have become the principal form of communication in today's corporate boardrooms.

Modification is the key word, for that is as much as is called for. Those who contemplate a conscious change in the expression of their arguments in no way wish to be defamatory or (less so) hurtful. But excessive restraint also has some drawbacks. To begin with, it is often false. The oft-used phrase 'with respect' is well known to indicate little or no respect by the speaker towards the person to whom the argument is addressed. Practising lawyers know that 'with great respect' suggests that the speaker regards the addressee of his comments with even less respect or admiration. Hypocrisy is part of social life; and it could be argued that it is not devoid of all value. Pretending to be one thing but being another is a phenomenon which we also find in nature; and here it assists self-preservation. Nature's rules can never be judged by reference to morality or elegance, only efficacy. There may be times when the same should apply to legal writing.

Over-restrained reaction can also make a lecture or text dull. Sometimes passion can be profitably displayed; opposition to an idea of theory strongly voiced; or humour injected to make a serious point more palatable or noticeable (though political correctness has nowadays almost banished humour from the lecture theatre given the many restrictions it has imposed even on well-intended speech). Contrasts in style also make the substance of the respective arguments and ideas stand out more sharply. The listener or the reader may be provoked to react; and in the classroom (more so than the courtroom) intellectual 'provocation' can be useful in so far as it pushes the audience to think and react.

In law the topics discussed, especially when related to political ideas, invite passion and can become more memorable if presented with some force. One can respect an (intellectual) opponent but utterly condemn his ideas as well as his attitude towards issues or people. The speaker should have the right to make such opposition clear; and in this book we have adopted this stance. In most cases we have been anxious to stress our respect for the intellectual talents of the colleague with whom we are disagreeing. But to tone down criticism, allow contrived subtlety to conceal legitimate strong feelings about our subject, its utility in the academic curriculum, and in the courtroom, would strike us as tantamount to letting it down. As Lord Justice Laws once put it so elegantly in an extra-judicial pronouncement, '[I]t is never enough to suppress free speech because its expression will hurt people's feelings'.[1]

We feel strongly about this; and it is strong feelings which, at times, have made our text hard-hitting or even acerbic. What mainly makes us say this is the fact that we have read many articles, essays, case notes and even books which are so bland and plainly descriptive that we felt we had to express these feelings in order to highlight the other side of the argument. To use the commercial language of a widely known advertisement—*where is the beef?* In our case, *where is the new contribution?* For too many comparatists see comparison as a mere description of a foreign system or even a summary of views expressed by others. Comparative law needs more than a description. It needs comparison, reflection, intuition, and further deductions following the exposition of foreign law. If stating this (and supporting it with illustrations) means being attacked ourselves, that, too, is acceptable. Justice Holmes was the first who spoke of a 'marketplace of ideas'[2]; and everyone who has had the remotest exposure to the 'market' as an investor, dealer, or advisor, knows that when economic interests clash, the gloves come off. The battle of ideas is no lesser struggle, so we have expressed our views accordingly. We would like to think that if those with whom we disagree object to what we say and how we say it, those who have no immediate stake in this debate will, on the other hand, enjoy the frankness of a robust text.

(b) Specialised Knowledge and Wider Culture

The ideas presented in this book are closely related to the aims of comparative law. What is the purpose of the subject? How can we best achieve it (or how can its aims be pursued effectively if it has more than one and if they are different)? Does the subject have a future in a shrinking world in which we are coming closer together, especially in some parts of the globe? Is harmonisation, once achieved, the death knell of comparative studies? These questions all need answers; and the answers they receive will also help shape the kind of education, learning, and experience those concerned with the subject ought to have. One issue in particular is that of language: can/should comparative law be limited only to systems that share the same language? Some would so argue.[3] Lack of imagination ('the Common law

[1] 'Judicial Remedies and the Constitution', 57 *MLR* 213, 225 (1994). The rest of the quotation deserves to be given here since it refers to political correctness. Thus, the learned judge continued: 'That is why any attempt to attach sanction against the use of what are called "politically incorrect" expressions, or to require the use of "politically correct" forms of speech, would be a neo-fascist exercise. Quite apart from the grotesque, if ludicrous, effects on the language created by claptrap of this kind, it is to my mind chilling that by the very phrase "politically correct" its proponents necessarily lay claim to a monopoly of wisdom as to where the truth lies'.

[2] *Abrams v United States* 250 US 616, 630–1 (1919).

[3] Jane Stapleton, 'Benefits of Comparative Tort Reasoning: Lost in Translation', (2007) *Journal of Tort Law*, vol 1, Issue 3, at p 11 of the online version at www.bepress.com/jtl/vol1/iss3/art6.

world seems, at least to me, rich enough'[4]) or caution (foreign-language comparative tort law is fraught with dangers'[5]) lie at the root of such attitudes. One cannot help the first, for one is born with or without it; but one must battle against the second since caution has always stopped innovation, progress, and improvement—courage, alone, having achieved the opposite. Besides, we have seen that worldwide experience suggests that the opposite from what is advocated by the conservatives is in fact practised by many courts—some of which have even found ways to reduce the risks that accompany inadequate knowledge of a foreign language—and, even more importantly, by commercial practice. Many academics share this analysis.[6]

Another issue is the extent of wider reading and interests which the comparatist should possess in order to carry out his task to the best advantage. The interlinking of these themes is, itself, a subject worthy of further exploration.

A legal sociologist—Roger Cotterrell—looked at some of the basic issues in one of his recent essays. He is not the only one to explore what are the subject's legitimate aims, for such enquiries have figured in comparative literature for almost the whole of the last century. One of the things that make his work interesting is that he has collected at least nine different aims or purposes for comparative law, and put them all in one paragraph. The richness of aims is, we shall suggest, more apparent than real. But Professor Cotterrell's meticulous notes (omitted from the following extract but valuable to anyone wishing to pursue the matter further) show that not everyone in our branch shares our emphasis on a more focused approach. Cotterell thus wrote:[7]

> The literature of comparative law suggests an immense range of possible justifications for the enterprise. Comparison of law might be pursued: (i) to find ideas useful in improving or clarifying one's own legal system; (ii) to aid detailed communication between lawyers of different systems, for example, in interpreting a uniquely common-law institution as the trust in civil law contexts; (iii) to explain legal development in particular systems by tracing lines of legal borrowing and influence; (iv) to harmonize or unify areas of law on a transnational basis to promote trade or economic activity across borders, or for other reasons; (v) to provide legal solutions to causes of international conflicts and so promote international understanding; (vi) to give law students and legal scholars a more distanced view of their own system, challenging the sense of naturalness and inevitability of its particular legal arrangement and promoting appreciation of 'difference'; (vii) to understand the power of legal cultures, for example, as barriers to harmonization of law; (viii) to find a 'common trunk' of legal ideas to express 'the awakening of an international consciousness'; or (ix) to contribute toward knowledge of the social world through study of its legal aspects.

Though Professor Cotterrell goes on to state 'that other professed aims of comparative law are found in the literature' one must ask oneself to what extent these are truly different aims or whether there is an overlap between all these causes, purposes, or aims. From our perspective Professor Vogenauer struck the right note when he wrote (not specifically referring to Cotterrell's summary) that all of the above really boil down to two essential aims. In his words:[8]

[4] *Ibid*, p 33.

[5] *Ibid*, p 44.

[6] James Gordley, When Is the Use of Foreign Law Possible? A Hard Case: The Protection of Privacy in Europe and the United States, 67 *Louisiana Law Review* 1073 (2007).

[7] Roger Cotterrell, 'Comparatists and Sociology', in Pierre Legrand and Roderick Munday (eds), *Comparative Legal Studies: Traditions and Transitions* (2003), pp 131, 134–5.

[8] 'Sources of Law and Method in Comparative Law' in Mathias Reimann and Reinhard Zimmermann (eds), *The Oxford Handbook of Comparative Law* (2006), pp. 869, 875 (emphasis added).

> There are, broadly speaking, two conceivable aims of comparative law. One possibility is to see the accumulation of comparative knowledge as an end in itself without further need of justification [reference to Rodolfo Sacco omitted]. Alternatively, comparative studies can be regarded as a means to another end, and a number of functions of comparative law are conventionally enumerated for this purpose. Some of these, *one might even argue the most important of these, are directly concerned with the creation, application, and interpretation of the law.*

Though one cannot deny the volume of literature serving the first purpose—the *Oxford Handbook* offers its own examples—we entirely agree with the italicised section of the quotation. Unlike others (including Professor Vogenauer), who have stressed this aim but failed to explain it or show to others how it should be achieved, we have devoted much time to this issue. This book, and our work as a whole, has thus been devoted to devising ways of using knowledge accumulated about a foreign system in one's own environment, be they related to court-induced or legislator-induced reform activities. For though we take for granted what Professor Vogenauer says, indeed accept the caution he urges in identifying the sources to be relied upon, we have also wished to go a step further and show how one can and should use this material in a foreign (ie different) setting. It is thus somewhat sad to observe that the general literature on comparative law has failed to address head-on this cardinal issue of methodology which even Professor Sacco, often cited as the strongest advocate of the pure scholarship, has admitted to exist.

This brings us back to culture (and not just legal education). Our own preference to serve the second cause should not be seen as demonstrating a neglect for cultural matters. The form in which we have presented the issues discussed in this book shows that the way we believe the study of foreign law should be pursued can only be practised properly by people who have a wider understanding of foreign culture. We have always subscribed to the view that education and culture are not the same, and have always supported initiatives (educational or societal) which encourage the acquisition of wider learning. Indeed, one of our most frequent complaints has been the fact that the modern educational system (as well as the family environment, which we regard as another very important source of education, training, and the shaping of character) does less and less to encourage and reward wider learning. We regard modern computer technology to have contributed to the decline of writing skills; and Professor David Gerber has discussed other issues related to the accumulation of information deriving from modern technologies.[9]

The above observations demonstrate an attempt on our part to discover or create a link between our emphasis on practical issues and the pursuit of knowledge for the sake of knowledge. We certainly hope that our work displays a reasonable awareness of the wider issues related to our subject as well as an awareness of the relevant literature. Yet what we are suggesting here is a *link*, not a wholesale adoption of the *ars gratia artis* approach. Our aim remains overwhelmingly practical. In the context of a law school curriculum, the command of wider knowledge is not called upon for the purposes of teaching and learning purely for the purpose of learning. In our view it is necessary for the understanding of legal rules, how they are affected by other (wider) societal but not necessarily legal factors, and how all of these taken together can show us how foreign law can be put to practical use.

It follows, therefore, that our approach to comparative law does not mean including within the law curriculum subjects which are unlikely to serve such aims. The statement by a learned French colleague that 'understanding French law requires knowledge and under-

[9] 'Globalization and Legal Knowledge: Implications for Comparative law', 75 *Tul L Rev* 949 (2001).

standing of French films' takes matters too far. Any attempt to integrate into one's study of foreign law all the elements of a foreign culture can only result (intentionally or not) in making comparison impossible. Learning to distinguish the relevant from the irrelevant is a matter of knowledge, experience, and (above all) common sense. No amount of legal sophistry, even of the kind in which law professors can indulge, can diminish the importance of this advice.

This, of course, includes the study of completely different legal cultures; and this is because they are of little practical use for the ultimate aim pursued. Sharia law should be an example; for the information so gleaned is in most cases irrelevant to our system (though our legal experience, say in matters of commercial law, may be of use even to religious systems). The same goes, perhaps with even greater force, for the anthropological study of customary or tribal law, which is too inaccessible but also too primitive to serve (at any rate in all but the most exceptional cases) as models for imitation or even inspiration. The chapters devoted to 'Religious Systems of African Customary Law' in the *Oxford Handbook* were thus read with interest but have done nothing to dissuade us from this belief. To put it differently, we can envisage an inquisitive (legal) mind reading parts of the anthropological work there described while 'on holiday' or during some other moment of leisure. But we doubt that it would ever be consulted during 'billable hours'.

There are other reasons why the pursuit of knowledge purely for the sake of knowledge is not what should be happening in law schools in the realm of comparative law. Though we do not subscribe to the 'ghetto view' mentioned at the beginning of this book, the fact is that the university curriculum, indeed even the school curriculum, is nowadays under many stresses, and these pressures are bound to affect our ability to teach and do research. Willingness to invest time and effort studying systems such as African customary law must be restrained by practical considerations. The study of subjects which are likely to give us few (if any) immediate returns are bound to wither on the vine, at least as far as law schools are concerned. Whether they should survive in other faculties is not for us to say or argue.

So what are these pressures?

First is the pressure to include new subjects which the 'market'—employers, governments, or even the students themselves—considers as necessary. This has, indeed, occurred more recently. The number of such new courses taught in Oxford and Cambridge has gone up dramatically. A rough guess suggests that something close to one third of the currently taught subjects—including Community law, human rights, and intellectual property law—were (virtually) untouched in Oxbridge until the late 1960s. Even commercial law appeared only in fragmented ways as part of advanced courses in contract and tort, company law, or isolated offerings such as agency. Banking law, financial services, insolvency, or securities were virtually ignored. And administrative law was for a long time treated as a mere appendix to constitutional law.

This enlargement of the curriculum is both necessary and intellectually enriching. But every time a new subject is added (whether as an obligatory offering or as a higher year option) something must come out or be relegated to a secondary position. For a law faculty can only ask its members to do so much; and in these days of constant assessments, unceasing laws and rules of conduct regulating administrative details (serious as well as trivial, but all requiring action—usually in the form of extra paperwork!), not to mention the growing pressures to fundraise, university teaching staff is over-stretched. Even less well treated is the administrative support staff, which also has to carry a growing volume of work and is paid substantially below the market rates. Finally, even students can only be asked to take on a limited number of subjects; and this number is getting smaller as the pressure to shorten the period of legal studies has reached the bone.

To the above realities add yet another and even more ominous one: money (or, rather, the lack of it). Demosthenes warned the Athenians a long time ago that without money nothing can be done. Lack of funds means that all institutions of higher education (and their law faculties) must make choices as never before in their long (or short) histories. That is one reason why Roman law, anthropology, and other such subjects are feeling the axe; and so they should. For if their prime reason for inclusion in a law curriculum—and, once again, we are expressing no view as to whether they should continue to exist, expand, or be restricted in other faculties since this of no immediate concern to our subject—is to give students a view of another system and/or a feel of a different way of addressing the same kind of problems, then these aims can be done just as well by teaching modern German, French, Italian or Spanish law. Indeed, teaching these subjects does more, since it informs our students about another living legal system and forces or encourages them to learn a *living* language which will be infinitely more useful to their careers than Latin (which, in any event, is quickly disappearing even as an A-level option). We do not expect those who, for a variety of legitimate reasons, object to these ideas to espouse ours—indeed, we even *expect* them to fight back. But however much people may fight, in the end these battles are won by what is dictated by the realities of their times. We made these points in this book; and for the reasons already explained we have made them strongly.

This does not solve the main problem of studying foreign law—which is not only to *find* it, but also to *understand* it and then *use* it constructively. We shall return to this point again further down; but, to begin with, we shall deal with it in accordance to the general stance thus far.

(c) Political Aims and Comparative Law

There was a time, especially after the Second World War, when comparatists tried to present their subject as being politically neutral. While one can understand why they took this view, especially those who were central European political émigrés and found themselves working in different countries (but especially in the United States[10]), such an approach is no longer tenable in our times. Indeed, the political element was as obvious to the previous generation as it is to the current one. Yet the underlying politics of times past seem different from those of today.

For one, the emphasis was on legal unification (which has, of course, its own political undertones), but it would be difficult to argue that the message was politically positioned on the 'Right' or the 'Left'. Nor was the intellectual debate ever meaningfully extended beyond the geographical limits of Europe and the United States. Both these points have been challenged by changing geopolitical developments and (especially) the politicisation of the subject by CLS. This shift shows a different kind of politics lying beneath (and sometimes even on the surface of) the subject. These express a distinct mistrust for 'establishment' thinking or strong left overtones, and display an attempt to include with the purview

[10] The influence that the Jewish-German émigrés had on American law is well documented. Thus, see EC Stiefel and F Mecklenburg, *Deutsche Juristen im amerikanischen Exil (1933–1955)* (1991) and, more recently, Lutter/Stiefel/Hoeflich (eds), *Der Einfluss deutscher Emigranten auf die Rechtsentwicklung in den USA und in Deutschland. Vorträge und Referate des Bonner Symposium im September 1991* (1994).

of comparative studies other legal systems, something which is often seen as yet another battle against political or cultural imperialism. There has also been a strong interest to bring within the walls of a law school disciplines like anthropology and sociology, which have interacted with comparative law but not often within the context of the same faculty.

All these shifts are understandable, even if they have failed to convince a substantial number of comparatists. But what has attracted most criticism for this new school of thought was not just its militant tone but also the unattractive language 'invented' by some of its members. The Utah Essays are widely seen as this group's political manifesto; and depending on which school of thought one belongs to, one will find in them justification for praise or criticism.

In intellectual terms, such a re-orientation of thinking and tone of argument is neither surprising nor unexpected, and (within measure) not even unwelcome. This is the stuff of which academic discourse is made; and it is based on an evolutionary theory of knowledge. For dogmas, doctrines, and theories must all succumb to the inevitable pressures brought about by societal change. They must all be constantly debated; and when they lose their theoretical or practical appeal, they must be modified or allowed to die. The debate, however, instituted by the CLS movement (in all its shapes and forms, including militant feminism), has become important and acrimonious for at least two reasons.

First, on a general level, the attempts of the 'political correctness movement' to impose its views on unwilling academics or, at the very least, subject them to a growing number of rules concerning university comportment, has led to a strong reaction against the will to impose a new academic ethos.[11] The objections are more strongly felt when the pressures are extended to university appointments on the grounds of some variant of reverse or positive discrimination. These divisions have become so serious that it is said that in one or two of the best law schools in the United States appointments proceed on the basis, 'camp A got one post so it is now the turn of Camp B to get its own'. If this is true, it seems more like political horse trading or, to put it more politely, a desire to keep a minimum of internal peace in an otherwise highly divided faculty. But it can hardly be described as the election of the most scholarly productive and original person to a vacant chair. This is not, in our view, just a condemnable development; it also defeats the real or apparent attempts made by most universities to claim that their selection processes are fair and transparent.

Secondly, as far as comparative law is concerned, this movement has tried to re-orient the direction of the subject, its aims, its targets, and even its language. Here the opposition to these innovations has been no less fervent. From the point of view of comparative law, it has also been motivated by the sincere belief that, if this new school were to prevail, it would seriously damage the future of the subject and the employment of the comparative method by practitioners. This book has concentrated on this theme and tried to show why its position is currently being vindicated in practice.

[11] For a wider criticism of these tendencies and their comparison with the Soviet Realist movement of the 1920s and 1930s, which did so much to degrade the quality of Russian literature, see Basil Markesinis, *Good and Evil in Art and Law* (2007), Ch 8 (h). More generally, see Ian Ward, *Law and Literature. Possibilities and Perspectives* (1995) where, after a detailed examination of the movement and its protagonists, the learned author observes (at p 22): 'The early socio-political CLS [Critical Legal Studies] movement began with the very best of motives. Its primary ambition was to educate law students about the politics of law. It has ended, not by reaching any particular goal or indeed identifying one, but by going round in ever-decreasing circles, using up its dissipating energies in a multitude of various internecine disputes, and in the invention of increasingly pretentious and ultimately useless language which, rather than educating, serves only to mystify and then to alienate all but the most fervent of believers'.

Why this movement and its ideas still remain outside the mainstream of comparative law was set out briefly in Chapters One and Two. More importantly, we also explained why we feel that it is contributing towards making comparative law an unattractive academic option (though some students may see it as a 'soft' one as well!). But, whether one likes this or not, the fact is that CLS has, undoubtedly, contributed to upping the political character of the debate about comparative law, and even brought back elements of a class battle which is obvious in the way some of its members have tried to caricature mainstream comparatists.

For present purposes, however, the orientation towards the Left of the political spectrum should not concern us too much. To be sure, it has to be mentioned; for if one section of our own academic community takes an overtly political position, those opposed to it are bound to react by taking the opposite direction. Yet the real attention should be given to another issue (or issues). By that we mean that the reaction should not be in terms of 'Right' or 'Left'—since both of these terms have lost, we feel, their original significance. For us the opposition should choose, instead, to focus (a) on the geographical centre of its own interests, and (b) decide upon the use which the ever-growing accumulation of information about foreign systems should be put to. This brings us back, via another route, to the question of Eurocentrism.

This last word should not, of course, be understood to mean that Europe is the political centre of the world as it was when the 1900 Congress of Paris launched comparative law into the public domain. For such political power as Europe had until the Second World War it has rapidly lost ever since. This weakening process will also, in our view, continue for as long as the European Union sees its future as lying in constant geographical expansion to include countries which are either not 'European' or not prepared in economic and social terms to join the older and more advanced nations instead of aiming at strengthening the internal cohesion of the Union and streamlining its unwieldy institutions.

Yet, though political power may have waned, Europe remains a hub of great intellectual activity, especially in the areas of law in general and comparative law in particular—and thus, along with the United States (with whom it has, in legal if not always political terms, many points of common reference), it is likely to remain an important source of legal influence on others. This richness of European activities is acknowledged even by those who wish to take American law 'out of the European shadow'.

This is especially true in certain important areas of the law—most notably commerce, financial services, intellectual property, and social welfare law. In those parts of the world which will soon become even greater centres of political power and influence, the impact of Eurocentric and US-centred law will exert huge influence, precisely because of the undoubted legal expertise found in these systems. These emerging political super powers—China, India and, eventually, one or two countries in South America such as Brazil and Argentina—will need this expertise if they are to hasten their transformation into modern economic and technological centres. They will not find it in the Critical Legal Studies literature.

That is where the political and economic power is shifting; and this slow shift of the political tectonic plates is already noticed by politicians, economists and businessmen. The shift is largely taking place because these countries possess rich resources of raw materials and (very) cheap labour. Leftist theorists may see this as fertile ground for their political views; business sees it as a great opportunity to create new wealth at the expense of the more socially conscious old world.

What about academics? Members of the Critical Legal Studies school have spent time telling Columbian law faculties how the movement can contribute to their legal and political development. One such research paper, by the *vieillard terrible* of the group, appeared in 2003 in printed form.[12] Its author refers to its 'sweeping assertions as supported by a minimal footnote apparatus that reflects the vagaries of [his own] interests and reading'. This is a shrewd confession to make; and it suggests either huge self-confidence or modesty (or both—if indeed these are compatible with each other). Yet is this really the way to attract the attention of these emerging economies, especially the ones who are leading in this race? We submitted to Professor Bryan Garner (among others) the above-cited passages from Professor Legrand's attack on Professor Kötz and invited his comments on language and style. His reply, unlike the endless text under scrutiny, was brief: 'parenthesis-filled, neologism-laden gibberish'. Those—many—who in America treat Professor Garner's *The Elements of Legal Style* (2002) or his *A Dictionary of Modern Legal Usage* (2001) as the Bible for the good legal American should take note, especially since they operate in that country and will be judged by the canons which prevail over there. As for England, we venture to suggest that the doubts about the text might be voiced in an even less appreciative way.

Academic lawyers should assess all these complex factors and their implications for the methodological approach. We have done just that; and we maintain that the above world developments do not affect our own theorising, our methodology, and those whom we should be targeting to proselytise to our ideas. Thus, in our view, the attempt of CLS in all its variants to shift attention to 'radically different cultures'—with or without its unattractive recourse to neologisms and its 'sweeping assertions'—will remain attractive only to certain groups of trendy academics but not the world we keep calling the 'real world'.

Were we alone in arguing this last-mentioned view, the proverbial observer from Mars might be entitled to count numbers and decide which academic school was gaining the upper hand: Hein Kötz, Ulrich Magnus, Walter van Gerven or Reinhard Zimmermann, one might argue, versus Duncan Kennedy, Ugo Mattei, Pierre Legrand or Anneliese Riles? That is four on either side, so is it a draw? CLS may be 'politically dead', as Professor Kennedy admitted in the above-cited article; but its legal branch at least is still striving to make itself heard. Yet that would be a wrong way to set about assessing the impact of this movement on the *creation and interpretation of the law.*

For one of the most interesting aspects of this debate about the purposes of comparative studies is the fact that nowadays it has also attracted the attention of leading judges from all over the world. It thus requires no great degree of ingenuity to see in the recent dialogue between the (then) First President of the French Court of Cassation, Guy Canivet, and Justice Stephen Breyer of the US Supreme Court a certain judicial preference for the positions we have been advocating for many years now. The published text of this debate thus shows a judicial agreement to stress the growing communality of values among the advanced industrial states, the need for co-operation between academics and practitioners, and the need to learn how to package the foreign information in order to make it usable by practitioners.[13] Moreover, both debaters seem to imply that it is the systematic and coherently developed ideas of these systems which will be used to help *les pays émergents* to move to a more advanced socio-economic and political level. Thus, as we argued in the earlier Chapters, it is Fiji, Romania or Columbia which will need to borrow from the most advanced and efficient systems of what was once called the 'Western world' and are

[12] Duncan Kennedy, 'Two Globalizations on Law & Legal Thought', 36 *Suffolk U L Rev 631* (2003).

[13] See the full text at http://www.culturedroit.com/pages/culture-droit-1-le-voisinage-des-cours-supreme-a-l-heure-du-village-mondial-stephen-breyer-guy-canivet.htm.

extremely unlikely to become, themselves, exporters of legal ideas. This idea of convergence, so crucial to our interrelated theses, also seems to have the support of some of Britain's top judges.[14]

Of course, one might return to the counting of voices or votes argument and claim that Canivet and Breyer each have one voice and one vote, and Legrand or Riles, likewise, have one—which, however, goes in the other direction. Our Martian observer might thus, again, be asked to call this a draw. Yet the emergence of the judge as comparatist combatant[15] means that the balance has now shifted decisively in favour of one side: that of the pragmatist school of thought. For a mere counting of voices would leave the issue we are addressing unresolved, besides being utterly misleading. *For though in a political contest each vote has the same weight, this is not so in the battle of ideas.* Here, *who* says something can often be more important than *what* he says; and, conversely (and regrettably perhaps), a good idea by an academic scholar can go unnoticed and unrewarded for a long time simply because of his lesser profile, status, or influence. So, if one is honest (rather than pretends to be polite or politically correct), one will admit that these two sets of voices—Canivet and Breyer—carry a very different weight in practice *for they reflect what is actually happening and how the ruling elites think and act.* Those who detest 'establishments' and make this a central part of their legal theorising should thus tell us, *in the context of the real world of legal practice and trade,* how they intend to change reality or interest the law makers in their cause. The recent case law of the French Court of Cassation, showing (as we suggested in Chapter Six) a growing interest in the legal experiences of other systems, totally ignores the views of those who do not find any utility in legal borrowings, even if they are based in France and write in French. No prophet, one might be tempted to say, in his own country.

This orientation towards American-European law will, in our view, thus not only remain strong in case law but will also be reflected in the legislative processes of these emerging super-powers (and other slowly industrialising states) as well as to the law creation processes of the European countries themselves. The information we have from the work of the Law Commission in England and the committee charged with the task of updating the German Civil Code confirms the above and demonstrates that such law-reforming bodies display no interest whatsoever in engaging in a dialogue with 'radically different cultures'. We would be surprised if the mandarins and other civil servants in charge of advising French or other ministers in matters of law reform spent much time reading CLS work or, come to that, Pompomius!

Adherents of opposing schools may dislike these positions; but to conceal from their audiences the views of real 'heavyweights' (like Canivet and Breyer)[16] who espouse the kind of pragmatic views we are advancing in this book can only tempt detached observers of this intellectual debate to devalue the credibility of the adherents of the modern schools. If the views of the latter thus prevail—to the extent that they are gaining acceptance in academic circles—this must be considered the prime reason for pushing comparative law into a ghetto.

[14] Thus see: Lord Irving of Lairg, 'The Influence of Europe on Public law on the United Kingdom' and Lord Bingham of Cornhill KG, 'A New Common Law for Europe', both in Basil S Markesinis (ed), *The Clifford Chance Millennium Lectures. The Coming Together of the Common Law and the Civil Law* (2000) at pp 11 *ff* and 27 *ff* respectively.

[15] On this see our 'The Judge as Comparatist', 80(1) *Tul L Rev* 11–167 and the responses that follow from seven leading judges representing important courts around the world.

[16] By refusing even to make reference to this literature, let alone engaging with it head on.

Statistics suggest as much—except that the support they offer to our themes is of the cold, unmoving, and difficult-to-challenge way in which numbers tend to tell their story. For our figures not only show what attracts attention; they support our view, fully endorsed by Breyer and Canivet, that judges, in most cases, can only become aware of important decisions if practitioners draw their attention to them; and they can only carry out this task properly if suitably prepared—'convinced' is the word used by the American justice—by the professors who do the ground work. All these are political messages if the word 'political' is given a wide meaning.

Do we find any trace of these ideas in any of the papers contributed to the very large volumes edited by Professors Reimann and Zimmermann or Legrand and Munday, and published in the last three years or so? In our view, both books (but especially the second!) display a certain preference for the opposite set of ideas which, of course, the editors are perfectly entitled to support. This preference could, of course, be presented through the (welcome) lens of objectivity, namely by arguing that they had to give full coverage to the existing literature on comparative law, including its sociological, anthropological, and post-modernist shades. Yet for those who study these books, their coverage is not really complete in the sense that even the doctrinally inclined contributors have failed (a) to 'take on' the new schools of thought, or (b) stress the practical importance of the subject to their readers. To put it differently—though the scholarly credentials of many of the contributors are not in doubt, the passions that the subject generates these days has almost been extinguished by the effect scholarly presentation can have on learned papers, a point deliberately stressed at the beginning of this Chapter.

Nor do these works of academic learning even hint at the fact that the two judges already mentioned above seem to stand in total opposition to some of their academic creeds. The adherents to 'culture' always warn us not to omit from our evaluation the variety of different factors which exist in different mixtures in different countries and make it possible to understand comparative law deeply and properly. We submit that the points we are making here about the 'weight' of some speakers go in the same direction, and help the readers of this book learn to appreciate the effect that academic works have *in reality*, and not the impression they may create through the pages of a book which contains essays which cite each other. Thus, it is also part of understanding French legal culture to be shown that what an academic advocates is totally ignored by his courts. This is the best description possible of 'law in action' as contrasted to the law of an individual law professor sitting in a secluded library.

The battle is thus engaged, and should be engaged, between reality and appearance of reality. That is where the figures come into play; and figures can crush theories and egos. This, however, does not mean that those who invoke them and those who contest their value must not also handle them with caution. Chapter Three shows how much care we lavished on these points, constantly voicing our doubts, our difficulties, and the dilemmas that confronted us, and we challenge our readers to present us with other examples where comparative methodologists have tried to be more detailed, more cautious, and more frank when describing how they have used their raw data as well as the difficulties which they have encountered while pursuing this laborious task. Notwithstanding the above, our continuing efforts to refine our method means that we, naturally, stand by to be corrected and to improve where possible our methods and prescriptions. But such a dialogue with those who take different views can only proceed if the latter study carefully our figures and are willing to proceed constructively in a discussion concerning details and not in a clash of generalisations. For what these figures suggest is more damning than the most severely phrased article.

(d) Political and Economic Structures and Comparative Law: A Postscript to the Previous Sub-Heading

In the previous sub-heading we talked about politics in general and the politicisation of the comparative law debate, largely because of the overt political agenda of CLS. Here we must refer to the importance of one's wider beliefs about the organisation and structure of the political system and the state, an issue which we have raised in those sections of the book which tried to explain the current ambivalence of the French towards their law. The message there was that there seems to be no clear consensus among the French population, so the law and its background structures remain largely determined by a static spirit which flows from a wider inability to reform State thinking both in terms of internal politics and social welfare, and externally in terms of appreciating the need to formulate a foreign policy which is more compatible with the different status of French diplomacy on the world scene. This interlinking of law and politics, however, naturally applies everywhere, not only to France; indeed, we showed this ourselves, albeit in a sketchy manner because of considerations of space, when we discussed American law. Here, however, we wish to return to this overlap of law and politics in a way appropriate to a concluding Chapter, and briefly explain why we think it is important and deserves more scholarly attention.

To say that political and economic beliefs will determine the shape and form of a country's government is obvious. To add that it will also affect that country's law is hardly any more original. What we argue, however, goes beyond the above, for we also stress the impact which this co-existence of law, economics and politics can have on comparative law in general and, more particularly, the convergence/divergence debate which has been so central to this book. We do so drawing on the learning of Professor Anthony Ogus who, in a short piece,[17] not only takes on the importance of adding an economic perspective to the study of comparative law (persistently championed by Professor Ugo Mattei[18] but, we submit, still in a somewhat embryonic state). We also use his piece as the main focus of our brief observations because it offers an excellent (and final) example of how one can raise general issues but at the same time combine them with specific points or observations in a manner that makes the academic thesis attractive even to non-academic lawyers. Ogus' piece, in other words, can also profitably be consulted to illustrate and test our wider complaints about the abstract and sweeping style which one often finds in the writings of sociologists and learned French colleagues.[19]

[17] 'Competition Between National and Legal Systems: A Contribution of Economic Analysis to Comparative Law', 48 *ICLQ*, 405 (1999).

[18] See his *Comparative Law and Economics* (1997); Ugo Mattei and Francesco Cafaggi, 'Comparative Law and Economics' in P Newman (ed), *The New Palgrave Dictionary of Economics and the Law* (1998), vol I, pp 346–51.

[19] An excellent (and quite revealing) contrast of the difference in choice of subjects and styles of expression between English and French comparative law writing can be found by comparing the piece of Professors Anthony Ogus with Professor Antoine Garapon's 'French Legal Culture and the Shock of "Globalization"', (1995) 4 *Social and Legal Studies*, 493 *ff.* We draw our readers' attention to these two texts (indicatively juxtaposed) and invite them to attempt their own comparison not because we think that the articles assist the claims of those who argue that cultures are 'separate' and 'unbridgeable' but because we feel it strengthens our own view that what is 'separate' (or different) is the written style and, in particular, the level of abstraction and generalisation which seems to appeal to many French lawyers, sociologists, or literary critics, but which will leave common lawyers with the overall impression of 'literary waffle'. More importantly, this 'type' of writing—and Professor Muir Watt's piece in the *Oxford Handbook* is another example—are precisely the kind of pieces which are likely to leave indifferent judges and practitioners.

Ogus' starting point is that[20]

> [I]f suppliers of a product or service have to compete with one another, consumers can choose according to the quality and price of what is offered. On certain assumptions, that should mean that consumer preferences are met at lowest cost. The corollary is that monopolistic suppliers will not necessarily meet consumer preferences and they lack incentive to constrain costs. These simple propositions can be applied to the supply of law within a single jurisdiction . . . More significantly for the purposes of this article, interaction with other jurisdictions may create external competition for the supply of law . . . [Thus] if domestic industries competing in international markets find that their national legal system imposes on them higher costs than those incurred by their foreign competitors operating under a different jurisdiction, they will apply pressure on their lawmakers to reduce costs. The demand will be threatened by the threat of migration to the more favourable jurisdiction, assuming that there are no barriers to the freedom of establishment and to the movement of capital . . . [or] as an alternative to physical migration, and to the extent that this is allowed by the private international law of their home jurisdiction, firms may be able to select the jurisdictions whose principles are to apply to their transaction or business.

It will be noticed that though the approach to comparative law is here attempted via economics and its language—and in our view of all the 'law and' approaches the 'comparative law and politics/economics school' can be the most profitable one to be pursued for the purposes of putting our subject to better use—our own thinking in terms of 'packaging' fits in very well. Indeed, when Ogus writes that 'free movement in goods and services may be matched by free movement in legal rules'[21] this comes very close to our ideas of the need to be 'practical' and 'useful' (for the 'impractical' and the 'useless' never travel but wither). For though our analysis was not economic in its language or thinking, the ideas of competition and survival of the best are implicit in our approach and form a kind of Wagnerian leitmotiv of this book. And it is this idea which gives birth to the accompanying condemnation of branches of the law which confuse the debate and divert comparative law from its main mission.

Professor Ogus' theory also points towards convergence of systems since the one most popular and suitable, especially for trade and commerce, will prevail in the end. Yet Ogus is much more subtle in his analysis on convergence (achieved through economic pressures) for he rightly distinguishes between those areas of the law which, like trade and financial services (and, we would add, intellectual property and internet technology), may need *homogenous legal practices* and the more interventionist areas of the law where internal pressures, regulatory tendencies and practices, and economic theory, do not favour such a convergence. To cite Ogus for the last time,[22]

> [T]he general conclusion . . . is that competition between national systems will not necessarily lead to a convergence of 'interventionist' law, since preference as to the content of the law may vary significantly.

It is here where French culture—the culture of protectionism, regulation, centralisation, and administrative interference (often in the form of excessive ministerial control over university affairs)—may prove a greater obstacle to legal convergence. It is also here where university education may suffer most, especially by being prevented from emulating American ways of funding research and pursuing new kinds of inter-disciplinary work.

20 Above note 17, pp 406–08.
21 Above note 17, at p 409.
22 Above note 17, at p 415.

More importantly, however, it is here where we may find the most important causes of that great country's further political decline. This last point is a political observation, no doubt influenced by the way this side of the Channel sees the politico-economic problems of its neighbour country, and can thus be ignored by the legal reader. To the extent that it supplements Professor Ogus' theory about where convergence is more likely to occur, it is, however, a point which must be kept firmly within our sights.

2. GROWING INTERACTION IN A SHRINKING WORLD—WILL IT HELP OR STUNT COMPARATIVE LAW?

(a) Globalisation—A Multi-Polar Source of Converging Law

The globalisation phenomenon has become in relatively recent times a topic of discussion and, naturally, the views about it have been coloured by the political beliefs and agendas of the speakers. The violent demonstrations that almost routinely take place when the G8 meet give an indication of how many on the extreme Left have come to see the phenomenon in politico-economic terms. Their view is that the poorer and developing states are being exploited. Thus seen, globalisation can be regarded as nourishing the ambitions (greed?) of multi-national corporations. This way of thinking goes further and, in fact, helps bring this rhetoric into the legal debate since CLS scholars see the expansion/extension of the influence of what was once summarily called 'Western' law as a means of extending old colonialism under the more attractive rubriques of economic liberalism, free trade, and enhanced human rights.[23] Recent American foreign policy has also revived fears of tendencies of world hegemony. The language is not only political, it is also emotional; and it dovetails well with the ideas of many of the demonstrators. In reality, of course, the phenomenon is a much more complex one and presupposes a degree of co-ordination between political, business and legal players (including judges) which is near-impossible to find in the real world.[24]

The lawyers who have discussed the above have, in various ways (and, we submit, rather unhelpfully) mixed all of these strands of thought in their exposés. Somewhat late in the day, some have even questioned the continued existence of comparative law given that more and more law and regulation is nowadays emanating from multi-national bodies, international treaties and conventions, European law, the growing importance of lex mercatoria, and even the cross-fertilisation of ideas which result from the growing number of judicial exchanges. That the sources of law are, nowadays, by- or multi-polar is a fact; the

[23] See, eg, Ugo Mattei, 'A Theory of Imperial Law: A Study on US Hegemony and the Latin Resistance', 10 *Ind J Global Legal Studies*, 383 (2003) and our own observations in *Judicial Recourse to Foreign Law. A New Source of Inspiration?* (2006), especially ch 6.

[24] See, eg, Ugo Mattei's piece mentioned in the previous note. Though not of a leftist persuasion, we have much sympathy with the critique of American exceptionalism and expansionism, which has reached new peaks under the neo-conservative influence of the last 10 years. It is the degree of co-ordination which he implies as being existent in this international 'conspiracy' that finds us especially sceptical. The hegemonic role attributed to the United States also seems to be based on the conviction that (a) Russia is 'exhausted' and (b) the new challenge which will come in the form of China is distant and not more immediate. We believe both assumptions to be over-simplistic, and the relationship of business interests and legal convergence exaggerated. Nonetheless, such works do escape from the purely descriptive character found in so much traditional comparative law writing.

wider conclusion drawn from this, coupled with the idea not just of convergence but uniformity, is exaggerated. Those who adopt the sweeping tone of generalisation may project (real or apparent) learning but they do not, we feel, convey a correct understanding of detail.

In at least one sense the first of the present writers feels a certain satisfaction by the invocation of this multi-polarity of sources as a reason of convergence. For he was one of the first to address this phenomenon in a series of seminars he organised in the early 1990s with Professor Ross Cranston QC FBA, the then Director of the Centre of Commercial Law Studies of Queen Mary College London. This was, to our knowledge, one of the earliest examples of a multi-national gathering taking place in England and investigating the effect of all of these factors in a legal context. Indeed, this may have been the first time that the phrase 'convergence' (and not 'uniformity' or even 'harmonisation') of systems appeared in the English legal jargon, and even the term 'Europeanisation of English Law' was coined[25] (as a phrase anathema at that time but by now also adopted in an extended form by Professor Zimmermann in his scholarly chapter on 'The Europeanisation of Private Law'[26]). This debate is not only one about semantics; it is about substance, for in many ways it put the older discussions about 'transplants' in a different context. Professor Legrand seems to be the only one still denying the phenomenon.

The lack of acknowledgment of the paternity of some of these ideas irks less than the way colleagues have subsequently used them (or re-invented them themselves). For as the piece in the *Oxford Handbook* contributed by Professor Muir-Watt shows,[27] the discussion of these issues is nowadays done in excessively sweeping terms—mixing law, economics, politics and history, and producing an end product which may project (to a few) the image of wide reading but is, we feel, unusable by anyone other than the purest of theoreticians. It is also intriguing because, amidst the invented vocabulary of CLS—'epistemic', 'directionality', 'normativity', and other such words are not to be found in the Shorter English Dictionary but abound in her text—one also finds ideas which lawyers need to address in a more down-to-earth and focused manner but which she fails to do. Why?

To us, this is as good an example as any for a lack of interest in specifics. Convergence, communality of values, the practical consequences of enhanced communication—all anathematic notions to trendy comparatists—are not even flagged up for further discussion by someone else. The result? The most original and significant exchange of ideas ever recorded between two senior judges—the Canivet-Breyer dialogue—is referred to in two-and-a-half lines, all part of the sweeping flow of generalities. The event and the contents of the debate are thus not fleshed out; nor are some of the weaknesses in the exchanges picked up and their reasons put under the microscope.

If, for whatever reason, Professor Muir Watt chose not to do this we, at least, feel obliged to single out the points which we believe deserve the attention of budding comparatists. We do this also because we feel that Anglophone readers, who will almost certainly have missed this exchange, will like to hear more about it and ponder over some of its strong and—inexplicable—weak points. Finally, we touch on some other features of Professor Muir Watt's text because we wish to emphasise the unattractive features of a writing (and thinking?)

[25] BS Markesinis, 'Learning from Europe and Learning in Europe' in BS Markesinis (ed), *The Gradual Convergence. Foreign Ideas, Foreign Influences, and English Law on the Eve of the 21st Century* (1994), pp 1, 20–32.

[26] Included in his *Oxford Handbook of Comparative Law* (2006), pp 539 *ff*—a theme more thoroughly explored by the learned author in *Die Europäisierung des Privatrechts und die Rechtsvergleichung* (2006).

[27] 'Comparative Law and the Process of Globalization' in M Reimann/R Zimmermann (eds), *The Oxford Handbook of Comparative Law* (2007), pp 579 *ff*.

style which, in our opinion, relies so heavily on 'effect' rather than substance, detail, and originality. To put this differently and more generally in the context of French academic comparative literature—being focused, specific, and practical are not virtues which are much valued by that country's contemporary comparative writers. The temptation to go for the magisterial, elegant, aphoristic, and broad-sweeping phrase (which confidently gives the impression of wide learning and a global vision) thus still seems to hold out much more attraction to our French colleagues than the devil who, we have always been told, resides in the detail. The contrast with the best of the current German and English writing thus remains stark. And, as we pointed out in Chapter Six, judicial writing on comparative law has largely avoided these faults.

The reader interested in the Canivet-Breyer debate, also available as a recording,[28] must thus look for the website reference[29] (since it is not given in the essay) and then draw specific conclusions for himself on what they have to say. In our view, at least three general issues arise for discussion: (a) substance, (b) methodology, and (c) the way judges speak when outside the courtroom. Indeed, one could also add a fourth point, namely (d) whether the contents of what judges say *when abroad* contain a twist or spin which is not evident in the debates back in their own home country. Such a rich analysis of this extraordinary material seems to be unsuited for Professor Muir Watt's confident but broad-brush approach to legal problems. We yield to no one in our admiration of the French culture and the crucial role it has played in what we may call European civilisation; but this kind of writing style, in our view, serves badly the science of law.

So let us start with Justice Breyer.

First, he tells us that the attention paid to foreign law is more and more important.[30] He uses the word 'nous'—ie 'we [pay] attention'. But, to begin with, it is not immediately clear whether 'we' refers to Americans in general, ie academics and judges, or whether he is speaking with the courts in mind. Reading the answers more carefully, the better view is that he is referring to the courts. Again, however, is he talking of the practices of his own court—the US Supreme Court—or courts in general? This vagueness could be fatal to his argument.

For if he is describing the US Supreme Court he is, we believe, giving a wrong impression to his readers, for the most exhaustive recent empirical study, which covers *all Federal Courts* (and not just the US Supreme Court), strongly suggests the opposite.[31] In any event,

[28] At www.radiofrance.fr/chaines/franceculture2/emissions/bien_commun/fiche.php?diffusion_id=49499.

[29] See note 11 above.

[30] The following assembled extracts give his own wording on points raised in our text, points we feel stress too much for the benefit of his French audience the similarities of views between France and the United States and conceal the very different views held by Justice Scalia and his followers. We thus submit that the French reader will not get through these texts an accurate view of the position in America—hence our own effort in Chapter Six to give a more balanced account of the complexities of American law. The extracts read as follows (the emphasis is ours): '*L'attention que nous portons aux systèmes étrangers est en effet de plus en plus importante.* En particulier parce que les sociétés se ressemblent de plus en plus du point de vue des valeurs: celles de la démocratie et des Droits de l'Homme. Nos sociétés font face à des problèmes similaires, *avec des textes similaires* et ont de la même façon recours à des juges pour interpréter ces textes. *Ainsi la liberté d'expression est-elle garantie pour le citoyen américain de la même façon que pour le citoyen européen* . . . J'ai participé aux célébrations du bicentenaire du code civil. Or, j'ai trouvé des similarités entre nos deux systèmes bien plus importantes qu'on ne le pense. Prenez cette citation de Portalis lorsqu'il explique que le travail du juge est de suivre le texte quand il est clair—il n'est jamais clair—et quand il n'est pas clair, d'approfondir le texte pour en trouver les valeurs. *Pour moi, Portalis décrit exactement le travail d'un juge à la Cour suprême des Etats-Unis*'.

[31] 'American courts rarely cite to foreign courts, they do so no more now than they did in the past, and on those few occasions where they do cite to foreign courts, it is actually not to help them interpret domestic law.' More on this with the aid of exhaustive statistics in David Zaring, 'The use of Foreign Decisions by Federal Courts: An Empirical Analysis', in 3 (2) *Journal of Empirical Studies*, 2970331 (2006).

while it is true to say that the use made of foreign law is friendly and welcoming by Breyer himself, as well as the two or perhaps three remaining liberal members of the court, it is unhesitantly rejected by the neo-conservatives led by Justice Scalia and dutifully followed by Justices Thomas and Alito, and (more often than not) Chief Justice Roberts. Not mentioning this hugely important and deep division in Justice Breyer's own court, discussed in greater detail in Chapter Six above,[32] cannot be justified by the inevitable brevity of responses in a radio debate. For it forms a crucial part of the American scene.

The same doubts can be voiced about his other claim—that American and French law take broadly the same view towards the value of speech. They do not, as hundreds of (successful) French defamation and privacy cases show. For the way they were decided in France, often against media defendants, would have been impossible in the United States because of the First Amendment. A less fortunate example to illustrate a point could thus not have been selected. But it was, and those who write about the understanding and use of foreign law have not, to our knowledge, picked it up.

Why these over-simplifications? They most certainly do not stem from ignorance, for Breyer is not only a respected judge but also a much admired former professor at the Harvard Law School. This being so, these 'slips'—or let us describe them more charitably as 'generalisations'—deserve not only to be noted but also investigated and explained. Querying what lies behind such over-simplifications is one thing; questioning the absence of response by French commentators who, after all, were the prime recipients of this broadcast, is another. Ignoring them out of a wish to 'sanitise' the debate is academically speaking unacceptable. And if the reason for the silence is due to the fact that no academic commentator picked up their significance (or potential errors or 'generalisations'), then it could be seen as a lack of imagination, inattention to detail, or even sloppiness.

Believing, as we do, in the need to *address* difficult issues and not merely to describe the available material, we offer as a starting point the simple but thought-provoking question: what psychological effect does an invitation to address an elite French legal audience have on a distinguished American judge? Practising amateur psychology (which, of course, we should not) might lead us to shallow suggestions. But the issue remains—why did Justice Breyer 'trim his sails' in order to produce such an impression of American law with his audience?

Was he simply being polite to them? Trying to impress? Wishing to round off some of the unpleasant edges of American law? Supreme Court Justices are powerful, even arrogant, personalities; and they are not known to subject their answers to rules of etiquette or adapt them to the (possible) demands of diplomacy. Was he then subconsciously expressing the hope and belief that his ideas about the utility of foreign law will finally prevail in the US Supreme Court?

This, at the very least, is debatable. So, if he was trying to convey this idea, he should have, at the very least, drawn attention to the necessary nuances. This is particular true in the case of his reference to Portalis (where that great jurist suggested that when the wording of the text is not clear we must search for its purpose and underlying value). To claim that this is a uniform rule of interpretation, adopted in the US Supreme Court as it is in France, is to write out of the American picture with one stroke of the pen his brother Justice Scalia and the originalist school of thought. So, was Mr Justice Breyer behaving as a politician—in the sense that he is conscious of the damage that American exceptionalism and expansionism

[32] See also our *Judicial Recourse to Foreign Law. A New Source of Inspiration?* (2006) with further references.

has caused to the image of his country and its law, and that he felt the need to present a better image of it? We have put on record our multiple objections to Scalia's interpretative techniques; but we feel that the French readership and audience of this interview were, again, denied the chance to realise how divided the American legal (and political) scene actually is.

It is for our readers to decide which—if any—of the above reasons best explains Justice Breyer's statements. At present we can do no more than offer some options for consideration. Yet one thing remains, we think, indisputable. The kind of randomly selected observations/reactions to the aforementioned judicial exchanges should have been touched upon by Professor Muir Watt and other French authors. The questions put to Justice Breyer can also be addressed to French academics. Why this silence? Is it due to politeness, writing style, ignorance of detail, lack of space, or some other reason which we have not thought of? But whatever the explanation, the fact is that Professor Muir Watt's readers were deprived of the opportunity to read the views of senior judges who believe in a growing communality of values, a growing convergence of ideas, and a growing need to present foreign material in a way that can be used by courts.

Lawyers, like anyone else, have the right to adopt and express different opinions. They can also decide what they include and what they omit form their texts. We are likewise free to comment on such omissions. Our reading of this extraordinary debate leaves us with the impression (setting aside any explanation for the omissions of both speakers and commentators) that the two debating justices are extremely close to our ideas about how foreign law should be used in the courtroom and the classroom, and how the two should collaborate with each other.

So what is the wider conclusion that any impartial reader might reach after reading such a text and also considering the omissions, accidental or deliberate? We suggest two.

The first, in our view, is that the elliptical, anodyne, descriptive presentation of such material as we have about foreign law is not likely to be used by anyone—judge, practitioner, legislator, or mandarin—who is remotely involved in making, shaping or interpreting law in the way that, for instance, Professor van Gerven's Casebook Series has been. Our view thus is that volumes that include such material will only make the contributors' CVs look fuller and their credentials appear to be in tune with contemporary thought, but is unlikely to help grade their musings as being more than a descriptive summary of thoughts currently banded around in the academic world.

Secondly, the feisty and polemical style of Professor Legrand makes his work stand out by a mile compared to the purely descriptive efforts of most of his compatriots. This is true not only because his ideas are 'unorthodox' but also because he puts them forward forcefully, and sometimes even rudely! The same is true of Professor Mattei's leftist ideas, and this despite his flirtation with the trendy language of the CLS. Both—ideas and language—may be unattractive to us. But like Legrand, Mattei (as so many other Italian comparatists) is being *different*—he is not descriptive in the use of the material he meticulously collects; and he often finds an original slant for his approach. We can, as repeatedly stressed, have a high regard for people with whom we disagree and yet feel no need to call them 'delusional' or 'deliberately misguided'.

Despite such praise, we insist upon our view that this work, if unchanged in the years to come, will have no impact on the real world. The real significance of the Canivet-Breyer debate is how two senior judges, coming from different systems and possessing very different characters and career patterns, can come so close to endorsing the kind of ideas which we have been advocating (indeed, to the point of exaggerating the similarities between their two systems). Incidentally for us, it makes absolutely no difference if our work helped shape their views or whether they came to them independently.[33] We do not see this as a battle for influence but rather one of different conceptions of what comparative law is really all about. And, on this score, we feel that our views are edging ahead. And we no longer feel we are alone in fighting from this corner. For in making our observations, we also note how American colleagues (Professor David Gerber for instance) have also stressed the view that such works (as the ones we are objecting to) 'obviously [have] little utility either to the process of epistemological self-examination or to the development of interpretative tools'.[34]

The views expressed in the previous paragraphs are personal and, as our readers will have noted, also strongly held. They will undoubtedly exasperate but not convert our colleagues. So let us see what, in our view, are the conclusions that those who write about the effect that globalisation may have on comparative law. In particular let us look at the claim that the multiplicity of international sources creating homogenous law alongside state-enacted law is leading to a convergence which may make comparative law superfluous (back again, in other words, to downgrading the methodological study of foreign law). Again, we disagree. For the convergence may be growing but it remains patchy, unsystematic, and deprived of any agreement as to underlying common principles. The multi-volume effort of the group led by Professor Helmut Koziol to discover these principles for European tort and insurance law falls in this category; and we are among those who find it more pragmatic and more useful than other attempts to draft model European codes.

(b) Will the Increase of Available Information Make Comparison Superfluous?

We may or may not be right about the above predictions, but the emergence of a new kind of transnational law, the product of many non-state related courts, agencies, or other groupings, coupled with the enhanced availability of information about national law, raises one further question. Will the proliferation of such activities and the increasing transnational material, often applicable across borders, render the study of foreign law redundant? In short, can we (as comparatists) move from being marginal to being useless simply because we are suddenly faced with so much law which is no longer emanating from the traditional sovereign state model or because new technologies have given us access to more information about other systems than we ever had before, and which make us aware of our similarities? Though even addressing this question can give us new topics to reflect about, we do not think that these developments, predicted by some, will place the subject under any kind of risk.

There are various reasons why we feel so confident in making our predictions but main among them is the following. The proliferation of material emanating from state or inter-state bodies is considerable but still difficult to digest, explain, adapt, and make usable in different countries and different contexts. As Professor David Gerber has put it in an admirably succinct manner: 'Globalisation not only renders legal information more

[33] Our suspicion, based on some evidence, is that it may have had some impact on the work of Canivet. As far as Breyer is concerned we have not the slightest clue as to whether he has read any of our work (though for years he has been on the Committee of Patronage of the Institute of Global Law at University College London, founded by the first of us and now directed by the second).

[34] 'Globalization and Legal Knowledge: Implications for Comparative Law', 75 *Tul L Rev* 949, 969.

readily available, but often also considerably more opaque'.[35] The distinction, as he makes clear in many parts his article, must be drawn between 'information and knowledge'.

This is partly because this material still reflects differing conceptualism, terminologies, and structures—to some extent because it has been uniformised in an ad hoc way without being accompanied by an organic growth of underlying principles,[36] and, equally important, because the legislators, judges and practitioners who have to work with it remain (despite all these changes) still in many respects parochial in their approach to this material. The website which the first of us has created[37] and which is directed by the second offers a good example of how the availability of information has gone up, but that so much work still needs to be done when it comes to its understanding.

Created some three and a half years ago, this website contains nearly one thousand leading French and German cases. As Professor Gerber suggests in the aforementioned article, it is not enough to make such material available in another—in this case English—language; one must also organise it efficiently. To achieve this end, and in order to facilitate the users of the site to 'pad' the raw translated material, we have presented it under headings which correspond to those found in the two major treatises already referred to (written by the first of us in collaboration with other colleagues), thus enabling users of the site to have easy access to additional, amplifying, and explanatory material which accompanies most of the reproduced decisions.

The French private law cases are also already equipped with short notes giving some indication to the reader of the subsequent fate of the translated case, namely telling him whether it is has been approved, distinguished, or overruled. This material is summary; and given the fact that the enterprise is an individual one, operating with a very limited budget, the updating is not done as frequently and as extensively as one would like. Still, it is made clear from the outset to all users of the site that this is not a tool meant for practitioners (who must do their own research and remain alive to the rapid changes in the law these days—a challenge to which the website cannot respond for as long as it remains a two-man band) but an instrument mainly intended to help students and teachers of comparative law. Eventually, however, it is hoped that the annotating material will go one step further and provide in summary form contrasting information about the Anglo-Saxon alternatives or parallel solutions. Thus, notwithstanding its many shortcomings—Professor Gerber rightly describes 'intercultural communication [as] a complicated process'[38]—this research tool has already proved its high value, at any rate if one is to judge it by the hundreds of thousands of hits it has received during its short life.[39]

3. WHAT SHOULD WE BE DOING?

It is the strange combination of past and present which TS Elliot refers to in a famous poem[40] that makes it possible to attempt—putting it any stronger than that would be

[35] Globalization and Legal Knowledge: Implications for Comparative Law', 75 *Tul L Rev* at 954.

[36] A point made beautifully, and with the necessary detail to back it, by Professor Walter van Gerven, 'Community and National Legislators, Regulators, Judges, Academics and Practitioners: Living together Apart' in Basil S Markesinis (ed), *Law Making, Law Finding and Law Shaping. The Diverse Influences* (1997), pp 13 *ff.*

[37] See http://www.utexas.edu/law/academics/centers/transnational/work_new.

[38] 'Globalization and Legal Knowledge: Implications for Comparative Law', 75 *Tul L Rev* 949, 957 (2001).

[39] This was also the view expressed by Canivet in the radio debate with Breyer (see note 11 above).

[40] TS Elliot, *Four Quartets, Burnt Norton.*

wrong—to predict the future. The endeavour can be tempting but it is perilous; and the dangers are that much greater if we attempt to predict the future by imagining it as a kind of linear projection of the present. For if there is one thing more likely than anything else, it is that the future will be different; and those who wrote about the subject or taught it 40 or more years ago may be hard-pressed to find in their works even the seeds of what was to come.[41] If this sounds unnecessarily cautious or even pessimistic it is because of the underlying belief—hurtful, no doubt, to the egos of academic writers including ourselves (but correct nonetheless)—that time spares only a few works of an even smaller number of academic writers from its obliterating force.[42] The statistical information given in this edition about the appeal that the work of comparatists has had on others of their kind shows that it is small, at any rate whenever they pursue a certain genre of scholarly work. This evidence, limited though it is in terms of numbers of scholars reviewed and journals and courts considered, offers convincing evidence that even the comparatist scholars—that is, the scholars who are appealing to lawyers from different systems—have, with only one or two exceptions, themselves had very limited geographical appeal. The few exceptions that our figures support only help bolster the validity of the general observation.

This preceding paragraph contains some of the building blocks which might prove useful to anyone trying to predict the future of the study and use of foreign law both in the classroom and the courtroom and, for the reasons explained in various parts of this work, by extension in the legislative chambers coping with law reform. They are, we feel, all strongly linked with the phenomenon of globalisation, especially of trade and tastes and fashions, but they are also connected to the philosophies and outlook of those who will carry a large part of this burden in the future. Though the two points interact (and, indeed, it could be argued that the first will largely dictate the shape the second will take), it might make for clearer reading if we tried to keep them apart.

Our specific suggestions and remedies, having been discussed in the preceding Chapters both in the context of different systems but also with respect to different branches of the law, should give a fair idea of how we think one should proceed. Should any colleague choose to use our book as a teaching tool he should, of course, use it merely as a starting point for discussion, adding his own material as well as his own criticisms, and then encouraging his students to consider all of the above and decide for themselves how much is convincing and how much is in need of further refinement. If this book offers, arguably, any advantages over the larger collection of essays which emanate from many authors it is that it presents its material around a set of themes which both authors share and which others, they believe, can use in order to agree, to refine, or to reject. In short, it can lead to the discussion of notions, ideas, and factual situations that are also addressed in other books but are here 'packaged'[43] in a thematic, more unified, and more provocative manner. In the light of the above, can we venture any concluding thoughts about what the future may hold for all of us? This, as stated, is a perilous endeavour but for that reason

[41] Gaston Berger, *Phénoménologie du temps et prospective* (1964). Berger, one of the fathers of futurology in France, argues that tomorrow will not be like yesterday; nor will it be a projection of yesterday into tomorrow but it will be something entirely new.

[42] The idea is, of course, more beautifully expressed by the chorus in Sophocles' *Fabulae*, Ajaz, 645 *ff* (Oxford Classical Texts, edited and annotated by AC Pearson).

[43] Professor Gerber uses the same terminology as the first of us has been doing for years when he states in no uncertain terms that '[H]ow senders [of information] package and structure messages influences the effectiveness of communication'. See 'Globalization and Legal Knowledge: Implications for Comparative Law', 75 *Tul L Rev* 949, 966 (2001).

alone worth attempting, for as Milton put it so well at the beginning of his great epic poem *Paradise Lost*—one must from time to time 'pursue things unattempted yet in prose or rhyme'.[44]

4. PROPHESYING THE FUTURE—A WORLD OF DIFFERENT SPEEDS

Notwithstanding our efforts to find a common ground, *de lege lata* our study has suggested a division between the practice of US courts (which is, at best, divided and, at worst, insular) and those of other countries which could, using the terminology loosely, be called 'advanced' or 'developed' and which are internationalist in spirit and deed. This concluding section of the book may thus call for a similar division. We start with the internationalists and then turn to the isolationists.

(a) Shades of Internationalism

The courts of all of the major systems reviewed in this book display, or so it seems to us, a growing interest in the development of legal ideas and solutions by sister courts and, occasionally, by foreign academics. To be sure, the interest varies in intensity, from the serious study of the foreign solution to the modest (but growing) amateurish curiosity to learn what others are doing. This curiosity is sometimes concealed rather than openly displayed. Except for countries such as, for instance, Canada, South Africa, and the United States, judges tend to hide their academic sources; and in some systems (such as the French and the Italian) they are by law even expected to do so—at any rate in the judgments proper. The full extent of the influence of foreign law is thus often a matter of speculation.

Our study, likewise, shows that the open use of foreign law also ranges from the mere citation of foreign information as supporting material to the genuine attempt to take advantage of foreign experience for the sake of achieving the best possible solution to the national problem. The French homosexual marriage case shows that this is particularly appropriate whenever the local system lacks a clearly phrased provision or precedent and is facing a problem which is geographically widespread. The fear that inspiration, even borrowing, is in these cases made difficult by local societal, religious or cultural reasons, though deserving to be taken seriously, seems to be losing its strength in a shrinking world.

In between, we find instances which are, from an academic point of view, just as interesting and important, and these include the cases where foreign law was considered but then rejected as inappropriate to national conditions. These cases can even be the most interesting if the rejection of the foreign idea (or text) reveals the wider reasons why the national system cannot adopt it. Though we oppose the death penalty, we draw special attention to Justice Scalia's way of 'degrading' the expert evidence submitted to him in *Roper v Simmons*.[45] His judgment is an excellent tool of how we (who do not share his views) can learn from his skills and improve our presentation of foreign law. Once again, therefore, we feel obliged to praise an intellectual opponent, and do so because we believe that the pre-

[44] *Paradise Lost I*, 16.
[45] *Roper v Simmons* 125 S Ct, 1183,1222 *ff* (2005).

sentational skills with respect to foreign law can be improved more from such a study than they can ever benefit from the reading of abstract, generalised, and descriptive essays of academics.

There is a third point which emerges from studies such as the one we have attempted here, and it refers to the human factor. The internationalist trend is the result of political, economic, and technological forces; and the way it has been expressed and encouraged has depended upon individuals—individuals who happened to hold key posts in the judicial systems of their countries at a crucial moment of the development. Few can deny the fact, especially those who knew the individuals mentioned, that Guy Canivet was a very different kettle of fish from Pierre Dret, as was Robert Goff from Harry Keith or Tom Bingham from Lenny Hoffmann. One is not talking of raw ability, but of imagination, open-mindedness, and intellectual adventurism (in the best sense of this term). Just as there are great artists and good artists so are there great judges and 'just' clever judges.

What makes a 'good' judge is an unexplored question in academic literature; only 'snippets' of the issue have been addressed. But a judge who is willing to innovate is more likely to be remembered than the one who remains wedded with what is a well-tried solution dictated by his conservative consciousness or his chauvinistic or cosmopolitan temperament. For creative centuries, which invariably coincide with periods of transition, do not think in terms of history nor attachment to established practice. 'It never occurred to the architects of Chartres or Reims or Notre Dame to build in the Romanesque style, any more than it occurred to Bramante or Michelangelo to return to the Gothic style for Saint Peter's, although the Gothic style is supposed to be 'more pious' than that of the Renaissance.'[46] This, of course, is even more true of scientists; but it is also true of lawyers, accustomed by their training to pay true (or lip) service to precedent since, by definition, during moments of transition the 'dying past' is ceding its place to the 'new future'.

One might be tempted to argue the same for academics, though their role in shaping the law is really so minor that they may not even deserve to be entered into such a race and their input in the creation of law studied any further. But academics can take part in a different competition on the basis of how timid, cautious, and unadventurous they are or not, and be classed as innovative thinkers or 'preservers of established dogma'. These characteristics will help determine their originality; but originality comes at a price, and thus even those who may be capable of attaining it will be encouraged to be timid, trendy and conformist, especially if they seek professional advancement. How this affects their approach to the study of foreign law has been pointed out several times in this book, and nothing further need be added except to note the sad phenomenon of promotions often going to those who opt for trendy causes. Feminism, for instance, especially the militant variety, seems a fairly good passport to 'distinction' in the sense of reward since it seems to confer credit and suggest originality and courage both for the person so 'recognised' and the person awarding the 'recognition'—and 'woe' to those who even suggest such things!

At an institutional level one must note that whatever form it may take, the interest in foreign law may be prompted by different motives.

At one end of the spectrum national constitutions may permit or encourage it. South Africa may be the best illustration of this category. This approach finds, these days, continued support not only in section 39(1) (c) of the 1996 Constitution but also in the 'duty to

[46] Alfred Einstein, *Mozart, His Character, His Work* (1962), p 320.

promote the values that underlie an open and democratic society based on human dignity, equality, and freedom'.[47]

Beyond this constitutional authorisation, it seems that comparative law was also particularly attractive due to the hybrid character of the legal system, which is rooted not only in Roman-Dutch but also in the English Common law. The mixed jurisdiction of the country thus seems to help it in adopting an open mind (and, of course, the mixture was there even greater for, alongside the so-called 'western' influences, one found and had to cope with indigenous, often customary ideas and notions). It is a tribute to this country and the lawyers who have been at its helm that it has managed its legal transition from a state of isolation and racial backwardness to one of intellectual leadership so well.

In other cases, the nature of the court or the law it generates—transnational—can stimulate such interest and make mutual exchanges of varying intensity necessary. The European Court of Justice and the European Court of Human Rights fall into this category subject to a number of caveats. A similar example can be found in cases where a national court has to interpret a European directive and, in the absence of a ruling from the ECJ, will naturally strive towards reaching a commonly acceptable meaning. The comparative exercise undertaken by the English High Court in the blood contamination case offers such an illustration. That the result may not appeal to a particular academic is neither here nor there; for us, it is the nature of the exercise and how it was carried out that holds lessons for the future.

Finally, a few words about another reason prompting interest in foreign law. The bulk of national courts seem to be developing this internationalist spirit because of enhanced contacts between judges, courts, universities and, of course, the part of the legal profession that finds itself at the cutting edge of the globalisation phenomenon and deals with an array of commercially flavoured issues which have strong international elements. Individually and taken together, these factors will go on enhancing this trend, and we see no signs of a reverse movement developing that would push courts back to a state of intellectual self-sufficiency.

Is the majority trend we detect threatening to local pride, local history, cultural diversity, and the individuality of each traditional legal system? This is a question that is more likely to cause concern to old, major, and established legal orders than to new ones, keen to learn from the experience of others. It is also often coloured by the views an individual observer or judge might hold about the political process of integration that may be taking place in a particular part of the world, notably modern Europe. Though we understand the American fears, we dismiss them as essentially unfounded for two reasons.

First, the intellectual exchanges we have reviewed are not leading to one system absorbing the other but, at best, attempts to encourage organic harmonisation (not unification!) and, at worst, result in a mere exchange of ideas. Thus, Israel has not, in our view, suffered any serious loss in the richness of its own intellectual and religious past by modernising its law, especially in the domain of human rights, by borrowing from Canada or the United States. South Africa has been catapulted into international legal prominence and gained almost universal praise by selectively using foreign law to transform what was once a legally discredited regime, and has often done so by invoking its own local, native traditions and, indeed, showing them to be in many respects more human than those of the 'advanced' world. Canada has not been as Americanised in its law as it has been in other parts of its daily life. Germany has achieved in law, especially in the area of human rights, a feat

[47] Section 39(1) (a) of the 1996 Constitution.

equivalent to its well-known and much vaunted post-War 'economic miracle' (made possible by its own determination and hard work as much as by American money), though the modernisation of its legal system may be partly due to constitutional and statutory reform and partly to judicial activity, which has been both bold and pragmatic.[48] The former First President of the French Supreme Court is on record as saying that 'comparative law indisputably widens the horizons of a jurist as comparative law multiplies the approaches [one can take towards a particular problem] and enlarges the interpretative options'. Even England has attained a truly dominant position in the domain of international legal services by modernising (not much internal foot-dragging here!) a legal profession that carries with it its English professionalism wherever it goes. Romantics and prophets of gloom are the only ones who fear this internationalisation which, in the British Isles, takes the threatening shape of Europe. Their cries are often couched in patriotic language, and their texts, replete with literary references, make for attractive reading. But they are unable to stop the new world which is *ante portas*, and this makes their calls more strident.

Who are the agents of these changes which 50 or even 30 years ago would have been unthinkable? Indisputably, it is the wider globalisation of trade and, to a secondary extent, the moves towards European integration, both of which have stimulated these developments. Additionally, the flowering of international human rights, the growing linkage of financial aid with improvements in their status, and the painfully slow dismantling of beliefs in race superiority, have all contributed to this willingness to consider good ideas whatever their origin.

We have already mentioned the role of charismatic, imaginative and determined judges. We must not forget how in this role they have been aided and abetted by practitioners engaged in international practice. It is painful to assert (but nonetheless true) that in this movement academics have followed, not led. Preoccupation with the past, more euphemistically referred to as interest in legal history or, at the other end of the spectrum, a newly acquired interest in trendy ideas, have all played a part in securing to modern academic comparatists the third and last place in this race—however valuable some of the tenets they hold may be. We must not tire saying that both have facilitated their own downfall by espousing the repellent language which CLS feels proud to have invented.

Those are reasons that may explain a 'slump' in comparative initiatives in England, especially in the 1970s and 1980s. Similar and other (more local) reasons may explain the 'decline'—relative or absolute—of comparative law in the academic circles of other countries. We have already mentioned the French comparatist attributing the 'crisis' in his country to the 'ethnocentricity' of many of his compatriots and of their main governmental and educational institutions. Likewise, we have mentioned how the language is deployed to create effect but is not used enough to promote concrete arguments. French comparative texts thus often sound beautiful to the ear but, when studied (not read) can be almost vacuous. If one tries to summarise them a day after one has read them, one will be hard pressed to remember what they said. These are phenomena which some French observers—and not only lawyers—regard as seriously affecting the progress of French society as a whole. However, important as these reasons may be, for us they recede into the background when compared with judicial efforts to rekindle interest in the study of foreign law; and it has

[48] On this see the very useful observations of Justice Brun-Otto Bryde of the German Constitutional Court in 'Constitutional Courts in Constitutional Transition', in F Van Loon and K Van Aeken (eds), *60 maal recht en 1 mall wijn, Liber Amicorum prof dr Jean Van Houtte* (1999), pp 235 *ff*.

been an important thesis of this book to note this phenomenon, and to urge its study more deeply than we have been able to do on this occasion.

Our overall conclusion thus is that the situation we describe in this book will, in the systems bracketed under this heading, strengthen and not weaken with the passage of time. We regard this almost as an historical inevitability and thus do not feel the need to defend it further even though we have in several Chapters and sub-sections stressed the *indisputable* difficulties that come with this exercise. So we call on colleagues to realise the trend and to work with one another to shape it in a controlled and systematic way rather than leave it to the piecemeal form in which progress is achieved whenever it is in the hands of practitioners alone rather than theoreticians working with them for a common aim. In other words, what we call for is a mix or collaboration of the different parts of the legal profession for the benefit of all. Again we were thus delighted to see a theme stressed for many years now by the first of us appear in one of Breyer's responses in the radio programme alluded to earlier on—judges *will* respond to comparative law if practitioners draw their attention to foreign ideas; and this they can only do with the help of academics. Our entire Chapter Nine depends on this thesis; and it is nice to know that, in essence, Justice Breyer also espouses it.

(b) *Introspection or Arrogant Self-Sufficiency?*

How does one predict the future of the American model? Though the justices of the US Supreme Court do not speak with one voice (and some recent cases such as *Lawrence v Texas*[49] and *Roper v Simmons*[50] suggest, thanks to shifting alliances, a greater—if temporary?—willingness to look abroad), our overall impression is that the isolationists still have the *louder* voice. Their numbers on the Supreme Court may also have been increased with the addition of the new Chief Justice and Justice Alito. Whether this potential shift to the Right can be slowed down when the next vacancy is filled by a democratic President is too soon to predict. The current numbers suggest that we are still in for a long winter and it will take a very strong personality to return American law more to the centre of the road. The question thus arises, how does one characterise this trend and, more intriguingly, how does one explain it?

The frame of one's mind is crucial to matters as varied as dealing with adversity (including physical illness) or reaching a conclusion on a legal conundrum. The way we speak reflects the way we think; and this, in turn, is shaped not only by the tools and arguments of our craft but by other factors including our wider culture at a particular moment of its historical evolution. Whether a court uses foreign law as part of its arguments in justifying its decision, as occasionally it must in all democratic systems, will also be determined by such factors. 'Isolationism', 'introverted attitudes', 'self-sufficiency', or 'arrogance' may all lead an individual judge to a denial of even a dialogue with foreign ideas; and it is hardly necessary to remind the reader that we are *not* talking here of treating foreign law as binding precedent but only as a source of *inspiration*, which might prompt local change or adaptation.

Such a state of mind can be justified, or should we say be 'disguised', by resorting to legal or legalistic arguments. Or, alternatively, it can be explained by exploring openly the above-

[49] 539 US 558 (2003).
[50] 125 S Ct 1183 (2005).

mentioned notions—isolationism, self-sufficiency, personal culture, and arrogance—and deciding whether they can explain the use or non-use of foreign law in general and the comparative method in particular. So which of these justifications is mostly relevant to America at the present juncture of its political and legal history? More likely, we need a combination of legal and legalistic reasons if we are to understand the complex American scene (as, indeed, we said we do if we try to understand other national scenes).

The second of these justifications is both more unusual to assert and more difficult to prove. For, though linking politics and law may not be fortuitous (especially these days), combining it with an attempt to understand the particular judge's mentality may thus be crucial to the understanding of what is happening in the United States these days. We talked about this issue in Chapter Six, so here we need not go into it again in any detail.

There is little doubt, however, that American law, especially constitutional law, is much more self-sufficient than, say, South African law, which has a relatively new presence in this field. To use this argument in order to explain the greater willingness of the South African judges to borrow from abroad can only go so far. For it does not help explain Canada, which in the field of human rights may, arguably, have been a (relative) novice at the time of the enactment of the 1982 Charter and needed guidance but can no longer be treated as an 'importer' only of ideas.

For the Canadian experience shows that what may have started as a need—looking at foreign law because it was richer, arguably more advanced—has now become a habit, and one which not only is accepted locally but also lends to Canadian case law an international aura and appeal. The import of Canadian ideas to Israel surely illustrates how extended the reach can be, both in terms of distance travelled and cultures bridged. The same can, probably, be said of the case of the South African Constitutional Court which can no longer be dismissed as a 'novice'. And just as success breeds success, internationalism breeds more internationalism.

If American law is, or sees itself, as self-sufficient these days, the United States as a political power is neither self-sufficient nor insular. It is, instead, a state that is enjoying a *phase* of political and military dominance which is unparalleled in historical terms and which is giving it the means and the excuse to express views (often externalised through the use of force thinly disguised behind rules of law) about events happening all over the globe. Yet it is this unparalleled technological power which encouraged the American leadership to launch in such a badly prepared manner into the invasion of Iraq, which, five years later, has shown the extent of the American reliance on the support of its friends. Indeed, America's true allies have served their friend badly by being so submissive to the imposed views of American neo-conservatives. Once again, law has followed political trends.

Can such political dominance be linked with the *current* introverted unilateralism of the Supreme Court? In one sense, it should not since (as Professor Henkin has not tired of saying) the American 'neglect' towards international law has, alas, a long tradition. Equally disturbing is America's willingness to get agitated about human rights violations if found in countries which are not close to it politically, but willing to ignore them if found in countries who serve its interests (often of a purely economic nature). Though this behaviour is not new (and not limited to the United States) the country may be going through a new phase of acute paroxysm.

The danger of personal political ideologies 'tarnishing' legal reasoning—especially that of public international lawyers—must be obvious from what has already been hinted; and it applies to us as authors of this book (and to our explanations) as much as to everyone else.

But then law is not (and cannot be) removed from the wider political debate that is taking place around it at a given political time and place. We thus tentatively suggest that there are signs of 'world-wide hegemony'[51] in the American air, and that this tendency can be found in all forms of human endeavour—including law.

American law is good for exportation as are American ideas of government and Wall Street's unbridled version of capitalism. The importation of foreign ideas is, however, another matter. In this atmosphere, it is *almost* tempting to argue that the country's respected (but old) Constitution is not only a reason for an introverted interpretation; it is also a helpful pretext for not opening the system up to new ideas. In making this assertion we stress again that the ideas we are floating are not new,[52] though the post-9/11 climate may have made it more obvious.

Current American law is not just divided over the utility of foreign law; it has also succumbed to the temptation to tolerate a lesser respect for human rights, at home and abroad. Dean Koh of the Yale Law School, an international lawyer with an experience at the State Department, had this to say about the effects of the current doctrine of unfettered executive power based on an extraordinarily broad interpretation of Article II of the Constitution. Speaking to the American Law Institute he thus said:[53]

> What does this mean in real terms? We now have law-free zones, let's call them Guantanamo or Diego Garcia. We have law-free practices, let's call them 'extraordinary rendition'. We have law-free courts, let's call them 'military commissions'. And we have law-free persons, let's call them 'enemy combatants', who can be detained indefinitely on executive say-so, largely free from judicial oversight.

Later in the text, Dean Koh quoted Dr Henry Kissinger who was reported[54] as having said that in contemporary America, '[T]he illegal we do immediately. The unconstitutional takes a little longer.'

Yet in looking at foreign events as a possible factor of internal legal attitudes, we are careful not to forget the fact that the current (sometimes desperate) attempt to get constitutional interpretation under control is fuelled more strongly by the intensity of the conflict between the religious 'Right' and the secular 'Left' over cultural issues such as abortion, gay rights, and the like, than it is determined by a suspicion or dislike of European ideas which are often seen by the American Right as 'woolly' and 'leftist'. What we are suggesting, however, is that in this wider context the post-9/11 climate and the European (if not the world's) reaction to America's current foreign policy may be strengthening further the in-built reasons for the self-sufficient approach to legal (especially statutory) interpretation in addition to leading to a weaker protection of human rights.

We note, secondly (and with regret), that (contemporary) Americans find the notion that they 'should be governed by ideas from foreign sources [un]congenial'[55] is spreading

[51] Professor Ackerman used the words (and asked the question) as far back as 1997; see (1997) 83 *Virginia L Rev* 771, 772.

[52] We see germs of this thinking in Professor McCrudden's 'A Common Law of Human Rights? Transnational Judicial Conversations on Constitutional Rights', 20 *Ox J of Legal Studies* 499, especially at pp 520 *ff* and (even earlier) in Louis Henkin's 'The US and International Human Rights' in *Justice for a Generation*, papers presented in London on 15–19 July 1985 at the meetings of the ABA and the Senate of the Inns of Court and the Law Society of England and Wales (at p 377).

[53] Address by Harold Hongju Koh, 17 May 2006, 66 at p 72, printed by the ALI in its Remarks and Addresses at the 83rd Annual Meeting, May 15–17, 2006.

[54] *The New York Times*, 28 October 1973. Koh, above note 54, at p 73.

[55] Louis Henkin, 'Constitutionalism and Human Rights', in L Henkin and AJ Rosenthal (eds), *Constitutionalism and Rights: The Influence of the US Constitution Abroad* (1990).

to private law even though here history suggests different attitudes in days gone by—and even though in this case one is not faced with the textual constitutional obstacles one encounters in the area of human rights. We think it would be too facile to explain this 'neglect' of foreign (and mainly) European ideas to a surfeit of local law.

Take, for instance, Professor Mathias Reimann, a German scholar who has made a substantial contribution to both comparative law and comparative (German/American) legal history. If his learning is not in dispute, his opinions deserve to be questioned. Thus, we have already cited one of his articles entitled 'Stepping out of the European *Shadow*: Why Comparative Law in the United States *Must* Develop its Own Agenda'.[56] That America should have and, indeed, already has its own agenda is both understandable and reasonable. Yet to refer to the European cultural influence on American law as having cast (or still casting) a *shadow* strikes one as an unfortunate exaggeration of (a) the past intellectual debt that America has towards Europe and (b) a serious underestimation of the intellectual vitality of modern European law especially that generated during the last 20 years. To put it differently, we doubt whether the likes of Oliver Wendell Holmes, Benjamin Cardozo, Roscoe Pound, Karl Llewellyn, Max Rheinstein, Jack Dawson, Fritz Kessler, John Fleming, Arthur von Mehren, Mary Ann Glendon, Ann Marie Slaughter, or James Godley could ever use such terms to describe a legal culture that shaped their thought in so many ways. And we doubt even more whether those by now dead would, if still alive, be ignoring the outpourings from such European courts as those sitting in Luxembourg and Strasbourg. Reimann, however, is not alone.

Strangely, to us at least, other American lawyers of recent European vintage have also taken this anti-European stance, expressing themselves in language that touches on the verbose.[57] Judge Guido Calabresi is one of the relative few who have voiced in one of his judgments the opposite view and, of course, has done so in his usual restrained and elegant manner[58]; but then in him we find that mixture of cultures and breadth of knowledge that tends to dispose one towards the universal rather than the particular—a combination of European style with American dynamism.

Yet even in America, where cultures mix, the trend may be going in the other direction. Thus, a public lawyer of some repute has not only echoed thoughts similar to those which we condemn here (with concern) but also indicated the reason why foreign ideas may be becoming less relevant to contemporary Americans. Quite simply, he feels indigenous ones are the ones that nowadays matter most. The idea makes some sense, though Professor Bruce Ackermann (the scholar we have in mind) may have expressed the thought in too extreme a manner (and one which misrepresents his own wide reading) when he wrote in the mid-1990s another of these 'prophetic' texts which show that America was getting ready for its 'intellectual imperialism' as the end of the cold war deprived it of its only world

[56] (1998) 46 *Amer J Comp L* 637 (our emphasis).

[57] See, eg, N Demleiter, 'Challenge, Opportunity and Risk: An Era of Change in Comparative Law', (1998) 46 *The Amer J Comp L* 647, 653: 'Colonialism and Social Darwinism were the primary contributors to the ethnocentric illusion of the superiority of . . . Western law . . . Today, the presumption seems to be that legal systems . . . jostle with one another in a market place of possibilities.' Are we really talking of an 'illusion' of (intellectually) superiority of the European systems or a very actual reality? And are these systems not the progenitors of the American and Canadian systems (and still influence the latter)? And which systems are 'jostling' for the role of 'inspirer' beyond the European, Canadian, and (contemporary) South African constitutional models (the latter precisely because it has proved itself so open to learning from the others)? This low regard for European ideas is also evident from the wording adopted by Professor Fletcher in his article 'Constitutional Identity', (1993) 14 *Cardozo L Rev* 737.

[58] *US v Then*, 56 Fed Rep (3rd) 464, 469 (1995).

competitor and in the trauma of 9/11 may have simply found the latest reason for expressing this confidence more openly.[59] Ackerman thus wrote:

> America is a world power, but does it have the strength to understand itself? Is it content, even now, to remain an intellectual colony, borrowing European categories, to decode the meaning of national identity? . . . To discover the Constitution, we must approach it without assistance of guides imported from another time and place. Neither Aristotle nor Cicero, Montesquieu nor Locke, Harrington nor Hume, Kant nor Weber will provide the key. Americans have borrowed much from such thinkers, but they have also built a genuinely distinctive pattern of constitutional thought and practice.

Such statements may sit uncomfortably with other writings by the same author, who is known not only for his liberal views but also his impressive awareness of what other systems are doing in his own field of law.[60] They also seem to be unconvincing in a subject—constitutional law—where basic ideas such as justice, equity, equality, liberty and so on are not only the lawyer's daily tools but also tools deeply fashioned by the classics Ackerman seems to be asking his young (new?) readers not to bother to read.

To our minds, the analysis of the different types of justice has thus not been bettered since Aristotle wrote his Nichomachean Ethics; and it will be a shame if new scholars, with the apparent blessing of their teachers, no longer feel the need to read such works. This is an area where jurisprudence can have a direct bearing on the understanding of key legal and constitutional concepts and notions. This is not like studying dead ideas developed by dead systems; this is understanding contemporary political and legal developments with the aid of basic notions which were first examined by the classics. The neglect of the past must be selective and based on evidence that it has lost its relevance for the present.

Yet in this book we are not concerned in reconciling real or apparent contradictions in the published views of certain serious contemporary scholars such as Ackerman nor, indeed, attempting to belittle the autochthonous contribution of the American legal and philosophical mind, but merely trying to detect and describe an emerging trend; and we are trying to do this by looking at it from as many angles as we can.

So this, really, is our main concluding point. A system that wishes to inspire and influence others—indeed, even export its legal ideas (as many American academics and judges[61] openly say they do)—cannot do this in a *sustained* manner (however good these ideas may be) if it simultaneously expresses its newly found confidence in a form which would strike potential 'importers' as bordering on the excessive or even arrogant. It may well be that this was the image of contemporary America and American law that Breyer was trying to dispel in his recorded dialogue with Canivet. Frankly, who would not wish to do the same?

Indeed, one might call this trend not merely excessive but an *historically unprecedented arrogance* given that, in their heyday, neither the English jurists (nor, before them, the Romans) were so closed to foreign ideas when at the peak of their own power. To be sure, when making such comparisons one must remember that in both of these worldly and cultural 'empires' the perceived sources of law were different; and neither faced the kind of problems which in the United States the founding document seems to generate.

Yet law and its interpretation is not entirely dependent on rules and structures. Imagination and confidence (or lack of it) can play a part in the shaping of the national or

[59] *We The People: Foundations* (1991), p 3.

[60] See, eg, 'The Rise of World Constitutionalism', (1997) 83 *Virginia L Rev* 771.

[61] Eg, Sandra Day O'Connor, Keynote Address in Proceedings of the 96th Annual Meeting of the American Society of International Law, pp 348 *ff*.

judicial mentality, especially in times of transition and change. And the Victorians, much more than the contemporary English, were a confident lot, riding on the crest of the industrial revolution and thus willing not just to read but also to say how much they admired the Germans, while the Roman debt to Greek thought was just as willingly acknowledged in public by Roman thinkers of the calibre of Cicero. We find nothing strange in this since we believe that power, well entrenched and not ephemeral, can inspire the kind of confidence that tolerates, if not actively welcomes, new ideas and comparative discussion.[62] Yet this is not the kind of *confidence* that one encounters in the United States today. On the contrary, in a country constantly advocating the merits of free trade we find the best example of protectionism in the realm of indigenous ideas through attempts to exclude in a blanket manner any active consideration of alternatives. Invoking the US Constitution, when both its text (and its founding fathers) are silent or in disagreement, is unconvincing. Unconvincing it is and—to us at least—unrealistic to believe that if reform is to come it will come only through changing the federal Constitution or State legislation. For would the States have acted on their own if there had not been *Brown v Board of Education*?[63]

Now we do not think that it involves a great logical leap to argue that American academics and judges who think in this (introverted) way may, in some respects, be in tune with the political realities which have gripped the United States in the post-9/11 era. For this terrible date inaugurated a new phase in geopolitical strategy and military thinking. It has also set in motion the passing of a variety of statutes, regulations, and the introduction of practices that have the laudable aims of protecting us against the scourge of terrorism, but also have the potential of being abused to intrude into domains not really related to this threat. Last but not least, through fear and other reasons, these events have led scholars, even of a liberal predisposition, to come close to turning a blind eye to horrible practices such as torture,[64] the maintenance of prison camps, and the waging of pre-emptive wars which the (few?) remaining adherents of classical international law may find difficult to comprehend.

Ultimately, all this is possible since the ruling classes believe that America's technological might enables it to go alone on the world scene, be it in matters of war, the environment, and now, apparently, even justice. However much American liberal thinkers may disagree with the conservative philosophies of the current ruling elites, the fact is that they do not seem—as yet—to have found a well-articulated voice on most of the matters discussed in this book.[65] We say that because we note that numerically judicial coalitions between Left and moderate Right may, in fact, be denting the conservative agenda. And the same people, if to be judged by their writings (admittedly brief and often conclusionary in tone), seem closer to the view here presented than one might think. Nevertheless, it is the Right's position that comes across more articulated and more forcefully argued, and may (with the help of some well-targeted judicial appointments) prevail for the foreseeable future. This is what we are singling out for discussion, for this is what we see happening in law. It is to this debate that this book has tried to make a modest contribution.

[62] See Brian Simpson, 'Innovation in the Nineteenth Century Contract Law', (1975) 91 *LQR* 247. Likewise CHS Fifoot, *Judge and Jurist in the Reign of Victoria* (1959) *passim*. The theme of openness coming with confidence is explored in a wider context by the late Lord Annan, 'The Victorian Intellectual Aristocracy' in JH Plumb (ed), *Studies in Social History: A Tribute to GM Trevelyan* (1955), ch 8.

[63] 347 US 483 (1954), overruling *Plessy v Ferguson*, 163 US 537 (1896).

[64] For a collection of essays on this topic see Sanford Levinson (ed), *Torture. A Collection* (2004).

[65] Justice Scalia brings this point out clearly (and we think convincingly) in his article 'Originalism: The Lesser Evil', (1989) 57 *Cincinnati L Rev* 849, esp at 855 ff.

Now this new American thought, in politics often referred to as 'neo-conservatism', may well be the path to the future. Equally, it may well be that the writers of this book represent—if not the 'old Europe'—the thinking of the world of yesterday (much as they proclaim their interest in the study of modern law and not the study of the law of past generations). And it may well be that the autochthonous ideas of contemporary America are sufficient (as undoubtedly they are often interesting and, occasionally, even inspiring) in that they do not need any cross-fertilisation from abroad. But in our view the case for such propositions has not yet been made out; and until it is, we at least feel much admiration for what our Canadian, South African, and, to a lesser extent, English, French and German judges are doing, and hope that the growing globalisation of our universe will encourage them to re-double their efforts.

Appendix I

CORRESPONDENCE BETWEEN LORD ATKIN AND PROFESSOR HC GUTTERIDGE

Confidential

The Rydings
Sylvester Road
Cambridge

27th November 1932

Dear Lord Atkin,

I enclose M's letter. I agree with most of his statements, but I think that he is unduly pessimistic.

He is troubled by a state of affairs which I have always regarded as a great misfortune, namely, the almost complete lack of contact between the practitioner and the academic lawyer in England. The gulf between the two is very wide—much wider than it is in America or on the Continent. The reason for this is no doubt the historical development of the teaching of English law and the fact that the Universities were late in the field, but it has led to the development of an inferiority complex on the part of the teacher which is bad for the teaching of law and also inimical to the future of English law. There is so much that the Judge and the practitioner cannot do because they have not got the time to spare, but which ought to be done and can only be done by the academic lawyer. I mean such tasks as the production of legal treatises: the study and development of certain departments of the law which are unremunerative to a practitioner e.g. Public and Private International Lawyers. There are only five in the Institute of International Law: Brierly, Pearce, Higgins, McNair and Fischer Williams. The result is that we cannot make our weight felt in any of the discussions which are constantly taking place, and the French have dug themselves in so thoroughly that it will be difficult to turn them out. English law is losing ground on the Continent because we cannot conduct the necessary propaganda: the Germans are hard at work trying to push it out of the Corn Trade and the other bulk trades as they pushed it out of Japan. I regard this movement as being somewhat serious for us now that we are no longer in a position of economic predominance.

It cannot be disputed that the University lawyer is regarded with benevolent contempt in England. This seems to be due to the following causes:—

a) The difficulty of recruiting first rate men as law teachers
b) The absence of contact between the teacher and the practitioner
c) The prevalence of the erroneous idea that there is something which is to be termed "practical" as opposed to theoretical law.

As regards a) and b) the situation is improving. The law faculties at Oxford and Cambridge are growing in strength and have great influence in their Universities. London is also on the upgrade. I doubt if much can be done at the provincial Universities for financial reasons. The teaching staffs are very small and they are constantly losing their best men because the stipends only provide a base livelihood. We have nearly a thousand students at Oxford and Cambridge doing law in some form or other, which is several times more than all the other Universities combined, if one leaves out the articled clerks. We can give a man a good prospect of making £1,000 a year or so before he is too old. But even with us it is difficult to hold the right type of man. The reason is not money but the lack of prestige attaching to law reading. The remedy seems to me to be a wider recognition of the importance of the work which is being done by teachers. Several of us "quorum pars minima fui" have received the honour of silk and this has helped a very great deal. I often wonder if it would not be a good thing if each Inn of Court appointed a teacher to the Bench if the right kind of man of sufficient standing were available. This should be an exception to the convention that only persons actively engaged in practice are eligible, and would only be adopted in the case of a very small number of teachers of real eminence. This would bring teachers and practitioners into contact and would much improve the status of the law teacher without causing any serious dislocation of existing traditions.

I must also feel that the moribund rule that the works of legal authors must not be cited in argument unless they are defunct is rather derogatory to academic lawyers. It is more honoured in the breach than otherwise but its formal abrogation would be a step towards the recognition of the work of academic lawyers.

Academic lawyers might also be made more use of by Government Departments than at present. As Committee men and investigators they have the advantage of being able to devote more time to their duties, and they are independent of vested interests such as Trade Organisations and the like. But above all, the recognition of some part of University examinations as exempting from the professional tests would do more than anything else to close the gulf, and this brings me to point c).

c) It is true that law can and should be taught as a living thing and not as an abstraction. This does not mean however that there is such a thing as practical law, unless one applies the term as one of reproach to certain topics where the law is entirely a matter of detail without any principle behind it. The law teacher, whether he be a practitioner or a don, must teach principles and given the right type of teacher the result will be the same in both cases except perhaps in the case of certain technical subjects which are not taught by the Universities. I think that every law teacher should have practical experience as early in his career and as much of it as possible, but I do not think that it is necessary for him to be actually in practice when he teaches. I am convinced of this as the result of my experience in London University where some of the teachers devoted the majority of their time to practice, whilst others made teaching their chief duty. It is not difficult for a teacher to find out what is going on, and sometimes he is more up to date than a busy advocate who cannot spare the time to investigate certain movements in the law.

Some subjects are best taught by practitioners e.g. Procedure Probate and Divorce, certain branches of Commercial law etc. I feel that such subjects are the peculiar province of the professional law schools and should not be attempted except in bare outline by the

Universities. But Contract, Tort, Property, Criminal Law can really be dealt with best by an experienced teacher who knows how to present the matter. The Council of Legal Education have recognised this in appointing Holdsworth for instance as one of their readers. If we could only get rid of this idea that University lecturers teach something which is different in kind from what the legal apprentice ought to know, a very great step in advance will have been made. It may have been true in the past that University teaching was unsuitable but it is certainly not so now.

Lastly, if something could be done to bring judges, practitioners and teachers together in a body charged with proposals for the reform and improvement of the law, we should have still further bridged over the gulf. Next to increased recognition of University examinations this seems to me to be the most likely method of counteracting the present—very unfortunate—isolation of the University teacher from the rest of the legal community.

I hope I have not bored you, but as M. very truly says you are the one person to whom one can unbosom oneself on this matter.

Yours very sincerely,
H. C. Gutteridge

4 Verulam Buildings
Gray's Inn
WC1

Dec. 4 1932

My dear Gutteridge,

It was kind of you to write to me fully on the subject of ( )'s letter. I agree with both of you in a good many respects. I think with you that the position is improving. One thing that is doing English law harm is the absence of public criticism by men who know: and the abundance of criticism by the ill-informed. It is largely due to the rule which prevents practising barristers from efforts which appear to be self-advertising, and prevents judges from writing at all. It seems to me to be particularly within the province of law teachers. I would include suggestions on and criticisms of the existing body of the law, the administrations of the law from time to time, refutation of all ill-informed criticism and suggestions for reform based on comparative law.

It would help the position of teachers very much if some of them showed up at times as discriminating champions of the profession.

As to the difference between academic teaching and practice I quite agree that ideally there should be none. In fact there is. You with your own experience don't feel it; but one only has to look at some articles and notes in the law magazines to see how impractical the writers are. Personally I am inclined to think that ( )'s is one of them. However I quite agree that many or perhaps I should say some teachers with only academic experience have a lively enough imagination or sympathy to be admirable guides in the appreciation of principles.

We can more fully discuss these and other topics at another time. I only sat down to thank you for your valuable letter.

With best wishes.

Always yours,

Atkin

Appendix II

THE LAW COMMISSION AND COMPARATIVE LAW DURING THE YEARS 1996–2006

Prepared by

Mr Raymond Youngs

Senior Research Fellow at the Institute of Global Law, University College London

Lawyer at the Law Commission from 2002 to 2005

This is a survey of those reports which appear online on the Law Commission website (i.e. those from 1996 to 2006 inclusive). Comparative law references have been identified either from the section headings in the reports or from a search for German. To make it easy to spot immediately which systems have been consulted, they have been printed in bold. The use of the foreign material is, as one may have expected, un-even, varying from a generic reference to Commonwealth or American law to proposals made by various Law Reform bodies, as well as isolated judicial decisions, codal provisions or foreign academic literature. References to the following terms were searched: comparative, foreign, Scottish, Ireland, Irish, Jersey, Guernsey, Commonwealth, Canada, Australia, New Zealand, Hong Kong, South Africa, India America, civil law, Europe, France, French, law. References to common law jurisdictions far outweigh references to modern civil law. Among these, France and Germany hold pride of place.

(Where the report is a joint one with the Scottish Law Commission, no mention will be made of any allusions to Scottish law.)

2006 Reports

Post-legislative Scrutiny (LC302)

Para 4.5 mentions the position in Scotland as to delegated legislation. Appendix B refers to post-legislative scrutiny in other jurisdictions. The consultation paper had mentioned some; responses are described from **Scotland** and **Switzerland**, and guidance from the former Law Reform Commission of Canada.

Trustee Exemption Clauses (LC301)

Paras 2.13 and 2.15 refer respectively to a **Jersey** decision and **Scottish** law. Para 4.20 refers to a test supported by the **New Zealand** Law Commission. Paras 5.78 and 6.53 refer respectively to the law of and codes of practice in Jersey and Guernsey. Appendix A (options rejected in the consultation paper) paras A.20 to A.27 consider a form of regulation recommended by the New Zealand Law Commission, paras A.29 to A.37 a model put forward by the **British Columbia Institute**, and paras A.43 to A.48 an example from Jersey, **Guernsey** and Scotland.

Inchoate Liability for Assisting and Encouraging Crime (LC300)

In para 2.23 a reference is made to the nature of punishments in **America.** Paras 3.6, 5.73 and 5.74 refer to **Canadian** decisions. Para 3.13 refers to a **Northern Irish** decision. Allusion is made in para 4.2 to legislation in **Canada** and **New Zealand**, and in para 4.3 to **Macaulay's Indian Code** and the **American Law Institute's Model Penal Code.**

Renting Homes: The Final Report (LC297)

Para 2.47 refers to the concept of abandonment and paras 2.55 and 7.10 to 7.12 to the rules about succession as both being inspired by **Scottish** law.

2005 Reports

Company Security Interests (LC 296)

Para 1.8 refers to a registration system based on the **American Uniform Commercial Code** (UCC) which has been adopted in part of **Canada** and **New Zealand** (see also para 3.3 as to the influence of these on scope). (There are numerous references to the Personal Property Security Acts in New Zealand and Canada.) Paras 1.42 to 1.44 relate to **Scottish law** and the Scottish Law Commission report (see also paras 3.177, 3.254 and 3.255). Para 1.67 mentions statute law in North America and New Zealand (see also paras 3.168, 3.247, 3.249 and 5.23). Paras 2.9, 2.12 and 3.96 refer to the New Zealand electronic scheme. Paras 2.30 and 2.31 consider the EU's interest in harmonising the law of personal property security interests not to be a reason for delay. Paras 3.18, 5.13 and 5.98 mention the UCC and Canadian proposals. Para 3.28 refers to a New Zealand and an Australian case. Para 3.62 refers to the registrability of charges in other countries (in view of its implications for private international law). Para 3.305 cites the absence of problems on the US and Canada as an argument.

The Forfeiture Rule and the Law of Succession (LC 295)

Para 3.22 refers to the position in **Commonwealth** and **US jurisdictions** and para 2.5 to the position in Scotland. Para 3.26 refers to the view of the Law Reform Advisory Committee for Northern Ireland.

Unfair Terms in Contracts (LC 292)

(with the Scottish Law Commission)

None.

2004 Reports

Towards a Compulsory Purchase Code: (2) Procedure: Final Report (LC 291)

Reference is made to a Northern Irish decision in para 2.41. An Australian statutory model is considered in paras 5.62 and 5.65, and a proposal of the **Australian Law** Reform Commission in para 5.66.

Partial Defences to Murder (LC 290)

Para 1.5 refers to accounts obtained, as part of the consultation process, of the law in the **USA, France** and **Germany**. Reference is made in para 2.49 to the law of Scotland. Paras 2.53 and 2.54 contain a brief overview of the law of murder in **Scotland**, the **USA, Canada, Cyprus, Denmark, France, Germany, Italy, Luxembourg, Malta, the Netherlands, Norway, Spain, Sweden, Switzerland and Turkey**. Paras 3.47 to 3.59 consider a defence under the **American Law Institute Model Penal Code**. In para 3.110 reference is made to the law in **Australia, Canada and New Zealand** and a provisional recommendation by the **Irish Law Reform Commission**, and in para 3.136 to the position in Canada and the **Northern Territory of Australia**. Para 3.44 refers to a recommendation by an Australian committee and the New Zealand Law Commission, para 3.73 to the provisions of the **Western Australian Criminal Code** and para 3.143 to an Australian decision. Para 3.75 refers to New Zealand legislation and para 3.148 to a Scottish decision. Para 4.3 refers to Australian law. Para 4.9 mentions the **Indian Penal Code.** Para 5.8 refers to the position as to diminished responsibility in Canada, New Zealand, Australia and Ireland. Para 5.22 refers to the proposals of the **New South Wales Law Reform Commission** (see also para 5.80) and the **New Zealand Law Commission.** Paras 5.57 to 5.63 describe a Scottish Law Commission report (also mentioned in other paras) on insanity and diminished responsibility, and the existing law there. Appendix F sets out the **USA Model Penal Code** provocation proposal and its reception in the state legislatures and courts.

In the Public Interest: Publication of Local Authority Inquiry Reports (LC 289)

Para 5.60 refers to an **Australian** decision and paras 5.64 to 5.71 to a **New Zealand** decision. A **Scottish** statutory provision is mentioned in para 8.64.

Pre-Judgment Interest on Debt and Damages (LC287)

The position in **Canada** is mentioned in para 3.24. Proposals by the **Law Reform Commission of Hong Kong** are mentioned in paras 3.34, 6.19 and 6.23. Para 5.9 mentions that the Consultation Paper referred to the stance of several foreign jurisdictions.

2003 Reports

Towards a Compulsory Purchase Code: (1) Compensation (LC286)

Para 2.4 refers to an **Australian decision,** paras 2.12 and 5.22 to an Australian statute, para 5.5 to an Australian Code, and para 5.12 to an Australian Law Reform Commission Report. Paras 4.12 to 4.14 describe an **Irish** court decision on disturbance and consequential loss. Para 7.23 refers to a suggestion by the Scottish executive. Two **Canadian** decisions are mentioned in para 8.5 and an Australian decision in para 10.14. The law in Australia and Canada is considered in para 11.11. Appendix D makes comparisons with Australia, Canada, **South Africa, California and France** in respect of the no-scheme rule.

Renting Homes (LC284)

In para 16.29 the police exclusion order is based on an **Australian** procedure. In paras 9.66 to 9.77 **Scottish** legislation is used as a model for abandonment. In paras 11.26, 11.27 and

11.38 Scottish legislation is used as a model in relation to notices. In para 14.28 the Scottish approach to succession is considered, and in paras 14.35 to 14.40 the Scottish concept of carer is employed.

Partnership Law (LC283)

(with Scottish Law Commission)

Para 5.1 states that **Commonwealth** countries have adopted or adapted the English approach, but the **USA** has moved to the entity approach (see also paras 2.5, 3.24, 4.16, 4.50, 5.7, 5.20. 5.21, 5.31 to 5.36, 6.10, 6.55, 6.77, 6.96, 6.98, 6.102, 7.53, 7.55, 8.26, 8.27, 8.66 to 8.68, 8.70, 8.122, 8.141, 8.142, 8.149, 9.28, 9.31, 10.27, 11.47, 11.49, 12.15, 14.5, 14.15 and 16.26 as to the American approach). Para 5.17 refers to an academic opinion on **Australian** and **New Zealand** law and para 6.96 to the law itself in these countries. Para 5.30 describes the extent to which partnerships have separate legal personality in eight European jurisdictions (**France, Luxembourg, Norway, Sweden, Belgium, Germany, the Netherlands and Switzerland**), and paras 5.31 to 5.36 consider the nature of partnerships in the USA. Para 8.37 refers to the **Law Reform Advisory Committee of Northern Ireland**. Paras 11.21 and 11.35 refer to Canadian cases, para 11.29 to an Irish case, para 11.7 to a New Zealand case, para 11.46 to an Australian case, and para 11.58 to a **Jersey** case. Para 15.27 refers to the law of Jersey, para 16.27 to the law of Jersey and **Guernsey**, para 17.6 to the law of Jersey and **Delaware,** para 17.21 to the law of Jersey, 17.34 to the law of Jersey, **Ontario** and Delaware, para 17.38 to the law of Jersey, Guernsey and Delaware and para 19.3 to the law of the **Netherlands** and Guernsey. Para 19.7 refers to the tax treatment of foreign bodies in Belgium, **Australia**, France and Germany.

Children: Their Non-Accidental Death or Serious Injury (Criminal Trials) (LC282)

None.

Land, Valuation and Housing Tribunals (LC281)

None.

2002 Reports

Sharing Homes: A Discussion Paper (LC278)

Paras 1.32, 4.29 and 5.45 mention the law in **Australia** and **New Zealand.** Paras 4.3 to 4.23 consider the approach of Australia, **Canada** and New Zealand to determining beneficial interests. Reference is made to the law in Scotland in para 5.6 and to proposals of the **Scottish Law Commission** and the **Northern Ireland Advisory Reform Committee** in para 5.12. Paras 5.18 to 5.22 describe the approach of Australia and New Zealand to unmarried couples. In paras 5.25 to 5.28 reports on the subject by the Scottish Law Commission and the Law Reform Advisory Committee for Northern Ireland are referred to. In paras 5.30 to 5.34 the concept of the registered partnership in certain European countries (especially **Denmark** and **France**) is described.

Effective Prosecution of Multiple Offending (LC277)

Para 3.16 refers to an **Australian** case. In paras 3.22 to 3.38 the approach of common law jurisdictions generally (and in particular in **Canadian** and Australian) is described. Reference is made in paras 7.39 and 7.82 to the courts in **Northern Ireland.**

Fraud (LC276)

Para 5.32 refers to the law of **Hong Kong** and **Scotland.** In paras 5.45 to 5.56 the approach of **Canada,** Hong Kong and **New Zealand** is considered and other common law jurisdictions (of which only Scotland and the **USA** are named). Para 7.19 refers to the law of Hong Kong.

2001 Reports

Evidence of Bad Character in Criminal Proceedings (LC273)

Para 3.32 refers to a **New Zealand** case and para 3.28 to a **Canadian** case. Paras 4.4, 4.27, 7.9 to 7.12, 8.25, 9.8, 9.9, 9.14 and 13.13 refer to **Australian** law. Para 7.14 mentions **American** law. Para 9.19 refers to the position in Australia, New Zealand and **Scotland.** Para 6.30 refers to the views of the Australian and New Zealand Law Commissions, paras 7.8, 9.16, 9.18, 9.22, 10.3 and 11.25 to the view of the former and paras 7.13, 9.15 and 11.44 to the view of the latter. Para 6.35 refers to **Dutch** cases and **French** law. In relation to admission of bad character evidence going to the matter in issue, two of the options canvassed are Australian common law (paras 11.11 to 11.13) and the Australian Evidence Act (paras 11.14 to 11.19 and 11.22 to 11.24).

Third Parties—Rights against Insurers (LC272)

(with the Scottish Law Commission—and recommending parallel reform in Northern Ireland, so no mention here of allusions to **Northern Irish law**)
Para 3.12 refers to the **Australian** model, and para 7.26 mentions an aspect of **American** and **Australian** law. Appendix F sets out third party rights in other jurisdictions (App F not in electronic version).

Land Registration for the 21st Century: A Conveyancing Revolution (LC271)

Para 2.37 refers to the abolition of the feudal system by the **Scottish** Parliament. Para 2.73 mentions that registration in Commonwealth states has led to changes in the law about adverse possession, and the **Queensland** model is considered. Para 14.12 refers to a **Hong Kong** case.

Limitation of Actions (LC270)

Para 3.103 refers to a **Canadian** case. Para 3.150 refers to a recommendation of the **New Zealand Law Commission,** and para 5.9 to a recommendation of this body and of the **Alberta Law Reform Institute.** Para 4.45 mentions **Scottish** law, and para 5.43 the view of the Law Reform Advisory Committee for **Northern Ireland.**

Bail and the Human Rights Act 1998 (LC269)

Paras 1.22 and 1.23 consider **Canadian, South African and New Zealand** constitutional law. Para 1.25 refers to a **New Zealand** case. Para 8.6 mentions the position in **Scotland.**

Double Jeopardy and Prosecution Appeals (LC267)

Para 3.2 refers to the stance of all **European states** in relation to res judicata. Para 5.1 refers to a paper by the **New Zealand Law Commission.** Paras 6.10 and 7.28 refer to **Scottish** law.

2000 Reports

Damages under the Human Rights Act 1998 (LC266)

(with the Scottish Law Commission—and dealing with an issue of relevance to Northern Ireland, so no mention here of allusions to Northern Irish law)

In para 1.6, it says a comparative study in common law and other jurisdictions was not requested, but 'certain common law cases' which seemed significant are referred to. Paras 3.6 to 3.8 describe the approach of **German, Dutch, French and Belgian** law to damages. Para 3.38 refers to **South African law** (see also para 4.29). Para 4.14 refers to an **American** case and a **Canadian** case as to the purpose of tort compensation, and paras 4.16 to 4.20 refer to remedies for human rights breaches in other **Commonwealth jurisdictions**, giving examples from **Trinidad and Tobago** and **New Zealand.** In para 4.25 a Canadian case is quoted to demonstrate the limits of analogy with tort. Para 4.66 contains a quotation from an English case about **Canadian** law. Para 4.72 refers to South African, New Zealand, American and Canadian law (see also para 4.88). Para 6.217 quotes from an ECHR judgment about American law.

1999 Reports

Claims for Wrongful Death (LC263)

Para 1.11 refers to a review of **Northern Ireland** criminal injuries compensation. Para 2.13 refers to a Northern Irish case. Para 2.66 refers to the approach of the **Scottish Law Commission.** Para 6.20 mentions the view of the Law Reform Advisory Committee for Northern Ireland, and Scottish judicial criticism). Para 6.22 refers to the approach of some **Canadian** jurisdictions.

Damages for Personal Injury: Medical, Nursing and Other Expenses: Collateral Benefits (LC262)

Para 2.19 refers to an **Australian** case. Paras 2.29 and 2.30 refer to number of Australian decisions (see also para 3.73). Reference is made in para 9.10 to a report of the **Irish Law Commission.** Paras 2.20 and 2.21 refer to the position in Scotland, and a proposal of the **Scottish Law Commission** is referred to in paras 3.4 and 3.15. Paras 3.44, 3.54, 3.56, 3.60 and 10.14 mention Scottish law. Australian law is referred to again in para 3.77. Para 5.13 alludes to a feature of the **Canadian** legal system. In para 11.6 option 1 contains a proposal suggested by the **American Law Institute.** Para 12.16 refers to a device used in **France** and **Germany.**

Company Directors: Regulating Conflict of Interest and Formulating a Statement of Duties (LC261)

(with the Scottish Law Commission—in co-operation with the Law Reform Advisory Committee for Northern Ireland, so no mention here of allusions to Northern Irish law)

Paras 1.23, 1.37, 4.9, 4.43, 5.10, 5.23, 5.24. 5.31, 8.75, 8.86 and 8.89 make reference to the law in **Australia**, and para 5.31 to legislative proposals in Australia, **New Zealand and Canada.** Para 2.7 refers to regulation in Canada and other states of the EC. Para 4.14 refers to **German law.** Para 4.22 mentions **Canadian law.** Para 4.37 refers to **South African law.** Para 5.5 refers to the law in Australia, Canada, Germany and **America.** Para 5.11 mentions the law in New Zealand. Para 5.22 refers to American law and para 5.23 to Australian (and American) law (see also para 5.25). Paras 5.24 and 5.31 mention a **Hong Kong** report. Para 5.30 mentions New Zealand and Canadian law. Para 8.10 refers to other common law jurisdictions, in particular Australia and New Zealand (see also para 8.18). Para 6.12 mentions Canadian law.

Trustees' Powers and Duties (LC260)

(with the Scottish Law Commission)

Para 3.19 refers to an **American** model. Para 3.24(4) mentions American and **Australian** models. Appendix C mentions Australian law in para 24, **Northern Irish law** in para 26 and Irish and Australian law in para 42.

Damages for Personal Injury: Non-pecuniary Loss (LC257)

Paras 2.4 to 2.7 consider whether the **Canadian** 'functional approach' should be adopted. Para 2.61 mentions **Scottish law.** Para 3.10 refers to Canada judicial practice. Para 3.87 refers to the level of awards in **North America, Australia, Europe and the Far East.** Paras 3.85 to 3.107 consider approaches in other jurisdictions, and mention the **USA, Australia, France, EU and EFTA countries,** and in particular **Scotland, Northern Ireland** and also the **Republic of Ireland.** Para 3.134 refers to **New Zealand** experience and para 3.155 refers to **Canadian** case law. Para 3.147 mentions a **Hong Kong** decision. Para 3.197 refers to attempted computer assessment of damages in **British Columbia** and Scotland. Para 4.5 mentions Australian decisions.

1998 Reports

Consents to Prosecution (LC255)

None.

Land Registration for the 21st Century: A consultative document (LC254)

Para 1.6 refers to legal systems in the **Commonwealth.** Para 3.40 mentions the law in **Australia and New Zealand.** Para 5.53 refers to the treatment of squatters in civil law systems. Para 10.1 refers to the stance of the Scottish and continental systems on adverse possession. Para 10.11 refers to the approach in other Commonwealth systems, in particular **Tasmania.** Para 10.17 refers to the position as to adverse possession in **New Zealand,**

Australia and Canada. Para 10.25 mentions an **Irish** decision. Para 11.2 refers to the system of electronic transfer in **Ontario.**

The Execution of Deeds and Documents by or on behalf of Bodies Corporate (LC253)

Mention is made of civil law in para 3.15.

The Rules against Perpetuities and Excessive Accumulations (LC251)

Appendix D gives examples of alteration of the rule in **America** and the **Commonwealth** (see also para 2.11). Paras 2.33 to 2.38 describe the position in **Scotland.** Paras 7.43 and 7.44 consider the **American** model for excluding commercial transactions and para 7.50 considers a model in **Canadian** states. In para 8.11 the American approach to perpetuity periods is considered. Para 10.2 describes the approach to accumulations in **Jersey, Northern Ireland** and certain states in Canada, **Australia** and the **USA**, and in **New Zealand**; and paras 9.28, 10.14 and 10.17 do the same for **Scotland.**

Liability for Psychiatric Illness (LC249)

Paras 2.28, 2.49, 2.61, 2.62 and 2.66 mention **Australian** decisions. Para 2.26 mentions **Scottish** law, and a Scottish decision is referred to in para 2.40. Para 2.51 mentions a trend in **American** and **Australian** courts. Paras 5.7, 5.9 and 8.5 refer to legislation in three Australian jurisdictions. Para 5.30(4) refers to the law in other jurisdictions, including Australia and **Canada.** Para 6.14 refers to the experience of Australian jurisdictions.

Legislating the Criminal Code: Corruption (LC248)

Paras 1.16 to 1.20 refer to a number of initiatives taking place to consider corruption, including **European, Commonwealth** and **American** ones (see also paras 5.31 to 5.35). In para 1.23 reference is made to the position in Scotland (see also paras 4.65 and 4.75). Para 2.26 refers to a **Scottish** case. Paras 4.55 to 4.58 consider the **Hong Kong** option for reform (see also para 4.29).

1997 Reports

Aggravated, exemplary and restitutionary damages (LC247)

(Part IV) Para 1.20 refers to an **Australian** case. Para 1.89 makes reference to the law in Australia, **Canada and New Zealand.** See also paras 1.119, 1.152, 1.164, 1.165 (including the USA), 1.185, 1.190, 1.191, *(Part V)* 1.38 (including the USA and civil law jurisdictions), 1.42, 1.46 (including the **USA**), 1.49, 1.53, 1.54, 1.55, 1.82, 1.94 (including the USA) 1.99, 1.100, (1.130 and 1.145 on American law), 1.160 (including the USA), 1.192, 1.193 (including **Ireland**), (1.231 on American law), 1.235 (including the USA), 1.239 (Australian case), 1.274 and 1.276 (including the USA). The view of the **Ontario Law Reform Commission** is also mentioned in a number of places.

Shareholder remedies (LC246)

(in consultation with the Scottish Law Commission and the Law Reform Advisory Committee for Northern Ireland which agree with the report—so no mention here of allusions to Scottish or Northern Irish law)

Paras 1.13, 6.8 and 6.9 refer to developments in **Australia, Canada, Hong Kong, Japan, South Africa and New Zealand.** Para 4.25 refers to foreign jurisdictions. Paras 3.64 and 3.67 refers to New Zealand, 4.25 to Australia, New Zealand and Canada, 6.13, 6.33, 6.41 and 6.45 to Canada, 6.52 to Canada, New Zealand and Australia, 6.50 to the **Cayman Islands**, and 6.99, 7.4 and 7.11 to Australia.

Evidence in Criminal Proceedings: Hearsay and Related Topics (LC245)

Para 1.4 sets out the view of the **Scottish Law Commission.** Para 3.17 mentions a **New Zealand** decision. Para 3.22 mentions jury studies in **Australia** and **America.** Para 3.30 refers to hearsay evidence by anonymous witnesses in **Denmark**, the **Netherlands** and **Germany.** Para 3.4 mentions New Zealand and American law. Paras 4.8, 10.8 and 10.13 refer to Australian decisions. Para 3.36 alludes to the position in **Scotland.** Para 4.11 mentions a Scottish decision. Para 4.25 refers to Scottish law. Para 5.10 refers to the method of examination of witnesses in **France, Germany** and other countries. Para 5.11 mentions the Canadian approach. Paras 5.21, 6.38 and 10.89 mention **Canadian** cases. Para 5.34 refers to the practice of 'many European countries'. In para 6.17 option 3 is based on the German approach (see also paras 6.19, 6.29 and 6.30). Para 7.22 refers to the law in Scotland and Australia, and proposals in Canada and **New Zealand** about the hearsay rule. Para 8.27 mentions American law and reform proposals in Scotland and Canada. Paras 10.30, 11.21 and 11.24 refer to Scottish law. Para 10.91 refers to legislation in Australia and America. Paras 11.16 and 11.17 refer to American and Australian law. Para 11.36 mentions New Zealand law. Paras 12.5 and 12.7 refer to a Scottish Law Commission Report. Para 12.15 mentions a feature of Scottish law and the view of a Northern Ireland advisory commission. Para 13.12 mentions the position on computer evidence in Scotland, some Australian states, New Zealand, the USA and Canada.

1996 Reports

Offences of Dishonesty: Money Transfers (LC243)

None.

Privity of Contract: Contracts for the Benefit of Third Parties (LC242)

Para 1.9 mentions **Australian** law. Para 2.28 refers to Australian law (and British **Columbian, Kenyan and New Zealand** law). Paras 2.31 and 2.32 mentions a Canadian decision. Para 2.34 refers to this decision and an Australian decision. Paras 2.67 and 2.68 refer again to Canadian and Australian law. Para 3.7 refers to the position in the common law world including the US, New Zealand and parts of Australia. Para 3.8 sets out the stance taken by EU states in particular **France, Germany, Italy, Austria, Spain, Portugal, the Netherlands, Belgium, Luxembourg, Greece, Scotland, Denmark, Northern Ireland and the Republic of Ireland.** Para 3.31 mentions **New Zealand** law. Para 3.26 mentions

Australian law. Para 41 refers to the reports of the **Manitoba** and **Ontario** Law Reform Commissions. Paras 4.5 to 4.21 describe the position in greater detail in Western Australia, **Queensland** and New Zealand (see also Appendix B for legislation here, including the Commonwealth of Australia), and the USA. (Reference is also made to Law Reform Commission reports in Canada). Para 5.7 refers to the approach in **Western Australia,** Queensland, New Zealand, and recommended in Manitoba. Para 6.9 refers to Australian and New Zealand law, and paras 6.17, 7.5, 7.17, 7.22, 7.24, 8.3, 8.4, 8.11, 8.13, 8.14, 9.7, 9.31, 9.35, 9.36, 9.37, 9.39, 9.48, 10.8 (referring also to the Manitoba Law Reform Commission), 10.10, 11.11 and 14.1 to New Zealand law. Paras 7.14 and 7.15 refer to the view of the **Scottish Law Commission** (see also para 9.10). Para 7.25 refers to German law and para 7.53 to American law. Para 7.50 mentions Australian law. Para 9.2 refers to Australian and New Zealand law and para 9.17 to Australian law. Para 9.44 mentions Australian and New Zealand law and para 9.45 to American law. Para 11.1 refers to New Zealand and Queensland law, and the Manitoba Law Reform Commission. Paras 10.5 to 10.7 describe the precedents for reform of defences etc in Western Australia, Queensland, the USA and New Zealand. (The Manitoba Law Reform Commission is also referred to after this). Para 11.21 refers to an American case. Paras 12.22 to 12.26 refer to Australian law. Para 14.1 mentions Australian and New Zealand law. Para 14.18 refers to French law.

Legislating the Criminal Code: Involuntary Manslaughter (LC237)

Para 1.18 refers to a Hong Kong decision, para 6.43 to a New Zealand decision and para 8.6 to an Australian decision. The comparative law position is mentioned in para 2.2 and foreign jurisdictions are mentioned in para 2.10.

Appendix III

DESCRIPTION OF DATABASES SEARCHED

Citations in Academic Literature (United States)—Westlaw JLR. A large database of about 825 law reviews, continuing legal education (CLE) course materials, and bar journals (mostly American). The results from non-American sources included in the JLR database (such as the *Melbourne University Law Review*, *Oxford Journal of Legal Studies*, *Singapore Journal of Legal Studies*, and *Vindobona Journal of International Commercial Law and Arbitration*) were manually excluded.

Citations by Courts (Australia)—Westlaw AU-ALLCASES. A database containing the judgments of the High Court of Australia and the Federal Court of Australia, both reported and unreported, with coverage beginning in 1903.

Citations by Courts (Canada)—Westlaw CAN-ALLCASES. A comprehensive database of judgments of federal and provincial Canadian courts, including all decisions ever published in Carswell law reports, with coverage beginning in 1876.

Citations by Courts (England)—Westlaw UK-RPTS-ALL. A comprehensive database of judgments of United Kingdom courts, including *The Law Reports* and many specialised series of reports, with coverage beginning in 1865.

Citations in Academic Literature and by Courts (Germany)—*beck-online*. A database provided by the publishing house CH Beck in Munich.

Citations by Courts (United States)—Westlaw ALLCASES. A comprehensive database of all reported and unreported federal and state judicial decisions from 1945, containing all available case law from earlier years, with coverage beginning in 1658.

The Search in England

The search in England was limited to five legal journals: *The Cambridge Law Journal*, *The International and Comparative Law Quarterly*, *The Law Quarterly Law Review*, *The Modern Law Review* and the *Oxford Journal of Legal Studies.* It was done manually by Mr Stephen Underwood of the London School of Economics and limited to the period 1980–2001.

The Search in Germany

Owing to the absence of adequate databases, the search in Germany was restricted to the commentaries and journals available at *beck-online* (a database of the publishing house CH Beck in Munich) in 2007. Further limitations result from the fact that authors are not cited with their first names in German legal literature. If the name of the author is common (as is the case, for example, with Lutter, Lorenz and Zimmermann), it is thus difficult to identify false positives. Finally, names of German authors that are similar or even identical to terms used in everyday German language (as is the case with von Bar) result in a high number of false hits, invalidating the results. A search by using the function 'by author' will, in turn, only reveal the works themselves, not citations in footnotes. In order to obtain at least some hard data, a limited number of the works of these authors were directly searched for. The most important sources searched by *beck-online* are the *Neue Juristische Wochenschrift* (1981–2005) and the *Münchner Kommentar zum Bürgerlichen Gesetzbuch.*

The Search in Italy

Dr Marino manually conducted a search of the following journals for the years 1980–2001: *Contratto e Impressa, Carriera giuridica, Digesto IV sul diritto comparato, Foro Italiano, Revue Internationale de droit comparé, Rivista diritto civile, Rivista diritto processuale civile.*

Formulations of Searches

Each Westlaw search was date-restricted to return results for only the relevant time period. The 1980–2000 searches contained these terms at the end of the author-name search string: & DA(AFT 12/31/1979 & BEF 1/1/2001); the 2001–2005 searches included these terms: & DA(AFT 12/31/2000 & BEF 1/1/2006). Because citations use various forms of names, it was necessary to construct searches using all variants of names likely to be found in citations. We made an effort to include misspelled forms of the authors' names as well. Some journal articles cited authors by only surname; in an effort to gather all true positives, the searches for authors with less common surnames were constructed using only that name—for example, the search string for Otto Kahn-Freund read: KAHN-FREUND & DA(AFT 12/31/1979 & BEF 1/1/2001). Works of other authors with the same surname were manually excluded from surname-only searches. The following is a list of the formulations of the variants of names used to construct searches.

American authors

Hans W. Baade
Hans Baade
H.W. Baade
H. Baade
Baade

George A. Bermann
George A. Berman
George Bermann
George Berman
G.A. Bermann
G. Bermann
Bermann

John P. Dawson
John Dawson
J.P. Dawson
J. Dawson

John G. Fleming
John Fleming
J.G. Fleming

Mary Ann Glendon
Mary Anne Glendon
Mary Glendon
M.A. Glendon
M. Glendon

James R. Gordley
James Gordley
J. Gordley

John Langbein
Langbein

Ugo Mattei
U. Mattei
Mattei

John Henry Merryman
John H. Merryman
John Merryman
J.H. Merryman
J. Merryman
Merryman

Mathias Reimann
M. Reimann
Reimann

Rudolf B. Schlesinger
Rudolf Schlesinger
R.B. Schlesinger
R. Schlesinger

Arthur Taylor von Mehren
Arthur T. von Mehren
A.T. von Mehren
A. von Mehren
von Mehren

Alan Watson

British authors

John Bell[i]

Tony Honoré
Honoré
Honore

J.A. Jolowicz
Jolowicz

Otto Kahn-Freund
O. Kahn-Freund
Kahn-Freund

Frederick Henry Lawson
Frederick H. Lawson
Frederick Lawson
F.H. Lawson

Kurt Lipstein
Lipstein

Frederick A. Mann
Frederick Mann
F.A. Mann

Basil S. Markesinis
B.S. Markesinis
B. Markesinis
Markesinis

Barry Nicholas
B. Nicholas

Bernard Rudden
B. Rudden
Rudden

John Antony Weir
J.A. Weir
Tony Weir
T. Weir

German authors

Ulrich Drobnig
U. Drobnig
Drobnig

Erik Jayme
Eric Jayme
E. Jayme
Jayme

[i] Because of the number of false positives, it was not possible to search on the name 'J Bell'. This means that inevitably some true positives were missed. This search was conducted by Mr Jonathan Pratter, Tarlton Law Library, University of Texas School of Law.

German authors (*cont.*)

Hein Kötz
Hein Koetz
H. Kötz
H. Koetz

Werner Lorenz
W. Lorenz

Marcus Lutter
M. Lutter
Lutter

Peter-Christian Müller-Graff
Peter-Christian Müller-Graf
Peter Müller-Graff
Peter Müller-Graf
P. Müller-Graff
P. Müller-Graf
Müller-Graff
Müller-Graf

Peter Schlechtriem
P. Schlechtriem
Schlechtriem

Christian von Bar
Christian v. Bar
Chr. von Bar
Chr. v. Bar
C. von Bar
von Bar

Reinhard Zimmermann
Reinhard Zimmerman
R. Zimmermann
R. Zimmerman

Konrad Zweigert
K. Zweigert
Zweigert

French authors

Xavier Blanc-Jouvan
X. Blanc-Jouvan
Blanc-Jouvan

René David
R. David

Mireille Delmas-Marty
Mireille Delmas Marty
M. Delmas-Marty
M. Delmas Marty
Delmas-Marty
Delmas Marty

Pierre Legrand
P. Legrand

Horatia Muir-Watt
Horatia Muir Watt
H. Muir-Watt
H. Muir Watt
Muir-Watt
Muir Watt

Denis Tallon
D. Tallon
Tallon

André Tunc
A. Tunc

Italian authors

Guido Alpa
G. Alpa

Michael Joachim Bonell
M.J. Bonell
Bonnell

Italian authors (*cont.*)

Mauro Bussani
Mauro Busani
M. Bussani
M. Busani
Bussani
Busani

Mauro Cappelletti
M. Cappelletti

Antonio Gambaro
A. Gambaro
Gambaro

Gino Gorla
G. Gorla
Gorla

Maurizio Lupoi
M. Lupoi
Lupoi

Rodolfo Sacco
R. Sacco

Appendix IV

JOURNALS INCLUDED IN WESTLAW'S JLR DATABASE: 825 JOURNALS

ABA Journal E-Report	ABA J E-Report
Administrative & Regulatory Law News	Admin & Reg L News
Administrative Law Journal of the American University (formerly: Administrative Law Journal)	Admin LJ Am U; Admin LJ
Administration Law Review	Admin L Rev
Advocate	Advocate (Idaho)
AIPLA Quarterly Journal	AIPLA QJ
Air & Space Lawyer	Air & Space Law
Air Force Law Review	AF L Rev
Akron Law Review	Akron L Rev
Akron Tax Journal	Akron Tax J
Alabama Law Review	Ala L Rev
Alabama Lawyer	Ala Law
Alaska Law Review	Alaska L Rev
Albany Law Journal of Science & Technology	Alb LJ Sci & Tech
Albany Law Review	Alb L Rev
Albany Law Environmental Outlook Journal (formerly: Albany Law Environmental Outlook)	Alb L Envtl Outlook J; Alb L Envtl Outlook
American Bankruptcy Institute Journal	Am Bankr Inst J
American Bankruptcy Institute Law Review	Am Bankr Inst L Rev
American Bankruptcy Law Journal	Am Bankr LJ
American Business Law Journal	Am Bus LJ
American Criminal Law Review	Am Crim L Rev
American Indian Law Review	Am Indian L Rev
American Journal of Criminal Law	Am J Crim L
American Journal of Comparative Law	Am J Comp L
American Journal of International Law	Am J Int'l L
American Journal of Jurisprudence	Am J Juris
American Journal of Law & Medicine	Am JL & Med
American Journal of Legal History	Am J Legal Hist
American Journal of Tax Policy	Am J Tax Pol'y
American Journal of Trial Advocacy	Am J Trial Advoc
American Law and Economic Review	Am L & Econ Rev
American Law Institute-American Bar Association Continuing Legal Education	ALI-ABA
American Review of International Arbitration	Am Rev Int'l Arb
American Society of International Law Proceedings	Am Soc'y Int'l L Proc

American University International Law Review formerly: American University Journal of International Law & Policy	Am U Int'l L Rev; Am U J Int'l L & Pol'y
American University Journal of Gender, Social Policy & the Law (formerly: American University Journal of Gender & the Law)	Am U J Gender Soc Pol'y & L; Am U J Gender & L
American University Journal of International Law & Policy	Am U J Int'l L & Pol'y
American University Law Review	Am U L Rev
Animal Law	Animal L
Annals of Health Law	Annals Health L
Annals of the American Academy & Political & Social Science	Ann Am Acad Pol & Soc Sci
Annual Review of Banking & Finance Law (formerly: Annual Review of Banking Law)	Ann Rev Banking & Fin L; Ann Rev Banking L
Annual Survey of International & Comparative Law	Ann Surv Int'l & Comp L
Antitrust	Antitrust
Antitrust Law Journal	Antitrust LJ
Appalachian Journal of Law	Appalachian JL
Arizona Attorney (formerly: Arizona Bar Journal)	Ariz Att'y (Ariz BJ)
Arizona Journal of International & Comparative Law	Ariz J Int'l & Comp L
Arizona Law Review	Ariz L Rev
Arizona State Law Journal	Ariz St LJ
Arkansas Law Notes	Ark L Notes
Arkansas Law Review	Ark L Rev
Arkansas Lawyer	Ark Law
Army Lawyer	Army Law
Asian American Law Journal (formerly Asian Law Journal)	Asian Am LJ
Asian Journal of WTO & International Health Law & Policy	Asian J WTO & Int'l Health L & Pol'y
Asian Pacific American Law Journal (formerly: Asian American Pacific Islands Law Journal)	Asian Pac Am LJ; Asian Am Pac Islands LJ
Asian Pacific Law & Policy Journal	Asian-Pac L & Pol'y J
Ave Maria Law Review	Ave Maria L Rev
Banking & Financial Services Policy Report (formerly Banking Policy Report)	Banking & Fin Services Pol'y Rep
Banking Law Journal	Banking LJ
Barry Law Review	Barry L Rev
Baylor Law Review	Baylor L Rev
Bench & Bar of Minnesota	Bench & B Minn
Berkeley Business Law Journal	Berkeley Bus LJ
Berkeley Journal of African-American Law & Policy (formerly African-American Law & Policy Report)	Berkeley J of Afr-Am L & Pol'y; Afr-Am J L & Pol'y Rep

Berkeley Journal of Criminal Law (formerly Boalt Journal of Criminal Law and California Criminal Law Review)	Berkeley J Crim L
Berkeley Journal of Employment & Labor Law (formerly: Industrial Relations Law Journal)	Berkeley J Emp & Lab L; Indus Rel LJ
Berkeley Journal of Gender, Law & Justice (formerly Berkeley Women's Law Journal)	Berkeley J Gender L & Just
Berkeley Journal of International Law (formerly: International Tax & Business Lawyer)	Berkeley J Int'l L; Int'l Tax & Bus Law
Berkeley La Raza Law Journal (formerly: La Raza Law Journal)	Berkeley La Raza LJ; La Raza LJ
Berkeley Technology Law Journal (formerly: High Technology Law Journal)	Berkeley Tech LJ; High Tech LJ
Beverly Hills Bar Association Journal	Beverly Hills B Ass'n J
Biotechnology Law Report	Biotechnology L Rep
Boalt Journal of Criminal Law (formerly California Criminal Law Review)	Boalt J Crim L
Boston Bar Journal	B BJ
Boston College Environmental Affairs Law Review	BC Envtl Aff L Rev
Boston College Intellectual Property & Technology Forum	BC Intell Prop & tech F
Boston College International & Comparative Law Review	BC Int'l & Comp L Rev
Boston College Law Review	BC L Rev
Boston College Third World Law Journal	BC Third World LJ
Boston University International Law Journal	BU Int'l LJ
Boston University Journal of Science & Technology Law	BU J Sci & Tech L
Boston University Law Review	BU L Rev
Boston University Public Interest Law Journal	BU Pub Int LJ
Brandeis Law Journal (formerly: Brandeis Journal of Family Law, University of Louisville Journal of Family Law, and Journal of Family Law)	Brandeis LJ; Brandeis J Fam L; U Louisville J Fam L, and J Fam L
Brief	Brief
Bringham Young University Education & Law Journal	BYU Educ & LJ
Brigham Young University International Law & Management Review (formerly International Law & Management Review)	BYU Int'l L & Mgmt Rev; Int'l L & Mgmt Rev
Brigham Young University Law Review	BYU L Rev
British Journal of Criminology	Brit J Criminology
Brooklyn Journal of Corporate, Financial & Commercial Law	Brook J Corp Fin & Comm L
Brooklyn Journal of International Law	Brook J Int'l L
Brooklyn Law Review	Brook L Rev
Buffalo Criminal Law Review	Buff Crim L Rev
Buffalo Environmental Law Journal	Buff Envtl LJ

Buffalo Human Rights Law Review	Buff Hum Rts L Rev
Buffalo Intellectual Property Law Journal	Buff Intell Prop LJ
Buffalo Law Review	Buff L Rev
Buffalo Public Interest Law Journal	Buff Pub Int LJ
Buffalo Women's Law Journal (formerly: Circles: The Buffalo Women's Journal of Law & Social Policy)	Buff Women's LJ; Circles: Buff Women's JL & Soc Pol'y
Business Law Today	Bus L Today
Business Lawyer	Bus Law
BYU Journal of Public Law	BYU J Pub L
California Bankruptcy Journal	Cal Bankr J
California Law Review	Cal L Rev
California Regulatory Law Reporter	Cal Reg L Rep
California Western International Law Journal	Cal W Int'l LJ
California Western Law Review	Cal W L Rev
Campbell Law Review	Campbell L Rev
Canada-United States Law Journal	Can-US LJ
Capital Defense Journal	Cap Def J
Capital University Law Review	Cap U L Rev
Cardozo Arts & Entertainment Law Journal	Cardozo Arts & Ent LJ
Cardozo Journal of Conflict Resolution (formerly: Cardozo Online Journal of Conflict Resolution)	Cardozo J Conflict Resol; Cardozo Online J Conflict Resol
Cardozo Journal of International & Comparative Law (formerly: New Europe Law Review)	Cardozo J Int'l & Comp L; New Eur L Rev
Cardozo Journal of Law & Gender	Cardozo JL & Gender
Cardozo Law Review	Cardozo L Rev
Cardozo Public Law, Policy and Ethics Journal	Cardozo Pub L Pol'y & Ethics J
Case Western Reserve Journal of International Law	Case W Res J Int'l L
Case Western Reserve Law Review	Case W Res L Rev
Catholic University Law Review	Cath U L Rev
Cato Supreme Court Review	Cato Sup Ct Rev
CBA Record (formerly: Chicago Bar Record)	CBA Rec; Chi B Rec
Champion	Champion
Chapman Law Review	Chap L Rev
Chicago Journal of International Law	Chi J Int'l L
Chicago-Kent Journal of Intellectual Property	Chic-Kent J Intell Prop
Chicago-Kent Journal of International and Comparative Law	Chic-Kent J Int'l & Comp L
Chicago-Kent Law Review	Chi-Kent L Rev
Chicana/o-Latina/o Law Review (formerly: Chicano-Latino Law Review and Chicano Law Review)	Chicana/o-Latina/o Law Review; Chicano-Latino L Rev; Chicano L Rev
Chinese Journal of International Law	Chinese J Int'l L
Cleveland State Law Review	Clev St L Rev
Clinical Law Review	Clinical L Rev
Colorado Journal of International Environmental Law & Policy	Colo J Int'l Envtl L & Pol'y

Colorado Lawyer	Colo Law
Columbia Business Law Review	Colum Bus L Rev
Columbia Human Rights Law Review	Colum Hum Rts L Rev
Columbia Journal of Asian Law (formerly: Journal of Chinese Law)	Colum J Asian L; J Chinese L
Columbia Journal of Environmental Law	Colum J Envtl L
Columbia Journal of European Law	Colum J Eur L
Columbia Journal of Gender & Law	Colum J Gender & L
Columbia Journal of Law & Social Problems	Colum JL & Soc Probs
Columbia Journal of Law & the Arts (formerly: Columbia-VLA Journal of Law & the Arts)	Colum JL & Arts; Colum-VLA JL & Arts
Columbia Journal of Transnational Law	Colum J Transnat'l L
Columbia Law Review	Colum L Rev
Columbia Science and Technology Law Review	Colum Sci & Tech L Rev
CommLaw Conspectus	CommLaw Conspectus
Communication Law & Policy	Comm L & Pol'y
Communications Lawyer	Comm Law
Comparative Labor Law & Policy Journal (formerly: Comparative Labor Law)	Comp Lab L & Pol'y J; Comp Lab LJ
Connecticut Bar Journal	Conn BJ
Connecticut Insurance Law Journal	Conn Ins LJ
Connecticut Journal of International Law	Conn J Int'l L
Connecticut Law Review	Conn L Rev
Connecticut Public Interest Law Journal	Conn Pub Int L J
Constitutional Commentary	Const Comment
Construction Lawyer	Construction Law
Consumer Finance Law Quarterly Report	Consumer Fin LQ Rep
Cornell International Law Journal	Cornell Int'l LJ
Cornell Journal of Law & Public Policy	Cornell JL & Pub Pol'y
Cornell Law Review	Cornell L Rev
Creighton Law Review	Creighton L Rev
Crime and Justice	Crime & Just
Criminal Justice	Crim Just
Criminal Law Forum	Crim LF
Cumberland Law Review	Cumb L Rev
Currents: International Trade Law Journal	Currents: Int'l Trade L J
DCBA Brief	DCBABR
Defense Counsel Journal	Def Couns J
Delaware Journal of Corporate Law	Del J Corp L
Delaware Law Review	Del L Rev
Delaware Lawyer	Del Law
Denver Journal of International Law & Policy	Denv J Int'l L & Pol'y
Denver University Law Review (formerly: Denver Law Journal)	Denv U L Rev; Denv LJ
DePaul Business & Commercial Law Journal (formerly: Commercial Law Journal and DePaul Business Law Journal)	DePaul Bus & Com LJ; Com LJ DePaul Bus LJ

DePaul International Law Journal (formerly: DePaul Digest of International Law)	DePaul Int'l LJ; DePaul Dig Int'l L
DePaul Journal of Health Care Law	DePaul J Health Care L
DePaul Journal of Sports Law & Contemporary Problems	DePaul J Sports L & Contemp Probs
DePaul Law Review	DePaul L Rev
DePaul-LCA Journal of Art and Entertainment Law	DePaul-LCA J Art & Ent L
Developments in Mental Health Law	Dev Mental Health L
Dispute Resolution Journal (formerly: Arbitration Journal)	Disp Resol J; Arb J
Drake Journal of Agricultural Law	Drake J Agric L
Drake Law Review	Drake L Rev
Duke Environmental Law & Policy Forum	Duke Envtl L & Pol'y F
Duke Journal of Comparative & International Law	Duke J Comp & Int'l L
Duke Journal of Gender Law & Policy	Duke J Gender L & Pol'y
Duke Law & Technology Review	Duke L & Tech Rev
Duke Law Journal	Duke LJ
Duquesne Law Review	Duq L Rev
Duquesne Business Law Journal	Duq Bus L J
Ecology Law Quarterly	Ecology LQ
Elder Law Journal	Elder LJ
Election Law Journal	Election LJ
Emerging Issues in State Constitutional Law (ceased publication)	Emerging Issues St Const L
Emory Bankruptcy Developments Journal (formerly: Bankruptcy Developments Journal)	Emory Bankr Dev J; Bankr Dev J
Emory International Law Review (formerly: Emory Journal of International Dispute Resolution)	Emory Int'l L Rev; Emory J Int'l Disp Resol
Emory Law Journal	Emory LJ
Employee Rights & Employment Policy Journal	Employee Rts & Emp Pol'y J
Energy Law Journal	Energy LJ
Entertainment & Sports Lawyer	Ent & Sports Law
Entertainment Law Review	Ent LR
Environmental Law	Envtl L
Environmental Lawyer	Envtl Law
Environs Environmental Law & Policy Journal	Environs Envtl L & Pol'y J
ERISA Litigation Reporter	ERISA Litig Rep
EU Focus	EU Focus
European Competition Law Review	ECLR
European Journal of International Law	Eur J Int'l L
Experience	Experience
Family Advocate	Fam Advoc
Family Court Review (formerly: Family & Conciliation Courts Review)	Fam Ct Rev; Fam & Conciliation Cts Rev
Family Law Quarterly	Fam LQ
Federal Bar Association Section of Taxation Report	Fed BA Sec Tax'n Rep
Federal Circuit Bar Journal	Fed Circuit BJ

Federal Communications Law Journal	Fed Comm LJ
Federal Courts Law Review	Fed Cts L Rev
Federal Lawyer (formerly: Federal Bar News & Journal)	Fed Law; Fed B News & J
Federal Probation	Fed Probation
Federal Rules Decisions (articles from the West reporter)	FRD
First Amendment Law Review	First Amend L Rev
Fletcher Forum of World Affairs	Fletcher F World Aff
Florida Bar Journal	Fla BJ
Florida Coastal Law Review (formerly: Florida Coastal Law Journal)	Fla Coastal L Rev; Fla Coastal LJ
Florida Journal of International Law (formerly: Florida International Law Journal)	Fla J Int'l L; Fla Int'l LJ
Florida Law Review (formerly: University of Florida Law Review)	Fla L Rev; U Fla L Rev
Florida State University Business Review	Fla St U Bus Rev
Florida State University Law Review	Fla St U L Rev
Florida Tax Review	Fla Tax Rev
Food & Drug Law Journal (formerly: Food Drug Cosmetic Law Journal)	Food & Drug LJ; Food Drug Cosm LJ
Fordham Environmental Law Review (formerly: Fordham Environmental Law Journal)	Fordham Envtl L Rev; Fordham Envtl LJ
Fordham Intellectual Property, Media & Entertainment Law Journal (formerly: Fordham Entertainment, Media & Intellectual Property Law Forum)	Fordham Intell Prop Media & Ent LJ; Fordham Ent Media & Intell Prop LF
Fordham International Law Journal	Fordham Int'l LJ
Fordham Journal of Corporate & Financial Law (formerly: Fordham Finance, Securities & Tax Law Forum)	Fordham J Corp & Fin L; Fordham Fin Sec & Tax LF
Fordham Law Review	Fordham L Rev
Fordham Urban Law Journal	Fordham Urb LJ
Franchise Law Journal	Franchise LJ
Gaming Law Review	Gaming Law Rev
George Mason Law Review (formerly: George Mason University Law Review; merger of: George Mason University Law Review and George Mason Independent Law Review)	Geo Mason L Rev; Geo Mason U L Rev; Geo Mason Indep L Rev
George Mason University Civil Rights Law Journal	Geo Mason U Civ Rts LJ
George Washington International Law Review (formerly: George Washington Journal of International Law & Economics)	Geo Wash J Int'l L Rev; Geo Wash J Int'l L & Econ
George Washington Law Review	Geo Wash L Rev
Georgetown Immigration Law Journal	Geo Immigr LJ
Georgetown International Environmental Law Review	Geo Int'l Envtl L Rev

Georgetown Journal of International Law (formerly: Law & Policy in International Business)	Geo J Int'l L; Law & Pol'y Int'l Bus
Georgetown Journal of Legal Ethics	Geo J Legal Ethics
Georgetown Journal on Poverty Law & Policy (formerly: Georgetown Journal on Fighting Poverty)	Geo J on Poverty L & Pol'y; Geo J on Fighting Poverty
Georgetown Law Journal	Geo LJ
Georgetown Public Policy Review	Geo Pub Pol'y Rev
Georgia Journal of International & Comparative Law	Ga J Int'l & Comp L
Georgia Law Review	Ga L Rev
Georgia State University Law Review	Ga St U L Rev
Glasser LegalWorks Seminars	Glasser CLE
Golden Gate University Law Review	Golden Gate U L Rev
Gonzaga Journal of International Law	Gonz J Int'l L
Gonzaga Law Review	Gonz L Rev
Great Plains Natural Resources Journal	Great Plains Nat Resources J
Green Bag	Green Bag 2d
Hamline Journal of Public Law & Policy	Hamline J Pub L & Pol'y
Hamline Law Review	Hamline L Rev
Harvard BlackLetter Law Journal (formerly: Harvard Blackletter Journal)	Harv BlackLetter L J; Harv Blackletter J
Harvard Civil Rights-Civil Liberties Law Review	Harv CR-CL L Rev
Harvard Environmental Law Review	Harv Envtl L Rev
Harvard Human Rights Journal (formerly: Harvard Human Rights Yearbook)	Harv Hum Rts J; Harv Hum Rts YB
Harvard International Law Journal	Harv Int'l LJ
Harvard Journal of Law & Gender (formerly Harvard Women's Law Journal)	Harv JL & Gender; Harvard Women's LJ
Harvard Journal of Law & Public Policy	Harv JL & Pub Pol'y
Harvard Journal of Law & Technology	Harv JL & Tech
Harvard Journal on Legislation	Harv J on Legis
Harvard Latino Law Review	Harv Latino L Rev
Harvard Law Review	Harv L Rev
Harvard Law Review Forum	Harv L Rev F
Harvard Negotiation Law Review	Harv Negot L Rev
Hastings Business Law Journal	Hastings Bus L J
Hastings Communications & Entertainment Law Journal (Comm/Ent)	Hastings Comm & Ent LJ
Hastings Constitutional Law Quarterly	Hastings Const LQ
Hastings International & Comparative Law Review	Hastings Int'l & Comp L Rev
Hastings Law Journal	Hastings LJ
Hastings West-Northwest Journal of Environmental Law and Policy & Policy (formerly: West-Northwest: Journal of Environmental Law, Policy, Thought)	Hastings W-NW J Envtl L; West-NW
Hastings Women's Law Journal	Hastings Women's LJ
Hawai'i Bar Journal	Haw BJ

Health Lawyer	Health Law
Health Matrix: The Journal of Law-Medicine	Health Matrix
Hofstra Law Review	Hofstra L Rev
Hofstra Labor & Employment Law Journal (formerly: Hofstra Labor Law Journal)	Hofstra Lab & Emp LJ; Hofstra Lab LJ
Hofstra Law & Policy Symposium	Hofstra L & Pol'y Symp
Hofstra Property Law Journal	Hofstra Prop LJ
Hong Kong Law Journal	Hong Kong LJ
Houston Business & Tax Law Journal	Hous Bus & Tax LJ
Houston Journal of Health Law & Policy	Hous J Health L & Pol'y J
Houston Journal of International Law	Hous J Int'l L
Houston Law Review	Hous L Rev
Houston Lawyer	Hous Law
Howard Law Journal	How LJ
Howard Scroll: The Social Justice Law Review (formerly Howard Scroll: The Social Justice Review)	How Scroll Soc Just L Rev; How Scroll
Human Rights	Hum Rts
Human Rights Brief	Hum Rts Brief
Human Rights Law Review	Hum Rts L Rev
Idaho Law Review	Idaho L Rev
IDEA: The Intellectual Property Law Review (formerly IDEA: Journal of Law & Technology)	IDEA
Illinois Bar Journal	Ill BJ
ILSA Journal of International & Comparative Law (formerly: ILSA Journal of International Law)	ILSA J Int'l & Comp L; ILSA J Int'l L
Indiana Health Law Review	Ind Health L Rev
Indiana International & Comparative Law review	Ind Int'l & Comp L Rev
Indiana Journal of Global Legal Studies	Ind J Global Legal Stud
Indiana Law Journal	Ind LJ
Indiana Law Review	Ind L Rev
Industrial & Labor Relations Review	Indus & Lab Rel Rev
Industrial Law Journal	Indus LJ
In the Public Interest	In Pub Int
Intellectual Property Law Bulletin	Intell Prop L Bull
Intellectual Property Law Newsletter	Intell Prop L Newsl
International & Comparative Law Quarterly	ICLQ
International Dimensions	Int'l Dimensions
International Journal of Constitutional Law	Int'l J Const L
International Journal of Law and Information Technology	Int'l JL & Info Tech
International Journal of Law, Policy and the Family	Int'l JL & Pol'y & Fam
International Journal of Legal Information	Int'l J Legal Info
International Journal of Refugee Law	Int'l J Refugee L
International Law & Management Review	Int'l L & Mgmt Rev
International Law Practicum	Int'l L Prac
International Lawyer	Int'l Law

International Legal Perspectives	Int'l Legal Persp
International Legal Theory	Int'l Legal Theory
International Review of Law & Economics	Int'l Rev L & Econ
Iowa Law Review	Iowa L Rev
Issues in Law & Medicine	Issues L & Med
IUS Gentium	IUS Gen
John Marshall Journal of Computer & Information Law merger of the former: Computer/Law Journal Computer/LJ	J Marshall J Computer & Info L
and Software Law Journal	Software LJ
John Marshall Law Review	J Marshall L Rev
John Marshall Review of Intellectual Property Law	J Marshall Rev Intell Prop L
Journal of Affordable Housing & Community Development Law	J Affordable Housing & Community Dev L
Journal of Air Law & Commerce	J Air L & Com
Journal of American Arbitration	J Am Arb
Journal of Animal Law & Ethics	J Animal L & Ethics
Journal of Appellate Practice & Process	J App Prac & Process
Journal of Bankruptcy Law & Practice	J Bankr L & Prac
Journal of Business & Securities Law	J Bus & Sec L
Journal of Catholic Legal Studies (formerly: Catholic Lawyer)	J Cath Legal Stud; Cath Law
Journal of Chinese & Comparative Law	J Chinese & Comp L
Journal of College & University Law	JC & UL
Journal of Competition Law and Economics	J Competition L & Econ
Journal of Conflict & Security Law	J Conflict & Security L
Journal of Contemporary Health Law & Policy	J Contemp Health L & Pol'y
Journal of Contemporary Law	J Contemp L
Journal of Contemporary Legal Issues	J Contemp Legal Issues
Journal of Corporation Law	J Corp L
Journal of Criminal Law & Criminology	J Crim L & Criminology
Journal of Dispute Resolution	J Disp Resol
Journal of Environmental Law	J Envtl L
Journal of Environmental Law & Litigation	J Envtl L & Litig
Journal of Ethics & Social Philosophy	J Ethics & Soc Phil
Journal of Forensic Document Examination	J Forensic Document Examination
Journal of Gender, Race & Justice	J Gender Race & Just
Journal of Health Care Law & Policy	J Health Care L & Pol'y
Journal of Health Law	J Health L
Journal of Health Politics, Policy & Law	J Health Pol Pol'y & L
Journal of High Technology Law	J High Tech L
Journal of Intellectual Property Law	J Intell Prop L
Journal of International Business and Law	J Int'l Bus & L
Journal of International Criminal Justice	J Int'l Crim Just
Journal of International Economic Law	J Int'l Econ L
Journal of International Law & International Relations	J Int'l L & Int'l Rel

Journal of International Legal Studies	J Int'l Legal Stud
Journal of Juvenile Law	J Juvenile L
Journal of Land Use & Environmental Law	J Land Use & Envtl L
Journal of Land, Resources & Environmental Law (formerly: Journal of Energy, Natural Resources & Environmental Law; Journal of Energy Law & Policy)	J Land Resources & Envntl L; J Energy, Nat Resources & Envtl L; J Energy L & Pol'y
Journal of Law & Commerce	JL & Com
Journal of Law & Economics	JL & Econ
Journal of Law & Education	JL & Educ
Journal of Law & Family Studies	JL & Fam Stud
Journal of Law & Health	JL & Health
Journal of Law & Policy	JL & Pol'y
Journal of Law & Politics	JL & Pol
Journal of Law & Religion	JL & Religion
Journal of Law & Social Challenges	JL & Soc Challenges
Journal of Law & Technology (ceased publication)	JL & Tech
Journal of Law, Economics & Organization	JL Econ & Org
Journal of Law, Economics & Policy	JL Econ & Pol'y
Journal of Law in Society	JL Soc'y
Journal of Law, Medicine & Ethics	JL Med & Ethics
Journal of Legal Advocacy & Practice	J Legal Advoc & Prac
Journal of Legal Aspects of Sport	J Legal Aspects Sport
Journal of Legal Economics	J Legal Econ
Journal of Legal Medicine	J Legal Med
Journal of Legal Studies	J Legal Stud
Journal of Legal Technology Risk Management	J Legal Tech Risk Mgmt
Journal of Legislation	J Legis
Journal of Maritime Law & Commerce	J Mar L & Com
Journal of Medicine & Law	J Med & L
Journal of National Security Law & Policy	J Nat'l Security L & Pol'y
Journal of Natural Resources & Environmental Law (formerly: Journal of Mineral Law & Policy)	J Nat Resources & Envtl L; J Min L & Pol'y
Journal of Pharmacy & Law	J Pharmacy & L
Journal of Refugee Studies	J Refugee Stud
Journal of Technology Law & Policy	J Tech L & Pol'y
Journal of the American Academy of Matrimonial Lawyers	J Am Acad Matrim Law
Journal of the Association of Legal Writing Directors	J Ass'n Legal Writing Directors
Journal of the Center for Families, Children, & the Courts (formerly: Journal of the Center of Children, & the Courts)	J Center for Families, Child & Cts; J Center for Child & Cts
Journal of the Copyright Society of the USA	J Copyright Soc'y USA
Journal of the Institute for the Study of Legal Ethics	J Inst for Study Legal Ethics
Journal of the Institute of Justice and International Studies	J Inst Just Int'l Stud
Journal of the Kansas Bar Association	J Kan BA

Journal of the Legal Profession	J Legal Prof
Journal of the Missouri Bar	J Mo B
Journal of the National Association of Administrative Law Judges	J Nat'l Ass'n Admin L J
Journal of the Patent & Trademark Office Society	J Pat & Trademark Off Soc'y
Journal of Transnational Law & Policy	J Transnat'l L & Pol'y
Jurimetrics Journal	Jurimetrics J
Justice System Journal	Just Sys J
Kansas Journal of Law & Public Policy	Kan JL & Pub Pol'y
Kentucky Children's Rights Journal	Ky Child Rts J
Kentucky Law Journal	Ky LJ
Labor Lawyer	Lab Law
Law & Business Review of the Americas (formerly: NAFTA: Law & Business Review of the Americas)	L & Bus Rev Am; NAFTA: L & Bus Rev Am
Law & Contemporary Problems	Law & Contemp Probs
Law & Inequality	Law & Ineq
Law & Literature (formerly: Cardozo Studies in Law & Literature)	Law & Literature; Cardozo Stud L & Literature
Law and History Review	Law & Hist Rev
Law, Probability & Risk	Law, Probability & Risk
Law and Human Behavior	Law & Hum Behav
Law & Psychology Review	Law & Psychol Rev
Law & Sexuality: A Review of Lesbian & Gay Legal Issues	Law & Sexuality
Law & Social Inquiry	Law & Soc Inquiry
Law Department Management	Law Dep't Mgmt
Law Library Journal	Law Libr J
Law Practice (formerly: Law Practice Management; Legal Economics)	Law Prac; Law Prac Mgmt; Legal Econ
Lawyers Journal (formerly: Pittsburgh Legal Journal)	Lawyers J; Pittsburgh Legal J
Legal Affairs	Legal Aff
Legal Malpractice Report	Legal Malpractice Rep
Legal Tech Newsletter	Legal Tech Newsl
Legal Writing: The Journal of Legal Writing Institute	Legal Writing: J Legal Writing Inst
LERC Monograph Series	LERC Monograph Ser
Lewis and Clark Law Review	Lewis & Clark L Rev
Litigation	Litigation
Los Angeles Lawyer	LA Law
Louisiana Bar Journal	La BJ
Louisiana Law Review	La L Rev
Loyola Consumer Law Review (formerly: Loyola Consumer Law Reporter)	Loy Consumer L Rev; Loy Consumer L Rep
Loyola Journal of Public Interest Law (formerly: Loyola Poverty Law Journal)	Loy J Pub Int L; Loy Poverty LJ
Loyola Law Review	Loy L Rev
Loyola Maritime Law Journal	Loy Mar LJ

Loyola of Los Angeles Entertainment Law Review (formerly: Loyola of Los Angeles Entertainment Law Journal and Loyola Entertainment Law Journal)	Loy LA Ent L Rev; Loy LA Ent LJ; Loy Ent LJ
Loyola of Los Angeles International & Comparative Law Review (formerly: Loyola of Los Angeles International & Comparative Law Journal)	Loy LA Int'l & Comp L Rev; Loy LA Int'l Comp LJ
Loyola of Los Angeles Law Review	Loy LA L Rev
Loyola University New Orleans School of Law—Law & Technology Annual	Loy U New Orleans Sch L—L & Tech Ann
Loyola University of Chicago International Law Review	Loy U Chi Int'l L Rev
Loyola University of Chicago Law Journal	Loy U Chi LJ
Maine Bar Journal	Me BJ
Maine Law Review	Me L Rev
Marquette Law Review	Marq L Rev
Marquette Elder's Advisor	Marq Elder's Advisor
Marquette Sports Law Review (formerly: Marquette Sports Law Journal)	Marq Sports L Rev; Marq Sports LJ
Marquette Intellectual Property Law Review	Marq Intell Prop L Rev
Maryland Bar Journal	Md BJ
Maryland Journal of Contemporary Legal Issues	Md J Contemp Legal Issues
Maryland Journal of International Law & Trade	Md J Int'l L & Trade
Maryland Law Review	Md L Rev
Massachusetts Law Review	Mass L Rev
McGeorge Law Review (formerly: Pacific Law Journal)	McGeorge L Rev; Pac LJ
Media Law & Policy	Media L & Pol'y
Medical Law Review	Med L Rev
Medicine & Law	Med & L
Melbourne University Law Review	Melbourne U L Rev
Mental & Physical Disability Law Reporter	Mental & Phys Disab L Rep
Mercer Law Review	Mercer L Rev
Michigan Bar Journal	Mich BJ
Michigan Journal of Gender & Law	Mich J Gender & L
Michigan Journal of International Law	Mich J Int'l L
Michigan Journal of Race & Law	Mich J Race & L
Michigan Law & Policy Review	Mich L & Pol'y Rev
Michigan Law Review	Mich L Rev
Michigan State Law Review (formerly: Michigan State DCL Law Review; Law Review of Michigan State University Detroit College of Law; Detroit College of Law at Michigan State University Law Review; Detroit College of Law Review)	Mich St L Rev; Mich St DCL L Rev; L Rev Mich St U Det CL; Det CL Mich St UL Rev; Det CL Rev
Michigan State Journal of International Law (formerly: Michigan State University-DCL Journal of International Law; Journal of International Law & Practice)	Mich St L Int'l L; MSU-DCL J Int'l L; J Int'l L & Prac

Michigan State University Journal of Medicine & Law (formerly: Journal of Medicine & Law)	Mich St U J Med & L; J Med & L
Michigan Telecommunications & Technology Law Review	Mich Telecomm & Tech L Rev
Military Law Review	Mil L Rev
Minnesota Journal of International Law (formerly: Minnesota Journal of Global Trade)	Minn J Int'l L; Minn J Global Trade
Minnesota Journal of Law, Science & Technology (formerly: Minnesota Intellectual Property Review)	Minn JL Sci & Tech; Minn Intell Prop Rev
Minnesota Law Review	Minn L Rev
Mississippi College Law Review	Miss C L Rev
Mississippi Law Journal	Miss LJ
Missouri Environmental Law & Policy Review	Mo Envtl L & Pol'y Rev
Missouri Law Review	Mo L Rev
Montana Law Review	Mont L Rev
Montana Lawyer	Mont Law
NAELA Journal	NAELA J
Nanotechnology Law and Business	Nanotechnology L & Bus
National Black Law Journal	Nat'l Black LJ
Natural Resources & Environment (formerly: Natural Resources Lawyer)	Nat Resources & Env't; Nat Resources Law
Natural Resources Journal	Nat Resources J
Naval Law Review	Nav L Rev
NBA National Bar Association Magazine	NBA Nat'l B Ass'n Mag
Nebraska Law Review	Neb L Rev
Nevada Law Journal	Nev LJ
Nevada Lawyer (formerly: Inter Alia)	Nev Law; Inter Alia
New England Journal of International & Comparative Law	New Eng J Int'l & Comp L
New England Journal on Criminal & Civil Confinement	New Eng J on Crim & Civ Confinement
New England Law Review	New Eng L Rev
New Jersey Lawyer	NJ Law
New Mexico Law Review	NM L Rev
New York City Law Review	NY City L Rev
New York International Law Review	NY Int'l L Rev
New York Law School Journal of Human Rights	NYL Sch J Hum Rts
New York Law School Journal of International & Comparative Law	NYL Sch J Int'l & Comp L
New York Law School Law Review	NYL Sch L Rev
New York State Bar Journal	NY St BJ
New York University Annual Survey of American Law (formerly: Annual Survey of American Law)	NYU Ann Surv Am L; Ann Surv Am L
New York University Environmental Law J Journal	NYU Envtl LJ
New York University Journal of International Law & Politics	NYU J Int'l L & Pol

New York University Journal of Legislation & Public Policy	NYU J Legis & Pub Pol'y
New York University Law Review	NYU L Rev
New York University Review of Law & Social Change	NYU Rev L & Soc Change
New Zealand Business Law Quarterly	NZBLQ
New Zealand Journal of Public and International Law	NZ J Pub & Int'l L
New Zealand Universities Law Review	NZU L Rev
NEXUS: A Journal of Opinion	NEXUS
North Carolina Banking Institute	NC Banking Inst
North Carolina Central Law Journal	NC Cent LJ
North Carolina Journal of International Law & Commercial Regulation	NC J Int'l L & Com Reg
North Carolina Journal of Law & Technology	NC J L & Tech
North Carolina Law Review	NC L Rev
North Dakota Law Review	ND L Rev
Northern Illinois University Law Review	N Ill U L Rev
Northern Kentucky Law Review	N Ky L Rev
Northwestern Journal of International Law & Business	Nw J Int'l L & Bus
Northwestern Journal of Law & Social Policy	NW J L & Soc Pol'y
Northwestern Journal of Technology & Intellectual Property	Nw J Tech & Intell Prop
Northwestern University Journal of International Human Rights	Nw U J Int'l Hum Rts
Northwestern University Law Review	Nw U L Rev
Norton Annual Survey of Bankruptcy Law	NRTN-ASBL
Notre Dame Journal of Law Ethics & Public Policy	Notre Dame JL Ethics & Pub Pol'y
Notre Dame Law Review (formerly: Notre Dame Lawyer)	Notre Dame L Rev; Notre Dame Law
Nova Law Review (formerly: Nova Law Journal)	Nova L Rev; Nova LJ
NYU Journal of Law & Business	NYU J L & Bus
NYU Journal of Law & Liberty	NYU J L & Liberty
Ocean & Coastal Law Journal (formerly: Territorial Sea Journal)	Ocean & Coastal LJ; Terr Sea J
Ohio Northern University Law Review	Ohio NU L Rev
Ohio State Journal of Criminal Law	Ohio St J Crim L
Ohio State Journal on Dispute Resolution	Ohio St J on Disp Resol
Ohio State Law Journal	Ohio St LJ
Oklahoma City University Law Review	Okla City U L Rev
Oklahoma Journal of Law & Technology	Okla J L & Tech
Oklahoma Law Review	Okla L Rev
Orange County Lawyer	Orange County Law
Oregon Law Review	Or L Rev
Oregon Review of International Law	Or Rev Int'l L
Oregon State Bar Bulletin	Or St B Bull
Oxford Journal of Legal Studies	Oxford J Legal Stud
Pace Environmental Law Review	Pace Envtl L Rev

Pace International Law Review (formerly: Pace Yearbook of International Law)	Pace Int'l L Rev; Pace YB Int'l L
Pace Law Review	Pace L Rev
Pacific McGeorge Global Business & Development Law Journal (formerly: Transnational Lawyer)	Pac McGeorge Global Bus & Dev LJ; Transnat'l Law
Pacific Rim Law & Policy Journal	Pac Rim L & Pol'y J
Penn State Environmental Law Review (formerly: Dickison Journal of Environmental Law & Policy)	Penn St Envtl L Rev; Dick J Envtl L & Pol'y
Penn State International Law Review (formerly: Dickison Journal of International Law)	Penn St Int'l L Rev; Dick J Int'l L
Penn State Law Review (formerly: Dickinson Law Review)	Penn St L Rev; Dick L Rev
Pennsylvania Bar Association Quarterly	Pa BA Q
Pennsylvania Lawyer	Pa Law
Pepperdine Dispute Resolution Law Journal	Pepp Disp Resol LJ
Pepperdine Law Review	Pepp L Rev
Pierce Law Review	Pierce L Rev
Pittsburgh Journal of Environmental and Public Health Law	Pitt J Envtl Pub Health L
Pittsburgh Legal Journal	Pittsburgh Legal J
Pittsburgh Tax Review	Pittsburgh Tax Rev
Practising Law Institute	PLI
Private Client Business	PCB
Probate & Property	Prob & Prop
Procurement Lawyer	Procurement Law
Products Liability Law Journal	Prod Liab LJ
Prosecutor	Prosecutor
Psychology, Public Policy & Law	Psychol Pub Pol'y & L
Public Contract Law Journal	Pub Cont LJ
Public Interest Law Review	Pub Int L Rev
Public Land & Resources Law Review (formerly: Public Land Law Review)	Pub Land & Resources L Rev; Pub Land L Rev
QLR (formerly: Bridgeport Law Review)	QLR; Bridgeport L Rev
Quinnipiac Health Law Journal	Quinnipiac Health LJ
Quinnipiac Probate Law Journal (formerly: Connecticut Probate Law Journal)	Quinnipiac Prob LJ; Conn Prob LJ
Race & Ethnic Ancestry Law Digest	Race & Ethnic Anc L Dig
Race & Ethnic Ancestry Law Journal	Race & Ethnic Anc LJ
Real Estate Law Journal	Real Est LJ
Real Estate Law Report	Real Est L Rep
Real Property, Probate & Trust Journal	Real Prop Prob & Tr J
Regent Journal of International Law	Regent J Int'l L
Regent University Law Review	Regent U L Rev
Res Gestae	Res Gestae
Review of Litigation	Rev Litig
Revista de Derecho Puertorriqueno	Rev Der PR

Revista Juridica de la Universidad Interamericana de Puerto Rico	Rev Jur UIPR
Revista Juridica Universidad de Puerto Rico	Rev Jur UPR
Rhode Island Bar Journal	RI BJ
Richmond Journal of Global Law & Business	Rich J Global L & Bus
Richmond Journal of Law & Technology	Rich JL & Tech
Risk: Health, Safety & Environment (formerly: Risk: Issues in Health & Safety)	RISK; Risk: Issues Health & Safety
Roger Williams University Law Review	Roger Williams U L Rev
Rutgers Business Law Journal (formerly: Rutgers Bankruptcy Law Journal)	Rutgers Bus LJ; Rutgers Bankr LJ
Rutgers Computer & Technology Law Journal	Rutgers Computer & Tech LJ
Rutgers Journal of Law & Public Policy (formerly Rutgers Journal of Law and Urban Policy)	Rutgers JL & Pub Pol'y; Rutgers JL & Urb Pol'y
Rutgers Journal of Law and Religion	Rutgers JL & Religion
Rutgers Law Journal	Rutgers LJ
Rutgers Law Record	Rutgers L Rec
Rutgers Law Review	Rutgers L Rev
Saint John's Journal of Legal Commentary	St John's J Legal Comment
Saint John's Law Review	St John's L Rev
Saint Louis University Law Journal	St Louis U LJ
Saint Louis University Public Law Review	St Louis U Pub L Rev
Saint Louis-Warsaw Transatlantic Law Journal	St Louis-Warsaw Transatlantic LJ
Saint Mary's Law Journal	St Mary's LJ
Saint Thomas Law Review	St Thomas L Rev
San Diego International Law Journal	San Diego Int'l LJ
San Diego Law Review	San Diego L Rev
San Joaquin Agricultural Law Review	San Joaquin Agric L Rev
Santa Clara Computer & High Technology Law Journal	Santa Clara Computer & High Tech LJ
Santa Clara Journal of International Law	Santa Clara J Int'l L
Santa Clara Law Review	Santa Clara L Rev
Scholar: St Mary's Law Review on Minority Issues	SCHOLAR
Seattle Journal for Social Justice	Seattle J for Soc Just
Seattle University Law Review	Seattle U L Rev
Sedona Conference Journal (formerly: University of Puget Sound Law Review)	Sedona Conf J; U Puget Sound L Rev
Seton Hall Circuit Review	Seton Hall Circuit Rev
Seton Hall Constitutional Law Journal	Seton Hall Const LJ
Seton Hall Journal of Sports and Entertainment Law (formerly: Seton Hall Journal of Sport Law)	Seton Hall J Sport & Ent L; Seton Hall J Sport L
Seton Hall Law Review	Seton Hall L Rev
Seton Hall Legislative Journal	Seton Hall Legis J
Shidler Journal of Law, Commerce & Technology	Shidler J L Com & Tech
Singapore Year Book of International Law (formerly: Singapore Journal of International & Comparative Law)	SYBIL; Sing J Int'l & Comp L

Singapore Journal of Legal Studies	Sing J Legal Stud
SMU Law Review (formerly: Southwestern Law Journal)	SMU L Rev; Sw LJ
Social Security Reporting Service (articles from the West Reporter)	Soc Security Reporting Service
South Carolina Law Review	SC L Rev
South Carolina Lawyer	SC Law
South Dakota Law Review	SD L Rev
South Texas Law Review (formerly: South Texas Law Journal)	S Tex L Rev; S Tex LJ
Southeastern Environmental Law Journal (formerly: South Carolina Environmental Law Journal)	Southeastern Envtl LJ; SC Envtl LJ
Southern California Interdisciplinary Law Journal	S Cal Interdisc LJ
Southern California Law Review	S Cal L Rev
Southern California Review of Law & Social Justice (formerly: Southern California Review of Law and Women's Studies)	S Cal Rev L & Soc Just; S Cal Rev L & Women's Stud
Southern Illinois University Law Journal	S Ill U LJ
Southern University Law Review	SU L Rev
Southwestern Journal of Law & Trade in the Americas	Sw J L & Trade Am
Southwestern University Law Review	Sw U L Rev
Sports Lawyers Journal	Sports Law J
Stanford Environmental Law Journal	Stan Envtl LJ
Stanford Journal of Civil Rights & Civil Liberties	Stan J Civ Rts & Civ Liberties
Stanford Journal of International Law	Stan J Int'l L
Stanford Journal of Law, Business & Finance	Stan JL Bus & Fin
Stanford Law & Policy Review	Stan L & Pol'y Rev
Stanford Law Review	Stan L Rev
Stanford Technology Law Review	Stan Tech L Rev
Statute Law Review	Statute L Rev
Stetson Law Review	Stetson L Rev
Suffolk Journal of Trial & Appellate Advocacy	Suffolk J Trial & App Advoc
Suffolk Transnational Law Review (formerly: Suffolk Transnational Law Journal)	Suffolk Transnat'l L Rev; Suffolk Transnat'l LJ
Suffolk University Law Review	Suffolk U L Rev
Supreme Court Economic Review	Sup Ct Econ Rev
Supreme Court Review	Sup Ct Rev
Sustainable Development Law & Policy	Sustainable Dev L & Pol'y
Syracuse Journal of International Law & Commerce	Syracuse J Int'l L & Com
Syracuse Journal of Legislation & Policy	Syracuse J Legis & Pol'y
Syracuse Law Review	Syracuse L Rev
Syracuse Science & Technology Law Reporter	Syracuse Sci & Tech L Rep
Tax Law Review	Tax L Rev
Tax Lawyer	Tax Law
Temple International & Comparative Law J	Temp Int'l & Comp LJ

Temple Journal of Science, Technology & Environmental Law (formerly: Temple Environmental Law & Technology J)	Temp J Sci Tech & Envtl L; Temp Envtl L & Tech J
Temple Law Review (formerly: Temple Law Quarterly)	Temp L Rev; Temp LQ
Temple Political & Civil Rights Law Review	Temp Pol & Civ Rts L Rev
Tennessee Bar Journal	Tenn BJ
Tennessee Law Review	Tenn L Rev
Texas Bar Journal	Tex BJ
Texas Hispanic Journal of Law & Policy (formerly: Hispanic Law Journal)	Tex Hispanic J L & Pol'y; Hispanic LJ
Texas Intellectual Property Law Journal	Tex Intell Prop LJ
Texas International Law Journal	Tex Int'l LJ
Texas Journal of Business Law (formerly: Bulletin of the Business Law Section of the State Bar of Texas)	Tex J Bus L; Bull Bus Sec St B Tx
Texas Journal of Women & the Law	Tex J Women & L
Texas Journal on Civil Liberties & Civil Rights (formerly: Texas Forum on Civil Liberties & Civil Rights)	Tex J on CL & CR; Tex F on CL & CR
Texas Law Review	Tex L Rev
Texas Review of Entertainment & Sports Law	Tex Rev Ent & Sports L
Texas Review of Law & Politics	Tex Rev L & Pol
Texas Tech Administrative Law Journal (formerly: Texas Tech Journal of Texas Administrative Law)	Tex Tech Admin LJ; Tex Tech J Tex Admin L
Texas Wesleyan Law Review	Tex Wesleyan L Rev
Texas Tech Law Review	Tex Tech L Rev
The Trademark Reporter	Trademark Rep
Thomas Jefferson Law Review	T Jefferson L Rev
Thomas M Cooley Journal of Practical & Clinical Law	TM Cooley J Prac & Clinical L
Thomas M Cooley Law Review (formerly: Cooley Law Review)	TM Cooley L Rev; Cooley L Rev
Thurgood Marshall Law Review	T Marshall L Rev
Tort Trial & Insurance Practice Law Journal (formerly: Tort & Insurance Law Journal and Forum)	Tort Trial & Ins Prac LJ; Tort & Ins LJ Forum
Touro Environmental Law Journal	Touro Envtl LJ
Touro International Law Review (formerly: Touro Journal of Transnational Law)	Touro Int'l L Rev; Touro J Transnat'l L
Touro Law Review	Touro L Rev
Transactions: The Tennessee Journal of Business Law	Transactions: Tenn J Bus L
Transnational Law & Contemporary Problems	Transnat'l L & Contemp Probs
Transportation Law Journal	Transp LJ
Trial	Trial
Trial Advocate Quarterly	Trial Advocate Quarterly
Trinity Law Review	Trinity L Rev

Tulane European & Civil Law Forum (formerly: Tulane Civil Law Forum)	Tul Eur & Civ LF; Tul Civ LF
Tulane Environmental Law Journal	Tul Envtl LJ
Tulane Journal of International & Comparative Law	Tul J Int'l & Comp L
Tulane Journal of Technology & Intellectual Property	Tul J Tech & Intell Prop
Tulane Law Review	Tul L Rev
Tulane Maritime Law Journal (formerly: Maritime Lawyer)	Tul Mar LJ; Mar Law
Tulsa Journal of Comparative & International Law	Tulsa J Comp & Int'l L
Tulsa Law Review (formerly: Tulsa Law Journal)	Tulsa L Rev; Tulsa LJ
UC Davis Business Law Journal	UC Davis Bus L J
UC Davis Journal of International Law & Policy	UC Davis J Int'l L & Pol'y
UC Davis Journal of Juvenile Law & Policy	UC Davis J Juv L & Pol'y
UC Davis Law Review	UC Davis L Rev
UCLA Entertainment Law Review	UCLA Ent L Rev
UCLA Journal of Environmental Law & Policy	UCLA J Envtl L & Pol'y
UCLA Journal of International Law & Foreign Affairs	UCLA J Int'l L & Foreign Aff
UCLA Journal of Islamic & Near Eastern Law	UCLA J Islamic & Near E L
UCLA Journal of Law & Technology	UCLA J L & Tech
UCLA Law Review	UCLA L Rev
UCLA Pacific Basin Law Journal	UCLA Pac Basin LJ
UMKC Law Review	UMKC L Rev
United States-Mexico Law Journal	US-Mex LJ
University of Arkansas at Little Rock Law Review	U Ark Little Rock L Rev
University of Baltimore Intellectual Property Law Journal	U Balt Intell Prop LJ
University of Baltimore Journal of Environmental Law	U Balt J Envtl L
University of Baltimore Law Forum	U Balt LF
University of Baltimore Law Review	U Balt L Rev
University of Chicago Law Review	U Chi L Rev
University of Chicago Law School Roundtable	U Chi L Sch Roundtable
University of Chicago Legal Forum	U Chi Legal F
University of Cincinnati Law Review	U Cin L Rev
University of Colorado Law Review	U Colo L Rev
University of Dayton Law Review	U Dayton L Rev
University of Denver Water Law Review	U Denv Water L Rev
University of Detroit Mercy Law Review (formerly: University of Detroit Law Review)	U Det Mercy L Rev; U Det L Rev
University of Florida Journal of Law & Public Policy	U Fla JL & Pub Pol'y
University of Hawaii Law Review	U Haw L Rev
University of Illinois Journal of Law, Technology & Policy	U Ill JL Tech & Pol'y
University of Illinois Law Review	U Ill L Rev
University of Kansas Law Review	U Kan L Rev

University of Maryland Law Journal of Race, Religion, Gender and Class (formerly MARGINS: Maryland's Law Journal on Race, Religion, Gender and Class and MARGINS: Maryland's Interdisciplinary Publication on Race, Religion, Gender and Class)	U Md LJ Race, Religion, Gender & Class
University of Memphis Law Review (formerly: Memphis State University Law Review)	Mem St U L Rev
University of Miami Business Law Review (formerly: University of Miami Business Law Journal)	U Miami Bus L Rev; U Miami Bus LJ
University of Miami Entertainment & Sports Law Review	U Miami Ent & Sports L Rev
University of Miami Inter-American Law Review (formerly: Lawyer of the Americas)	U Miami Inter-Am L Rev; Law Am
University of Miami International & Comparative Law Review (formerly: University of Miami Yearbook of International Law)	U Miami Int'l & Comp L Rev; U Miami YB Int'l L
University of Miami Law Review International Law	U Miami L Rev
University of Michigan Journal of Law Reform	U Mich JL Reform
University of Pennsylvania Journal of Constitutional Law	U Pa J Const L
University of Pennsylvania Journal of International Economic Law (formerly: University of Pennsylvania Journal of International Business Law)	U Pa J Int'l Econ L; U Pa J Int'l Bus L
University of Pennsylvania Journal of Labor & Employment Law	U Pa J Lab & Emp L
University of Pennsylvania Law Review	U Pa L Rev
University of Pittsburgh Journal of Technology Law and Policy	U Pittsburgh J Tech L Pol'y
University of Pittsburgh Law Review	U Pitt L Rev
University of Richmond Law Review	U Rich L Rev
University of San Francisco Law Review	USF L Rev
University of San Francisco Maritime Law Journal	USF Mar LJ
University of the District of Columbia Law Review (formerly: District of Columbia Law Review)	U DC L Rev; DC L Rev
University of Toledo Law Review	U Tol L Rev
Urban Lawyer	Urb Law
Utah Bar Journal	Utah BJ
Utah Law Review	Utah L Rev
UWLA Law Review	UWLA L Rev
Valparaiso University Law Review	Val U L Rev
Vanderbilt Journal of Entertainment & Technology Law (formerly: Vanderbilt Journal of Entertainment Law & Practice)	Vand J Ent & Tech L; Vand J Ent L & Prac
Vanderbilt Journal of Transnational Law	Vand J Transnat'l L
Vanderbilt Law Review	Vand L Rev

Vermont Bar Journal	Vt BJ
Vermont Journal of Environmental Law (formerly Res Communes: Vermont's Journal of the Environment)	Vt J Envtl L
Vermont Law Review	Vt L Rev
Victoria University of Wellington Law Review	Vict U Wellington L Rev
Villanova Environmental Law Journal	Vill Envtl LJ
Villanova Law Review	Vill L Rev
Villanova Sports and Entertainment Law Journal (formerly: Villanova Sports and Entertainment Law Forum)	Vill Sports & Ent LJ; Vill Sports & Ent LF
Vindobona Journal of International Commercial Law & Arbitration (formerly: Vindobona Journal)	VJ; Vindobona J
Virginia Environmental Law Journal	Va Envtl LJ
Virginia Journal of International Law	Va J Int'l L
Virginia Journal of Law & Technology	Va JL & Tech
Virginia Journal of Social Policy & Law	Va J Soc Pol'y & L
Virginia Journal of Sports & Entertainment Law Journal (formerly: Virginia Journal of Sports & the Law)	Va J Sports & Ent LJ; Va J Sports & L
Virginia Law Review	Va L Rev
Virginia Tax Review	Va Tax Rev
Wake Forest Law Review	Wake Forest L Rev
Washburn Law Journal	Washburn LJ
Washington & Lee Journal of Civil Rights and Social Justice (formerly: Washington & Lee Race & Ethnic Ancestry Law; Race & Ethnic Ancestry Law; Journal and Race & Ethnic Ancestry Law Digest)	Wash & Lee J Civil Rts & Soc Just; Wash & Lee Race & Ethnic Anc LJ; Race & Ethnic Anc LJ; Race & Ethnic Anc L Dig
Washington & Lee Law Review	Wash & Lee L Rev
Washington Law Review	Wash L Rev
Washington University Global Studies Law Review	Wash U Global Stud L Rev
Washington University Journal of Law & Policy (formerly: Washington University Journal of Urban & Contemporary Law)	Wash U JL & Pol'y; Wash U J Urb & Contemp L
Washington University Law Review (formerly Washington University Law Quarterly)	Wash U L Rev
Wayne Law Review	Wayne L Rev
West Virginia Law Review	W Va L Rev
West Virginia Lawyer	W Va Law
West's Education Law Reporter (articles from the West reporter)	Educ L Rep
Westchester Bar Journal	Westchester BJ
Western New England Law Review	W New Eng L Rev
Western State University Law Review	W St U L Rev
Whittier Journal of Child & Family Advocacy	Whittier J Child & Fam Advoc
Whittier Law Review	Whittier L Rev

Widener Law Journal (formerly: Widener Journal of Public Law)	Widener LJ; Widener J Pub L
Widener Law Review Formerly: Widener Law Symposium Journal	Widener L Rev; Widener L Symp J
Willamette Journal of International Law & Dispute Resolution	Willamette J Int'l & Disp Resol
Willamette Law Review	Willamette L Rev
William & Mary Bill of Rights Journal	Wm & Mary Bill Rts J
William & Mary Environmental Law & Policy Review	Wm & Mary Envtl L & Pol'y Rev
William & Mary Journal of Women and the Law	Wm & Mary J Women & L
William & Mary Law Review	Wm & Mary L Rev
William Mitchell Law Review	Wm Mitchell L Rev
Wisconsin Environmental Law Journal	Wis Envtl LJ
Wisconsin International Law Journal	Wis Int'l LJ
Wisconsin Law Review	Wis L Rev
Wisconsin Lawyer (formerly: Wisconsin Bar Bulletin)	Wis Law; Wis B Bull
Wisconsin Women's Law Journal	Wis Women's LJ
Women's Rights Law Reporter	Women's Rts L Rep
World Arbitration and Mediation Report	World Arb & Mediation Rep
Wyoming Law Review (formerly: Land & Water Law Review)	Wyo L Rev; Land & Water L Rev
Wyoming Lawyer	Wyo Law
Yale Human Rights & Development Law Journal	Yale Hum Rts & Dev L J
Yale Journal of Health Policy, Law & Ethics	Yale J Health Pol'y, L & Ethics
Yale Journal of International Law	Yale J Int'l L
Yale Journal of Law & Feminism	Yale J L & Feminism
Yale Journal of Law & Technology (formerly: Yale Symposium on Law & Technology)	Yale J L & Tech; Yale Symp on L & Tech
Yale Journal of Law & the Humanities	Yale J L & Human
Yale Journal on Regulation	Yale J on Reg
Yale Law & Policy Review	Yale L & Pol'y Rev
Yale Law Journal	Yale L J
Yale Law Journal Pocket Part	Yale L J Pocket Part

BIBLIOGRAPHY OF SELECTED PUBLICATIONS

A

Andenas, M and Jacobs, F (eds), *European Community Law in the English Courts* (Oxford University Press, 1998)

Andenas, M, Norton, J J and Footer, M (eds), *The Changing World of International Law in the Twenty-First Century In Memoriam Ken Simmonds* (Kluwer Law International,1998)

Andenas, M and Jareborg, N, *Anglo-Swedish Studies in Law* (Upsala-King's College London Colloquium, 1999)

Andenas, M and Rider, B A K, *Developments in European Company Law: The Quest for an Ideal Legal Form for Small Businesses* (Kluwer Law International, 1999)

Andenas, M and Türk, A (eds), *Delegated Legislation and the Role of Committees in the EC* (Kluwer Law International, 2002)

—— *Directors' Conflicts of Interest: Legal, Socio-Legal and Economic Analyses Developments in European Company Law* (Kluwer Law International, 2000)

Andenas, M and Wintemute, R (eds), *Legal Recognition of Same-Sex Partnerships* (Hart Publishing, 2001)

Andenas, M and Norton, J (eds), *International Monetary and Financial Law upon Entering the New Millennium: A Tribute to Sir Joseph and Ruth Gold* (BIICL, 2002)

Andenas M, *English Public Law and the Common Law of Europe* (Key Haven, 1998)

Andenas, M, 'Tort Liability for Educational Malpractice: the *Phelps* case' (1999) 10 *King's College Law Journal* 210

Andenas, M and Fairgrieve D, 'Securing Progress in Collateral Law Reform: The EBRD's Regional Survey of Secured Transactions Laws', (2000) *Law in Transition* 28

Andenas, M and Roth, W-H (eds), *Services and Free Movement in EU Law* (Oxford University Press, 2002)

Andenas, M and Fairgrieve, D (eds), *Judicial Review in International Perspective, Liber Amicorum in Honour of Lord Slynn of Hadley* (Kluwer Law International, 2000)

Andenas, M and Fairgrieve, D, 'Misfeasance in Public Office, Governmental Liability, and European Influences', (2002) 51 *International & Comparative Law Quarterly* 757

Annan N G, *The Dons: Mentors, Eccentrics and Geniuses* (HarperCollins Publishers Ltd, 1999)

Atiyah, P and Summers, R S, *Form and Substance in Anglo-American Law: A Comparative Study of Legal Reasoning, Legal Theory and Legal Institutions* (Clarendon Press, 1987)

Atiyah, P, *Vicarious Liability in the Law of Torts* (Butterworths, 1967)

——, 'Negligence and Economic Loss', [1967] 83 *Law Quarterly Review* 248

——, *The Rise and Fall of Freedom of Contract* (Oxford University Press, 1979)

——, 'Judges and Policy', [1980] 15 *Israel Law Review* 346

——, *Accidents, Compensation and the Law* 3rd edn (Cambridge University Press, 1980)

——, *Promises, Morals and Law* (Oxford University Press, 1981)

——, 'Common Law and Statute Law', [1985] 48 *Modern Law Review* 1

——, 'Tort Law and the Alternatives: Some Anglo-American Comparisons' (1987) *Duke Law Journal* 1002

——, *Pragmatism and Theory in English Law* (Sweet & Maxwell, 1987)

——, 'Judicial Legislative Relations in England' in Katzman, R (ed), *Judges and Legislators: Towards Institutional Comity* (Brookings Institution, 1988)

Atiyah, P, *Essays on Contract* (Clarendon Paperbacks, 1990)
——, *An Introduction to the Law of Contract* 5th edn (Clarendon Press, 1995)
——, 'Personal Injuries in the 21st Century: Thinking the Unthinkable' in Birks, P (ed), *Wrongs and Remedies in the 21st Century* (Clarendon Press, 1996)
——, *The Damages Lottery* (Hart Publishing, 1997)
Atiyah, P, Adams, J N, and MacQueen, H L, *The Sale of Goods* 10th edn (Longman, 2001)

B

Bagshaw, R, 'Monetary remedies in public law—misdiagnosis and misdescription', (2006) 26 *Legal Studies* 4
Beale, H, Hartkamp, A, Kötz, H, and Tallon, D (eds), *Cases, Materials and Texts on Contract Law* (Hart Publishing, 2002)
Bell, J, Boyron, S and Whittaker, S, *Principles of French Law* (Oxford University Press, 1998)
Bell, J, *Policy Arguments in Judicial Decisions* (Oxford University Press, 1985)
——, 'The Expansion of Judicial Review and Discretionary Powers in France', [1986] *Public Law* 99
——, *Modern Law of Personal Property in England and Ireland* (Butterworths, 1989)
——, 'Religious Observance in Secular Schools: A French Solution', (1990)2 *Education Law Journal* 121
——, *French Constitutional Law* (Clarendon Press, 1992)
——, 'English Law and French Law—Not So Different?' (1995)69 *Current Legal Problems* 70
——, 'Governmental Liability in Tort', [1996] 6 *National Journal of Constitutional Law* 97
——, J, *French Legal Cultures* (Cambridge University Press, 2001)
——, J, 'Comparative Administrative Law' in Reimann, M and Zimmermann, R (eds), *The Oxford Handbook of Comparative Law* (Oxford University Press, 2006) pp 1259 *ff*
Beltramo, M, Lango, G and Merryman, J H, *The Italian Civil Code* (Oxford, 1969)
Berger, K P, *The Creeping Codification of the Lex Mercatoria* (Kluwer Law International, 1999)
——, *The Practice of Transnational Law* (Kluwer Law International, 2000)
Berger, K P, Dubberstein H, Lehmann, S and Petzold, V, 'The CENTRAL Enquiry on the Use of Transnational Law in International Contract Law and Arbitration—Background, Procedure and Selected Results' in Berger KP (ed), *The Practice of Transnational Law* (Kluwer Law International, 2000), pp 91 *ff*
Bermann, G A, de Vries, H P and Galston, N M (eds), *French Law: Constitution and Selective Legislation* (Juris Pub Inc, 1994)
Bernhardt, R and Jolowicz, J A, *International Enforcement of Human Rights* (Springer-Verlag, 1987)
Birks, P B H and Pretto, A (eds), *Breach of Trust* (Hart Publishing, 2002)
Birks, P B H and Yin, C N, 'On the Nature of Undue Influence' in Beatson and Friedman (eds), *Good Faith and Fault in Contract Law* (Oxford University Press, 1995)
Birks, P B H and Rose, F (eds), *Restitution and Equity (Vol 1): Resulting Trusts and Equitable Compensation* (Informa Pub, 2000)
——, *Lessons of the Swaps Litigation* (Mansfield Press, 2000)
Birks, P B H and Chambers R, *The Restitution Research Resource* 2nd edn (Mansfield, 1997)
Birks, P B H (ed), *English Private Law* (Oxford University Press, 2000)
——, 'Harassment and Hubris: The Right to an Equality of Respect', [1997] 32 *Irish Jurist* 1
——, 'The Academic and the Practitioner', [1998] 18 *Legal Studies* 397
Bolton, J, 'Should We Take Global Governance Seriously?'(Fall 2000) vol 1 no 2 *Chicago Journal of International Law* 206
Booth, C and Squires, D, *The Negligence Liability of Public Authorities* (2006)
Bonell, M J, 'Vertragsverhandlungen und culpa in contrahendo nach dem Wiener Kaufrechtsübereinkommen' (1990) *Recht der Internationalen Wirtschaft* 693
——, 'Die UNIDROIT-Prinzipien der internationalen Handelsverträge—Eine neue Lex Mercatoria?' (1996) 37 *Zeitschrift fur Rechtsvergleichung, Internationales Privatrecht und Europarecht* 152

——, 'The UNIDROIT Principles of International Commercial Contracts and the Principles of European Contract Law—Same Rules for the Same Purposes?' (1996) *Uniform Law Review* 229
——, 'The UNIDROIT Principles of International Commercial Contracts and the Principles of European Contract Law, a Comparison' in *Essays in Honour of Roy Goode* (1997)
——, 'The UNIDROIT Principles and Transnational Law', *Uniform Law Review* (2000) 5 199
——, 'A "Global" Arbitration Decided on the Basis of the Unidroit Principles' in *Aufbruch nach Europa—Festschrift 75 Jahre Max-Planck-Institut* (2001) pp 771 *ff*
——, 'UNIDROIT Principles 2004' (2004) *Uniform Law Review* 5
Bork, R, *Slouching Towards Gomorrah* (Regan Books, 2002)
——, *Coercing Virtue: The Worldwide Rule of Judges* rev edn (AEI press, 2003)
Brown, G M, 'Changing Models in Corporate Governance—Implications of the US Sarbanes-Oxley Act' in Hopt, KJ, Wymeersch, E, Kanda, H and Baum, H (eds), *Corporate Governance in Context* (Oxford University Press, 2005) pp 160 *ff*
Brown, N and Bell, J, *French Administrative Law* 5th edn (Oxford University Press, 1998)

C

Cairns, J W and Robinson, O F (eds), *Critical Studies in Ancient Law, Comparative Law and Legal Theory: Essays in Honour of Alan Watson* (Hart Publishing, 2002)
Cane, P, *Tort Law and Economic Interests* 2nd edn (Clarendon Press, 1996)
Calabresi, G, *A Common Law in an Age of Statutes* (Harvard University Press, 1985)
——, 'Des "Professeurs-Juges" aux "Juges-Professeurs"' in *La Cour de cassation, L' université et le droit, Etudes en l'Honneur de A Ponsard* (Litec, Paris, 2003), pp 115 *ff*
——, 'La Cour de cassation et la doctrine'in *Propos sur les obligations et quelques autres thèmes fondamentaux du droit Mélanges offerts à Jean-Luc Aubert* (Dalloz-Sirey, 2005) pp 373 *ff*
——, 'Le juge entre le progrès scientifique et mondialisation', 33 No 1 *Revue Trimestrielle de Droit Civil* (Dalloz, 2005)
Canivet, G, Andenas, M and Fairgrieve, D (eds), *Comparative Law before the Courts* (BIICL, 2004)
Cappelletti, M and Jolowicz, J A, *Public Interest Parties and the Active Role of the Judge in Civil Litigation* (Oceana Publications Inc,1975)
Cappelletti, M (ed), *New Perspectives for a Common Law of Europe* (Springer, 1978)
Carnwath, R, 'The Thornton Heresy Exposed: Financial Remedies for Breach of Public Duties' [1998] *Public Law* 407
——, 'Welfare Services—Liabilities in Tort After the Human Rights Act', [2001] *Public Law* 21
——, 'Welfare Services—Liabilities in Tort after the Human Rights Act: A Postscript', [2001] *Public Law* 475
Chapus, R, *Droit Administratif Général* 13th edn (Montchrestien, 1999)
Chase, O G, and Bruner, J, *Law, Culture, and Ritual Dispute Systems in Cross-Cultural Context* (NYU Press, 2005)
Clinquennois, M, 'Essai sur la responsabilité de l'Etat du fait de ses activités de contrôle et de tutelle' No 98, 16 August 1995 *Les Petites Affiches* 4
Colley, L, *Britons Forging the Nation 1707–1837* (Vintage, 1992)
Cooke, R, 'An Impossible Distinction' (1991) 107 *Law Quarterly Review* 46
Craig, P and Fairgrieve, D, 'Barrett, Negligence and Discretionary Powers' [1999] *Public Law* 626

D

Dannemann, G, 'Comparative Law: Study of Similarities or Differences?' in Reimann, M and Zimmermann, R (eds), *The Oxford Handbook of Comparative Law* (Oxford University Press, 2006) pp 395 *ff*
David, R and Brierley, J E C, *Major Legal Systems in the World Today* (The Free Press, 1985)
David, R, *English Law and French Law* (Stevens & Sons, 1980)
——, *Arbitration in International Trade* (Kluwer Law International, 1985)

David, R and Jauffret-Spinosi, C, *Les Grands Systèmes de Droit Contemporains* 11th edn (Dalloz, 2002)

Dawson, J P, *Unjust Enrichment: A Comparative Analysis* (Little Brown, 1951)

——, *The Oracles of the Law* (Little Brown, 1968)

Deguergue, M, *Jurisprudence et Doctrine dans l'Elaboration du Droit de la Responsabilité Administrative* (LGDJ, 1994)

Delmas-Marty, M and Spencer, J (eds), *European Criminal Procedures* (Cambridge University Press, 2002)

Delmas-Marty, M, 'The *Juge d'Instruction*: Do the English Really Need Him?' in Markesinis, B S (ed), *The Gradual Convergence* (Oxford University Press, 1994)

——, *Pour un droit commun* (Editions de Seuil, 1994)

—— (ed), *The Criminal Process and Human Rights: Towards a European Consciousness* (Springer, 1995)

——, *The European Union and Penal Law; What kind of criminal policy in Europe?* (Kluwer Law International, 1996)

——, *Toward a Truly Common Law* (Cambridge University Press, 2002)

Dewees, D, Duff, D and Trebilock, M, *Exploring the Domain of Accident Law Taking the Facts Seriously* (Oxford University Press, 1996)

Dezalay Y and Garth, B G, *Dealing in Virtue: International Commercial Arbitration and the Construction of a Transnational Legal Order* (University of Chicago Press, 1996)

Dickson, B, 'Has the Charter Americanised the Canadian Judiciary?', (1992) 26 *University of British Columbia Law Review* 195

Drobnig, U, 'General Principles of European Contract Law' in Sarcevic, P and Volken, P (eds), *International Sale of Goods: Dubrovnik Lectures* (Oceana Publications Inc, 1986), pp 305 *ff*

Duxbury, N, *Jurists and Judges: An Essay on Influence* (Hart Publishing, 2001)

E

Ernst, W and Zimmermann, R (eds), *Zivilrechtswissenschaft und Schuldrechtsreform* (2001)

F

Fairgrieve, D, Andenas, M and Bell, J (eds), *Tort Liability of Public Authorities in Comparative Perspective* (BIICL, 2002)

Fairgrieve, D and Belloir, K, 'Liability of the French State for negligent Supervision of Banks', (1999) 10 *European Business Law Review* 17

Fairgrieve, D, *State Liability on Tort: A Comparative Law Study* (Oxford University Press, 2003)

Favoreu, L, Jolowicz, J A and Cappelletti, M (eds), *Le Contrôle Juridictionnel des Lois* (Economica, 1986)

Fedtke, J, *Die Rezeption von Verfassungsrecht Südafrika 1993–1996* (Baden-Baden, 2000)

——, 'Legal Transplants' in Smits, J M (ed), *Elgar Encyclopedia of Comparative Law* (Edward Elgar Publishing, 2006), pp 434 *ff*

Finer, S E, Bogdanor, V and Rudden, B, *Comparing Constitutions* (Oxford University Press, 1995)

Fleming, J G, *An Introduction to the Law of Torts* (Oxford University Press, 1967)

——, *The American Tort Process* (Oxford University Press, 1988)

——, *Law of Torts* 9th edn (Law Book Co of Australasia, 1998)

Flogaitis, S, *Adminstrative law et droit administrative* (LGDJ, Paris 1988)

——, *La notion de décentralisation en France, en Allemagne et en Italie* (LGDJ, Montchrestien 1979)

G

Glenn, H P, 'Comparative Law and Legal Practice: On Removing the Borders', (2001) 75 *Tulane Law Review* 977

——, *Legal Traditions of the World* 2nd edn (Oxford University Press, 2004)

——, 'Aims of comparative law', in Smits, J M (ed), *Elgar Encyclopedia of Comparative Law* (Edward Elgar Publishing, 2006), pp 62 *ff*
Glendon M-A, *The Transformation of Family State, Law and Family in the United States and Western Europe* (University of Chicago Press, 1977)
——, *The New Family and the New Property* (Butterworths, 1981)
——, *Rights Talk: The Impoverishment of Political Discourse* (Free Press, 1991)
——, *Comparative Legal Traditions* (with Gordon and Osakwe) (West, 2nd edn 1994)
——, *A Nation under Lawyers: How the Crisis in the Legal Profession is Transforming American Society* (Farrar, Straus and Giroux, 1996)
——, *Hire Purchase, Law and Practice* 2nd edn (Butterworths, 1970)
——, 'The Right to Trace and its Impact on Commercial Transactions', [1976] 92 *Law Quarterly Review* 360
——, 'The Death of Insolvency Law', [1980] 1 *Company Lawyer* 123
——, *Introduction to the Law of Restitution* (1985)
——, *Legal Problems of Credit and Security* 2nd edn (Sweet & Maxwell, 1988)
—— (ed), *Consumer Credit Law* (Butterworths, 1989)
——, *Commercial Law* 2nd edn (Penguin, 1995)
——, 'International Restatements of Contract and English Contract Law', [1997] 2 *Uniform Law Review* 231
——, *Principles of Corporate Insolvency Law* 2nd edn (Sweet & Maxwell, 1997)
——, 'Security in Cross-Border Transactions', [1998] 33 *Texas International Law Journal* 47
——, *Commercial Law in the Next Millennium* (Sweet & Maxwell, 1998)
——, 'The Law of Restitution at the End of an Epoch', [1999] 28 *University of Western Australia Law Review* 13
——, 'Insularity or Leadership? The Role of the United Kingdom in the Harmonisation of Commercial Law', [2001] 50 *International & Comparative Law Quarterly* 751
Gordley J and von Mehren, A T, *The Civil Law System: An Introduction to the Comparative Study of Law* 2nd edn (Cambridge University Press, 1977)
Gordley J, *The Philosophical Origins of Modern Contract Doctrine* (Oxford University Press, 1991)
——, 'Common law und civil law: Eine überholte Unterscheidung' 1993 *Zeitschrift für Europäisches Privatrecht* 498
——, 'Myths of the French Civil Code', (1994) 42 *American Journal of Comparative Law* 459
——, 'Is Comparative Law a Distinct Discipline' (1998) 46 *American Journal of Comparative Law* 607
——, 'The Common Law in the Twentieth Century: Some Unfinished Business' (2000) 88 *California Law Review* 1815
——, *Foundations of Private Law: Property, Tort, Contract, Unjustified Enrichment* (Oxford University Press, 2006)
Guenassia H, 'Overview of the new French Insolvency Law' (2007) no 1 *International In-house Counsel Journal*, vol 1 pp 50 *ff*
Guettier C, *La Responsabilité Administrative* (LGDJ, Montchrestien 1996)

H

Halpérin J-L, *L' impossible Code Civil* (Presses Universitaires de France, 1992)
Handford P, 'Psychiatric Damage Where the Defendant is the Immediate Victim' [2001] 117 *Law Quarterly Review* 397
Harding, S K, 'Comparative reasoning and Judicial Review', (2003) 28 *Yale Journal of International Law* 409
Harlow, C, *State Liability—Tort Law and Beyond* (Oxford University Press, 2004)
Harris, D and Tallon, D (eds), *Contract Law Today: Anglo-French Comparisons* (Oxford University Press, 1989)

Hélin, J C, *Faute de Service et Préjudice dans le Contentieux de la Responsabilité pour Illégalité* (Thesis, L'Universite de Nantes, 1969)
Hoffmann (Lord), 'Human Rights and the House of Lords', (1999) 62 *Modern Law Review* 159
Holmes, O W, *The Common Law* (Dover Publications, 1991)
Honoré T, *Tribonian* (Gerald Duckworth & Co Ltd, 1978)
——, *Ulpian* (Oxford University Press, 1982)
——, 'Responsibility and Luck: The Moral Basis of Strict Liability', [1988] 104 *Law Quarterly Review* 530
——, 'The Dependence of Morality on Law', [1993] 13 *Oxford Journal of Legal Studies* 1
——, *Responsibility and Fault* (Hart Publishing, 1999)
——, 'The Necessary Connection between Law and Morality', [2002] 22 *Oxford Journal of Legal Studies* 489

I

Ignatieff, M (ed), *American Exceptionalism and Human Rights* (Princeton University Press, 2005)

J

Jayme, E (ed), *Ein Internationales Zivilverfahrensrecht für Gesampteuropa* (1992)
Jayme, E, 'Identité Culturelle et Integration: Le Droit Privé Post Moderne', [1995] 251 *Recueil de Cours* 9
Johnston, D and Zimmermann, R (eds), *Unjustified Enrichment: Key Issues in Comparative Perspective* (Cambridge University Press, 2002)
Jolowicz, J A, *Roman Foundations of Modern Law* (Greenwood Press Reprint, 1957)
——, *Lectures on Jurisprudence* (The Athlone Press, 1963)
——, *The Division and Classification of the Law* (Butterworth, 1970)
——, J A, 'The Judicial Protection of Fundamental Rights Under English Law', *Cambridge-Tilburg Law Lectures*, 2nd Series 1979 (Wolters Kluwer BV Juridische Boeken en Tijdschriften, 1980)
——, 'The Woolf Report and the Adversary System', (1996) 15 *Civil Justice Quarterly* 198
——, *On Civil Procedure* (Cambridge University Press, 2000)

K

Kahn-Freund, O and Hepple, B A, *Laws Against Strikes* (Fabian Society, 1972)
Kahn-Freund O, Levy, C and Rudden, B, *A Source Book on French Law* (Oxford University Press, 1973)
Kahn-Freund O, 'English Contracts and American Anti-Trust Law—The Nylon Patent Case', [1955] 18 *Modern Law Review* 65
——, *The Growth of Internationalism in English Private International Law* (Oxford University Press, 1960)
——, *Labour Relations and the Law: A Comparative Study* (Stevens, 1965)
——, 'Comparative Law as an Academic Subject', [1966] 82 *Law Quarterly Review* 40
——, 'On Uses and Misuses of Comparative Law', [1974] 37 *Modern Law Review* 1
——, 'Common Law and Civil Law—Imaginary and Real Obstacles to Assimilation' in Cappelletti, M (ed), *New Perspectives for a Common Law of Europe* (Brill, 1978), pp 137 *ff*
——, *Selected Writings* (Stevens & Sons, 1978)
Kersting, C and Schindler, C P, 'The ECJ's Inspire Art Decision of 30 September 2003 and its Effects on Practice' (2203) 4 *German Law Journal* No 12, pp 1277 *ff*
Kieninger, E-M, 'The Legal Framework of Regulatory Competition Based on Company Mobility: EU and US Compared' (2004) 6 *German Law Journal* No 4, pp 741 *ff*
Kiikeri, M, *Comparative Legal Reasoning and European Law* (Springer, 2001)
Kötz, H and Wagner, G, *Deliktsrecht* 10th edn (Luchterhand, 2006)
Kötz, H, *Trust und Treuhand* (1963)

——, *Haftung für besondere Gefahr* (1970) 170 *Archiv fur die civilistische Praxis* 1 *ff*
——, *Sozialer Wandel im Unfallrecht* (Muller, 1976)
——, 'Rechtsvereinheitlichung—Nutzen, Kosten, Methoden, Ziele' (1986) 50 *Rabels Zeitschrift fur Auslandisches und Internationales Privatrecht* 1 *ff*
——, 'Taking Civil Codes Less Seriously', [1987] 50 *Modern Law Review* 1
——, 'Scholarship and the Courts: A Comparative Survey' in Clark, D S (ed), *Comparative and Private International Law: Essays in Honour of John Henry Merryman on his Seventieth Birthday* (Duncker & Humboldt, 1990) pp 183 *ff*
——, 'The Doctrine of Privity of Contract', [1990] 10 *Tel Aviv University Studies in Law* 195
——, 'Ziele des Haftungsrechts', in *Festschrift Steindorff* (1990), pp 643 *ff*
——, *European Contract Law Volume 1: Formation, Validity and Content of Contracts; Contract and Third Parties* (Oxford University Press, 1997)
Kramer, L D, 'The Supreme Court 2000 Term Foreword: We the Court', (2001) 115 *Harvard Law Review* 4, 130

L

Lando O, 'Comparative Law and Lawmaking', (2001) 75 *Tulane Law Review* 1015 *ff*
Langbein J, *Comparative Criminal Procedure: Germany* (West Group, 1977)
——, 'The German Advantage in Civil Procedure', 52 *University of Chicago Law Review* 823 (1985)
Law, D S, 'Generic Constitutional Law' (2005) 89 *Minnesota Law Review* 652
Lawson, F H and Markesinis, B S, *Tortious Liability for Unintentional Harm in Common Law and the Civil Law* (Cambridge University Press, 1982)
Lawson, F H, 'The Duty of Care in Negligence: A Comparative Study' (1947) 22 *Tulane Law Review* 111
——, *Negligence in the Civil Law* (Clarendon Press, 1950)
——, *The Rational Strength of English Law* (Stevens & Sons, 1951)
——, *A Common Lawyer Looks at the Civil Law* (Oxford University Press, 1953)
——, *The Oxford Law School (1850–1965)* (Oxford University Press, 1968)
——, *Many Laws: Selected Essays* (North Holland, 1977)
——, *Remedies of English Law* 2nd edn (Penguin, 1980)
Legrand, P and Munday, R (eds), *Comparative Legal Studies: Traditions and Transitions* (Cambridge University Press, 2003)
Legrand P, 'Comparative Legal Studies and Commitment to Theory', [1995] 58 *Modern Law Review* 262
——, 'Questions à Rodolfo Sacco' [1995] *Revue Internationale de Droit Comparé* 943
——, *Comparatists-at-Law and the Contrarian Challenge* (Inaugural Lecture, University of Tilburg, 1995)
——, 'European Legal Systems are not Converging', [1996] 45 *International & Comparative Law Quarterly* 761
——, 'How to Compare Now', [1996] 16 *Legal Studies* 23
——, 'Against a European Civil Code', [1997] 62 *Modern Law Review* 44
——, 'The Impossibility of "Legal Transplants"', (1997) 4 *Maastricht Journal of European and Comparative Law* 111
——, 'Are Civilians Educable?', [1998] 18 *Legal Studies* 216
——, *Fragments on Law-as-Culture* (Tjeenk Willink, 1999)
——, *Le Droit Comparé* (Presses Universitaires France, 1999)
——, 'The Same and the Different' in Legrand P and Munday R (eds), *Comparative Legal Studies: Traditions and Transitions* (Cambridge University Press, 2003) pp 240 *ff*
Lequette, Y, 'Quelques remarques à propos du projet de code civil européen de M von Bar',2002, no 8, *Dalloz, chron* 2202
Lester, A, 'The Overseas Trade in the American Bill of Rights' (1988) 88 *Columbia Law Review* 537

Levinson, S, 'Looking Abroad When Interpreting the US Constitution Some Reflections', (2004) 39 *Texas International Law Journal* 353
Limbach, J, *Das Bundesverfassungsgericht als politischer Machtfaktor* (Humboldt Forum Recht, 1996)
Lipstein, K, 'Protected Interests in the Law of Tort', [1963] *Cambridge Law Journal* 85
—— (ed), *Harmonisation of Private International Law by the EEC* (AbeBooks, 1978)
Llewellyn, K, 'A Lecture on Appellate Advocacy' (1962) 29 *University of Chicago Law Review* 627
Lloyd, D, 'Reason and Logic in the Common Law' [1948] 62 *Law Quarterly Review* 468
LoPucki, L, 'The Death of Liability', (1996) 106 *Yale Law Journal* 1
Lorenz, W and Markesinis, B S, 'Solicitors' Liability Towards Third Parties: Back into the Troubled Waters of the Contract/Torts Divide' (1993) 56 *Modern Law Review* 558
Lorenz, W, Witz, W and Salger, H C, *Internationales Einheitliches Kaufrecht* (Recht und Wirtschaft, 2000)
Lorenz, W, 'Contracts and Third Party Rights in German and English Law' *in* Markesinis, B S (ed), *The Gradual Convergence* (Oxford, Clarendon Press, 1994)
Lupoi, M, *Trusts: A Comparative Study* (Cambridge University Press, 2000)
Lutter, M, 'Die Auslegung angeglichenen Rechts' 1992 *Juristenzeitung* 593
——, 'Perspektiven eines europäischen Unternehmensrechts' 1992 *Zeitschrift fur Unternehmens- und Gesellschaftsrecht* 435
——, *Der Einfluß deutscher Emigranten auf die Rechtsentwicklung in den USA und in Deutschland* (Mohr Siebeck, 1993)
——, *Konzernrecht im Ausland* (de Gruyter, 1994)
——, *Gestaltungsfreiheit im Gesellschaftsrecht: Deutschland, Europa und USA* (de Gruyter, 1996)
——, *Der Letter of Intent: zur rechtlichen Bedeutung von Absichtserklärungen* (Heymanns, 1998)

M

MacKinnon, C, *Towards a Feminist Theory of State* (Harvard University Press,1989)
Magnus, U (ed), *The Impact of Social Security Law on Tort Law* (Springer, 2003)
Mallat, C, *Introduction to Middle Eastern Law* (Oxford University Press, 2007)
Mann, F A, 'Outlines of a History of Expropriation', [1959] *Law Quarterly Review* 188
——, 'The Doctrine of Jurisdiction in International Law', (1964) 111 *Recueil des Cours* 9
——, 'Lex Facit Arbitrum' in Sanders P (ed), *International Arbitration: Liber Amicorum for Martin Damke* (Martinus Nijhoff, 1967)
——, 'Eingriffsgesetze und IPR' in *Festschrift Wahl* (1973) pp 139 *ff*
——, *Studies in International Law* (Oxford University Press, 1973), 'The Doctrine of International Jurisdiction Revisited After Twenty Years',(1984) 186 *Recueil des Cours* 9
——, 'The Effect in England of the Compulsory Acquisition by a Foreign State of the Shares in a Foreign Company', [1986] *Law Quarterly Review* 191
——, *Foreign Affairs in English Courts* (Oxford University Press, 1986)
——, 'L'exécution internationale des droits publics' (1988) 77 *Revue Critique de Droit International Privé* 1
——, *Further Studies in International Law* (Oxford University Press, 1990)
——, 'Conflict of Laws and Public Law' (1991) 132 *Recueil des Cours* 107
Markesinis, B S, Coester, M, Alpa, G and Ullstein, A, *Compensation for Personal Injury in England, Germany and Italy* (Cambridge University Press, 2005)
Markesinis, B S and von Bar, C, *Richterliche Rechtspolitik im Haftungsrecht* (JCB Mohr, 1981)
Markesinis, B S and Unberath, H, *The German Law of Torts: A Comparative Treatise* 4th edn (Hart Publishing, 2002)
Markesinis, B S and Fedtke, J, 'The Judge as Comparatist' (2005) 80 *Tulane Law Review* no 1, 11–167
——, *Judicial Recourse to Foreign Law: A New Source of Inspiration?* (Routledge, 2006)
Markesinis, B S and Nolte, N, 'Some Comparative Reflections on the Right of Privacy of Public Figures in Public Places' in Birks, P (ed), *Privacy and Loyalty* (Clarendon Press, 1997)

Markesinis, B S and Deakin, S, 'The Random Element of their Lordships' Infallible Judgment: An Economic and Comparative Analysis of the Tort of Negligence from Anns to Murphy', [1992] 55 *Modern Law Review* 619

Markesinis, B S, O'Cinneide, C, Fedtke, J and Hunter-Henin, M, 'Concerns and Ideas about the Development of the English Law of Privacy (And How Knowledge of Foreign Law Might be of Help)' (2004) 52 *American Journal of Comparative Law* 133

Markesinis, B S, Auby, J-B, Coester-Waltjen, D and Deakin, S, *Tortious Liability of Statutory Bodies: A Comparative and Economic Analysis of Five English Cases* (Hart Publishing, 1999)

Markesinis, B S, Unberath, H and Johnston, A, *The German Law of Contract: A Comparative Treatise* (Hart Publishing, 2006)

Markesinis, B S, Lorenz, W and Dannemann, G, *The German Law of Obligations, vol 1: The Law of Contracts and Restitution* (Clarendon Press, 1997)

Markesinis, B S, *The French Law of Contract* 2nd edn (Clarendon Press, 1972)

——, *The English Law of Torts: A Comparative Introduction* (E Bruylant, 1976)

——, 'The Not So Dissimilar Tort and Delict', [1977] 93 *Law Quarterly Review* 78

——, 'Fundamental Rights and Judicial Review in France' [1978] *Public Law* 82

——, 'La Politique Jurisprudentielle et la Réparation du Préjudice Economique en Angleterre: Une Approche Comparative' [1983] *Revue Internationale de Droit Comparé* 31

——, 'Conceptualism, Pragmatism and Courage: A Common Lawyer Looks at Some Judgments of the German Federal Court', 34 *American Journal of Comparative Law* (1986)

——, 'An Expanding Tort Law—The Price of a Rigid Contract Law', [1987] 103 *Law Quarterly Review* 354

——, 'Negligence, Nuisance and Affirmative Duties', [1989] 105 *Law Quarterly Review* 104

——, 'Comparative Law—A Subject in Search of an Audience'(1990) 53 *Modern Law Review* 1

——, 'Compensation for Negligently Inflicted Pure Economic Loss: Some Canadian Views', [1993] 109 *Law Quarterly Review* 5

——, 'A Matter of Style', [1994] 110 *Law Quarterly Review* 607

—— (ed), *Gradual Convergence: Foreign Ideas, Foreign Influences, and English Law on the Eve of the 21st Century* (Oxford University Press, 1994)

——, 'Five Days in the House of Lords: Some Reflections on *White v Jones*', [1995] 3 *Torts Law Journal* 169

——, 'Why a Code is Not the Best Way to Advance the Cause of European Legal Unity', (1997) 5 *European Review of Private Law* 519

——, *Foreign Law and Comparative Methodology: A Subject and a Thesis* (Hart Publishing, 1997)

—— (ed), *Law Making, Law Finding and Law Shaping* (Oxford University Press,1997)

—— (ed), *The Impact of the Human Rights Bill on English Law* (Oxford University Press,1998)

—— *Protecting Privacy* (Oxford University Press,1999)

——, 'Privacy, Freedom of Expression and the Horizontal Effects of the Human Rights Bill: Lessons from Germany' (1999) 115 *Law Quarterly Review* 47

——, 'Judicial Style and Judicial Reasoning in England and Germany' [2000] *Cambridge Law Journal* 294

——, 'Plaintiff's Tort Law or Defendant's Tort Law? Is the House of Lords Moving Towards a Synthesis?' [2001] 9 *Torts Law Journal* 3

——, *Always on the Same Path Essays on Foreign Law and Comparative Methodology* (Hart Publishing, 2001)

——, 'Réflexions d'un comparatiste anglais sur et à partir de l'arrêt Perruche', *Revue Trimestrielle de Droit Civil* (1) janv-mars 2001, 77

——, 'Lessons from *Greatorex v Greatorex*', [2002] *Cambridge Law Journal* 405

——, *Comparative Law in the Courtroom and the Classroom The Story of the Last Thirty Five Years* (Hart Publishing, 2003)

——, 'Deux cents ans dans la vie d'un code célèbre. Réflexions historiques et comparatives à propos des projets européens' (2004) *Revue Trimestrielle de Droit Civil* 45

Markesinis, B S, *Rechtsvergleichung in Theorie und Praxis* (Sellier European Law Publishing, 2004)
——, 'French System Builders and English Problem Solvers: Missed and Emerging Opportunities for Convergence of French and English Law' (2005) 40 *Texas International Law Journal* 663
——, 'The Enduring (Double) Legacy of the Code Napoléon', (2005) *Law Quarterly Review* 80
——, 'Judicial Mentality: Mental Disposition and Outlook as a Factor Impeding recourse to Foreign Law' (2006) 80 *Tulane Law Review* 1325–75
——, 'Understanding American Law by Looking at it Through Foreign Eyes—Towards a Wider Theory for the Study and Use of Foreign Law' (2006) 81 *Tulane Law Review* 125
Mattei, U and di Robilant, A, 'The Art and Science of Critical Scholarship: Postmodernism and International Style in the Legal Architecture of Europe' (2001) 75 *Tulane Law Review* 1053
Mattei, U and Reimann, M, 'Introduction' (Symposium on New Directions in Comparative Law) (1998) 46 *American Journal of Comparative Law* 597
Mattei, U, 'Three Patterns of Law: Taxonomy and Change in the World's Legal Systems' (1997) 45 *American Journal of Comparative Law* 5
——, *Comparative Law and Economics* (University of Michigan Press, 1997)
McCormick, N and Birks, P, *The Legal Mind Essays for Tony Honoré* (Oxford University Press, 1986)
Meier, S and Zimmermann, R, 'Judicial Development of the Law, Error Iuris, and the Law of Unjustified Enrichment—A View from Germany', [1999] 115 *Law Quarterly Review* 556
Merryman, J H and Elsen, A E, *Law, Ethics and the Visual Arts* 4th edn (Kluwer Law International, 2002)
Merryman J H and Pérez-Perdomo R, *The Civil Law Tradition: An Introduction to the Legal Systems of Europe and Latin America* 3rd edn (Stanford University Press, 2007)
Merryman, J H, *Comparative Law: Western European and Latin American Legal Systems* (Bobbs-Merrill, 1978)
——, 'On the Convergence (and Divergence) of the Civil Law and the Common Law', (1981) 17 *Stanford Journal of International Law* 357
——, 'Two Ways of Thinking about Cultural Property' (1986) 80 *American Journal of International Law* 831
——, 'The French Deviation' (1996) 44 *American Journal of Comparative Law* 109
——, *The Loneliness of the Comparative Lawyer and Other Essays in Foreign and Comparative Law* (Kluwer Law International, 1999)
——, *Thinking About the Elgin Marbles: Critical Essays on Cultural Property, Art and Law* (Springer, 2000)
Meyer, G J, 'International Commercial Arbitration' in Kopenol-Laforce, M et al (eds), *International Contracts: Aspects of Jurisdiction, Arbitration and Private International Law* (Sweet & Maxwell, 1996) pp 86 *ff*
Meyer, J-A and Schleus, R (eds), *Erfahrungen mit der Limited—Tagungsreader* (EUL, 2006)
Michelman, F, 'Integrity Anxiety?' in Ignatieff, M (ed), *American Exceptionalism and Human Rights* (Princeton University Press, 2005),pp 241 *ff*
Moréteau, O, 'Ne tirez pas sur le comparatiste' *Dalloz* 2005, no 7, 452
Moss, G C, 'International Contracts between Common Law and Civil Law: Is Non-state Law to Be Preferred? The Difficulty of Interpreting Legal Standards such as Good Faith', *Global Jurist* vol 7: Iss 1 (Advances), Article 3
Muchlinski, P T, *Multinational Enterprises and the Law* 2nd edn (Oxford University Press, 2007)
Müller-Graff, P-C, 'EC Directives as a Means of Private Law Unification' in Hartkamp, A et al (eds), *Towards a European Civil Code* 2nd edn (Kluwer Law International, 1998)

N

Nelken, D and Feest, J (eds), *Adapting Legal Cultures* (Hart Publishing, 2001)
Nicholas, B, *Introduction to Roman Law* (Oxford University Press, 1962)

——, 'Unjustified Enrichment in the Civil Law and Louisiana Law' (1962) 36 *Tulane Law Review* 605
——, 'Rules and Terms—Civil Law and Common Law' (1974) 48 *Tulane Law Review* 946
——, 'Fundamental Rights and Judicial Review in France' [1978] *Public Law* 82
——, 'The Vienna Convention on International Sales Law' [1989] 105 *Law Quarterly Review* 201
——, *French Law of Contract* 2nd edn (Oxford University Press, 1992)
——, 'Unjust Enrichment and the Law of Restitution: A Comparison' in Schrage, E J H (ed), *Unjust Enrichment—the Comparative Legal History of the Law of Restitution* (Kluwer Law International, 1995)

O

Örücü, E and Nelken, D, *Comparative Law* (Hart Publishing, 2007)

P

Paillet, M, *Responsabilité Adminsitrative* (Dalloz, 1996)
Parrish, A L, 'Storm in a Teacup: The US Supreme Court's Use of Foreign Law', [2007] 2 *Illinois Law Review* 637
Portalis, J-E-M, *Ecrits et discourse juridiques et politiques* (PU, 1988)
Posner, R A, *Cardozo A Study in Reputation* (University of Chicago Press, 1990)

R

Ramsey, M D, 'International Materials and Domestic Rights: Reflections on Atkins and Lawrence' (2004) 98 *American Journal of International Law* 69
Reimann, M and Zimmermann, R (eds), *The Oxford Handbook of Comparative Law* (Oxford University Press, 2006)
Reimann, M, 'A Career in Itself: The German Professoriate as a Model for American Legal Academia' in Reinmann, M (ed), *The Reception of Continental Ideas in the Common Law World 1820–1920* (Duncker & Humboldt, 1993)
—— (ed), *The Reception of Continental Ideas in the Common Law World 1820–1920* (Duncker & Humboldt, 1993)
——, 'A Human Rights Exception to Sovereign Immunity: Some Thoughts on *Princz v Federal Republic of Germany*' (1995) 16 *Michigan Journal of International Law* 403
——, *Conflict of Laws in Western Europe: A Guide Through the Jungle* (Transnational Publishers, 1995)
——, 'The End of Comparative Law as an Autonomous Subject' (1996) 11 *Tulane European and Civil Law Forum* 49
——, 'Stepping Out of the European Shadow: Why Comparative Law in the United States Must Develop Its Own Agenda' (1998) 46 *American Journal of Comparative Law* 637
——, 'Towards a European Civil Code: Why Continental Jurists Should Consult Their Transatlantic Colleagues'(1999) 73 *Tulane Law Review* 1337
——, 'Savigny's Triumph? Choice of Law in Contract Cases at the Close of the Twentieth Century' (1999) 39 *Virginia Journal of International Law* 571
Reimann, M, 'The Progress and Failure of Comparative Law in the Second Half of the Twentieth Century' (2002) 50 *American Journal of Comparative Law* 670
Rheinstein, M and Glendon, M-A, *The Law of Decedents' Estates* (Foundation Press, 1971)
Rials, S, *Le Juge Administratif Français et la Technique du Standard* (LGDJ, 1980)
Riles, A (ed), *Rethinking the Masters of Comparative Law* (Hart Publishing, 2001)
Rudden, B, 'Soviet Tort Law' (1967) 42 *New York University Law Review*
——, 'Courts and Codes in England, France, and Soviet Russia' 48 *Tulane Law Review* (1974)
——, 'Consequences' (1980) *Judicial Review* 194
——, 'Correspondence' (1990) 10 *Oxford Journal of Legal Studies*
——, 'Civil Law, Civil Society, and the Russian Constitution' (1994) 110 *Law Quarterly Review*

S

Sacco, R, *La Comparaison Juridique au Service de la Connaissance du Droit* (Economica, 1991)

——, 'Legal formants: A Dynamic Approach to Comparative Law' 39 *American Journal of Comparative Law* 395 (1991)

——, *Introduzione al diritto comparator* 5th edn (Torino, 1992)

——, 'Mute Law', [1995] 43 *American Journal of Comparative Law* 455

——, *Einführung in die Rechtsvergleichung* (Nomos, 2001)

Scalia, A, 'Originalism: The Lesser Evil', (1989) 57 *University of Cincinnati Law Review* 849

——, 'The Rule of Law as a Law of Rules', (1989) 56 *University of Chicago Law Review* 1175

——, 'Assorted Canards of Contemporary Legal Analysis', (1990) 40 *Case Western Reserve Law Review* 581

——, *A Matter of Interpretation Federal Courts and the Law* (Princeton University Press, 1997)

Schlechtriem, P, *Restitution und Bereicherungsrecht in Europa* (Mohr Siebeck, 2000)

Schlesinger, R B, *Formation of Contracts: A Study of the Common Core of Legal Systems* (Oceana, 1968)

——, 'The Past and Future of Comparative Law' (1995) 43 *American Journal of Comparative Law*

Schwartze, J (ed), *Administrative Law Under European Influence* (Sweet & Maxwell, 1996)

Selden, B S, 'Lex Mercatoria in European and US Trade Practice: Time to Take a Closer Look' (1995) 2 *Annual Survey of International and Comparative Law* 111

Shapiro, F, 'The Most Cited Law Review Article' (1985) 73 *California Law Review* 1540

——, 'The Most Cited Legal Scholars', 29 *J Legal Studies* 409 (2000)

Shavell, S, 'Economic Analysis of Law', (1999) (Spring) *NBER Reporter* 12

Simons, T, 'European and International Uniform Law' 1/2-2007, *The European Legal Forum* I-4

Singh, M, *German Administrative Law in a Common Law Perspective* 2nd edn (Springer, 2001)

Snell, J and Andenas, M, 'Exploring the Outer Limits' in Andenas, M et al (eds), *Services and Free Movement in EU Law* (Oxford University Press, 2002)

T

Tallon, D, 'Grandeur et décadence du Code civil français', in *Mélanges offerts à Marcel Fontaine* (Larcier, 2003) pp 279 *ff*

Teubner, G, '"Global Bukowina": Legal Pluralism in the World Society', in Teubner, G (ed), *Global Law Without a State* (Dartmouth Publishing Group, 1997), p 3 *ff*

Toobin, J, *The Nine: Inside the Secret Weapon of the Supreme Court* (Doubleday, 2007)

Tunc, A, 'Les Cours Suprêmes: Synthèse' [1978] 30 *Revue Internationale de Droit Comparé* 5

V

Vedel, G, *Droit Administratif* 2nd edn (Presses Universitaires France, 1961)

von Bar, C, *Gemeineuropäisches Deliktsrecht* (CH Beck, 1996)

——, *The Common European Law of Torts, Vol 2 Part 1* (Oxford University Press, 2000)

von Mehren, A T and Trautmann, D T, *The Law of Multistate Problems* (Transnational Publishers, 1965)

W

Watson, A (ed), *Daube Noster: Essays in Legal History for David Daube* (Scottish Academic Press Ltd, 1974)

——, *Legal Transplants: An Approach to Comparative Law* (University Of Georgia Press, 1974)

——, 'Comparative Law and Legal Change', [1978] 37 *Cambridge Law Journal* 313

——, *The Making of the Civil Law* (Harvard University Press, 1981)

——, *Sources of Law, Legal Change and Ambiguity* (University of Pennsylvania Press, 1984)

——, *The Evolution of Law* (The Johns Hopkins University Press, 1985)

——, *Legal Origins and Legal Change* (Hambledon Press, 1991)

——, *Roman Law and Comparative Law* (University of Georgia Press, 1991)

——, 'The Importance of "Nutshells"' (1994) 42 *American Journal of Comparative Law* 1
——, 'Aspects of Reception of Law', (1996) 44 *American Journal of Comparative Law* 345
——, *Completing the World Trading System* (Springer, 1999)
——, *Comparative Law: Law, Reality and Society* (Vandeplas Publishing, 2007)
Weir, T, 'Governmental Liability', [1989] *Public Law* 40
——, 'Die Sprachen des europäischen Rechts: Eine skeptische Betrachtung' (1995) *Zeitschrift für Europäisches Privatrecht* 368
——, 'Difficulties in Transposing Directives' (2004) *Zeitschrift für Europäisches Privatrecht* 595

Z

Zimmermann, R and du Plessis, J, 'Basic Features of the German Law of Unjustified Enrichment', [1994] *Restitution Law Review* 14
Zimmermann, R and Whittaker, S (eds), *Good Faith in European Contract Law* (Cambridge University Press, 2000)
Zimmermann, R, *The Law of Obligations: Roman Foundations of the Civilian Tradition* (Clarendon Press, 1990/1992)
——, 'Der europäische Charakter englischen Rechts' (1993) *Zeitschrift für Europäisches Privatrecht* 4
——, 'Civil Code and Civil Law The 'Europeanisation' of Private Law Within the European Community and the Re-emergence of a European Legal Service' (1994/95)1 *Columbia Journal of European Law* 77
——, 'Konturen eines Europäischen Vertragsrechts', [1995] *Juristenzeitung* 477
——, *Roman law, contemporary law, European law: The civilian tradition today* (Oxford University Press, 2001)
Zweigert, K and Kötz, H, *Einführung in die Rechtsvergleichung* 3rd edn (Mohr, 1996)
Zweigert, K, 'Some Reflections on the Sociological Dimensions of Private International Law or What is Justice in the Conflict of Laws?' (1973) 44 *Colo Law Review* 283

INDEX